Decentering America

Explorations in Culture and International History
General Editor: Jessica C. E. Gienow-Hecht

Volume 1
Culture and International History
Edited by Jessica C. E. Gienow-Hecht and Frank Schumacher

Volume 2
Remaking France
Brian Angus McKenzie

Volume 3
Anti-Americanism in Latin America and the Caribbean
Edited by Alan McPherson

Volume 4
Decentering America
Edited by Jessica C. E. Gienow-Hecht

DECENTERING AMERICA

Edited by
Jessica C. E. Gienow-Hecht

Berghahn Books
New York • Oxford

Published in 2007 by
Berghahn Books
www.berghahnbooks.com

©2007 Jessica C. E. Gienow-Hecht

All rights reserved. Except for the quotation of short passages for the purposes of criticism and review, no part of this book may be reproduced in any form or by any means, electronic or mechanical, including photocopying, recording, or any information storage and retrieval system now known or to be invented, without written permission of the publisher.

Library of Congress Cataloging-in-Publication Data

Decentering America / edited by Jessica C. E. Gienow-Hecht.
   p. cm. — (Explorations in culture and international history series)
   Includes bibliographical references and index.
   ISBN 978-1-84545-205-6 (hbk. : alk. paper)
   1. United States—Historiography. 2. United States—History—Philosophy. 3. United States—Foreign relations—Research. 4. International relations—Research. 5. United States—Civilization—Foreign influences. 6. Internationalism. 7. Transnationalism. 8. Non-governmental organizations. 9. Cultural relations. 10. Diplomacy—Social aspects. I. Gienow-Hecht, Jessica C. E., 1964-

E175.7.D43 2007
973.072—dc22

                                                    2007023972

British Library Cataloguing in Publication Data

A catalogue record for this book is available from the British Library

ISBN 978-1-84545-205-6 hardback, 978-1-84545-499-9 paperback

Contents

List of Illustrations   vii
Editor's Preface   ix
List of Contributors   xi

Introduction
Decentering American History   1
Jessica C. E. Gienow-Hecht

Part I: Inverting Americanization

Chapter 1
Who Said "Americanization"? The Case of Twentieth-Century Advertising and Mass Marketing from a British Perspective   23
Stefan Schwarzkopf

Chapter 2
Die antideutsche Welle: The Anti-German Wave, Public Diplomacy, and Intercultural Relations in Cold War America   73
Brian C. Etheridge

Part II: Internationalism

Chapter 3
Chinese Debates on Modernization and the West after the Great War   109
Dominic Sachsenmaier

Chapter 4
"For the Genuine Culture of the Americas": Musical Folklore, Popular Arts, and the Cultural Politics of Pan Americanism, 1933–50   132
Corinne A. Pernet

Part III: Non-governmental Influences

Chapter 5
"The Other Side of the War": Memory and Meaning at the War Remnants Museum of Vietnam 171
Scott Laderman

Chapter 6
Americanized Protests? The British and West German Protests against Nuclear Weapons and the Pacifist Roots of the West German New Left, 1957–64 210
Holger Nehring

Part IV: Cultural Violence

Chapter 7
Misperceptions of Empire: How Berlin and Washington Misread the "Ordinary Germans" of Latin America in World War II 255
Max Paul Friedman

Chapter 8
Rape and Murder in the Canal Zone: Cultural Conflict and the US Military Presence in Panama, 1955–56 277
Michael E. Donoghue

Part V: Decentering the World? The Culture of Diplomacy

Chapter 9
The Marriage of Thames and Rhine: Reflections on the English-Palatine Relations 1608–32 and the Culture of Diplomacy in Early Modern Europe 315
Magnus Rüde

Chapter 10
Self-Perception, the Official Attitude toward Pacifism, and Great Power Détente: Reflections on Diplomatic Culture before World War I 345
Friedrich Kießling

Index 381

Illustrations

Figure 1.1.	"The American Invasion," 1910	25
Figure 1.2.	Advertising poster by Aubrey Beardsley	36
Figure 1.3.	Advertising poster by Aubrey Beardsley	36
Figure 1.4.	Typical advertisement for Chrysler cars	40
Figure 1.5.	"Buy a British Motor" advertisement	42
Figure 1.6.	"Dunlop as British as the flag" advertisement	42
Figure 1.7.	Wells-Brimtoy stamp	42
Figure 1.8.	*Daily Express,* 22 March 1927	43
Figure 1.9.	*Advertising World,* April 1924	44
Figure 1.10.	Erwin, Wasey & Company Ltd. advertisement, 1924	45
Figure 1.11.	Associated American Newspapers advertisement, 1924	46
Figure 1.12.	J. Walter Thompson office, Alexandria	51
Figure 1.13.	J. Walter Thompson office, Berlin	51
Figure 1.14.	J. Walter Thompson office, London	51
Figure 1.15.	"Hut ab vor dem Neuen Chrysler" advertisement	53
Figure 1.16.	Crawford's advertisement 1928	54
Figure 1.17.	Crawford's advertisement 1937	54
Figure 5.1.	Tanks and planes in courtyard	174
Figure 5.2.	Military hardware inside museum complex	177
Figure 5.3.	Entrance to exhibition space	179

Figure 5.4.	Quote at entrance	181
Figure 5.5.	Nakamura Goro, Japanese photographer	183
Figure 5.6.	Tiger Cage	185
Figure 5.7.	Guillotine	187
Figure 5.8.	Donated articles from American war veterans	192
Figure 5.9.	*Mother,* work of art constructed of bomb fragments	195
Figure 5.10.	Fetuses, the alleged result of Agent Orange	198
Figure 6.1.	Easter March	216
Figure 6.2.	CND Peace Sign	217
Figure 6.3.	Easter March Badge	219
Figure 9.1.	Triumphal column erected by the city of Frankenthal to welcome the Elector Palatine Friedrich V and his wife Elizabeth, June 1613	331
Figure 9.2.	Friedrich V alias Jason on his ship Argo during a procession in Heidelberg, June 1613	333
Figure 9.3.	Frontispiece of a triumphal arc erected by the city of Oppenheim to welcome the Elector Palatine and his wife, June 1613	334

Editor's Preface

In the best-case scenario, an edited volume is an expression of team spirit. Authors compose and submit drafts, reviewers suggest revisions, editors mediate between both, and everyone tries to be as cooperative as possible. I consider myself extremely fortunate that the "players" in this volume have done exactly that. Hence my foremost gratitude goes to the contributors of the individual essays. Each one went out of their way to compose and then revise their essays, sometimes more than once. Via email and telephone we conceptualized the central idea and framework of this volume, exchanged criticism and suggestions, and read final drafts. This experience and the ensuing result has indeed been a collective labor of love.

The essays originate in the symposium Culture and International History II, which took place at the Stiftung Leucorea, Martin-Luther-Universität Halle-Wittenberg in Germany, in December 2002. Many thanks are due to the staff of the foundation; above all Christine Grabbe, who has the unique gift of finding solutions in seemingly hopeless situations. Generous support came from the Stifterverband für die deutsche Wissenschaft and the Kulturabteilung of the US embassy in Berlin. Many thanks in particular to Renate Semler, who has dedicated a good part of her life to the promotion and support of transAtlantic relations. I also wish to thank the Leucorea Foundation for sponsoring the index in this book.

Finally, Berghahn Books has once again proven to be a good sport. Many thanks to our copy editor, Mike Dempsey, who did a stellar job and even took this manuscript on a vacation to Mexico. Thank you also to our indexer, Wayne Moquin. I personally wish to express my gratitude to Marion Berghahn for her open mind, critical perspective, and faith in our project throughout the years. If our series *Explorations in Culture and*

International History has evoked more interest than we could anticipate, much of this is due to her support.
I would also like to thank the Zentrum for Nordamerika forschung for its continuing support of my research and for providing a stimulating intellectual environment.
   Jessica C. E. Gienow-Hecht, Frankfurt, July 2006

Contributors

MICHAEL E. DONOGHUE is an assistant professor of US foreign relations history at Marquette University. He received his BA and MA in history at the University of Rhode Island. He earned his doctorate from the University of Connecticut at Storrs under the direction of Frank Costigliola. Donoghue was a recipient of a Fulbright Overseas Research Grant for the year 2002 in the Republic of Panama. He has also received the Stuart Bernath Research Travel Grant and the W. Stull Holt Dissertation Fellowship from the Society of Historians of American Foreign Relations (SHAFR). Donoghue is currently transforming his dissertation *Imperial Sunset: Race, Identity, and Gender in the Panama Canal Zone 1939–1979* into a book.

BRIAN C. ETHERIDGE earned his doctorate under the direction of Michael Hogan and Peter Hahn at the Ohio State University. Currently, he is an assistant professor of history at Louisiana Tech University, where he also works as Director of Graduate Studies and Research Director of the American Foreign Policy Center. Etheridge also serves as Roster and Research List Coordinator for the Society of Historians of American Foreign Relations. He is busy preparing his manuscript "Nazis and Berliners: Representing Germany in Cold War America" for publication.

MAX PAUL FRIEDMAN is associate professor of history at American University in Washington, DC. His book *Nazis and Good Neighbors: The United States Campaign against the Germans of Latin America in World War II* (Cambridge, 2003) won the Herbert Hoover Award in US History and the A. B. Thomas Award in Latin American Studies. His articles have appeared in *Diplomatic History, German Life and Letters, Holocaust and Genocide Studies, Journal of Policy History, Journal of Social History, Oral*

History Review, Procesos: Revista Ecuatoriana de Historia, and The Americas: A Quarterly Review of Inter-American Cultural History. He is coeditor with Padraic Kenney of Partisan Histories: The Past in Contemporary Global Politics (Palgrave Macmillan, 2005).

JESSICA C. E. GIENOW-HECHT is a Heisenberg fellow teaching at the Johann Wolfgang Goethe-Universität Frankfurt am Main. She has previously taught at the University of Virginia, Universität Bielefeld, Martin-Luther-Universität Halle-Wittenberg, and Harvard University. Her field of interest is the interplay of culture and international relations since the early modern period. Gienow-Hecht's study *Transmission Impossible: American Journalism as Cultural Diplomacy in Postwar Germany, 1945–1955* (Baton Rouge, 1999) was co-awarded the Stuart Bernath Book Prize (best first book in diplomatic history) as well as the Myrna Bernard Prize (best book in diplomatic history written by a woman), both given by the Society for Historians of American Foreign Relations. Her study *Sound Diplomacy: Music and Emotions in German-American Relations since 1850* is under contract with the University of Chicago Press.

FRIEDRICH KIEßLING is Wissenschaftlicher Assistent at Friedrich-Alexander-University Erlangen-Nuremberg. He was educated at the universities of Munich and Erlangen, where he received his PhD in 2001. He specializes in the history of international relations and modern German intellectual history. Among his publications are his study of great power détente before World War I (*Gegen den großen Krieg? Entspannung in den internationalen Beziehungen 1911–1914*, Munich, 2002) and an edition of primary sources of Nazi-Germany foreign policy (*Quellen zur deutschen Außenpolitik 1933–1939*, Darmstadt, 2000, in *Ausgewählte Quellen zur deutschen Geschichte der Neuzeit*, vol. XXXIV).

SCOTT LADERMAN is an assistant professor of history at the University of Minnesota, Duluth. His first book, *An All Year Round Vacation Land: History, Tourism, and Memory in Postcolonial Vietnam*, is currently being prepared for publication. His second book, which he is currently researching, is tentatively entitled *A World Made Safe for Discovery: Surfing, Surf Culture, and U.S. Foreign Relations*.

HOLGER NEHRING is a lecturer in contemporary European history at the University of Sheffield, UK. He obtained his DPhil as a Rhodes Scholar at University College, University of Oxford, with a comparative study on the British and West German protests against nuclear weapons in the late 1950s and early 1960s. Before coming to Sheffield, he held research and teaching positions at University College, Pembroke College, and St. Peter's College; all at the University of Oxford. He has published several articles on twentieth-century peace protests, social movements, and Cold War history and is currently converting his DPhil thesis into a book.

CORINNE A. PERNET received her PhD in Latin American history from the University of California, Irvine, in 1996. Besides *Mobilizing Women in the Popular Front Era: Feminism, Class, and Politics in the Movimiento Pro-Emancipación de la Mujer Chilena, 1935–1950* (1997) she has published articles on the connections between national and transnational women's movements and on US–Latin American relations in the twentieth century. She currently teaches at the University of Zurich.

MAGNUS RÜDE studied history, political science, and law in Heidelberg and Berlin, where he graduated in 2001. As a PhD student at the history department of the Humboldt University Berlin, he worked on the English-Palatine relations from 1608–32. His research in German, English, and French archives and libraries was funded by scholarships from the German National Academic Foundation and the German Historical Institutes in London and Paris. After completing his doctorate in 2004 he currently works for the German Science Council.

DOMINIC SACHSENMAIER is an assistant professor of transcultural and Chinese history at Duke University. He has published a book in the field of 17th-century Sino-Western cultural relations (in German). Dominic Sachsenmaier is also the main editor of the 2002 book *Reflections on Multiple Modernities. European, Chinese, and Other Perspectives,* and he is the co-editor of *Competing Visions of World Order. Global Moments and Movements, 1880s – 1930s,* which was published in 2007. His current research focuses on approaches to global history in China, Germany and the United States as well as on worldwide political movements during the Interwar Period.

STEFAN SCHWARZKOPF studied modern history and history of science at the University of Jena (where he received his MA in

2000) and is now a lecturer in global marketing and business history at Queen Mary College, University of London. He completed his PhD at Birkbeck College, where he focused on the political, cultural, and social dimensions of early twentieth-century British advertising. Schwarzkopf's interests in the history of commercial and political propaganda resulted in a book he edited on German social-democratic advertising and public relations between the late 1960s and the late 1990s (*Die Anatomie des Machtwechsels*, Leipzig University Press, 2002). He has published widely on the trans-Atlantic co-evolution of a modern advertising service industry, on the history of motivation research, and the impact of the Cold War on the making of post-war marketing thought.

INTRODUCTION
Decentering American History

Jessica C. E. Gienow-Hecht

This is a book about one of the most recent directions in the research of culture and international history. Specifically, it addresses the attempt to decenter the United States in the history of culture and international relations both in times when the United States has been assumed to take center place. Recent debates among scholars of American history have postulated a critical analysis of the field; we have been asked to broaden our horizons, internationalize our perspective, and adopt analytical techniques where the analysis of national history does not necessarily assume a center position. Decentering is fast becoming a dynamic approach to the study of American cultural and diplomatic history. But what precisely is decentering, how should we apply it to the study of history, and why has it risen to such prominence? This book seeks to address these issues: rather than contributing more theoretical perspectives, it offers a variety of examples of how one can look at the role of culture in international history without assigning the central role to the United States. Collectively, these essays pragmatically demonstrate how the study of culture and international history can help us to rethink and reconceptualize US history today.

Decentering American history requires scholars to either replace the traditional centrist viewpoint with something else or abandon the notion of a center altogether, similar to recent developments in the field of Atlantic and Transatlantic Studies.[1] Since the 1990s, US diplomatic historians have made a major

---

Notes for this section begin on page 14.

contribution to this idea by broadening the study of US foreign relations to include issues of gender, race, religion, sports, the arts, and many other cultural factors.[2] In doing so, they have not only paved the way for a new generation of junior diplomatic historians, they have also inspired scholars from neighboring fields such as American Studies and literature.[3]

Ironically, those scholars who have contributed so much to the decentering of US history—diplomatic historians—have at the same time reaffirmed the central position of the United States in the study of culture and international history. Most of the research dedicated to cultural diplomacy, non-governmental organizations, and informal relations focuses on the twentieth century and the cold war, a period during which the nation emerged as a hegemonic power in the diplomatic, military, and cultural arenas.[4]

But if the United States is not at the core of this process, a book on decentering begs the question what or where the new center should be or whether there should be one at all? There is a certain irony in the fact that in a volume about decentering we should continue to search for a "central" paradigm. Decentering the nation means to focus less on the central actor and more on the nature of interaction, the process, the forum, the milieu, and the arena. To some of the authors presented here, decentering signifies the attempt to deemphasize the roles of American agents or institutions in international crises. To others, it entails the effort to transform a concept typically attributed to US agents into a different chronological or geographical context. Regardless of their focus, all authors adhere to the cultural turn in that they privilege cultural dynamics over political intentions and strategy.

This book seeks to supplement the existing scholarly approach by providing empirical demonstrations rather than yet more theoretical perspectives. It is designed to introduce students and scholars to some of the most novel approaches involving a more thorough attempt to resituate the American past in the context of International History. The volume offers five different sections with a total of ten contributions focusing on some of the most important developments in the field: the United States as a recipient of cultural trends (inverted Americanization), internationalism and transnational currents, NGOs, cultural forms of interaction (violence), and the culture of diplomacy.

The point of this book is not to show how one can deemphasize the roles of American agents and institutions for its own sake. Nor do we wish to suggest that decentering American history can encompass any work that does not have the United States at its center. Instead, the essays seek to demonstrate in practice how and where to shift the balance because this can help us understand history in a new and interesting way. Decentering America implies decentering the nation as the main field for diplomatic historians, both on the geographical as well as the chronological level. There is definitely some tension in this book between the "American" contributions and the contributions from outside US history. This tension manifests the need for outside perspectives to generate a more balanced idea of American history and its implications for the rest of the world.

* * *

National historiographies develop along specific lines and paradigms. "We arouse and arrange our memories," says the historian Michael Kammen, "to suit our psychic needs."[5]

What, then, are our psychic needs? History offers a way to affirm national identity. National identity still matters for the wider public. Both facts explain the continued attraction of national perspectives in historical writing. European as well as US historians have long used history to derive lessons for improving the present and forge national bonds. Academic postulations for new theoretical outlines, a broader intellectual horizon, and more contacts abroad ignore the fact that historiographies do not lead a life of their own. Instead, history and historiography entail what people want to believe about their past and their present.[6]

Take the historiography of American culture: for the longest time it has remained oblivious to the long-term legacy of foreign influences with little improvement in sight. Every year, a profusion of books in the United States with titles like "The Rise of" or "The Origins of," flood publishers' catalogs and university bookshelves. Such titles foreshadow a story that retraces how Americans came to arrive in the present. They tell a national story of progress, one that begins in America and ends or culminates in the present.[7] This historiographical vision has received powerful bipartisan support from Washington, DC. Congress has recently debated and passed several proposals dedicated to the creation of a "traditional American history."[8]

This tendency is notably explicit in the history of American culture. Here, historians occasionally pay lip service to ethnic European art and artists before uncovering the richness of a presumably independent mass culture. While mass culture counts as genuinely American, elitist aspirations that have no room in the anti-elitist history of the United States are typically labeled as European. The continuing search for a peculiarly American culture, the lack of a dialogue between diplomatic and cultural historians, and the antagonism against everything that seems remotely connected to high culture have all contributed to this silence. Hampered by language constraints, the ignorance of books by non-English-speaking authors, and the vision of an exceptional people, many historians have remained hesitant to reframe the nation's history in an international context where the United States poses as one among many actors.

In 1996 the Organization of American Historians and New York University initiated a project titled "Internationalizing the Study of American History." The organizers hoped to respond to what they perceived as the growing isolation of American history from the history of other nations, other regions, and other people. Four years later the project issued the so-called La Pietra Report, named after the Italian renaissance villa in Florence where four conferences dedicated to this theme took place. The report advised that US historians should modernize and internationalize American history, both in their research and in their teaching.[9] Shortly thereafter, Thomas Bender, professor of history at New York University, edited select samples of presentations given by the seventy-five international participants at La Pietra under the title *Rethinking American History*. In his introduction he argued that transnational history sought to establish a global history of the United States. By decentering the United States, US historians might spruce up the increasingly boring historiographical discourse, which, as Bender put it, "has become too familiar, too technical and predictable."[10] The volume contained the works of eighteen scholars of American history, many of them international, who investigated the theoretical significance of the project and presented tentative examples of such an approach. Prasenjit Duara, Marilyn Young, Rob Kroes, Walter Johnson, Daniel Rodgers, Winfried Fluck, Ian Tyrrell, Karen Ordahl Kupperman, Daniel Rodgers, and others grappled with substories, transnational concepts, hidden agendas, and, most importantly, the unrecognized influence of foreign agents and artifacts.

Most of the resulting reviews of *Rethinking American History* sounded positive and hopeful. "For decades American historians have been urging one another to place our culture in comparative or transnational perspective," James Kloppenberg announced on the jacket cover. Reading the book, added Linda Kerber, "one emerges invigorated, ready to welcome a new American history for a new international century." "De-centering the United States allows for a thicker analysis of social, cultural, political, and economic interactions," Jeremi Suri marveled in *Reviews in American History*. "De-centering the U.S. in these terms makes us explain the transmission of ideas and influences in a truly international light."[11]

Surprisingly, the project has evoked little controversy. Unlike innovative concepts in previous decades, such as gender or race, the international approach does not appear to irritate many scholars. Instead of triggering passionate debates, it has resulted in broad compliance. Most historians agree with or at least pay lip service to the suggestion that the time is ripe for historiographical change. But what has come of this effort? We may ask to see some results of the debate on decentering, both within and outside the United States.

It is no coincidence that the term decentering along with the postulation for analytical change does not originate in American historiography but among other subjects and other fields: the sciences, the arts, and, above all, literary criticism. For centuries scientists have developed concepts designed to decenter the core beliefs of their respective disciplines in order to either reassign the center to another field or to obliterate the notion of a center altogether.[12] In the contemporary study of the sciences, laws are no longer absolute and unchallengeable but, instead, determined by statistical analysis or probabilistic assumptions.

During the past decade, indeterminacy and decentralization have inspired a host of scholars in the humanities. How else to explain religious warfare and ideologically motivated manslaughter if not by the absence of a center of laws, customs, mores, and beliefs? In his study of the nexus between the sciences and the humanities, *Air Craft Stories,* John Law insists that in the contemporary Euro-American world, "many have lost their faith in big theories or 'grand narratives'" as well as "grand projects and plans." "Nuclear power, medical practices, food safety, the environment, everywhere ... experts are doubted, and people are skeptical of the claims made by authorities." And that, of course, includes academic authorities.[13]

Scholars working in the humanities have introduced and applied the term long before historians became interested in this subject. Literary critics have followed postmodernism's journey to decenter subjects, topics and narratives since the late 1970s.[14] Here, scholars talk about decentering as an attempt to remove the boundaries between production and consumption, and deemphasize "privileged centers" of narratives and analysis. Such efforts include, ironically, the center position of poststructuralism, which originally formed the cradle for the idea of decentering.[15] Writing on the Latin American literary scene, Nelly Richard and Carlos Rincón have criticized the ethnocentrism of poststructruralism and called for a decentered approach, such as feminism, that allows the periphery to receive its fair share of critical attention.[16]

Since then, decentering has assumed a central position in deconstructionalist and postmodernist thought and related fields.[17] Focusing on issues of distinctiveness, scholars of ethnicity like Catherine Hodeir, Ralph Premdas, and Marios Constantinou have stressed since the 1990s how difficult it is to define the core identity of presumably homogenous ethnic groups such as "the Carribeans," "the Cypriotic population," or even the colonial gaze on Africans at large.[18] Political scientists have called for an increasing regionalization of analysis outside of the Western hemisphere.[19] Scholars of geography like Ash Amin and Doreen Massey argue for an entirely new geography of the nation, one that features a dispersed rather than a spatial center.[20]

In the arts, decentering has likewise risen to prominence. Visual artists talk about the decentering of the artist whose many identities offer no single avenue to the understanding of his or her art. Musicologists have begun to decenter the notion of a musical canon: juggling thinkers from Michel Foucault to Richard Rorty, Kevin Korsyn's *Decentering Music* seeks to examine and then question the power to analyze certain genres of music at the expense of others.[21] Students of Asian film such as Peter Feng talk about how Chinese-American directors "decenter" the Middle Kingdom in their bicultural films.[22] And in philosophy, Uma Narayan and Sandra Harding have suggested the abandonment of the center in favor of an approach that caters to a "multicultural, postcolonial and feminist world."[22]

All these analyses employ the terminology of decentering albeit in different ways, ranging from questions of identity to investigations of institutionalization. Most scholars seem to use it in one of two ways: either to abandon a preponderant narrative, agent, or topic, such as the "Anglo-American point of view," the western perspective, or the prevalence of classical music research; or they attempt to broaden the identity of the subject, for example by drawing attention to the multitude of voices, egos, and personalities within a national unit. For our purposes, the attempt to decenter America has to do with both: it seeks to move the United States and its perspective away from the center of the historical narrative. Furthermore, it entails the attempt to point to the fractured identities of American actors within both US and global history.

What does the evidently highly malleable term decentering signify in historiographical research and debates? In contrast to literary critics, historians never regarded their attempt to broaden the field as an effort to radicalize their interest in indeterminacy, subjectivity, or contingency. While the 1990s saw a brief debate on the issue of whether or not diplomatic historians could or should see themselves as writers of fiction and as subjects involved in a world of text,[24] such efforts were mostly meant to counter the traditional historiography and the prevalence of presumably elitist perspectives.

Now, the effort to decenter America has also reached the field of international history in the United States. Here decentering attempts to retrace the meaning of American history in relation to the experience of other countries, people, regions, and ideas involved with the United States, the American people, and American culture. It also endeavors to dethrone the United States as a principal agent in international history, including during the crises and periods prior to 1914. Such efforts are not altogether new. Other countries and other fields have had their fair share of decentering debates in the past. Historians of Modern Europe, for example, have argued for years that "Germany is not an island" even though much of the current historiography on the nation's past foreign relations still seems to be based on that premise. Some, such as Jürgen Osterhammel and Johannes Paulmann, have begun to retrace the global visions dictating much of German social, economic, and cultural life since 1871,[25] while others such as David Blackbourn and Ute Frevert have grappled with the idea of "Europeanizing" German history.[26]

Our volume seeks to present some of the most recent research emerging as a result of the decentering discourse. The book is subdivided in five sections, each of which highlights a particular topic, ranging from conservative debates on modernity and the West in China to violence in Panama. While some essays use US history as a departure point for the analysis of international conflicts, others address concepts that have been connected with American history and investigate them in a different geographical context. Collectively, they offer an alternative to the prevailing research on the role of culture in international history and relations. The approaches offered in this book deliberately recast or even marginalize US history, be it in relation to the perception of time and space, issues and agents, or simply in the context of historical events typically associated with the United States such as the coming of modernity or the invention of advertising.

The most obvious effort to decenter the United States concerns situations in which contrary to traditional analysis, the nation features as a target, a victim, or a passive agent rather than as a hegemonic power. Accordingly, the two essays in the first section focus on the inversion of the term "Americanization," i.e., the United States as a recipient or marginal agent rather than exporter of cultural values. Stefan Schwarzkopf reassesses the idea of an Americanization of British advertising and consumer culture in the twentieth century. Instead of merely importing American advertising and its product imagery, Britain also exported advertising innovations to the United States and produced the primary rivals of American agencies in the competition for international advertising clients. Rejecting the notion of modern mass advertising as an American invention, Schwarzkopf suggests that the transfer and hybridization of advertising styles, institutions, and methods characterized the emergence of a common, trans-Atlantic market culture. In doing so, he questions the existing interpretation of twentieth-century advertising and marketing history, above all in the context of US "cultural imperialism."

In "Die antideutsche Welle," Brian Etheridge explores the tension in the United States over the nature of the German people in the 1950s and 1960s. To discuss these larger issues, the essay focuses on the outbreak of the anti-German wave during those years. Etheridge examines how Germans attempted to control images of Germany in the United States and how Americans received those representations. He concludes that the anti-German wave in particular and the concept of an "inverted Americanization" in general change our understanding of the origins of western cultural diplomacy.

Some of the empirical basis for the decentering approaches originates in studies of transnational processes, actors, and networks that transcend national boundaries. To make this point, part II turns to an analysis of the term "internationalism"—the idea of a multilateral forum of ideas, debates, and tastes. In one of the most radical departures from past investigations of modernity, Dominic Sachsenmaier looks at global debates on modernity after World War I with a particular emphasis on China. The purpose of his essay is to show the ambiguity of the discourse on modernity. Chinese thinkers agreed that in order to hinder the colonization of their country, they needed to look to a stereotyped "West" as a positive and negative landmark for China's future development. In a sense, then, all debates about the future of China were also debates about how to understand and evaluate "the West." As Sachsenmaier argues, there existed not one, western, concept of modernity but multiple (or alternative) modernities, which, like in the case of China, Europe, and the United States, borrowed heavily from each other. Just like Europeans projected their worst fears and greatest expectations on the United States, Chinese intellectuals looked to Europe when outlining various concepts for the future of their society.

In a similar vein, Corinne Pernet retraces the emergence of a trans-cultural folklore movement in the Americas from the 1930s to the 1950s. As she shows, in Latin America as well as the United States, this period witnessed a flourishing productivity in popular culture and folklore. Beginning in the late 1930s, the promotion of folklore also formed part of US cultural policies aimed at "Americanizing the Americas" in a desire to distance the United States from Europe, a continent sliding into war. Pernet's essay examines how a transnational community of scholars and professionals from the North and South shaped the cultural policy of the United States and probes the modes of interaction between US Americans and Latin Americans. But in an ironic twist, the institutionalization of folklore in Latin America nourished musical traditions that were put to use in protests against US imperialism beginning in the late 1950s.

The field of transnational history has yielded a number of important studies dedicated to the role of non-governmental organizations, international non-governmental organizations, and non-governmental currents the world over. Together, they reveal the occasional frequent marginalization and retreat of the nation state in the international arena and, thus, contribute to the decentering of the United States in international history. Section III, therefore, addresses non-governmental influences in Asia and Europe. Scott Laderman explores the manner in which the War Remnants Museum in Ho Chi Minh City emerged as a repository of memory and as a site of discourse on competing narratives of the American war in Vietnam. Unlike American sites of remembrance, the War Remnants Museum places the Vietnamese at the center of its constructed narrative, sparking contrition from countless visitors as well as frustration from foreign tourists accustomed to considering the war as a distinctly *American* tragedy. Drawing on the museum's exhibits, interviews with staff and visitors, travel reports, and comment books scattered throughout its display areas, the essay provides a "bottom up" analysis of the passions aroused by a representation of the war that refuses to focus on the American point of view.

Holger Nehring, meanwhile, investigates the importance of "culture" in the relations between two social movements, the British and West German protests against nuclear weapons during their peak in the late 1950s and early 1960s. Based on recent studies of international migration and social movements, Nehring shows that the culture of the Cold War in Britain and West Germany both impeded and facilitated communications between the two protest movements. Moreover, this chapter highlights the importance of actions and emotions in generating cross-cultural communications between the movements. Finally, Nehring provides a snapshot on important precursors to the student protests of the later 1960s: he suggests that pacifist traditions, rather than diffusion of ideas from the United States, played a crucial role in the emergence of the West German New Left.

The analysis of cultural forms of behavior provides another avenue to decenter the role of the United States in the context of international history. Here, scholars stress mutual perceptions, interactions, and receptions balancing the voices of two or more parties involved with one another. To exemplify this approach, the fourth part of this volume investigates the issue of violence triggered by cultural antagonism in international relations. In his case study of "ordinary Germans" in Latin America during World War II, Max Friedman shows how many US officials were convinced that Latin Americans were incapable of managing their domestic and foreign affairs. Some mid-level Nazi Party officials, meanwhile, combined a disdain for Latin Americans with a misunderstanding of the emigrant experience in preparing an unsuccessful effort to enlist large numbers of German expatriates for the war effort. These two sets of ideological blinders and assumptions of superiority persuaded officials in Berlin and Washington that Latin America was a fertile field for the seeds of Nazi intrigue, producing a clash that resulted in the internment of some four thousand German emigrants.

In an essay addressing perhaps the most graphic and gruesome topic of this collection, Michael Donoghue turns to cultural conflicts in the Panama Canal Zone under US occupation. Before an era of crisis in the US-Panamanian relations, in 1955–56, both sought to adjust problems of inequality in their relations and to confer greater economic benefits from the Canal and its workers on Panama. Egyptian president Nasser's 1956 nationalization of the Suez Canal refocused Panama's desire for sovereignty over the Canal Zone and ignited a resurgence of Panamanian nationalism among a younger generation of students, activists, and politicians. Beneath this "official transcript" of the US-Panamanian dispute, widespread Panamanian frustration over the US presence on the isthmus erupted following a series of shocking rapes, murders, and assaults by US servicemen against Panamanian citizens. Such cultural conflicts, Donoghue argues, registered "beneath the radar screen" of high-status diplomatic events. Yet at the same time they resonated powerfully in the consciousness of the colonized, highlighting the centrality of race, gender, and culture in the US-Panamanian conflict.

In the last and perhaps most groundbreaking section, we ask whether the need for decentering constitutes an American peculiarity. The present series, *Exploration in Culture and International History,* seeks to internationalize the study of history; it internationalizes individual topics, including, in this case, the idea of "decentering." To emphasize this point, we have selected two case studies from a different region and, in one case, a different time frame, in order to show how the cultural approach decenters our understanding of the inner workings of modern diplomacy, American-style. These chapters are exemplary; they make the point that spatial and temporal decentering is, in fact, a most appropriate notion.

Magnus Rüde seeks to broaden the decentering thesis in a genuine historical sense by applying a twentieth-century concept typically associated with US history to early modern history. His essay represents a useful approach to contextualize the history of twentieth-century American international relations. Taking the role of religious strives in diplomacy, Rüde elaborates a set of implications when dealing with the political dimensions of militant Protestantism. His study on the English-Palatine relations and the culture of diplomacy in Early Modern Europe focuses on processes, structures, and cultural dimensions at the "starting point" of international relations in a modern sense. Studying the marriage of Elizabeth Stuart, King James I's only daughter, and the young Count Palatine Friedrich V in February 1613, the essay concentrates on theatrical productions and representative performances linked to this dynastic alliance in London and Heidelberg, inside the courts as well as on the public stage. To Rüde, the symbolism generated during these events eventually led to the escalation of religious tensions and the outbreak of the Thirty Years War. On a broader level, Rüde challenges a number of "truths" such as the modern state as central actor of diplomacy. Although the power of religion as a driving force in diplomacy temporarily retreated in the face of modern ideological concepts such as nationalism and communism, it retained its influence on policy in the "third world" before it recently emerged as a powerful international issue in the Middle East. In other words, religion has been a driving force in modern diplomacy from the seventeenth to the twenty-first century.

In a similar vein, Friedrich Kießling seeks to broaden the decentering thesis in a genuine historiographical sense by applying a concept attributed to US diplomacy to European actors. Kießling sheds light on a different and more recent aspect of European diplomatic culture by looking at self-perceptions, official attitudes toward pacifism, and Great Power détente prior to World War I. Like Rüde's essay, this approach reflects the attempt to analyze diplomacy as a distinct cultural phenomenon. In studying the worldviews of diplomats and politicians engaged in European diplomacy before World War I it provides an insight into diplomatic culture before 1914. Kießling thus challenges observations on the "peculiarity" of American diplomatic culture; according to him, international historians should label all diplomatic cultures as "peculiar" and in need of decentering because diplomatic cultures are always driven by regional and local special interests.[27]

Collectively, the essays allow an insight into some of the most recent research in culture and international history, broadening or even sidestepping the American perspective. Most importantly, they demonstrate how decentering can help us understand history in a fresh and dynamic way. The contributors show how decentering is not only interesting in and of itself but how it can help transform our understanding of American history. We may begin to be able to see the United States as a recipient rather than an exporter of culture. Transnational debates and currents marginalize the US contribution to foreign debates and cultural trends. Non-governmental influences force Americans to accept or at least live with viewpoints other than their own. Cultural forms of interactions manifest the limits of US hegemonic power and democratic persuasion. And on the theoretical level, the concept of twentieth-century US diplomacy is not peculiar to the United States. In other words, decentering not only destabilizes but also helps redefine—or transform—the center. Because at the center is not the nation but the interaction of nations, organizations, private individuals, and cultural flows.

There remain, of course, challenges regarding the broadening and decentering of the American perspective and they might well inspire future research in this field. The most obvious concern is the detailed investigation of areas and individuals involved with the United States and its culture that have not been studied extensively before, above all Eastern Europe and the Middle East. Furthermore, the decades prior to the Great War remain a historiographical wasteland.

On a more theoretical level, we need to be continuously aware of the politics of any scholarly discourse. Even decentering runs the risk of turning into a new dogma. A few years ago, Chana Kronfeld postulated in her study on literary dynamics that for all the efforts to deconstruct the subject, there will always remain a center deciding which voices will achieve prominence and who will remain beyond investigation. The "invisible center," Kronfeld believes, "has a vested interest in periodically revising the canon, both diachronically and synchronically." The center can only survive if a periodic influx of controlled "counter narratives" dismisses any fundamental criticism of mainstream culture.²⁸ The challenge for historians of culture and international history, then, is to resist the current drive to annihilate some forms of marginality while highlighting others. Many philosophers believe that the authenticity of the self will rise, like Phoenix from the ashes, out of the blazes of postmodernism. Of course, a subject—and a nation—can have many souls and selves. But it is still a subject, regardless of how much it suffers from of a tormented, multiple, and—to use a medical term—disassociative identity disorder.²⁹

In offering this selection of essays this book attempts to look at the role of culture in international history without putting the United States in the center of the stage. The idea of decentering America has, in a way, reaffirmed the centrality of the United States in the study of culture and international history. Yet, notwithstanding the prevailing preponderance of analyses pertaining to the influence of U.S. culture, cultural imperialism, cultural transfer, cultural diplomacy and cultural transnationalism, we are witnessing in Europe, Asia, Australia, Africa and in the Americas the emergence of a new and international cast of scholars who are reapplying the concepts developed in the 1990s to regions and topics outside the traditional transatlantic one-way street. Their work will go a long way to help us understand where the United States is situated in a global world, regardless of how fractured, marginalized and internationalized the nation, its culture and its history may be.

Notes

Thank you to Friedrich Kießling, Holger Nehring, Volker Berghahn, Heiko Hecht, Gregory Glova, the anonymous reviewer of Berghahn Books, and the participants of Hans-Jürgen Puhle's research colloquium at the Johann Wolfgang Goethe-Universität Frankfurt am Main for their comments and suggestions on this essay.

1. For an introduction see Bernard Bailyn, *Atlantic History: Concept and Contours* (Cambridge, MA: Harvard University, 2005).
2. See Jessica C. E. Gienow-Hecht, "On the Division of Knowledge and the Community of Thought: Culture and International History," *Culture and International History*, eds. Jessica C. E. Gienow-Hecht and Frank Schumacher (Oxford and New York: Berghahn Books, 2003), 3–26; Michael Hogan and Thomas Patterson, eds., *Explaining the History of American Foreign Relations* (Cambridge: Cambridge University Press, 2004).
3. Alexandra Epstein, "The Last Word," *Passport: The Newsletter for the Society for Historians of American Foreign Relations* 36, 2 (August 2005): 59;

Eckart Conze, Guido Müller, and Ulrich Lappenküper, eds., *Erneuerung und Erweiterung: Themen und Perspektiven einer Geschichte der internationalen Beziehungen* (Cologne and Vienna: Böhlau, 2004); Wilfried Loth and Jürgen Osterhammel, eds. *Internationale Geschichte: Themen—Ergebnisse—Aussichten* (Munich: Oldenbourg Wissenschaftsverlag, 2000).

4. Since the 1990s, the journal *Diplomatic History* has commendably published a number of influential articles along these lines. See also Gienow-Hecht and Schumacher, *Culture and International History.*
5. Michael Kammen, *Mystic Chords of Memory: The Transformation of Tradition in American Culture* (New York: Alfred Knopf, 1991), 9.
6. I am indebted to Holger Nehring for this suggestion. For at recent study on this phenomenon, see Peter Fritzsche, *Stranded in the Present: Modern Time and the Melancholy of History* (Cambridge, MA: Harvard University Press, 2004).
7. See, e.g., Max M. Edling, *A Revolution in Favor of Government: Origins of the United States and the Making of the American State* (New York: Oxford University Press, 2003); Jane Hunter, *How Young Ladies Became Girls: The Victorian Origins of American Girlhood* (New Haven: Yale University Press, 2002); Mark F. Bernstein, *Football: The Ivy League Origins of an American Obsession* (Philadelphia: University of Pennsylvania Press, 2001); Michael A. Bellesiles, *Arming America: The Origins of a National Gun Culture* (New York: Alfred Knopf, 2000); Donald Miller, *City of the Century: The Epic of Chicago and the Making of America* (New York: Simon & Schuster, 1996).
8. Among these proposal are the "Teaching American History" initiative of Senator Robert C. Byrd (D-WV) and the "American History and Civics Education Act" by Senator Lamar Alexander (R-TN), and they all of these focus on the "March of Progress" perspective, obstructing "anything that smacks of comparative world history." Bruce Craig, "The Politics of 'Traditional' American History," *Perspectives: Newsmagazine of the American Historical Association* 41, 8 (November 2003): 13–17; Bruce Craig, "The Battle Continues," *Perspectives* (April 2004). <www.historians.org/Perspectives/Issues/2004/0404/0404nch1.cfm> (accessed 9 June 2005).
9. "The La Pietra Report: Project on Internationalizing the Study of American History: A Report to the Profession," (N.p., 2000), 17. See also Louis A. Pérez Jr., "We are the World: Internationalizing the National, Nationalizing the International," *Journal of American History* 89 (2002/03): 558–68.
10. Thomas Bender, "Introduction: Historians, the Nation, and the Plenitude of Narratives," in *Rethinking American History in a Global Age,* ed. Thomas Bender (Berkeley: University of California Press, 2002), 1–21, quote p. 11.
11. Jeremi Suri, "The Significance of the Wider World in American History," *Reviews in American History* 31, 1 (2003): 1–13, quote p. 9. See also Peter Fritzsche, "Global History and Bounded Subjects: A Response to Thomas Bender 18," *American Literary History* 18 (2006): 283–287.
12. Copernicus taught us that the Earth was not the center of the universe, Darwin proved that the creation of humankind was not a special project apart from the rest of animal life, and Freud wiped out the notion that people were cognizant masters of their own lives. In the late twentieth century, Stephen Hawking has rekindled the debate with the proclamation of a narrow set of "basic laws" that he feels might explain just about everything. Stephen W. Hawking, *The Universe in a Nutshell* (New York: Bantam Books, 2001); Hawking, *A Brief History of Time: From the Big Bang to Black Holes* (Toronto and New York: Bantam Books, 1988).

13. John Law, *Aircraft Stories: Decentering the Object in Technoscience* (Durham: Duke University Press, 2002), 1–11, quotes 1, 2. Law suggests to evade the dilemma between modernism and postmodernism by claiming that the two can exist side by side: "Fractional coherence," he argues, "is *about drawing things together without centering them.*" "Euro-American language," he concludes, "just does not have the language yet to imagine this possibility of coexistence between the center and the decentering of the subject."
14. "What began to displace both modernization and dependency models," write John Beverley and José Oviedo, "was an interrogation of the interrelation between the respective 'sphere' (culture, ethics, politics, etc.) of modernity, an interrogation that required of social scientists a new concern with subjectivity and identity as well as new understandings of, and tolerance for, the cultural, religious, and ethnic heterogeneity of Latin America in the 1970s." John Beverley and José Oviedo, "Introduction," in The *Postmodernism Debate in Latin America,* eds. John Beverley, Michael Aronna, and José Oviedo (Durham: Duke University Press, 1995), 7.
15. Theo L. D'haen, "Magical Realism and Postmodernism: Decentering Privileged Centers," in *Magical Realism: Theory, History, Community,* eds. Lois Parkinson Zamora and Wendy B. Faris (Durham: Duke University Press, 1995), 191–208; Michael Bérubé, excerpt from *Public Access: Literary Theory and American Cultural Politics* (1994), in *Postmodern American Fiction: A Norton Anthology,* eds. Paula Geyh, Fred G. Leeborn, and Andrew Levy (New York and London: W. W. Norton, 1998), 595–603. For a general introduction to postmodernism in contemporary art forms such as painting, photography, architecture, film, video, and literature, see Frederic Jameson, *Postmodernism, or, The Cultural Logic of Late Capitalism* (Durham: Duke University Press, 1991); Silvio Gaggi, *From Text to Hypertext: Decentering the Subject in Fiction, Film, the Visual Arts, and Electronic Media* (Philadelphia: University of Pennsylvania Press, 1997).
16. Nelly Richard, "Cultural Peripheries: Latin America and Postmodernist De-centering," in *The Postmodernism Debate in Latin America,* eds. John Beverley, Michael Aronna, and José Oviedo (Durham: Duke University Press, 1995), 217–22; Carlos Rincón, "The Peripheral Center of Postmodernism: On Borges, Garcia Márquez, and Alterity," in ibid., 223–40. See also Gaggi, *From Text to Hypertext,* 98–139, 152.
17. Postmodernism postulates a view of humans as polycentric and fluid, who only hold limited autonomy over their choices and informed by a multitude of diverse perspectives. As a concept, it essentially describes a mode of thought that rejects notions of centering, a point of reference or an essence. As Pirkko Moisala puts it, "Decentering aims to expose contractions and fluctuations inherent in concepts and structures." Pirkko Moisala, "Decentering the term 'woman composer,'" in *Frau Musica (nova): komponieren heute = composing today,* ed. Martina Homma (Sinzig: Studio, 2000), 84; Charles B. Guignon, *On Being Authentic* (London and New York: Routledge, 2004), 109.
18. Ralph R. Premdas, *Ethnic Identity in the Caribbean: Decentering a Myth* (Toronto: Robert F. Harney Professorship and Program in Ethnic Immigration and Pluralism Studies, University of Toronto, 1995); Marios Constantinou, "The Cavafian Poetics of Diasporic Constitutionalism: Toward a Neo-Hellenistic Decentering on the Kyp(riot)ic Experience," in *Cyprus and Its People: Nation, Identity, and Experience in an Unimaginable Community,*

1955–1997, ed. Vangelis Calotychos (Boulder: Westview Press, 1998), 171–203 (plus notes); Catherine Hodeir, "Decentering the Gaze at French Colonial Exhibitions," in *Images and Empires: Visuality in Colonial and Postcolonial Africa,* eds. Paul S. Landau and Deborah D. Kaspin (Berkeley: University of California Press, 2002), 233–52.

19. Jeffrey Rubin, for example, has developed a theoretical approach designed to decenter the analysis of regime, state, and contestation in Mexico by focusing on subregions such as Juchitán. Jeffrey W. Rubin, *Decentering the Regime: Ethnicity, Radicalism, and Democracy in Juchitán, Mexico* (Durham: Duke University Press, 1997), 238–64.
20. Ash Amin, Doreen Massey, and Nigel Thrift, eds., *Decentering the Nation: A Radical Approach to Regional Inequality* (London: Catalyst Forum, 2003).
21. Kevin Korsyn, *Decentering Music: A Critique of Contemporary Musical Research* (Oxford and New York: Oxford University Press, 2003), 5–31, 176–88.
22. Peter X. Feng, *Identities in Motion: Asian American Film and Video* (Durham and London: Duke University Press, 2002), 103–27.
23. Uma Narayan and Sandra Harding, eds., *Decentering the Center: Philosophy for a Multicultural, Postcolonial and Feminist World* (Bloomington: Indiana University Press, 2000). See, in particular, Alison M. Jaggar's essay on "Globalizing Feminist Ethics" (1–25), in which the author argues that "inequities of power are even more conspicuous in global and local contexts" and then goes on to retrace the emergence of a "global discourse community" among feminists that feeds on small communities (1). Even the public discourse has now seen its fair share of lingual revisions. Educators grapple with the challenge of decentering charter schools which, albeit supported by the government, operate autonomously and offer inventive pedagogy. Meanwhile, the London School of Economics has announced to "decenter the Cold War Programme" in order to stimulate a broader research perspective. The full title of the program is: "Decenter the Cold War Programme: Conflicts and Currents in Europe and the Third World, 1965–1990." Funded by a grant from the Arts and Humanities Research Board and launched in October 2001, the program seeks to produce "high quality historical research for publication, to translate and make more widely available a range of key documents and to stimulate further historical research in this rapidly evolving field." See also Judith Plaskow, "Decentering Sex: Rethinking Jewish Sexual Ethics," in *God Forbid: Religion and Sex in American Public Life,* ed. Kathleen M. Sands (Oxford and New York: Oxford University Press, 2000), 23–41; Bruce Fuller, ed., *Inside Charter Schools: The Paradox of Radical Decentralization* (Cambridge, MA: Harvard University Press, 2000), esp. 230–54; Peter McLaren, "Decentering Whiteness: In Search of a Revolutionary Multiculturalism," *Multicultural Education* 5, 1 (Fall 1997).
24. See the debate between the two presidents of the Society for Historians of American Relations (SHAFR) in 1995 and 1998 respectively: Melvyn P. Leffler, "New Approaches, Old Interpretations, and Prospective Reconfigurations," *Diplomatic History* 19 (Spring 1995): 173–96; Emily S. Rosenberg, "Revisiting Dollar Diplomacy: Narratives of Money and Manliness," *Diplomatic History* 22 (Spring 1998): 155–76.
25. Johannes Paulmann, ed., *Auswärtige Repräsentationen: Deutsche Kulturdiplomatie nach 1945* (Cologne and Vienna: Böhlau, 2005); Sebastian Conrad and Jürgen Osterhammel, "Einleitung," in *Das Kaiserreich transna-*

tional: Deutschland in der Welt, 1871–1914, eds. Sebastian Conrad und Jürgen Osterhammel (Göttingen: Vandenhoeck & Ruprecht, 2004), 7. See also David Blackbourn, "Das Kaiserreich transnational: Eine Skizze," in ibid., 302–24.
26. Ute Frevert and David Blackbourn, "Europeanizing German History," *Bulletin of the German Historical Institute* 36 (Spring 2005): 9–31.
27. For a comparison, see Fred Logevall, "A Critique of Containment," *Diplomatic History* 28, 4 (September 2004): 473–99.
28. Chana Kronfeld, *On the Margins of Modernism: Decentering Literary Dynamics* (Berkeley: University of California Press, 1996), 225, 226–27.
29. Guignon, *On Being Authentic*, 110, 125. Disassociative Identity Disorder involves a disturbance in a patient's memory and identity. The patient uses defense mechanisms such as idealization, splitting, denial, or taking on the personality of another in order to cope with a childhood trauma. <www.cmhawrb.on.ca/disassociation.htm> (accessed 20 March 2006).

Bibliography

Amin, Ash, Doreen Massey, and Nigel Thrift, eds. *Decentering the Nation: A Radical Approach to Regional Inequality*. London: Catalyst Forum, 2003.

Bailyn, Bernard. *Atlantic History: Concept and Contours*. Cambridge, MA: Harvard University, 2005.

Bellesiles, Michael A. *Arming America: The Origins of a National Gun Culture*. New York: Alfred Knopf, 2000.

Bender, Thomas. "Introduction: Historians, the Nation, and the Plenitude of Narratives." In *Rethinking American History in a Global Age*, ed. Thomas Bender. Berkeley: University of California Press, 2002, pp. 1–21.

———, ed. *Rethinking American History in a Global Age*. Berkeley: University of California Press, 2002.

Bernstein, Mark F. *Football: The Ivy League Origins of an American Obsession*. Philadelphia: University of Pennsylvania Press, 2001.

Bérubé, Michael. *Public Access: Literary Theory and American Cultural Politics* (excerpt, 1994). In *Postmodern American Fiction: A Norton Anthology*, eds. Paula Geyh, Fred G. Leeborn, and Andrew Levy. New York and London: W. W. Norton, 1998, pp. 595–603.

Beverley, John, and José Oviedo. "Introduction." In *The Postmodernism Debate in Latin America*, eds. John Beverley, Michael Aronna, and José Oviedo. Durham: Duke University Press, 1995.

Blackbourn, David. "Das Kaiserreich transnational: Eine Skizze." In *Das Kaiserreich transnational: Deutschland in der Welt, 1871–1914*, eds. Sebastian Conrad and Jürgen Osterhammel. Göttingen: Vandenhoeck & Ruprecht, 2004, pp. 302–24.

Conrad, Sebastian, and Jürgen Osterhammel, eds. *Das Kaiserreich transnational: Deutschland in der Welt, 1871–1914*. Göttingen: Vandenhoeck & Ruprecht, 2004.

Constantinou, Marios. "The Cavafian Poetics of Diasporic Constitutionalism: Toward a Neo-Hellenistic Decentering on the Kyp(riot)ic Experience." In *Cyprus and Its People: Nation, Identity, and Experience in an Unimaginable Community, 1955–1997*, ed. Vangelis Calotychos. Boulder: Westview Press, 1998, pp. 171–203 (plus notes).

Conze, Eckart, Guido Müller, and Ulrich Lappenküper, eds. *Erneuerung und Erweiterung: Themen und Perspektiven einer Geschichte der internationalen Beziehungen.* Cologne and Vienna: Böhlau, 2004.

Craig, Bruce. "The Politics of 'Traditional' American History." *Perspectives: Newsmagazine of the American Historical Association* 41, 8 (November 2003): 13–17.

———. "The Battle Continues: Advisory boards and the Title VI Higher Education Act." *Perspectives* (April 2004). <www.historians.org/Perspectives/Issues/2004/0404/0404nch1.cfm> (accessed 9 June 2005).

D'haen, Theo L. "Magical Realism and Postmodernism: Decentering Privileged Centers." In *Magical Realism: Theory, History, Community*, eds. Lois Parkinson Zamora and Wendy B. Faris. Durham: Duke University Press, 1995, pp. 191–208.

Edling, Max M. *A Revolution in Favor of Government: Origins of the United States and the Making of the American State.* New York: Oxford University Press, 2003.

Epstein, Alexandra. "The Last Word." *Passport: The Newsletter for the Society for Historians of American Foreign Relations* 36, 2 (August 2005): 59.

Feng, Peter X. *Identities in Motion: Asian American Film and Video.* Durham, London: Duke University Press, 2002, pp. 103–27.

Fritzsche, Peter. "Global History and Bounded Subjects: A Response to Thomas Bender 18." *American Literary History* 18 (2006): 283–287.

Fritzsche, Peter. *Stranded in the Present: Modern Time and the Melancholy of History.* Cambridge, MA: Harvard University Press, 2004.

Fuller, Bruce, ed. *Inside Charter Schools: The Paradox of Radical Decentralization.* Cambridge, MA: Harvard University Press, 2000.

Gaggi, Silvio. *From Text to Hypertext: Decentering the Subject in Fiction, Film, the Visual Arts, and Electronic Media.* Philadelphia: University of Pennsylvania Press, 1997.

Gienow-Hecht, Jessica C. E. "On the Division of Knowledge and the Community of Thought: Culture and International History." In *Culture and International History,* eds. Jessica C. E. Gienow-Hecht and Frank Schumacher. Oxford, New York: Berghahn Books, 2003, pp. 3–26.

Guignon, Charles B. *On Being Authentic.* London and New York: Routledge, 2004.

Hawking, Stephen W. *A Brief History of Time: From the Big Bang to Black Holes.* Toronto and New York: Bantam Books, 1988.

———. *The Universe in a Nutshell.* New York: Bantam Books, 2001.

Hodeir, Catherine. "Decentering the Gaze at French Colonial Exhibitions." In *Images and Empires: Visuality in Colonial and Postcolonial Africa,* eds. Paul S. Landau and Deborah D. Kaspin. Berkeley: University of California Press, 2002, pp. 233–52.

Hogan, Michael, and Thomas Patterson, eds. *Explaining the History of American Foreign Relations.* Cambridge: Cambridge University Press, 2004.

Hunter, Jane. *How Young Ladies Became Girls: The Victorian Origins of American Girlhood.* New Haven: Yale University Press, 2002.

Jaggar, Alison M. "Globalizing Feminist Ethics." In *Decentering the Center: Philosophy for a Multicultural, Postcolonial and Feminist World,* eds. Uma Narayan and Sandra Harding. Bloomington: Indiana University Press, 2000, pp. 1–25.

Jameson, Frederic. *Postmodernism, or, The Cultural Logic of Late Capitalism.* Durham: Duke University Press, 1991.

Kammen, Michael. *Mystic Chords of Memory: The Transformation of Tradition in American Culture.* New York: Alfred Knopf, 1991.

Korsyn, Kevin. *Decentering Music: A Critique of Contemporary Musical Research.* Oxford and New York: Oxford University Press, 2003.

Kronfeld, Chana. *On the Margins of Modernism: Decentering Literary Dynamics.* Berkeley: University of California Press, 1996.

"The La Pietra Report: Project on Internationalizing the Study of American History. A Report to the Profession." N.p., 2000.

Law, John. *Aircraft Stories: Decentering the Object in Technoscience.* Durham: Duke University Press, 2002.

Leffler, Melvyn P. "New Approaches, Old Interpretations, and Prospective Reconfigurations." *Diplomatic History* 19 (Spring 1995): 173–96.

Loth, Wilfried, and Jürgen Osterhammel, eds. *Internationale Geschichte: Themen—Ergebnisse—Aussichten.* Munich: Oldenbourg Wissenschaftsverlag, 2000.

McLaren, Peter. "Decentering Whiteness: In Search of a Revolutionary Multiculturalism." *Multicultural Education* 5, 1 (Fall 1997).

Miller, Donald. *City of the Century: The Epic of Chicago and the Making of America.* New York: Simon & Schuster, 1996.

Moisala, Pirkko. "Decentering the Term 'Woman Composer.'" In *Frau Musica (nova): komponieren heute = composing today,* ed. Martina Homma. Sinzig: Studio, 2000, pp. 83–94.

Narayan, Uma, and Sandra Harding, eds. *Decentering the Center: Philosophy for a Multicultural, Postcolonial and Feminist World.* Bloomington: Indiana University Press, 2000.

Pérez, Louis A., Jr. "We Are the World: Internationalizing the National, Nationalizing the International." *Journal of American History* 89 (2002/03): 558–68.

Plaskow, Judith. "Decentering Sex: Rethinking Jewish Sexual Ethics." In *God Forbid: Religion and Sex in American Public Life,* ed. Kathleen M. Sands. Oxford and New York: Oxford University Press, 2000, pp. 23–41.

Premdas, Ralph R. *Ethnic Identity in the Caribbean: Decentering a Myth.* Toronto: Robert F. Harney Professorship and Program in Ethnic Immigration and Pluralism Studies, University of Toronto, 1995.

Richard, Nelly. "Cultural Peripheries: Latin America and Postmodernist Decentering." In *The Postmodernism Debate in Latin America,* eds. John Beverley, Michael Aronna, and José Oviedo. Durham: Duke University Press, 1995, pp. 217–22.

Rincón, Carlos. "The Peripheral Center of Postmodernism: On Borges, Garcia Márquez, and Alterity." In *The Postmodernism Debate in Latin America,* eds. John Beverley, Michael Aronna, and José Oviedo. Durham: Duke University Press, 1995, pp. 223–40.

Rosenberg, Emily S. "Revisiting Dollar Diplomacy: Narratives of Money and Manliness." *Diplomatic History* 22 (Spring 1998): 155–76.

Rubin, Jeffrey W. *Decentering the Regime: Ethnicity, Radicalism, and Democracy in Juchitán, Mexico.* Durham: Duke University Press, 1997, pp. 238–64.

Suri, Jeremi. "The Significance of the Wider World in American History." *Reviews in American History* 31, 1 (2003): 1–13.

Part I
INVERTING AMERICANIZATION

Chapter 1

WHO SAID "AMERICANIZATION"?
The Case of Twentieth-Century Advertising and Mass Marketing from a British Perspective

Stefan Schwarzkopf

> "We were Britain's colony once, she will be our colony before she is done."
>
> Ludwell Denny (1930)[1]

Advertising and International History

The twentieth century was characterized by a breathtaking rise of new marketing and advertising techniques and an even more dramatic profusion of new media and material wealth. A large number of social, cultural and business historians have interpreted this success story of modern advertising and consumer culture as originating in the United States and from there "conquering" the rest of the world. The concept of Americanization, the triumphant spread of American products, movies and "consumerist" values, has been at the heart of these accounts. The idea of an all-pervasive Americanization has offered a seemingly self-evident narrative of twentieth-century global cultural convergence and influenced a multitude of accounts regarding British, French or German society. Recently, German historiography has resorted to the notion of Americanization and employed it as an analytic tool for the understanding of post-war German history.[2] English historiography, on the other hand, has experienced a boom of studies on the notions of

---

Notes for this section begin on page 58.

"Englishness" and "Britishness" and the role of collective identities in twentieth-century British social and political history. This, in turn, has triggered a similar interest in the cultural influence of the United States on twentieth-century British society.[3]

This chapter is concerned with the question of the influences of allegedly "American" advertising and mass marketing techniques on British consumer society in the early twentieth century. I will present a journey through a number of examples which show that twentieth-century European and, in particular, British consumer culture cannot be framed by vague allusions to Americanization. As an alternative to that perception, the idea of a long-term trans-Atlantic dialogue between the advertising and consumer worlds in America and Britain is introduced. In relation to this argument, I will show that the Americanization narrative underestimates the level of globalization which the advertising industry had reached well before World War II. This argument will be accompanied by a demonstration of the significance of the *politico-economic* Empire as a point of *cultural* reference for the British advertising industry and important corrective for the ability of American advertisers to expand into the British market.

A number of critical studies on the concept of Americanization as cultural imperialism have shown that this concept ignores that cultural transfers work differently from economic takeovers or the monopolization of markets.[4] Working on the notion of American cultural imperialism has made historians oblivious to the considerable amount of disagreement among different groups in non-American societies over the appropriate level of receptiveness shown toward US models of product marketing and consumer culture. Looking at the rise of modern product marketing from "below," from the perspective of advertisers and consumers—thus without immediately connecting this rise to meta-narratives of the "American century"—helps us gain an understanding for the interconnectedness of various developments in consumption, advertising, and product design on both sides of the Atlantic. Instead of reinforcing dichotomies of center and periphery, of the powerful and the powerless, my approach analyzes the ascent of modern forms of mass marketing not as the outcome of an "American Empire" spreading across territories and borders, but that of social interactions between economic competitors in spaces of commercial interaction which defy the political geographies of nation states.[5]

Twentieth-century British consumer culture for example saw a changing receptiveness for American products and American advertising sloganeering. The parameters for the change in the success of some campaigns in the United Kingdom were more often than not out of the reach of American salesmen and advertisers. The Americanization thesis fails to recognize the difficulties American agencies had in finding acceptance in the United Kingdom for their services and methods. The second part of the paper is devoted to a discussion of two advertising

Figure 1.1
In July 1910, the Lancaster Guardian points at the growing number of American business and sales people crossing the Atlantic by using a very common term: the "The American Invasion." (*Lancaster Guardian,* 30 July 1910. The British Newspaper Library, Colindale, London.)

agencies in the 1920s and 1930s: the expansion of the American advertising agency J. Walter Thompson to London in 1919 and that of the British agency W. S. Crawford's to Berlin in 1927. By juxtaposing the cases of two expanding advertising agencies, I will attempt to further undermine the thesis of an innate global "cultural imperialism" of the American advertising industry.

Arguments about the "American century" (Harold Evans, Oliver Zunz) and the global spread of American consumption habits and popular culture have often been linked to the growth of American advertising abroad. This chapter will build upon this narrative in a way that questions the idea of an American dominance over twentieth-century global convergence of consumer cultures. The consequences of this reassessment for the methodology of studying culture and international history can be far reaching. Rather than applying terms such as Americanization, I suggest that the study of twentieth-century consumer culture in terms of cultural transfer and globalization might provide us with a more complex and comprehensive grasp of all phenomena which accompany the expansion of consumer society since the eighteenth century.

International Relations and the Political Rhetoric of "Americanization"

Perceptions of the Americanization of British consumer culture were always related to contemporary politics in the United Kingdom as well as debates about the position of Britain within global political power structures. The political propaganda and sociocultural agendas behind notions of Americanization were at times very palpable, but also, in some cases, hidden. Cultural cross traffic between the United States and Britain has a long history dating back to the seventeenth century. Items such as food, the selling and merchandizing of agricultural produce and industrial goods, etc., played an important part in shaping these relationships.[6] For at least the last two centuries, managing and contesting the progress of American habits, management methods, foodstuffs, brands, etc., within British society has been part and parcel of Britain's attempt to define itself as a nation.

Around the turn of the last century, this British culture of self-observation changed into a siege mentality. Journalists and businessmen began to alert the British public to the menacing activities of American industries in Britain and the danger of British consumers being enslaved by the aggressive marketing of American products.[7] In his 1909 novel, *Tono Bungay*, H. G. Wells, for example, portrayed the remarkable rise and sudden fall of Edward Ponderevo, a small London patent medicine manufacturer. Ponderevo's dishonest methods of selling overprized, but "slightly injurious rubbish" through massive advertising are introduced to readers as an American invention. In *Tono Bungay*, focusing on the sales of pills rather than their product quality is accompanied by slogans such as "Not a drug, but a Live American Remedy."[8]

A few years earlier, this humorous literary representation of a hostile takeover of British marketing and product culture by American industries and their business methods became bitter reality for British tobacco manufacturers. In 1901, James Buchanan Duke's American Tobacco Co. began to embark on an "invasion" course in Britain by purchasing the Liverpool-based cigarette manufacturer Ogden's. This move sparked an unprecedented advertising war in the UK with British tobacco firms and American Tobacco stuck in a battle over promotional offers and price cuts. One advertisement in the ensuing struggle for dominance in the British cigarette market featured the slogan "Don't be gulled by Yankee Bluff. Support John Bull with every puff." The advertisement showed John Bull discharging his gun in the air at the American gull. Other advertisements showed Uncle Sam plunging a dagger into the back of John Bull. The same firm, Godfrey Phillips, devised an advertisement with the British lion crouching defensively over a display of the firm's "Guinea Gold Cigarettes" and snarling at a top-hatted and star-spangled octopus in the sea. In the background of the advertisement stood the Statue of Liberty with the word "TRUSTS" radiating across the sky. In November and December 1901, the London evening papers were abound with American advertisements trying to assure British smokers of the superior quality of imported cigarettes. British advertisements retaliated by reminding smokers of the thousands of British workers whose employment depended upon each and every purchase.[9]

In December 1901 the leading British firms reacted to the threat of the American Tobacco Company by forming a trade alliance, the Imperial Tobacco Co. In advertisements announcing the formation of Imperial Tobacco to the British public, the company again activated patriotic emotions and an anti-American rhetoric of foreign trusts and monopolies subjugating the free-born Englishman: "Americans, whose markets are closed by prohibitive tariffs against British goods, have declared their intention of monopolizing the tobacco trade of this country. It is for the British public to decide whether British labour, capital and trade are to be subordinate to the American system of Trust Monopoly and all that is implied therein."[10]

In 1902, the British journalist William Thomas Stead even prophesied the "Americanisation of the World."[11] His account still carried the optimism of the progressive nineteenth century with its belief in the positive outcomes of the free trade of goods and a free exchange of ideas. Some of his British contemporaries, however, framed their criticism of the United States in a cultural pessimism which bears the hallmark of the ensuing anti-American discourses of the twentieth century. In 1914, for example, the Cambridge professor G. Lowe Dickinson concluded his impressions about the United States in this way: "All America is Niagara. Force without direction, noise without significance, speed without accomplishment."[12]

Observations according to which the identity of the British people and their enlightened spirit were threatened by the rising influence of American mass culture were a common feature of twentieth-century British cultural and political discourse. Contemporaries of the inter-war period saw themselves beleaguered by attempts to infiltrate the minds of the British people. The cinema correspondent of the *Daily Express*, G. A. Atkinson, wrote in March 1927 about the London filmgoers: "the bulk of our picture-goers are Americanised.... They talk America, think America, and dream America; we have several million people, mostly women, who, to all intents and purposes, are temporary American citizens."[13] Only a few months after that scornful depreciation of American film culture in London, the English advertising man Frith Milward complained in Britain's most important advertising trade journal, the *Advertising World*, about "these awful, high-powered, Americanised super-salesmen, so prevalent today."[14] According to Milward, this new generation of salesmen tried to apply "American" advertising methods but eventually failed, as the British consumer wanted to *buy* goods rather than *be* sold.

Apart from British journalists and advertising men who mainly feared American professional and business competition, a fiercely anti-American attitude was also quite characteristic of the British literary intelligentsia and the political feature pages both in the inter-war period as well as in the post-war "age of affluence."[15] The anti-American impetus and bitter cynicism of Aldous Huxley's *Brave New World* is as well known and oft quoted as is the work of author J. B. Priestley. Priestley's inter-war and post-war stories are often centered around concerns of an uncritical takeover of the "American way of life" by the British.[16] His book *Journey Down the Rainbow*, a mix of social observations and travel impressions he and his wife collected in the United States in the mid 1950s, is a powerful intellectual attack on a seemingly shallow and materialistic way of life which was about to spread its tentacles to Europe, the and last refuge of culture and enlightenment. In his perception, the United States and all its entourage of advertising and mass marketing was the "Great Invader" which created an "admass" society wherever it was allowed to set its feet.[17]

Similarly, the British author George Orwell, known for his literary defenses of the individual against the mind-controlling super state, also saw the arrival of American advertising and consumer culture as the first step toward the final decline of human dignity. In his 1936 novel *Keep the Aspidistra Flying*, Orwell describes the emotional struggles of a young man, Gordon Comstock, stuck between the need to earn money as an advertising copywriter and his dreams of becoming an independent author. Eventually, Gordon returns to his job at the agency "New Albion" to feed his wife and newborn child. At the "New Albion" agency, Orwell's synonym for what he saw to be an Americanized and feminized new England, Gordon helps in marketing "The Queen of Sheba Toilette Requisites." His fellow employees are characterized by Gordon as "the hard-boiled, Americanised, go-getting type—the type to whom nothing in the world is sacred, except money."[18]

Thus, in the perception of the majority of British intellectuals in the twentieth century, "America" and its cultural policies and material values posed a threat to the balanced British way of life. After World War II, such anti-American cultural criticism was a phenomenon especially among the British left. The Labour Party activist and journalist Francis Williams, for example, warned of an "American Invasion" which endangered British culture and its sense of civilized restraint.[19]

Historical accounts of twentieth-century European-American encounters in areas such as media, culture, and commerce now tend to move away from the stark visions of an "invasion" and "takeover" expressed by contemporary observers until well into the 1960s. Instead, a number of international social, cultural, and business historical studies have stressed the limits of Americanization and focused on how American values and ideas were resisted and/or reworked within European contexts.[20] Historians such as Jonathan Zeitlin, Jessica C. E. Gienow-Hecht, Uta Poiger, Heide Fehrenbach, Reinhold Wagnleitner, Rob Kroes, and Richard Kuisel have also highlighted the significance of mediators in processes of cultural transfer.[21] By subscribing to the idea of a fragmented global cultural order with no discernible center, these studies have powerfully undermined the simplistic "sender—receiver" approach of the Americanization thesis. Instead, they offered a new frame for historians of twentieth-century European societies in terms of studying international cultural convergence and cultural transfers.

On the other hand, the standard account of the history of the advertising industry and mass marketing in Britain, but also countries such as Sweden, Finland, and West Germany, still portrays "American" advertising methods as dominant "new" inventions, as something outlandish and virulent that beset these countries like a virus. This narrative works on the idea of two waves of Americanization. A first wave in the 1920s and 1930s, with the first American advertising agencies arriving in Europe, carried the promises of American levels of productivity and consumerism. This wave then provided the ground for a second wave following in the post-war era, which eventually ensured the victory for American consumerist values embodied in a refrigerator and a car for every family. In this perspective, the "American dream" of consumerism appears to be a social ideology invented in the United States and subsequently exported in its entirety to Europe. Several influential studies on West-German advertising history,[22] Finish and Swedish consumer culture,[23] tourism and mass consumption of literature in France,[24] Italian advertising history,[25] and the history of mass marketing and retailing in Britain[26] work on this basic narrative of an "Americanized" European consumer culture.

Fallacies of the Americanization Thesis

Thus, a great number of studies into European consumer, marketing, and advertising cultures still follow the paradigm of

Americanization in the belief of merely describing and analyzing existing phenomena. Some of these oft-quoted "historical facts" are the advent of American advertising agencies in Western Europe in the early twentieth century or the arrival of icons of consumer culture after World War II, such as Coca Cola, comics, jeans, sunglasses, American car designs, or jazz and rock and roll. In this section of my essay I wish to question these positions; by doing so I will show that simply pointing at the arrival of American products or advertising methods in Europe is not sufficient to support the thesis of an "Americanized" consumer culture.

The misconceptions of the Americanization thesis are twofold. At first, using this paradigm necessarily essentializes notions of "America" and "culture." To argue in terms of "Americanization" entails the impression that nations, cultures, and societies are single, undisrupted entities—seemingly fixed items like parcels which can be ex- or imported in their entirety. In the case of Anglo-American cultural relations, however, eminent voices such as David Reynolds already reminded us to think twice about the application of such simplified models: "Americanization is a crude concept that glosses over the complexities of British society. Moreover, it conceals the fact that the United States was not as 'American' as movie-mad Britons imagined. We need to reflect on the Americanization of America as well."[27] Along these lines, Rob Kroes has demonstrated that notions of Americanization are blind to the fact that America itself is everything but a country characterized and glued together by a fixed set of habits or values.[28] On the contrary, American culture, like all other societies and cultures in history, is constantly reshaped, fragmented, torn apart, and rebuilt in the image of competing ideals and utopias. Moreover, the term Americanization itself eventually reduces historic actors and individuals to extreme positions: either they pose as dominating modernizers of mass culture and "Americanized" cultural values or as traditionalists protecting nations from imminent cultural colonization.

There are examples which throw a skeptical light on the assumption that European advertisers, marketing experts, and consumers represented just passive objects of an overwhelming process of Americanization. Most European advertisers showed a remarkable creativity in absorbing and emulating some of the marketing impulses coming from the United States, while at the same time rejecting others. In a number of essays, Frank

Mort, for example, has offered the example of the British manufacturer and retailer of suits and men's-wear Montague Burton.[29] Burton, the UK's market leader in men's wear between 1930 and the late 1950s, traveled the United States widely and studied American sales methods in detail. Nevertheless, he decided that a typical "British" habit of selling suits to male customers should be retained: although the suits were actually factory made, the individual customer at Montague Burton's was still measured with the whole ritual of an established, "old-fashioned" tailor. It was indeed this ability of mixing seemingly new "American" production, advertising, and retail methods with established British habits that gave Burton's its competitive advantage over American retailers in the UK for much of the early twentieth century. Thus, European retail, advertising, and marketing cultures negotiated American influences rather than simply subscribing to every bit coming from across the Atlantic.[30]

The second fallacy hidden in the "Americanization" thesis comes in the form of a deeply unhistoric argument. The vast majority of the accounts discussing trans-Atlantic influences on European consumer cultures see "Americanization" as a one-way transfer of cultural and economic habits and institutions with one starting point and one trajectory only. In this view, the starting point of the "Americanization" of European market cultures usually coincides with the decline of the European powers after 1914. Yet this view ignores a number of important questions, above all how modern advertising and mass marketing came to America in the first place. Quite often, the implicit assumption remains unquestioned that mass marketing as well as "modern" advertising and retailing methods were American inventions.

Yet virtually all modern advertising techniques were European inventions. The artistic advertising poster, for example, had its origins in the entertainment boom of Fin-de-Siècle Paris. Jules Chéret (1836–1932) and Henri de Toulouse-Lautrec (1864–1901) have been credited for the idea of developing the plain announcement poster into an art form with mass-selling appeal.[31] In the last decades of the nineteenth century, Europe's foremost advertising artists were using the poster to sell everything from bicycles, sterilized milk, books, dance performances, oral hygiene products, to French champagne, perfume, tobacco, and biscuits.[32] The genuinely transnational origins of poster advertising is reflected in the fact that the Frenchmen Chéret learned the craft of painting and poster lithography in England and first applied his skills in 1867 to advertise an American actress, Sarah Bernhardt.[33] Similarly, the illustrated advertising postcard was invented by Europeans. The first advertising postcard appeared in the United Kingdom in 1872. Later, Continental European design movements such as the Wiener Werkstätte further developed the modern style of the applied art of painting advertising postcards.[34]

Both artistic innovations, the advertising poster and postcards, eventually made their way into the marketing cultures of Europe and America in the late 1880s. Also, the early history of the advertising movie supports the idea of a parallel, transnational emergence of modern advertising media and marketing methods on both sides of the Atlantic. The first advertising films appeared at the same time in 1897–98 in Paris and New York.[35] Moreover, the department store is a nineteenth-century marketing and retailing novelty which is deeply rooted in European commercial cultures. Literary representations of the department store, like in Emile Zola's *Au Bonheur des Dames* (1883), were modeled after stores in Paris, London, Brussels, Milan, and Moscow, where the most interesting and most up-to-date department stores at that time were to be found. Historians such as Lisa Tiersten and Serge Jaumain have shown that the commercial space of the department store has been part and parcel of the urban, cosmopolitan cultural experience of European capitals since the mid-nineteenth century.[36] Thus, retail advertising—the proper marketing of a department store—was a craft the Americans learned from the European department stores, decades before Woolworth's and Macey's became the embodiment of typical "modern" retail empires.

The arrival of modern American department stores in the United Kingdom, such as the case of the American businessman Gordon Selfridge and his department store opening in London in 1909, could be seen as an example of successful "Americanization" of British consumer culture. Mica Nava and Erika Rappaport have suggested an alternative reading of these developments. Their research points at an emerging international and cross-Atlantic "cosmopolitan" modernity which was brought about by an expanding and more inclusive consumer and leisure life both in the United States and in Europe in the first decades of the twentieth century. Their investigation of the role of department stores like Selfridge's in the transformation of gender stereotypes again underpins the importance of studying the social processes of the acculturation of perceived "otherness." In a number of essays, Nava and Rappaport have shown that London's female shoppers around 1900 utilized the success of Selfridge's on Oxford Street for the sake of their own sociocultural agenda of extending social spaces available to and governed by women. Thus Selfridge's became part of an emerging mix of cosmopolitan values and habits rather than the driver of a flattening Americanization of British shopping and consumer cultures.[37]

This argument about the multifold sources of twentieth-century shopping and consumer modernity has recently been buttressed by Kristin Hoganson's essay about the uses of European products in late nineteenth-century American households.[38] Hoganson has shown how eagerly late nineteenth-century American middle-class women acquired a taste for furniture, carpets, and sofas coming from European interior designers and manufacturers in Paris and London. Hoganson's research also suggests that this development has to be understood as both a class and a gender statement as "modern" American middle-class women actively turned to European—instead of American—interior designs and products in kitchens and bathrooms. These developments were accompanied by critical voices warning that British products would eventually threaten the "Americanness" of female shoppers. Nineteenth-century American politicians, producers, and shopkeepers campaigned against the buying and selling of British products in the United States by pointing out that only American products were produced by free people and a free nation. British products, on the other hand, came under ethical suspicion of being produced under conditions of sweat labor in British colonies.[39]

Nava's, Rappaport's, and Hoganson's research does not seem to fit easily into a picture which presents "modern" consumer culture as an American invention exported to the rest of the world. Following David Reynolds' argument about the "Americanization of America," it has to be said again that US consumer culture itself is the product of strong European influences and inner-American discussions as to how much "consumerism" could be endured in the light of the ethical and political spirit of the founding fathers. For much of the nineteenth and early twentieth century, Europe (especially its capitals such as Paris, London, Berlin, and St. Petersburg) was the epitome of "crazy" and unethical consumerism, whereas America saw itself at the receiving—sometimes suffering—end of the crazes and stunts in European advertising and consumer life. European advertising art played an important role in this framework of American self-interpretations, which run counter to all simplistic narrations of Americanization.

One of these European advertising fashions, which swept the United States around 1900, was the Art Nouveau advertising poster. The most important cultural diplomat who helped establish this new detail of late nineteenth-century European consumer culture in the United States was Aubrey Beardsley (1872–98). The poster designs of this young London-based English artist became so fashionable in the US that he literally caused something of a poster craze. Throughout the United States, his posters were sold in galleries, at auctions, and in shops at the highest prices. Cases are reported where his posters and other Art Nouveau-style advertising posters—for books, magazines, music shows, operas, etc.—were stolen from billboards by American devotees of European advertising culture (see figures 1.2–3). Aubrey Beardsley, as well as the brothers-in-law William Nicholson (1872–1949) and James Pryde (1866–1941), known as the Beggarstaff brothers, were later emulated by Will Bradley (1868–1964), the "Paladin of Art Noveau in the United States."[40] American advertisers went into the new Beardsley poster style with such a vengeance that this Englishman can justifiably be identified as one of the most eminent "Americanizers" of America.[41] From the perspective of a global advertising and marketing history, which works on notions of multidimensional cultural transfer, Art Nouveau was the first completely international design style that "merchandized" artwork for the sake of profits and clearly began to think of advertising as a legitimate art form. The origin of this development which merged art and individual creativity with the techniques of modern mass marketing was the European metropolis: Paris, London, Berlin, and Vienna.

The 1920s and 1930s then saw the rise of Art Deco as a global design and consumer style, succeeding Art Nouveau and outmaneuvering the rather cold and intellectual Functionalism. Here again, a new style in producing interiors, fashion, and commodities ushered in a new generation of advertising designs and marketing ideas. As such, Art Deco was a European "invention" which was successfully sold to American consumers. When the organizers of the 1925 Paris "Exposition Internationale des Arts Décoratifs et Industriels Modernes," which gave Art Deco its name and kick-started Art Deco movements

Figures 1.2 and 1.3
Advertising Posters by Aubrey Beardsley. (Victoria and Albert Museum, London, Poster Collection.)

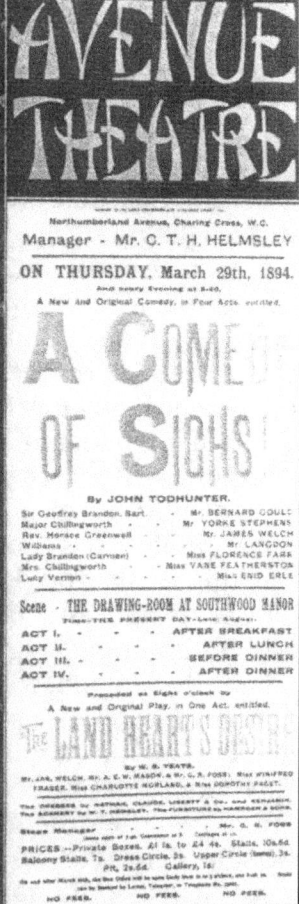

all over the world, asked American producers to take part in the exhibition, they received polite replies which pointed out that there was no modern design in the United States. After the exhibition however, American producers realized that there was an immense demand for European Art Deco designs on their home market. In the past, historians have tended to interpret the 1939 New York World's Fair, with its towering Art Deco exhibits, as the new beginning of an American century of unprecedented levels of designed and streamlined consumerism. In reality, the show was nothing more than the emulation of a European development which had started to "Europeanize" the United States some fourteen years earlier. Seen from the perspective of design history, it was in the 1930s only that the United States had been brought on a par with European cultures of commodity design and advertising style.[42]

"Britishing" US Consumer Culture

In the 1920s, British businesses began to "sell" the Empire and the Empire ideal to British consumers at home. One of the best-known cooperative institutions charged with the task to mould an Empire-conscious body of consumers in inter-war Britain was the Empire Marketing Board (1926–32).[43] At the same time, the British state began to see the projection of a positive image of Britain and the British Empire to consumers abroad as an important means to improve the competitiveness of British industries on international markets and, in particular, in the United States.[44] Inter-war American consumers were increasingly exposed to British trade propaganda and cooperative advertising for British products. In the search for a market position for British-made products, marketing experts within industry and state realized that the cultural and historical background of the British Empire provided a unique selling point with strong appeal for American consumers.

The Indian Tea Grower's Association was only one among a considerable number of such cooperative trade bodies poised to build up the sales of specific British and Empire produce. In 1923–24, the Association decided to spend more than one million dollars in a five-year advertising campaign which was to promote Indian tea and tea drinking in the United States. In January 1924, Charles Higham, the founder of the Charles F. Higham Advertising Agency Ltd., went on a three-week tour through the United States in order to inaugurate the campaign before American businessmen. Higham, as director of one of the most dynamic British advertising agencies in the inter-war years and certainly the most dazzling and colorful British advertising man at the time, spent twenty days in the United States and addressed over six thousand advertising men, newspaper publishers, tea importers, merchants, grocers, wholesalers, and department store managers and probably thousands of American radio listeners about the delights of tea drinking. In his own words, this campaign was "the entering of the wedge in a publicity drive on American markets on behalf of British industry throughout the Empire."[45]

In a remarkable tour de force, he gave addresses and radio talks on an almost daily basis and specifically picked out American retailers as a target audience. Amongst others, the Retail Grocers' Associations of Philadelphia, New York, and Boston and the Sales Managers of Austin & Nichols in New York were subjected to Higham's "Anglicizing" propaganda machinery.[46] Such cooperative British advertising efforts in the United States not only raised expectations of opening up new markets, but also of a "counter-invasion" of American popular culture by typically British products. The British marketing journal *Advertiser's Weekly* jubilantly reported Higham's claim that he had "instituted the four o'clock [sic] tea habit in American offices."[47] As evidence of the results his trade propaganda had yielded in the United States, Higham brought back a folder of some sixteen hundred press cuttings from US newspapers. In contrast to oft-reiterated clichés about 1920s America as heading a global "Fordist," streamlined consumer modernity, American middle-class consumers were delighted by what they saw as the classical Victorian tea ritual. As a result of the cooperative marketing efforts of the tea growers, American tea consumption increased by three million pounds in 1924 alone. In 1922, there were only as few as three hundred teashops in the principal cities of America; after Higham's tour, the number rose to over eight thousand by 1926.[48]

In the wake of this success of British marketing in the US, the cinema correspondent of the *Daily Express* suggested that the Empire could be sold to Americans via film. As he observed on his many trips to the United States, the American audience was indeed crazy about English movies, which were full of knights, castles, and old villages. He concluded in May 1927: "There is hardly anything in America for which Americans have such attachment as this sentimental aspect of the traditional connection with Britain. They may not have a drop of English blood in them.... But now that they are all rich enough to buy culture they will assuredly buy it from England. Every native-born American wants to visit Europe, and the first place in Europe that he wants to visit is England, so that he can see for himself all that he has read of, heard of, thought and dreamed. We can meet that ambition half-way by selling England to him on the screen."[49]

In the inter-war era, therefore, the British saw themselves in a position of being able to counter the American influence on an emerging global media, entertainment, and consumer culture. American consumers' craving for Anglo-Saxon history and "Englishness" provided a springboard for British attempts to regain lost markets in the United States. At the same time, however, state officials and representatives of the British movie industry watched with horror the rising impact of Hollywood movies on British consumers and moviegoers. After the proportion of British films shown in the United Kingdom had fallen from a level of 25 percent in 1914 to about 5 percent in 1926, a new Act of Parliament introduced a system of quotas. The 1927 Cinematograph Films Act introduced a quota of 5 percent of British films on cinema exhibitors, rising to 20 percent in 1935. The main protagonists of this law explained this move by pointing at the alleged cultural impact of American movies on British consumers and their tendency to favor American products. A higher ratio of English films was thought to ensure that British consumers would find British-made products—as featured in the movies—just as glamorous and attractive a choice.[50]

While British advertising agencies and other marketing specialists sold "Britain" and a fabricated picture of English traditionalism to Americans, car advertisements in the UK, drawn up by exactly the same agencies, used the "American theme" of modern, clean, streamlined, and functional designs: "American" meant the latest fashion and must-have in the 1920s (see figure 1.4). But by the late 1920s it became clear that successful sales campaigns for American cars in Britain had to strike a "British" chord or even conceal the American origins of the very cars they were selling.

At that time, more and more advertisements appeared in British newspapers and magazines which advocated the purchase of British cars and British products in general. These adverts promoted the idea that British consumers should con-

Figure 1.4
A typical advertisement for Chrysler cars in Britain by the British advertising agency of William S. Crawford (late 1920s). (Victoria and Albert Museum, London, Poster Collection.)

sciously choose British-made products to provide permanent employment for British workers. In the late 1920s and early 1930s, the Empire Marketing Board engaged in heavy national advertising campaigns such as the "Buy British" campaign and staged "Buy British" weeks in London and in other major cities of the Empire. In this climate, Charles Higham's advertisements for Dunlop tires produced in Birmingham began to feature the slogan, "As British as the flag!" (see figures 1.5–8). The American J. Walter Thompson advertising agency, operating in London since 1919, noticed this development quite early. In their house journal, the agency therefore published an article under the heading, "Outbritishing the Britisher," which explained that American cars had to be sold to the British under the disguise of "Britishness." J. Walter Thompson advised his American client General Motors to use lordships and retired brigadier generals as testimonials for the British campaign as well as giving some of the Buick models names such as "Empire" and "Regent."[51] This shift in attitudes during the late 1920s shows the difficulties which some American advertisers and merchants faced in finding acceptance in Britain. In a cultural climate of a continuously struggling British economy, Britain's advertisers began to draw on the cultural resource of "Britishness" and "Englishness" which acted as barriers to the success of American products in "Americanizing" British consumption habits.

The examples of inter-war tea and car advertising discussed here demonstrate how consumers on both sides of the Atlantic were actively using images and clichés of "Britishness" and "Americanness" in order to buy into certain lifestyles. British consumers in the inter-war years purchasing an American telephone, radio, or cigarette were offered the expression of aspirations to social and economic success. Similarly, American inter-war consumers were led to believe that the purchase of British shirts, cars, and cutlery expressed similar hopes of achievement and wealth. Recognizing this, the British advertising journal *Advertising World* explained to its readers in April 1924 that there was ample scope and opportunity especially for upmarket and traditional "homemade" British products on the US market:

> the demand for British-made branded products in the States is an increasing one. There are two principal reasons promoting this demand. One is that British goods are essentially quality goods, and the other that British goods are the 'vogue'. Among the articles particularly in demand at present are woolen wear, men's clothing, and certain foodstuffs, such as marmalade, which is regarded in America as a British institution.... An extraordinary instance of the demand for our goods in the U.S.A. is the case of Dunhill pipes. The amazing vogue for these pipes in America is solely due to the fact that the American looks upon the Englishman as one who knows and appreciates a good pipe. Lever Bros. (whose advertising appropriation is one of the largest in America) and Lipton's teas (the widest selling and best-known in the States) are other examples of the demand for our goods on the other side of the Atlantic.[52]

Figures 1.5–8
British inter-war advertising culture promotes "Britishness" and the Empire (1927–28).

Figure 1.5
The Times, 8 March 1928. (The British Newspaper Library, Colindale, London.)

Figure 1.6
The Times, 14 March 1928. (The British Newspaper Library, Colindale, London.)

Figure 1.7
Stamp issued by Royal Mail Ltd. (United Kingdom, September 2003.)

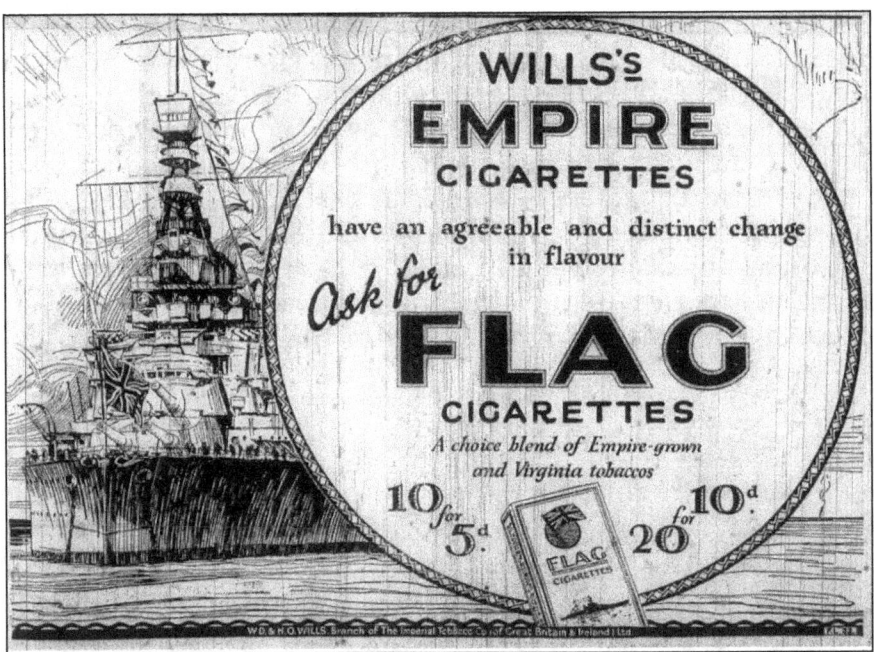

Figure 1.8
Daily Express, 22 March 1927. (The British Newspaper Library, Colindale, London.)

The example of British advertising agencies such as Charles F. Higham being active both at home and in the US suggests that a mutual dialogue between European and the American consumer culture characterized the twentieth century from the turn of the last century onward. It is this dialogue, rather than a simple "export-import" process, which accounts for the emergence of a global consumer culture well before the age of Microsoft, Levi's 501, and Nike. The reality of a transatlantic exchange of ideas as regards advertising and marketing is illustrated by a number of cases from the inter-war and post-war era. Advertising gurus of the 1950s, such as David Ogilvy and Ernest Dichter, are exemplary for the genuinely transnational and global origins of modern advertising. Both were probably the leading advertising thinkers of the post-war period and, more importantly, both were Europeans.

David Ogilvy's name is connected to the concept of the brand image, which is part and parcel of today's culture of Western mass marketing. Ogilvy introduced the idea that brands, such as Schweppes, Rolls-Royce, or Hathaway Shirts, are personalities with an individual character and so should be linked to a face, a human being, or a striking character in order to make the brand itself recognizable and distinguishable from its competitors. It was the idea of the brand image which gave birth to so many of the typical post-war advertising characters, which turned some American products into icons of an allegedly "Americanized" consumer culture, such as the Marlboro Cowboy or the Shell Tiger.[53] Even though Ogilvy made his name in America, he took his first steps at the London advertising agency Mather & Crowther in the 1930s after he had

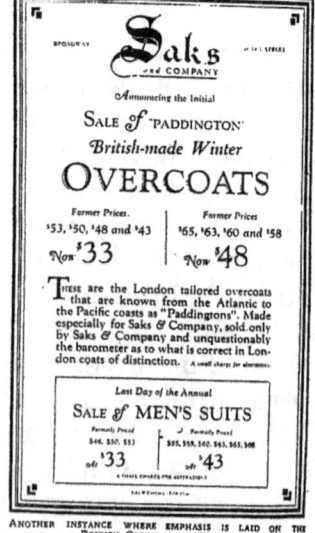

Figure 1.9

The *Advertising World* explains how to increase the sales power of British advertising in the US (1924). (*Advertising World*, April 1924, Overseas Marketing Supplement. The British Newspaper Library, Colindale, London.)

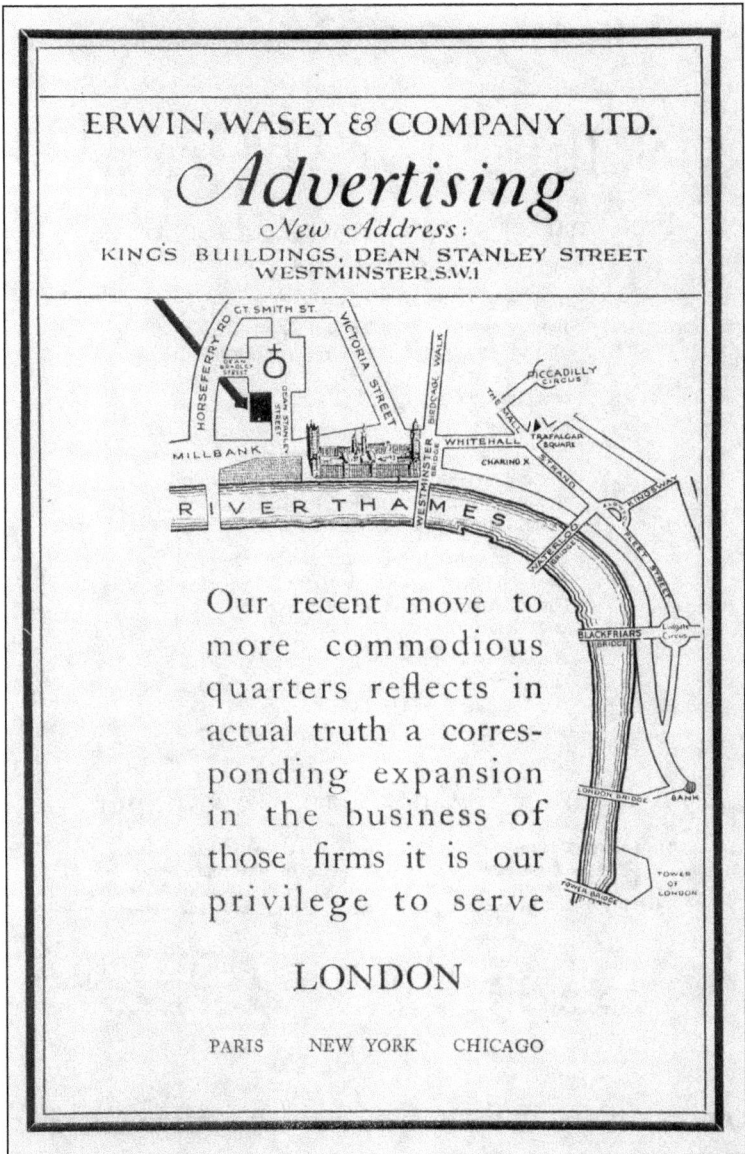

Figure 1.10
American media and agencies advertise in London, 1924. (*Advertising World*, June 1924. The British Newspaper Library, Colindale, London).

worked for years as a salesman in Britain. It was the British advertising executives at Mather & Crowther who first sent Ogilvy to the United States in 1938. Upon his return, Ogilvy challenged some of the old approaches of the agency in London.[54] After the war, during which he served as Embassy secretary in Washing-

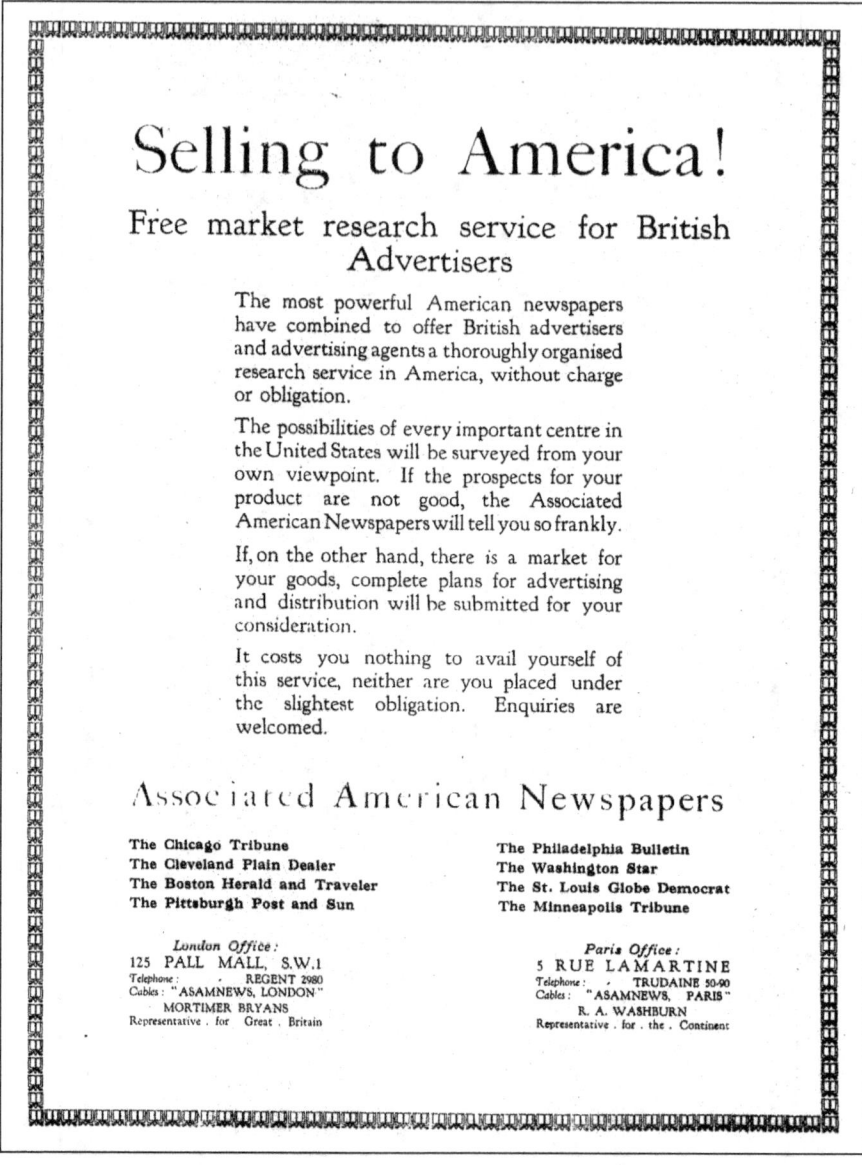

Figure 1.11
American media and agencies advertise in London, 1924. (*Advertising World*, March 1924. The British Newspaper Library, Colindale, London).

ton, DC, the large British advertising agency S. H. Benson Ltd. contributed forty-five thousand dollars to help Ogilvy in setting up his own agency in New York: Hewitt, Ogilvy, Benson & Mather, which later became Ogilvy & Mather.[55] The fact that the marketing idea and creative value of the brand image sprung from a British head underlines the necessity for historians of modern consumer culture to take into account the real existence of a transcultural framework within which advertisers acted since about 1900, rather than artificial ideas of societies and nations as secluded entities.

The legacy of Ernest Dichter, in turn, consists of his research into the sometimes hidden motives that drive people to desire or reject certain products. Dichter had studied psychology and sociology with Charlotte Bühler and Paul Lazarsfeld in Vienna before 1938. In the 1950s, he pioneered motivational studies in market research and the use of psychoanalysis and depth interviews for the sake of defining selling points for products such as cars, chocolate, or detergent powder. In the wake of Vance Packard's bitter criticism of Dichter's consumer research, historians have interpreted the application of psychoanalytical models and the search for hidden emotions behind consumer behavior as one of the typically "American" novelties in postwar European consumerism.[56] Dichter, however, was an Austrian immigrant who fled the Nazis first to New York. His theoretical work at the Institute of Motivational Research in Croton-on-Hudson combined the traditions of European dynamic psychology and psychoanalysis with the requirements and questions of a developed Western consumer society such as the United States. Even though both Ogilvy and Dichter worked in the United States, there is nothing specifically "American" about their ideas on advertising practices as both successfully merged their European heritage with the new challenges of a global market for advertising services.[57]

J. Walter Thompson in London and Crawford's in Berlin—Or Again: What Is "Americanization"?

The arrival of American advertising agencies in Europe has often been applied by historians as a measuring device for the level of "Americanization" of consumer societies. In some interpretations, as we have seen, these agencies feature as the main drivers of Americanization. Since the British advertising scene proved to be more resistant to their American competitors,[58] the German advertising market is one of the favorite examples cited by the advocates of the Americanization thesis. Harm Schroeter for example has argued that the move of the J. Walter Thompson agency and the Erwin, Wasey & Co. advertising agency to West Germany in the 1950s is sufficient evidence to describe Germany's post-war advertising industry as essentially Americanized. More recently, Alexander Schug has followed this argumentation and studied the Americanization of the German advertising market in the inter-war years.[59] Case studies on the expansion of American advertising agencies to Europe and Great Britain already exist in sufficient number to allow an assessment of different views and opinions about the alleged Americanizing impact of these ventures.[60] Below, I concentrate on the case of the J. Walter Thompson agency in London and juxtapose this example with the case of the expansion of the British W. S. Crawford advertising agency to the European continent in the inter-war years.

The activities of American advertising agents in London began in the late nineteenth century. The first American advertisement offices, as representatives of American newspapers, appeared in London in the 1870s and 1880s. One of the first American advertising agents was Paul E. Derrick, who moved to London in 1896. In 1905, the American agency Dorland opened its offices in London. In 1919, J. Walter Thompson and Erwin, Wasey & Co. did the same. In 1922, Lord & Thomas and McCann-Erickson became the next American multinational advertising agencies to move their offices to London.[61] After his arrival, Paul E. Derrick became fully involved in British advertising affairs and was perceived as a British rather than a specifically "American" advertising agent. In the First World War, he supported the British government with their propaganda efforts and the drafting of poster designs. In the 1930s, Derrick's agency merged with the British Crawford agency. Dorland London, in turn, was sold to the managing director George Kettle, an Englishman from Liverpool, in 1917 and, thus, became a British advertising agency.[62]

All other American agencies arriving in Britain followed the expansion of their American clients who demanded advertising services in the United Kingdom and on the European continent. By opening offices in London and subsequently in Paris, Brussels, or Berlin, American agencies were able to deliver better services to their major clients. Those of the larger British agencies that wanted to follow this example simply formed joint ventures with American agencies. Charles Higham's agency, for example, formed such an association with the Chicago-based William H. Rankin agency. Under this agreement, Higham handled the accounts of Rankin's American clients in the United

Kingdom and Europe, whereas Rankin delivered advertising services to Higham's British clients in the United States. Another British advertising agency that moved into international markets in the inter-war years was W. S. Crawford's. Crawford's agency network began to open offices in Europe, South America, and the Commonwealth and handled accounts for both British and American clients. It is worth pointing out again that only four American advertising agencies entered the British market in the inter-war years. Other American competitors were either bought up by the British or became involved in joint ventures and business associations. Moreover, the largest British agencies, such as S. H. Benson, the London Press Exchange, W. S. Crawford, Mather & Crowther, and others, proved to be powerful and prosperous enough to compete with the American newcomers.

Until well into the 1930s, American agencies in London relied on a very small number of American clients that provided the mainstay of turnover needed to run a profitable business.[63] While large British agencies in London usually counted several hundreds of employees, J. Walter Thompson's London office staff at Bush House remained limited to fourteen between 1919 and the mid-1920s. In 1926 and 1927 only, major new British and American accounts were gained and the London office of JWT expanded considerably as new clients such as Pond's, Horlicks, Lux, and General Motors were picked up. For advertising services on the European continent, JWT often relied on affiliated British, German, French, and Belgian agencies.[64] It was only the enormous advertising expenditure of General Motors which allowed JWT to open several company-owned offices on the European continent. The advertising contract which enabled JWT to embark on this expansion stated that JWT would agree to open an office in every country where General Motors had an assembly plant or distributor. In return, General Motors would place all its US and international advertising with JWT.[65] Between 1927 and 1929, JWT opened ten offices in Europe (Paris, Berlin, Stockholm, Madrid, etc.) and one in Egypt (Alexandria), while another eleven offices were opened in South Africa, India, Australia, the East Indies, Canada, New Zealand, and South America.[66]

The London office played a major role in orchestrating the expansion of JWT to Europe. Rather than planning the "Americanization of the world" from the American headquarters in New York, it was the London office which organized JWT's

European advertising expansion. Douglas West's research on the JWT office in London has shown that most of the advertising for General Motors was planned and written in London and then translated by Continental and overseas offices in the respective home markets. London also served as the training center for American and Continental staff who were to work on the account in the overseas offices. Moreover, the London office, and likewise the Continental and overseas offices, were staffed by "locals," not Americans. By 1933, only three non-senior staff members of JWT's London office were American.[67] In 1929, JWT London hired a British Director, the Cambridge graduate Douglas Saunders and in 1946, the London office had an all-British top management team.[68] Thus, the local knowledge of "native" business and advertising people was seen as crucial by J. Walter Thompson's New York headquarters. This serves as a reminder to take modes of autonomy and the independence of JWT's worldwide offices into account when studying the expansion of American advertising.

Early on, JWT London recognized the need to adapt their advertising messages to local and national conditions in order to ensure the success of the campaigns. Not only did the London office realize that "Britishers" demanded at least a British-looking advertising symbol when considering an automobile purchase, but the director of JWT's Berlin office, Clement Watson, too, reminded his international colleagues to pay attention to the local side of global trade when he remarked in 1928 that "markets are people—not places."[69] Rather than dominating international consumer cultures from their New York headquarters, J. Walter Thompson at times even struggled to "blend in" with British consumer culture. On various occasions between the early 1930s and the late 1960s, JWT London failed to win over British and international advertising clients due to the fact that it was seen as "too American" or "too global" and not enough in tune with "local" British consumer tastes. These problems increased in particular after the economic crisis in 1930–31, when both Guinness ("Guinness is good for you") and the British Beer Brewers Association ("Beer is best") told JWT that it could not compete for their multi-million pound advertising accounts on the grounds of it being part of an American advertising corporation. Senior British staff at the JWT offices at Bush House were told that any advertising money spent through JWT would eventually end up in American hands. Eventually, JWT was told, this could put the reputation

Figures 1.12–1.14
J. Walter Thompson offices in Europe and Egypt in 1927–28. (The *J. Walter Thompson News Bulletin* 123, March 1928. The British Library, London.)

of the beer brewers at risk. JWT encountered similar precautions even with American multinational manufacturers of consumer durables such as Kodak and Ford. Both companies ran a policy of leaving their local European subsidiaries free to determine the advertising strategies. The heads of the British subsidiaries of both companies decided in 1937 and in 1961, respectively, that large British advertising agencies could deliver similar services at a lower price and were better adjusted to the specific necessities of the British market. JWT went to great lengths to "prove" its "Britishness" to the outside world, for example by handing over the financial ownership of its London subsidiary to local senior members of staff and therefore avoiding any official financial connection to the JWT headquarters in New York appearing on paper. In 1933, JWT revamped its market research department and its new head John Rodgers specifically advised his seniors to call the new organization the *British* Market Research Bureau (BMRB). Along the same lines, JWT connected its name with various charitable causes in London and gave considerable financial support to St. Paul's Cathedral and various art galleries in order to create a sense of "connectedness" to British culture and the British way of life.[70]

Another example that allows us to look at global consumer cultures in the early twentieth century from a different angle is the case of the British advertising agency W. S. Crawford. Crawford's, one of the largest British advertising agencies throughout the first half of the twentieth century, handled Chrysler advertising in Britain and Europe since 1925. Following the same business policy as General Motors—that of having an advertising agency in all countries where production plants were built—Chrysler encouraged Crawford's to move to Berlin in May 1927. From London and Berlin, Crawford managed the advertising account of Chrysler for countries like Germany, the Netherlands, Austria, the Czech Republic, Slovakia, Poland, Yugoslavia, Greece, Belgium, Sweden, Denmark, etc.[71]

In May 1927, Crawford's opened an office in Berlin's Kraussenstraße. The staff consisted of four German and two British advertising men. The office was led by the Englishman Herbert Broadley, who formerly worked in the British government as Secretary to the Imperial Economic Committee. In October 1928, Crawford's moved to Potsdamer Straße with a staff of forty designers, researchers, accountants, and secretaries. Just before the stock markets crashed, Crawford's employed sixty-

Figure 1.15
Crawford's German poster, "Hut ab vor dem neuen Chrysler," 1929. (Printed by Crawford's Berlin, 1929. The Wolfsonian, FIU 87.1126.4.1)

seven people in its Berlin office alone. In 1928, it opened an office in Paris, from where it handled Chrysler advertising for France, Belgium, Spain, Italy, and other South European countries. In Berlin, Crawford worked closely with the powerful German Ullstein Presse and was invited to handle the sales of advertising space in all Ullstein publications on behalf of the German company.[72]

In 1930, following the collapse of the international stock markets, both the French and the German offices of Crawford's were heavily reduced. In order to keep the advertising work at the Berlin office profitable, Crawford started a joint venture with the German office of Dorland in Berlin. J. Walter Thompson encountered the same fate due to falling automobile sales in the wake of the depression after 1930. By 1935, half of the new JWT overseas offices had been closed. Thus, even though the ability of British agencies to expand was limited in comparison to their American competitors, the mechanisms of expanding and contracting advertising business were the same for both JWT and Crawford's. Both advertising agencies were more or less pushed into the European expansion in order to retain their clients—American automobile manufacturers. Both agencies retreated from their expansion as soon as their major clients (General Motors and Chrysler, respec-

Figures 1.16 and 1.17
Crawford advertisement (above) in *Gebrauchsgraphik*, a German advertising journal, 1928. (Printed by Crawford's Berlin, 1929. The Wolfsonian, FIU 87.1126.4.1) The advertisement at right is from 1937.

tively) closed down factories and construction plants on the Continent and overseas.

Thus, by the late 1920s, the market for advertising services had been effectively globalized: American as well as British agencies worked side by side and competed for the same advertising clients. Until at least the late 1950s, British agencies enjoyed a competitive advantage over American agencies in the UK market due to their ability to exploit the idea of "British culture," which acted as a powerful barrier to the growth of American agencies in the UK. The impression of a transatlantic service advertising environment emerging in these years is supported by the fact that both the British as well as the American advertising world benefited from a unique cross fertilization of market cultures and individual biographies. While the British Unilever company employed J. Walter Thompson, an American agency, to cover the global market, including its British homeland, an American company such as Chrysler employed a British agency. This British agency, W. S. Crawford, in turn employed amongst others an advertising artist, Ashley Havinden (1903–73), who, together with the agency director William Crawford, focused the creative output of the agency explicitly on modernist German and French designs. Havinden found support among both British and American advertising clients in the United Kingdom, who also offered a great deal of patronage to another modernist advertising designer of that time, Edward McKnight Kauffer (1891–68). Kauffer, in turn, was an American designer who spent most of his professional life in London after having learned his craft in France. Kauffer helped to create a peculiarly British style of modernist poster advertising in the 1920s and 1930s. His clients were both British advertisers, such as the London Underground and a number of railway companies, as well as international industrial conglomerates, such as Shell.[73]

Taking the case of internationally expanding British advertising agencies such as Dorland and Crawford's into consideration, the simple idea of an Americanization of European advertising in the inter-war years does not seem to suggest itself that easily.[74] What becomes apparent in these examples is that the Americanization thesis somehow misses the full grasp of the logic of the market conditions in the early twentieth century and the change of global markets in that era. The case of the British advertising agency Crawford's demonstrates that the change of global markets and the spending power of the

German consumer in the 1920s made it attractive for large advertising agencies to move their offices to Berlin. Thus, it was the changing character of the global economy in the 1920s which provided for the existence of American, but also British and French advertising agencies in Berlin, London, Amsterdam, and Paris. The Americanization thesis puts this logic in reverse and explains the change in the German, French, and English markets by the "advent of American marketing methods." Instead of an Americanization, the European national markets underwent a profound globalization and internationalization of their product and consumer culture in the first decades of the twentieth century.

Cultural Mediation and Asymmetry: Advertising as Global Culture

This study has been driven by the argument that modern mass marketing advertising was not an "idea" or an "ideology" which originated in the United States and then spread across the world via means of cultural domination or hegemony. The dynamics of change within the world of advertising and mass marketing affected the United States as much as it affected those European countries which saw themselves as victims of Americanization. The processes of appropriation and redefinition of American advertising in the United Kingdom were preceded by forms of "Europeanization" of the American market and commodity culture before World War I. After World War I, cross-Atlantic cultural and economic transfer in the area of advertising and mass marketing further intensified. This process, in turn, led to the emergence of a globalized advertising service market well before World War II. The complexity of interchange within this global market therefore evades cultural Americanization as an explanatory concept. Rather, advertising since the 1890s can, itself, be interpreted as a form of global culture. As such, advertising since that time has become what Uta Poiger referred to as a "site" in the formation of international relations as well as a cultural force that is constantly being renegotiated in the context of uneven power relations.[75] Moreover, at least until World War II the British Empire served as an important springboard for the internationalization of British advertising services, which often preceded that of the

American agency networks. Despite anxieties about the "Americanization" of Britain expressed by British cultural commentators, America did not play the most important role in shaping early twentieth-century British advertising.

I argue that the modernization of advertising and mass marketing in the United Kingdom in the early twentieth century was fed by a multitude of sources. As genuinely British and Continental European institutions and innovations merged with American influences, American advertising became selectively appropriated and redefined in the European context. The case study of American advertising agencies expanding to the United Kingdom points toward the significance of social agents in this process of cultural transfer. Advertising practitioners, as cultural intermediaries, are often determining the fate as well as contesting the meaning of new, seemingly dominant styles and artifacts entering other social and cultural spaces. In the case of American products and marketing styles in the United Kingdom, an artifact such as an American automobile could then—depending on the economic, political, or cultural angle of the contemporary cultural mediator—be interpreted as a foreign, American competitor to British-made automobiles or a globally acceptable engineering success that simply needed to be appropriated to different target cultures of consumers.[76]

The global growth of British and American advertising agencies also suggests an asymmetry between the history of states on the one side and the sphere of culture and economy on the other.[77] Thus, if historians are to follow their interest in transatlantic cultural and market relations, they cannot necessarily rely on paradigms and narratives provided by diplomacy-centered approaches to international history. The study of the emergence of global mass marketing proposed here also indicates the fruitfulness of further comparative studies into the circumstances and the uniqueness of appropriations of American advertising styles within different European societies throughout the twentieth century. In this respect, the narrative offered in this chapter cries out for more study of advertising and marketing networks emerging at a global level in the early twentieth century as well as further research into the global entanglement of product manufacturers, brands, consumers, and international advertising agencies such as J. Walter Thompson, Dorland, or W. S. Crawford before the 1950s.

Notes

I would like to thank Johannah Latchem of Goldsmiths College, Peter Clark of Queen Mary College, and Frank Trentmann of Birkbeck College (all London) for their help and criticism.

1. Ludwell Denny, *America Conquers Britain: A Record of Economic War* (New York: Alfred Knopf, 1930). Quoted in John E. Moser, *Twisting the Lion's Tail: American Anglophobia between the World Wars* (Basingstoke: Macmillan, 1998).
2. See, e.g., Volker Berghahn, *The Americanization of West German Industry, 1945–1973* (Leamington Spa: Berg, 1986); Michael Ermarth, ed., *America and the Shaping of German Society, 1945–1955* (Oxford: Berg, 1993); Alf Luedtke, Inge Marssolek, Adelheid von Saldern, eds., *Amerikanisierung: Traum und Alptraum im Deutschland des 20. Jahrhunderts* (Stuttgart: Steiner, 1996); Konrad Jarausch and Hannes Siegrist, eds., *Amerikanisierung und Sowjetisierung in Deutschland, 1945–1970* (Frankfurt: Campus, 1997); Anselm Doering-Manteuffel, *Wie westlich sind die Deutschen? Amerikanisierung und Westernisierung im 20. Jahrhundert* (Göttingen: Vandenhoeck & Ruprecht, 1999); Philipp Gassert, "Amerikanismus, Antiamerikanismus, Amerikanisierung: Neue Literatur zur Sozial-, Wirtschafts- und Kulturgeschichte des amerikanischen Einflusses in Deutschland und Europa," *Archiv für Sozialgeschichte* 39 (1999), 531–61. See also the wide-ranging case study by Christian Kleinschmidt, *Der produktive Blick: Wahrnehmung amerikanischer und japanischer Management- und Produktionsmethoden durch deutsche Unternehmer 1950–1985* (Berlin: Akademie Verlag, 2001), and more recently Egbert Klautke, *Unbegrenzte Möglichkeiten: "Amerikanisierung" in Deutscland und Frankreich, 1900–1933* (Stuttgart: Steiner, 2003); Susanne Hilger, *"Amerikanisierung" deutscher Unternehmen: Wettbewerbsstrategien und Unternehmenspolitik bei Henkel, Siemens und Daimler-Benz, 1945/49–1975* (Stuttgart: Steiner, 2004); Alexander Stephan, ed., *Americanization and Anti-Americanism: The German Encounter with American Culture after 1945* (New York and Oxford: Berghahn Books, 2004).
3. Richard Weight, *Patriots: National Identity in Britain, 1940–2000* (Basingstoke: Macmillan, 2002); Krishan Kumar, *The Making of the English National Identity* (Cambridge: Cambridge University Press, 2003); Robert Colls, *The Identity of England* (Oxford: Oxford University Press, 2002); Philip Dodd, Robert Colls, eds., *Englishness: Politics and Culture, 1880–1920* (London: Croom Helm, 1986); Philip Dodd, *The Battle over Britain* (London: Demos, 1996); Stephen Caunce et al., eds., *Relocating Britishness* (Manchester: Manchester University Press, 2004); Allan Ward, *Britishness since 1870* (London: Routledge, 2004); Wendy Webster, *Englishness and Empire, 1939–1965* (Oxford: Oxford University Press, 2005).
4. John Tomlinson, *Cultural Imperialism: A Critical Introduction* (London: Continuum, 1991).
5. For the analysis of networks and spaces of social interaction as opposed to closed nation states, see John W. Burton, *World Society* (Cambridge: Cambridge University Press, 1972); Manuel Castells, "Materials for an Exploratory Theory of the Network Society," *British Journal of Sociology* 51 (2000): 5–24.
6. T. H. Breen, *The Marketplace of Revolution: How Consumer Politics Shaped American Independence* (Oxford: Oxford University Press, 2004).

7. Fred A. McKenzie, *The American Invaders: Their Plans, Tactics and Progress* (London: Grant Richards, 1902).
8. H. G. Wells, *Tono Bungay,* (London: Macmillan, [1909] 1953), 136, 208.
9. "The real British Bulldog, not the sham!," *Daily Mail,* 19 December 1901, 8; "Who said 'Gull'?," *Daily Mail,* 30 November 1901, 8; see also Player's Cigarettes calling on "British Patriots" to smoke Players, *Daily Mail,* 1 November 1901, 8. For a more detailed analysis, see Stefan Schwarzkopf, "From Barnum to 'Organization Man': Images of 'America' in the British Advertising Discourse, 1850s–1950s," in *America in the British Imagination,* ed. Catherine Armstrong (Cambridge: Cambridge Scholar Press, 2007), pp. 132–52.
10. *The Times,* 2 December 1901, 12.
11. William Thomas Stead, *The Americanisation of the World, or the Trend of the Twentieth Century* (London: H. Markley, 1902). See also John Franklin Carter, *Conquest: America's Painless Imperialism* (New York: Harcourt, Brace, 1928), and Albert Weisbord, *The Conquest of Power: Liberalism, Anarchism, Syndicalism, Socialism, Fascism and Communism* (London: M. Secker & Warburg, 1938), which both studied the spread of American political and economic power in inter-war Europe.
12. G. Lowes Dickinson, *Appearances: Being Notes of Travel* (London: J. M. Dent & Sons, 1914), 160.
13. *Daily Express,* 3 March 1927, 6.
14. Frith Milward, "Those Awful Supersalesmen," *Advertising World* 52, 3 (July 1927): 428.
15. As an overview to the British debates about the detrimental impact of "America" on British "culture" see Dominic Strinati, "The Taste of America: Americanization and Popular Culture in Britain," in *Come on Down? Popular Media Culture in Post-war Britain,* eds. Dominic Strinati and Stephen Wagg (London: Routledge, 1992), 46–81, and George H. Knoles, *The Jazz Age Revisited: British Criticism of American Civilization during the 1920s* (Oxford: Oxford University Press, 1955).
16. Aldous Huxley, *Brave New World* (London: Chatto & Windus, 1932); J. B. Priestley, *English Journey* (London: Victor Gollancz, 1934).
17. J. B. Priestly and Jacqueta Hawkes, *Journey Down the Rainbow* (London: Heinemann-Cresset, 1957), 43–44.
18. George Orwell, *Keep the Aspidistra Flying* (London: Victor Gollancz, 1936), 66.
19. See, e.g., Francis Williams, *The American Invasion* (London: Anthony Blond, 1962); and James McMillan and Bernard Harris, *The American Take-Over of Britain* (London: Frewin, 1968).
20. Jessica C. E. Gienow-Hecht, "Shame on US? Academics, Cultural Transfer and the Cold War—A Critical Review," *Diplomatic History* 24, 3 (Summer 2000): 465–93; and Jonathan Zeitlin, "Introduction: Americanization and its Limits: Reworking US Technology and Management in Post-war Europe and Japan," in *Americanization and Its Limits: Reworking US Technology and Management in Post-war Europe and Japan,* eds. Jonathan Zeitlin and Gary Herrigel (Oxford: Oxford University Press, 2000), 1–50; as well as the excellent discussion of how labels such as "modern," "American," and "French" were negotiated in inter-war France in Stephen Harp, *Marketing Michelin: Advertising and Cultural Identity in Twentieth-Century France* (Baltimore: John Hopkins University Press, 2000), 187–224.

21. See Heide Fehrenbach, Uta G. Poiger, eds., *Transactions, Transgressions, Transformations: American Culture in Western Europe and Japan* (New York and Oxford: Berghahn Books, 1999), which points out the way for de-essentializing notions of "American" and "the Native." This is more concentrated in Poiger, "Beyond 'Modernization' and 'Colonization,'" *Diplomatic History* 23, 1 (Spring 1999): 45–56. See Rob Kroes, "American Empire and Cultural Imperialism: A View from the Receiving End," *Diplomatic History* 23, 3 (Fall 1999): 463–77; Kroes, "Among the Receivers: American Culture Transmitted Abroad," *European Contributions to American Studies* 22 (1991): 1–10; Kroes, "The Reception of American Films in the Netherlands: The Interwar Years," *American Studies International* 28, 2 (1990): 37–51; Richard Kuisel, "'Americanization' for Historians," *Diplomatic History* 24, 3 (Fall 2000): 509–15. Useful critical introductions to the field are to be found in Luisa Passerini, ed., *Across the Atlantic: Cultural Exchanges between Europe and the United States* (New York: Campus, 2000); Neill Cambell et al., eds., *Issues in Americanization and Culture* (Edinburgh: Edinburgh University Press, 2004); Robert Rydell and Rob Kroes, *Buffalo Bill in Bologna: The Americanization of the World, 1869–1922* (Chicago: Chicago University Press, 2005).
22. Harm Schroeter, "Die Amerikanisierung der Werbung in der Bundesrepublik Deutschland," *Jahrbuch für Wirtschaftsgeschichte* (1997): 93–115; Alexander Schug, "Wegbereiter der modernen Absatzwerbung in Deutschland: Advertising Agencies und die Amerikanisierung der deutschen Werbebranche in der Zwischenkriegszeit," *Werkstatt Geschichte* 12, 1 (2003): 29–52; David F. Crew, "Gender, Media and Consumerism in Germany, 1920s–1950s," *Journal of Social History* 32, 2 (1998), 395–402; Berghahn, *Americanization*. See also the more general argument in Harm Schroeter and Eli Moen, "Americanization as a Concept for a Deeper Understanding of Economic Changes, 1945–1970," *Entreprise et Histoire* 19 (1998): 5–13.
23. Visa Heinonen, "Professionalisation and Institutionalisation of the Finnish Advertising Business," in *Business and Society: Entrepreneurs, Politics and Networks in a Historical Perspective,* eds. Anne Marie Kuijlaars, Kim Prudon, and Joop Visser (Rotterdam: Center of Business History, 2000), 361–70; Visa Heinonen and Mika Pantzar, "Little America: the Modernization of the Finnish Consumer Society in the 1950s and 1960s," in *Americanisation in Twentieth-Century Europe: Business, Culture, Politics,* eds. Matthias Kipping and Nick Tiratsoo (Lille: Centre de Recherche sur l'Histoire de l'Europe du Nord-Ouest, 2002); Visa Heinonen, "Mainonnan amerikkalaiset juuret ja muita naekoekulmia mainonnan historiaan" [The American Roots of Advertising and Other Viewpoints to the History of Advertising], *Kansantaloudellinen aikakauskirja* [The Finnish Economic Journal] 2 (1999): 373–84.
24. Christopher Endy, "Travel and World Power: Americans in Europe, 1890–1917," *Diplomatic History* 22 (Fall 1998): 565–94; Brian McKenzie, *Remaking France: Americanization, Public Diplomacy, and the Marshall Plan* (New York and Oxford: Berghahn Books, 2005); Ellen Furlough, "Selling the American Way in Inter-war France: Prix Uniques and the Salon des Arts Ménagers," *Journal of Social History* 26 (1993): 491–519; Richard Kuisel, "Learning to Love McDonald's, Coca-Cola and Disneyland Paris," *Tocqueville Review* 21, 2 (2000): 129–49; Richard F. Kuisel, "Coca-Cola and the Cold War: The French Face of Americanization, 1948–1953," *French Historical Studies* 17, 1 (1991): 96–116; and Richard Kuisel, *Seducing the*

French: The Dilemma of Americanization (Berkeley: University of California Press, 1993). Kuisel refuses to subscribe to simplified views of Coca-Cola completely "Americanizing" France, yet "Americanization" remains the operative concept in his accounts.

25. Adam Arvidsson, "Between Fascism and the American Dream: Advertising in Inter-war Italy," *Social Science History* 25, 2 (Summer 2001): 151–86; Adam Arvidsson, "The Therapy of Consumption: Motivation Research and the New Italian Housewife, 1958–62," *Journal of Material Culture* 5, 3 (2000): 251–74; Arvidsson, *Marketing Modernity: Italian Advertising from Fascism to Postmodernity* (London: Routledge, 2003), 44–63; Victoria de Grazia, *Irresistible Empire: America's Advance through 20th-Century Europe* (Cambridge, MA: Belknap, 2005), has a lot of material on the case of Italy.

26. Gareth Shaw, Andrew Alexander, Louise Curth, "Selling Self-service and the Supermarket: The Americanisation of Food Retailing in Britain, 1945–60," *Business History* 46, 4 (October 2004): 568–82.

27. David Reynolds, *Rich Relations: The American Occupation of Britain, 1942–1945* (London: Harper Collins, 1996), 431.

28. Rob Kroes, *If You've Seen One You've Seen the Mall: Europeans and American Mass Culture* (Urbana: University of Illinois Press, 1996). See also his "Americanisation: What are We Talking About?" *European Contributions to American Studies* 25 (1993): 302–18. Also Indispensable for this argument is Richard Pells, *Not Like Us: How Europeans have loved, hated, and transformed American Culture since World War II* (New York: Basic Books, 1997).

29. Frank Mort, "The Commercial Domain: Advertising and the Cultural Management of Demand," in *Commercial Cultures: Economies, Practices, Spaces,* eds. Peter Jackson, Michelle Lowe, Daniel Miller, and Frank Mort (Oxford: Berg, 2000), 35–54. Recently, the biography of the German Volkswagen-boss Heinz Nordhoff has shown quite the same: rather than slavishly following American production methods and systems of organization in industrial relations at Volkswagen, Nordhoff studied the examples of his American parent companies and made his name by carefully selecting certain elements of American production and management life and adapting these to the traditions and necessities of post-war West German car manufacturing at Volkswagen in Wolfsburg, Lower Saxony. See Heidrun Edelmann, *Heinz Nordhoff: ein deutscher Unternehmer im amerikanischen Jahrhundert* (Göttingen: Vandenhoeck & Ruprecht, 2003).

30. See for this approach and accompanying criticism Victoria de Grazia "Nationalizing Women: The Competition between Fascist and Commercial Cultural Models in Mussolini's Italy," in *The Sex of Things: Gender and Consumption in Historical Perspective,* ed. Victoria de Grazia (Berkeley: University of California Press, 1996), 337–58; Jessica C. E. Gienow-Hecht, *Transmission Impossible: American Journalism as Cultural Diplomacy in Post-war Germany, 1945–1955* (Baton-Rouge: Louisiana State University Press, 1999). Gienow-Hecht discusses the significance of agents in manipulating the transfer of icons, messages, and habits and shows how, in the process of transfer, social and cultural artifacts are being transformed and entirely changed on the "receiving end."

31. Charles Hiatt, *Picture Posters* (London: G. Bell & Sons, 1895); Charles Higham, "Posters," *Encyclopedia Britannica* (Cambridge: Cambridge University Press, 1910), vol. 22, 196–97.

32. Cyril Sheldon, *A History of Poster Advertising* (London: Chapman & Hall, 1937); Alston W. Purvis, "A Century of Posters," in *A Century of Posters,*

eds. Martijn F. LeCoultre and Alston W. Purvis (London: Lund Humphries, 2002), 8–19; and John Barnicoat, *A Concise History of Posters* (London: Thames and Hudson, 1972), 29–47.
33. Purvis in LeCoultre and Purvis, *A Century of Posters,* 9.
34. See Richard Carline, *Pictures in the Post: The Story of the Picture Postcard and its Place in the History of Popular Art* (London: Gordon Fraser, 1971); Frank Staff, *The Picture Postcard and its Origins* (London: Lutterworth Press, 1979).
35. See Terry Ramsaye, *A Million and One Nights: a History of the Motion Picture* (New York: Simon & Schuster, 1926).
36. Lisa Tiersten, *Marianne in the Market: Envisioning Consumer Culture in Fin-de-Siècle France* (Berkeley: University of California Press, 2001); Geoffrey Crossick, Serge Jaumain, eds., *Cathedrals of Consumption: The European Department Store, 1850–1939* (Aldershot: Ashgate, 1998).
37. See Mica Nava, "Cosmopolitan Modernity: Everyday Imaginaries and the Register of Difference," *Theory, Culture & Society* 19, 1–2 (2002): 81–99; Nava, "The Cosmopolitanism of Commerce and the Allure of Difference: Selfridges, the Russian Ballet and the Tango 1911–14," *International Journal of Cultural Studies* 1, 2 (1998): 163–96; Nava, "Modernity's Disavowal: Women, the City and the Department Store," in *Modern Times: Reflections on a Century of English Modernity,* eds. Mica Nava and Alan O'Shea (London: Routledge, 1996), 36–76. See also Erika Rappaport, *Shopping for Pleasure: Women in the Making of London's West End* (Princeton: Princeton University Press, 2000); and Rachel Bowlby, *Carried Away: The Invention of Modern Shopping* (London: Faber, 2000), 94–95, 155–57.
38. Kristin Hoganson, "Cosmopolitan Domesticity: Importing the American Dream, 1865–1920," *American Review* (February 2002): 55–83.
39. For a discussion about anti-consumerism in the US since Thoreau's *Walden,* see Paul L. Wachtel, "Alternatives to the Consumer Society," in *Ethics of Consumption: The Good Life, Justice and Global Stewardship,* eds. David A. Crocker and Toby Linden (Oxford: Rowman & Littlefield, 1997), 198–217; Daniel Horowitz, *The Morality of Spending: Attitudes Toward the Consumer Society in America: 1675–1940* (Baltimore: John Hopkins University Press, 1985); and Daniel Horowitz, *The Anxieties of Affluence: Critiques of American Consumer Culture, 1939–1979* (Amherst: University of Massachusetts Press, 2004).
40. Purvis in LeCoultre and Purvis, *A Century of Posters,* 12; and Terrence Nevett, *Advertising in Britain: A History* (London: Heinemann, 1982), 86–92. Bradley himself asserted that his most profound inspiration came from the English artist-reformer William Morris. See Clarence P. Hornung, *Bill Bradley: His Graphic Art* (New York: Dover Publications, 1974).
41. See the American advertising journal *Printer's Ink* (28 July 1938): 122–23; Jane Haville Desmarais, *The Beardsley Industry: The Critical Reception in England and France, 1893–1914* (Aldershot: Ashgate, 1998); Stephen Calloway, *Aubrey Beardsley* (London: V & A Publications, 1998); and Matthew Sturgis, *Aubrey Beardsley: A Biography* (London: Harper Collins, 1999). On the European Art Nouveau advertising poster art and its influence on the US, see Jacquelyn Days Serwer, "The American Artistic Poster of the 1890s" (PhD diss., City University of New York, 1980); Edgar Breitenbach, "The Poster Craze," *American Heritage* 13, 2 (1962): 26–31; and Victor Margolin, *American Poster Renaissance* (New York: Castle Books, 1975). The opposing "Americanization = Subversion" story is told by Victoria de

Grazia, "The Arts of Purchase: How U.S. Advertising Subverted the European Poster," in *Remaking History,* eds. Phil Mariani and Barbara Kruger (Seattle: Bay Press, 1989), 221–57.
42. On Art Deco as international "consumerist" design style being imported to the United States from Europe, see Jonathan M. Woodham, *Twentieth-century Design* (Oxford: Oxford University Press, 1997), 76–81, 87–9, 107–9; Bevis Hillier, *The Style of the Twentieth Century* (New York: Herbert, 1998), 97–99; Tag Gronberg, *Designs of Modernity: Exhibiting the City in 1920s Paris* (Manchester: Manchester University Press, 1998); Maurice Dufrene, *Authentic Art Deco Interiors from the 1925 Paris Exhibition* (Woodbridge: Antique Collectors' Club, 1989); and Charlotte Benton, Tim Benton, Ghislaine Wood, eds., *Art Deco, 1910–1939* (London: V & A Publications, 2003).
43. On the EMB's activities, see Stephen Constantine, "Bringing the Empire Alive: The Empire Marketing Board and Imperial Propaganda, 1926–1933," in *Imperialism and Popular Culture,* ed. John MacKenzie (Manchester: Manchester University Press, 1986), 192–231; and Stephen Constantine, *Buy and Build: The Advertising Posters of the Empire Marketing Board* (London: HMSO, 1986).
44. The "projection" of Britain and England became a hotly debated issue in the 1930s as the British elite tried to sell the "right" picture of Britain as a modern nation, especially to United States citizens. See, for the origin of the idea of overseas Public Relations, Stephen Tallents, *The Projection of England* (London: Faber & Faber, 1932). As an introduction into this discourse, see Fred M. Leventhal, "The Projection of Britain in America before the Second World War," in *Still More Adventures with Britannia: Personalities, Politics and Culture in Britain,* ed. Wm. Roger Louis (London: I. B. Tauris, 2003), 195–209; Fred M. Leventhal, "Public Face and Public Space: The Projection of Britain in America before the Second World War," in *Anglo-American Attitudes: From Revolution to Partnership,* eds. Fred M. Leventhal and Ronald Quinault (Aldershot: Ashgate, 2000), 212–26; Nicholas J. Cull, *Selling War: The British Propaganda Campaign Against American "Neutrality" in World War II* (Oxford: Oxford University Press, 1995); and Cull, "Overture to an Alliance: British Propaganda at the New York World's Fair, 1939–1940," *Journal of British Studies* 36, 3 (1997): 325–54.
45. "Tea Consumption in the United States," *The Times,* 14 January 1924, 15; H. J. Rudglen, "Changing the Customs of a Continent: Putting Tea at the End of Publici-Tea," *Advertising World* (February 1924): 388–94.
46. *Advertiser's Weekly,* 4 January 1924, 14; *Advertiser's Weekly,* 25 January 1924, 116.
47. "Sir Charles Sells Tea," *Advertiser's Weekly,* 8 February 1924, 172.
48. On Higham's campaign, see also Percy Bradshaw, *Art in Advertising: A Study of British and American Pictorial Publicity* (London: Press Art School, 1926), 114–15.
49. G. A. Atkinson, "Forty British Films this Year," *Daily Express,* 16 May 1927, 6. Christopher Hitchens has argued that these debates were part of a more continuously running "transmission belt" by which the British consciously infected Americans with nostalgic ideas about Empire and class and tempted them to "think with blood." See Christopher Hitchens, *Blood, Class and Nostalgia: Anglo-American Ironies* (London: Chatto & Windus, 1990), 5.
50. See Jeffrey Richards, *The Age of the Dream Palace: Cinema and Society in Britain, 1930–1939* (London: Routledge, 1984); Sarah Street, "British Film

and the National Interest, 1927–1939," in *The British Cinema Book*, ed. Robert Murphy (London: British Film Institute, 2002), 32–41; Tom Ryall, *Britain and the American Cinema* (London: Sage, 2001); H. M. Glancy, *When Hollywood Loved Britain: The Hollywood "British" Film, 1939–1945* (Manchester: Manchester University Press, 1999); I. Harvie, *Hollywood's Overseas Campaign: The North-Atlantic Movie Trade, 1920–1950* (Cambridge: Cambridge University Press, 1995); John Trumpour, *Selling Hollywood to the World: U.S. and European Struggles for Mastery of the Global Film Industry, 1920–1950* (Cambridge, MA: Cambridge University Press, 2002); Victoria de Grazia, "Mass Culture and Sovereignty: The American Challenge to European Cinemas, 1920–1960," *Journal of Modern History* 61 (1989): 53–87; and Peter Stead, "Hollywood's Message for the World: The British Response in the 1930s," *The Historical Journal of Film, Radio and Television* 1, 1 (1981): 18–32.

51. "Out-Britishing the Britisher," *The J. Walter Thompson News Bulletin* 136 (November 1928): 11–15. The article quotes the Coventry-based British advertising agency Heritage Peters: "In the face of the £1,000,000-a-year Government campaign to 'Buy British Goods', and the smaller but no less insistent campaign of the Society of British Motor Manufacturers to 'Buy a British Car', it is becoming increasingly difficult for American manufacturers to market their cars in our country."
52. "America is Buying British Goods," *Advertising World* (April 1924, Overseas Market Supplement): ii–vi.
53. On Ogilvy's invention of the brand image and its application in the US, see Ogilvy, *Ogilvy on Advertising* (London: Pan, 1983), 9–16; and Ogilvy, *Confessions of an Advertising Man* (New York: Atheneum, 1963), 24–45. For a more detailed analysis see Stefan Schwarzkopf, "Transatlantic Invasions or Common Culture? Modes of Cultural and Economic Exchange between the American and the British Advertising Industries, 1951–1989," in *Anglo-American Media Interactions*, eds. Joel H. Wiener and Mark Hampton (London: Palgrave, 2007), pp. 254–74.
54. See David Ogilvy "A New Deal for Our Clients," *Journal of Advertising History* 3 (March 1980): 6–11. The original typescript (dated 9 February 1939) can be found at the History of Advertising Trust Archive, Norwich.
55. Oddly, Schroeter, "Die Amerikanisierung der Werbung," 108, refers to Ogilvy as an "American agency owner."
56. The best-known attack on advertising ever published, Vance Packard's *Hidden Persuaders* (New York: D. McKay, 1957), was actually written in order to damage Ernest Dichter's work and him personally. On Dichter's biography, see Dichter, *Motivforschung – mein Leben: die Autobiographie eines kreativ Unzufriedenen* (Frankfurt, Main: Lorch, 1977). His most important books on motivational research are *The Strategy of Desire* (New York: Doubleday, 1960), and *Handbook of Consumer Motivations: The Psychology of the World of Objects* (New York: McGraw-Hill, 1964). A useful interpretation of his life and work can be found in Daniel Horowitz, "The Emigré as Celebrant of American Consumer Culture: George Kantona and Ernest Dichter," in *Getting and Spending: European and American Consumer Society in the Twentieth Century*, eds. Susan Strasser, Charles McGovern, and Matthias Judt (Cambridge: Cambridge University Press, 1998), 149–66; and Stefan Schwarzkopf et al., "Ernest Dichter and Motivation Research: An International Perspective," *Medien und Zeit* 20 (2005): 40–49.

57. See a similar argument being made by Daniel T. Rodgers, *Atlantic Crossings: Social Politics in the Progressive Age* (Cambridge, MA: Belknap, 1998).
58. By 1964, only 40 percent of the top twenty British advertising agencies were controlled by American firms. See Douglas C. West, "Multinational Competition in the British Advertising Agency Business, 1936–1987," *Business History Review* 62 (Autumn 1988): 467–501.
59. See Schroeter, "Die Amerikanisierung der Werbung," and Schug, "Wegbereiter der modernen Absatzwerbung."
60. On J. Walter Thompson's expansion to Italy and Spain, see, e.g., Arvidsson "Between Fascism." See also James P. Woodard, "Marketing Modernity: The J. Walter Thompson Company and North American Advertising in Brazil, 1929–1939," *Hispanic American Historical Review* 82, 2 (2002): 257–90; Julio Moreno, "Marketing in Mexico: Sears, Roebuck Company, J. Walter Thompson, and the Culture of North American Commerce in Mexico City during the 1940s," *Enterprise & Society* 1 (2000): 683–92; Moreno, "J. Walter Thompson, the Good Neighbor Policy, and Lessons in Mexican Business Culture," *Enterprise & Society* 5, 2 (2004): 254–80; Clark Eric Hultquist, "Americans in Paris: The J. Walter Thompson Company in France, 1927–1968," *Enterprise & Society* 4, 3 (2003): 471–501; and Jonathan Silva, "The Marketing Complex: The J. Walter Thompson Company, 1916–1929," *Essays in Economic and Business History* 14 (1996): 207–18.
61. For an early history of American agencies in Britain, see Albert Teele, *Ideal Advertising* (London: A. L. Teele, 1892); *Advertising World* (July 1902): 88–89, 113; *Advertising World* (September 1916), 250–54, 260–61; Douglas West, "From T-Square to T-Plan: The London Office of the J. Walter Thompson Advertising Agency, 1919–1970," *Business History* 29 (1987): 199–217; and Terrence Nevett, "American Influences on British Advertising before 1920," in *Historical Perspectives in Marketing*, eds. Terrence Nevett and Ronald Fullerton (Lexington, MA: Lexington Books, 1988), 223–40.
62. On the Dorland agency in London, see Elizabeth Hennessy and Ian Keil, "Dorland: Its Origin and Growth Until 1939," *European Journal of Marketing* 22, 8 (1988): 49–67.
63. See Douglas West, *The Growth and Development of the Advertising Industry Within the United Kingdom, 1920–1970* (PhD diss., University of Leeds, 1984), 189ff.
64. Transcripts of interview with James Webb Young (November 1963), in Sidney Bernstein Papers, Box 1; Report, "The London Office," in Sidney Bernstein Papers, Box 5, International Office Histories. All at JWT Archive, Hartman Center, Duke University.
65. Letter by General Motors to Stanley Resor (JWT), 26 January 1927, Sidney Bernstein Papers, Box 9 (chapter files), JWT Archive, Hartman Center, Duke University; Jeffrey L. Merron, *American Culture Goes Abroad: J. Walter Thompson and the General Motors Export Account, 1927–1933* (PhD diss., University of North Carolina at Chapel Hill, 1991).
66. *The J. Walter Thompson News Bulletin* 133 (March 1928): 12–13; *JWT News* 12, 49 (April 1930): 3.
67. *Advertiser's Weekly*, 5 October 1933.
68. West, *The Growth and Development*, 201–4.
69. Clement H. Watson, "Markets are People – Not places," *The J. Walter Thompson News Bulletin* 135 (July 1928): 3–23.

70. Letter by Rae Smith (London) to Earl Clark (NY), 4 April 1933, folder, "British Research Bureau"; letter by Sinclair (London) to Clark (NY), 15 February 1935, folder, "Incorporation," both in Treasurer's Office Records, Box 7; and folder "Kodak (1934–35)," Box 8, all at JWT Archive, Hartman Center, Duke University. John Downham, *British Market Research Bureau: the First Sixty Years, 1933–1993* (London: British Market Research Bureau, 1993), 23; Graham Turner, John Pearson, *The Persuasion Industry* (London: Eyre & Spottiswoode, 1966), 9–21; and my forthcoming thesis, Stefan Schwarzkopf, *The Quest for Legitimacy: Service Advertising Agencies and Consumer Culture in Britain, 1900–1951* (Birkbeck College, University of London, 2008).
71. See G. H. Saxon Mills, *There is a Tide... The Life and Works of Sir William Crawford, K.B.E., Embodying an Historical Study of Modern British Advertising* (London: Heinemann, 1954), 82–85.
72. *Advertising World* (May 1927), and W. S. Crawford's *Chairman's Report for 1964* (London: W. S. Crawford's, 1965), History of Advertising Trust Archive, CWS Agency Box; *Advertiser's Weekly*, 22 July 1974.
73. For this international network of advertising design emerging in the inter-war years, see Michael Havinden et al., eds., *Advertising and the Artist: Ashley Havinden* (Edinburgh: National Galleries of Scotland, 2003); Mark Haworth-Booth, *E. McKnight Kauffer: A Designer and His Public* (London: Gordon Fraser, 1979); Naomi Games et al., eds., *Abram Games, Graphic Designer: Maximum Meaning, Minimum Means* (Aldershot: Lund Humphries, 2003); Steven Heller and Louise Fili, *British Modern: Graphic Design between the Wars* (San Francisco: Chronicle Books, 1998); D. L. LeMahieu, *A Culture for Democracy: Mass Communication and the Cultivated Mind in Britain between the Wars* (Oxford: Oxford University Press, 1988), 164, 208–10; and Jeremy Aynsley, *A Century of Graphic Design: Graphic Design Pioneers of the Twentieth Century* (London: Mitchell Beazley, 2001), 46–49.
74. Moreover, the existence of an American advertising office in a European or Asian city in the inter-war or post-war era does not necessarily mean these offices were successful or even dominated the market of their new countries. Hultquist, "Americans in Paris," has shown that the JWT office in Paris severely struggled for its economic existence throughout the period between 1927 and the 1960s. Hultquist names factors such as cultural clashes between Americans and the French, the protected French advertising and media market, anti-Americanism amongst French businessmen, and severe cases of cultural condescension and insensitivity on the American side as reasons for JWT's failure in France.
75. See Uta Poiger's epilogue in Sabrina R. Ramet and Gordana P. Crnkovic, eds., *Kazaam! Splat! Ploof! The American Impact on European Popular Culture since 1945* (New York: Rowman & Littlefield, 2003).
76. See also Anne Cronin, "Regimes of Mediation: Advertising Practitioners as Cultural Intermediaries," *Consumption, Markets and Culture* 7, 4 (2004): 349–69.
77. See, for a discussion of new models in international history, Antoinette Burton, ed., *After the Imperial Turn: Thinking with and through the Nation* (Durham: Duke University Press, 2003); Werner, Michael, and Bénédicte Zimmermann, "Penser l'histoire croisée: entre empirie et réflexivité," *Annales* 58 (2003): 7–36; Tony McGrew, "A Global Society," in *Modernity and its Futures*, eds. Stuart Hall et al. (Cambridge: Polity, 1993), 61–102; Arjun Appadurai, "Disjuncture and Difference in the Global Cultural Economy,"

in *Global Culture: Nationalism, Globalization and Modernity*, ed. Mike Featherstone (London: Sage, 1990), 295–310; Garcia Nestor, *Hybrid Cultures: Strategies for Entering and Leaving Modernity* (Minneapolis: University of Minnesota Press, 1995); Mike Featherstone et al., eds., *Global Modernities* (London: Sage, 1995); Peter Jackson, Philip Crang, Claire Dwyer, eds., *Transnational Spaces* (London: Routledge, 2004); Rebekka Habermas and Rebekka von Malinckrodt, eds., *Interkultureller Transfer und nationaler Eigensinn: Europäische und anglo-amerikanische Positionen der Kulturwissenschaften* (Göttingen: Vandenhoeck & Ruprecht, 2004); Wolf Lepenies, *Entangled Histories and Negotiated Universals: Centers and Peripheries in a Changing World* (Frankfurt: Campus, 2003); Michael Geyer, Charles Bright, "World History in a Global Age," *American Historical Review* 100, 4 (1995): 1034–60; Shmuel Eisenstadt, *Comparative Civilizations and Multiple Modernities: A Collection of Essays* (Leiden: Brill, 2003); as well as his seminal essay, Eisenstadt, "Multiple Modernities," *Daedalus* 129, 1 (2000): 1–30.

Bibliography

Arvidsson, Adam. "Between Fascism and the American Dream: Advertising in Inter-war Italy." *Social Science History* 25, 2 (Summer 2001): 151–86.
———. *Marketing Modernity: Italian Advertising from Fascism to Postmodernity*. London: Routledge, 2003.
———. "The Therapy of Consumption: Motivation Research and the New Italian Housewife, 1958–62." *Journal of Material Culture* 5, 3 (2000): 251–74.
Aynsley, Jeremy. *A Century of Graphic Design: Graphic Design Pioneers of the Twentieth Century*. London: Mitchell Beazley, 2001.
Bowlby, Rachel. *Carried Away: The Invention of Modern Shopping*. London: Faber, 2000.
Breen, T. H. *The Marketplace of Revolution: How Consumer Politics Shaped American Independence*. Oxford: Oxford University Press, 2004.
Burton, Antoinette, ed. *After the Imperial Turn: Thinking with and through the Nation*. Durham: Duke University Press, 2003.
Burton, John W. *World Society*. Cambridge: Cambridge University Press, 1972.
Calloway, Stephen. *Aubrey Beardsley*. London: V & A Publications, 1998.
Campbell, Neil, et al., eds. *Issues in Americanisation and Culture*. Edingburgh: Edinburgh University Press, 2004.
Castells, Manuel. "Materials for an Exploratory Theory of the Network Society." *British Journal of Sociology* 51 (2000): 5–24.
Caunce, Stephen, et al., eds. *Relocating Britishness*. Manchester: Manchester University Press, 2004.
Constantine, Stephen. *Buy and Build: The Advertising Posters of the Empire Marketing Board*. London: HMSO, 1986.
Cronin, Anne. "Regimes of Mediation: Advertising Practitioners as Cultural Intermediaries." *Consumption, Markets and Culture* 7, 4 (2004): 349–69.
Crossick, Geoffrey, and Serge Jaumain, eds. *Cathedrals of Consumption: The European Department Store, 1850–1939*. Aldershot: Ashgate, 1998.
Cull, Nicholas J. "Overture to an Alliance: British Propaganda at the New York World's Fair, 1939–1940." *Journal of British Studies* 36, 3 (1997): 325–54.
———. *Selling War: The British Propaganda Campaign against American "Neutrality" in World War II*. Oxford: Oxford University Press, 1995.

Days-Serwer, Jacquelyn. "The American Artistic Poster of the 1890s." PhD diss., City University of New York, 1980.
de Grazia, Victoria. "The Arts of Purchase: How U.S. Advertising Subverted the European Poster." In *Remaking History,* eds. Phil Mariani and Barbara Kruger. Seattle: Bay Press, 1989, pp. 221–57.
———. "Mass Culture and Sovereignty: The American Challenge to European Cinemas." *Journal of Modern History* 61 (1989): 53–87.
———. "Nationalizing Women: The Competition between Fascist and Commercial Cultural Models in Mussolini's Italy." In *The Sex of Things: Gender and Consumption in Historical Perspective,* ed. Victoria de Grazia. Berkeley: University of California Press, 1996, pp. 337–58.
———. *Irresistible Empire: America's Advance through Twentieth-Century Europe.* Cambridge: Belknap, 2005.
Dichter, Ernest. *The Strategy of Desire.* New York: Doubleday, 1960.
———. *Handbook of Consumer Motivations: The Psychology of the World of Objects.* New York: McGraw-Hill, 1964.
———. *Motivforschung – Mein Leben: Die Autobiographie eines kreativ Unzufriedenen.* Frankfurt: Lorch, 1977.
Dickinson, G. Lowes. *Appearances: Being Notes of Travel.* London: J. M. Dent & Sons, 1914.
Downham, John. *British Market Research Bureau: The First Sixty Years, 1933–1993.* London: British Market Research Bureau, 1993.
Edelmann, Heidrun. *Heinz Nordhoff: Ein deutscher Unternehmer im amerikanischen Jahrhundert.* Göttingen: Vandenhoeck & Ruprecht, 2003.
Eisenstadt, Shmuel. "Multiple Modernities." *Daedalus* 129, 1 (2000): 1–30.
———. *Comparative Civilizations and Multiple Modernities: A Collection of Essays.* Leiden: Brill, 2003.
Endy, Christopher. "Travel and World Power: Americans in Europe, 1890–1917." *Diplomatic History* 22 (Fall 1998): 565–94.
Fehrenbach, Heide, and Uta G. Poiger, eds. *Transactions, Transgressions, Transformations: American Culture in Western Europe and Japan.* New York and Oxford: Berghahn Books, 1999.
Furlough, Ellen. "Selling the American Way in Inter-war France: Prix Uniques and the Salon des Arts Ménagers." *Journal of Social History* 26 (1993): 491–519.
Geyer, Michael, and Charles Bright. "World History in a Global Age." *American Historical Review* 100, 4 (1995): 1034–60.
Gienow-Hecht, Jessica C. E. *Transmission Impossible: American Journalism as Cultural Diplomacy in Post-war Germany, 1945–1955.* Baton-Rouge: Louisiana State University Press, 1999.
———. "Shame on US? Academics, Cultural Transfer and the Cold War – A Critical Review." *Diplomatic History* 24, 3 (Summer 2000): 465–93.
Gronberg, Tag. *Designs of Modernity: Exhibiting the City in 1920s Paris.* Manchester: Manchester University Press, 1998.
Habermas, Rebekka, and Rebekka von Malinckrodt, eds. *Interkultureller Transfer und Nationaler Eigensinn: Europäische und Anglo-amerikanische Positionen der Kulturwissenschaften.* Göttingen: Vandenhoeck & Ruprecht, 2004.
Harp, Stephen. *Marketing Michelin: Advertising and Cultural Identity in Twentieth-century France.* Baltimore: John Hopkins University Press, 2000.
Haville-Desmarais, Jane. *The Beardsley Industry: The Critical Reception in England and France, 1893–1914.* Aldershot: Ashgate, 1998.

Heinonen, Visa. "Professionalisation and Institutionalisation of the Finnish Advertising Business." In *Business and Society: Entrepreneurs, Politics and Networks in a Historical Perspective,* eds. Anne Marie Kuijlaars, Kim Prudon, and Joop Visser. Rotterdam: Centre of Business History, 2000, pp. 361–70.

Hennessy, Elizabeth, and Ian Keil. "Dorland: its Origin and Growth until 1939." *European Journal of Marketing* 22, 8 (1988): 49–67.

Hilger, Susanne. *"Amerikaniserung" deutscher Unternehmen: Wettbewerbsstrategien und Unternehmenspolitik bei Henkel, Siemens und Daimler-Benz, 1945/49–1975.* Stuttgart: Steiner, 2004.

Hillier, Bevis. *The Style of the Twentieth Century.* New York: Herbert, 1998.

Hitchens, Christopher. *Blood, Class and Nostalgia: Anglo-American Ironies.* London: Chatto & Windus, 1990.

Hoganson, Kristin. "Cosmopolitan Domesticity: Importing the American Dream, 1865–1920." *American Review* (February 2002): 55–83.

Hornung, Clarence P. *Bill Bradley: His Graphic Art.* New York: Dover Publications, 1974.

Horowitz, Daniel. *The Morality of Spending: Attitudes toward the Consumer Society in America: 1675–1940.* Baltimore: John Hopkins University Press, 1985.

———. "The Emigré as Celebrant of American Consumer Culture: George Kantona and Ernest Dichter." In *Getting and Spending: European and American Consumer Society in the Twentieth Century,* eds. Susan Strasser, Charles McGovern, and Matthias Judt. Cambridge: Cambridge University Press, 1998, pp. 149–66.

———. *The Anxieties of Affluence: Critiques of American Consumer Culture, 1939–1979.* Amherst: University of Massachusetts Press, 2004.

Hultquist, Clark Eric. "Americans in Paris: The J. Walter Thompson Company in France, 1927–1968." *Enterprise & Society* 4, 3 (2003): 471–501.

Jarausch, Konrad, and Hannes Siegrist, eds. *Amerikanisierung und Sowjetisierung in Deutschland, 1945–1970.* Frankfurt: Campus, 1997.

Kipping, Matthias, and Nick Tiratsoo, ed. *Americanisation in Twentieth-century Europe: Business, Culture, Politics.* Lille: Centre de Recherche sur l'Histoire de l'Europe du Nord-Ouest, 2002.

Klautke, Egbert. *Unbegrenzte Möglichkeiten: 'Amerikanisierung' in Deutschland und Frankreich, 1900–1933.* Stuttgart: Steiner, 2003.

Kroes, Rob. "The Reception of American Films in the Netherlands: The Interwar Years." *American Studies International* 28, 2 (1990): 37–51.

———. "Among the Receivers: American Culture Transmitted Abroad." *European Contributions to American Studies* 22 (1991): 1–10.

———. "Americanisation: What Are We Talking about?" *European Contributions to American Studies* 25 (1993): 302–18.

———. *If You've Seen One You've Seen the Mall: Europeans and American Mass Culture.* Urbana: University of Illinois Press, 1996.

———. "American Empire and Cultural Imperialism: A View from the Receiving End." *Diplomatic History* 23, 3 (Fall 1999): 463–77.

Kuisel, Richard F. "Coca-Cola and the Cold War: The French Face Americanization, 1948–1953." *French Historical Studies* 17, 1 (1991): 96–116.

———. *Seducing the French: The Dilemma of Americanization.* Berkeley: University of California Press, 1993.

———. "'Americanization' for Historians." *Diplomatic History* 24, 3 (Fall 2000): 509–15.

———. "Learning to Love McDonald's, Coca-Cola and Disneyland Paris." *Tocqueville Review* 21, 2 (2000): 129–49.
LeMahieu, D. L. *A Culture for Democracy: Mass Communication and the Cultivated Mind in Britain between the Wars.* Oxford: Oxford University Press, 1988.
Lepenies, Wolf. *Entangled Histories and Negotiated Universals: Centers and Peripheries in a Changing World.* Frankfurt: Campus, 2003.
Leventhal, Fred M. "The Projection of Britain in America before the Second World War." In *Still More Adventures with Britannia: Personalities, Politics and Culture in Britain,* ed. Wm. Roger Louis. London: I. B. Tauris, 2003, pp. 195–209.
Leventhal, Fred M., and Ronald Quinault, eds. *Anglo-American Attitudes: From Revolution to Partnership.* Aldershot: Ashgate, 2000.
MacKenzie, John. *Imperialism and Popular Culture.* Manchester: Manchester University Press, 1986.
Margolin, Victor. *American Poster Renaissance.* New York: Castle Books, 1975.
McKenzie, Brian. *Remaking France: Americanization, Public Diplomacy, and the Marshall Plan.* New York and Oxford: Berghahn Books, 2005.
McKenzie, Fred A. *The American Invaders: Their Plans, Tactics and Progress.* London: Grant Richards, 1901.
McMillan, James, and Bernard Harris. *The American Take-Over of Britain.* London: Frewin, 1968.
Merron, Jeffrey L. "American Culture Goes Abroad: J. Walter Thompson and the General Motors Export Account, 1927–1933." PhD diss., University of North Carolina at Chapel Hill, 1991.
Moreno, Julio. "Marketing in Mexico: Sears, Roebuck Company, J. Walter Thompson, and the Culture of North American Commerce in Mexico City during the 1940s." *Enterprise & Society* 1 (2000): 683–92.
———. "J. Walter Thompson, the Good Neighbor Policy, and Lessons in Mexican Business Culture." *Enterprise & Society* 5, 2 (2004): 254–80.
Mort, Frank. "The Commercial Domain: Advertising and the Cultural Management of Demand." In *Commercial Cultures: Economies, Practices, Spaces,* eds. Peter Jackson, Michelle Lowe, Daniel Miller, and Frank Mort. Oxford: Berg, 2000, pp. 35–54.
Moser, John E. *Twisting the Lion's Tail: American Anglophobia between the World Wars.* Basingstoke: Macmillan, 1998.
Nava, Mica. "Modernity's Disavowal: Women, the City and the Department Store." In *Modern Times: Reflections on a Century of English Modernity,* eds. Mica Nava and Alan O'Shea. London: Routledge, 1996, pp. 36–76.
———. "The Cosmopolitanism of Commerce and the Allure of Difference: Selfridges, the Russian Ballet and the Tango 1911–14." *International Journal of Cultural Studies* 1, 2 (1998): 163–96.
———. "Cosmopolitan Modernity: Everyday Imaginaries and the Register of Difference." *Theory, Culture & Society* 19, 1–2 (2002): 81–99.
Nevett, Terrence. *Advertising in Britain: A History.* London: Heinemann, 1982.
———. "American Influences on British Advertising before 1920." In *Historical Perspectives in Marketing,* eds. Terrence Nevett and Ronald Fullerton. Lexington: Lexington Books, 1988, pp. 223–40.
Ogilvy, David. *Confessions of an Advertising Man.* New York: Atheneum, 1963.
———. "A New Deal for Our Clients." *Journal of Advertising History* 3 (March 1980): 6–11.
———. *Ogilvy on Advertising.* London: Pan, 1983.
Orwell, George. *Keep the Aspidistra Flying.* London: Victor Gollancz, 1936.

Osterhammel, Jürgen. *Geschichtswissenschaft jenseits des Nationalstaats: Studien zu Beziehungsgeschichte und Zivilisationsvergleich.* Göttingen: Vandenhoeck & Ruprecht, 2001.
Packard, Vance. *Hidden Persuaders.* New York: D. McKay, 1957.
Passerini, Luisa, ed. *Across the Atlantic: Cultural Exchanges between Europe and the United States.* New York: Campus, 2000.
Pells, Richard. *Not Like Us: How European Loved, Hated and Transformed American Culture since World War II.* New York: Basic Books, 1997.
Priestley, J. B. *English Journey.* London: Victor Gollancz, 1934.
Priestley, J. B., and Jacqueta Hawkes. *Journey Down the Rainbow.* London: Heinemann-Cresset, 1957.
Purvis, Alston W., and Martijn F. LeCoultre, eds. *A Century of Posters.* London: Lund Humphries, 2002.
Ramet, Sabrina R., and Gordana P. Crnkovic, eds. *Kazaam! Splat! Ploof! The American Impact on European Popular Culture since 1945.* New York: Rowman & Littlefield, 2003.
Ramsaye, Terry. *A Million and One Nights: A History of the Motion Picture.* New York: Simon & Schuster, 1926.
Rappaport, Erika. *Shopping for Pleasure: Women in the Making of London's West End.* Princeton: Princeton University Press, 2000.
Reynolds, David. *Rich Relations: The American Occupation of Britain, 1942–1945.* London: Harper Collins, 1996.
Richards, Jeffrey. *The Age of the Dream Palace: Cinema and Society in Britain, 1930–1939.* London: Routledge, 1984.
Rodgers, Daniel T. *Atlantic Crossings: Social Politics in the Progressive Age.* Cambridge, MA: Belknap, 1998.
Ryall, Tom. *Britain and the American Cinema.* London: Sage, 2001.
Rydell, Robert, and Rob Kroes. *Buffalo Bill in Bologna: The Americanization of the World, 1869–1922.* Chicago: Chicago University Press, 2005.
Saxon-Mills, G. H. *There is a Tide... The Life and Works of Sir William Crawford, K.B.E., Embodying an Historical Study of Modern British Advertising.* London: Heinemann, 1954.
Schroeter, Harm. "Die Amerikanisierung der Werbung in der Bundesrepublik Deutschland." *Jahrbuch für Wirtschaftsgeschichte* (1997): 93–115.
Schroeter, Harm, and Eli Moen. "Americanization as a Concept for a Deeper Understanding of Economic Changes, 1945–1970." *Entreprise et Histoire* 19 (1998): 5–13.
Schug, Alexander. "Wegbereiter der modernen Absatzwerbung in Deutschland: Advertising Agencies und die Amerikanisierung der deutschen Werbebranche in der Zwischenkriegszeit." *Werkstatt Geschichte* 12, 1 (2003): 29–52.
Schwarzkopf, Stefan. "Ernest Dichter and Motivation Research: An International Perspective." *Medien und Zeit* 20, 4 (2005): 40–49.
———. "From Barnum to 'Organization Man': Images of 'America' in the British Advertising Discourse, 1850s–1950s." In *America in the British Imagination,* ed. Catherine Armstrong. Cambridge: Cambridge Scholar Press, 2007, pp. 132–52.
———. "The Quest for Legitimacy: Service Advertising Agencies and Consumer Culture in Britain, 1900–1951." PhD thesis, Birkbeck College, University of London, 2008.
———. "Transatlantic Invasions or Common Culture? Modes of Cultural and Economic Exchange between the American and the British Advertising

Industries, 1951–1989." In *Anglo-American Media Interactions,* eds. Joel H. Wiener and Mark Hampton. London: Palgrave, 2007, pp. 254–74.

Shaw, Gareth, Andrew Alexander, and Louise Curth. "Selling Self-Service and the Supermarket: The Americanisation of Food Retailing in Britain, 1945–60." *Business History* 46, 4 (October 2004): 568–82.

Sheldon, Cyril. *A History of Poster Advertising.* London: Chapman & Hall, 1937.

Silva, Jonathan. "The Marketing Complex: The J. Walter Thompson Company, 1916–1929." *Essays in Economic and Business History* 14 (1996): 207–18.

Staff, Frank. *The Picture Postcard and its Origins.* London: Lutterworth, 1979.

Stead, Peter. "Hollywood's Message for the World: The British Response in the 1930s." *The Historical Journal of Film, Radio and Television* 1, 1 (1981): 18–32.

Stead, William Thomas. *The Americanisation of the World, or the Trend of the Twentieth Century.* London: H. Markley, 1902.

Stephan, Alexander, ed. *Americanization and Anti-Americanism: The German Encounter with American Culture after 1945.* New York and Oxford: Berghahn Books, 2004.

Strinati, Dominic. "The Taste of America: Americanization and Popular Culture in Britain." In *Come on Down? Popular Media and Culture in Post-war Britain,* eds. Dominic Strinati and Stephen Wagg. London: Routledge, 1992, pp. 46–81.

Tallents, Stephen. *The Projection of England.* London: Faber & Faber, 1932.

Teele, Albert. *Ideal Advertising.* London: A. L. Teele, 1892.

Tiersten, Lisa. *Marianne in the Market: Envisioning Consumer Culture in Fin-de-Siècle France.* Berkeley: University of California Press, 2001.

Tomlinson, John. *Cultural Imperialism: A Critical Introduction.* Baltimore: John Hopkins University Press, 1991.

Turner, Graham, and John Pearson. *The Persuasion Industry.* London: Eyre & Spottiswoode, 1966.

Ward, Allan. *Britishness since 1870.* London: Routledge, 2004.

Wells, H. G. *Tono Bungay.* London: Macmillan, 1909.

Webster, Wendy. *Englishness and Empire, 1939–1965.* Oxford: Oxford University Press, 2005.

West, Douglas. "The Growth and Development of the Advertising Industry within the United Kingdom, 1920–1970." PhD diss., University of Leeds, 1984.

———. "From T-Square to T-Plan: the London Office of the J. Walter Thompson Advertising Agency, 1919–1970." *Business History* 29 (1987): 199–217.

———. "Multinational Competition in the British Advertising Agency Business, 1936–1987." *Business History Review* 62 (Autumn 1988): 467–501.

Williams, Francis. *The American Invasion.* London: Anthony Blond, 1962.

Woodard, James P. "Marketing Modernity: The J. Walter Thompson Company and North American Advertising in Brazil, 1929–1939." *Hispanic American Historical Review* 82, 2 (2002): 257–90.

Woodham, Jonathan M. *Twentieth-Century Design.* Oxford: Oxford University Press, 1997.

Zeitlin, Jonathan, and Gary Herrigel, eds. *Americanization and Its Limits: Reworking US Technology and Management in Post-war Europe and Japan.* Oxford: Oxford University Press, 2000.

Chapter 2

DIE ANTIDEUTSCHE WELLE
The Anti-German Wave, Public Diplomacy, and Intercultural Relations in Cold War America

Brian C. Etheridge

On 14 December 1961, Governing Mayor of West Berlin Willy Brandt spoke before an international assemblage of military figures, diplomats, and journalists at the Congress Hall of West Berlin. Although the event was located only a few hundred yards from the newly erected Berlin Wall, Brandt's speech did not concern international politics or the status of his beleaguered city. Instead, Brandt delivered an address at the world premiere of Stanley Kramer's controversial film, *Judgment at Nuremberg*. Warning that "it will be difficult for some of us to watch and hear this film," Brandt nevertheless argued that "Berlin as the center of spiritual conflict" was the best place to begin wrestling with Germany's past.[1]

For Kramer, landing Brandt to personally host the premiere was only the beginning. Kramer and United Artists had spared no expense in planning and funding this event. They had reserved the Congress Hall of West Berlin, flown reporters from around the world into West Berlin, and invited representatives from one hundred different nations stationed in the divided city to the premiere. In addition to Kramer, the production crew, and most of the stars, correspondents from Berlin, Germany, the United States, and around the world attended, as did General Lucius Clay, President Kennedy's personal representative in Berlin, Major General Albert Watson, the American commandant, twenty ambassadors from various countries, and

Notes for this section begin on page 101.

officials of the Bonn government. As one American reporter put it, "Mr. Kramer and his associates found themselves in the ideal position of having an attraction and a locale of unparalleled interest."[2]

Indeed, in planning the premiere the previous year, Kramer and United Artists had targeted Berlin to capitalize on the ongoing crisis regarding the status of the city. But they could not have foreseen the fortuitous constellation of events (from a publicity standpoint) that would take place in the intervening months to make their premiere international news. In addition to the continuing drama surrounding the newly constructed Berlin Wall, the Adolf Eichmann trial was rapidly reaching its conclusion in Israel. For these reasons, Kramer's film seemed especially timely. *Judgment at Nuremberg* told the story of a fictitious American judge (played by Spencer Tracy) who in the late 1940s was entrusted with the task of presiding over the trial of four German judges from the Nazi period. As Tracy's character struggles to understand the roots of National Socialism, the onset of the Berlin Blockade in the middle of the trial generates pressure on the prosecuting attorney and judge to be lenient on the Germans, with the argument frequently made that the United States needs Germany on its side in the developing Cold War.[3] In this way, *Judgment at Nuremberg* was a film that addressed the guilt of the German people for their crimes against the Jews, while at the same time suggesting that the Cold War, and specifically the conflict over Berlin in the late 1940s, had helped whitewash that guilt.

Aware of both the film's content and Kramer's plans, representatives from both the German and American governments sought to prevent the premiere. In the short term, they feared that the film could have serious repercussions in a delicate international environment. In the long term, they worried that the film would damage the image of Germany in the world. Since the late 1940s, American and German representatives had worked assiduously to rehabilitate Germany's image. The United States had labored to rebuild their new Cold War allies in a democratic mold, and American officials desperately wanted the American people to believe that all of their hard work had paid off. The West Germans, for their part, believed that continued American goodwill was essential to the Federal Republic's survival, and had sought to convince Americans that the country had been democratized and reconstructed. Both sides feared that *Judgment at Nuremberg* could unravel years of difficult labor.[4]

What was more, German officials worried that the release of *Judgment at Nuremberg* was only part of a larger pattern of anti-German material coming from film, television, and the print media in the United States, a phenomenon that they called the *antideutsche Welle,* or the anti-German wave. In addition to *Judgment at Nuremberg,* officials cited the televised trial of Adolf Eichmann and the publication of William Shirer's *The Rise and Fall of the Third Reich* as major elements in this push. Fearful that such programs and images would poison American attitudes toward the Federal Republic, they sought means to neutralize or mitigate their effects.

In this way, the world premiere of *Judgment at Nuremberg* in the Congress Hall of West Berlin dramatized two conflicting narratives of the German people in the American imagination. On the one hand, the film about the Nuremberg trials helped resurrect a World War narrative of the German people that painted them as arrogant, servile, cruel, and ultimately unrepentant for their crimes in World War II. On the other hand, the spectacle associated with the location and host of the premiere—West Berlin and its governing mayor, Willy Brandt, respectively—presented a Cold War narrative that portrayed the Germans as heroic people standing firm on the front line. This event represented in microcosm the larger conflict in American collective memory over the nature and meaning of the German people.

This essay explores the tension in the United States over the nature of the German people in the 1950s and 1960s, examining both how Germans attempted to control representations of Germany in the United States and how Americans received those representations. To discuss these larger issues, the chapter centers its analysis around the outbreak of the anti-German wave during the late 1950s and 1960s. The essay begins with a brief history of German *"Kulturpolitik"* and *"Öffentlichkeitsarbeit"* (public relations and propaganda) work in the United States before moving on to outline German responses and reactions to the perceived onset of an anti-German wave. It then transitions to a discussion of the American reception of one of the primary elements *(Judgment at Nuremberg)* of the anti-German wave. Finally, it offers some conclusions on what can be gleaned from this phenomenon as far as public diplomacy is concerned.

Broadly speaking, this essay suggests that an examination of the anti-German wave in the United States illuminates the benefits that inverting Americanization can have for the study of cultural transfer. Most discussions of intercultural relations between the United States and Germany focus on the impact of American culture in Germany. In this way, these studies fall within the general realm of Americanization studies. The conclusion highlights in a general way how examining public diplomacy *in* the United States (rather than *from* the United States) opens up new vistas and challenges associated with the study of intercultural relationships.

"Kulturpolitik" and "Öffentlichkeitsarbeit"

Although much of the fear and apprehension about Germany in Cold War America focused on the Nazi period, previous regimes had done little to help win American friendship. The imperial regime, in particular, left a lasting negative legacy. Much of what passed for public diplomacy during Wilhelmian Germany consisted of private, academic, and religious initiatives. And much of it was based on assumptions of cultural and racial superiority. To German intellectuals (as well as to those of Britain and France), the United States, in the words of Jessica C. E. Gienow-Hecht, "represented a cultural wasteland ready to be civilized but also a convenient battlefield where the European powers would fight their last battle for global colonial preponderance." German professors, as a group one of the most visible agents of German cultural transfer, sought to enlighten Americans about their own primitiveness by trumpeting the superiority of the German model of higher education.[5]

This sense of superiority was most evident in the conduct of the Kaiser. Frank Trommler has illustrated how Wilhelm II "transformed [the German nation] into a mere appendage of an odd personality." With the Kaiser's help, the Germans became "arrogant," "power-mad," "militaristic and imperialistic," and "fond of vainglory and conquest" in the eyes of many Americans. Intended as tokens of friendship, imperial gifts, such as a Wilhelm's present of a bronze statue of Frederick the Great, instead came across as ominous. As a result, German cultural activities in the imperial period often did not solidify the latent respect that many Americans had for German culture and education. Many times, with the help of misguided public diplomacy, traditionally positive German characteristics such as "hard working" and "efficient" took on terrifying militaristic dimensions. This was especially true after the outbreak of World

War I. With the help of British propaganda, previous German initiatives appeared even more sinister.[6]

American impressions before the Nazi period therefore were already unfavorable. But the conduct of the Nazis sharpened and heightened these fears and anxieties. In the hands of Goebbels and others, public diplomacy became a feared weapon. Nazi Germany used propaganda to help subvert governments in Austria, Czechoslovakia, Poland, Belgium, Denmark, Norway, and France. The size of the Nazi bureaucracy demonstrated the importance that the party placed on propaganda. In addition to Goebbel's Ministry for Popular Enlightenment and Propaganda, von Ribbentrop's Foreign Office contained foreign press and broadcast monitoring stations, and the party itself maintained its own organs for domestic and foreign propaganda. The Nazis conceived of propaganda as an integral part of their drive for world domination.[7]

In the United States, the Nazi party hoped to galvanize German-Americans. Party theorists estimated that between seven and eight million German-Americans still spoke German as their primary language, and that fully a quarter of the American population was of German extraction. In fact, party leaders believed that the American population was as much German as it was Anglo-Saxon. The Nazi Party believed that these German elements in the United States remained "uncontaminated" by the corruptive Jewish influences. Nazi race theorists went so far as to label the "melting pot" philosophy a "Jewish invention." During the first half of the 1930s, the German government attempted to re-awaken *Deutschtum* or Germanness in the German-American segment of the population. They sought to make German-Americans aware of their racial heritage and encouraged them to think of themselves as Germans exclusively.[8]

The Nazis sought to achieve this goal, as well as the general goal of weakening American democracy, through propaganda using a number of front organizations. The German National Railway, the Tourist Information Bureau, and the Library of Information were formal outlets, eventually closed down by the Justice Department for their activities. The Nazis also sent material to specific individuals such as George Sylvester Viereck and Friedrich E. F. Aufhagen. Many other right-wing anti-Semitic organizations were suspected of Nazi influence, such as the Knights of the White Camellia, the American Nationalist Confederation, and the Silver Shirts.[9] The most notorious of these groups, however, was the German-American Bund, whose leader

Fritz Kuhn, with "his thick foreign accent, his Nazi-style uniform, his repeated statements of allegiance to Hitler, and above all, his apparent misuse of his recently acquired American citizenship," accomplished, in the words of Sander Diamond, what "a host of other Americans had failed to do in the years immediately following Hitler's consolidation of power: he made numerous Americans aware of the fascist challenge." Obsessed with him and his Bund, American observers often exaggerated the strength and popularity of his organization.[10]

Following Germany's defeat after World War II, the nature of the power-political relationship between the United States and the German people, as well as the moral ruin associated with the Nazi period, brought great changes to German public diplomacy in the United States. For five years following World War II, Germany's public diplomacy was virtually nonexistent. Once the Federal Republic emerged in 1949, the new German state did not enjoy the relative parity with the United States that its predecessors had. Rather, the new Federal Republic was dependent on the United States in a number of very obvious ways. This dependence demanded a transformation in the approach of the Federal Republic to the United States.[11]

Rather than attempting to introduce *Kultur* to the United States or awaken *Deutschtum* among German-Americans, then, the Federal Republic pursued a much more modest objective. It sought to ingratiate itself with the American people, to convince Americans that West Germany was different from Nazi Germany, and to demonstrate that the nation was now a dependable ally of the West. As for America's allies, the Federal Republic's goal was, according to historian Manuela Aguilar, "to establish a positive image in those countries and to convince them that Germany was oriented toward peace and international cooperation and thus worthy to become a member of the community of western democratic nations." In these efforts, the West Germans attempted to carefully navigate around the debris left by their predecessors. In particular, West German activities were hamstrung by American fears of fifth-column activity. German officials proceeded carefully, always aware of the activities of anti-German groups, such as the Society for the Prevention of World War III, that were determined to prove to Americans that Nazis remained in power in the Federal Republic. German officials were also concerned about sensitive Jewish groups in the United States.[12]

Through his early institutional initiatives, Chancellor Konrad Adenauer demonstrated his understanding of the importance of public diplomacy. Beginning with the hiring of Rudolf Salat to work in the Chancellor's Office Liaison Department to the Allied High Commission, Adenauer emphasized the necessity of reestablishing cultural relations with the Federal Republic's western allies. One of his most important early actions was the creation of a new institution, the Federal Press and Information Office, designed to handle such affairs. In 1951, the Foreign Office and the Federal Press and Information Office together established Inter Nationes, a semi-private institution entrusted with the responsibility of creating information for distribution abroad.[13]

In the United States, much of the informational work of the Federal Republic during the 1950s was conducted by an American public relations firm. Several German officials observed that public opinion played an uncommonly large role in the formulation of American foreign policy, and thus reasoned that the manipulation of representations of Germans in the United States should constitute a major element of their broader plan to win American friendship. Therefore, in addition to the resumption of *Kulturpolitik,* officials realized that they needed to coordinate the dissemination of information in the United States. Public relations firms, several officials argued, were simply needed to coordinate all of the "multi-faceted" propaganda activities of an organization. Dr. Heinz Krekeler, then consul general of New York, found that an "especially important" arm of activity was the "placement" of information and pictures in periodicals. The employment of a public relations firm would also help sidestep American fears about renewed German propaganda in the United States. Employing an American public relations firm became a priority of the new Federal Republic.[14]

After entertaining several bids by American public relations firms,[15] the Federal Republic of Germany entered into a contract with the Roy Bernard Company, a firm that secured the German contract through its pitch, "Germany belongs in the Western world." That the principal partners, Roy Blumenthal and Bernard Gittelson, were Jews with German backgrounds unquestionably helped them prevail over more seasoned public relations firms. The contract stipulated that Roy Bernard should be "public relations counsel within the general area of public-relations that shall be considered by the Government of the Federal Republic of Germany conducive to the promotion of harmony, understanding and industrial and cultural intercourse between the nations of West Germany and the United States." Part of this responsibility included the preparation of literature, pamphlets, and brochures, as well as the general charge to do whatever it could and whatever the German government thought was necessary to promote German interests. A decade later, Roy Bernard entered into a similar arrangement with the City of West Berlin to conduct the same kinds of informational policies.[16]

In addition to serving as a source of information on West Germany and West Berlin, Roy Bernard functioned as public relations counsel in a number of other ways. One of its main charges was to serve as the conduit between the press and visiting dignitaries. Roy Bernard also advised on West German and West Berlin propaganda efforts. Most importantly, Roy Bernard admirably fulfilled its reputation for placing articles in major newspapers and periodicals, "planting" pieces in such popular magazines as *Life, Atlantic Monthly, Holiday,* and *Collier's*. Additionally, Roy Bernard successfully suppressed or neutralized negative representations of Germans, such as silencing a planned anti-German piece by popular radio host Walter Winchell.[17] For the most part satisfied with the work of the firm, the Federal Republic renewed its contract with Roy Bernard through the 1970s.

Despite these successes, the PR firm's expertise did not, admittedly, extend to film and television.[18] In these areas, the Germans continued to worry over anti-German products during the 1950s. In 1952, for example, Heinz Krekeler reported that a "disproportional" amount of entertainment films with negative German stereotypes still appeared on American television in the evening. Cautiously estimating the nightly viewing population at fifty to sixty million Americans, he wrote that the "tasteless" content of these films was "extraordinarily distressing" from a German standpoint.[19] Krekeler noted that on one evening he saw a film which featured a "brutal shooting" of French freedom fighters by the SS and another that centered around German spies and saboteurs. Observing that many of these programs owed their origins to wartime Britain, however, German officials believed that over time they would disappear as new programming was produced. To counter these negative images in the interim, German officials considered various ways to place positive images of Germans on television, including the synchronization of German films as well as the production of new films by American companies.[20]

But West German officials were not so patient with Hollywood. Despite the fact that several pro-German films were produced (among the most egregious was Nunnally Johnson's pro-Rommel film *The Desert Fox*), Germans worried that Hollywood continued to churn out products that defamed the German people. As the consul general from Chicago put it, actual hate films *(Hetzfilme)* were rare. What was far more common, however, were otherwise "harmless" films that left a subconscious impression through individual characters that Germans were "back-stabbing, brutal, criminal, in short: villains." This official pointed out such tendencies in *The African Queen, The Greatest Show on Earth,* and *Rope of Sand.*[21] The first contained scenes of brutal German soldiers from World War I, while the latter two featured villainous players with German characteristics. Officials in the Federal Republic targeted Paramount, United Artists, and Metro-Goldwyn-Mayer as the three most consistent producers of films with anti-German undertones, and considered various ways to retaliate.

Such was the tenuous environment, when a series of international events brought, from the German perspective, a new wave of anti-German propaganda.

The Anti-German Wave

In retrospect, pinpointing the onset of the anti-German wave was a difficult task for German officials. Some traced it to the publication of Anne Frank's diary,[22] others to the desecration of a rededicated synagogue in Cologne on Christmas Eve in 1959 and the subsequent swastika daubings of Jewish institutions and cemeteries throughout the rest of the year. Whatever the trigger, most agreed that the capture of Eichmann and his subsequent trial were the most important events in terms of generating and sustaining anti-German sentiment.[23]

As a result of these events, many journalists in the United States began to question the dependability and nature of the Federal Republic. With Israel's "forthcoming trial of Adolf Eichmann ... forcing attention again on the enormity of what the Nazis were," Edward Gruson, chief of the *New York Times* bureau in Bonn, wondered, "who speaks for the new Germany?" Was it Konrad Adenauer and others, "conscious as they write that their readership includes watchful foreigners," or was it "swastika daubers and the furtive souls who creep anonymously into cemeteries to smash tombstones and wreak still more vengeance on the dead?" Officially, he noted, Germans appear determined to confront their past, bombarding their children with facts about the Third Reich. But he uneasily observed that another crisis could renew German nationalism.[24] This unease was amplified five years later, when the Nationaldemokratische Partei Deutschlands (NPD), the new rightist party of Germany, gained a significant 2 percent of the popular vote. British journalist James Cameron interviewed Adolf von Thadden, leader of the NPD movement, for *New York Times Magazine*. Von Thadden charged that the Germans had been puppets in the hands of the Americans and Soviets and that the theory of collective guilt had been paralyzing.[25]

In *New York Times Magazine* Richard Lowenthal reported that the "Germans are beginning to feel like Germans again." Lowenthal pointed out that after the war, Germans had subordinated everything to economic reconstruction. In the process, they tried to fill the "spiritual void" left by the collapse of the "Nazi myth" with the hope of Western European integration. When de Gaulle destroyed that hope, the Germans began to think in national terms again. Other factors such as the reestablishment of contacts with Eastern Germans following the Berlin crisis, and the "dramatized" meaning of national partition in the Berlin Wall bolstered this trend. Lowenthal feared that if the United States did not take a firm stand in settling the European problem, the Germans might pursue a neutral course.[26]

From the perspective of German officials, one of the most troubling news reports was CBS's "The Germans," which premiered in 1967. It incensed even Joseph Thomas, the Director of the German Information Center, who did not express the same level of concern that other Germans did over the anti-German wave. "The Germans" focused on life in Nuremberg, and drew a number of controversial conclusions from its examination of the city. Among them, it painted the Germans as backward, provincial, nationalistic, politically immature, and concerned primarily with swilling beer and consuming potatoes (the producers claimed that each German consumed about two pounds daily). German officials found much of the factual reporting to be tendentious. Joseph Thomas wrote a detailed letter to CBS outlining their grievances against the program.[27]

German officials were joined in their outrage by the citizens of Nuremberg, who did not take kindly to the implications of the program.

German officials noted that present-day events were not the only source of fodder for *die antideutsche Welle*. They also observed that Germany's past became a fertile ground for historical and fictional works on German nature. German officials argued that William Shirer's *The Rise and Fall of the Third Reich* had, and continued to have, a far more negative impact on American public opinion than any exhibition of an atrocity film could ever exert. After its publication at the beginning of the decade, they believed that Shirer's book, in the minds of many, became the standard work on the Nazi period. The most disastrous parts of the book, from the point of view of the German Foreign Office, came not from the descriptions of the Nazis, but from the opening sections, in which Shirer argued that the Nazi regime was the logical outgrowth of the German national character. As a correspondent in Berlin during the Third Reich, Shirer enjoyed a great deal of credibility in his writing on the Germans and the Third Reich, and his book and opinions were disseminated widely.[28]

While Shirer's work tended to resonate with the general public, Fritz Fischer's *Griff nach der Weltmacht* appealed more to professional historians. Based on a staggering amount of archival work, Fischer's book contained a relatively simple argument: the Central Powers were responsible for the outbreak of World War I. In this way, Fischer's thesis rehabilitated the war guilt clause of the Versailles treaty, angering many Germans who preferred to think of their involvement in World War I as morally equivalent at worst and morally superior at best. It offered a powerful revision to the American understanding of World War I, which also tended to blame the Allies for the Great War. Unsurprisingly, Fischer encountered a great deal of criticism in both Germany and America, but the strength of his research led many to reevaluate their understanding of World War I.[29]

While German officials found that the "anti-German wave" manifested itself in virtually all outlets in American society, they worried most about its effects in film and television. *Judgment at Nuremberg* was only the most worrisome in this regard. German officials also fretted over films like *The Battle of the Bulge*, *The Blue Max*, *Is Paris Burning*, and *The Ship of Fools*. They objected to the ways in which these films stereotyped the Germans. Since these stories often took place during World War II, they more often than not appeared to equate Nazism with Germanism. German officials railed against films that seemed to impute that Nazism formed a constitutive part of German culture.[30]

The German Foreign Office and the Federal Press Office were most concerned about anti-German products in American television, however. They believed that programs like *Combat!*, *Rat Patrol*, and *Hogan's Heroes* portrayed the Germans as a dumb, vicious, and cruel people. They were especially concerned about the effect that these television programs were having on children. Having banked on the hope that wartime portrayals of the Germans would fade away with time in the 1950s, they were alarmed to see the creation of new programs that started the defamation all over again. They also worried about the effect that these programs were having in the Third World. On a number of occasions, German officials reported that these programs were breeding hatred against the Germans in Latin America.[31]

German officials offered a variety of reasons for the anti-German wave. Most believed that Americans for some reason still nurtured a lingering hatred of the Germans, who, despite their steadfast alliance with the United States, could convince Americans that they were trustworthy. Others blamed powerful Jews in the United States, arguing that Jews exercised a "great influence in the modern communication industry." But officials in the embassy put forth the most reasonable explanation. They thought that the recent revival of interest in Nazism was a byproduct of a greater discovery of World War II. Stories that dealt with World War II would naturally portray the enemy in an unfavorable light. The Eichmann trial and the victory of the NPD, officials in the Embassy pointed out, only spurred this revival along.[32]

German officials tried a number of tactics to stem the tide of the anti-German wave. Because they feared that official protests would only give the anti-German wave more attention, German officials preferred to work behind the scenes. The German Foreign Office encouraged German-American groups to protest the defamation of Germans in the American media. Along these lines they supported the idea of a German Anti-Defamation League. They wrote private letters of protest to executives of media outlets, asking for their cooperation in improving the image of Germans on television. And in at least one instance, Joseph Thomas offered powerful Hollywood columnist Hedda Hopper the idea for an anti-Communist movie (as opposed to an anti-Nazi film) that could be passed along to producers in Hollywood.[33]

The Federal Republic's primary response to the anti-German wave was to step up German cultural and social representation in the United States through the creation of the German Information Center (GIC) in 1961. West German officials did not believe that their public relations firm Roy Bernard was doing enough to stem the tide of the anti-German wave, and so the proposed GIC took on many of the duties and responsibilities of the Roy Bernard Company. Jointly administered by the Foreign Office and the Federal Press Office, the GIC's primary function was to serve as a source of information on the Federal Republic. But it was also expected to place information in major American periodicals. German officials chose Dr. Joseph Thomas as its director, a German who had served as Press Officer as well as Deputy Chief Director of the American Desk in Bonn. The GIC began operations in late 1960 and continues to serve as a source of information for American journalists. In this new configuration, Roy Bernard's role was reduced to advisor to the Federal Republic.[34]

When West German officials moved more forcefully to counteract the anti-German wave, it sometimes ended in disaster. Such was the case when the Foreign Office cut funding for a lecture circuit planned by Fritz Fischer. As one American official put it, "the controversy over Fischer has unquestionably undone years of effort by the representatives of the Federal Republic in the United States to encourage a favorable image of the new Germany." The basic contours of the story are clear. Fischer had received funding from the Goethe-Institut to present a series of papers in the United States on his recent work *Griff nach der Weltmacht*. In the fall of 1963, the German government informed the universities that Fischer had refused the invitation. Since he was personally in contact with some of the members of the faculty, the lie was readily discovered. The Goethe-Institut then informed Fischer and the universities that a mistake had been made, and that funds were unavailable. Professor William Langer of Harvard University joined other American professors in protest, embarrassing even Fischer with the strident tone of their missives to the German Foreign Office. In due course, these American professors convinced the American Council of Learned Societies to fund Fischer's trip.

Once it became aware of the availability of these funds, the Foreign Office dispatched a high official to Hamburg to plead with Fischer not to go. According to the American report, "he made a strong appeal to Fischer's German patriotism and tried to show Fischer that his trip to America would harm the favorable image the Germans had been trying to create in the United States." Fischer tried to convince him that at this point it would be more damaging not to go. Eventually Fischer came to the United States and gave his lectures. The American consulate in Hamburg was left to conclude that "one can only agree with the general evaluation of the American professors on the stupidity and lack of comprehension of the German Foreign Office demonstrated by its activities in the Fischer affair.... Now, too many Americans will agree with William Shirer, that 'the Germans never change.'"[35]

Despite their damaging experience in the Fischer controversy, Foreign Office officials considered even more drastic measures to bring American film and television producers to heel. They strongly considered an embargo on firms or sponsors such as Alka Seltzer, General Electric, and Union Carbide who were affiliated anti-German products. Yet before they took this radical step, they needed proof of the negative effect that these films were having on the American people.[36]

What evidence did the Federal Republic already possess, and what did it say? Did these cultural products serve as sites of collective memory in which Americans reflected on the barbarism of the German people? Anecdotal evidence to this effect trickled into the Press and Information Office (BPA) and the Foreign Office (AA). A concerned German passed along a letter from his son who was studying in the United States. His son reported that his classmates often asked him if he was a Nazi or a Communist, despite the fact that he was born in 1949. His son blamed American television, which contained several programs on the World War II era that, according to him, portrayed the Germans as "hard, unscrupulous, vicious, and always ready to say 'Heil Hitler' or 'Jawohl.'" In a later letter, he expressed frustration for having to carry this heavy burden, when he himself had "done nothing bad." A German-American living in California warned Chancellor Kiesinger that American children were being educated by the television, and that the television was teaching children that the German was a "stupid, brutal animal. No other land in the world is similarly propagandized in the US as the Germans."[37]

The German Foreign Office decided that anecdotal evidence was not enough to move forward with serious measures, however. They wanted to know when anti-German programs were shown on television, where on television they could be found, and who was sponsoring them. And more importantly, they sought to discover if American attitudes had changed as a result of these cultural products. Officials in the embassy wanted concrete data before they decided to recommend economic sanctions or suggest that the Chancellor speak with President Johnson about the matter.[38]

The results of this survey were a great relief to German officials. The poll found that the Germans were second only to the British of "best-liked" people. Most encouraging to the BPA was evidence that the anti-German wave had virtually no effect on public opinion. A mere 7 percent of respondents said that the anti-German programs reflected their true feelings. Twenty-four percent said that there was no relationship between the depictions of the programs and present-day Germany. The other 76 percent apparently had not even recognized a possible connection. Dr. Graf Schweinitz of the BPA proudly claimed that this poll, and not the apparent anti-German wave, revealed the true feelings of the American people. He declared that the results confirmed the outstanding success of the Press and Information Office in promoting a positive image of the German people during the post-war period. By the end of the decade, Joseph Thomas was reporting that *Rat Patrol* and *Combat!* had been canceled, and that humorous depictions of Germans in *Hogan's Heroes* and *Laugh-In* did not have an adverse effect on the image of Germany. The anti-German wave apparently had not affected the American understanding of Germany.[39]

Contextualizing the Anti-German Wave

Was Graf Schweinitz's analysis accurate? Was the American resistance to the anti-German wave simply a product of persistent public relations work? Or was the situation more complex? Other public opinion polls from the period offer some clues. The Survey Research Center at the University of Michigan surveyed thirteen hundred people on their attitudes toward the Germans in the late spring–early summer of 1962, just after the publication of *The Rise and Fall of the Third Reich*, the trial of Adolf Eichmann, and the release of *Judgment at Nuremberg*.

The results were remarkably similar. Sixty percent of respondents had a good impression of the Germans, while only 15 percent held a negative view. When asked if their opinions of the Germans had changed over the last few years, 72 percent said no, 15 percent said it had improved, and only 4 percent said that it had become worse. Only three people mentioned the Shirer book, and only one discussed the Eichmann trial. A majority of Americans thought that the Germans were dependable allies, and an overwhelming majority thought that the United States should stay in Berlin.[40] This survey also suggested a hardy resistance to the anti-German wave.

But this survey probed deeper, asking respondents to explain their answers. What is remarkable in these explanations is the towering shadow that the Cold War cast across the American understanding of West Germany. The most popular reason for liking Germany? Germany's role in the Cold War. The most popular reason for trusting Germany as an ally? "They know and dislike Communism and Russia." The second most popular reason? "They know and like us." The most popular reason for defending West Berlin? Four out of five said to stop communism.[41]

From these responses it is clear that in the early 1960s, just as in the 1950s, the Cold War remained the decisive prism through which Americans understood the world around them. Indeed, the onset of the Cold War, more so than any public diplomacy work, was responsible for the rehabilitation of the Germans in the eyes of many Americans. Many factors helped knit Western Germany into the fabric of America's Cold War consensus. One was Berlin, the erstwhile German capital itself. As Thomas Schwartz has observed, "the struggle over the city helped to change American perceptions of Germans, whose determination to resist the Soviet action evoked widespread admiration."[42] Another important element was the concept of totalitarianism. Totalitarianism rested in large part on the belief that, in the words of Abbott Gleason, "the Soviet threat was similar to the German threat and was its lineal successor."[43] Tracing lineage along ideological rather than national lines certainly facilitated the work of West Germany's public diplomacy. Yet credit must be given to the Federal Republic and its proxies for realizing and capitalizing on these larger cultural forces. Roy Bernard's campaign "Germany Belongs in the Western World" exemplified the savvy and intelligence of this effort.

The extent to which West Germany was woven into the fabric of the Cold War consensus can easily be seen in some of the knee-jerk reactions to the anti-German wave. Perhaps the most hysterical in this regard was conservative *Wall Street Journal* columnist William H. Chamberlain's attack on the producers of some anti-German products in an article entitled, "The Revival of Anti-Germanism." Claiming that the American public "has been the target of the most intensive 'Hate Germany' campaign since the war and immediate postwar years," Chamberlain denounced "a movement which is clearly injurious to the interests of American foreign policy, which defames an ally and gratifies an enemy, [and] which misrepresents and distorts the most heartening European postwar development, the emergence of a reconstructed prosperous Germany as a reliable ally in the Western camp." In this way, Chamberlain and others contended that to be anti-German was to be anti-American.[44]

In the 1960s, however, the mainstream common understanding of the Cold War and America's place in it began to break down. As Gleason has written, "the young radicals who were creating the New Left began to disagree" with many aspects of the Cold War consensus, especially the notion that "that there really was a huge gulf between the Western democracies, led by the United States, and Soviet imperialism."[45] Young idealistic Americans who watched white supremacists brutalize peacefully demonstrating African-Americans began to question the supposed superiority of their civilization. The Vietnam War, in particular, convinced many that American imperialism was equally or perhaps more odious that that of the Soviet Union. By the end of the 1960s, politics in the United States had polarized.

If Americans understood the Cold War differently during the 1960s, then that would mean that they understood West Germany differently too. During the early years of the Cold War, the heyday of the Cold War consensus, Americans understood West Germany as a nation in transition from despotism to democracy. The Cold War consensus saw the United States as the highest form of government, and, according to this worldview, Americanizing West Germany was the best means of reconstructing it. In the 1960s, that understanding remained, but as the Cold War consensus fractured, the ways in which Americans understood Germans fractured as well. Both present and past German experiences provided a language and set of metaphors that were increasingly appropriated by the Left as well as by mainstream America. The more and more polysemic nature of American discourse on Germany helps explain how increasingly negative images of Germany could still coexist with general public approval. Either Americans approved of West Germany because they continued to subscribe to the Cold War consensus and therefore resented the implication of many of these anti-German texts; or Americans did not disapprove of West Germany because they saw no reason to single out the Federal Republic when it was clear that their own nation was not any better.

Judging the Germans

This fracturing consensus can be witnessed in American responses to one of the principal elements of the feared "anti-German wave," and in the process help explain how Nazi Germany was highly visible in the United States during the 1960s without blackening West Germany's image.[46] In particular, an examination of the reactions to Stanley Kramer and Abby Mann's *Judgment at Nuremberg* (hereafter *Judgment*) illustrates how anti-Nazi and indeed anti-German texts functioned as sites of memory in which Americans remade relations between Nazis, Germans, and their own society.[47]

With *Judgment,* scriptwriter Abby Mann and director-producer Stanley Kramer said that they wanted to challenge prevailing American attitudes toward the Federal Republic of Germany. When Mann first began writing *Judgment* in the 1950s he remembered, "it was considered a breech of good manners in polite society to bring up the subject of German guilt or the victims of the Third Reich."[48] For Mann, this repression stemmed from an American desire to whitewash the German people in the name of Cold War expediency. As evidenced in his screenplay, Mann believed that there was no "ground zero" in which German democracy was reborn. Most of the Germans portrayed in his film come across as servile, arrogant, or cruel. For example, in one of the most powerful moments of the film, the German defense attorney approaches Judge Haywood after the conviction of his clients and informs him that, despite his ruling, his clients will go free in five years. Haywood compliments the young lawyer for his logical mind, but lectures him that because it is logical does not mean that it is right. In the script, Mann writes that the defense attorney "is a little stunned. Haywood has stopped him for a moment, making him think. But only for a moment. It is not long until the old rationalizations come into his face. He is indeed the symbol of the new Germany."[49] In these ways, Mann's screenplay makes little distinction between Nazi Germany and the Federal Republic.

And yet Mann maintained later that the film was not even really about Germany. In a sense, Mann believed that he failed in his effort, because, as he said later in an interview, "I wasn't writing about Germany, I was writing about patriotism, to say that patriotism is evil." This intent is evident in the way that the film juxtaposes unsavory episodes in American history with elements of Nazism. Perhaps the most obvious (and the one that several German viewers noticed) was the German defense lawyer's invocation of the widespread American belief in eugenics, as propounded by Oliver Wendell Holmes, in the early twentieth century. Another was the willingness of American military personnel to subvert justice for national advantage in the Cold War. Read this way, Mann's film conformed to the New Left's indictment against American hypocrisy and moral bankruptcy. For Mann, as for many others in the New Left, Germany provided powerful images, symbols, metaphors, and lessons that could be used to criticize the current domestic and foreign policies of the United States.

An advanced preview of *Judgment* held on 12 August 1961 (coincidentally, the day before construction began on the Wall) illustrates how Americans understood the film in the early part of the 1960s. Although a few respondents focused on the misdeeds of the Americans, the overwhelming number of spectators concentrated on the degree of guilt that average everyday Germans bore for the Holocaust. Many of these viewers believed that the message of the film, as one put it, "*did* need to be said." For those who interpreted the film as a righteous effort to tackle the issues of the Holocaust, *Judgment* "outlined and detailed the German character perfectly in their denial of knowledge and or responsibility." On the other hand, others believed that this was an "old story revisited," a "rehashment [sic]" that "many would like to forget." They believed that World War II and the Holocaust should remain in the past, that there was no need to dredge up these awful memories. One spectator summarized this sentiment when he wrote, "Why not save resentment for the communist[s], instead of a party that is no longer in power? Let us live in the present not in the past."[50]

Yet despite these sharp differences over the responsibility that contemporary Germans bore for the Holocaust, these spectators shared a remarkable homogeneity in their interpretation of the main issue. For the most part, these Americans were still part of the Cold War consensus that evinced confidence in the supremacy of American ideals and the desirability of the American way of life. For them, the Holocaust remained a German event, and the main terms of the debate revolved around how much progress the Germans were making in shedding their past and reaching that exalted state of American-style democracy and capitalism. As evidenced by these responses, some believed that the Germans were still unrepentant Nazis, others believed that Nazism died out a long time ago, but all believed that Nazism, if it was a problem at all, was a German problem.

In contrast to this screening of *Judgment* in San Francisco (which was likely more representative for most Americans) was the world premiere in Berlin. The meaning that American reporters drew from this event was heavily conditioned by the environment created by Kramer and Brandt. As previously noted, Brandt warned that it would be difficult to watch the film, but he maintained that "the roots of the present position of our people, our country and our city lie in this fact, that we did not prevent right from being trampled underfoot during the time of Nazi power." He welcomed the premiere of this difficult film, calling it an "important political event" and believing that its occurrence in West Berlin underscored the importance of "Berlin as a center of spiritual conflict." Through such powerful rhetoric, Brandt made a pitch for Berlin as the place of reconciliation, the place where Germans were willing to come to grips with the sins of their past. Moreover, by comparing the brutality of the Nazis with the evident brutality of the East German regime in the construction of the Berlin Wall, he cast the East Germans as the heirs to Hitler's National Socialism.[51] Buttressed by tours of the Wall and East Berlin given to foreign visitors by the Berlin Senate, Brandt's words colored the interpretation of American reporters in attendance, drawing their attention to the city—and present-day Germany by extension—as much as the film itself.

As a result of their environment, American reporters explicitly related context with text. For them, this exhibition of *Judgment* became a litmus test for the political maturity of the

Germans, and they, along with Kramer and the rest of his staff, curiously awaited the response of the Germans. On the whole, they were impressed with the willingness of most Germans to face up to the damning film. Reporters noted that the Germans were "grim," or sat through the film in "stoic silence." Others described the Germans as "stunned" or "dazed" by the film. Although a few Berliners denounced the film, according to the reviewers, most hailed it for its "piercing honesty." Discussed in the context of Brandt's speech and the circumstances of the city of Berlin itself, these reports of the German reaction suggested that Berliners would lead the rest of the country into an honest appraisal of the German past.[52] In this reading of *Judgment,* then, the emphasis on the bravery of present day Germans in facing the Communists and their own horrific past suggested that Germany had made substantial progress in its effort to become like the United States.

Both the San Francisco and Berlin screenings of the film demonstrated the hold that the Cold War consensus continued to have on Americans. They differ sharply from the responses generated by the television broadcast of *Judgment* on Sunday night, 7 March 1965. This Sunday, "Bloody Sunday," as observers of the Civil Rights came to know it, witnessed a shocking clash between peaceful marchers and brutal Alabama state troopers at a bridge in Selma, Alabama. Millions of viewers received their first images of "Bloody Sunday" when *Judgment* was interrupted by ABC News that night to display footage of the carnage. Many viewers believed that the footage of Selma was actually a part of the film. Andrew Young, a member of the Southern Christian Leadership Conference, wrote that "the violence in Selma was so similar to the violence in Nazi Germany that viewers could hardly miss the connection." The meaning that many Americans drew from this exhibition of *Judgment* disturbed them greatly. "The pictures from Selma were unpleasant," wrote Warren Hinckle and David Welsh of the publication *Ramparts.* "The juxtaposition of the Nazi Storm Troopers and the Alabama State Troopers made them unbearable."[53]

As a result of this accident of programming, those who saw *Judgment at Nuremberg* that evening drew a radically different meaning from it than did previous viewers. Rather than use the film as a basis to judge Germans, they used the film as a basis to judge themselves. As one concerned citizen from Wisconsin wrote to his senator, "Are we seeing the days of Hitler lived in our own country? Disregard politics—fight for human rights, stop all Federal money going to Mississippi and Alabama." Partly as a result of this meaning drawn from the film, mainstream Americans began to view the civil rights struggle in terms not unlike those used to describe World War II and the Cold War. Walter Mondale, senator from Minnesota, worried that "this is totalitarian oppression at its worst—it is what we fought against in World War II and it is what we are fighting against in the cold war today."[54] In the increasingly difficult decade of the 1960s, Americans stopped worrying about Germany becoming like America and started worrying about America becoming like Nazi Germany. In this sense, World War II narratives of Germany provided an international perspective that framed understanding of American politics in a new and powerful way.

These different understandings of Germans from the same cultural document illustrate that American attitudes toward themselves were changing. While some Americans continued to understand Germany in terms of the Cold War consensus, more Americans began to universalize the Nazi experience as the decade wore on and their own flaws became more apparent. This process of universalizing the Nazi experience was aided in part by German public diplomacy and the power of Berlin to make Germans appear like Americans. It was also assisted by the increasing unrest in American society and the growing power of Vietnam to suggest alternative narratives of American participation in the world.

In this sense, then, larger cultural forces and structures determined the response of Americans to anti-German propaganda, forces and structures that the West Germans were largely unable to influence. This conclusion might lead some to regard the public diplomacy of West Germany as inconsequential. They would be wrong. For one, the hard work of the United States, the Federal Republic, and Roy Bernard, and their coordinated strategy to make Germany part of "the Western world," facilitated and shaped this rapprochement. For another, and more importantly, an examination of German efforts to combat the increase in anti-Nazi products during the 1960s touches on a whole host of issues related to the study of intercultural relationships. Among the most important of these, perhaps, is that it demonstrates the benefit of emphasizing questions of meaning over questions of causation when discussing public diplomacy.

The Anti-German Wave and the Study of Public Diplomacy

What does all of this say about our understanding of public diplomacy? More importantly, perhaps, for the purposes of this volume, what can an analysis of the anti-German wave contribute to our understanding of public diplomacy and intercultural relationships? This analysis of the anti-German wave illustrates the many benefits that can be gained from an effort to dislodge the privileged place of Americanization in the study of cultural relationships. "Inverting Americanization" enables students of intercultural relationships, and especially of America's place in the world, to revisit some of the assumptions that Americanization brings to the study of intercultural relationships.

Exploring the public diplomacy of the Federal Republic and its effort to combat the anti-German wave in this context is especially fruitful. First, there is a substantial literature on Americanization in Germany, so this offers a useful point of comparison. Excellent works by Jessica C. E. Gienow-Hecht, Ralph Willet, Petra Goedde, Uta Poiger, Maria Hoehn, and Volker Berghahn illustrate the various ways that America sought to remake Western Germany in an American image.[55] Second, the Germans had attempted, prior to their defeat in World War II, to remake cultures abroad or to Germanize them, so Germany's changed power position following its destruction in World War II highlights the importance of power to method and aims in the conduct of public diplomacy.

One of the major assumptions that Americanization brings to the study of public diplomacy and intercultural relationships is that cultural influence is a function of power. In his highly influential and engaging *Coca-colonization and the Cold War,* Reinhold Wagnleitner notes that the tale of the "global success of U.S. culture," which represents "one of the most important chapters of history in this century," is not a story "only about a cultural process in a narrow sense but also about an economic and eminently political phenomenon, namely, the phenomenon of symbolic power, the power over cultural capital." Wagnleitner goes on to note that American cultural products did not "automatically penetrate foreign countries" but rather formed part of a larger web of American imperialism, of which culture was one of the most important facets. Others, such as Emily Rosenberg, have made similar observations.[56]

In this vein, several scholars have explored the role of the American state in facilitating or taking advantage of Americanization. Wagnleitner has observed that one of the major elements of the "global success story of U.S. culture" has been "the massive direct and indirect support that the export of this culture received from the government of the United States." As Walter Hixson, Richard Pells, and host of others have described it, American public diplomacy in the Cold War was an effort to take advantage of the power and appeal of American mass culture to persuade other nations to be "like us," and not like the Soviet Union.[57]

If we examine the relationship between culture and power from the perspective of public diplomacy in America rather than from or of it, we encounter a different understanding of that relationship. As previously stated, the German strategy regarding cultural relations with the United States changed dramatically in light of the power differential between the two countries following World War II. The new Federal Republic abandoned any designs of significantly altering American culture, focusing its energy instead on producing and maintaining positive representations of Germany in the United States. The methods of German public diplomacy changed to meet these different demands. Because German officials no longer sought to Germanize American culture, but rather work within the structures of American culture to maintain positive representations of Germans, they needed professional American advice. To this end, they employed an American public relations firm to coordinate and advise on their activities. Roy Bernard did this by using its knowledge of and contacts within the media to exploit dominant trends in American culture.

German officials were worried about the anti-German wave precisely because they understood their dependence on the United States. And in this dependence, the Federal Republic was not alone. In fact, the power position and public diplomacy of the Federal Republic vis-à-vis the United States was far more common than the power position and public diplomacy of the United States vis-à-vis other nations in the Cold War. In these relationships, the United States was the only nation that could seriously entertain designs of remaking the culture of the other. In their relationship with the United States, other nations often had a much more modest aim: currying favor with the American people.

Another major assumption that Americanization brings to the study of public diplomacy and intercultural relationships is that public diplomacy is the process by which one nation is remade in the image of another. As Rob Kroes has noted, Americanization, to the extent that it is a useful concept at all, serves as a "shorthand reference to what is essentially a black box in the simple diagram of cultural transmission and reception." The primary point of debate in this framework is the degree to which Americanization has successfully transformed other cultures. In her excellent review "Shame on US?" Gienow-Hecht has outlined this debate, demonstrating how it has become entangled with political issues. On the one side, there exist the "cultural imperialists" who assert (and complain) that American culture has destroyed national cultures and sought to homogenize international norms and culture. The other side seeks to restore agency to natives in target countries by illustrating how American culture has been adapted to meet needs not originally intended. Regardless of an individual's position on this issue, however, most do not question the fact that Americanization is the most important form of intercultural relations to study. In this sense, they constitute a hegemonic force the likes of which they deplore in the subject that they study.[58]

Again, examining public diplomacy in the United States rather than from it yields a different perspective on this issue. Because West Germany understood that it could not long survive without political, economic, and military assistance from the United States, the fundamental aim of West German public diplomacy was not to remake America in Germany's image, but to remake Germany, at least in the eyes of Americans, in America's image. Roy Bernard's strategy, "Germany Belongs in the Western World," echoed this belief. Roy Bernard sought to wipe out thirty-six years of negative publicity brought about by two world wars by stressing both idyllic nineteenth-century perceptions of Germany as well as emphasizing the role of such popular figures as "Mr. Germany," Konrad Adenauer. In carrying out this campaign, Roy Bernard emphasized the similarities between the Federal Republic and the United States.[59]

Comparing American public diplomacy to that of West Germany suggests that the aims of American public diplomacy during the Cold War era were unique, especially when considering the enormous disparities present in international power. It is highly likely that a great deal of the public diplomacy conducted during the Cold War had aims more similar to that of West Germany in the United States than that of the United States in West Germany. Abandoning the efforts of previous regimes to significantly affect American culture, West German public diplomacy was limited to efforts to convince Americans of the similarities between Germany and the United States.

The third assumption that Americanization brings to the study of public diplomacy and intercultural relationships is that cultural influence only matters in one direction. This is in part a factor of the magnitude of Americanization. The prevalence of Coca-cola, McDonald's, Nike, Michael Jordan, and other American icons in foreign lands underscores the importance of this influence. Americanization is such an inescapable fact of modern life that it logically suggests the study of American public diplomacy abroad.

But the tendency to study public diplomacy in one direction is also due in large part to the history of the discipline in the United States. Many of the early American pioneers in the integration of culture and international history, scholars like Frank Ninkovich, Emily Rosenberg, and Frank Costigliola, felt compelled to justify their inclusion of culture into the study of diplomacy by tracing the effects that it could have on US foreign policy more broadly defined. In other words, the raison d'être of the field was, and for many continues to be, the explication of American foreign policy. In this formulation, American public diplomacy was the natural expression of the marriage between culture and international history.

The net result of these twin factors is that Americanization, the process by which American culture is transmitted, has become the focus of study, and Americanism, that is the constellation of ideas that constitute the American culture that is being transmitted, remains relatively static or given. Hixson frankly states in his study: "I make no systematic effort to analyze how the Cold War shaped American society." Kroes nicely articulates the role of Americanism in Americanization studies when he says that Americanism, for most, remains "a short-hand reference to America's hallowed repertoire of guiding ideals, explaining the nation's course and destiny to the American people while at the same time providing an inspiration to non-Americans abroad."[60]

Exploring public diplomacy in America rather than from America, in this last perspective, enables us to transform our relationship between American culture and foreign relations. Rather than viewing Americanism as content to be transferred, we can, if we examine cultural activity in the other direction, recapture the dynamism inherent in American culture in the post-war period. Just as so many works on Americanization have begun by studying the reception of American culture in a particular country (and thus exploring the dynamism of the host country's culture), examining the efforts of other countries to influence American culture recovers the crosscurrents and contestations inherent in post-war American culture. This essay demonstrates this last point. It highlights the role that representations of Germans played in American discourse on its foreign and domestic policies. In particular, it illustrates the role that Germany's past and present played in the construction and destruction of America's Cold War consensus.

All of this brings us to the last major benefit that inverting Americanization can have for our understanding of intercultural relationships. In large part because of its curious development (at least in the United States), the study of public diplomacy, and especially Americanization, has been obsessed with measuring the impact of cultural initiatives. With its origins in the study of diplomacy and not in the study of culture, the scholarship in public diplomacy has largely been concerned with assessing causation and gauging effectiveness, rather than dealing with questions of meaning. Gienow-Hecht has ably recounted how much of the scholarship on Americanization and public diplomacy has centered on how much, if any, culture has "transferred" in these initiatives. To crudely paraphrase Shakespeare (and Richard Pells): like us, or not like us: that has been the question.

As this study of the anti-German wave shows, however, understanding the reception or usage of German representations is far more complex and nuanced than the simplistic effective/ineffective dichotomy used by German officials allows. In fact, it suggests that the whole approach, founded as it is in the diplomat *manqué* tradition of diplomatic history, focuses inquiry along a very narrow course. The polysemic nature of German representations, the welter of representational activities, the sheer complexity of America's mass media—all these obstacles and more indicate that making claims, in any national context, about the impact or effectiveness of cultural initiatives is so fraught with epistemological difficulties as to make any such claims inherently problematic. While this is particularly evident in this context—the Germans clearly did not possess the requisite power to transform American culture—the same kinds of obstacles nevertheless plague claims about the effectiveness of American public diplomacy or Americanization also. What's more, an overemphasis on effectiveness has also obscured some of the other ways that public diplomacy can be used.

Instead, I would like to submit that one of the most important reasons for studying public diplomacy is not so much that it opens another window onto power relations between states, but that it provides new ways for studying a particular nation's culture, and specifically how that culture understands or constructs the nation conducting public diplomacy within its borders. In other words, the study of public diplomacy offers new sources of evidence for historians interested in exploring domestic culture. First, through reports, studies, public opinion polls, and the like, representatives of a nation-state in the host country provide information on the attitudes, debates, and cultural products that illuminate the contours of the host nation's society and culture. Because these representatives are often most concerned with how their nation is represented or talked about, public diplomacy more specifically gives an excellent avenue for exploring how the host country understands their nation. Second, propaganda and other fruits of information work offer historians additional primary sources with which to understand how people receive and understand cultural products from and about the nation-state in question. As this study of the anti-German wave demonstrates, the greatest value of the German efforts to analyze and combat the anti-German wave lay not in gauging the effectiveness of their public diplomacy work but in providing us with additional material to understand how Americans at the time understood the Germans. Indeed, German officials cited and generated evidence that ultimately contradicted their own conclusions. Their evidence suggests that the cultural products and reactions that made up the anti-German wave were, in the end, not primarily about Germany. Instead, Americans used Germany as a metaphor and framing device for talking about and understanding themselves and their society.

In conclusion, the anti-German wave is an event that confirms the importance of the study of German public diplomacy (and the public diplomacy of other nations on the cultural periphery), even if it does not necessarily confirm the efficacy of that diplomacy (as the Germans claimed). As we seek to internationalize the study not only of American foreign relations history but of American history itself, it is necessary to adopt an international perspective regarding public diplomacy. Comparing the effects of Americanization in different countries is not enough. We must begin working with the public diplomacy of other nations, not only to understand what is unique about American cultural activity but also to understand what makes it unique—in other words, to understand what has passed for more "common" public diplomacy in the post-World War II period. Once we do this, we will be on the road to creating a truly international history of public diplomacy.

Notes

Thanks go the Deutsche Akademische Austauschdienst (DAAD), the Graduate School at Ohio State University, and the Mershon Center for research support. I would also like to thank Michael Hogan, Peter Hahn, Matt Masur, Jennifer Walton, Ken Osgood, Jason Parker, and Jessica C. E. Gienow-Hecht for their comments on previous versions of this essay and Barbara Glenn for going over key German documents with me and confirming my translations.

1. Address of Governing Mayor Brandt at World Premiere of *Judgment at Nuremberg*, Publicity—Horwits, Al Correspondence, Stanley Kramer Papers, Department of Special Collections, UCLA, Los Angeles, CA, USA (hereafter SKP).
2. Martin Quigley, "An Important Political Event," *Motion Picture Herald*, 27 December 1961, 7–9, *Judgment at Nuremberg* Clippings File, Margaret Herrick Library, Academy of Motion Pictures Arts and Sciences, Beverly Hills, CA, USA (hereafter MHL).
3. Stanley Kramer, *Judgment at Nuremberg* (USA: United Artists, 1961).
4. Minutes and assignments of meeting, 24 October 1961, Berlin Task Force Minutes of Meetings, Records Relating to the Berlin Crisis, 1961–62, Executive Secretariat, Record Group 59, National Archives II, College Park, MD, USA (hereafter NA); minutes and assignments of meeting, 30 October 1961, Berlin Task Force Minutes of Meetings, Records Relating to the Berlin Crisis, 1961–62, Executive Secretariat, RG 59, NA; Roeber to Schiffer, 1 December 1961, B 106/903, Bundesarchiv, Koblenz, Germany (hereafter BAK); letter, Wrasmann to Roeber, 23 November 1961, B 106/903, BAK.
5. Jessica C. E. Gienow-Hecht, "Trumpeting Down the Walls of Jericho: the Politics of Art, Music, and Emotion in German-American Relations, 1870–1920," *Journal of Social History* 36, 3 (Spring 2003): 585.
6. The lone exception to this tale of ineptitude, according to Gienow-Hecht, was the diplomacy of music. Frank Trommler, "Inventing the Enemy: Germany-American Cultural Relations, 1900–1917," in *Confrontation and Cooperation: Germany and the United States in the Era of World War I, 1900–1924*, ed. Hans-Jürgen Schröder (Providence and Oxford: Berg, 1993), 100–4.
7. See Brett Gary, *The Nervous Liberals: Propaganda Anxieties from World War I to the Cold War* (New York: Columbia University Press, 1999) for a discussion of the fight against Nazi influence in the United States.
8. Sander A. Diamond, *The Nazi Movement in the United States, 1924–1941* (Ithaca: Cornell University Press, 1974), 24–29.

9. Gary, *The Nervous Liberals*, 79–81. Also see Clayton D. Laurie, *The Propaganda Warriors: America's Crusade against Nazi Germany* (Lawrence: University Press of Kansas, 1996).
10. Diamond, *The Nazi Movement in the United States*, 204.
11. For a very useful overview of Federal Republic cultural diplomacy, see Manuela Aguilar, *Cultural Diplomacy and Foreign Policy: German-American Relations, 1955–1968* (New York: Peter Lang, 1996).
12. The Society for the Prevention of World War III often lodged complaints with the US government over its lenient treatment of Germans. See, for example, C. Monteith Gilpin to Robert Patterson, 22 July 1946, 2, Society for the Prevention of World War III collection, Rare Book and Manuscript Library, Columbia University, New York, NY, USA. Many of their fears are publicly expressed in their publication, *Prevent World War III*. For the relationship between Germans and American Jews after World War II, see Shlomo Shafir, *Ambiguous Relations: The American Jewish Community and Germany since 1945* (Detroit: Wayne State University Press, 1999).
13. Aguilar, *Cultural Diplomacy and Foreign Policy*, 33–35.
14. Aufzeichnung, 18 July 1951, B 90-KA/71, Politisches Archiv des Auswärtigen Amts., Berlin, Germany (hereafter AA). Krekeler to AA, 20 August 1951, B 145/775, BAK.
15. Krekeler to AA, 18 October 1951, B 145/775, BAK. Von Lilienfeld to Walter Gong, 17 October 1951, B 145/775, BAK. Aufzeichnung, 18 October 1951, B 145/775, BAK. Aufzeichnung, 25 June 1951, B 11/297, AA.
16. Contract between Federal Republic of Germany and Roy Bernard 1951, B 145/775, BAK. Report, "Activities of the Berlin Department of the Roy Bernard Company, Inc." 1963, B 145/9764, BAK.
17. Roy Bernard to von Lilienfeld, October 1952, B 145/775, BAK. This report ably illustrates the kinds of activities that Roy Bernard performed for the Federal Republic.
18. This is somewhat surprising, given that Blumenthal for a brief time represented the American Jewish Congress on the Motion Picture and Mass Media Committee of the National Community Relations Advisory Council. See, for example, his participation in Meeting of the Motion Picture and Mass Media Committee, 6 October 1949, Box 49, National Jewish Community Relations Advisory Council, American Jewish Historical Society, Center for Jewish History, New York, NY, USA.
19. Krekeler to von Lilienfeld, 16 April 1952, B 145/775, BAK.
20. Aufzeichnung, 24 June 1953, B 145/531, BAK. Krekeler to AA, 11 February 1954, B 145/531, BAK. Aufzeichnung, Mönnig, 16 July 1953, B 145/531, BAK.
21. Riesser to AA, 21 July 1952, B 106/903, BAK.
22. Anne Frank's diary, and especially the play and movie that were based on it, captured the emotions of Americans with its depiction of the Holocaust through the eyes of a young Jewish girl.
23. On the importance of these events, see Shafir, *Ambiguous Relations*.
24. Sydney and Flora Gruson, "Have the Germans Learned?" *New York Times Magazine*, 29 January 1961, 8.
25. James Cameron, "Shadow No Larger Than a Crooked Cross," *New York Times Magazine*, 11 September 1966, 94.
26. Richard Lowenthal, "Germans Feel Like Germans Again," *New York Times Magazine*, 6 March 1966, 40.
27. Aufzeichnung, 24 May 1968, B 145/2873, BAK. Thomas to Leonard, 5 October 1967, B 145/2873, BAK.

28. Aufzeichnung, 24 January 1966, B 145/2873, BAK.
29. Fritz Fischer, *Griff nach der Weltmacht: die Kriegszielpolitik des kaiserlichen Deutschland, 1914/18* (Düsseldorf: Droste, 1961). Fischer's work was translated and published in the United States as *Germany's Aims in the First World War*. For a discussion of Fischer, please see Richard Bosworth, *Explaining Auschwitz and Hiroshima: History Writing and the Second World War, 1945–1990* (London: Routledge, 1993), 53–72.
30. Generalkonsulat Boston to the German Embassy, 10 February 1966, B 97/356, AA.
31. Botschaft Guatemala to AA, 3 May 1967, B 145/3003, BAK.
32. Aufzeichnung, Bauer to Thomas, 15 October 1965, B 145/2873, BAK. Graf Schweinitz to von Lilienfeld, 1 December 1965, B 145/2873, BAK.
33. Aufzeichnung, 19 October 1965, B 145/2873, BAK. *New York Times* article, "German Americans Provoked by Portrayal of Germans on TV," 25 February 1968, B 145/3005, BAK. Thomas to Leonard H. Goldenson, 21 April 1964, B 145/3004, BAK. Thomas to Hedda Hopper, 19 November 1965, B 145/2140, BAK. Graf Schweinitz to Sellier, 18 January 1966, B 145/2873, BAK.
34. Report, 11 June 1959, B 145/1304, BAK. Von Eckardt to AA, 3 August 1960, B 145/1304, BAK. Grewe to AA, 21 October 1960, B 145/1304, BAK. News release, "Germany Opens Information Center in New York City," 6 May 1961, B 145/3255, BAK. Botschaft to AA, 6 February 1962, B 145/3255, BAK.
35. Report, Amconsul Hamburg to Department of State, 22 June 1964, EDX GER W-US, Subject Numeric Files, RG 59, NA. Schröder to Dr. Fritz Fischer, 7 March 1964, B 96 (IV 7)/783, AA.
36. Vermerk, 25 August 1967, B 145/3003, BAK. Krapf, Botschaft in Tokyo, to BPA, 14 February 1968, B 145/3005, BAK. Kramer to Bundestag 28 October 1965, B 145/2873, BAK.
37. Fehr to Diehl, 23 November 1965, B 145/2873, BAK. Auszug aus einem Brief von Michael Fehr, Salem, MA, USA, 24 October 1965, B 145/2873, BAK. Auszug aus einem Brief von Michael Fehr, z. Zt. Salem, MA, USA, 14 November 1065, B 145/2873, BAK. Fritz F. W. Krohn to Bundeskanzler Georg Kiesinger, 3 January 1968, B 145/3005, BA. Arthur Sellier to BPA, 10 December 1965, B 145/2873, BAK.
38. Von Lilienfeld to Diehl, 4 November 1965, B 145/2873, BAK. Vermerk, 23 November 1965, B 145/2873, BAK.
39. Ausschnitt, "Germans Relish Popularity Gain, New U.S. Image," *Inquirer*, 30 June 1966, B 145/9869, BAK. Graf Schweinitz to W. Simon, 16 February 1966, B 145/2873, BAK. Thomas to GIC, 22 July 1969, B 145/6444, BAK.
40. Report, "American Attitudes Toward West Germany," 29 June 1962, B 145/9764, BAK. Von Lilienfeld to AA, 20 July 1962, B 145/9869, BAK. Survey Research Center, University of Michigan Report "American Attitudes toward West Germany," 29 June 1962, B 145/9869, BAK.
41. Report, "American Attitudes Toward West Germany."
42. Thomas Alan Schwartz, *America's Germany: John J. McCloy and the Federal Republic of Germany* (Cambridge, MA: Harvard University Press, 1991), 32.
43. Abbott Gleason, *Totalitarianism: The Inner History of the Cold War* (New York: Oxford University Press, 1995). See also Les K. Adler and Thomas G. Paterson, "Red Fascism: The Merger of Nazi Germany and Soviet Russia in the American Image of Totalitarianism, 1930's–1950's," *American Historical Review* 75, 4 (1970): 1046–64.

44. William H. Chamberlain, "The Revival of Anti-Germanism," *Modern Age*, Summer 1962, 277–83.
45. Gleason, *Totalitarianism*, 128–29.
46. For works on the reception of Eichmann, see Deborah E. Lipstadt, "America and the Memory of the Holocaust, 1950–1965," *Modern Judaism* 16, 3 (1996): 195–214, and Peter Novick, *The Holocaust in American Life* (Boston: Houghton Mifflin, 1999). For a work on the reception of Shirer, see Gavriel Rosenfeld, "The Reception of William L. Shirer's *The Rise and Fall of the Third Reich* in the United States and West Germany, 1960–1962," *Journal of Contemporary History* 29, 1 (1994): 95–128.
47. There is a broad literature on reception. Some of the most important works are Janet Staiger, *Interpreting Films: Studies in the Historical Reception of American Cinema* (Princeton: Princeton University Press, 1992), and John Fiske, *Understanding Popular Culture* (Boston: Unwin Hyman, 1989).
48. Souvenir Program from Berlin Premiere, *Judgment at Nuremberg* Clippings File, MHL.
49. Abby Mann, "Judgment at Nuremberg," SKP.
50. Audience Preview Cards, August 1961, SKP.
51. Address of Governing Mayor Brandt at World Premiere of *Judgment at Nuremberg*, Publicity—Horwits, Al Correspondence, SKP.
52. Quigley, "'An Important Political Event'"; Al. Steen, "Germans are Grim at Preview of 'Judgment at Nuremberg,'" *Boxoffice*, 25 December 1961, *Judgment at Nuremberg* Clippings File, MHL; David Binder, "World Premiere for 'Nuremberg,'" *New York Times*, 15 December 1961, *Judgment at Nuremberg* Clippings File, MHL.
53. Andrew Young, *An Easy Burden: The Civil Rights Movement and the Transformation of America*, (New York: HarperCollins Publishers, 1996), 358. Warren Hinckle and David Welsh, "Five Battles of Selma," *Ramparts* 4 (June 1965): 36.
54. Congress, Senate, Senator Mondale speaking about shocking brutality in Selma, Ala., 89th Congress, 1st session, *Congressional Record*, 111, pt. 4 (3 March 1965): 4351. Congress, Senate, Senator Proxmire reads Wisconsin protests against brutality in Selma, Ala., 89th Congress, 1st session, 111, pt. 4 (9 March 1965): 4639.
55. Volker R. Berghahn, *America and the Intellectual Cold Wars in Europe: Shepard Stone between Philanthropy, Academy, and Diplomacy* (Princeton: Princeton University Press, 2001); Jessica C. E. Gienow-Hecht, *Transmission Impossible: American Journalism as Cultural Diplomacy in Postwar Germany, 1945–1955* (Baton Rouge: Louisiana State University Press, 1999); Petra Goedde, *GIs and Germans: Culture, Gender and Foreign Relations, 1945–1949* (New Haven: Yale University Press, 2003); Maria Hoehn, *GIs and Fraeuleins: The German-American Encounter in 1950s West Germany* (Chapel Hill: University of North Carolina Press, 2002); Uta G. Poiger, *Jazz, Rock, and Rebels: Cold War Politics and American Culture in a Divided Germany* (Berkeley: University of California Press, 2000); and Ralph Willett, *The Americanization of Germany, 1945–1949* (London: Routledge, 1989).
56. Reinhold Wagnleitner, *Coca-colonization and the Cold War: The Cultural Mission of the United States in Austria after the Second World War*, (Chapel Hill: University of North Carolina Press, 1994); Emily Rosenberg, *Spreading the American Dream: American Economic and Cultural Expansion, 1890–1945* (New York: Hill and Wang, 1982).

57. Wagnleitner, *Coca-colonization and the Cold War;* Walter L. Hixson, *Parting the Curtain: Propaganda, Culture, and the Cold War, 1945–1961* (New York: St. Martin's Press, 1997); Richard H. Pells, *Not Like Us: How Europeans Have Loved, Hated, and Transformed American culture since World War II* (New York: Basic Books, 1997).
58. Kroes, *If You've Seen One You've Seen the Mall: Europeans and American Mass Culture* (Urbana: University of Illinois Press, 1996), xi. Jessica C. E. Gienow-Hecht, "Shame on US?" *Diplomatic History* 24, 3 (2000): 465–94.
59. Aufzeichnung, 17 January 1951, B 11/297, AA.
60. Frank Ninkovich, *The Diplomacy of Ideas: U.S. Foreign Policy and Cultural Relations, 1938–1950* (Cambridge: Cambridge University Press, 1981); Rosenberg, *Spreading the American Dream;* Frank Costigliola, *Awkward Dominion: American Political, Economic, and Cultural Relations with Europe, 1919–1933* (Ithaca: Cornell University Press, 1984); Kroes, *If You've Seen One You've Seen the Mall,* x.

Bibliography

Adler, Les K., and Thomas G. Paterson. "Red Fascism: The Merger of Nazi Germany and Soviet Russia in the American Image of Totalitarianism, 1930's–1950's." *American Historical Review* 75, 4 (1970): 1046–64.
Aguilar, Manuela. *Cultural Diplomacy and Foreign Policy: German-American Relations, 1955–1968.* New York: Peter Lang, 1996.
Berghahn, Volker R. *America and the Intellectual Cold Wars in Europe: Shepard Stone between Philanthropy, Academy, and Diplomacy.* Princeton: Princeton University Press, 2001.
Bosworth, Richard. *Explaining Auschwitz and Hiroshima: History Writing and the Second World War, 1945–1990.* London: Routledge, 1993.
Costigliola, Frank. *Awkward Dominion: American Political, Economic, and Cultural Realtions with Europe, 1919–1933.* Ithaca: Cornell University Press, 1984.
Diamond, Sander A. *The Nazi Movement in the United States, 1924–1941.* Ithaca: Cornell University Press, 1974.
Gary, Brett. *The Nervous Liberals: Propaganda Anxieties from World War I to the Cold War.* New York: Columbia University Press, 1999.
Gienow-Hecht, Jessica C. E. *Transmission Impossible: American Journalism as Cultural Diplomacy in Postwar Germany, 1945–1955.* Baton Rouge: Louisiana State University Press, 1999.
———. "Shame on Us?" *Diplomatic History* 24, 3 (2000): 465–94.
———. "Trumpeting Down the Walls of Jericho: The Politics of Art, Music, and Emotion in German-American Relations, 1870–1920." *Journal of Social History* 36, 3 (Spring 2003): 585–613.
Gleason, Abbott. *Totalitarianism: The Inner History of the Cold War.* New York: Oxford University Press, 1995.
Goedde, Petra. *GIs and Germans: Culture, Gender and Foreign Relations, 1945–1949.* New Haven: Yale University Press, 2003.
Hixson, Walter L. *Parting the Curtain: Propaganda, Culture, and the Cold War, 1945–1961.* New York: St. Martin's Press, 1997.
Höhn, Maria. *GIs and Fräuleins: The German-American Encounter in 1950s West Germany.* Chapel Hill: University of North Carolina Press, 2002.

Kroes. Rob. *If You've Seen One You've Seen the Mall: Europeans and American Mass Culture.* Urbana: University of Illinois Press, 1996.
Laurie, Clayton D. *The Propaganda Warriors: America's Crusade against Nazi Germany, Modern War Studies.* Lawrence: University Press of Kansas, 1996.
Lipstadt, Deborah E. "America and the Memory of the Holocaust, 1950–1965." *Modern Judaism* 16, 3 (1996): 195–214.
Ninkovich, Frank. *The Diplomacy of Ideas: U.S. Foreign Policy and Cultural Relations, 1938–1950.* Cambridge: Cambridge University Press, 1981.
Pells, Richard H. *Not Like Us: How Europeans Have Loved, Hated, and Transformed American Culture since World War II.* New York: Basic Books, 1997.
Poiger, Uta G. *Jazz, Rock, and Rebels: Cold War Politics and American Culture in a Divided Germany.* Berkeley: University of California Press, 2000.
Rosenberg, Emily. *Spreading the American Dream: American Economic and Cultural Expansion, 1890–1945.* New York: Hill and Wang, 1982.
Rosenfeld, Gavriel. "The Reception of William L. Shirer's *the Rise and Fall of the Third Reich* in the United States and West Germany, 1960–1962." *Journal of Contemporary History* 29 (1994): 95–128.
Schwartz, Thomas Alan. *America's Germany: John J. McCloy and the Federal Republic of Germany.* Cambridge, MA: Harvard University Press, 1991.
Shafir, Shlomo. *Ambiguous Relations: The American Jewish Community and Germany since 1945.* Detroit: Wayne State University Press, 1999.
Staiger, Janet. *Interpreting Films: Studies in the Historical Reception of American Cinema.* Princeton: Princeton University Press, 1992.
Trommler, Frank. "Inventing the Enemy: Germany-American Cultural Relations, 1900–1917." In *Confrontation and Cooperation: Germany and the United States in the Era of World War I, 1900–1924,* ed. Hans-Jürgen Schröder. Providence, Oxford: Berg, 1993, pp. 99–125.
Wagnleitner, Reinhold. *Coca-Colonization and the Cold War: The Cultural Mission of the United States in Austria after the Second World War.* Chapel Hill: University of North Carolina Press, 1994.
Willett, Ralph. *The Americanization of Germany, 1945–1949.* London: Routledge, 1989.

Part II
INTERNATIONALISM

Chapter 3

CHINESE DEBATES ON MODERNIZATION AND THE WEST AFTER THE GREAT WAR

Dominic Sachsenmaier

The Decentering of China and Calls for a New Culture in early Twentieth-Century China

Around the turn of the twentieth century international debates on local order had become intrinsically connected with visions of world order. In an age of imperialism, an internationalizing economy, and mass migration only wishful thinking could assume that local politics operated largely autonomously and independent from the world at large. The political debates within industrialized societies such as the United States, several Western European countries, and Japan were profoundly shaped by the question of what role the nation was supposed to play on a global level. Furthermore, the rising influence of ideologies such anarchism, socialism, and liberalism implied competing visions of global order, even though these political struggles largely took place within national boundaries. Within certain political cultures, most notably the United States, Britain, France, and Germany, there were powerful political forces claiming that their own respective nation could actually serve as a role model for the world at large. However, such claims to represent the cultural, civilizational, or political center of the world tended to be accompanied by a heightened sense of international competition and fears of outside influences.

Notes for this section begin on page 127.

Also on the other end of the widening global hierarchies—the colonized and semicolonized societies—levels of global consciousness were growing within elite circles. For instance, in an age of empire and worldwide transformations it was no longer an option to regard India, China, or the Islamic World as their own cultural centers. In the case of China, the increasing presence of the Western powers and Japan had ushered in a period of severe domestic crises and political instability. In the years following a failed attempt at moderate reforms in 1898 it became increasingly clear to the most influential circles in China that profound changes were necessary to ensure the country's survival as an independent polity. The new geopolitical and geocultural environment made it clear that it was not possible for China to assume itself to be a fully equal member in a world that seemed cruelly restless. In the eyes of its neighbors, most notably Japan, the international standing of the former Middle Kingdom had degenerated to the position of a sleeping giant in danger of becoming colonized by superior powers. The feeling grew that any kind of society that would not react to the new international and domestic constellations was doomed to be swept away by the new age.

As time progressed in the twentieth century, the forces of change became more apparent. In the eyes of Chinese observers, "modernity" spread from the coastal cities and treaty ports to the most remote hinterlands. Steamships patrolled the rivers, railways crossed the land, and city life started to change with daily newspapers, international fashion, and even shopping malls. However, the most central historical ruptures were the fall of the dynastic order and the demise of the literati class as the political and cultural pillars of the Middle Kingdom. The last Chinese dynasty fell with the Chinese Revolution of 1911, when a constitutional republic based on a parliamentary system was founded. However, the decline of the literati class, which had been the sociocultural backbone of Imperial China, was not as clear cut. Already during the last years of the nineteenth century Western-style education had provided an alternative social ladder to that of the Confucian system of education. The hereditary education system was finally stripped of its political significance in 1905 when the state examinations to recruit new scholar-officials were abolished. In the years before and after 1905 fields such as engineering and the natural sciences enjoyed ever-increasing social and cultural prestige. This trend was reflected in the growing number of engineers and foreign-trained experts in Chinese government positions. Whereas the traditional scholar-officials, which constituted the core of the old literati elite, had still been the main force behind the reform movements of 1898, the vast majority of the first post-revolutionary Chinese parliamentarians and administrators of the Chinese Republic had been predominantly trained in modern fields of study.[1]

The extent, degree, and pace of these transformations prompted Liang Qichao (1873–29)—one of the reformers of 1898, a historian, and a leading intellectual—to conclude that for the first time in its history, China was undergoing a wide-reaching revolution. In the past, Liang had argued that there had been alterations of dynastic governments though no profound changes in China's political, cultural, and social structures.[2] Liang's assessment was widely shared by many of his contemporaries, especially after the Chinese Revolution and the failed attempt by Yuan Shikai to restore a Chinese monarchy in 1916. It was evident that China would be forced to give up long established traditions and institutions due to the impact of outside influences. And even though China imported a number of modern technologies and even neologisms via Japan, the modernizing visions of the Chinese elites tended to be fixated on the West. For most educated Chinese the transformations of their time emanated from a Western epicenter. Consequently, in Chinese intellectual discourse terms such as "West" *(xifang)* quickly became a symbol of modernity that generated feelings of hope and despair, admiration and fear. This being said, in the ardent debates on modernization and modernity it should not surprise us to find the concept of the West serving as a reference space in the searches for China's future. As time progressed, one started to define the meaning of being Chinese in relation to the conceptualized notion of the West. Parallel to symbols of "the West," "modernity," and "Europe," one can find a wealth of quintessential national images in Chinese sources dating from the early twentieth century. Stereotypes such as the German authoritarian, the French romantic, or the pragmatic national culture of the British resulted from the enculturation of Western discourses that had found their way into China. To the best of my knowledge, there was no methodological attempt in China at the time to integrate images of Europe in general and stereotypes of single European nations into a coherent intellectual system. Both images and discourses coexisted on different levels, with little reflection on their compatibility.

Around the time of World War I there seemed to be different directions in which to channel China's rapid transformations and to envision the country's future. In many of the hundreds of new journals mushrooming in China all kinds of political positions were represented. A look at some of the key journals of the era reveals that Chinese intellectual and political currents had not yet fully crystallized into rivaling camps with distinct public organs. The new models for China that were being discussed included anarchism, liberalism, and—after the Bolshevik Revolution—socialism and communism. Many intellectual biographies of the time reveal individual jumps between different ideological visions; all in the midst of a climate that Mao Zedong later characterized as a "search for truth from the West."

Yet hardly anyone expected that China would eventually shed off all local characteristics and become a full copy of the West. By the beginning of the Chinese Republic (if not even before), it had become clear that many of the transformations China was undergoing were both inevitable and irreversible. During that time almost all intellectual and ideological camps shared a strong sense of nationalism, which was partly based on strong feelings of national humiliation *(guochi)* and a sense of urgency.[3] If China could not respond quickly and aptly to the challenges of the time, it would be bullied in the international environment, which educated Chinese[4] increasingly understood through the lenses of Social Darwinism.[5]

There was a consensus that China was no longer the center of its own cultural universe but a mere latecomer in an international race for development.[6] Despite this basic commonality, however, the search for "truth from the West" left important issues unresolved. There was not only the question of what truth China should try to find from the West, but also the daunting list of possible answers ranging from American liberalism to Soviet communism. There was also the problem of how deep the ongoing transformative processes should eventually penetrate Chinese society and culture—for example, whether foreign influences should also alter social mores or local religious traditions. Was, as Western colonial rhetoric tended to suggest, Europe the spearhead of a great global development, destined to imbue other cultures with the same dynamism and energy that seemed to make the Occident so powerful?

At the time when Europe became entrapped in the Great War a powerful movement emerged in China, arguing that it was essential to overcome key aspects of tradition in order to embark on a project of national development and progress. The belief in complete Westernization was particularly popular among the younger generation of students,[7] who in many cases had access to foreign doctrines through translations or attending Western-style institutions of higher learning. In addition, a mass migration of students brought tens of thousands of students mainly to Japan but also to Europe and the United States.[8] This new generation of urban intellectuals with access to foreign thinking began to regard almost all traditional institutions and sociocultural mores as impediments to progress. According to their opinion it was impossible for China to follow its own trajectories—retaining one's cultural roots was regarded as tantamount to stagnating in a world in which only dynamism and progressivism would promise social betterment and international dignity.

To these young pro-Westernization forces, nationalism did not necessarily mean defending heritages of the past.[9] In a rough, dynamic international environment Confucianism—and the Chinese tradition in general—now looked stale and seemed to carry no promises for the creative social and cultural energy now deemed necessary to sustain the country. In one of his many articles for the journal *New Youth (Xin Qingnian)*, Chen Duxiu expressed this common sentiment: "All our traditional ethics, law, scholarship and customs are survivals of feudalism. When compared with the achievements of the white race, there is a difference of a thousand years in thought, although we live in the same period. [Unless we improve], our people will be turned out of the 20th century world, and be lodged in the dark ditches fit only for slaves, cattle and horses. ... I would much rather see the past culture of our nation disappear than to see our nation die out now because of its unfitness for living in the modern world."[10]

Chen cited the disappearance of the Babylonians as a lesson to be learned from, and he warned that the possession of an ancient culture was no guarantee of survival. Ironically, with the use of terms such as "race," "feudalism," and "modern world," we see that Chen's entire system of evaluating China's backwardness was based on Western concepts. Even grasping the dangers for China seemed to require a foreign system of thought and evaluation. Positing Chinese culture in terms of polar opposites to modern Western countries, Chen's method of evaluating China's backwardness emanates from his interpretation of the West. Compared to the dynamic, ever-expanding powers of the West, Chen Duxiu paints China as a suppressive apparatus, stifling creativity and paralyzing its creative potential.

In the same article Chen Duxiu calls on the Chinese youth to be progressive and not conservative. Chen encourages Chinese youth to be their own masters and not slaves, to have an open worldview and not be isolationist, and to rely on scientific evidence and not on hereditary teachings. Similar ideas were subsequently published in a series of articles by authors such as Gao Yihan, who in 1918 joined the editorial board of *New Youth*.[11] In essence, the New Youth Movement (1915) put great faith in younger Chinese intellectuals with access to foreign thinking and in that sense it can be seen as the precursor to the May Fourth Movement of 1919. Its adherents believed that only the educated segments of China's younger generation would be able to create a new culture and follow in the footsteps of the European Enlightenment. Analogous to their understanding of the European revolutions of the eighteenth and nineteenth centuries, the leaders of the New Youth Movement hoped to create a culture that was based on the power of reason and the methodology of doubt. Chen Duxiu and likeminded thinkers hoped that old traditions and customs would eventually crumble under the scrutiny of scientific analysis and applied reason. Freed from its traditional shackles China would emerge triumphantly as a young and forceful nation.

For the iconoclasts of the New Youth Movement the new generation was destined to solve the double crises of meaning and sociopolitical order that had been disrupting China for a considerable period of time. The younger generation would basically destroy many of the Middle Kingdom's customs and mores, and on this tabula rasa a new political and economic system could be set. For the May Fourth Movement and its predecessors "youth" thus acquired a double-revolutionary connotation. On a domestic level it promised to break traditional hierarchies based on age and social status by arguing that only the new generation could sweep away the repressive, stagnant, and paralyzed domestic culture. On an international level a "Young China" could turn its status as a developing country, as a latecomer, into an asset by learning from the mistakes of advanced societies.

Young China was usually envisioned as a movement toward a powerful nation state. Some intellectuals, though, regarded "young China" as a new supranational spirit that would in the future reach Western societies as well as the rest of the world. One of the prime examples of this trend is the chief librarian of Beijing University, Li Dazhao, who later became one of the founding members of the Chinese Communist Party. Influenced by early Soviet rhetoric he wrote in the journal *Young China* (Shaonian Zhongguo): "We should recognize that the movement of loving people is more important than loving one's country. The range of our young China is not limited to China; sometimes we need to shake hands with the youth of Asia and make it a common Asian youth movement. Sometimes we need to shake hands with the youth of the world and make it a common world youth movement.... The movement of Young China is a movement of changing the world: the youth of young China should be all the youth of the world."[12]

The new Chinese youth were supposed to achieve these ambitious aims by awakening the masses. For example, in 1919 the editorial note of the first issue of the newly founded journal *New Wave* (Xinchao) encouraged its young readers to make the Chinese understand the backwardness of traditional knowledge as well as the great beauty and potential of Western knowledge. The editors also pledged to make the Chinese population recognize the great impediments posed by traditional institutions and arouse the masses' interest in new scholarship.[13]

Along these lines Zong Zhikui argued in *Young China* that young people should work on creating new personalities and "new selves" *(xin wo)* as a precondition for creating a new culture.[14] In premodern China there was no real equivalent to this great faith in the revolutionary power of knowledge and the notion of the intellectual as an instigator of the masses.[15] Only in the late Qing Dynasty do we see that significant parts of the educated gentry families had begun to perceive their own social responsibilities no longer primarily as the institutional carriers of the Middle Kingdom.[16] As already mentioned, the disentanglement of scholarship and power was deepened with the abolition of the Confucian state examination in 1905, opening the way for scientists, engineers, and foreign-trained experts into the civil administration.[17] Cultural, philosophical, and historical knowledge thus found itself at the margins of

China's political system—a necessary precondition for the radicalization of large parts of the new Chinese intellectuals.[18]

Modern Traditionalism and Conservatism in China

The emergence of a new milieu of independent intellectuals during the second decade of the twentieth century did not just produce radical iconoclasts. Another important and highly influential grouping were moderate liberal voices advocating gradual reform. One of their chief exponents was Hu Shi, a US-trained scholar and professor of philosophy at Beijing University. In addition, the so-called "conservative" or "traditionalist" milieu also had to adapt its intellectual agenda to the new place of scholarship within the sociocultural pattern of China. For the European context it has already been long established that traditionalism and conservatism are modern phenomena that have no real equivalent in earlier historical epochs.[19] Both terms are rather vague and only loosely describe a wide variety of currents that can range from philosophical approaches to political movements. Yet all varieties of conservatism share a spirit of preserving or revitalizing indigenous traditions, which are part of the somewhat critical attitude toward modernization processes and discourses.

Since traditionalism appeared as a reaction to ideologies of modernization and Westernization, it is no coincidence that it did not remain confined to the West. Whereas European conservatism turned into an organized and coherent force during the time of the French Revolution, a genuine Chinese conservatism did not appear before the turn of the twentieth century. It was intrinsically connected with the pro-modernization forces in China and, later, the emergence of the New Culture and New Youth movements. Against the iconoclastic progressivism of the latter, conservatives upheld the value of history as a living force that would be absolutely relevant for the future. Against the program of freeing man from irrational authorities, conservatives maintained the importance of organic or primordial ties. In sharp contrast to the Enlightenment creed in the sole power of reason, conservatives defended the importance of human bonds and responsibilities. This does not mean that all conservative thinkers were inimical to change, but for them change had to occur through moderate reforms and organic growth rather than through the quantum leaps of revolutionary developments.

In the face of all its varieties and branches it is very hard to define the meaning of Chinese conservatism or traditionalism. Its parameters could range from Liang Qichao's calls for moderate forms of Westernization to the protofascist New Life Movement under president Chiang Kai-Shek during the 1930s. It is safe to say that after the Chinese Revolution the number of those who argued that China could remain free from all foreign influence was extremely small. None of the traditionalists with a public voice were naïve enough to advocate a staunch cultural isolationism.

Looking at the more academic branches of Chinese conservatism during the Early Republic, one can observe that scholars holding a traditionalist worldview had begun to reconstitute themselves as intellectuals. The traditional status of scholar-officials, that is, administrators who derived their social status and political weight from Confucian learning, had been irretrievably lost. One clear indication of the emergence of a conservative type of intellectual was the declining influence of the Confucian state orthodoxy in the tradition of Zhu Xi, a twelfth-century thinker on whose concepts the official state examinations had been largely based. Among traditionalist thinkers, the more inward-looking Lu-Wang school of Confucianism became more prominent. Within these branches of the Confucian tradition, which had received a certain influence from Buddhism and Taoism, the meaning of being a Confucian was not inseparably connected with political responsibilities and aspirations. Based on these traditions it was possible to defend Confucianism as a religion rather than as China's state doctrine or official orthodoxy.[20] As part of the same process, concepts such as "national essence" became very prominent for conservatives at a time when institutional traditions such as the imperial Confucian schools were being dismantled.

To a large extent the conservative milieu in China consisted of individuals who could not hope to gain from the benefits of modernization. The bulk of conservatives were older scholars or students, who still went through traditional education systems with a heavy emphasis on Confucianism.[21] In addition to the marginalization of China within the world order, and the marginalization of Confucian teaching within China, this group experienced a personal marginalization within society.[22] This constellation made this social milieu particularly sensitive to the cultural losses caused by modernization and internationalization. Among these circles, which saw their previously privileged status declining, one could expect little sympathy for modernization processes. Many educated Chinese with a conservative worldview translated their personal nostalgia into a cultural agenda. Still, one ought to understand these social roots of conservatism only as general tendencies, since personal mobility did not necessarily determine an individual's political outlook. Those profiting from modernization and internationalization could also adhere to a conservative school.

Chinese Interpretations of World War I

During the second decade of the twentieth century all political and intellectual milieus referred to "the West" as a stereotyped reference space that symbolized the hopes and threats of modernity. In a certain sense all debates about the future of China were also debates about how to understand and evaluate "the West." In addition to the West as a geographical symbol there could also be temporal reference points in the debates on modernization—events that were global in the sense that they had a major impact on political cultures in many societies around the world. The way one understood such global moments was largely determined by one's political outlook and intellectual position.

A global moment of this kind was World War I. Without a doubt, the Great War had almost worldwide economic and political dimensions, but also its cultural implications reached far beyond the war theatre. In the Chinese media there were vivid portraits of the slaughters on various fronts, the difficult domestic-supply situations, and the political turmoil that started in many European societies when the war approached its end.[23] Ironically, the news about the suffering in Europe was accompanied by a short economic boom in China caused by the drastic reduction of exports on the side of the war-torn European countries.[24] Due to the ensuing rise of living standards, Western influences on urban cultures in China were even accelerated by the Great War in Europe.

Still, World War I became a major factor in the general political climate of China. A principal paradigm had been shaken: Europe, the previously unchallenged source of modern transformations and the world's political center, had plunged into a deep crisis.[25] In that manner the Great War meant hope for societies that had found themselves at the very margins of a rapidly progressing world. The trembling of Europe gave the prospect for new dignity, and it seemed as if the gap between the advanced and the backward countries, the difference between the colonizers and the colonized, could now be significantly narrowed or even reversed. Partly encouraged by the demise of the nimbus of White Man's Burden, anti-colonial and nationalist movements were emerging in many parts of the world.[26]

For China the end of World War I became a major cultural landmark. The aftermath of the Great War witnessed one of the most effervescent intellectual periods in modern Chinese history. The May Fourth Movement gained its name from the student protests and strikes following the day when news of the humiliating conditions for China in the Versailles Peace Treaty reached the public. The Wilsonian hopes for full national sovereignty were shattered by the fact that Japan had been secretly promised the German colonies in Shandong province, even though China had supported the allies. For many students this disillusionment with the new international system also turned into anger with Chinese tradition, which many held responsible for the country's weakness.

Most of the younger Chinese intellectuals remained committed to the profound Westernization of Chinese society and culture, which they saw as an essential aspect of national awakening. Some went as far as to interpret the Great War as another indication of European superiority, namely, its martial spirit. Liu Shuya, for instance, held that the war had heightened national sentiments in the West, which—when combined with materialism and industrialization—could provide societies with the necessary strength to survive in a merciless world.[27] Others continued to argue that the West remained superior because of its revolutionary energy, its individual commitment, and its scientific, progressive culture. In the liberal camp intellectuals such as Hu Shi and Cai Yuanpei,[28] the director of Beijing University, shared the interpretation of the war as a triumph of democracy over militarism, authoritarianism, and imperialism. In many cases one predicted that the United States would succeed Europe as the world's political center and most influential reference culture.

Nevertheless, most Chinese advocates of profound modernization acknowledged that European triumphalism had taken a dent in the years from 1914 to 1918. For example, in an article written in 1919 Wei Siluan, a member of the Young China Association's centrist-right wing, mentioned that World War I had caused some doubts in China about progressivism and the prospect of sustained development. The physical destruction and economic crisis in Europe, Wei held, were almost outweighed by the ethical and political benefits of the war such as the foundation of the League of Nations or the global waves of democratization following the truce of 1918.[29] On the left, people like Li Dazhao also argued that the Great War actually further enhanced the progress of humanity. In an article entitled the "Victory of the People," he followed Lenin by portraying the end of the war as a triumph over despotism and capitalism. Now, Li Dazhao argued, a higher and better stage of the human condition was within reach.[30] Thus, a variety of groups in China, ranging from free-trade liberalists to early Marxists, still saw the Great War as part of a teleological history. Since—expressed in Hegelian terms—European history had a purpose, so did the events after August 1914. Depending on their political and intellectual positions, Chinese intellectuals interpreted this facet of the war either as the triumph of democratic nationalism, the precursor to a world revolution, or yet another manifestation of European aggressiveness and thus fitness for survival.

However, for a considerable number of Chinese intellectuals the Great War was not yet another, admittedly bloody, stage on the way of human progress. Quite the contrary, for them the war cast shadows of doubt onto the belief in a better global future emanating from Europe. There was a whole genre of articles painting a picture of total economic decline and social instability.[31] Many intellectuals referred to such accounts in their assessments of the future of Europe in particular and modernity in general. For example, in the journal *Young China,* which also published articles in the spirit of the New Culture Movement, Shen Yi wrote the following thoughts from his travels in Europe: "Since I am abroad I realize that there is no other nation in the world as good as the Chinese in regards to morality, tolerance, and love for others.... Following these great qualities we should be able to contribute to the coming of world peace. The others might be awakened, the path towards the future might still be unpaved, but I firmly believe that the day will come when our nation will be able to demonstrate its own ability and to achieve its ideals."[32]

After World War I, a group of thinkers rose to prominence who held that Western modernity was not only a promise but also a danger. In fact, the war had become a turning point in many intellectual biographies. Now some major figures on the intellectual scene such as Liang Qichao[33] or Yan Fu, who is commonly known as having introduced Social Darwinism to China,[34] became highly doubtful of the promises of Westernization, since the international conflict had revealed a Faustian process that had spun out of control. Yan Fu, for example, experienced a major paradigm shift from the "Weberian" question of what elements of the West were missing in other cultures, to asking what elements in other cultures were missing in the West.[35] Some thinkers held that the contemporary West could no longer symbolize the future of the world, since its civilization had failed. Rather, the tradition and history of the East could assist the European presence.

Quite a substantial number of Chinese scholars had the privilege of acquiring a personal impression of Europe in the years after 1918. Some of them were visiting scholars at European universities and others were accompanying diplomatic missions. Liang Qichao and the philosopher Zhang Junmai (otherwise know as Carson Chang) were among the cultural delegates of the Chinese mission to Versailles. During their stay in Europe both traveled extensively through various countries and met intellectuals such as Romain Rolland, René Guénon, and Thomas Mann. These leading intellectuals shared their doubts about the viability of the modern European path of continued industrial development, political revolutions, and social transformations. Critical voices arguing that modernity was not much more than an empty, materialistic process were doubtlessly as old as modernity itself and had intensified around the fin de siècle. Still, the experience of World War I further accentuated this partly romanticist, partly conservative tradition in European intellectual life. For many thinkers the events between 1914 and 1918 seemed to prove that the West's claim to civilizational superiority was futile since they had revealed the destructive potential of modernity.[36]

Now an increasing number of poets and thinkers called for the salvation of Europe from a modernity that was seen as superficial, purely technological, rational, and dangerously naïve and brutal. Seeing the source of this salvation increasingly in cultures outside Europe, many intellectuals turned their attention to Asia. In a speech during his stay in China in the summer of 1920, Bertrand Russell addressed his audience: "The Great War showed that something is wrong with our civilization.... The Chinese have discovered, and practiced for many centuries, a way of life, which, if it could be adopted by all the world, would make all the world happy. We Europeans have not. Our way of life demands strife, exploitation, restless change, discontent, and destruction. Efficiency directed to destruction can only end in annihilation, and it is to this consummation that our civilization is tending, if it cannot learn some of that wisdom for which it despises the East."[37]

One of the most productive contacts between Chinese and European critics of Western modernity resulted from the exchanges between Zhang Junmai and Rudolf Eucken, a philosopher at the University of Jena and Nobel Prize laureate in literature.[38] Eucken tirelessly asserted that society needed to balance materialism and progressivism with self-cultivation and spiritual growth. Zhang Junmai was so impressed with Eucken's approach that he decided to stay in Jena for several years in order to work on several common projects. He and Eucken even coauthored a book entitled *The Problem of Life in China and Europe,* which was published in both Germany and China.[39] In essence, the work called for German idealism and Chinese Confucianism to join forces and serve as bulwarks against materialism. Like other works by Zhang Junmai and Rudolf Eucken, this joint publication advocated a continued modernization but warned of blindly following the British and the American way. It depicted both nations as unwilling to accept any alternative approaches to modernity.

After his return to China Zhang Junmai continued to pursue his intellectual agenda. In later writings, such as an essay on his political impressions derived from a stay in postwar Europe[40] or an article entitled "The Crisis of European Culture and the Trend Towards a New Chinese Culture"[41] Zhang warned contemporaries of copying European ideas and realities. Pointing to the fact that Europe experienced a "kind of cultural crisis," he held that conscious choice and selection should be the guiding spirits for the modernization of China. For him China was now in the privileged position to have an insightful perspective into the constructive and destructive potentials of European modernity. The Chinese now had the option to import only those elements that were compatible with their own situation and beneficial for the future. Zhang argued that such cultural eclecticism was possible since the idea of coherent Eastern and Western cultures were nothing but gross generalizations. Zhang believed that one should look at individual elements within different civilizations and decide whether they would be compatible with one's visions for the future. In that manner there was an alternative route for China between either wholesale Westernization or the complete denial of any European influence. Consequently, for Zhang the crisis-ridden Europe of his time could now consider elements of Chinese society and culture as sources of inspiration.

The idea that Europe could learn from China was now also advocated by Liang Qichao. In his historical writings before the Great War Liang had depicted the history of the European civilization as a history of continuous innovations and transformations.[42] Like many of his contemporaries he had portrayed China as diametrically opposed to Europe, his major reference system. In comparison to the civilization of the West, Liang had held, China was not only rather stagnant and isolated but also stricken by blindness since it could not even recognize the great new civilization emanating from the epicenter in the West. He had added that while European societies were characterized by mature political cultures and civil societies, the Chinese masses would have to be led slowly toward liberalism and socially responsible individualism. Even though Liang had warned that one should not be too naïve about the possibility of a shortcut to European modernity, he had assumed that all cultures would eventually adopt the basic parameters of the Western model.

The war in Europe led Liang to a revision of his previously rather teleological understanding of European civilization. After returning home from his travels in Europe from 1919–20 Liang Qichao published a book entitled *Impressions of [My] Travels in Europe* (Ouyou Xinying Lu). The first part of this book, "Europe before and after the Great War," contains an account of Liang's travels in Europe and delivers an analysis of the situation there. The second, "The Self-Awakening of the Chinese People," outlines the implications of the European crisis and the new geopolitical constellation for China and its future course. In the first part Liang provides some rather graphical accounts of the conditions in Europe, describing, for example, his arrival in London in the following way: "As soon as we landed, nothing but images of poverty and destruction opened up in front of our eyes."[43]

Liang goes on to recount that despite the winter season, his hotel room had no heat and that during breakfast sugar was "so precious" that the Chinese delegation had to negotiate with half-empty stomachs. Already these images of hunger and despair in a Chinese description of Europe indicated a revision of an otherwise dominant trope of European superiority in material advancement and living standards. In the same text he addresses his readers with the following question: "Who would have expected European countries and their populations to suffer the fate of poverty as we do? And who could have imagined those wealthy English, French, and Germans would also start crying out about their poverty and in their lives would start depending on high-interest loans?"[44]

Undeniably there is a certain triumphalism in Liang's account—the alleged center of the world was in crisis, and its overall situation had deteriorated to the conditions of the periphery. The previously privileged nations now experienced a crisis worse than most other parts of the world. In a similar way one can understand Liang's detailed accounts of the widespread pessimism among European intellectuals. He actually regarded Europe's overall dark cultural and intellectual climate as a more severe symptom of crisis than the material shortage from the destructions of war. Before the war he had always praised Europe's endless resources of ambitious energies and its continuous endeavor to discover the new and unknown as major advantages over China.

But now, for him, Europe was a continent out of breath, desperately searching for a new direction. In the following reflections Liang problematizes Europe's fate from different angles. Each of these angles leads back to a common line of interpretation—a dynamic process that had gotten out of control. According to Liang, Europe's revolutionary restlessness (which he had praised before) was now in the process of dissecting itself into a multitude of national and class-related protest movements, which in essence meant that the revolutionary energy had started to turn against itself. In the same text Liang predicts that in the near future, national and socialist movements would once again lead the continent into severe domestic and international conflicts. Liang adds that it was mainly the method and the mentality of systematic scientific doubt that had robbed Europe of its spiritual stronghold. He further states that the consequences of a scientific culture such as industrialization, urbanization, and proletarization had largely disintegrated the communal spirit of European societies, resulting in great personal and collective imbalances.

According to Liang Qichao, the dream of a human-made, scientific golden age had revealed itself as a nightmare, and the previously pursued form of modernity had destroyed itself in a pathological process. Its main symptoms were the growth of violent forces, of extreme contradictions, and the loss of any kind of social cohesion. In *Impressions from [My] Travels in Europe,* such passages are followed by descriptions of the social fragmentation of European cities, the growing gaps not only between the social classes, but also between urban and rural areas. For Liang the consequence of these extremely contradictory forces was the spread of Social Darwinism on all levels, among social classes, religions, and nations.

In the eyes of Liang Qichao the world could no longer learn from Europe but rather from Europe's fall. China's status of a "latecomer" as a developing country now became an advantage; a rich culture of values and communal ties could be revitalized before it was completely dried out by the processes of modernization. According to Liang, such communal values and traditional ties had the potential to enrich a culture focused on science and progress, possibly preventing the modernizing forces from turning against themselves. Still, he did not simply prophesize the decline of the West. On the contrary, he predicted that European culture would eventually turn around and approach a more cautious, humble, and gentle form of modernity. Europe would learn to listen to the voices of less expansive and dynamic cultures. For Liang, Europe had not only been dethroned as the world's sole teaching civilization, but was now placed in the role of the student, having to learn from other world regions that were supposed to be culturally more intact. Such thoughts provided the background for Liang's appeal to Chinese students: "Our beloved youth! Please pay attention! March on! On the other side of the great landmass, in Europe, millions are suffering from the bankruptcy of material culture and are desperately calling for help. They are waiting for you to come and save them."[45]

It is interesting to note that Liang and many other conservatives believed that "youth" could inject new energy and spirit into a decaying world. Despite all ideological differences, Liang shared this vision with the proponents of the New Culture Movement. The concepts of youth as a generational identity and a symbol of transformation were thus not only important to the New Culture Movement but also to more conservative groupings. This trend reflected the experience with a young

Chinese generation, which was the first generation to gain access to foreign resources—a new body of knowledge that proved to be advantageous for social mobility. The young generation could thus symbolize the budding force in a tumultuous period; all political and intellectual camps deemed change and transformation to be necessary.

But the telos of this change remained heavily contested, and together with it the interpretation of the very stereotyped "West," which stood for the potentials of modernity. In China, just as in many other societies around the globe, all significant political groupings understood World War I as a global moment, from which a new era would emerge. Despite great ideological differences, almost all political camps assumed that now East and West were presented with the opportunity to reach out to each other in new ways. Many leading public figures even assumed that now the East would be able to play a more proactive role in a global context. Yet despite these common assumptions, the visions for this new role of the "East" varied as much as the connotations of "East" and "West" did. For example, rather conservative voices argued that Europe and the project of modernity could benefit from a revitalized Chinese past. Quite the contrary, the progressive forces saw a new potential for China to step into the position of a forerunner of revolutionary developments that had originated in the West.

In any case, the constructed geography, epitomized by the concepts of "East" and "West," was only reconfigured but not completely abandoned under the impact of the Great War. It is important to note that Chinese liberals, socialists, and traditionalists maintained tight networks of exchanges with like-minded intellectuals in Europe, the United States, and other world regions. For historians of the Atlantic World, the Chinese example demonstrates that the changes in Western political and intellectual cultures during and after the Great War were tied to global transformations. Concepts such as the "West," the "East," or "modernity" were close to the core of worldwide debates on such topics as the future of international order and the relationship between progress and tradition. To a certain extent these contestations centered on the West as both a political and cultural symbol. Yet at the same time the scope, agents, and parameters of these debates were decentered: they were globally entangled yet primarily located in regional settings.

Notes

1. Hui Huang, "The Chinese Construction of the West, 1862–1922: Discourses, Actors and the Cultural Field" (PhD diss., University of North Carolina at Chapel Hill, 1996).
2. Generally on the topic: Jürgen Osterhammel, *Shanghai, 30. Mai 1925: Die chinesische Revolution* (Munich: Deutscher Taschenbuch-Verlag, 1997), 22ff.
3. The concepts and categories for the new nation states such as ethnos, citizenship, or territorial sovereignty were taken from transnational discourses. For China, see, for example, Prasenjit Duara, "Transnationalism in the Era of Nation States: China, 1900–1945," *Development and Change* 29, no. 4 (1994): 647–670, and Lowell Dittmer and Samuel S. Kim, "In Search of a Theory for National Identity," in *China's Quest for National Identity*, eds. L. Dittmer and S. S. Kim (Ithaca: Cornell University Press, 1993), 1–31.
4. See Paul Cohen, "Remembering and Forgetting National Humiliation in Twentieth-Century China," *Twentieth-Century China* 27, no. 2 (2002): 1–39.
5. The widely read interpretative translation by the scholar Yan Fu expressed an even more ruthless and merciless Darwinism than the original account by Herbert Spencer. See James Reeve Pusey, *China and Charles Darwin* (Cambridge, MA: Council on East Asian Studies, Harvard University, 1983).
6. About the emergence of conceptions of world order and the notion of international hierarchies see Sebastian Conrad, and Dominic Sachsenmaier, eds., *Competing Visions of World Order: Global Moments and Movements, 1880s–1930s* (New York: Palgrave, 2007).
7. See, for example, Vera Schwarcz, *The Chinese Enlightenment: Intellectuals and the Legacy of the May Fourth Movement of 1919* (Berkeley: University of California Press, 1986).
8. A statistical analysis is provided in Hui Huang, "Chinese Construction of the West."
9. About the competing visions of Chinese history and tradition, and their relation to national tropes see Prasenjit Duara, *Rescuing History from the Nation. Questioning Narratives of Modern China* (Chicago: University of Chicago Press, 1997). See also Axel Schneider, "Reconciling History With the Nation?—Historicity, National Particularity, and the Question of Universals," In *Historiography East and West* 1, no.1 (2003): 117–136.
10. Chen Duxiu, "Jinggao Jinnian" [A Call to Youth], Xin Qingnian 1, no. 1 (1915). Quoted in Susan Daruvala, *Zhou Zuoren and an Alternative Response to Chinese Modernity* (Cambridge, MA: Harvard University Press, 2000), 47.
11. For example, Gao Yihan, "Gonghe quojia yu qingnian zhi zijue" [The Republic and the Self-Consciousness of Youth], *Xin Qingnian* 1, no. 1 (1915); Gao Yihan, "Qingnian yu quojia zhi qiantu" [Youth and the Future of the Nation], *Xin Qingnian* 1, no. 5 (1916); Gao Yihan, "Qingnian zhi di" [The Enemies of Youth], *Xin Qingnian* 1, no. 6 (1916). Also, other authors have argued along similar lines. See, for example, Tao Lügong, "Xin Qingnian de xin daode" [New Youth's New Morals], *Xin Qingnian* 4, no. 2 (1918).
12. Li Dazhao, "Shaonian zhongguo de shaonian yundong" [The Youth Movement of Young China], *Shaonian Zhongguo* 3 (September 1919).

13. *Xinchao* 1, no. 1 (1919).
14. Zong Zhikui, "Zhongguo qingnian de fendou shenghuo yu chuangzao shenghuo" [The Struggling Life and Creative Life of China's Youth], *Shaonian Zhongguo* 1, no. 5 (1919).
15. Cf. Wang Ermin, "Qingji zhishifenzi de zijue" [Self-Awareness of Intellectuals During the Qing Period], in *Zhongguo jindai sixiangshi shilun*, ed. Jinyu Wang (Taibei: Tawain Shan wu yin shu guan, 1995): 95–164.
16. Joseph W. Esherick and Mary B. Rankin argue that since the 1860s the traditional distinction between merchant *(shang)* and political elites *(shi)* had become blurred in local gentry circles. See Joseph W. Esherick and Mary B. Rankin, "Introduction," in *Chinese Local Elites and Patterns of Dominance*, eds. J.W. Esherick and M. B. Rankin (Berkeley: University of California Press, 1990).
17. Hui Huang, "The Chinese Construction of the West."
18. Cf. Yü Ying-shih, "The Radicalization of China in the Twentieth Century," *Daedalus: China in Transformation* 122, no. 2 (1993): 125–50.
19. See, for example, the classic work by Karl Mannheim, *Konservatismus: Ein Beitrag zur Soziologie des Wissens*, eds. David Kettler and Volker Meja (Frankfurt: Suhrkamp, 1984).
20. See Charlotte Furth, "Culture and Politics in Modern Chinese Conservatism," in *The Limits of Change: Essays on Conservative Alternatives in Republican China*, ed. C. Furth (Cambridge, MA: Harvard University Press, 1976): 31–37.
21. Compare Hui Huang, "Chinese Construction of the West," 179ff.
22. Cf. Yü Ying-shih, "The Radicalization of China," 125–50, who speaks of a "double marginalization" (excluding personal marginalization).
23. See Xu Guoqi, *China and the Great War: China's Pursuit of a New National Identity and Internationalization* (Cambridge: Cambridge University Press, 2005).
24. See Osterhammel, *Shanghai, 30. Mai 1925*.
25. See Michael Adas, "The Great War and the Decline of the Civilizing Mission," in *Autonomous Histories, Particular Truths: Essays in Honor of John R. W. Small*, ed. L. J. Sears (Madison: University of Wisconsin, Center for Southeast Asian Studies, 1993): 101–21.
26. See, for example, Ali Mirsepassi, *Intellectual Discourse and the Politics of Modernization: Negotiating Modernity in Iran* (Cambridge, MA: Cambridge University Press, 2000).
27. Liu Shuya, "Ouzhou zhanzheng yu qingnian zhi juewu" [World War One and the Awakening of Youth], *Xin Qingnian* 2, no. 2 (1919): 119–26.
28. Cai Yuanpei, "Ouzhan yu zhexue" [The War and Philosophy], *Xin Qingnian* 5, no. 5 (1918): 491–96. A similar argument is provided by Tao Lügong, "Guanyu Ouzhan de yanshuo san pian - Ouzhan yi hou de zhengzhi" [Three Lectures about the European War—Politics after the European War], *Xin Qingnian* 5, no. 5 (1918): 470–72.
29. Wei Siluan, "Renlei jinhua de geminghuang" [Aspects of Human Evolution], *Shaonian Zhongguo* 1, no. 1 (1919): 14–34.
30. Li Dazhao, "Shumin zhi shengli" [The Victory of the People], *Xin Qingnian* 5, no. 5 (1918): 467–69. The article is part of a series entitled "Three Lectures On the European War."
31. For example, Wang Guangqi, "Quan'ou geguo caizheng gaiguan" [A brief Summary of the Fiscal Situation in the Whole of Europe], *Shaonian Zhong-*

guo 4, no. 3 (1923): 1–7. In the following three issues of *Young China*, Wang published a series of articles on the situation in Europe.
32. Shen Yi, "Zhanhou deguo zhi zhenxiang" [The real condition of Germany after WWI], *Shaonian Zhongguo* 6 (1922): 24–34. Shen Yi was one of the regular contributors to *Shaonian Zhongguo*.
33. For an intellectual biography, see Tang Xiaobing, *Global Space and the Nationalist Discourse of Modernity: The Historical Thinking of Liang Qichao* (Stanford: Stanford University Press, 1996).
34. See David Wright, "Yan Fu and the Tasks of the Translator." In *New Terms for New Ideas. Western Knowledge & Lexical Change in Late Imperial China*, ed. M. Lackner, I. Amelung & J. Kurtz (Leiden: Brill, 2001): 235–256.
35. Still an important intellectual biography: Benjamin Schwartz, *In Search of Wealth and Power: Yen Fu and the West* (Cambridge, MA: Belknap Press, 1964), 235ff.
36. See Michael Adas, *Machines as the Measure of Men: Science, Technology, and Ideologies of Western Dominance* (Ithaca: Cornell University Press, 1989).
37. Bertrand Russell, *The Problem of China* (New York: Century, 1922), 46. Quoted in Stephen N. Hay, *Asian Ideas of East and West: Tagore and His Critics in Japan, China, and India* (Cambridge, MA: Harvard University Press, 1970), 140.
38. See Werner Meißner, *China zwischen nationalem 'Sonderweg' und universaler Modernisierung: Zur Rezeption westlichen Denkens in China* (Munich: W. Fink, 1994). Eucken's works later became prominent in the early German fascist movement.
39. Published by Reclam Leipzig in 1922. See Meißner, *China*.
40. Zhang Junmai, "1919 zhi 1921 nian lü Ouzhong zhizhi zhengzhi yinxiang ji wuren suo de zhi jiaoxun" [The Political Impressions I arrived at During my Stay in Europe from 1919 to 1921 and the Lessons that I have Learned], *Xinlu* 5, no. 1 (1928): 19–27.
41. Zhang Junmai, "The Crisis of European Culture and the Trend Towards a New Chinese Culture," *Dongfang Zazhi* 19, no. 3 (1922).
42. Cf. Tang, *Liang*, chapter 2.
43. Liang Qichao, *Ouyou Xinying Lu* [Impressions from (My) Travels in Europe] (Beijing, 1921), 2961.
44. Ibid., 2969
45. Liang Qichao, *Ouyou Xinying Lu*, 2979.

Bibliography

Adas, Michael. *Machines as the Measure of Men: Science, Technology, and Ideologies of Western Dominance*. Ithaca: Cornell University Press, 1989.
———. "The Great War and the Decline of the Civilizing Mission." In *Autonomous Histories, Particular Truths: Essays in Honor of John R. W. Small*, ed. L. J. Sears. Madison: University of Wisconsin, Center for Southeast Asian Studies, 1993: 101–21.
Cai, Yuanpei. "Ouzhan yu zhexue" [The War and Philosophy]. *Xin Qingnian* 5, no. 5 (1918): 491–96.
Chen, Duxiu. "Jinggao Jinnian" [A Call to Youth]. *Xin Qingnian* 1, no. 1 (1915).

Cohen, Paul. "Remembering and Forgetting: National Humiliation in Twentieth-Century China." *Twentieth-Century China* 27, no. 2 (2002): 1–39.

Conrad, Sebastian, and Dominic Sachsenmaier, eds. *Competing Visions of World Order: Global Moments and Movements, 1880s–1930s*. New York: Palgrave, 2007.

Daruvala, Susan. *Zhou Zuoren and an Alternative Response to Chinese Modernity*. Cambridge, MA: Harvard University Press, 2000.

Dittmer, Lowell, and Samuel S. Kim. "In Search of a Theory for National Identity." In *China's Quest for National Identity*, eds. L. Dittmer and S.S. Kim. Ithaca: Cornell University Press, 1993.

Duara, Prasenjit. "Transnationalism in the Era of Nation States: China, 1900–1945." *Development and Change* 29, no. 4 (1994).

———. *Rescuing History from the Nation. Questioning Narratives of Modern China*. Chicago: University of Chicago Press, 1997.

Esherick, Joseph W., and Mary Backus Rankin. "Introduction." In *Chinese Local Elites and Patterns of Dominance*, eds. J.W. Esherick and M. B. Rankin. Berkeley: University of California Press, 1990, 1–25.

Furth, Charlotte. "Culture and Politics in Modern Chinese Conservatism." In *The Limits of Change: Essays on Conservative Alternatives in Republican China*, ed. C. Furth. Cambridge, MA: Harvard University Press, 1976: 22–56.

Gao, Yihan. "Gonghe quojia yu qingnian zhi zijue" [The Republic and the Self-Consciousness of Youth]. *Xin Qingnian* 1, no. 1 (1915).

———. "Qingnian yu quojia zhi qiantu" [Youth and the Future of the Nation]. *Xin Qingnian* 1, no. 5 (1916).

———. "Qingnian zhi di" [The Enemies of Youth]. *Xin Qingnian* 1, no. 6 (1916).

Hay, Stephen N. *Asian Ideas of East and West: Tagore and His Critics in Japan, China, and India*. Cambridge, MA: Harvard University Press, 1970.

Huang, Hui. "The Chinese Construction of the West, 1862–1922: Discourses, Actors and the Cultural Field." PhD diss., University of North Carolina, 1996.

Iriye, Akira. *Cultural Internationalism and World Order*. Baltimore, London: Johns Hopkins University Press, 1997.

Li, Dazaho. "Shumin zhi shengli" [The Victory of the People]. *Xin Qingnian* 5, no. 5 (1918): 467–69.

———. "Shaonian zhongguo de shaonian yundong" [The Youth Movement of Young China]. *Shaonian Zhongguo,* 3 (September 1919).

Liang, Qichao, *Ouyou xinying lu* [Impressions from [My] Travels in Europe]. Beijing, 1921.

Liu, Shuya. "Ouzhou zhanzheng yu qingnian zhi juewu" [World War One and the Awakening of Youth]. *Xin Qingnian* 2, no. 2 (1919): 119–26.

Mannheim, Karl. *Konservatismus: Ein Beitrag zur Soziologie des Wissens*. Eds. David Kettler and Volker Meja. Frankfurt: Suhrkamp, 1984.

Meissner, Werner. *China zwischen nationalem 'Sonderweg' und universaler Modernisierung: Zur Rezeption westlichen Denkens in China*. Munich: W. Fink, 1994.

Mirsepassi, Ali. *Intellectual Discourse and the Politics of Modernization: Negotiating Modernity in Iran*. Cambridge, MA: Cambridge University Press, 2000.

Osterhammel, Jürgen. *Shanghai, 30. Mai 1925: Die chinesische Revolution*. Munich: Deutscher Taschenbuch-Verlag, 1997.

Pusey, James Reeve. *China and Charles Darwin*. Cambridge, MA: Council on East Asian Studies, Harvard University, 1983.

Russell, Bertrand. *The Problem of China*. New York: Century, 1922.

Schneider, Axel. "Reconciling History With the Nation?—Historicity, National Particularity, and the Question of Universals." *Historiography East and West,* 1, no. 1 (2003): 117–136.
Schwarcz, Vera. *The Chinese Enlightenment: Intellectuals and the Legacy of the May Fourth Movement of 1919.* Berkeley: University of California Press, 1986.
Schwartz, Benjamin. *In Search of Wealth and Power: Yen Fu and the West.* Cambridge, MA: Belknap Press, 1964.
Shen, Yi. "Zhanhou deguo zhi zhenxiang" [The Real Condition of Germany after WWI]. *Shaonian Zhongguo* 6 (1922): 24–34.
Tang, Xiaobing. *Global Space and the Nationalist Discourse of Modernity: The Historical Thinking of Liang Qichao.* Stanford: Stanford University Press, 1996.
Tao, Lügong. "Guanyu Ouzhan de yanshuo san pian - Ouzhan yihou de zhengzhi" [Three Lectures about the European War—Post-War European Politics]. *Xin Qingnian* 5, no. 5 (1918): 470–72.
Wang, Ermin. "Qingji zhishifenzi de zijue" [Self-Awareness of Intellectuals During the Qing-Period]. In *Zhongguo jindai sixiangshi shilun,* ed. Jinyu Wang. Taibei: Tawain Shan wu yin shu guan, 1995: 95–164.
Wang, Guangqi. "Quan'ou geguo caizheng gaiguan" [A Brief Summary of the Fiscal Situation in the Whole of Europe]. *Shaonian Zhongguo* 4, no. 3 (May 1923): 1–7.
Wang, Hui. *Xiandai zhongguo sixiang de xingqi* [The Rise of Modern Chinese Thought]. 4 vols. Peking: Sanlian Shudian, 2004.
Wei, Siluan. "Renlei jinhua de geminghuang" [Aspects of Human Evolution]. *Shaonian Zhongguo* 1, no. 1 (1919): 14–34.
Wright, David. "Yan Fu and the Tasks of the Translator." In *New Terms for New Ideas. Western Knowledge & Lexical Change in Late Imperial China,* ed. M. Lackner, I. Amelung, and J. Kurtz. Leiden: Brill, 2001: 235–256.
Xu, Guoqi. *China and the Great War: China's Pursuit of a New National Identity and Internationalization.* Cambridge: Cambridge University Press, 2005.
Yü, Ying-shih. "The Radicalization of China in the Twentieth Century." *Daedalus: China in Transformation* 122, no. 2 (1993): 125–50.
Zhang, Junmai. "The Crisis of European Culture and the Trend Towards a New Chinese Culture." *Dongfang Zazhi* 19, no. 3 (1922).
———. "1919 zhi 1921 nian lü Ouzhong zhizhi zhengzhi yinxiang ji wuren suo de zhi jiaoxun" [The Political Impressions I arrived at During my Stay in Europe from 1919 to 1921 and the Lessons that I have Learned]. *Xinlu* 5, no.1 (1928): 19–27.
Zong, Zhikui. "Zhongguo qingnian de fendou shenghuo yu chuangzao shenghuo" [The Struggling Life and Creative Life of China's Youth]. *Shaonian Zhongguo* 1, no. 5 (1919).

Chapter 4

"FOR THE GENUINE CULTURE OF THE AMERICAS"
Musical Folklore, Popular Arts, and the Cultural Politics of Pan Americanism, 1933–50

Corinne A. Pernet

In 1942 the Silver Burdett Company, one of the leading textbook and music publishers in the United States, collaborated with the Pan American Union to publish a "Pan American Songbook," the *Cancionero Pan Americano*. The book contained folklore songs from all countries of the Americas, and was lavishly illustrated with photos and drawings of picturesque rural scenes. Its cover supposedly showed a *huaso,* a Chilean cowboy, but the handsome man appeared to be decidedly caucasian and was dressed in the holiday version of a *huaso* costume: shiny leather boots, elegant checkered woolen pants, and a colorful *manta* over a white shirt. It was a glossy production with a tendency to romanticize rural life and poverty while its Pan-American rhetoric thinly veiled US wartime political interest in a united Western hemisphere. Most of the photographic material in the book appeared courtesy of Grace Line, a US company that dominated the shipping lanes to South America. This songbook could well serve as a symbol for the problematic aspects of cultural diplomacy: A decade after its publication, the former director of the Pan American Union's Music Division, Charles Seeger, felt he had to beg for forgiveness for having published the book.[1]

Notes for this section begin on page 156.

Such a vignette might very well introduce a chapter on how various actors in the United States appropriated, misrepresented, and misused Latin American folklore during the era of the Good Neighbor policy. Similar arguments have long been made about the cultural aspects of the Good Neighbor policy as far as cinematic representations of Latin America were concerned, be they feature movies or Walt Disney's animated films.[2] These analyses are doubtless interesting and convincing, but they only speak to one side of this cultural interaction as they privilege North American agents and tend to render the Latin Americans hapless victims of US power.

To denounce the spread of US ideologies, values, and culture, Latin American scholars themselves have for decades engaged the notion of cultural imperialism supported by economic power. Ariel Dorfman and Armand Mattelart's *How To Read Donald Duck,* for instance, detailed how Disney comics undermined Latin American identities. First published in Chile in 1973, it became one of the best-selling book in Latin America in the 1970s.[3] With regards to film, scholars have pointed out that even if Latin American film industries could survive the onslaught of American movies in the 1930s and 1940s, they did so by producing movies that were "slavishly emulative of foreign models."[4] Recently Jean Franco referred to the cultural politics as an "apparently benevolent form of imperialism," but emphasized that the "formidable propaganda machine" of the United States flooded Latin American media with its version of reality.[5]

One reason for this somewhat limited view is that historians have often reduced the cultural aspects of the Good Neighbor policy to the activities of the Office of the Coordinator of Inter-American Affairs (OCIAA), a wartime creation headed by Nelson A. Rockefeller. Rockefeller is certainly an intriguing figure in US-Latin American relations,[6] and his OCIAA cofinanced several notorious "cultural exchanges," such as Orson Welles' film-making trip to Brazil, the grand South American tours of *maestro* Arturo Toscanini, and the "caravans" of the Kirstein Ballet. It also supported the Mexican film industry and brought Brazilian star composer Heitor Villa-Lobos and countless other artists to the United States.[7] Moreover, it was apparently Rockefeller's idea to call on Walt Disney to help improve relations between the North and the South in the Americas. But the cultural aspects of the Good Neighbor policy should not be reduced to the OCIAA, as many other actors were involved. For instance, we should not neglect the activities of the Cultural Division of the State Department that was established in 1938 and started a variety of programs before Rockefeller entered the arena of cultural foreign policy.

In the past decade or so, the history of US-Latin American cultural relations has been greatly enriched by new analyses that are informed by postcolonial theory.[8] Positioning myself among scholars intent on refining the analyses of US-Latin American interactions, I propose a different approach that takes Latin Americans—their motivations and actions—seriously as actors in their relations with the United States. I will unravel the complicated fabric of international intellectual currents and national expediencies in cultural politics, taking as my example the field of musical folklore. By focusing on the arena of cultural networks and transnational institutions, this chapter will demonstrate that the long-held dichotomies between center/periphery, exploiters/victims cannot always provide a good framework for examining the impact of the United States in Latin America. Certainly, inequality was an element of the "encounter" between Northern and Southern protagonists, but my examination of the inter-American politics of the vogue of folklore that swept the Americas in the 1930s and 1940s will show that a considerable space for negotiation existed.

In the 1930s, the attempts of the Latin American[9] cultural avant-garde to emancipate itself from overly Eurocentric views were joined by the efforts of many educators and bureaucrats. The latter wished to create national cultures that would be rooted in popular culture and would find resonance with large parts of the population. At the same time, state educational institutions for all population groups expanded greatly across Latin America. "Cultural extension" projects played an important role in this expansion, as did the increased integration of intellectuals and cultural workers into these institutions. The rise of fascism in Europe and the aggressive politics of Hitler's Germany posed a dilemma for the New World. Even as some political leaders across the hemisphere flirted with fascism during the 1930s (most prominently the Brazilian Getulio Vargas and his Estado Nôvo), the countries of the Western hemisphere started to present themselves as the bedrock of occidental democracy in the 1940s. While Europe descended into turmoil, "the Americas" would be a safe haven for civilization and democracy. In this situation, the New World could not simply hold fast to the dominant culture of the now-decadent Europe, because operating a democratic system implied taking seriously all non-European cultures and national traditions. Thus the international political situation gave the countries of the Western hemisphere an additional reason to explore their own cultures and investigate the notion of a distinct "American" culture.

Intellectuals and artists from North and South America were able to convince the political establishment that the cultivation and investigation of folklore contributed significantly to the cultural emancipation of the Americas. Yet this essay is not concerned with the "content" of folklore, its performers, nor does it aim to provide a deep analysis of how the field of folklore developed in the Americas or in individual countries. It does not address the question of why and how the binary system of a distinction between "the folk" and high culture developed or changed.[10] Rather, it will examine how cultural workers and folklore specialists used the national and international political constellations of the 1930s and 1940s to further their goals on the transnational level. The convergence of folklore projects on a national scale with trends in the international arena provides the backdrop to this study of the interactions between Latin American proponents of folklore and their counterparts in the United States.

My work thus focuses on the establishment of a transnational cultural network of professionals in a period of international upheaval. Most of the protagonists in my account were not career diplomats but academics and artists who sought transnational interactions for professional rather than political reasons. The focus on a transnational network of folklore specialists does not mean that the state—or international organizations of states—were not important. Both provided important employment niches for folklorists and arenas for their activities. Indeed, in some cases it is not always clear if a protagonist represented either the state or civil society at any given moment. In the case of the United States, some folklore specialists started working for the State Department during the war years, while others collaborated in an advisory capacity. In Latin America, the relations between cultural workers and the state have traditionally been rather close (if not unproblematic).[11] The strengthening of a transnational cultural network indicates that nationalism and national power were only factors among others in the politics of folklore. Despite partially divergent goals, folklorists from North and South actively built a transnational professional community—and used the cultural diplomacy of their governments to further their ends.

Given the preexisting interest in folklore across the hemisphere, the new US cultural policies reinforced a transnational community of scholars. Records of Latin American institutes of popular arts and folklore, from scholarly societies, as well as materials from the Pan American Union, the Library of Congress, and the State Department all indicate that the US initiatives and resources resulted in increased networking activities among folklore scholars and helped to bring about the institutionalization of popular arts and folklore studies at museums and universities across the Americas. Funds from the United States opened possibilities for research previously not existing. It is difficult to assess whether or not this process served to divulge US political values or ideological frameworks. Folklore and popular arts specialists publicly presented their subjects in a Pan American discourse of a distinct popular culture of the Western hemisphere. Certainly, in a final ironic twist, the institutionalization of popular arts and folklore in Latin America nourished cultural traditions that were effectively put to political use against "US imperialism" of the cultural sort beginning in the late 1950s.

Cultural Nationalism and Americanism in Latin America

Once independent from Spain and Portugal, Latin American countries continued to look toward Europe for societal models. Latin American elites sought to escape the "barbarism" they perceived in their countries (particularly among the indigenous populations, Afro-Americans, or plain rural people) through Europeanization. Europeanization meant not only the whitening of the population through immigration programs but also the replication of European cultural institutions.[12] A "nativist" cultural movement developed among Latin American artists and intellectuals only in the final years of the nineteenth century. Cuban poet José Martí was among the first to question the inferiority of the *mestizo,* while Ruben Darío and Enrique Rodó elaborated on a Latin American identity that was distinct from that of Europe or the United States. As Richard Morse has convincingly argued, the quest for a Latin American identity began in full force during the twentieth century, "amid the disintegration of Western rationales and received understandings."[13]

Even in their quest for a Latin American identity, intellectuals remained in close contact with developments abroad, especially with the European avant-garde, and allowed an intensive cross-fertilization of ideas.[14] By the 1920s, disenchantment with the US imperialist adventures combined with the devastation of World War I to challenge the notion of European or North American cultural superiority. Thus the 1920s became a decade of reconsideration of Latin America's cultural heritage, particularly as far as the indigenous or African legacy was concerned. In Mexico, Minister of Education José Vasconcelos predicted that Latin America was leading the way into a new age, in which the "cosmic race," the mix of the indigenous, African, and European population would transcend the narrow limits of Western cultures. In Peru, the political leader and essayist José Carlos Mariátegui combined his Marxist stance on economic issues with a steadfast defense of indigenous rights and culture. These are just the best-known exponents of the tendency.[15] At the same time, the social scientists both in Europe and in the United States (there under the influence of German-born Franz Boas) started to engage in comparative studies. With cross-cultural fieldwork, they sought to delineate the relationships between cultures. Intellectuals in Mexico, Brazil, and Argentina were well aware of these trends and started to develop programs of research in this direction as well.[16]

Studying folklore and folkloric music was part and parcel of the Latin American trend toward cultural nationalism. The Cuban government proposed in 1926 a congress on "Music as a means to tighten relations between the American peoples," and particularly recommended "the study of Pan-American folklore."[17] Revolutionary Mexico also made pioneering efforts in the investigation of folklore. Mexican rural culture and folklore even turned into a fashionable trend in the United States, but the emphasis was placed less on music than on popular arts.[18] In Brazil, avant-garde artists and writers became important promoters of the folklore movement. They questioned the long-standing fascination of Brazilians with all things French in particular and European in general, and demanded that Brazilian art address Brazilian realities.[19] The vanguard's notion of *brasilidade* (Brazilianness), was pitched against that of traditionalists, who sought a Brazilian identity rooted in the eighteenth-century baroque.[20] Apart from appropriating the folk, modern *brasilidade* included the possibility of dynamically interacting with outside cultural forces, as in the figure of Oswald de Andrade's celebrated cannibal that consumes and transforms the other.

The avant-gardists, with their interest in afro-Brazilian and indigenous music forms, played a most important role in Brazilian musical culture. Composer Heitor Villa-Lobos (1887–59) even claimed in Paris that "le Folklore, c'est moi"—because his compositions were diffused with Brazilian themes and styles that he had been exposed to during his long years as an itinerant musician. Writer and critic Mário de Andrade devoted himself to ethnographic projects in northeastern Brazil in 1928 and started to write on musical folklore shortly thereafter.[21] As director of the Department of Culture of the City of São Paulo, he initiated the collection of Afro-Brazilian and Northeastern folklore in 1937. He financed a research group that traveled for six months through Brazil's northeast and returned with about fifteen hundred items for the Discoteca Pública Municipal. Though funds were limited, records of this sound archive were distributed to music schools and cultural organizations. De Andrade also founded a short-lived Society for Ethnography and Folklore (1936–39), which produced cartographic representations of folkloric traditions in Brazil, another pioneer effort in Latin America.[22] The government of Getúlio Vargas took up folklore for its own aims, recording over one hundred disks of folk music in the late 1930s.[23] The government station broadcast a weekly program where the moderator brought in folk performers from all over Brazil to tell their stories and explain the pieces performed.[24] Brazilian folklore researchers were also well connected internationally, participating in congresses and travelling abroad as well as within Latin America.[25]

In Chile the transition to a cultural nationalism was not as closely linked with the avant-garde. Research on Chilean folklore, especially on folk literature, began during the late nineteenth century and was inspired by the German tradition. Contracted by the Chilean government in 1890, the German scholar Rudolf Lenz (1863–38) founded the Sociedad del Folklore Chileno in 1909. The Sociedad organized regular talks and published its own journal.[26] In the first decades of the twentieth century, a generation of *criollista* (nativist) writers favored themes on the Chilean countryside but kept a rather conservative outlook. They spoke about or, at best, for the rural underclass, and romanticized an unchangeable if inegalitarian community.[27]

Parallel to the literary interest in rural culture, there was also a movement that sought to revalidate Chilean folkloric music.

By the 1920s, modern Chilean composers such as Pedro Humberto Allende, Carlos Isamitt, and Carlos Levin took an interest in folk traditions as well.[28] In 1938, university circles (gathered in the Chilean Commission on Intellectual Cooperation) organized a large exposition on Chilean popular art in Santiago that turned into a resounding success. One year later, at the American Congress on Intellectual Cooperation, the Chilean delegation presented a report on folklore studies, which recommended that all countries organize their folklore societies.[29] The Commission's brochure, "What is Folklore and What is it Good For?" explained that folklore could provide interesting study materials on Chilean society and ethnicity. Created in a private setting, folklore was perceived as a way to understand how *el pueblo,* the common people, viewed the world.[30] Several departments at the University of Chile focused on different aspects of folklore investigations, and Chilean students went to Brazil to perfect their studies by the early 1940s.[31]

Interest in Chilean folklore had spread beyond the bounds of art, music, and academe to educators and cultural critics at large. Promoters of Chilean musical traditions claimed that they would contribute to the cultural uplift of all classes and criticized sharply that radio stations broadcast so much foreign music. Musician Pablo Garrido, for instance, lamented that "decadent *tangones*" killed the spirit of Chileans. As a counter-measure, he wrote a popular book on the Chilean national dance, the *cueca*. It was the first book wholly dedicated to the national dance, and newspapers and weeklies reviewed it widely.[32] Other writers concurred that the tangos, boleros, Mexican *rancheros,* and foxtrots that dominated radio broadcasts amounted to "continuous attacks against culture."[33] The promotion of folklore aimed at erecting a barrier to stop this invasion because "authentic" Chilean culture was under attack from all sides. After the progressive Popular Front government had taken power in 1938, the revalidation of common people's culture became an important aspect of fostering *chilenidad* (Chileanness). By the late 1930s, folk songbooks received enthusiastic reviews in middle-class magazines, which also started to feature articles on provincial fiestas and the customs of peasants and miners.[34]

In academe as well as in cultural politics, folklore had definitely become a concern across Latin America in the 1940s. Even poor countries like El Salvador established a National Committee for Folklore Research in 1941. The committee asked local priests, teachers, and mayors to participate in the initiative. Within three years it managed to publish a four hundred-page compilation of popular art and songs.[35] In 1946, Colombia established a National Folklore Commission that started to issue its biannual journal one year later. In Venezuela, the efforts of individual researchers and writers were consolidated in 1946 in a special division of the Ministry of Education.[36]

Of course, folklore did have its commercial dimensions. Some countries quickly attracted tourists with folkloric displays—traditional fiestas, music, dances, and rodeos—when air travel and the lack of European destinations after 1939 had turned Latin America into a viable option at least for elite tourists. In Brazil, state organizations directed the transformation of Afro-Brazilians' carnival and other festivals into tourist-worthy performances.[37] In Mexico, the Ballet Folklórico that performed the *jarabe tapatío* dance rose to stardom among Mexican foreign tourists thanks to the alliance of the governmental Tourism Department and the Institute of Fine Arts.[38] The Chilean tourist service sponsored lavishly and distributed abroad illustrated booklets on the Chilean *huasos,* the cowboys it presented as "a handsome and energetic representative of the race."[39] In Brazil, interest in musical folklore was so strong that record companies such as Victor RCA and Columbia offered folklore collections to native buyers.[40] Though these commercial aspects did have their effects on certain forms of popular culture (as Nestor García Canclini expounded in a pioneering book),[41] they do neither explain nor represent the vogue of folklore as a whole and are of little importance in this chapter.

Folklore appealed to different groups in North and South for varied reasons—even if the mere definition of the term was contested among specialists. Some defined folklore narrowly as the popular arts of supposedly isolated "traditional communities." In this view, folklore figured as a distilled expression of the "collective soul" (of a region or nation) that needed to be saved because it was on the verge of disappearing. Others employed a broader concept that included the popular culture of different professional groups (such as miners and fishermen) and even urban sectors. Both groups, however, engaged in documentation and research, although they might apply different standards and approaches.[42] Composers wrote scores on folkloric themes, incorporated folk melodies, indigenous instruments, and rhythms to express national or regional identities. Among many others, Heitor Villa-Lobos or the Mexican composer Carlos Chávez were two of the most prolific nationalist composers.[43]

For educators and officials working in the new departments of ethnography, musicology, or linguistics, folklore contributed to a scientific analysis of regional and national cultures. They advocated the promotion of folklore to foster a sense of community (on different levels from local to supranational), maintain traditional skills, and fill leisure hours in a sensible fashion. As in Europe, governments and political parties attempted to instrumentalize folk culture in different ways. In Argentina, some government institutions like the Federal Commission on Folklore and Natives clearly subscribed to a conservative agenda as they attempted to resist the cultural disintegration brought about by the "immigrant floods."[44] In Mexico, Chile, and Colombia, the promotion of folk stood for the valorization of the common people's culture. Governmental institutions would not only focus on highbrow culture, but dedicate themselves to popular art as well. In these countries, "democratic culture" was a key to the building of the national popular state.[45]

Despite the importance of popular art for building the national states, a transnational network of music professionals in Latin America promoting "musical Americanism" attracted leading figures in the music world of the 1930s. One of the main promoters of "musical Americanism" was the German-born and trained architect and musicologist Francisco Curt Lange, who arrived in Uruguay in 1930 and within a few years had helped to establish the national radio station, the sound archives, as well as a graduate program in musicology. He also founded the prestigious journal *Boletín Latinoamericana de Música* in 1935.[46] Citing the Mexican philosopher José Vasconcelos, he encouraged musicians and music educators in Latin America to draw on their own cultural resources and to emancipate themselves from the slavish adoration of European music. In view of the "hecatomb" he saw coming in Europe, he asked music specialists to request the collaboration of the state in fostering "musical Americanism." Lange evidently conceived of cultural politics as a means to defend peace, as one of the goals of "musical Americanism" was to contribute to a more-united Latin America.[47]

Lange had contacts all across Latin America and established especially close links with the Brazilians Mario de Andrade, Heitor Villa-Lobos, Luiz-Heitor Corrêa de Azevedo, and Camargo Guarneri during a trip in 1934. The fact that each issue of the

Boletín Latinoamericana de Música showcased a Latin American country with the help of a coeditor from that same country also helped to form a community of music professionals, many of whom had a strong interest in folklore as one of the bases for "American" music.[48] The leading music journal in Latin America, the *Boletín* soon found an echo abroad, as it had subscribers from forty-six countries. By the time that the United States entered the arena of folklore studies, networks among Latin American proponents of musical Americanism were already in place.

The Vogue of Folk and Cultural Diplomacy in the USA

The United States was not exempt from this nationalist turn in music in the early twentieth century. Folk symbolized emancipation and democracy during the 1939 US visit of the British majesties, King George VI and Queen Elizabeth. The Roosevelts entertained the king and queen during the state dinner at the White House mostly with black spirituals, cowboy songs, folk dances, and only two performances of "art music."[49] This expressed the slow retreat from the long-lasting dominance of classical music, especially German orchestral music, in the United States.[50] Though the folk music movement had emerged prior to World War I, the Depression heightened its promise. As Peter Filene put it in his recent book: "America's fascination with folk culture challenged the status quo: it registered dissatisfaction with the emptiness of mass culture and the sterility of high culture, the corruption of power politics, and the vicissitudes of the industrial economy."[51] Emphasizing the folk took on political overtones shortly before World War II, as it stood for democratic sentiments as well as the proud American nation.

The Depression not only fostered the interest in folklore, but the Work Program Administration (WPA) also provided ways and means to collect folklore from different regions and population groups. Harvard-educated avant-garde composer Charles Seeger, who took charge of the music program at the WPA, instructed his field workers to organize folklore events and collect songs rather than try to force art music on people who did not want to hear it.[52] The Library of Congress began to collect folk music, and founded the "Archive of American Folk Song" in 1928. This institution was the first to record Woody

Guthrie and Leadbelly (Huddie William Leadbetter), for instance. Moving beyond their initial focus on US music, the archivists started to collect folklore from all over the world in the mid 1930s. Latin American material became an important subject in 1938.[53]

Also in the 1930s, universities across the country started to offer courses in folklore studies. Ralph Steele Boggs, a professor of Spanish with a profound interest in Latin American folklore, founded the first graduate program in folklore studies at the University of North Carolina in 1939. An avid bibliographer and publisher of Spanish language bibliographies on folklore, he was well aware of the work done by folklorists south of the border. He managed to unite prominent researchers, such as Vicente T. Mendoza of Mexico or the Argentine Carlos Vega, in an association called Folklore Americas that started a journal by the same name in 1941.[54] Thus important researchers in the field of folklore had already established ties in the 1930s.

The US government had traditionally left cultural diplomacy to private initiatives. As the clouds of war gathered on the European horizon, US diplomats and politicians started to worry about the expansionist aspirations of Germany with regards to Latin America. They were alarmed by the overtures the fascist Italian government made to Latin American countries. The apparent success of German and Italian cultural missions (binational institutes, magazine publications, tours of theater troupes) became a preoccupation in Washington circles.[55] The Roosevelt administration had made efforts to improve relations with Latin America in 1933 when it renounced unilateral interventions in the internal affairs of its southern neighbors and proclaimed "the policy of the good neighbor." But only in 1938 did the president create the Cultural Division of the State Department, with Latin America as a special focus.

A newcomer in the field of international cultural relations, the State Department drew on the experience of other organizations such as the (private) United States National Committee for Intellectual Cooperation or the American Library Association. The Cultural Division assembled its staff by bringing in people from outside of the State Department.[56] The first director of the Division of Cultural Relations, Ben Cherrington, was a social scientist who had directed a program of international relations at the University of Denver. He first appointed advisory committees and invited representatives of Latin America for a series of four conferences on the state of hemispheric cultural relations that covered education, art, music, publications, and libraries.[57] Some of these new government appointees were critical of the notion of cultural diplomacy; they warned that cultural politics had their own dynamics and constituted a complex field. Historian Lewis Hanke, an advisor to the State Department, cautioned U.S. Americans not to be offended if Latin Americans would not follow U.S. models in their search for cultural identity.[58] The first generation of cultural foreign policymakers thus kept a certain distance from instrumentalist politics. But with the advent of World War II, many actors in the field, public as well as private organizations, came to believe that the United States should act to create a sense of unity among the nations of the Americas and to develop schemes to intensify cultural relations.

At times it seemed that the Division of Cultural Relations was a step behind the professional or academic organizations in terms of implementing policy. In 1939, the American Musicological Society had already invited a number of prominent Latin American music specialists to international congress that was taking place in New York in September.[59] The newly formed advisory committee on music of the Cultural Division then decided to appeal to some of these specialists to stay for a "Conference on the Inter-American Relations in the Field of Music" taking place in October.[60]

Conference participants discussed topics ranging from school music, radio exchanges, and folk music collections, but also wrote a memorandum on copyrights—a great concern for the Latin Americans, who complained about the lack of copyright protection their work suffered in the United States. The conference resolved to appoint an organizing committee that drew up a plan for a clearinghouse for music exchanges. Having gained financial support for its plan from Nelson Rockefeller's Office of the Coordinator of Inter-American Affairs and from the Carnegie Endowment, the committee asked the Pan American Union to accept the Inter-American Music Center under its umbrella.[61] The PAU, which had maintained a financially strapped, but continually expanding cultural division since the late 1920s, accepted what must have appeared to be a good deal.[62] Led by Charles Seeger, the new center opened at the PAU headquarters in Washington, DC in early 1941.[63]

The appointment of Seeger as head of the PAU Music Center was a victory for those in Inter-American cultural relations who favored a focus on folklore and popular culture—as opposed to "serious" music championed by Howard Hanson, Director of the Eastman School of Music and member of the Cultural Division's advisory committee on music—in the new cultural diplomacy. Indeed, a strong lobby for folklore studies shaped the policies of the Cultural Division of the State Department. Charles Seeger argued that folklore would be a good tool in "trying to reach people, peoples of countries, not just ruling classes"—poorer people who would not attend a concert or an evening at the ballet.[64] The report of the 1939 conference on music recommended that researchers make an effort to find folk songs that were "connected" with people's lives, songs of "birth and death, heroic deeds, work, of beggars, muleteers, *vaqueros*...." Such a focus would also counterbalance the notion that Latin American music was "very gay and sometimes spicy entertainment"—very likely a reference to Carmen Miranda, the scantily-dressed, samba-dancing "Brazilian bombshell" who was at the time sweeping New York off its feet.[65] Carleton Sprague Smith, the head of the music division of the New York Public library, toured South America in 1940 on behalf of the State Department. In his report, he argued that the music of the Western Hemisphere was "not as reflective, as ponderous, as metaphysical" as European music, but rather rough, humorous, exaggerated, as well as sentimental. He wrote that exchanging popular and folk music was more important for "fundamental cultural understanding" than tours by "operatic and other musical stars."[66] Smith claimed that the cultural understanding brought about by promoting the Americas' musical heritage contributed significantly to defending freedom in the Western Hemisphere.[67]

Folklore scholars from North and South were quick to jump on the bandwagon, hoping to find sponsors for their subject within and outside the United States. For the renowned folklorist Stith Thompson (University of Indiana), the concept of a "Folklore of the Americas" offered great opportunities to unite folklorists who he considered "scattered and often ineffective." He pleaded for coordination of national efforts and dreamed of a Pan American Folklore archive. He hoped that the Americas would catch up to European countries like Sweden and Denmark, where folklore studies were advanced.[68] Ralph Steele Boggs saw in the government efforts a validation of his endeavors with Folklore Americas. The Music Educators' National Conference that met in the Fall of 1942 agreed that teaching Latin

American folk music in US schools was needed to "Americanize the Americas." The meeting attractions included a radio connection to Brazil, where star composer Heitor Villa-Lobos answered questions about the importance of folklore.[69]

Thus the consensus among music specialists was to encourage Latin Americans to showcase their own democratic traditions and find their artistic inspiration in "American" traditions instead of looking to the decadent aristocratic European culture. Latin Americans should make the most of the "golden opportunity to establish their own music-cultural independence of Europe."[70] Certainly, Francisco Curt Lange and many other Latin American music specialists favoring "Musical Americanism" could not have agreed more.

Behind the overly optimistic rhetoric about the potential of folklore lay a more realistic assessment of cultural diplomacy as well as a good deal of concern about the current political situation. Seeger, for instance, was not entirely blue eyed about the potential of music as an agent of international understanding per se. As he put it, "[e]ven when in the best of faith we try to put music at the service of broad cultural policies, we cannot assure our non-musical collaborators that we know what we are doing." A few years later, he declared music to be "a highly competitive field and can be used as a medium for aggression as easily as any other."[71] Political motives and context were also plainly evident in Carleton Sprague Smith's report on his tour of South America. He pointed out that the German, Italian, and Japanese governments had managed to invite hundreds of intellectuals annually and noted that German and Italian businesses generously donated books to libraries. Reflecting an attitude that might have still been prevalent in the 1930s, Smith considered propaganda as "foreign to our nature." But in view of fascist activities, the US government had no choice but to adopt more aggressive measures.[72] Having met with many radio station managers in Latin America, he urged the United States to produce records with its own folk and popular music, accompanied with scripts in Spanish and Portuguese, so that the US "might thus have Propaganda Half Hours (free of charge) in important Radio Stations ... with very little effort." Among the people he met, he designated "Inter-American key people" who were "friendly to the United States and may be counted on to do what they can to further inter-American exchange," suggesting that the State Department invite them to tour the US. The worst the United States could do, he warned, was to issue vague promises about common cultural projects and then not follow up.[73]

In announcing the creation of the Cultural Division of the Department of State on 27 July 1938, Sumner Welles had called on educational institutions and private organizations to assist the government in developing and implementing its program of cultural diplomacy. Indeed, many of the men and women who were now developing government policy came from and remained active in universities, professional organizations as well as private foundations. To cite just one example, the head of the PAU's Music Division, Charles Seeger, served on the Advisory Committee on Music of the State Department's Cultural Division and on the American Council of Learned Societies' Committee on Musicology. He was a board member of the Music Education Research Council and a consultant to the Carnegie Endowment. As one of the leading members of the American Musicological Society, he participated in a publication project, "Monuments of Music in the Western Hemisphere," which was in turn financed by the American Council of Learned Societies. Seeger's ties also extended to broadcasting companies since he was on the advisory committee for NBC's program "Music of the New World."[74] The financial schemes to fund the different cultural initiatives were equally complex. As mentioned above, Seeger's Music Division of the Pan American Union was funded by the State Department and the Carnegie Endowment in its early years, but still the PAU's music division was able to raise $33,970 from private institutions for its operations in its first year.[75] When the initial subsidy ran out in 1944, projects continued to be cosponsored by entities ranging from the Music Educators National Conference to the Library of Congress and private foundations.[76] Appreciating the opportunity of receiving official validation of their engagement, professional organizations and philanthropies were eager to collaborate with the government. Thus with public and private funding, US folklore specialists working through different agencies and institutions were ready by the early 1940s to engage in the folklore offensive.[77]

Policies in Practice

Though there were quite a few voices demanding reciprocity and warning against the danger of arrogance, there is no denying that many US protagonists regarded Latin Americans as the junior partner in the enterprise of cultural exchange. Archibald MacLeish, librarian of Congress, found himself pressed to point out to the Conference on Inter-American Relation in the Field of Music in 1939 that Latin American audiences were "a very sophisticated, highly intelligent group of people"; North Americans should not think that they were "going to do the giving." William Berrien, already a bit more patronizing, stated that there was a "surprising amount of good music available in Latin America to be performed...."[78] Also regarding folklore studies, US attitudes were initially rather paternalistic. Thus Seamus Doyle, director of the Folk Archive of the Library of Congress, reported in 1941 that "the value of encouraging, preserving and demonstrating [sic] the oral tradition of folk song is not yet recognized or appreciated," despite the fact that Latin American folklorists had started to record folk songs and organize archives many years ago.[79] Neither did Charles Seeger note any contradictions in calling the Latin American music resources "disorganized" at the same time that he tried—rather desperately—to convince Uruguayan Francisco Curt Lange to let him guest edit a special issue of the renowned *Boletín Latinoamericana de Música* on the music of the United States.[80] Moreover, when it came to establishing the Inter-American Music Center, the power of the US and its desire to be at the center of cultural initiatives was palpable in the decision to completely ignore Lange's Inter-American Institute of Musicology in Montevideo and establish the center in Washington, DC. At least it seems that once the communication had improved between the folklore specialists of the Western Hemisphere, the attitude of the North Americans tended to change. Lewis Hanke, eminent historian who worked for the State Department, was well aware of the "tremendous handicaps" Latin American folklorists worked under and marveled, "How they accomplish what they do is beyond me."[81]

Rather understandably, folklorists in South America, who sometimes had spent years assembling their collections under difficult conditions, were at times suspicious of the sudden interest on the part of the North Americans in their folklore. One model of interaction that was likely to be fraught with difficulty was the "recording mission"—in which North Americans traveled around Latin America trying to record folklore music. One such mission took place in June 1941, when Seamus Doyle joined the American Ballet Caravan (a venture of Lincoln Kirstein and George Balanchine)[82] during its South America tour with the task to bring back folk material. In every city that the Ballet appeared, Doyle consulted with local specialists for access to information and material, but often found that they were not willing to provide either. The Brazilian intellectual Gilberto Freyre, for instance, was "pleasant and courteous" but did not help Doyle in finding recordable folklore. When Doyle asked the producers of the Brazilian radio program *La Hora Nacional* (The National Hour) about the possibility of recording some of the folk singers that had appeared on their program, the inquiry "did not produce an enthusiastic reaction." Doyle and his crew were not much more fortunate at the municipal sound archive in São Paulo. The US Americans were impressed with the institution, "a most attractive place and very well stocked, cataloged and efficiently managed." Director Oneyda Alvarenga provided Doyle with copies of the latest publications (classifications of Brazilian folk songs) but despite the "cordial" relations, she was apparently reluctant to share some recent recordings with Doyle and his crew.

Even the Chilean music professor Domingo Santa Cruz, who normally maintained the most cordial relations with the United States, was annoyed about Doyle's recording tour. Santa Cruz thought that the approach of the recording tour was not "serious" enough and announced to Doyle that he was going to submit a protest in writing to the Library of Congress. Finally, Santa Cruz and Eugenio Pereira Salas choose two performers ("two gypsyish looking females who required a little cognac to put them in a singing mood") with whom Doyle could record a few songs. Doyle acknowledged that Santa Cruz, who was trying to receive funding for a large-scale folk music recording project from the Chilean government, might be "a little uneasy about collectors, especially from the States, who might mess up the idea by doing a superficial research without adequate qualifications for it."[83]

Most explicit in his reaction was the Argentine folklore specialist Carlos Vega, who had worked in the field since the 1920s and had good contacts in Europe. He flatly refused to let Doyle copy any of his records on the spot, but "indicated that he would be interested in an offer" from the Library of Congress Music Division for the duplication of his recordings.[84] The Library's Archive of American Folksong would try for years to collect the funds necessary to make Vega an offer for duplication, worrying that they might lose "the opportunity to acquire one of the best collections of Latin American folk music."[85] Evidently, Latin American folklorists started to view popular art as a resource that should not simply be given away, but rather something that could be used to bargain with, especially vis-a-vis the United States.

The more the local folklore community was involved in recording projects of the various US agents, the more successful they tended to be. In Mexico, the Inter-American Institute of Indigenous Studies received money from the PAU to prepare eight broadcasts on the subject of musical folklore. Most of the people involved were Mexicans, and the production went ahead speedily. The Archive of American Folk Song also sponsored collection projects in Cuba. For the Archive, this was a convenient way of adding to its collection even during the war years, when field trips within the United States were out of the question because of the rationing of gasoline and tires. The Folk Archive also started producing records with the specific purpose of "exchange with cultural institutions in the other American republics." By 1944, the Archive reported that its services were in great demand "because of the ever growing importance of American folk song in the consciousness of our people."[86] Another possibility were exchange contracts satisfactory to both parties. Thus the Sound Archive of São Paulo, which had not wanted to share recordings with Seamus Doyle, made duplicates available on an exchange basis to the Library of Congress only a few years later.[87]

Latin American folklore researchers did not shy away from opportunities that they deemed beneficial. Indeed, for some Latin American folk specialists, the new US policies provided much-needed technical resources to engage in their research. In 1941, for instance, the US State Department invited the Chilean historian Eugenio Pereira Salas and the composer Domingo Santa Cruz, both specialists of folklore, to tour the United States.[88] Once in Washington, DC, Charles Seeger of the PAU Music Division asked Pereira Salas to write a short booklet on the state of music in Chile, to be distributed through the PAU. Pereira Salas and Santa Cruz also met with the folklorists of the Library of Congress and exchanged views on different ways to collect material. They managed to convince the American Council of Learned Societies to purchase recording equipment for the Institute of Musical Extension in Chile, a university affiliate concerned with the collection and diffusion of folklore. With the help of the Coordinator of Inter-American Affairs, Nelson Rockefeller, the ACLS was able to circumvent war-time shipping restrictions. The state of the art recording machines (one portable and one for studio use) with a value of $4,900 arrived in 1943 in Chile where they were immediately put to use.[89]

Other folklore researchers were able to use the networks they built during the heyday of the vogue of folklore as a springboard to an international career. This was certainly the case of Luiz Heitor Corrêa de Azevedo, the Brazilian musicologist and folklorist. Corrêa had just finished his doctoral thesis on the music of Brazilian indigenous people in 1938 and was working at the School of Music of the University of Rio de Janeiro when the Music Division of the PAU hired him for six months on the recommendation of William Berrien and Carleton Sprague Smith of the New York Public Library.[90] During his six months in the United States, Corrêa visited many universities and gave talks on Brazilian music at meetings of professional organizations.[91] When he returned to Brazil in February 1942, he took along more than just good memories. He carried with him a State Department voucher for over one thousand dollars, to be disbursed by the US Embassy, and three boxes of recording equipment. The money and the equipment were used during a two-month field trip to record folk music in the Brazilian Northeast.[92] The agreement with Corrêa was simple: the Archive of American Folk Song at the Library of Congress organized the shipment of empty disks and recording machines; the original recordings Corrêa made went back to the Library of Congress, while the National School of Music in Rio de Janeiro could retain a copy. Corrêa had a free hand in deciding which material to record and how to spend the allotted money. The agreement was productive as Corrêa sent back almost two hundred records to the Library of Congress over the next six years—and kept two hundred records in Rio.

The correspondence between Corrêa and the Library of Congress reveals the modes of interaction between the two parties. All in all, Corrêa presented himself as an energetic, hard-working, and resourceful young researcher who wanted to "improve the standard of the school" despite the opposition of a conservative majority. In doing so, he represented the kind of forward-looking person the US cultural diplomats and professionals were looking to collaborate with.[93] When he remitted the first records, Corrêa complained that he had no staff whatsoever and was forced to do "everything" himself, including typing the catalogs and even packing the records and bringing them to the post office. His working environment was abysmal since he he was given a small room where the custodian of the schools also kept cleaning equipment. He announced that he was fighting for better conditions despite his marginal position in the school.

In his correspondence, Corrêa was at times apologetic for Brazilian "deficiencies," most of them of financial or logistical nature. Corrêa asked the US Americans' indulgence for being late, but insisted he was not lazy (by contrast, he chastised the new editors of the *Revista Brasileira de Música*, who let the publication of the journal lapse rather than surveying the printing and mailing the issues themselves, as he had done as its previous editor). Also, in the description of his field trips, Corrêa tried to align himself with his colleagues in Washington, DC. From the villages of the Northeast he reported that recording conditions were difficult as the unreliable electrical supply sometimes damaged the machines. As to lodging, Corrêa mused, "You cannot imagine in what kind of hotels we have to stay.... It is just like in the old books of travels in colonial times."[94]

Deference to notions of US efficiency and travel comfort not withstanding, Corrêa was at complete liberty to decide where and what to record with the US funding. He had not received any directions from the Archive of American Folk Song or the trustful Library of Congress. When the Library of Congress started to issue a "Folk Music of the Americas" series in 1944, the producers were anxious to receive Corrêa's recommendations for a selection of five titles, and asked him to provide a brief note on the songs.[95] Corrêa thus helped define the official canon of Brazilian folk music in the United States, at least as far as these research institutions were concerned.

The invitation to the United States and the resulting collaboration with the Library of Congress helped to promote Corrêa's career significantly. Within two years after his return from the United States, his standing in Brazil had become such that he was able to found the Center for Folklore Research at the School of Music, which gave him an extra room as well as an assistant.[96] Carleton Sprague Smith, chief of the Music Division of the New York Public Library and one-time member of the State Department advisory committee on Music, was present at the opening session. Later, the Center would hold regular conferences on folklore that attracted the most prominent specialists in Brazil. Though funding from the US government for recording missions dried out by 1945,[97] Corrêa's international connections helped to open other doors. The North American periodical *Musical America,* for instance, solicited and published Corrêa de Azevedo's opinions on the role music should play in UNESCO, which had just been established. UNESCO's division of arts and letters had at first been led by Gustavo Durán, and afterward by Vanett Lawler. Lawler, with the support of Charles Seeger and others, then appointed Corrêa as director of the newly created Music Division of UNESCO in 1947. He held this position until returning to Brazil in 1965 and remained a most active folklorist, also taking leading positions in the International Folk Music Council.[98]

Conclusion

Let us return now to the more general questions of cultural diplomacy in the era of the Good Neighbor policy. There is no denying that the folklore initiatives were motivated by and to some extent served US short-term political interests. The more substantial collections of folklore available in the United States and the newly acquired knowledge about it were used for propaganda purposes during and after World War II. Even the personnel of the Pan American Union's Division of Music— an international body, after all—was "at all times available for consultation" to the US State Department. The War and Navy Departments frequently asked the PAU's Music Divison for "information, advice, etc." on material that they could broadcast abroad, on scores for folk music they would like to play abroad, and the like.[99] The Library of Congress assisted in the development of folklore radio shows and broadcast them in the United States as well as in Latin America. Not only the government, but also the mass media profited from the many resources on folklore. Both Walt Disney and Metro Goldwin Mayer requested duplicates of the Folk Archive's holdings and asked for guidance on appropriate music for their Latin American films.[100]

In the post-war period, the shifting political concerns of the US government brought about a dramatic geographic reorientation of cultural policy. As the United States emerged victorious from World War II and assumed its role as a superpower, conflicts in Europe and wars in China, Korea, and the Middle East absorbed the attention of policy makers. Initiatives in cultural diplomacy focused on these areas as well.[101] In the Organization of American States, which superseded the

Pan American Union in 1948, cultural relations were a low priority once the security issues had been clarified with the mutual defense pact.[102] All of a sudden, Latin America played but a minor role in the Cold War battle for hearts and minds.

The nascent folklore research community of the Americas complained in vain to the OAS because of the lack of funding for recording projects.[103] They also found that the Library of Congress reoriented its activities, intensifying relations with the European International Commission on Folk Arts and Folklore while also engaging in projects in Japan and Iraq. Though the State Department continued to finance the production and distribution overseas of US folk music, financial support for folklore collection in Latin America was halted.[104]

Folklore specialists from the South who, like Luis Heitor Corrêa de Azevedo, had benefitted from US government largesse were forced to look to other sources. In the post-war period, US foundations such as the Guggenheim Foundation, the Ford Foundation, and others provided some opportunities for continued exchanges, though the field of folklore was not a priority for them.

The politically motivated decision made by the US government to engage in cultural diplomacy after 1938 thus injected important resources for folklore researchers into a variety of exchange and collection projects. Since folklorists in many Latin American countries had already engaged in significant research and also networking, they were in an excellent position to profit from travels, equipment, and financial resources provided in the context of US cultural policy. Researchers, educators, and the interested public profited from bibliographies and recordings that the experts compiled and made available internationally.[105] This contributed to the institutionalization of folklore research in the North and the South, and helped expand collections. Within the Inter-American organizations, the Committee on Folklore attached to the Pan-American Institute of Geography and History (established in 1928 with its seat in Mexico City) started to publish its journal *Folklore Americano* in 1953. The US-based journal *Folklore Americas,* a project of Ralph Steele Boggs, continued publication until 1968.

The improved networking led to the standardization and professionalization of folkloric research as far as universities, libraries, and government agencies were concerned. Folklore specialists worked hard to establish permanent networks through mutual visits, correspondence, and the exchange of publications. They freely shared advice, if not their collections. Argentines trained by Carlos Vega introduced their methodologies to Uruguay and Venezuela. In 1947, US folklorist Stith Thompson worked for six months as a consultant in Venezuela where he advised on the structure of the National Service for Folklore Investigation at the Ministry of Education.[106] Moreover, folklorists from North and South profited from the greater international recognition and visibility outside their own countries. Engagement in the transnational arena helped Latin American folklore specialists gain leverage against their employers and earn prestige in their own countries.

The ten years of intense US efforts to promote folkore in the Americas had certainly invigorated transnational collaboration. Through initiatives developed in the Cultural Division of the State Department, personal contacts and professional networks were strengthened, organizations and publications established. But despite the collaboration and the cordial relationships that had developed between US and Latin American folklorists, US influence was not hegemonic. European folklore research had also informed Latin American institutions. In Colombia, a Frenchman organized and led the Archive of Folklore in the Museum of Ethnology.[107] The Brazilians had cultivated their ties to Portugal, as some of the former Spanish colonies did with their parent country. Latin American folklorists took an active part not only in hemisperic ventures, but also in Europe-based international organizations such as the International Folk Music Council (IFMC, founded in 1947 in London). It was a triumph for Brazilian folklorists to host the 1954 World Conference of the IFMC in conjunction with a Folklore Congress organized to celebrate the 400th anniversary of the city.[108] Also UNESCO, especially its music division headed by Corrêa de Azevedo, provided another transnational platform for folklore scholars and sponsored a number of projects.[109]

As much as folklore specialists from North and South America talked about their desire to create a "genuine culture of the Americas," the outcome of their venture differed starkly from that vision. Much more Latin American folklore was propagated in the United States than vice-versa. Latin Americans were too concerned with promoting their own national or regional cultures to be truly fascinated by folk influences from the United States. The US government, in turn, remained lukewarm in its efforts to export American folk culture, diverse as it may have been.[110]

In the long run, the constant referral to notions of Pan American Folklore and the traditions of "the Americas" was not enough to bind Anglo- and Latin American popular cultures together. Beginning in the late 1950s, the folklore resources assembled with US encouragement during the 1930s and 1940s would be used by a new generation of music artists to promote a common Latin American identity. In the 1950s, precursors such as Chile's Violeta Parra worked with schools and universities. By the late 1960s, the so-called New Song movement *(nueva canción)* encompassed artists from many Latin American countries who combined traditional musical forms with socially relevant texts. They protested social inequalities and imperialism, and challenged the cultural and economic domination of the United States—thus revindicating the doubters Lewis Hanke and Charles Seeger, who had warned all along about the uncertain outcomes of cultural diplomacy.[111]

Notes

I would like to thank the Helen Bieber Fund (adminstered through the University of Zurich) for research funding and I am grateful for Jakob Tanner's invitation to present the paper on which this essay is based at the social history colloquy at the University of Zurich. Finally I would like to acknowledge the stimulating comments of Philippe Forêt, Sandie Holguín, and Jessica C. E. Gienow-Hecht.

1. Charles Seeger, "Memorandum to Dr. Lima," 1953, 4, Columbus Memorial Library, Box "Music," Washington, DC.
2. See, for instance, Julianne Burton, "Don (Juanito) Duck and the Imperial Patriarchal Unconscious: Disney Studios, the Good Neighbor Policy, and the Packaging of Latin America," in *Nationalism and Sexualities,* eds. Andrew Parker et al. (New York: Routledge, 1992), 21–41.
3. Ariel Dorfman and Armand Mattelart, *Para leer al Pato Donald,* 2nd ed. (Valparaíso: Ediciones Universitarias de Valparaíso, Universidad Católica de Valparaíso-Chile, 1973). Translated into English as, Ariel Dorfman and Armand Mattelart, *How to read Donald Duck: imperialist ideology in the Disney comic* (New York: International General, 1975). The book has since been translated into fifteen languages. In Chile, a new edition was published in 2002, almost thirty years after the first edition.
4. John Mosier, "Film," in *Handbook of Latin American Popular Culture,* eds. Harold E. Hinds and Charles M. Tatum (Westport, London: Greenwood Press, 1985), 176.
5. Jean Franco, *The Decline and Fall of the Lettered City: Latin America in the Cold War* (Cambridge, MA, and London: Harvard University Press, 2002), 23.
6. The standard works on the development of governmental cultural policy are Frank A. Ninkovich, *The Diplomacy of Ideas: U.S. Foreign Policy and Cultural Relations, 1938–1950* (Cambridge: Cambridge University Press,

1981), and J. Manuel Espinosa, *Inter-American Beginnings of U.S. Cultural diplomacy, 1936–1948: Cultural Relations Programs of the U.S. Department of State,* Historical Studies, 2 (Washington, DC: Bureau of Educational and Cultural Affairs, US Dept. of State, 1977).

7. See Donald C. Meyer, "Toscanini and the Good Neighbor Policy: The NBC Symphony Orchestra's 1940 South American tour," *American Music,* 18, 3 (2000): 233–56; Seth Fein, "Transnationalization and Cultural Collaboration: Mexican Film Propaganda during World War II," *Studies in Latin American Popular Culture* 17 (1998): 105–28; and Ursula Prutsch, "Machtlegitimierung durch kulturelle Inszenierung am Beispiel Brasilien - interamerikanische Perspektiven," *Wiener Zeitschrift zur Geschichte der Neuzeit* 2, 1 (2002): 41–61. There is no solid, comprehensive account of Rockefeller's engagements with Latin America, but Elizabeth Cobbs Hoffman, *The Rich Neighbor Policy: Rockefeller and Kaiser in Brazil* (New Haven: Yale University Press, 1992), and Darlene Rivas, *Missionary Capitalist: Nelson Rockefeller in Venezuela,* The Luther Hartwell Hodges Series on Business, Society, and the State (Chapel Hill: University of North Carolina Press, 2002), shed light on him.
8. G. M. Joseph, Catherine LeGrand, and Ricardo Donato Salvatore, *Close Encounters of Empire: Writing the Cultural History of U.S.-Latin American Relations,* American Encounters/Global Interactions (Durham: Duke University Press, 1998).
9. "Latin America" is here defined as the former colonies of Spain or Portugal; "the Americas" refers to the entire Western Hemisphere, from Alaska to Patagonia.
10. *Radical History Review,* 84 (Fall 2002) is a special issue on "The Uses of Folk" edited by Karl Hagstrom Miller and Ellen Noonan. For a critical account of the history of folklore studies, see Regina Bendix, *In Search of Authenticity: The Formation of Folklore Studies* (Madison: University of Wisconsin Press, 1997).
11. For a stimulating discussion on the relationship between intellectuals and the state in Argentina, Chile, Peru, Mexico, and Cuba, see Nicola Miller, *In the Shadow of the State: Intellectuals and the Quest for National Identity in Twentieth Century Latin America* (London: Verso, 1999).
12. To cite just two examples: The architecture department of the University in Chile was headed by French Architects from its founding in 1849 into the 1870s. In Costa Rica, a Swiss professor appointed in the 1880s to build educational and scientific institutions brought a slew of European colleagues to Central America. Marshall C. Eakin, "The Origins of Modern Science in Costa Rica: The Instituto Físico-Geográfico Nacional, 1887–1904," *Latin American Research Review* 34, 1 (1999): 123–50.
13. Richard M. Morse, "The Multiverse of Latin American Identity, c.1920–c.1979," in *The Cambridge History of Latin America: Latin America since 1930: Ideas, Culture, and Society,* ed. Leslie Bethell (Cambridge, New York: Cambridge University Press, 1995), 8–10. Scholars have established a similar cultural roster for the United States. See MacDonald Smith Moore, *Yankee Blues: Musical Culture and American Identity* (Bloomington: Indiana University Press, 1985), and Christine Stansell, *American Moderns: Bohemian New York and the Creation of a New Century,* 1st ed. (New York: Metropolitan Books, 2000).
14. Vicky Unruh dealt with the relations between the European and the Latin American vanguards in *Latin American Vanguards: The Art of Contentious*

Encounters (Berkeley: University of California Press, 1994). See also Francine Masiello, "Rethinking Neocolonial Esthetics: Literature, Politics, and Intellectual Community in Cuba's Revista de Avance," *Latin American Research Review* 28, 2 (1993): 3–31.

15. Jesús Chavarría, *José Carlos Mariátegui and the Rise of Modern Peru, 1890–1930* (Albuquerque: University of New Mexico Press, 1979); Ricardo Pérez Montfort, *Avatares del Nacionalismo Cultural: Cinco Ensayos* (México: Centro de Investigación y Docencia en Humanidades del Estado de Morelos: Centro de Investigaciones y Estudios Superiores en Antropología Social, 2000).

16. Mauricio Tenorio Trillo, "Stereophonic Scientific Modernisms: Social Science between Mexico and the United States, 1880s–1930s," *Journal of American History* 86, 3 (1999): 1156–87.

17. This is from the program of a planned "First Pan-American Congress of Music" which was supposed to meet in Havana in February 1928. However, I have been unable to find more information on the congress.

18. Helen Delpar, *The Enormous Vogue of Things Mexican: Cultural Relations between the United States and Mexico, 1920–1935* (Tuscaloosa: University of Alabama Press, 1992).

19. For the Brazilian fascination with France, see Jeffrey D. Needell, *A Tropical Belle-Epoque: Elite Culture and Society in Turn-of-the-Century Rio de Janeiro*, Cambridge Latin American Studies 62 (Cambridge, New York: Cambridge University Press, 1987). Brazilians rediscovered the modernists in the 1980s; hundreds of books on the subject, biographies, and editions of letters of protagonists have since appeared in Brazil. There has been less of a boom in English publications. See K. David Jackson, *One Hundred Years of Invention: Oswald de Andrade and the Modern Tradition in Latin American Literature* (Austin: Abaporu Press, 1992), and Wilson Martins, *The Modernist Idea: A Critical Survey of Brazilian Writing in the Twentieth Century* (Westport: Greenwood Press, 1979).

20. The traditionalists enjoyed a strong influence in architecture, where they promoted a neocolonial style, while the moderns dominated in literature and music. For a discussion of the different exponents, see Daryle Williams, *Culture Wars in Brazil: The First Vargas Regime, 1930–1945* (Durham: Duke University Press, 2001), 26–51.

21. His relevant writings on music include Mário de Andrade, *Ensaio sobre Musica Brasileira* (São Paulo: I. Chiarato & Cia., 1928), *A Música e a Canção Populares no Brasil* (Rio de Janeiro: Ministério das Relações Exteriores Divisão de Cooperação Intelectual, 1936), *Cultura Musical* (São Paulo: Departamento municipal de cultura, 1936). Many of his works were translated into Spanish within a few years of their initial publication. The Brazilian literature on Andrade includes more than two hundred biographies, collections of letters, and the like (around half of them published after 1990), but unfortunately no biography is available in English. From the context of musicology, Vasco Mariz, *Três Musicólogos Brasileiros: Mário de Andrade, Renato Almeida, Luiz Heitor Corrêa de Azevedo*, Coleção Retratos do Brasil, vol. 169 (Rio de Janeiro: Civilização Brasileira, 1983). Andrade and Almeida gave important impulses to folklore studies at the time, but later ethnomusicologists have revised some of their theories. See Gérard Béhague, "Recent Studies on the Music of Latin America," *Latin American Research Review* 20, 3 (1985): 220.

22. Modern composer Mozart Camargo Guarnieri also engaged in research during the second Afro-Brazilian Congress in Bahia, 1937. Arquivo Folclórico da Discoteca Pública Municipal, *Catálogo Ilustrado do Museu Folclórico,* 2nd vol. (São Paulo: Secreataria de Educação e Cultura, 1950), IX.
23. Evans Clark, *Brief Notes on Music in Eight Countries of Latin America: A Report of a Flying Trip to Brazil, Costa Rica, Honduras, Guatemala, Mexico, Nicaragua, Panama, and El Salvador for the Coordinator of Inter-American Affairs,* Washington, DC: United States Office of Inter-American Affairs, 1941, 16, Library of Congress, Music Division.
24. Seamus E. Doyle, "Report on the Collection of Folk Music in South America," 1–2, 1941, Library of Congress, Archive of American Folk Song.
25. Brazil was one of the few non-European countries that participated in the International Folklore Congress that ran concurrently to the 1937 Universal Exposition in Paris. The League of Nations' Institute of Intellectual Cooperation cosponsored the congress. See Nicanor Miranda, *O Congresso Internacional de Folklore* (São Paulo: Departamento de Cultura, 1940); Musée National des Arts et Traditions Populaires (France) and Georges Maurice Huisman, *Travaux du 1er Congrès International de Golklore, Tenu à Paris, du 23 au 28 août 1937 à l'Ecole du Louvre* (Tours: Arrault et cie imprimeurs, 1938).
26. Lenz was professor at the Pedagogical Institute of the University of Chile. Soon after his arrival, he developed a great interest in the Mapuche language and culture as well as popular poetry. Also in U.S. universities, German émigré musicologists became prominent in the 1930s. See Richard Crawford, *The American Musicological Society, 1934–1984* (Philadelphia, n.p: 1984), 10; and Reinhold Brinkman and Christoph Wolff, eds., *Driven Into Paradise: The Musical Migration from Nazi Germany to the United States* (Berkeley: University of California Press, 1999).
27. Patrick Barr-Melej, *Reforming Chile: Cultural Politics, Nationalism, and the Rise of the Middle Class* (Chapel Hill: University of North Carolina Press, 2001).
28. Pedro Humberto Allende for instance was the Chilean representative at the 1928 Prague Conference of Popular Arts that was sponsored by the League of Nations' Division for Intellectual Cooperation.
29. The exposition was organized by the Chilean Commission on Intellectual Cooperation, an affiliate with the League of Nations. Museo de Bellas Artes, *Catálogo de la Exposición Americana de Artes Populares* (Santiago: n.p., 1943).
30. Julio Vicuña Cifuentes, *Qué es el Folklore y para qué Sirve?* (Santiago: Comisión Chilena de Cooperación Intelectual, 1940), 4. His colleague Abdón also considered folklore to be a window on "the feelings and the thinking of the people at large" (el pueblo mismo), the "soul of the people." Abdón Andrade Coloma, "Introducción," *Archivos del Folklore Chileno* 1 (1940): 7.
31. Oreste Plath, who went on to become one of Chile's most prolific folklorists, was one of the Chilean students in Brazil in 1943. The Brazilian foreign ministry and the Chilean Commission on Intellectual Cooperation funded his stay.
32. Garrido was not a traditionalist per se since he worked mainly as a jazz musician for many years and wrote hundreds of articles on its positive aspects. *Ercilla,* 16 September 1941, 16. By 1947, Garrido was in charge of

the Music Department of the Dirección de Informaciones y Cultura, a government agency coordinating and implementing cultural policy.
33. "Hay que Perfeccionar los Programas," *Ecrán*, 18 February 1947, 30; Mirón Callejero, "La Radio y sus Absurdos," *Hoy*, 14 January 1937, 16; Juan Pez, "Onda Larga: Nueva Temporada," *Ecrán*, 25 April 1944, 25; John Reed, "Lista Negra," *Ecrán*, 8 January 1946.
34. Plath wrote many articles on folklore in magazines such as *Hoy*, *Eva*, *Ercilla* and the newspaper *La Nación*. For a sample see "Aspectos del Folklore," *Hoy*, 17 December 1942, 63; and "Animalismo Oceánico y Campero en el Hablar del Pueblo Chileno," *Hoy*, 11 March 1943, 59.
35. Interestingly enough, the founding document made reference to the League of Nations' 1928 conference on Folklore and Popular Arts that took place in Prague. Comité de Investigaciones del Folklore Nacional y Arte Típico Salvadoreño, *Planes para la Investigación del Folklore Nacional y Arte Típico Salvadoreño* (n.p.), 3–11. The resulting book was Comité de Investigaciones del Folklore Nacional y Arte Típico Salvadoreño, *Recopilación de Materiales Folklóricos Salvadoreños* (San Salvador: América Central Imprenta Nacional, 1944).
36. For an interesting discussion on the uses of folk in Venezuela, see David M. Guss, *The Festive State: Race, Ethnicity, and Nationalism as Cultural Performance* (Berkeley: University of California Press, 2000), 15–18. The Revista de Folklore was the official organ of the Colombian Folklore Commission, which depended from the Ministry of Education.
37. Alison Raphael, "From Popular Culture to Microenterprise: The History of Brazilian Samba Schools," *Latin American Music Review* 11, 1 (June 1990): 73–83; see also Bryan McCann, *Hello, Hello Brazil: Popular Music in the Making of Modern Brazil* (Durham: Duke University Press, 2004).
38. Pérez Montfort, *Avatares del Nacionalismo Cultural: Cinco Ensayos*, 28–34.
39. Carlos Del Campo, *Huasos Chilenos: Folklore Campesino Autorizado por la Dirección del los Servicios de Turismo del Ministerio de Fomento* (Santiago de Chile: Lito Leblanc, 1939).
40. Carleton Sprague Smith, *Musical Tour through South America, June–October, 1940* (Washington, DC: n.p., 1940), 43.
41. Néstor García Canclini, *Las Culturas Populares en el Capitalismo*, 1st ed., Serie El Arte en la Sociedad (México City: Editorial Nueva Imagen, 1982), translated into English as *Transforming Modernity: Popular Culture in Mexico*, Translations from Latin America Series (Austin: University of Texas Press, 1993).
42. Space does not allow a comprehensive listing of the major tendencies. For the traditionalist approach, see, e.g., Félix Coluccio and Gerardo Schiaffino, *Folklore y Nativismo* (Buenos Aires: Editorial Bell, 1948); for the broader definition, Julio Vicuña Cifuentes, *Qué es el Folklore y para qué Sirve?* (Santiago: Comisión Chilena de Cooperación Intelectual, 1940).
43. This nationalist turn in music also took place in Europe, where Bela Bartok, Antonin Dvorak, Charles Debussy, Sibelius, and Grieg all attempted to compose specifically national music.
44. Félix Coluccio and Gerardo Schiaffino, *Folklore y Nativismo* (Buenos Aires: Editorial Bell, 1948), 7. For a comparison to European folklore studies, see Felix J. Oinas, *Folklore, Nationalism, and Politics* (Columbus: Slavica Publishers, 1978), and James R. Dow and Hannjost Lixfeld, *The Nazification of an Academic Discipline: Folklore in the Third Reich*, Folklore Studies in Translation (Bloomington: Indiana University Press, 1993). The

example of Nazi Germany has contributed strongly to the identification of folklore with fascist politics.
45. I argued this for the case of Chile in Corinne A. Pernet, "The Popular Fronts and Folklore: Chilean Cultural Institutions, Nationalism and Pan-Americanism, 1936–1948," in *The Norte-Americanización of Latin America?* eds. Hans-Joachim König and Stefan Rinke (Stuttgart: Heinz Verlag 2004), 253–77. See also Alan Knight, "Popular Culture and the Revolutionary State in Mexico, 1910–1940," *Hispanic American Historical Review* 74, 3 (August 1994): 393–444.
46. A good overview of Lange's career can be found in Luis Merino Montero, "Francisco Curt Lange, 1903–1997: Tributo a un Americanista de Excepción," *Revista Musical Chilena* 52, 187 (January 1998): 9–36. Lange was not the only immigrant who adamantly defended his adopted country's culture. A few decades earlier, composer Antonin Dvorak had similarly admonished US Americans to return to their own musical sources, especially African-American gospel and American-Indian music. See Jessica C. E. Gienow-Hecht, "Trumpeting Down the Walls of Jericho: The Politics of Art, Music, and Emotion in German-American Relations, 1870-1920," *Journal of Social History* 36, 3 (2003): 602.
47. Francisco Curt Lange, "Americanismo Musical," *Boletín Latino-Americano de Música* 2 (April 1936): 117–30. The first issue of the *Boletín* included contributions from the United States. Beginning with the second issue, separate sections were kept for "Studies on the United States" and "European Studies," usually with more articles in the latter section. Keeping the Latin American and the Anglo-American heritage strictly apart was a strong tendency throughout the hemisphere. See Pérez Montfort, *Avatares del Nacionalismo Cultural: Cinco Ensayos,* 29–30.
48. Chilean Domingo Santa Cruz and Brazilian Heitor Villa-Lobos were both classical composers who strongly supported folklore investigations.
49. Franklin Delano Roosevelt Library and Museum, Great Britain Diplomatic Files, Box 38. The program of the evening is available online, <http://www.fdrlibrary.marist.edu/psf/box38/folo343.html>, consulted 22 September 2002.
50. See Gienow-Hecht, "Trumpeting Down the Walls of Jericho," 600–5.
51. Benjamin Filene, *Romancing the Folk: Public Memory and American Roots Music* (Chapel Hill and London: University of North Carolina Press, 2000).
52. Ann Marie Pescatello, *Charles Seeger: A Life in American Music* (Pittsburgh: University of Pittsburgh Press, 1992), 136–50.
53. "Archive of American Folk Song: A History, 1928–1939," 63, Library of Congress, Archive of American Folk Song. Unfortunately, the yearly reports of the archive do not reveal much on this expansion of the collection. During the war years, the efforts to collect material within the United States were seriously hampered, but the acquisition of foreign materials did not suffer much. "Annual Report, 1943–44," 1–2, Library of Congress, Archive of American Folk Song. See also Peter Bartis, "A history of the Archive of Folk Song at the Library of Congress: The First Fifty Years: A Dissertation in Folklore and Folklife" (PhD diss., University of Pennsylvania, 1984).
54. The original but clumsy journal title, *Folklore of the – de las – das Americas* was changed to *Folklore Americas* in 1943. It remained in existence until 1968.
55. Stefan H. Rinke, *"Der letzte freie Kontinent": Deutsche Lateinamerikapolitik im Zeichen Transnationaler Beziehungen, 1918–1933,* Historamericana

(Stuttgart: Heinz, 1996). Many contemporaries made reference to German and Italian activities; see also Charles Seeger et al., "Reminiscences of an American Musicologist," 1972, 303–4, Library of Congress, Music Library.
56. Temperance Smith, National Committee of the United States of America on International Intellectual Cooperation to Cherrington, 18 April 1939, National Archives, RG 59, 111.46/117. On the collaboration between the State Department and the American Library Association see Gary E. Kraske, *Missionaries of the Book: The American Library Profession and the Origins of United States Cultural Diplomacy,* Contributions in Librarianship and Information Science (Westport: Greenwood Press, 1985).
57. All four conferences took place in late 1939. For a good overview on the debates surrounding the implementation of cultural diplomacy, see Ninkovich, *The Diplomacy of Ideas: U.S. Foreign Policy and Cultural Relations, 1938–1950.*
58. Lewis Hanke, "Americanizing the Americas," *The Inter-American Monthly* 1, 1 (May 1942): 8.
59. Carleton Sprague Smith of the Music Division of the New York Public Library told the Cultural Division of the State Department that he had already received a grant of five thousand dollars from the Carnegie Corporation to that end, and that he was seeking further support from Rockefeller Foundation and the Pan American Union. "Memorandum: Interviews in New York City by Mr. Charles A. Thomson, March 24 and 25, 1939," US National Archives, RG 59, Box 237, 111.46/108, College Park, MD.
60. Francisco Curt Lange was the only Latin American who gave a formal address at the meeting. One Guatemalan conductor and the Brazilian musicologist Marx-Burle (in New York for the World's Fair) were present but did not contribute much to the discussion. Department of State, Division of Cultural Relations, "Conference on Inter-American Relations in the Field of Music. Digest of Proceedings. Principal Adresses," 1940, US National Archives, RG 353 Box 30, College Park, MD.
61. Willam Berrien, "Report of the Committee of the Conference on Inter-American Relations in the Field of Music," 4–8.
62. The long-time director of the PAU, Leo Stanton Rowe, was a strong proponent of cultural exchanges. Founded in 1928, the PAU's Division of Intellectual Cooperation initially organized academic exchanges, compiled lists of cultural societies, coordinated bibliographic exchanges, and informed cultural institutions across the Americas, as well as the League of Nations, of the relevant decisions taken by the Pan American Conferences. During the 1930s, the PAU issued bulletins like the *Panorama, Lecturas para Maestros,* and *Points of View* series (in English, Spanish, and Portuguese) that presented American issues and intellectual life. Pan American Union, Division of Intellectual Cooperation, *Report of the Division of Intellectual Cooperation of the Pan American Union* (Washington, DC: n.p., 1941). See also David Barton Castle, "Leo Stanton Rowe and the Meaning of Pan Americanism," in *Beyond the Inter-American Affairs,* ed. David Sheinin (Westport, London: Praeger, 2000), 33–44.
63. Charles Seeger, "Brief History of the Music Division of the Pan American Union," 1947, 1, Columbus Memorial Library, Washington, DC.
64. Seeger et al., "Reminiscences of an American Musicologist," 308–20.
65. Berrien, "Report of the Committee of the Conference on Inter-American Relations in the Field of Music," 88. This was in the suggestions of the

subcommittee on community and recreational music. Seeger was a member of the committee.
66. "Memorandum: Interviews in New York City by Mr. Charles A. Thomson, March 24 and 25, 1939," US National Archives, RG 59 111.46/108.
67. Carleton Sprague Smith, "Musical Tour through South America: June–October 1940," 1940, 289–90, Washington, DC, Library of Congress, Music Library.
68. Stith Thompson, "Folklore of the Americas: An Opportunity and a Challenge," 1940, Abstract of Paper read at the Eigth American Scientific Congress, Washington, DC, 1940, Columbus Memorial Library, Washington, DC.
69. Seeger et al., "Reminiscences of an American Musicologist," 303–12.
70. See Ralph Steele Boggs, "Folklore Democrático y Cultura Aristocrática," *Folklore Americas* 2, 2 (1942). See also Seeger, "Brief History of the Music Division of the Pan American Union," 3.
71. Charles Seeger, "Review of Inter-American Relations in the Field of Music, 1940–1943," 1943, 10, Columbus Memorial Library, Washington, DC; Charles Seeger, "Suggestions for a Music Program for UNESCO," 1946, Columbus Memorial Library, Washington, DC.
72. Smith also pointed to a persistent problem that hampered US efforts: unlike the Italians and the Germans, US Americans were reluctant to learn Spanish or Portuguese. Smith, "Musical tour through South America: June–October 1940," 280. Some of the steps the Italian government undertook, such as teaching and student exchanges, certainly were a cornerstone of all international cultural relations. Smith was also aware of the travels of fellow music specialist Antonio Lualdi, *Viaggio musicale nel Sud-America* (Milan: Istituto Editoriale Nazionale, Stampa, 1934).
73. He considered Mario de Andrade and Luiz Heitor Corrêa de Azevedo "key people" even though they spoke little English. Smith, "Musical Tour through South America: June–October 1940," 44, 286.
74. Seeger was a council member of the American Folklore Society, served as chairman of the committee on Inter-American relations of the Music Library Association, and sat on the executive committee of the Music Teachers National Association. Charles Seeger, "Inter-American Music Center: Report to the Carnegie Corporation for period from September 1, 1942, to August, 1943," 1943, 8–9, Columbus Memorial Library, Box "Music," Washington, DC; Seeger, "Brief History of the Music Division of the Pan American Union," 12–13. On the changing relations between philanthropic foundations and US foreign policy, see Volker R. Berghahn, "Philanthropy and Diplomacy in the 'American Century,'" *Diplomatic History* 23, 3 (1999): 393–419. Berghahn focuses only on US-European relations. Another member of the PAU's Inter-American Music Center fulfilled the same function for the "School of the Air of the Americas" of the rival Columbia Broadcasting System
75. Seeger, "Brief History of the Music Division of the Pan American Union," 11.
76. In an oral history transcript, Seeger says that Carnegie gave fifteen thousand dollars for three years, and that the first year of the center at the PAU was paid by the OCIAA. Seeger et al., "Reminiscences of an American Musicologist," 295.
77. Oliver Schmidt points to the same phenomenon in "Small Atlantic World: U.S. Philanthropy and the Expanding International Exchange of Scholars

after 1945," in *Culture and International History,* eds. Jessica C. E. Gienow-Hecht and Frank Schumacher (New York: Berghahn Books, 2003), 115–34.
78. "Adress of Archibald MacLeish," and "Adress of William Berrien," in Department of State, Division of Cultural Relations, "Conference on Inter-American Relations in the Field of Music: Digest of Proceedings: Principal Adresses," US National Archives, RG 353, Box 30.
79. Doyle, "Report on the Collection of Folk Music in South America," 6.
80. Seeger, "Brief History of the Music Division of the Pan American Union," 8.
81. Lewis Hanke to Gilbert Chase, 1 January 1943, AFS 7324–7398, Archive of American Folksong, Library of Congress.
82. The Kirstein-Balanchine American Ballet Caravan was one of the projects financed by Nelson Rockefeller's Office of the Coordinator of Inter-American Affairs. Interestingly enough, the pieces performed by the American Ballet Caravan were "Concerto Baroco," a Balanchine choreography set to *Bach's Concerto in D minor for Two Violins,* B.W.V. 1043, and the "Ballet Imperial," set Tchaikovsky's *Piano Concerto in G Major*—though the choreography might have been modern, the music was not. The OCIAA did favor contemporary compositions in other instances by promoting composers such as Aron Copland.
83. Doyle, "Report on the Collection of Folk Music in South America," 2.
84. Doyle, "Report on the Collection of Folk Music in South America," 3.
85. Since Peronist Argentina had fallen out of grace with the State Department, it became more and more difficult to obtain funding for this project. B. A. Botkin to Harold Spivacke, 22 February 1945, Archive of American Folk Song, Folder "Argentina," Library of Congress.
86. "Annual Report 1943–44," 2, Archive of American Folk Song Library of Congress.
87. "Annual Report 1942–43," 9, Archive of American Folk Song Library of Congress.
88. Pereira Salas had studied in the US as a Guggenheim Fellow in 1933 and was one of the founders of the Chile-United States Cultural Institite in November 1938.
89. Instituto de Investigaciones Musicales, *Estudios sobre folklore en Chile y labor del Instituto de Investigaciones Musicales* (Santiago: Universidad de Chile, 1950), 9; Seeger, "Inter-American Music Center: Report to the Carnegie Corporation for period from September 1, 1942, to August, 1943"; Charles Seeger, "Inter-American Music Center: Report to the Carnegie Corporation for period from September 1, 1942, to August, 1943," 1943, Columbus Memorial Library, Box "Music," Washington, DC, 5. It is most likely no coincidence that young composer Juan Orrego-Salas (the stepson of Domingo Santa Cruz who married Orrego-Salas' mother) studied in the United States from 1944 to 1946 with fellowships from the Rockefeller and Guggenheim foundations. Luis Merino, "Juan Orrego-Salas a los ochenta años," *Latin American Music Review* 21, 1 (2000): 4.
90. The title of Corrêas thesis was "Escala, ritmo e melodia na música dos índios brasileiros." Seeger et al., "Reminiscences of an American Musicologist," 300.
91. Charles Seeger, "Memorandum on the Work of the Music Division of the Pan American Union," 1941, Columbus Memorial Library, Washington, DC.
92. The money for this venture came from the State Department (Appropriation for Cooperation with American Republics). Memorandum Alan Lomax, Library of Congress, Archive of American Folk Song, AFS 7324–7398.

93. Corrêa de Azevedo to Harold Spivacke, 17 December 1942, AFS 7324–7398.
94. Luiz Heitor Corrêa de Azevedo to Harold Spivacke, 27 January 1943, AFS 7324–7398. In other ways, though, Corrêa adapted slowly. In January 1944, the Library of Congress wrote almost apologetically to remind Corrêa he had to turn in his accounting records on the funds and on the material shipped to Brazil: "Please do not misunderstand me. I do not desire to terminate our joint project. On the contrary, I hope that we shall be able to cooperate for many, many years to come. On the other hand, as a government official, you will understand why it is necessary for me to give these final accountings.... If you are willing to continue to work with us in the future, I must begin to arrange for an extension [of the funding]." Harold Spivacke to Corrêa de Azevedo, 28 January 1944, AFS 7324–7398.
95. B. A. Botkin to Corrêa de Azevedo, 16 November 1944, AFS 7324–7398.
96. Corrêa de Azevedo to Harold Spivacke, 7 January 1944, AFS 7324–7398.
97. Duncan Emrich, Chief, Archive of American Folk Song, to Luiz Heitor Corrêa de Azevedo, AFS 7324–7398.
98. Luiz Heitor Corrêa de Azevedo, *Minhas memórias da UNESCO (a música nas relações internacionais), 1947–1965* (Curitiba: Pró-Música, 1967), 3–7. One generation later, the Brazilian musicologist Vasco Mariz had a very similar international career, as president of the Inter-American Council on Music, secretary of the Brazilian National UNESCO commission on music, and vice-president of the Brazilian UNESCO commission.
99. Seeger, "Inter-American Music Center: Report to the Carnegie Corporation for period from September 1, 1942, to August, 1943," 9–10.
100. How folklore was used and rediffused by mass media and other cultural institutions in the United States is beyond the scope of this paper. "Annual Report 1945–46," 1, Library of Congress, Archive of American Folk Song.
101. See Jessica C. E. Gienow-Hecht, *Transmission Impossible: American Journalism as Cultural Diplomacy in Postwar Germany, 1945–1955,* Eisenhower Center Studies on War and Peace (Baton Rouge: Louisiana State University Press, 1999), Walter L. Hixson, *Parting the Curtain: Propaganda, Culture and the Cold War, 1945–1961* (Houndmills: Macmillan, 1997), and Melvyn P. Leffler, *A Preponderance of Power: National Security, the Truman Administration, and the Cold War* (Stanford: Stanford University Press, 1992).
102. The Pan American Union was demoted to being the "secretariat" of the OAS.
103. T. M. Pearce to William Dorson, 14 July 1948, US National Archives, RG 43, Lot 60D 665, Box 1b.
104. Archive of American Folk Song, "Annual Report 1952–53," 2–4, Library of Congress.
105. Library of Congress, *The Fine and Folk Arts of the Other American Republics* (Washington, DC: N.p., 1942).
106. Thompson, incidentally, considered Vega to be the one of the most able folk music specialists he knew. Stith Thompson, "Folklore in South America," *The Journal of American Folklore* 61, 241 (1948): 256–258.
107. This was due to the long-time presence of the eminent French ethnographer Paul Rivet (1876–58), the founder of the Musée de l'Homme in Paris. See Academia Colombiana de Historia, *Homenaje al Profesor Paul Rivet* (Bogotá: Editorial A.B.C., 1958).

108. *International Congress of Folklore, August 16th to 22d, 1954, São Paulo, Brazil* (N.p., n.d.), microform.
109. In the late 1950s, Corrêa de Azevedo hired Francisco Curt Lange to study the folklore of Minas Gerais in Brazil. Merino M., "Francisco Curt Lange, 1903–1997," 29.
110. Members of the State Department's advisory committee had recognized this issue early on. Olga Samaroff Stokovski, for instance, argued that Latin Americans were predisposed to suspect "self-interest or desire to dominate on our part." She cautioned that exchanges needed to happen "on a footing of equality" and that the United States should not use economic power to force recognition of their music by other countries. US National Archives, RG 59, 111.46 Music/3-245, Olga Samaroff Stokovski to Charles Childs, 2 March 1945.
111. This is not the place to discuss current musical cultures in Latin America, but I would like to point out that music life is less dominated by US groups than the neoliberal policies of their respective governments would lead one to believe. New Song is still an important genre. Jane Tumas-Serna, "The 'Nueva Canción' Movement and its Mass-mediated Performance Context," *Latin American Music Review* 13, 2 (Fall/Winter 1992): 240–256.

Bibliography

Andrade, Mário de. *Cultura Musical.* São Paulo: Departamento municipal de cultura, 1936.

Barr-Melej, Patrick. *Reforming Chile: Cultural Politics, Nationalism, and the Rise of the Middle Class.* Chapel Hill: University of North Carolina Press, 2001.

Bartis, Peter. "A History of the Archive of Folk Song at the Library of Congress: The First Fifty Years: A Dissertation in Folklore and Folklife." PhD diss.: University of Pennsylvania, 1984.

Bendix, Regina. *In Search of Authenticity: The Formation of Folklore Studies.* Madison: University of Wisconsin Press, 1997.

Berghahn, Volker R. "Philanthropy and Diplomacy in the 'American Century.'" *Diplomatic History* 23, 3 (1999): 393–419.

Brinkman, Reinhold, and Christoph Woolff, eds. *Driven into Paradise: The Musical Migration from Nazi Germany to the United States.* Berkeley: Stanford University Press, 1999.

Castle, David Barton. "Leo Stanton Rowe and the Meaning of Pan Americanism." In *Beyond the Ideal: Pan Americanism in Inter-American Affairs,* ed. David Sheinin. Westport, London: Praeger, 2000, pp. 33–44.

Cobbs Hoffman, Elizabeth. *The Rich Neighbor Policy: Rockefeller and Kaiser in Brazil.* New Haven: Yale University Press, 1992.

Corrêa de Azevedo, Luiz Heitor. *Minhas Memórias Da Unesco (a Música Nas Relações Internacionais), 1947–1965.* Curitiba: Pró-Música, 1967.

Delpar, Helen. *The Enormous Vogue of Things Mexican: Cultural Relations between the United States and Mexico, 1920–1935.* Tuscaloosa: University of Alabama Press, 1992.

Dow, James R., and Hannjost Lixfeld. *The Nazification of an Academic Discipline: Folklore in the Third Reich.* Folklore Studies in Translation. Bloomington: Indiana University Press, 1993.

Espinosa, J. Manuel. *Inter-American Beginnings of U.S. Cultural Diplomacy, 1936-1948.* Cultural Relations Programs of the U.S. Department of State. Historical Studies, 2. Washington, DC: Bureau of Educational and Cultural Affairs, US Dept. of State, 1977.
Fein, Seth. "Transnationalization and Cultural Collaboration: Mexican Film Propaganda During World War II." *Studies in Latin American Popular Culture* 17 (1998): 105-28.
Filene, Benjamin. *Romancing the Folk: Public Memory and American Roots Music.* Chapel Hill, London: University of North Carolina Press, 2000.
García Canclini, Néstor. *Transforming Modernity: Popular Culture in Mexico.* Translations from Latin America Series. Austin: University of Texas Press, 1993.
Gienow-Hecht, Jessica C. E. *Transmission Impossible: American Journalism as Cultural Diplomacy in Postwar Germany, 1945-1955.* Eisenhower Center Studies on War and Peace. Baton Rouge: Louisiana State University Press, 1999.
———. "Trumpeting Down the Walls of Jericho: The Politics of Art, Music, and Emotion in German-American Relations, 1870-1920." *Journal of Social History* 36, 3 (2003): 585-613.
Guss, David M. *The Festive State: Race, Ethnicity, and Nationalism as Cultural Performance.* Berkeley: University of California Press, 2000.
Hixson, Walter L. *Parting the Curtain: Propaganda, Culture and the Cold War, 1945-1961.* Houndmills: Macmillan, 1997.
Jackson, K. David. *One Hundred Years of Invention: Oswald De Andrade and the Modern Tradition in Latin American Literature.* Austin: Abaporu Press, 1992.
Joseph, G. M., Catherine LeGrand, and Ricardo Donato Salvatore. *Close Encounters of Empire: Writing the Cultural History of U.S.-Latin American Relations.* American Encounters/Global Interactions. Durham: Duke University Press, 1998.
Knight, Alan, "Popular Culture and the Revolutionary State in Mexico, 1910-1940." *Hispanic American Historical Review* 74, 3 (1994): 393-444.
König, Hans-Joachim, and Stefan Rinke, eds. *The Norte-Americanización of Latin America?* Stuttgart: Heinz Verlag 2004.
Mariz, Vasco. *Três Musicólogos Brasileiros: Mário De Andrade, Renato Almeida, Luiz Heitor Corrêa De Azevedo.* Coleção Retratos Do Brasil, vol. 169. Rio de Janeiro: Civilização Brasileira, 1983.
Martins, Wilson. *The Modernist Idea: A Critical Survey of Brazilian Writing in the Twentieth Century.* Westport: Greenwood Press, 1979.
Masiello, Francine. "Rethinking Neocolonial Esthetics: Literature, Politics, and Intellectual Community in Cuba's *Revista De Avance.*" *Latin American Research Review* 28, 2 (1993): 3-31.
McCann, Bryan. *Hello, Hello Brazil: Popular Music in the Making of Modern Brazil.* Durham: Duke University Press, 2004.
Miller, Nicola. *In the Shadow of the State: Intellectuals and the Quest for National Identity in Twentieth Century Latin America.* London: Verso, 1999.
Moore, MacDonald Smith. *Yankee Blues: Musical Culture and American Identity.* Bloomington: Indiana University Press, 1985.
Morse, Richard M. "The Multiverse of Latin American Identity, c.1920-c.1979." In *The Cambridge History of Latin America: Latin America since 1930: Ideas, Culture, and Society,* ed. Leslie Bethell. Cambridge and New York: Cambridge University Press, 1995, pp. 8-10.

Needell, Jeffrey D. *A Tropical Belle Epoque: Elite Culture and Society in Turn-of-the-Century Rio De Janeiro.* Cambridge Latin American Studies, 62. Cambridge and New York: Cambridge University Press, 1987.

Ninkovich, Frank A. *The Diplomacy of Ideas: U.S. Foreign Policy and Cultural Relations, 1938–1950.* Cambridge: Cambridge University Press, 1981.

Oinas, Felix J. *Folklore, Nationalism, and Politics.* Columbus: Slavica Publishers, 1978.

Pérez Montfort, Ricardo. *Avatares Del Nacionalismo Cultural: Cinco Ensayos.* México: Centro de Investigación y Docencia en Humanidades del Estado de Morelos: Centro de Investigaciones y Estudios Superiores en Antropología Social, 2000.

Pernet Corinne A. "The Popular Fronts and Folklore: Chilean Cultural Institutions, Nationalism and Pan-Americanism, 1936–1948." In *The Norte-Americanización of Latin America?* eds. Hans-Joachim König and Stefan Rinke. Stuttgart: Heinz Verlag 2004, pp. 253–77.

Pescatello, Ann Marie. *Charles Seeger: A Life in American Music.* Pittsburgh: University of Pittsburgh Press, 1992.

Prutsch, Ursula. "Machtlegitimierung Durch Kulturelle Inszenierung Am Beispiel Brasilien - Interamerikanische Perspektiven." *Wiener Zeitschrift zur Geschichte der Neuzeit* 2, 1 (2002): 41–61.

Rivas, Darlene. *Missionary Capitalist: Nelson Rockefeller in Venezuela.* The Luther Hartwell Hodges Series on Business, Society, and the State. Chapel Hill: University of North Carolina Press, 2002.

Schmidt, Oliver. "Small Atlantic World: U.S. Philanthropy and the Expanding International Exchange of Scholars after 1945." In *Culture and International History,* eds. Jessica C. E. Gienow-Hecht and Frank Schumacher. New York: Berghahn Books, 2003, pp. 115–34.

Stansell, Christine. *American Moderns: Bohemian New York and the Creation of a New Century.* 1st ed. New York: Metropolitan Books, 2000.

Tenorio Trillo, Mauricio. "Stereophonic Scientific Modernisms: Social Science between Mexico and the United States, 1880s–1930s." *Journal of American History* 86, 3 (2000).

Unruh, Vicky. *Latin American Vanguards: The Art of Contentious Encounters.* Berkeley: University of California Press, 1994.

Williams, Daryle. *Culture Wars in Brazil: The First Vargas Regime, 1930–1945.* Durham: Duke University Press, 2001.

Part III
NON-GOVERNMENTAL INFLUENCES

Chapter 5

"THE OTHER SIDE OF THE WAR"
Memory and Meaning at the War Remnants Museum of Vietnam

Scott Laderman

When George H. W. Bush implored Americans during his inaugural address in 1989 to ignore one of the seminal events of twentieth-century international history, he connected his nation's greatness to its embrace of collective amnesia. "The final lesson of Vietnam is that no great nation can long afford to be sundered by a memory," he proclaimed. The president's plea—that the United States forget its (and, by implication, Vietnam's) history—would not be the last time he spoke of the Vietnam conflict. When the United States went to war with Iraq two years later, Bush promised that "this will not be another Vietnam." And when the war ended he was jubilant: "[B]y God, we've kicked the Vietnam syndrome once and for all."[1]

Yet with the more recent escalation of American warfare in Iraq and the ubiquitous allusions to "another Vietnam," not to mention the Southeast Asian conflict's omnipresence in the 2004 US presidential contest, it was made abundantly clear that Bush could not have been more wrong. The United States had not "kicked" the troubling memories to which the president referred. In the twenty-first century, Americans obviously remained conflicted about the meaning of the war and its continuing implications for national identity. For the Right, the Vietnam intervention was a "noble cause" for which its warriors were shamefully betrayed when Washington bureaucrats

---

Notes for this section begin on page 202.

and the antiwar movement hindered the American fighting machine. For liberals, the war represented a tragic "mistake" in which the United States deviated from its national values and ideals. And for the Left, the Americans invaded Vietnam in furtherance of Washington's post-World War II efforts to establish globally a system of liberal capitalism that furthered the interests of various elites. The irreconcilability of these interpretations ensured that the debates would continue.

Indeed, among tourists in Vietnam they had been raging for years. Whereas the war erupted in American political culture somewhat episodically, foreign travelers, who began arriving in Vietnam in exponentially greater numbers throughout the 1990s, never stopped disputing its memory. No site better captured the explosive emotions engendered by this popular conversation than the War Remnants Museum in Ho Chi Minh City. The institution provided a space in which foreigners often remarked about being exposed for the first time to a narrative of the war with which they were previously unfamiliar, a narrative that, in its most basic focus, placed Vietnamese rather than American experiences at its center. As a result of witnessing the suffering endured by millions of Vietnamese, many of these tourists sought contrition. "I am very sorry for what our country has done to [the Vietnamese] people," wrote a former Australian soldier in January 2002.[2] "I regret the part I played in it," added another. "Normally, I am proud, grateful, and even blessed to be an American living the good life that I do," a visitor from San Francisco commented. "However, today I feel a sense of shame at what my country did to this part of the world in pursuit of folly." Among the displays at the museum in 2002 was a set of combat medals donated by William Brown, a veteran from the United States. "To the people of a united Vietnam," he wrote, "I was wrong. I am sorry." He was far from alone. "This museum may be a hard pill for many American visitors to swallow," another returning American veteran noted in 1994, "but [the] truths underlying these exhibits [are] as important to our history as [they are] to that of the Vietnamese people."

Other tourists responded by defiantly expressing their rejection of the Vietnamese narrative, accusing the museum of bias and historical inaccuracy. "If you believe half of what you read here your [sic] a fool. U.S.A. all the way," an anonymous tourist, presumably an American, insisted in March 2002. "The war was a tragedy for everyone involved," commented an entry signed "Asian-American" that same month, "[b]ut what you see here is a bias [*sic*] viewpoint. Ho Chi Minh should not have invade [*sic*] South Vietnam. If the communist government is so wonderful, why would millions of Vietnamese flee Vietnam after the war[?] They don't talk about that. Think about it." The museum was "a little biased," another visitor—this one from Australia—believed in January 2002. "[T]he Americans were here to give freedom[;] they too lost a lot."

What the responses at the museum collectively reveal is both tourism's potential to briefly denationalize travelers, placing them within an ideological universe in which the power of their inherited beliefs becomes at least temporarily suspended, as well as many tourists' persistent hold on such beliefs as shields through which to fend off alternative historical perspectives. As such, an examination of the War Remnants Museum and visitors' responses to it enables a social history of international post-war memory. This intersection of memory and culture—in the present case, the culture of tourism—deserves the attention of international historians. Tourism as a practice can be implicated not just in diplomatic relations, as Linda Richter has ably shown, but also in sustaining or destabilizing the cherished myths of those nations from which many tourists originate.[3] Travel can allow, in other words, for a decentering of the United States from many Americans' understanding of the Vietnam War, introducing them (and others) to a narrative of the conflict that places Vietnamese experiences at its center.

The War Remnants Museum engages a popular audience whom most historians have clearly failed to reach, sparking reactions among tourists of various nationalities that arrive with a multitude of frequently conflicting experiential or acquired memories. By addressing these tourists' responses, as well as the ways that travel writers have mediated the site for them, this essay explores the continued potency of the war to notions of national identity nearly thirty years after the RVN's (Republic of Vietnam, or "South Vietnam") leadership surrendered to the revolutionaries in Saigon.

Mapping the Museum: Imperial Aggression from France to the United States

Once known as the Exhibition House of American and Chinese War Crimes, later rechristened the Exhibition House of Aggres-

Figure 5.1
Visitors examine tanks and planes in the courtyard of the museum compound. The entrance to the compound is visible in the distance. (Photograph by Scott Laderman.)

sion War Crimes, and now officially called the War Remnants Museum, the institution had become, by the turn of the twenty-first century, the most popular in the former Saigon, welcoming hundreds of thousands of visitors every year.[4] As of early 2003, according to the Vietnamese media, attendance at the War Remnants Museum had reached unprecedented numbers, with approximately thirteen hundred foreign visitors coming to the site every day.[5] Yet most Western tourists, judging from dozens of interviews I conducted in 2000 and 2002, arrived knowing little or nothing about the recent Vietnamese past.[6] Indeed, the effort after 1975 to essentially forget the conflict had left a void in historical understanding that became filled with popular culture representations (generally of US origin but made international by the global profusion of American culture), unfounded myths, and distorted memories rooted in the political battles and emotional pain that characterized postwar American life. For many of these tourists, tours of Vietnamese museums and historical sites thus provided not only a basic introduction to the history of the war (albeit one that many visitors found sorely deficient), but also a sobering revelation about the sacrifices borne by the Vietnamese people during their long struggle for national independence.

How foreigners ultimately viewed the museum was often determined by their moral assessment of the US intervention. Many of those inclined, like Ronald Reagan, to adjudge the campaign a "noble cause" rejected the photographs and other displays at the site that were inconsistent with their vision of American benevolence. Conversely, those tourists confused or undecided about the war found and often embraced a narrative to which they had previously not been privy. The museum's tone and emotional thrust were evident from the moment visitors entered the exhibits.[7] Adjacent to the entrance of a room designated "Historic Truths" that was intended to offer tourists background information on the war was a photograph of Robert McNamara, the US secretary of defense in the Kennedy and Johnson administrations; he was sitting alone and surrounded by empty chairs and a lectern. Below the photograph was a case containing English- and Vietnamese-language editions of *In Retrospect*, his controversial 1995 book. A glass plate next to the case rested between two jagged blocks, as if they were ripped or torn apart, symbolizing, perhaps, Vietnam's division for over twenty years. On the plate was transcribed probably the most famous lines from the publication: "Yet we were wrong, terribly wrong. We owe it to future generations to explain why."[8] "It was that mistake," the curators added, "that has caused severe results toward the country and people of Vietnam."

In a move replicated elsewhere, the museum staff employed American or other Western sources—in this case the concession by one of the war's major architects that the United States was "wrong"—as framing devices through which to examine the contested subjects being addressed. As such, it was not necessary for the curators themselves to inveigh against the war and consequently invite charges of "anti-Americanism"; quoting Robert McNamara, Representative William Clay, the US Declaration of Independence, or other prominent figures and documents sufficed for this purpose while, at the same time, rendering opposition to the intervention a decidedly American position.

What was perhaps most striking and ultimately divisive about the room devoted to "Historic Truths" was its departure from most popular Western accounts in either Hollywood films or Vietnam travel guidebooks. Whereas, to cite one recent production, Mel Gibson's character in *We Were Soldiers* (2002) explained the US intervention to his child as having to simply stop "some people" from "try[ing] to take the lives of other people," the curators located the Geneva accords of 1954, and their acknowledgment that Vietnam was a single nation, at the center of their rendition of the past. From this foundation the remainder of the exhibits were built. The displays covered wartime weaponry, the imprisonment of revolutionaries at Con Dao, the antiwar movement in the United States and around the world, and "hostile forces against the Vietnamese revolution," which was a euphemism for Vietnamese anti-Communists. There were also rooms devoted to the work of photojournalists killed in the conflict, to the photographs of Ishikawa Bunyo and Nakamura Goro, and to drawings by Vietnamese children on war and peace. For many tourists the most troubling portion of the museum was the room documenting the suffering of those whom a sign outside referred to as "war victims." The exhibits graphically illustrated the American atrocities at Son My (My Lai), where US forces massacred hundreds of unarmed women, men, and children; the widespread use of the herbicide Agent Orange and its alleged ongoing repercussions for Vietnamese and Americans; the US destruction of schools, hospitals, and other civilian structures; and the employment by the United States of napalm and white phosphorus bombs.

A sign recorded the government in Hanoi's 1995 findings on the human costs of the conflict to Vietnam: "Nearly 3 million people killed, [o]ver 4 million injured, [o]ver 2 million affected by chemicals, [a]bout 500,000 infants malformed," and, in one of those statistics that has rarely surfaced in scholarly accounts of the era, "170,000 old people [who] get lonesome" due to "their children or relatives [being] killed during the war." What was perhaps most shocking to many tourists about such numbers was that, as the anthropologist Victor Alneng observed, "[three] million Vietnamese *people* were killed—in the movies there were only gooks, V.C.s ["Viet Cong"], and hookers."[9]

Like all such institutions, the War Remnants Museum offered visitors a necessarily incomplete narrative. Beyond basic limitations of space and resources, the museum exemplified the struggles that have been waged for decades in Vietnam over issues of memory and narration. One could certainly find a "version of the past" that, as historian Hue-Tam Ho Tai characterized it, "inscribes [the Party] as the legitimate inheritor of the Vietnamese patriotic tradition and the dominant force in the recent history of the country," although such a narrative was less starkly evident than at other major historical sites, such as the Museum of Vietnamese Revolution in Hanoi.[10] At the War Remnants Museum, the strictures of official ideology accounted for only part of the publicly presented story. In fact, the demands of international tourist consumption had generated a historical narrative that was surprisingly nuanced in its treatment of the United States.

Visitors learned, for instance, of the American alliance with the Vietnamese revolutionary forces during World War II, including the cooperation of US intelligence with Ho Chi Minh. Since first emerging in 1993, moreover, there had been numerous displays on the American antiwar movement, both civilian and military. Several resisters were prominently featured, among them Michael Heck, a United States Air Force pilot who refused to bomb the Democratic Republic of Vietnam, or "North Vietnam"; Hugh Thompson and Lawrence Colburn, two of the three helicopter personnel who intervened in the American massacre of civilians at Son My (the third was Glenn Andreatta, who was killed in April 1968); and deserters Terry Whitmore, John Michael Barilla, Richard D. Bailey, Michael A. Lindner, and Craig W. Anderson. There was an exhibit devoted

Figure 5.2
Visitors examine military hardware inside the museum complex. (Photograph by Scott Laderman.)

to two Americans about whom most of their compatriots had almost certainly never heard: Norman Morrison and Roger LaPorte, both of whom immolated themselves in November 1965 to protest the war. Taken together, the exhibits on the antiwar movement served as a powerful institutional reminder that many Vietnamese recognized, although perhaps too simply, the distinction between the American political leadership and the American public.

Also given voice at the museum—without critical comment, it should be added—was what has been called the "official view," or the United States government's "public explanation," for the intervention; the English translation of a large quote said, "In August 1953, President Eisenhower, while briefing the Domino Doctrine, said Burma, India, and Indonesia would be easily oppressed if the Communists [achieved] victory in Indochina. He emphasized that the U.S. economic and military aid to the anti-Communist forces in Indochina was the best way [to combat] the severe threat [to] ... U.S. security." Elsewhere in the same room, visitors learned that "[t]he U.S. policy gradually strongly supported [the] Diem regime, eliminated French influence, and changed South Vietnam into a bunker against communism."[11]

Since 2000 and the installation of the Requiem exhibit featuring the work of photojournalists killed in the war, there had been numerous photographs and testimonials to the wartime suffering and pain of American combat troops, from Henri Huet's images of a wounded American medic assisting a fellow soldier to the photographs shot by Sam Castan minutes before the Vietnamese attack that claimed his life.[12] In the area of the museum devoted to Agent Orange, among the victims portrayed by the curators were a young American boy, a former US Air Force electrician, and two American parents and their young daughter. A sign noted that veterans from the United States, Australia, and New Zealand were awarded compensation for their exposure to Agent Orange, and it maintained that a "medical check carried out on Australian [v]ets confirmed that at least 10 [percent] of them were so seriously affected that their spouses suffered miscarriages and that [one quarter] of their new-born children had malformations." The sign also alluded to a demonstration for compensation by former Korean soldiers who served on behalf of the Americans in Vietnam, and claimed that, "[a]ccording to them, nearly 5,000 [v]eterans had been affected" by their exposure to chemical agents. And the museum's gallery

Figure 5.3
The entrance to the exhibition space, identified as "Historic Truths" by the curators, devoted to the historical background of the war. (Photograph by Scott Laderman.)

of photographs by Nakamura Goro contained an image from a 1994 demonstration by those referred to as "Agent Orange victims and war widows" in Washington, DC. The photograph was dominated by an American woman with the words "Widow of Agent Orange Victim" in large print across the front of her sweatshirt.

In other words, one found at the War Remnants Museum a remarkable willingness by the conflict's principal victims to acknowledge the human travails of their foreign adversaries. While certainly not identical as historical analogies, one might wonder, for instance, whether similar treatment has been afforded the Japanese invaders of China or the German occupiers of France at Chinese and French sites devoted to displaying the histories of those mid-twentieth-century imperial ventures, or whether in Kabul today one could locate exhibits on the undeniable hardships endured by Soviet troops in Afghanistan.

The Vietnamese museum was not without its problems, however. For example, a number of tourists complained about there being far too little historical context, including almost no attention to the origins, composition, and appeal to certain Vietnamese of the Republic of Vietnam and its anti-Communist government. The museum also failed to remind visitors that among those who perished before 1975 were tens of thousands of members of the RVN armed forces; killing, in other words, was attributable to all sides in the conflict. And while its absence should not have detracted from the force of the museum's exhibits, an examination of a number of the insurgents' gravest shortcomings, such as the execution by National Liberation Front insurgents of hundreds of noncombatants in Hue in 1968, would only have strengthened the site's historical richness.

Whereas the curators constructed a narrative that was remarkably nuanced in its acknowledgment of American suffering, they were less sympathetic to right-wing visions of the conflict as a necessary defense against Communist aggression. To the museum staff, the Vietnamese insurgents were fully justified in their resistance against France and the United States, which they depicted as a mass struggle for national liberation opposed by hostile foreign powers. It naturally followed that if there was merit in the revolutionary movement, as the exhibits suggested, then the moral basis for the American intervention was implicitly undermined. For visitors who were convinced that the US involvement was inspired by the enlightened support it lent to an embattled democratic government (i.e., the Republic of Vietnam), the unbridgeable tension between these interpretations was certain to generate conflict. That it did so was evidenced, as will be seen, by the reactions of numerous visitors. But first, it would be useful to map the ideological terrain traversed by foreigners in mediating their visit to the museum.

Mediating the Museum Experience

Any examination of tourists' displays of memory at the site must account for the fact that most visitors arrived there neither accidentally nor wholly uninformed. The museum was brought to tourists' attention by their guidebooks and other media, by tour companies (some of which still referred to it as the "War Crime [sic] Museum"), and by other travelers. What they learned from these sources contributed to their understanding of how the Vietnamese depicted the past. At a broader level, American films also performed a role in mediating tourists' firsthand experiences, providing the "Vietnam" template

Figure 5.4
Inside the "Historic Truths" room can be found this display featuring English- and Vietnamese-language editions of Robert McNamara's *In Retrospect: The Tragedy and Lessons of Vietnam*. Excerpted between the two jagged blocks are the following sentences from the book: "Yet we were wrong, terribly wrong. We owe it to future generations to explain why." Next to the excerpt the curators added, "It was that mistake that has caused severe results toward the country and people of Vietnam." (Photograph by Scott Laderman.)

against which reality would be judged.[13] Years of Hollywood fictionalizations had, after all, placed American combat and suffering at the center of post-war historical memory. Actual Vietnamese—be they combatants, politicians, or civilians—in most cases served as little more than backdrops through which to evaluate the strategic or moral quandaries of the accounts' American protagonists.

Probably no source was more important as a daily instrument of touristic mediation than Vietnam travel guidebooks. Their authors' synopses of the museum are themselves revealing markers of memory, recording the responses of some foreigners—none of the leading publishers used Vietnamese writers—to a narrative of the war not often seen or heard in cultural accounts outside of Southeast Asia. More crucially, however, interviews with numerous tourists attest to the guidebooks' importance in influencing tourists' itineraries and, in many cases, their perspectives. "[I]t is the travelers' (backpackers') 'Bible,'" confided a British woman in her early thirties in referring to the Lonely Planet volume for Southeast Asia.[14] The sentiment was reinforced by a young German who said she learned about the museum from the same publisher's guidebook to Vietnam: "Everything is from the guidebook," she emphasized.[15] Likewise, when a Briton in his late thirties noted that the site's exhibits displayed a "Vietnamese bias," he added that his opinion "probably comes through the guidebook."[16]

The extent to which tourists' reactions to the museum appear to have been colored by guidebook accounts was graphically demonstrated in 1998 in a comment book entry by a British tourist; the complaints about the site voiced by the Briton were almost identical to the language then being used by Lonely Planet in its synopsis of the institution. Whereas the tourist wrote that "[t]his museum really drives home the point that war is horrible and brutal," the guidebook claimed that "there are few museums in the world which drive home the point so well that modern warfare is horribly brutal...." When the tourist observed, "I do feel, however, that *this museum is one-sided,*" the statement paralleled the observation in the guidebook that many American tourists "complain that the museum is one-sided." And there was a remarkable similarity between the two sources on the issue of National Liberation Front atrocities. The Briton asked, "What about the thousands of people murdered and tortured by the Viet Cong? Where are the pictures?" According to the guidebook, "[O]f course, there is official amnesia when it comes to the topic of the many thousands of people tortured and murdered by the V.C."[17] The British tourist was certainly voicing a legitimate complaint, and it was one that other visitors had arrived at without mirroring the authors for Lonely Planet; however, the resemblance to the publication, suggesting that it may have impelled his displeasure, was striking.

While guidebooks have been crucial in mediating tourists' experiences in places other than Vietnam, their importance in understanding fin-de-siècle Vietnamese tourism and its relationship to American memory cannot be underestimated.[18] Most guidebook synopses of the museum, it should be noted, were characterized by a certain degree of ambivalence. All conceded—some explicitly, some implicitly—that the United States was responsible for terrible acts of violence during the war. However, several authors seemed to take umbrage at the Vietnamese curators for displaying this record. The Moon guidebook for Southeast Asia, for example, drew its readers' attention to the museum's "crudely rationalized propaganda."[19] Similarly, the author of *Fodor's Exploring Vietnam* warned, without elucidation, that the site was "an eye-opener on both the atrocities of war and on the manipulative language of propa-

Figure 5.5

The outdoor exhibition space devoted to the works of Japanese photographer Nakamura Goro. (Photograph by Scott Laderman.)

ganda," while the same publisher's Gold Guide suggested that "[y]ou'll probably come away with mixed feelings about the one-sided propaganda—ashamed of the U.S. actions, angry about the Vietnamese inaccuracies in depicting them, or both." Even with the facility's change of name to the War Remnants Museum, the guidebook insisted, the "coverage continues to be skewed."[20] The most popular guidebook among Western tourists in Vietnam, the country volume published by Lonely Planet, leveled its criticism by displacing it onto others: "The main objection to the museum," author Robert Storey wrote, "comes from, not surprisingly, American tourists, many of whom complain that the museum is one-sided."[21]

Ironically, while a number of guidebooks charged the museum with serving as a vehicle for official propaganda, the Vietnamese authorities apparently sought to minimize Western tourists' awareness of the institution's existence. The most recent editions of the English-language guidebook published by the Vietnam National Administration of Tourism (VNAT), a state entity that was created and placed directly under the prime minister in 1992, failed to acknowledge the War Remnants Museum either in their listings of sites of interest or on their maps of the city's principal tourist attractions, a strange omission given its position as the most popular museum in the metropolitan area.[22] However, the site *was* included in the Vietnamese-language edition of VNAT's guidebook.[23] The reason for the tourism officials' mixed record was presumably a desire to avoid exposing Western visitors to graphic reminders of the war and the potential discomfort such an exposure might engender. Tourism authorities had, in fact, made a conscious effort for years to revise Western perceptions of Vietnam as a holiday destination, for they were well aware that many tourists continued to view the country largely through the prism of the American war.[24] A publication launched by VNAT in 2002, for example, insisted on the first page of its inaugural issue that Vietnam is "More Than a War"; the second issue went further, implicitly pleading with foreigners to move "Beyond the War."[25]

The Western guidebooks for Vietnam posited various charges against the museum. For instance, according to Fodor's Gold Guide, "Conspicuous in its absence ... is any mention of the division of the country into South Vietnam and North Vietnam throughout the Vietnam War. (The Communist government

Figure 5.6
A replica in the museum of one of the "tiger cages" used by the Republic of Vietnam to imprison its enemies, both real and perceived. (Photograph by Scott Laderman.)

tends to overlook this division; instead it claims a puppet government backed by American imperialists illegally ruled in the South against the will of the people.)"[26] At a factual level the first sentence was demonstrably false.[27] Yet its truth or falsity is almost irrelevant; what is more fascinating is the much deeper anxiety concerning the popular memory of the war masked by the authors' perturbation. Their frustration was clearly rooted not in the museum's alleged failure to acknowledge the country's division for over twenty years, which it unambiguously did, but rather in the curators' seeming embrace of the sentiment expressed in the guidebook's second sentence.[28] Indeed, the fin-de-siècle travel literature often struggled in addressing the issue of the 1954 partition, as this reframed the nature of the American conflict. In order for the notion of Communist aggression to retain its plausibility, its adherents had to believe that the southern Vietnamese people supported the RVN authorities and opposed the revolutionary movement. The dilemma for those accepting this framework is that all credible evidence indicates just the opposite—that is, the United States and the successive Saigon governments consistently rejected a political settlement with the insurgents precisely because they knew that their popular support was minimal and could translate into an unfavorable agreement.[29] America, in other words, was fighting a counterrevolutionary rather than a defensive war. For a people whose nation was borne out of its own eighteenth-century revolution, this presented something of an ideological conundrum. To cloak the inherent contradiction between American rhetoric and the Vietnamese reality, US policymakers (and some travel writers) overlooked the RVN's lack of political appeal and ignored the recent past by minimizing the importance of the 1954 Geneva accords in favor of a more simplistic, but largely erroneous, narrative of Communist aggression.

The larger framework employed by Western guidebooks to mediate tourists' experiences at the museum was also evident in the volume published by Footprint, which criticized the omission of any "record of North Vietnamese atrocities to U.S. and South Vietnamese troops."[30] The observation, which was echoed elsewhere, implicitly subscribed to the view of the war as a conflict waged between a country called "North Vietnam" and a country called "South Vietnam." But this construction, as historian Robert Brigham argued, "gives primacy to north-

Figure 5.7
Guillotines such as this one were used by both the French and the regime of Ngo Dinh Diem to execute their opponents until 1960. (Photograph by Scott Laderman.)

erners within Vietnam's modern revolution and it inaccurately divides the struggle in Vietnam along geopolitical lines that have no cultural or historical precedent."[31] Similarly, the passage also defined "South Vietnamese troops" as those of the Army of the Republic of Vietnam, implying that the insurgents of the National Liberation Front—or even the Cao Dai, Hoa Hao, and Binh Xuyen militia units—were not "South Vietnamese." Perhaps most interestingly, however, the statement suggested that armed resistance to foreign invaders could credibly be classified as "atrocities."[32] Precisely what the authors had in mind is unclear, but they appeared to move beyond the criticism leveled by others regarding human rights violations against noncombatants by insinuating that any commission of violence against the so-called "Free World" forces was, ipso facto, an atrocity.

The comment suggests that Hollywood's depiction of American suffering as perhaps the central experience of the war had become so powerful that its alleged non-acknowledgement emerged as a legitimate criterion for gauging other accounts' historical credibility. Reflecting the degree to which a focus on the United States had become normative, however, this test did not seem to apply in the inverse. For instance, of the two exhibits dealing with the war at the National Museum of American History in Washington, DC, that same year, neither addressed the war's consequences for the Vietnamese people.[33] But this "one-sidedness" did not stimulate any guidebook objections. The same held for the Vietnam Veterans Memorial. While the Wall has been recognized by millions of Americans as a painful site of remembrance—indeed, "possibly the most poignant sight in Washington," one travel author observed—the absence of any Indochinese names from its compendium of "fallen heroes" was met only with silence in the guidebook literature.[34] In fact, it was virtually impossible to discern from guidebook accounts that museums in the capital had for years been contested political spaces. With respect to the highly publicized Enola Gay controversy at the National Air and Space Museum, for example, only one major guidebook acknowledged the debate that erupted over the proposed commemorative exhibit in 1994 and 1995.[35] What these dual standards suggest is the naturalization of American suffering as the symbolic embodiment of the Vietnam War. To situate the Vietnamese people at the center of the narrative was, for many from the West, to reveal an ideological bias. Yet to situate Americans at the center of this narrative was perceived as ideologically neutral—indeed, it was perfectly natural. As such, Vietnamese museums and historical sites were treated in the guidebook literature as highly political spaces. In contrast, American museums and historical sites did not merit a comparable degree of scrutiny.

At a more prescriptive level, the guidebooks' critiques of the War Remnants Museum collectively illustrate the extent to which many Westerners believed there was a need to somehow balance Vietnamese depictions of what was, by virtually all historical accounts, an inherently unbalanced war.[36] It is clear that this call for balance resonated with some American tourists. "Very graphic pictures. War is always full of these pictures," one wrote in a comment book in 1998. But "[t]here were a lot of casualties on both sides! Each country has a lot of horror stories." A Louisianan concurred. "A terrible war," he intoned. "I only wish that the displays had some balance."[37] The comment books often became interactive sites in which visitors, who regularly could be seen flipping through their pages and reading earlier remarks, disputed the sentiments of other travelers. In response to the Louisianan, for example, someone wrote, "Really? Four million dead vs. 55,000! Flechettes, napalm, phosphorous bombs—balance!!!"

It was not only in the relative anonymity of the comment books that complaints about "bias" were expressed. When tourists would volunteer their frustration during interviews at the site, I often would ask the interviewee what he or she would like to see changed. Prescriptions for improvement were usually lacking, however. Whereas a number of visitors were adamant that the museum was little more than an exercise in "anti-American propaganda," few were able to substantiate the charge with any degree of certainty. For instance, one American traveler, after decrying the "silly bias" of the museum, which he said was so "one sided" that "you don't take it seriously," explained in an interview that the site could have showed "the POWs in Hanoi," the "atrocities committed against the POWs." But he qualified his statement by adding that he was not actually certain that any such mistreatment occurred. The 31-year-old Navy veteran from California acknowledged that Hollywood movies had been the leading source in his own education on the conflict.[38]

While there in fact were instances of American prisoners being tortured by the Vietnamese prior to 1969, especially during periods of heavy US aerial bombardment, his comments nevertheless speak to the power of popular culture to shape Western historical consciousness, as American POWs have for years been a regular staple of cinematic treatments of the war. From *The Deer Hunter* (1978) and *The Hanoi Hilton* (1987) to *Uncommon Valor* (1983) and *Rambo: First Blood Part II* (1985), the plight of captured Americans has served in the United States as perhaps the most potent symbol of the suffering caused by the United States intervention. But this remembering—or, more accurately, reimaging—has found a necessary correlative in forgetting. With only two exceptions, no major American filmic productions have seriously addressed the hundreds of thousands of people imprisoned and tortured by the RVN authorities, many of whom were left physically crippled or psychologically devastated after years of confinement.[39] Indeed, one 43-year-old American woman told me that, before learning at the museum about the torture of Vietnamese insurgents and civilians, "in the past [she] probably would have thought it was just the opposite."[40]

History, Resistance, Contrition: A Touristic Dialogue

One of the most remarkable aspects of the War Remnants Museum is the extent to which the site has combined public history with international mourning and dialogue. Its comment books, in particular, allowed tourists to record their impressions for the curators, to respond to other travelers, to address the Vietnamese or American people, or to discuss larger global issues of war and peace. For some visitors the books were a means of expressing their deep emotional pain about the war and the suffering it caused. For others they provided a venue in which to decry the American intervention and, in some cases, the continued global exercise of American power. For a minority of visitors, the comment books allowed them to criticize what they believed to be the museum's skewed narrative of the war. Perhaps more than anything else, the books emerged as a site of witness. Countless visitors wanted to simply record their presence and their revulsion at the suffering caused by the American intervention. The Vietnamese people, they suggested, had admirably demonstrated why aggression should be denounced at every turn.

Contrition and U.S. Foreign Policy

Within the comment books a multitude of discourses emerged. Among these was some visitors' acknowledgement of a sense of culpability—generally national rather than personal—in the suffering of the Vietnamese people. While a number of Americans criticized the museum's focus on these Vietnamese hardships, many more tourists, including Americans, transformed their presence into an act of atonement. As one veteran pleaded, "May God forgive us." Another American simply wrote, "I'm sorry, Vietnam." Such expressions demonstrated the museum's potential for transnational reconciliation. While many Americans have focused since 1975 on healing the wounds caused by the war in domestic social life, many tourists, a group more traditionally associated with seeking pleasure rather than contrition, have sought to transcend the spatial constraints of national healing by using their holidays to request forgiveness from the Vietnamese. For a visitor from the Midwest, for example, the comment book afforded an opportunity to offer a collective apology: "I want to express the sorrow I feel for the horrors presented in this museum. On behalf of my prayer community in Chicago, Illinois, U.S.A., I want to apologize for the violence committed here in Vietnam."

Yet even among some Americans who expressed revulsion there could be seen the powerful post-war appeal of an exceptionalist national narrative. A young woman from Maryland, for instance, felt "terrible and responsible" even though "it all happened before I was born." But "anyone that thinks that America didn't learn much from these atrocities is sorely mistaken," she added. The comment illustrates the determined hope of some Americans, particularly those with no lived memory of the war, to believe that the conflict led to a fundamental alteration in US policies, a belated recognition by officials that the sanctity of human life had to be placed at the center of American foreign relations. It was precisely such optimism that led the Carter administration in the 1970s to declare itself wedded to the international promotion of human rights. But it is within the chasm between rhetoric and practice that the power of the post-war narrative can be evidenced.

Few would dispute that Jimmy Carter went further than his predecessors in invoking the language of human rights as a compass for American foreign policy. He presided over a nation that wished to forget the war in Vietnam and have its faith

Figure 5.8

A wall at the museum containing items donated by American veterans of the war. In the top right is a set of military awards given to the museum by Sgt. William Brown. Upon donating them in 1990 he wrote, "To the people of a united Vietnam. I was wrong. I am sorry." (Photograph by Scott Laderman.)

in America's self-proclaimed ideals restored, and the discourse of human rights provided just such an opportunity. Yet while publicly espousing moralistic language, the realpolitik necessary to further America's global ambitions persisted. The administration thus found itself abetting the Indonesian genocide in East Timor and the right-wing death squads of El Salvador. On the Southeast Asian mainland, the White House grew alarmed when Vietnam ousted the genocidal Pol Pot regime in Cambodia in the late 1970s, interpreting the invasion as an expansion of Soviet power. It thus "secretly supported efforts to resuscitate and sustain" the "remaining military forces" of the Khmer Rouge.[41] With the election of Ronald Reagan, US support for civilian dictatorships or military governments in Latin America, Asia, Africa, and the Middle East continued.

What one found among leading policymakers after 1975, in other words, was not a moral reckoning with America's history of support for the authoritarian regimes of Ngo Dinh Diem, Nguyen Van Thieu, and other RVN leaders, and thus a major redirection in American relations with the world; rather, American foreign policy, which since 1945 has nearly always enjoyed a bipartisan consensus, remained fairly constant. If there was a major lesson learned by US officials following the Vietnam conflict, it was to prevent the public from seeing unfavorable images of American warfare. Censorship and press controls were thus widely embraced by policymakers during the interventions of the 1980s and 1990s in Grenada, Panama, and Iraq.

Memories of the war sharply crystallized in the years after 1975. At the level of popular discourse, the Vietnam experience coalesced into, on the Right, a "noble cause" undermined by civilian bureaucrats and the antiwar movement and, among liberals, a tragic episode in which, as one American tourist wrote in January 2002, "We wanted to help your country and got lost along the way." To such Americans the war was a "mistake" rather than a symptom, a deviation rather than the norm. Although they continued to face resistance, it is clear that the ideological precepts that were shattered by the popular movements of the 1960s had been reembraced and renaturalized during the reactionary ascendance that followed the war's official end in 1975.

The extent to which much of the critical historiography on the Vietnam conflict had failed to reach a popular audience could be detected in the comment book entry of a woman from Massachusetts: "As an American, I am ashamed and appalled at the atrocities perpetrated on the Vietnamese people. The use of chemical *warfare,* the use of torture, the inconcievable [*sic*] hatred—I honestly don't understand how it could have come to this. My tears, my apologies are nothing, really, in the face of such destruction, but I give it [*sic*] anyway in the hopes that we will all be *vigilant* in the future & protect others from the *horrors* that out [*sic*] countries have perpetrated on one another in the name of fear & ignorance."[42]

While remarks such as this one were genuine and moving and reveal the painful recognition by many Americans of what their country had done in Vietnam, they also illustrate the manner in which many tourists viewed the war through a prism that ignored its larger historical context. That is, the United States intervention was rooted in "fear" and "ignorance"; if only policymakers had understood that the Vietnamese were fighting for their independence then the suffering could have been averted.[43] So marginalized had the deeper imperialist critique of many historians become in American popular discourse that many visitors appeared to be simply unaware of it. To numerous scholars, the intervention was best explained not by ignorance but by design: the United States sought to establish a liberal capitalist system that served American global interests after World War II, and it was the logic of these aspirations that led to the Vietnam conflict. But for tourists who had been taught that American wars were relatively bloodless (as in Iraq in 1991) or were waged on humanitarian grounds (as in Kosovo in 1999), the visitor's inability to "understand how it could have come to this" would not have seemed extraordinary. It had to be "ignorance" that led America into such a moral morass.

Not all tourists, however, accepted this interpretive framework. Indeed, a recurring theme among mostly non-American travelers was a perceptible continuity between the conflict in Vietnam and post-war US foreign policy. A February 2002 entry by an Italian visitor read, "Yesterday in Vietnam (Laos-Cambodia). Today in Afghanistan." The following month his comment was echoed by a German at the site: "Bush = Nixon? Afghanistan = Vietnam? Muslims = Communists? What's the difference? Never again?!" While there are, in fact, great differences between the wars in Vietnam and Afghanistan, American power and the country's continued resort to military force nevertheless left many tourists unsettled. Shortly after the invasion of Afghanistan, for example, one visitor lamented, "I am from the U.S., a country so proud & so ignorant. I leave here

Figure 5.9
"Mother," a work of art by Nguyen Hoang Huy that was constructed of bomb fragments. (Photograph by Scott Laderman.)

today saddened & confused why our country refuses to educate itself." The sentiment was mirrored by "An Anonymous American": "It[']s really sad to see that nearly forty years later my country and the world has not learned that killing is wrong." In its political ambiguity, the last comment reflected a pacifist strain that ran through many of the entries. While many tourists made pointed comments about the United States in the books, for others they provided a more metaphysical venue. "Can we live without killing each other?" asked an American traveler in January 2002. "No more war," wrote another.

That different interpretive lenses were employed by different people could be seen in the entries by visitors from states which had been colonizers in the twentieth century (or were settler states) and those from states which had been colonized. The former seemed more inclined to focus on the tragedy of war or the "mistakes" made by the Americans. Conversely, most of the comments celebrating the Vietnamese resistance—that is, foregrounding Vietnamese agency rather than the repercussions of the American intervention—were authored by individuals from the latter. Typical of the first group was the entry from an Australian woman: "Thank you for giving the new generations & those from other countries the opportunity to see the tradegic [sic] affects [sic] of such a brutal war. May we all learn & move on to make a better society." An Indian visitor was more representative of the second: "After viewing all these photographs, all my credit goes to the valiant people of Vietnam who had the courage and guts to face such a mighty military as a U.S. Army who always boast they are almighty. My kudos & best wishes to Vietnamese in their struggle to build up a strong nation." Likewise, the Vietnamese who faced "horrifying brutality committed by the aggressors," opined a Malaysian in July 1995, were "freedom fighters" on a quest "for unification and liberation." For a Singaporean immigrant to Canada, "To say no more war is naive," he wrote in March 2002. "You have to fight for your rights and freedom. I admire the Vietnamese people for defeating foreign powers to regain their dignity and stand proudly as an indipendent [sic] nation in the world."

The Museum as Symbol: A Multinational Dialogue

At times the entries in the comment books transcended the immediate focus of the Vietnam War, with the museum essentially becoming a site at which an international dialogue on justice and peace could be entertained. But unlike in most multinational forums, the discussion took place among ordinary people, not elites or the government officials who inhabit the United Nations, the Organization of American States, and other multilateral bodies. The museum, in other words, became a space more akin to the World Social Forum than the World Economic Forum. While the discussion was not truly representative—it was limited, after all, to people who could afford to be tourists—its broad international participation rendered it unusual by most standards. The focus of those remarks transcending the temporal and spatial boundaries of the Indochina wars was wide ranging.

A pressing concern among some visitors was that others would leave the museum horrified by the historical injustices displayed at the site but unable to make connections to what the commentators considered to be more contemporary global concerns. For example, an American born in 1974 pleaded, "Let us remember how colonialization [sic] has wreaked havoc on so many people and so many countries. While America is great in many ways[,] it can only be as great as its leaders and followers allow. Push education. And please think twice when you spend your money on that McDonald's cheeseburger or [C]oca-[C]ola." To her, democracy required personal commitment, and all actions had potentially unforeseen consequences. Purchasing a hamburger from McDonald's could be perceived as contributing to the destruction of the Amazonian rainforests cleared to create cattle farms from which the fast-food chain purchased much of its beef. Individuals thus became immediately responsible for improving the health of the planet.

Other visitors moved beyond issues of personal responsibility into discussions of war and peace. "I pray for a day," wrote an Israeli tourist in March 2002, "when words will replace weapons, kindness will replace killing, and compassion will replace conflict.... And I pray for an end to the Palestinian-Israeli conflict in my lifetime." Some travelers, with the American war in Afghanistan raging, used the past conflict in Vietnam to spotlight the ongoing conflict in central Asia. "The same thing is happening in Afghanistan! Shameful.... Stop it now!" insisted an Italian tourist. More humble was a visitor from Hong Kong: "I hope there won't be another museum in Afghanistan."

An overwhelming sentiment among visitors to the site was the pacifist conviction that war and aggression were immoral

Figure 5.10
Among the more disturbing exhibits at the museum are two jars containing fetuses whose deformities have been attributed by the curators to Agent Orange. (Photograph by Scott Laderman.)

and even ineffective. A Chicagoan wrote in March 2002, "War is, and always will be, hell on Earth. Let's all learn it never serves a positive purpose and move forward in peace." For some, the museum starkly highlighted the innocence of those who often bear the greatest costs in violent conflicts. "There is one lesson to be learned[:] military power will *not* solve the problems of this world but only increases the suffering of innocent people," declared an Israeli in February 2002.[44] It was time, believed a visitor from Australia that same month, for the world's people to reassert the centrality of human rights in international affairs. "If the choke in my throat is any indication of the emotion that boils on the sight of these pictures," the Australian wrote, "then there must too be hope that people know that fighting is never a solution. People everywhere should never ever stop thinking for themselves—you know what right is, and you know what wrong is. Support [h]uman [r]ights—Support [h]umans."

For at least one visitor, the horror expressed by the museumgoers over the past suffering of the Vietnamese seemed at least partially misdirected. Writing anonymously in March 2002, the tourist seemed frustrated that other travelers were neglecting contemporary oppression by the Vietnamese state, and thus sought to remind them of Vietnam's human rights violations: "Yes. This & Laos & Cambodia [are] heartbreaking—lest [sic] us not forget that at this very day Northern [sic] Hill Tribes are still fleeing to Cambodia (Mondilkiri [sic] Province) as refugees. One sided histories are the cause for history repeating itself— in the U.S. as well as elsewhere."[45] Indeed, national introspection or critical examinations by foreigners were requested both of Vietnamese and Americans. Another anonymous tourist wrote the same month, "Let's hope we never witness anything like this again. America stay out[;] it is unreal how they call on Saddam Hussein for using/stockpilling [sic] chemical weapons. Look at yourselves for god[']s sake. Hears [sic] to world peace."

What seemed to disturb many visitors was the hypocrisy of state power. Vietnamese, who were represented in the museum as the victims of American aggression, were taken to task for suppressing the rights of indigenous peoples in the interior mountainous provinces. And that twenty-first century American global ambitions were alleged by US officials to be humanitarian or pacific was mocked by countless tourists. From within this context a number of travelers reflected on the Western campaign that, by 2002, had replaced anti-Communism as the reigning orthodoxy in international affairs: the "war on terror." Thus wrote a Briton in March of that year: "I'm amazed and humbled by the tolerance, forgiveness, and pragmatism of the people I have met during my two visits to Vietnam. I hope that people seeing the exhibition can—each in their own small way—oppose our current surge of world domination, where atrocities are approved in Palestine, Kashmir, N. China, etc. under the guise/pretence of the 'War Against Terrorism.' And[,] in particular," he concluded, "to cry foul when the perpetrators (here the U.S.) claim the status of victims!" One of his compatriots felt similarly, stating at approximately the same time that "these photographs are an indictment of war, from whichever side you were on, and whatever way you choose to look at it. It didn't stop after Vietnam[;] it continues to this day. Why is it that people using car bombs and suicide bombers are terrorists and those using jets, tanks, etc. are soldiers[?]" he asked. In then suggesting that people "please always try to look at things from the two sides that exist, not just the one the media (in general) tells you about," the British tourist raised a troubling prospect. Just as decades earlier the war in Vietnam had been framed by policymakers and, in most instances, by the press as a war against Communist aggression, what if in 2002 the policies of the United States, the United Kingdom, and other Western powers were being misleadingly ascribed to anti-terrorism? Indeed, it was precisely the ease with which visitors viewing the museum's historical exhibits drew connections to the present that lent the site its symbolic potency.

What the comments illustrate is the transnational solidarity felt by many tourists with respect to issues of peace. Allegiance to humanistic principles was expressed by visitors on the basis of their shared beliefs, not their shared citizenship. In fact, in some cases travelers even urged others to resist the actions of their own governments, as when a Briton asked that the world "oppose our current surge of world domination" in March 2002. The objective was a peaceful coexistence that crossed national borders. How to achieve this peace was not always certain, but by engaging peoples from Vietnam and across the planet, the tourists in Ho Chi Minh City thought themselves to be taking a first step.

Competing Pasts, Competing Futures

History museums are inherently political spaces. In providing narratives about the past, they inevitably comment on both the present and the future. Visitors are exposed to not just artifacts and recorded experiences, but also implicit signals about history's contemporary meanings. When, in January 2004, officials at the National Museum of American History disclosed their plans to address the US experience in Vietnam within a larger exhibit called "The Price of Freedom: Americans at War," they seemed to be suggesting that the Indochina wars were a cost to be paid in defense of one of America's most cherished ideals.[46] To be sure, freedom is a fundamental tenet of American national identity, and it is one whose meaning has been vigorously contested since the country's inception.[47] But the struggle for freedom would strike many Vietnamese as a curious interpretive framework for the American campaign in Indochina. For them, the conflict was self-evidently an imperial crusade, one of several interventions—a painfully tragic one given that many revolutionaries had initially viewed the United States as a guarantor of self-determination—intended to undermine their decades-long quest for national liberation and unification. While these American and Vietnamese views would appear to be mutually incompatible, both countries do, however, share common experiential terrain.

It is this shared history that was on display at the War Remnants Museum. What made the site so disconcerting to a number of tourists was precisely these connections between the American military and the Vietnamese people. The curators decentered the United States from the conflict, reminding travelers that the war deeply affected millions of Vietnamese. The reminder shocked countless travelers whose views had been shaped by popular narratives that focused almost exclusively on the painful travails of the American invaders. "Finally I was able to see the other side of the war," an American visitor wrote in March 2002, signing his name next to a peace symbol. Or, as an Australian tourist observed in 1998, "A number of people who have written in this book have complained about this museum not providing a balanced view of the war. I, like most of them, come from a Western society and I can honestly say that after my visit here a balanced view is exactly what I *now* have."[48] The comments, which allowed for a multinational conversation among visitors who otherwise would probably never have conversed, were revealing for their implicit acknowledgement that tourists' views had previously been limited. While not offering a complete or total narrative, the museum nevertheless forced Western travelers to confront some of the realities of a conflict that for years has remained shrouded in fantasy and myth. No longer could Vietnamese perspectives be ignored.

More broadly, the museum provided a sobering reminder that war is much more than the technological spectacle, or what *Newsweek*, referring to the Persian Gulf conflict of 1991, called the "bloodless unreality of the Nintendo-game air war," that has seemed its defining feature on American television screens since at least 1991.[49] In actuality, the curators implied, war is an impersonal force that causes unspeakable destruction and death. It is bloody, it is ruthless, and it is indiscriminate. For travelers who embraced America's continued resort to militarism in international affairs, the museum was thus interpreted as a bastion of propaganda. For others, however, the site's images of suffering, both military and civilian, served as an indispensable and timeless corrective.

Notes

The author wishes to gratefully acknowledge Victor Alneng, H. Bruce Franklin, Jessica C. E. Gienow-Hecht, Fabian Hilfrich, Elaine Tyler May, Lary May, Viet Thanh Nguyen, an anonymous referee, and his graduate student colleagues at the University of Minnesota for their thoughtful comments on various drafts of this essay.

1. George Bush, "Inaugural Address," 20 January 1989, *Public Papers of the Presidents of the United States: George Bush, 1989* (Washington, DC: Government Printing Office, 1990), Book 1: 3; George Bush, "Address to the Nation Announcing Allied Military Action in the Persian Gulf," 16 January 1991, *Public Papers of the Presidents of the United States: George Bush, 1991* (Washington, DC: Government Printing Office, 1992), Book 1: 44; George Bush, "Remarks to the American Legislative Exchange Council," 1 March 1991, *Public Papers of the Presidents of the United States: George Bush, 1991*, Book 1: 197.
2. Unless otherwise indicated, all comments from visitors are from the "Impressions" books at the museum. I relied on the comment books used at the site in March 2002 (which contained entries from January through March), a comment book from 1998 that had earlier appeared in the room devoted to the photography of Ishikawa Bunyo, and a selection of comments from throughout the 1990s. I am grateful to the directors of the museum for making copies of these documents available to me.
3. Linda K. Richter, *The Politics of Tourism in Asia* (Honolulu: University of Hawaii Press, 1989), 4–11. As a research focus, tourism has only somewhat recently been embraced by historians of American foreign relations. See, for several of the best recent examples, Christopher Endy, *Cold War Holidays: American Tourism in France* (Chapel Hill: University of North Carolina Press, 2004); Dennis Merrill, "Negotiating Cold War Paradise: U.S. Tourism, Economic Planning, and Cultural Modernity in Twentieth-Century Puerto Rico," *Diplomatic History* 25, 2 (Spring 2001): 179–214; and Christina Klein, *Cold War Orientalism: Asia in the Middlebrow Imagination, 1945–1961* (Berkeley: University of California Press, 2003), 100–42.
4. Interview of Huynh Ngoc Van, Vice Director of the War Remnants Museum, Ho Chi Minh City, 12 March 2002. There is considerable confusion with respect to the institution's former English-language names. The site opened on 4 September 1975. According to Ms. Van, from 1975 until 1990 it was called, in Vietnamese, the Nha Trung Bay Toi Ac My Nguy, which roughly translates to the Exhibition House of Crimes of America and Its Puppet. However, I have been unable to confirm this English-language name from any contemporaneous source. A number of journalists and writers have reported that the institution was originally called the Museum of American War Crimes. However, to the Vietnamese there is a difference between an "exhibition house," the purpose of which is to exhibit, and a museum, which also engages in functions such as research and conservation. A short piece in the *Economist* was probably most accurate; it referred to the English-language name of the institution as the Exhibition House of American and Chinese War Crimes, claiming that "Chinese" was dropped in 1990. "Spot the Crime in Vietnam," *Economist,* 3 December 1994. The same claim is found in John Colet and Joshua Eliot, *Vietnam Handbook* (Bath: Footprint Handbooks, 1997), 242. It is doubtful, however, that "Chinese" existed in the name before the brief conflict between

Vietnam and China in 1979. Before its rechristening as the War Remnants Museum (Bao Tang Chung Tich Chien Tranh) in 1995, the institution was called the Exhibition House of Aggression War Crimes (Nha Trung Bay Toi Ac Chien Tranh Xam Luoc). This name appeared in the *Economist* article cited above, and was confirmed to me by the anthropologist Christina Schwenkel, who was in possession of a pre-1995 English-language pamphlet from the museum containing the appellation. Email correspondence with Christina Schwenkel, 4 August 2003. (A 1991 article in the *Los Angeles Times* used the slightly different Exhibition House of Aggressive War Crimes. Alvin Shuster, "20 Years Later, Back to Saigon," *Los Angeles Times*, 17 May 1991, Folder 07, Box 24, Douglas Pike Collection: Other Manuscripts – Current News, Vietnam Archive, Texas Tech University.) Ms. Van indicated that the name was most recently changed to make it suitable to the opinions of people everywhere, as Vietnam had opened itself to the world since 1990, she said. The museum has, since my last visit in 2002, undergone substantial renovation. According to Ms. Van, upon completion it was to contain displays on Vietnam's three major wars: against the French, against the Japanese, and against the Americans; she said the 1979 conflict with China was not a war but a border dispute, and she did not mention the war against the Khmer Rouge in Cambodia.

5. "Tourist Numbers Up at H.C.M. City's War Remnants Museum," *Viet Nam News*, 10 February 2003. <vietnnamnews.vnagency.com.vn/2003-02/10/Stories/04.htm> (accessed 24 June 2003).

6. While I base this claim on my interviews during 2000 and 2002 with over 170 tourists throughout Vietnam, I must caution, however, that my findings should not be construed as scientific, although I suspect they were reasonably accurate for independent Western travelers. I cannot claim to have interviewed a representative sample of Western visitors, if such was even possible, although I did make an effort to speak with as wide of a cross section of individuals as possible. One notable exception was my inability to interview large numbers of package tourists; their fixed, tight schedules made interviews logistically almost impossible, so with only a few exceptions they are not included in these findings.

7. Unless otherwise indicated, all references to the exhibits at the museum were recorded by me in March 2002. I also conducted research at the museum in June 2000, and I visited as an interested tourist in February 1998. There were a number of changes during that time—for example, by March 2002 the museum had begun displaying a series of drawings by Vietnamese children on war and peace and, by June 2000, had installed a large collection of photographs by Ishikawa Bunyo and the Requiem exhibit—but I did not discern a substantial difference in the exhibits' general tone.

8. Robert S. McNamara with Brian VanDeMark, *In Retrospect: The Tragedy and Lessons of Vietnam* (New York: Vintage Books, 1996 [1995]), xx. The quote also appeared in the pamphlet handed out to tourists when they purchased a ticket to the museum. McNamara's statement generated widespread debate, much of it inspired by the mistaken belief that he was making a moral judgment about the war. He was not. For one of the more insightful exchanges on the publication of *In Retrospect,* see the roundtable essays by Marilyn B. Young, Tom Wicker, Noam Chomsky, Edwin M. Yoder, Jr., Ward Just, and W. W. Rostow in *Diplomatic History* 20, 3 (Summer 1996): 439–71.

9. Victor Alneng, "'What the Fuck is a Vietnam?': Touristic Phantasms and the Popcolonization of (the) Vietnam (War)," *Critique of Anthropology* 22, 4 (December 2002): 476. There is scholarly uncertainty about the number of Vietnamese fatalities caused by the American war. The Vietnamese Ministry of Labor, War Invalids, and Social Affairs estimated in April 1995 that approximately three million soldiers and civilians had perished. More recently, drawing on Vietnam Life History Survey data, several scholars concluded (with important qualifications) that approximately one million Vietnamese suffered war-related deaths from 1965 to 1975. See Charles Hirschman, Samuel Preston, and Vu Manh Loi, "Vietnamese Casualties during the American War: A New Estimate," *Population and Development Review* 21, 4 (December 1995): 783–812.
10. Hue-Tam Ho Tai, "Introduction: Situating Memory," in *The Country of Memory: Remaking the Past in Late Socialist Vietnam,* ed. Hue-Tam Ho Tai (Berkeley: University of California Press, 2001), 3.
11. On the "official view" of the US intervention, see Jeffrey P. Kimball, ed., *To Reason Why: The Debate About the Causes of U.S. Involvement in the Vietnam War* (Philadelphia: Temple University Press, 1990), 25–50. The museum exhibits contained a number of grammatical errors, awkward statements, or inappropriate uses of tense which I have chosen to revise for purposes of clarity, consistency, and flow. By way of illustration, the original version of the first quote said, "In August 1953, President Eisenhower, while briefing the Domino Doctrine said Burma, India, and Indonesia would be easily oppressed if the communists got victory in Indo-China. He emphasized that the U.S. economic and military aid to the anti-communist forces in Indo-China was the best way against the severe threat toward the U.S. security." As both passages in this paragraph were attributed by the curators to Peter A. Poole's *The United States and Indochina: From F.D.R. to Nixon,* it is likely that the quotes were English translations of a Vietnamese translation of Poole's original English-language text. The study is Peter A. Poole, *The United States and Indochina: From F.D.R. to Nixon* (Hinsdale: Dryden Press, 1973).
12. In fact, Ishikawa Bunyo's photographs, installed in the museum in 1998, also portrayed the "in country" experiences of American soldiers, although not as extensively as the Requiem exhibit; the latter collection has been published as Horst Faas and Tim Page, eds., *Requiem: By the Photographers Who Died in Vietnam and Indochina* (New York: Random House, 1997).
13. As I base this analysis in part on my interviews of foreign tourists during research trips in 2000 and 2002, I wish to reemphasize the caveats contained in note 6. With respect to the limitations in interviewing package tourists expressed earlier, it should be noted that many tour companies did not place the War Remnants Museum on their regular itineraries, adding a visit only if specifically requested by those enrolled in the tour. Telephone interview of Tu Nguyen, US Representative for Trails of Indochina, 27 September 2001; and interview of the director of a Vietnamese tour company who requested confidentiality, Ho Chi Minh City, March 2002.
14. Interview No. 9, Hoa Lo Prison, Hanoi, 31 January 2002.
15. Interview No. 73, War Remnants Museum, 20 March 2002.
16. Interview No. 74, War Remnants Museum, 20 March 2002. He was using the Vietnam volume published by Rough Guides.

17. Robert Storey and Daniel Robinson, *Vietnam,* Fourth Edition (Hawthorn, Victoria: Lonely Planet Publications, 1997), 201. Emphasis in the original.
18. On the importance of guidebooks in Indonesia, see Andrew McGregor, "Dynamic Texts and Tourist Gaze: Death, Bones, and Buffalo," *Annals of Tourism Research* 27, 1 (2000), 27–50.
19. Carl Parkes, *Southeast Asia Handbook,* Third Edition (Chico: Moon Publications, Inc., 1998 [1999]), 960.
20. Fiona Dunlop, *Fodor's Exploring Vietnam,* Second Edition (New York: Fodor's Travel Publications, 2002), 176; Deborah Kaufman, ed., *Vietnam,* Second Edition (New York: Fodor's Travel Publications, 2001), 186.
21. Robert Storey and Daniel Robinson, *Vietnam,* Third Edition (Hawthorn, Victoria: Lonely Planet Publications, 1995), 198. The same language was used in the fourth and fifth editions but was altered when a new author, Mason Florence, revised the sixth edition.
22. Vu The Binh, ed., *Vietnam Tourist Guidebook,* Third Edition (Hanoi: Vietnam National Administration of Tourism, 2001). The first edition of the guidebook acknowledged the War Remnants Museum but did not, unlike with several other museums and historical attractions, provide any substantive information about it; the site's name ("War Crimes Exhibition"), address, and telephone number were simply listed in a catalog of museums in Ho Chi Minh City. Vu The Binh, ed., *Vietnam Tourist Guidebook,* First Edition (Hanoi: Vietnam National Administration of Tourism, 1998), 113. This information was excised in the guidebook's subsequent editions. Museum attendance rankings were provided in an interview with Trinh Thi Hoa, Director of the Museum of Vietnamese History – Ho Chi Minh City, 7 March 2002.
23. Vu The Binh, ed., *Non Nuoc Viet Nam: Sach Huong Dan Du Lich,* In Lan Thu Bon (Hanoi: Tong Cuc Du Lich Trung Tam Cong Nghe Thong Tin Du Lich, 2002), 559.
24. See, for example, Annabel Biles, Kate Lloyd, and William S. Logan, "'Tiger on a Bicycle': The Growth, Character, and Dilemmas of International Tourism in Vietnam," *Pacific Tourism Review* 3 (1999): 14–16.
25. Vietnam National Administration of Tourism, *Vietnam Discovery* (February 2002): 1; Vietnam National Administration of Tourism, *Vietnam Discovery* (March 2002): 1.
26. Kaufman, *Vietnam,* Second Edition, 186.
27. Among the numerous exhibits acknowledging Vietnam's wartime division was the earlier-cited large quotation in Vietnamese with an English caption that said, "The U.S. policy gradually strongly supported [the] Diem regime, eliminated French influence, and changed South Vietnam into a bunker against communism." Another exhibit noted of the Geneva accords: "All the sides participating in the conference, in principle, recognized the independence, unification, and the territorial integrity of Vietnam. The negotiation[s] between [the] two parts of the country began on July 20, 1955[,] and the general election would be held in July 1956. The 17th parallel was the temporary military border in Vietnam...." Also recognizing the country's division, a large painted map showed the "[a]rrangement of [the] U.S. Army and its allied forces in South Vietnam in April 1969." Adjacent to this map was a chart with a caption that began, "Forces of the United States, its allies, and the former Saigon government in South Vietnam during the highest phase (April 1969)."

28. I wrote "seeming embrace" because, while the larger narrative at the site implicitly accepted this framework, the curators did not use the jargon (i.e., "American imperialists," "puppet government") dismissively attributed to the "Communist government" by the writer for Fodor's. Other Vietnamese institutions have been blunter than the War Remnants Museum, however. For example, the Museum of Vietnamese Revolution in Hanoi, which is one of the country's seven national museums, contained numerous references in its exhibits to the "puppet regime" or "Ngo Dinh Diem clique" when I was conducting research at the site in February 2002. Whatever their merit, the sentiments expressed by such designations seriously conflict with many popular American representations of the war and thus, to some Western tourists, stimulated a considerable degree of cognitive dissonance.
29. Simply put, there was no basis in either Vietnamese history or in southern majority opinion for the establishment of a permanent sovereign entity south of the seventeenth parallel. Legally, the 1954 accords explicitly identified the "independence, unity, and territorial integrity" of a single Vietnamese state that was to be only temporarily divided into separate military "regrouping zones"—one for the French colonialist forces, the other for those of the Democratic Republic of Vietnam—until the country's reunification following a nationwide election in July 1956. The "military demarcation line" at the seventeenth parallel, the Final Declaration on Indochina decreed, was strictly "provisional" and "should not in any way be interpreted as constituting a political or territorial boundary." "The Final Declaration on Indochina," *Foreign Relations of the United States, 1952–1954,* Volume XVI: The Geneva Conference (Washington, DC: Government Printing Office, 1981), 1541.
30. Colet and Eliot, *Vietnam Handbook,* 242.
31. Robert K. Brigham, "Why the South Won the American War in Vietnam," in *Why the North Won the Vietnam War,* ed. Marc Jason Gilbert (New York: Palgrave, 2002), 97.
32. If the guidebook's authors were referring to violations of the laws of war by the Vietnamese revolutionary forces, they failed to identify them.
33. The two exhibits to which I am referring—both of which were viewed in October 2002—were the museum's displays on the Vietnam Veterans Memorial and a small section of "A Different Kind of War," an exhibit devoted to nuclear warfare and deterrence. The former included several statistics on the human cost of the war, although its focus was limited to the people of the United States.
34. Elise Hartman Ford, *Frommer's Washington, D.C. from $80 a Day,* Eleventh Edition (New York: Hungry Minds, Inc., 2002), 169; the reference to "more than 58,000 fallen heroes" was from Helen Sillett, et al., eds., *Moon Metro: Washington, D.C.* (Emeryville: Avalon Travel Publishing, 2002), 23. Also consulted for guidebook treatments of these American sites were Jules Brown and Jeff Cranmer, *The Rough Guide to Washington, D.C.,* Third Edition (London: Rough Guides, 2002); David S. Cashion, ed., *Fodor's U.S.A.,* Twenty-seventh Edition (New York: Fodor's Travel Publications, 2001); Jane Driesen, Julie Mazur, and Chris Swiac, eds., *Fodor's Washington, D.C.* (New York: Fodor's Travel Publications, 2002); Brian Wansley Flanagan, ed., *Let's Go: Washington, D.C.* (New York: St. Martin's Press, 2003); and Laura Harger, *Washington, D.C.* (Footscray, Victoria: Lonely Planet Publications, 2001).

35. Flanagan, *Let's Go: Washington, D.C.*, 113. For the list of guidebooks consulted, see note 34.
36. While most historians would acknowledge the war's imbalance, the same cannot be said of American political leaders. The most notorious utterance along these lines was probably that of Jimmy Carter, who claimed in a 1977 news conference that, referring to Vietnam and America, the "destruction was mutual." "The President's News Conference of March 24, 1977," *Public Papers of the Presidents of the United States: Jimmy Carter, 1977*, Book 1 (Washington, DC: Government Printing Office, 1977), 501.
37. Other tourists bemoaned the attention to Vietnamese suffering. "It's too bad that this museum is only showing how the Vietnamese people suffered," a visitor of unknown nationality complained in 1998. "The Americans suffered as well. Forced by their government! They came to help S[outh] Vietnam but after 'too' many years they lost it. It took too long and it was useless. Feel sorry for all the people who died and for the families who lost someone, houses, etc.!!"
38. Interview No. 41, War Remnants Museum, 13 March 2002.
39. The exceptions were Oliver Stone's *Heaven and Earth* (1993), which was based on the life of Le Ly Hayslip, and *Hearts and Minds* (1974), the award-winning documentary by Peter Davis.
40. Interview No. 60, War Remnants Museum, 17 March 2002.
41. National Security Adviser Zbigniew Brzezinski, "presumably with Carter's at least tacit approval," bore "primary responsibility" for the American policy of support for the Khmer Rouge, wrote historian Kenton Clymer. "[H]uman-rights considerations hardly entered into the administration's foreign-policy calculus," he maintained. Kenton Clymer, "Jimmy Carter, Human Rights, and Cambodia," *Diplomatic History* 27, 2 (April 2003): 246–47.
42. Emphases in the original.
43. The "ignorance" hypothesis was expressed well by an Australian visitor in January 2002. "Why did America not realize that Ho Chi Minh wanted independence[,] not the American bullshit 'domino theory'[?]" the tourist asked.
44. Emphasis in the original.
45. On the human rights violations in the Central Highlands, see Amnesty International, "Viet Nam," in *Amnesty International Report 2002* (Amnesty International Publications, 2002). <web.amnesty.org/web/ar2002.nsf/asa/viet+nam!Open> (accessed 14 October 2004).
46. On the announcement of the permanent exhibition, see Teresa Wiltz, "The Smithsonian's Military Bearing," *Washington Post*, 23 January 2004.
47. See, especially, Eric Foner, *The Story of American Freedom* (New York: W. W. Norton & Company, Inc., 1998).
48. Emphasis in the original.
49. Tom Morganthau with Douglas Waller, et al., "The Military's New Image," *Newsweek* (11 March 1991): 50.

Bibliography

Alneng, Victor. "'What the Fuck is a Vietnam?': Touristic Phantasms and the Popcolonization of (the) Vietnam (War)." *Critique of Anthropology* 22, 4 (December 2002): 461–89.

Amnesty International. "Viet Nam." *Amnesty International Report 2002.* Amnesty International Publications, 2002, <web.amnesty.org/web/ar2002.nsf/asa/viet+nam!Open>.

Biles, Annabel, Kate Lloyd, and William S. Logan, "'Tiger on a Bicycle': The Growth, Character, and Dilemmas of International Tourism in Vietnam." *Pacific Tourism Review* 3, 1 (1999): 11–23.

Brigham, Robert K. "Why the South Won the American War in Vietnam." In *Why the North Won the Vietnam War,* ed. Marc Jason Gilbert. New York: Palgrave, 2002.

Brown, Jules, and Jeff Cranmer. *The Rough Guide to Washington, D.C.* Third Edition. London: Rough Guides, 2002.

Cashion, David S., ed. *Fodor's U.S.A.* Twenty-seventh Edition. New York: Fodor's Travel Publications, 2001.

Chomsky, Noam. "Hamlet without the Prince of Denmark." *Diplomatic History* 20, 3 (Summer 1996): 450–55.

Clymer, Kenton. "Jimmy Carter, Human Rights, and Cambodia." *Diplomatic History* 27, 2 (April 2003): 246–47.

Colet, John, and Joshua Eliot. *Vietnam Handbook.* Bath: Footprint Handbooks, 1997.

Driesen, Jane, Julie Mazur, and Chris Swiac, eds. *Fodor's Washington, D.C.* New York: Fodor's Travel Publications, 2002.

Dunlop, Fiona. *Fodor's Exploring Vietnam.* Second Edition. New York: Fodor's Travel Publications, 2002.

Endy, Christopher. *Cold War Holidays: American Tourism in France.* Chapel Hill: University of North Carolina Press, 2004.

Faas, Horst, and Tim Page, eds. *Requiem: By the Photographers Who Died in Vietnam and Indochina.* New York: Random House, 1997.

Flanagan, Brian Wansley, ed. *Let's Go: Washington, D.C.* New York: St. Martin's Press, 2003.

Ford, Elise Hartman. *Frommer's Washington, D.C. from $80 a Day.* Eleventh Edition. New York: Hungry Minds, Inc., 2002.

Foner, Eric. *The Story of American Freedom.* New York: W. W. Norton & Company, Inc., 1998.

Foreign Relations of the United States, 1952–1954. Volume XVI: The Geneva Conference. Washington, DC: Government Printing Office, 1981.

Harger, Laura. *Washington, D.C.* Footscray, Victoria: Lonely Planet Publications, 2001.

Hirschman, Charles, Samuel Preston, and Vu Manh Loi. "Vietnamese Casualties during the American War: A New Estimate." *Population and Development Review* 21, 4 (December 1995): 783–812.

Just, Ward. "McNamara's Complaint." *Diplomatic History* 20, 3 (Summer 1996): 462–66.

Kaufman, Deborah, ed. *Vietnam.* Second Edition. New York: Fodor's Travel Publications, 2001.

Kimball, Jeffrey P., ed. *To Reason Why: The Debate About the Causes of U.S. Involvement in the Vietnam War.* Philadelphia: Temple University Press, 1990.

Klein, Christina. *Cold War Orientalism: Asia in the Middlebrow Imagination, 1945–1961.* Berkeley: University of California Press, 2003.

McGregor, Andrew. "Dynamic Texts and Tourist Gaze: Death, Bones, and Buffalo." *Annals of Tourism Research* 27, 1 (2000): 27–50.

McNamara, Robert S. with Brian VanDeMark. *In Retrospect: The Tragedy and Lessons of Vietnam.* New York: Vintage Books, 1996 [1995].

Merrill, Dennis. "Negotiating Cold War Paradise: U.S. Tourism, Economic Planning, and Cultural Modernity in Twentieth-Century Puerto Rico." *Diplomatic History* 25, 2 (Spring 2001): 179–214.
Morganthau, Tom, et al. "The Military's New Image." *Newsweek* (March 11, 1991): 50–51.
Parkes, Carl. *Southeast Asia Handbook*. Third Edition. Chico: Moon Publications, Inc., 1998 [1999].
Poole, Peter A. *The United States and Indochina: From FDR to Nixon*. Hinsdale: Dryden Press, 1973.
Public Papers of the Presidents of the United States: George Bush, 1989. Book 1. Washington, DC: Government Printing Office, 1990.
Public Papers of the Presidents of the United States: George Bush, 1991, Book 1. Washington, DC: Government Printing Office, 1992.
Public Papers of the Presidents of the United States: Jimmy Carter, 1977, Book 1. Washington, DC: Government Printing Office, 1977.
Richter, Linda K. *The Politics of Tourism in Asia*. Honolulu: University of Hawaii Press, 1989.
Rostow, W. W. "Vietnam and Asia." *Diplomatic History* 20, 3 (Summer 1996): 467–71.
Shuster, Alvin. "20 Years Later, Back to Saigon." *Los Angeles Times*. 17 May 1991.
Sillett, Helen, et al., eds. *Moon Metro: Washington, D.C.* Emeryville: Avalon Travel Publishing, 2002.
"Spot the Crime in Vietnam." *Economist*. 3 December 1994.
Storey, Robert, and Daniel Robinson. *Vietnam*. Third Edition. Hawthorn, Victoria: Lonely Planet Publications, 1995.
———. *Vietnam*. Fourth Edition. Hawthorn, Victoria: Lonely Planet Publications, 1997.
Tai, Hue-Tam Ho. "Introduction: Situating Memory." In *The Country of Memory: Remaking the Past in Late Socialist Vietnam,* ed. Hue-Tam Ho Tai. Berkeley: University of California Press, 2001.
"Tourist Numbers Up at HCM City's War Remnants Museum." *Viet Nam News*. 10 February 2003. <vietnnamnews.vnagency.com.vn/2003-02/10/Stories/04.htm>.
Vietnam National Administration of Tourism. *Vietnam Discovery* (February 2002).
———. *Vietnam Discovery* (March 2002).
Vu The Binh, ed. *Vietnam Tourist Guidebook*. First Edition. Hanoi: Vietnam National Administration of Tourism, 1998.
———, ed. *Vietnam Tourist Guidebook*. Third Edition. Hanoi: Vietnam National Administration of Tourism, 2001.
———, ed. *Non Nuoc Viet Nam: Sach Huong Dan Du Lich*. In Lan Thu Bon. Hanoi: Tong Cuc Du Lich Trung Tam Cong Nghe Thong Tin Du Lich, 2002.
Wicker, Tom. "A Theological War." *Diplomatic History* 20, 3 (Summer 1996): 445–49.
Wiltz, Teresa. "The Smithsonian's Military Bearing." *Washington Post*. 23 January 2004.
Yoder, Edwin M., Jr. "A Very Subdued Confession." *Diplomatic History* 20, 3 (Summer 1996): 456–61.
Young, Marilyn B. "The Closest of Hindsight." *Diplomatic History* 20, 3 (Summer 1996): 440–44.

Chapter 6

AMERICANIZED PROTESTS?
The British and West German Protests against Nuclear Weapons and the Pacifist Roots of the West German New Left, 1957–64

Holger Nehring

Since the break-up of the Soviet Union at the beginning of the 1990s, the perception that we live in a "globalized" world has become commonplace. Political and social scientists increasingly discuss the emergence of a "world society."[1] The perception of a globalized world has been particularly pronounced in the area of protest movements. One German newspaper recently described the protesters at an antiwar rally as "global kids."[2] The growth of non-state actors in international relations over the twentieth century is indeed so staggering that the historian Akira Iriye has labelled it the "century of NGOs."[3] While about 135 international non-governmental organizations (INGOs) existed in 1910, the number had grown to 375 in 1930 and to 427 in 1940. Yet, the biggest growth took place during the 1950s and 1960s. In 1950, 755 INGOs operated worldwide, in 1960 there were 1321, and in 1970 some 2296 international non-governmental organizations.[4] The analysis of such non-governmental actors affords unique insights into the workings of "culture" in international history, since the traditional framework of power politics can no longer serve as an adequate analytical tool.

Given the *global* character of these developments, it is surprising to what extent the history of European protest move-

---
Notes for this section begin on page 238.

ments in the post-1945 period has been written from an explicitly or implicitly American perspective. This is particularly true for protest movements in the Federal Republic of Germany: the dominant narrative of the history of these movements in the 1950s and 1960s describes how American forms of protest, stemming mainly from the civil rights movement, slowly gained ground in West Germany and helped to democratize and liberalize its political culture. To a large extent, such research relies on identifying transatlantic networks of student activists.[5] The United States' international hegemony is thus transferred to the politics of protest: the West European, and particularly the West German New Left and their student supporters become an outpost of their American colleagues. Such analyses rest upon a very narrow understanding of the protests of the 1950s and 1960s: they focus on a small group of student activists and assume, rather than prove, their influence.[6] They also concentrate on intellectual discussions, rather than the actual protests, and by and large ignore the contested nature of these debates.

This chapter seeks to decenter this American perspective by focusing on the role of cultural assumptions in the transnational relations between the most important and strongest movements against nuclear weapons during their peak in the late 1950s and early 1960s: the British and West German ones. It highlights the importance of transnational radical pacifist, rather than New Left, networks for the adoption of new forms of protest, such as sit downs, in West Germany, and shows the importance of Britain as a model for West German extra-parliamentary politics in this period. Not least, it demonstrates how contested and difficult the relationship between the two movements was.

Both movements responded to a global problem: the threat of thermonuclear war between the United States and the Soviet Union with weapons far more powerful than those which had annihilated the Japanese cities Hiroshima and Nagasaki at the end of World War II. The movements' responses, however, were not mere reactions to global threats. The different ways in which the protesters perceived the Cold War influenced their actions significantly. But rather than always facilitating their interactions, different cultural norms often hampered mutual understanding. By examining these interactions, this essay provides a snapshot on important precursors to the student protests of the later 1960s.

Historians have come to analyse the student protests in Europe and the United States from a global and transnational perspective.[7] More generally, research on cultural norms has highlighted how important perceptions of "global community" were in twentieth-century international history. Akira Iriye's work, in particular, demonstrates impressively how worldwide cultural norms permeated the framework of nation-states and transcended the "Iron Curtain" between the Western and the Communist world.[8]

Historians of transnational history have often neglected, however, that "culture" does not only facilitate, but may also impede communications across national boundaries.[9] This shortcoming is to a large degree due to a definition of "culture" which already implies the success of transmission processes. According to Akira Iriye's influential definition, "culture in the study of international relations may be defined as the sharing and transmitting of consciousness within and across national boundaries."[10] By drawing on recent social movement theories, this chapter seeks to advance a less straightforward reading of cross-cultural communication processes. It suggests that nuclear bombs were potent symbols for many domestic grievances. The ways in which the protesters defined these grievances depended on national, regional, or even local conditions and were only rarely translated into transnational actions.

Such an approach is based on a more dynamic definition of "culture." "Culture" is not naturally given and universal. Instead, "culture" entails shared meanings and values, which are "produced, exchanged, challenged, and altered by people operating within (and increasingly across) societies."[11] Culture influences actors' cognition by providing rules and models. Conversely, actors use culture to evaluate their environment through norms and values.[12] More recent theoretical analyses of social movements have highlighted the importance of the dynamic character of "culture." Social scientists have emphasized the ways in which social movements define their identity by creating their own cultural norms and expressions in their protest marches, in their writings, and in their symbols. A political crisis—such as the arms race—does not give rise to social movements, rather the perception of the crisis does. Social movement rhetoric is thus not merely the reflection of objective dangers. It also constitutes a specific "framing" of these problems. Framing is a highly complicated process in which current and historical experiences and specific cultural assumptions lead to the definition of problems. Framing processes are primarily acts of communication which are connected to specific audiences and which build on individual motives and commitments.[13]

Such a dynamic definition of "culture" allows us to move beyond the work of those historians and social scientists who have examined the diffusion of ideas between social movements and summarized some of the preconditions for the successful diffusion of ideas. According to Donatella della Porta, three main factors make such a diffusion of ideas between social movements possible: cultural and geographical proximity; shared institutions; and similar conditions in the interacting societies.[14] Yet diffusion theories are based on a very simplistic model of communication which only takes the sender and the receiver of messages into account, but which underestimates the autonomy of the receiver to reject or to reformulate the message. A more dynamic definition of "culture," by contrast, departs from the assumption that cross-cultural communication is extremely difficult. We cannot take its success for granted. And even if it occurs, it may be wrought with misperceptions and misunderstandings.[15] We therefore need to distinguish clearly between a rhetoric which suggests cross-cultural communications and its often more complicated practice. At the same time, we must not discount the possibility that "culture" was indeed defined in terms that transcended national, regional, or local perceptions.

After outlining the history of the protests against nuclear weapons in both countries, this chapter uses these theoretical insights for telling the story of how British and West German activists created and debated culture. Specifically, it investigates the workings of the European Federation against Nuclear Arms (EF), the International Confederation for Disarmament and Peace (ICDP), and the War Resisters' International (WRI) in the late 1950s and early 1960s. The first part traces the development of a global consciousness with regard to the dangers of nuclear weapons in Britain and West Germany up to the early 1960s. The following sections examine the debates within the transnational social space that the British and West German movements created and explore the successes and failures of communication within this transnational sphere. The concluding part makes some suggestions about how the results of this study differentiate our understanding of culture and international history and how they may change our reading of 1960s protest movements.[16] Methodologically, this is not an easy task.

Social movements defy handsome historical classifications. The following remarks therefore concentrate primarily on the interactions of the social movement organizations[17] and thus on the movement elites. Although this procedure leaves out a large number of social actors, it focuses on those who were most active in constructing the transnational society of anti-nuclear weapons protesters.

The Context

Before the concern about nuclear weapons found expression in extra-parliamentary movements in the mid and late 1950s, there was widespread unease all over the world about the potential dangers of nuclear warfare.[18] While atomic weapons had played a role in the works of science fiction, such as H. G. Wells's *The World Set Free* (1914), the dropping of atomic bombs on Hiroshima and Nagasaki by the American air force in early August 1945 turned these hopes and fears into despair. When the Soviet Union announced amid heightening Cold War tensions that it had developed its own atomic device in the late 1940s, the fear of nuclear war became global.[19] Yet concern in most post-war Western societies first focused on social and economic reconstruction.[20] This, together with the burgeoning Cold War, explains why organized protests against nuclear weapons emerged on a larger scale only in the mid 1950s. Then, concerns about fallout from weapons tests and the development of hydrogen bomb technology had heightened the awareness of the dangers of nuclear weapons further. Only with the development, testing, and deployment of hydrogen bombs by the United States, the Soviet Union, and Great Britain, did an awareness emerge that these weapons, when used, could destroy the whole world. Populations across the world felt that Hiroshima could now take place anywhere.[21]

These general developments formed the context in which protest movements against nuclear weapons emerged on a mass scale in Western countries in the late 1950s. Owing to specific political conditions, the movements in Britain and the Federal Republic were particularly strong.[22] In 1958, a group of British intellectuals founded the Campaign for Nuclear Disarmament (CND). CND's initial aim was to persuade the oppositional Labour Party to advocate the unilateral abandonment of nuclear tests and nuclear weapons. The Campaign succeeded various smaller movements that had campaigned against the dangers of nuclear war. The annual fifty-mile march between the British government's nuclear weapons research establishment, Aldermaston, and London, took place for the first time in 1958.[23] It soon became the trademark of the campaign: the protesters walked the whole or parts of the distance, carrying banners, shouting slogans, singing, or in silence in order to voice their opposition to British nuclear weapons. In autumn 1960, a more radical group of activists split off from CND and founded the Committee of 100. It took up the causes of the direct action groups and tapped revived traditions of radical pacifism and anarchism. The Committee of 100 also had some support from the younger New Left, a group which tried to find a way between Communist doctrines and social democratic values.[24]

The West German movement, by contrast, did not originate in a campaign to influence an oppositional Labour Party. It was the attempt by the oppositional Social Democrats and the trade unions to campaign against the Christian Democratic government under Chancellor Konrad Adenauer. This "Campaign against Atomic Death" (Kampagne Kampf dem Atomtod) protested against the Adenauer Government's plans to acquire nuclear-capable equipment of the West German army. It thus continued, on a broader basis, the campaigns against West Germany's conventional rearmament of the early 1950s and against Adenauer's plans.[25] After the SPD had lost several state-level elections and after it had adopted a more moderate party program in 1959, the SPD abandoned the Campaign against Atomic Death. This prompted a group of Hamburg Quakers around the teacher Hans-Konrad Tempel to found a new kind of campaign along British lines, with regular marches as the main focal point. The first of these marches took place in 1960 between Hamburg and the British military base Bergen-Hohne in Lower Saxony. From 1961 onward, there were marches all over West Germany. The protesters soon set up an organization called Easter March of Nuclear Weapons Opponents (Ostermarsch der Atomwaffengegner), which was later renamed Easter Marches—Campaign for Disarmament (Ostermarsch—Kampagne für Abrüstung) and, finally, turned into the Campaign for Democracy and Disarmament (Kampagne für Demokratie und Abrüstung). In the mid and late 1960s, the Easter Marches became a focus for the protests against the American military intervention in Vietnam and for parts of the student protests. Thus, unlike in Britain, there existed a direct continuity between

Figure 6.1
Easter March Bergen-Hohne Hamburg, 1961 (www.archivaktiv.org)

these protests against nuclear weapons and the extraparliamentary student protests in 1967–68.[26]

The Rhetoric of Internationalism

The fear and despair voiced in these movements were coupled with hopes for a lessening of Cold War tensions. These hopes found their expression in a language of global human brotherhood and community in both countries. National and international movements employed a language of "global community." This rhetoric identified the aims of the movements as the common cause of humankind. Protesters thus became part of a global family. Although protesters employed these arguments in both countries, they tapped different cultural traditions and assumptions.

The resurgence of ideas for "One World" during and immediately after the Second World War formed part of the international and intellectual background for this rhetoric. The idea of a global community had existed for a long time, but it had gained new significance during the Second World War, particularly in the United States. In 1941, Henry Luce, celebrating American efforts to achieve such a "global community," had written, "our world ... is one world, fundamentally indivisible."[27] This vision of "one world" took on a new importance with the advent of the nuclear age in weapons technology. In a collection of essays entitled *One World or None,* published in 1946, famous scientists warned that the only way to prevent nuclear war was by founding an international agency. The physicist Robert Oppenheimer claimed that "the common interest of all in the prevention of nuclear warfare would seem immensely to overshadow any purely national interest, whether of welfare or of security."[28]

This language of global community soon entered the statements of the anti-nuclear weapons movements all over the world. The philosopher Bertrand Russell, later President of the British CND and of the Committee of 100, appealed to his BBC audience in a radio broadcast on 23 December 1954: "Remember your humanity, and forget the rest. If you can do so, the way lies open to a new Paradise; if you cannot, nothing lies before you, but universal death."[29] At a conference organized by the pacifist War Resisters Resisters' International (WRI), the Canadian pacifist F. C. Hunnius proclaimed, "history today is world history. It affects every man, woman and child."[30] Consequently, pacifists argued for the abandonment of power politics and the adoption of "an idea and a philosophy of life."[31] Similarly, CND stated in its charter that it was concerned with "the common cause of mankind,"[32] and the British writer Robert Bolt concluded that "the brotherhood of man is no longer a notion, it's here."[33] Characteristically

Figure 6.2
CND sign.
(www.mdwg.org.uk)

blending the personal, national, and global spheres, a CND broadsheet proclaimed, "it matters to you and yours. To the present and the future. To Britain and the whole human race." The text continued: "Let's recognise the threat to all of us, like an invasion from Mars or a comet heading smack for the earth."[34] In their call for support for the Committee of 100, the octogenarian philosopher Bertrand Russell and the Rev. Michael Scott, a prominent British pacifist, demanded a "new realisation of the common destinies of the human family."[35] In one of the most popular songs sung at the annual British Easter Marches, the marchers declared, blending socialist and Christian languages of human brotherhood and socialist fraternity:

> I belong to a family, the biggest on earth ...
> I've got a sister in Melbourne, a brother in Paree
>   The whole wide world is dad and mother to me.
> Wherever you turn you will find my kin
>   Whatever the creed, or the colour of the skin.[36]

Despite this identification with a global community, most British protesters did not become internationalists. They continued to advocate nuclear disarmament as a specifically national policy. Some protesters regarded it as a way of maintaining British prowess in international affairs without nuclear weapons. Others saw nuclear disarmament as a beacon for the disintegrating British Empire, as a way through which Britain could show moral leadership: "Lift up your heads and be proud," a group of waiting supporters proclaimed through a loudspeaker on the first Aldermaston March in 1958: "The lead has been given to the English people. Britain must take up that lead in the world. 'England, arise, the long, long night is over.'"[37]

We can also find this language of a global community in West Germany. Like their British counterparts, West German activists referred to the interests of "humanity," defined as a single, undifferentiated entity. Yet, the protesters confronted a difficult situation in the Federal Republic. More than in other countries, "peace" had the reputation of being a term of communist propaganda. The German Democratic Republic and the Soviet Union tried to suggest to the West German population that the Adenauer government was militarist, whereas the countries of the Eastern bloc formed part of a peace camp.[38] Even some West German peace activists were therefore concerned that those who used the rhetoric of "peace," in reality "wanted to serve a political, sometimes even a military power."[39] Only tentatively, and much more hesitantly than in Britain, did non-Communist groups emerge which advocated "peaceful co-existence," first in the tradition of neutralist thinking,[40] then increasingly in the context of the emerging New Left.[41]

The language that West German protesters used was far more dramatic than that of their British counterparts. Where the British protesters campaigned for "unilateral disarmament," the West Germans stood up against "annihilation" and "atomic death," and for "naked existence."[42] This made their calls for "human brotherhood" and "global community" even more emphatic. Nevertheless, West German pacifists did not give up their identification with the West German nation. They remained concerned with the problem of German division; and most of them did not envision a world without nation-states.[43]

Figure 6.3

Easter March badge, 1962. Haus der Geschichte der Bundesrepublik Deutschland, Bonn, Germany. (www.dhm.de/lemo//objekte/pict/ NeueHerausforderungen_ buttonOstermarsch/index.html)

This language of a global community of humankind had two functions in West German discussions. By identifying the issue of "peace" with "brotherhood," "family," and belonging, the protesters tried to create a feeling of community against their governments, which they accused of seeking to destroy that community. More specifically, this language served to normalize social relations in West Germany after the horrors of World War II: it was meant to make horrors of the Second World War, which many had experienced at home and on the battlefield, disappear. By applying the values of the family to public affairs, they sought to keep the experiences of violence private.[44]

At the same time, this talk about human brotherhood fulfilled a redemptory function in West German public discourse: by appealing to the global community of humankind, the West German protesters sought to recreate the West German population as equals within the post-World War II world community, despite the heinous crimes which had been committed on German soil and by Germans during the National Socialist regime. The focus on the possible destruction of humankind by nuclear weapons shifted attention away from the genocide committed in the German name.[45]

In both countries, the languages of "global community" and "human brotherhood," therefore, had very specific national overtones, although they purported to transcend the framework of the nation-state. Activists at the time realised this.[46] This language was not a mere representation of historical reality, but it served specific functions. It was an attempt by the British and West German movements to build their own collective identities. First, internally, this rhetoric served to integrate the different movements into one movement.[47] Second, externally, it demonstrated strength by highlighting the transnational character of the protests.[48] Social movements, in particular, need to employ such rhetoric to maintain support as they are rather loosely structured and mostly lack hierarchies. At the same time, the movement elites do not have access to sanctioning mechanisms since they do not normally know formal membership.[49] The non-political and essentially moral character of this rhetoric was of great importance. It allowed the British and West German movements to bridge traditional political cleavages. It also made it possible to transcend those political differences which had emerged during the Cold War between communists and non-communists. And it was intimately connected to the aims of the movements to transcend the Cold War framework and to start the reconstruction of domestic societies under new auspices.

Culture and the Problems of Communication

The specific national aims and the functions that the language of global community had for the national movements suggest that cross-cultural communications between the British and West German movements was rather cumbersome. We will now see that national cultural traditions made the cooperation between the two movements often difficult, if not impossible. It appears that, during the Cold War, it was extremely difficult to set up new transnational peace organizations. This was partly due to the ideological ambiguities of the word "peace," which had become a propaganda term of the Soviet Union and its satellites. And it was due to the manifold political differences arising from the problem of coping with this situation. But we will also discover that, under certain conditions, cross-cultural communication could indeed take place, leading to the formation of a transnational social space which did not coincide with geographical boundaries.

Links between the British and West German "old" Left, the West German Social Democrats, and the British Labour Party were also wrought with difficulties. While the SPD campaigned against nuclear weapons in 1958–59, the Labour Party's official policy was in line with the British government's policy on nuclear weapons. This led to serious misunderstandings and disagreements among the two parties, making the coordination of activities impossible. Although the British and West German parties' executives agreed on the importance of multilateral efforts for disarmament, the term had different implications in each national context. This, in turn, led to different attitudes toward the protests. In Britain, the Labour executive's emphasis on *multi*lateral disarmament was diametrically opposed to CND's agenda of *uni*lateral nuclear disarmament. In the Federal Republic, the SPD's attitude toward multilateral disarmament in general and the arming of the Bundeswehr (Federal Army) with nuclear-capable equipment meant a general opposition to Adenauer's "policy of strength" and motivated the party to initiate its own protest organization, the Campaign against Atomic Death.[50] Thus, the contacts between the British and West German movements—apart from exchanging a few speakers and marchers—remained rare at the beginning when the SPD ran the campaign in West Germany.

The West German campaign headquarters did not even seem to have been aware of the existence of a counterpart in Britain until the summer of 1958, almost half a year after both campaigns had been founded. Thus, when the SPD-run campaign received a letter from the British CND asking for some information about the venture, the West German campaign office tried to gain information about its counterpart's credentials by writing to the International Department of the Labour Party. But the Labour Party was not keen to help since CND Transport House, the Labour Headquarters, regarded it as a divisive force. As a result, the Party warned the SPD to avoid cooperation. The SPD, in turn, classified CND as Communist.[51]

There existed also more fundamental reasons for why the cooperation between the two social-democratic parties was so cumbersome. Labour politicians had repeatedly put forward plans for a nuclear-free zone in Europe. The SPD felt increasingly embarrassed by these plans, as governments in the Eastern bloc had voiced similar proposals, particularly the Ulbricht regime in the German Democratic Republic. Moreover, the Labour Executive continued to allow Labour Members of Parliament (MPs) to visit Eastern bloc countries without reprimand, despite repeated requests by the SPD to take action against the left-wing MPs. The visits represented a welcome piece of propaganda which the Adenauer government could use against the SPD.[52]

The British and West German New Left, both active in the anti-nuclear weapons movements, were similarly unsuccessful in forming transnational links, although they aimed to bridge the two camps in the Cold War. In contrast to many neutralists in other countries, the New Left linked such proposals with demands for radical domestic social reforms in order to establish a socialist society.[53] Curiously, the protagonists of the British New Left took little interest in the activities of the West German movement. There were no reports on developments in the Federal Republic in the British *New Left Review*, the leading New Left journal.[54] Leading members of the British New Left complained about the "confusion" in international affairs and about the fact that "too many of our people regard these as personal contacts only," with the result that "we learn about what they say only in chance remarks and gossip."[55]

Personal links between the British and the West German New Left were virtually non-existent at the time, as the West German New Left was only emerging as a political force. Closely linked to the growing Easter Marches but grouped around the Socialist German Student Federation (Sozialistischer Deutscher Studentenbund, or SDS), the West German New Left showed a keen interest in British New Left ideas. But the mutual relationship was by far not as strong as the one between the British and the French New Left.[56] The conditions in the two countries and their cultural assumptions were too different. The British New Left had two main strands. The first had emerged around a group of socialist students in Oxford. The second was based primarily in Northern England and consisted of former members of the Communist Party. They had left the Communist Party in protest against the lack of internal discussion of the consequences of Khrushchev's Secret Speech (1956) which had revealed the horrors of the Stalinist purges in the 1930s, and in disgust about the Soviet invasion of Hungary in autumn

1956. The members of the West German New Left, by contrast, had been close to the SPD before, but were expelled from the party when they refused to support a more reformist party program.

The British and West German activists soon sought to found movements whose reach went beyond the national boundaries. Thus, in 1959 a group of West German and British protesters founded the European Federation against Nuclear Arms (EF). The Federation rapidly incorporated movements from other European countries as well, and in 1963–64 it was refounded as the International Confederation for Disarmament and Peace (ICDP) with a worldwide scope. The founders intended the ICDP to be the democratic equivalent of the communist World Peace Council.

These two transnational bodies never assumed a significant role for the communications between the British and West German movements. They did not even have enough funds to support a propaganda campaign which went beyond national boundaries. It was very difficult for the various national member movements to agree on common aims, especially since many national movements had difficulties finding a consensus at home. Discussions were hampered by serious misunderstandings, by a degree of ignorance of the conditions in the other country, and, finally, by the denial that these problems existed at all. Also, communication was by and large a one-way process: the British movement showed even less interest in trying to establish contacts to other anti-nuclear weapons movements than that of West Germany. The different national cultures of the Cold War prevented more thorough and wide-ranging discussions.

Significantly, the first West German movement which established links to CND was not the SPD-run Campaign against Atomic Death, but the Munich Committee against Nuclear Armaments (Komitee gegen Atomrüstung). This Committee was run by the German writer and intellectual Hans Werner Richter, founder of the Gruppe 47, the most important literary circle in post-World War II West Germany.[57] The Munich group was, as far as its social structure and organization were concerned, very similar to CND. It consisted mainly of intellectuals, it was governed by a committee structure, and it was, like the CND executive, initially not very keen on street protests. Instead, it emphasized the education of the public.[58]

Richter established first contacts to the president of CND, Bertrand Russell, through a British journalist he knew from one of the Gruppe 47 conferences.[59] Yet, even these contacts between two organizations with a very similar outlook—except for unilateralism, which the Munich Committee did not regard as problematic—did not lead to the establishment of a transnational community of protesters. Different cultural assumptions about movement aims prevented any such cooperation.

Richter, together with Collins, initiated the EF in London and Frankfurt in early 1959. Its aims were to prevent nuclear proliferation, to achieve general nuclear disarmament, and to campaign for the civilian use of atomic energy. The London headquarters of the Federation would coordinate joint campaigns in the future.[60] In striking contrast to its rhetoric of a "world community," there was unanimity at EF meetings that the Federation should *not* undermine the national position of the individual movements and should instead be sensitive toward different national issues: the EF was not allowed to interfere into the national campaign efforts and was not even allowed to produce statements which went beyond what had been agreed on the national level. Richter himself regarded the Federation as an answer to the alliance of nuclear powers. It is also striking that he, like others, used the traditional language of diplomacy rather than arguing for a global society without states.[61]

Fundamental disagreements about the aims and the purpose of the campaign impeded its activities greatly. Most importantly, the British and West German groups could not agree on a common policy toward the Communist World Peace Council. Different cultural assumptions about communism prevented any concurrence. British activists could voice sympathies toward policies advocated by the World Peace Council (WPC) relatively freely without endangering their cause. Due to the staunchly anti-communist political culture in the Federal Republic, West German protesters, by contrast, risked discrediting their whole campaign if they endorsed any of the WPC's aims.[62]

Although Hans Werner Richter's attitude was characterized by a relatively large degree of tolerance toward the GDR's and the Soviet Union's foreign policies, the building of the Berlin Wall in August 1961 shattered his hopes of peaceful change from Stalinism toward socialist democracy in the East. With the backing of his Munich Committee, Richter then withdrew his support from Canon Collins's plans for a joint conference with the WPC.[63] With Hans Werner Richter's support gone, there were no potent West German groups willing to support the EF.

When delegates of eighteen nations gathered in Oxford in January 1963 to found a worldwide successor organization for the European Federation, West German delegates played hardly any role.[64] The idea for founding this International Confederation for Disarmament and Peace (ICDP) had come from Canon Collins. He had hoped that such an organization would offer a democratic alternative to the communist WPC, while at the same time serving as a forum for discussions with the WPC. The ICDP's aims reflected this thinking. The Confederation sought "to demand and foster a fundamentally new way of thinking and to use new forces and means to counter the arms race in order to build an international community of values"[65] and thus to build a new "Peace International."[66] Yet even the ICDP's program stated that the "different views and sovereignty of the member organisations should not be infringed."[67]

Communication or even cooperation with the WPC was, however, unacceptable to the West German delegates. Due to the anti-communist political climate in the Federal Republic, the West German delegates felt unable to support these aims. For similar domestic political reasons, the American delegation did also not accept the invitation of WPC delegates.[68] From its inception, the ICDP therefore lacked the firm support of the most powerful anti-nuclear weapons movements at the time.

Very few conferences took place in the future,[69] and the ICDP's main role lay in informing its members of the activities of other movements.[70] It produced a quarterly newsletter which was sent out to the membership organizations. Since ICDP's offices were in London and many of the organizing staff, among them CND organizer Peggy Duff, were linked to CND, the ICDP served effectively as the international office of the British Campaign. Although CND was itself instrumental in founding and running ICDP, its approach to the latter was rather insular, as some of its own supporters pointed out.[71]

Communication as Observation: Pacifism, Emotions and Non-Violence

Much more important for the communication between the British and the West German movements than the newly founded transnational bodies EF and the ICDP was the War Resisters' International (WRI), which was able to provide the resources, logistics, and organization. It was mainly through the links of this organization that forms of protest, information about other campaigns, and ideas were transferred from one country to the other. The story of Anglo-German cooperation within the WRI shows that cross-cultural communication only worked when the discussants shared common cultural traditions. The traditions of radical, non-violent pacifism, which the WRI embodied, allowed West German and British activists to understand each other's motives. In the case of the WRI, communications were further facilitated by the existence of an institution which had existed since the 1920s. Common cultural traditions and institutions thus contributed to the emergence of a transnational social space of anti-nuclear weapons protesters.

The term "transnational social space" comes from anthropological and sociological migration studies. It addresses the problem that geographical spaces and the spaces for social interactions are not always identical.[72] The sociologist Ludger Pries has developed the concept of "transnational social spaces" in order to take account of the links between migrant communities which cross national boundaries. He defines such spaces as stable, intensive, and often circular interactions of all kind beyond national boundaries.[73] Such spaces do not just exist. People have to create them and they do so on the basis of specific cultural norms. This chapter thus seeks to stress the ways in which people create culture through their actions. These actions are not always framed in ways that transcend the national, regional, or even local context.[74] Transnational social spaces are, therefore, not characterized by the harmony of an international community, but by multiple conflicts between different actors over social, cultural, and political aspects of their joint campaign.[75] It is primarily created through intensive communication across national boundaries.

The traditions of radical pacifism which the WRI embodied seemed to offer a neutral framework for exchange and interaction. Kees Boeke and others founded the WRI in 1921 under the name "Paco" ("peace," in Esperanto) in the Netherlands. In 1923, the secretariat moved to Enfield, London, and the organization changed its name to "War Resisters' International."[76] During the 1920s and 1930s, the WRI was primarily concerned with assisting conscientious objectors. In the 1950s and 1960s, however, it became the central place for exchanging ideas about non-violent civil disobedience and non-violent direct action. It thus linked the American civil rights movement to the West European peace and anti-nuclear weapons campaigns even before the student protests and anti-Vietnam protests had developed. And it proved an important forum in which European peace movements could rediscover their own traditions of non-violent protest.

An examination of the connections between the British and West German nuclear weapons activists shows that the adoption of protest forms linked to direct action by the student protesters cannot be understood without reference to the WRI channels. Attributing the transfer of ideas simply to personal contacts between the West German and American student protesters does not suffice.[77] To be sure, there were debates within the WRI framework on how the different national movement should be represented at a transnational level, about the ways in which votes should be taken, and other such matters. But the fact that the basic rules had already been established gave the discussions a different character. Rather than evolving around the establishment of certain norms and rules, they tailored the modification of these rules to fit the developing interests of the member organizations.[78] These discussions, however, were nothing special. They were part of the committee work on a national level as well.[79]

The WRI was so efficient because its organization, conferences, summer schools, and seminars were already in place. Moreover, it was able to draw from various national traditions of protest, mainly in the pacifist and socialist fields, but also in connection to youth and life reform movements. As these traditions had lain dormant in West Germany during the Nazi dictatorship and since West Germany lacked an independent socialist grouping left of the SPD, the WRI connections had a far greater impact on the West German movement than it had on the British movement.

WRI conferences, workshops, and summer schools not only opened up a transnational social space by serving as exchanges for the dissemination of ideas and for making personal contacts. They were also chosen with an eye to "socialising." The WRI's Triennial Conferences, for example, offered four o'clock tea for selected delegates.[80] Before the conferences, elaborate discussions took place regarding the questions in which country and at what location the meeting or workshop was to take place. The 1957 Triennial Conference, for example, took place at the Froebel Institute for Education, a leading life-reform school in Roehampton near London. When the WRI's West German section, which was involved with planning a WRI study conference for 1964, suggested either Hamburg or the north German town Bückeburg as suitable locations, the WRI was disappointed. While the West Germans argued that it was much cheaper than the WRI secretary's first choice Berlin, WRI thought that Hamburg, was "too crowded," and Bückeburg was not good since it was "from a holiday point of view ... most uninteresting." Finally, Offenbach was chosen as a suitable location because it was close to Frankfurt but, at the same time, offered some natural environment for relaxation.[81] Often, national groups suggested conference venues because of their symbolic value. In autumn 1960, West German activists suggested holding the next annual summer school in Poland and asked the WRI to plan such a conference. Such a summer school, they hoped, would counter one of the most powerful arguments against the West German peace protesters: that the Easter Marches were not allowed to protest against the aggressive policies of the Soviet Union. In addition, such a conference would signal support for the "neutralist" policies, put forward by the Polish foreign minister Rapacki in the late 1950s.[82]

Much more efficiently than the EF and the ICDP, the WRI was able to distribute information through its West German branches, which, up to that point, had been primarily concerned with issues of conscientious objection: the WRI's German branch (Internationale der Kriegsdienstgegner—Deutscher Zweig, or IdK) and, from the early 1960s, the Association of Conscientious Objectors (Verband der Kriegsdienstverweigerer, or VK). These communication resources were crucial for the WRI's success. Unlike the European Federation and the ICDP, the WRI was able, through its affiliated movements, to communicate common aims effectively and efficiently. This was an important precondition for the mutual awareness of the movements and for formulating perspectives which went beyond the national framework. The WRI's publications carried reports from conferences, advice on reading, and registration forms for conferences in a form which was accessible to all supporters. In particular, the IdK and VK publications could tap the particular West German and British conditions by relying on local authors who translated the message into the local political climate and protest traditions.[83] Equally, British journals such as *Peace News* and, later, the CND's journal, *Sanity,* carried articles on campaigns abroad.

It was through the WRI's Triennial Conferences that the networks were built that gave rise to the idea that a West German Easter March could travel from Britain to West Germany. The links between the future organizers of the Easter March, Hans-Konrad Tempel, and his future wife, Helga Stolle, started in the early 1950s. Tempel had been involved in discussion circles on the application of Gandhian methods of civil disobedience in Hamburg since the early 1950s as well as in the local war resisters' organization. He was also active in the protests against conventional West German rearmament and in the neutralist All German People's Party (Gesamtdeutsche Volkspartei). At the WRI's eighth Triennial Conference in Paris in July 1954, Tempel became acquainted with activists from the British peace movement, such as Stuart Morris and Fenner Brockway and the later founder of the French New Left, Claude Bourdet.[84] Activists, such as Andreas Buro, who were later instrumental in turning the Easter Marches from moral protests into the crucible of the New Left, were present at these WRI conferences.

The conferences not only contributed to the formation of a transnational network of protesters, but they were also instrumental in allowing communication within the national movements by bringing the dispersed activities of the West German movement together. At the 1954 conference, Tempel met Ingeborg Küster, the later organizer of the Munich Easter Marches.[85] The circles around the WRI and its West German branches were also important in linking the Hamburg group which organized the first Easter Marches to a wider circle around Andreas Buro, then an official in the youth department at the Kassel city council.[86] Through his job, Buro, in turn, was in touch with various groups around the emerging New Left in West Germany, such as Klaus Vack of the youth organization Friends of Nature (Naturfreundejugend) and Herbert Faller of the socialist youth organization Socialist Youth—The Falcons (Sozialistische Jugend—Die Falken), which had both been linked to the SPD in the 1920s.[87] Vack himself, through his activities in the local branch of a conscientious objectors' association, became involved in the WRI later on.[88]

The conferences were also important in dispersing the theory of a "third camp," one of the central tenets of the British and West German New Left, among peace movements all over the world. At the 1954 conference, the American pacifist A. J. Muste gave a paper in which he linked the necessity for a Third Camp between the superpowers with the need for nonviolent forms of protest. Defining the polarization of power as the main problem of the time, he suggested that the "Third

Camp" could signify "a new way of life" and herald "a new socio-economic regime" in international relations which was "more genuinely fraternal and cooperative."[89] Particularly in Britain and West Germany, the conferences thus created the condition for the popularity of these ideas in a setting that was immune from Cold War suspicions: radical pacifism. When the dynamic of the Cold War seemed to be broken with Khrushchev's confessions of Stalinists sins at the twentieth congress of the Soviet Communist Party in spring 1956, when the British and French Suez invasion failed due to lack of American support for the operation, and when the coup in Hungary in 1956 signalled some movement in the Eastern bloc, this ideology spread more widely than the original teachings of the New Left, which had developed around Communist dissidents and dissatisfied Labour supporters.

In West Germany, this process began later. The fact that West Germany was a frontline state in Cold War made it harder for protesters and the population at large to perceive the changes in the Eastern bloc. Also, the Communist Party had been banned before the processes of disassociation could take off during 1956. The SPD was still riding a course of fierce opposition to the policies of the Christian Democratic Adenauer government. The conditions for the emergence of an independent socialist left outside the SPD only emerged after the dissatisfaction with the SPD had risen in the wake of Godesberg in 1959, after the student association SDS had been expelled from the party in 1961, and after the building of the Berlin Wall in August 1961 appeared to have cast German division in stone.

The Easter Marches soon turned into crucibles in which these groups of the "homeless left" met with the pacifist groups. Pacifist and socialist traditions thus creatively merged and developed further.[90] Buro, the future press secretary of the Easter Marches as well as Vack, now the campaign's organizing secretary, participated regularly in the triennial conferences, study conferences, workshops, and summer schools that the WRI organized.[91] West German activists first discussed the idea of internationalizing the marches first at the 1962 Study Conference in Denmark—and this although communication was hampered by the insufficient English language skills of one of the organizers, as he himself admitted.[92]

At the WRI conferences, activists from the American civil rights movements acquainted West Europeans with the practice of Gandhian-type civil disobedience, thus reinvigorating the theoretical discussions about these forms of protest, whose origins can be traced back to the 1920s. The 1957 conference in London was attended by Bayard Rustin, the future organizer of Martin Luther King's civil disobedience campaigns in the United States, and by the future activists of the Committee of 100, such as Christopher Farley, who were the first to transfer sit-downs and the occupation of military bases and government buildings systemically in a Western European setting.[93]

While particularly those groups who belonged to the anti-authoritarian wing of the emerging New Left and student movement adopted and adapted these protest forms, those with closer links to the Labour movement doubted the viability of a "non-violent society." Before the study conference in Offenbach in summer 1964, for example, an elaborate discussion took place between the WRI secretariat and the West German organizers. While the WRI was interested in debating the relevance of non-violence as a protest form and a way of life as well as its role in military defence, the West Germans preferred the title "Strategies of Political Pacifism." They feared that non-violence constituted too narrow a theme.[94]

Nevertheless, the conference went ahead with a program and with an impressive array of speakers ranging from the British pacifist April Carter to the West German left-wing intellectual Ossip K. Flechtheim, all of whom stressed non-violent direct action as a form of protest. The participants discussed topics such as non-violence as a means for the "creative solution of conflicts" as well as a means of civilian defence. Due to its proximity to Frankfurt, the conference was well attended by members of the Frankfurt SDS, one of the centers of the student association.[95]

The WRI not only helped the emergence of a transnational social space of anti-nuclear weapons protesters directly. The organization also contributed to its emergence in more indirect ways. Through the WRI secretary, Tony Smythe, there existed a strong connection between the Committee of 100 and the WRI. In 1962, Smythe used the WRI machinery to advertise for a conference which should bring about an "Anti-war International," based on civil disobedience and direct action on an international scale. The conference was organized with the help of the Dutch radical pacifists around the Comite 1952 voor de Vrede and the Japanese socialist student group Zengakuren. The West German student association SDS and the Dutch anarchists De Vrije were among its supporters.[96] Activists discussed methods of direct action and civil disobedience in some detail, even before the SDS activists had actively engaged with Martin Luther King's civil disobedience campaign in the United States.[97] A follow-up conference took place in Amsterdam at the end of February 1963.[98]

The conferences were mostly movement-elite and middle-class affairs. The costs of travelling at the time were still significant and at least a rudimentary knowledge of foreign languages was required. Some of the conferences took place on weekends, but most of the Triennial Conferences, summer schools, and study conferences lasted for five days, an entire week, or longer. They required both a high level of interest and commitment and the possibility to take time off from work. Although these conferences mainly took place in the summer months, it is probable that they primarily appealed to full-time activists, students, academics, and others who could afford the time and the money.[99]

It would nevertheless be wrong to conclude that these conferences were insignificant just because only a small fraction of activists took part in them. Rather, these activists acted as messengers of information in their local war resisters', Easter March, or student movement groups. They wrote articles in the relevant journals and thus helped to spread the information. This aspect becomes particularly obvious when considering the ways in which the WRI facilitated private contacts between protest movements in different countries. It supported the exchange of marchers, often through local affiliates.[100] It also assisted with supplying pictures for local exhibition and the dissemination of British marching songs to West Germany.[101] In 1964, the organizing secretary approached the WRI secretariat to establish a link to the American WRI section in order to discuss a visit of Martin Luther King to West Germany.[102]

In Britain, these radical pacifist groups only played a marginal role within the movement. The majority of those involved in CND and the British public did not regard the Committee of 100 as a respectable movement. It could never get beyond the status of a fringe group.[103] In West Germany, by contrast, the observation of the Committee of 100 helped West German activists to rediscover their own national protest traditions. These traditions initially had nothing to do with the Marxism of the Frankfurt School, but rather with the writings of the Indian Mahatma Gandhi and the American writer Henry David Thoreau. Radical German pacifists had discussed their ideas of non-violent civil disobedience since the 1920s. But the transnational social space around the WRI which developed in the late 1950s secured an audience for these ideas, which went beyond the peace protesters. Protest communication worked best through emotions. The WRI's ideas appealed to the West German protesters in search for new forms of protest through their emphasis on human solidarity, on actions, and on emotions, rather than through their precise political message. When the West German student protesters in the late 1960s resorted to campaigns of non-violent civil disobedience, to sit-downs and occupations of buildings, this was not so much due to a simple diffusion of ideas from the United States to West Germany. It was rather because the protesters in the early 1960s had managed to broaden the appeal of radical pacifism. The language of pacifist brotherhood and not the political rationality of socialism was at the root of West German extraparliamentary protests in the 1960s.[104]

As one of the speakers at a WRI conference elaborated, the transnational social space worked best not in the realm of ideas and conferences: "Co-operation works best on the basis of action rather than that of exchange of ideas or on the day-to-day work."[105] It was primarily through the WRI network that the long American-European march from San Francisco to Moscow in 1960–61 could take place. Its aim was to symbolize the importance of cooperation among the different peace movements and to demonstrate the global nature of the protests against nuclear weapons.[106] Other international initiatives included the establishment of an International Peace Brigade which was supposed to provide non-violent solutions to conflicts all over the world[107] and a "peace walk" from Vancouver to Berlin in 1964.[108]

Communications between the British and West German movements were more complex than most of the research on culture and international history has assumed. Common actions and the emotions generated on protest marches achieved much more for the emergence of a transnational social space. Cultural assumptions and ideas drove the national groups apart as they were deeply embedded into perceptions of different political, social, and cultural contexts. And the groups who agreed on the ideas of radical pacifism around which the WRI was based were rather small. What was far more important was the observation among the activists that they were not alone and that they were united along a common cause when marching together. The moral rhetoric of a world community and human brotherhood is the expression of this feeling. Communications between the two movements mostly took the form of mutual observation. These mutual observations served as powerful arguments. They demonstrated to the national publics that the protesters expressed the interests of people all over the world, and they also motivated their supporters.[109]

This internationalization was, by and large, symbolic. It was in the field of symbolic actions that the international links worked best.[110] As one activist put it at the time, internationalized marches "gave a powerful impression of solidarity and unity without much conscious liaison having been attempted."[111] Taken as a whole, the annual Marches at Easter, although held nationally in Britain, West Germany, and other West European countries, demonstrated the peaceful intentions of one's own nation toward others. Their immediate goals related to the national situation, yet the aims of ending the proliferation of nuclear weapons, ending the Cold War, and thus "halting and decreasing the militarisation of public life" were formulated as international aims. They found their practical expression in border meetings and the exchange of delegations.[112] Moreover, the information bulletins and personal meetings acquainted the West German activists in particular with new forms of protest: non-violent direct action "as the way in which peoples can defend their values and their way of life" and thus achieve "our ultimate aim[:] ... the elimination of violence from society."[113]

These exchanges were also important for making international symbols accessible to the various national movements. It was through the exchange of delegations and marchers as well as through the journals of the national peace movements that the symbol found its way into peace campaigns around the world. The sign was developed by a British artist from the "N" and the "D" in the semaphore alphabet (for nuclear disarmament), surrounded by a ring (figure 6.2). The ring was alternatively interpreted as signifying an "unborn child," the semaphore letters as a bent cross symbolising the "death of man."[114]

It is quite telling in this context, that the symbol of the EF, a kind of sun symbol, never found widespread acceptance beyond the immediate EF circles. The CND symbol, by contrast, could be found on West German Easter Marches since 1961. It made its way onto flyers and pamphlets from about 1962 or

1963 onward.[115] There also existed a demand for iconic figures. For example, the secretary of the Offenbach branch of the Verband der Kriegsdienstverweigerer was interested in obtaining a signed portrait of Bertrand Russell as a present for an old member. The former President of CND had become an icon for the global anti-nuclear weapons movements when he was arrested at a sit-down in the early 1960s.[116] Cross-cultural communication took place on a largely symbolic level, rather than on the level of the exchange of ideas. Yet this does not mean that it was not important. Communication through symbols and mutual observation was a part of movement politics, as it established the specific identities of the movements at once within and across national boundaries.

During the marches, however, the protesters never shed their national identities entirely. Even though their aim was to show the international character of the protest, instead of choosing to march in one column without any national symbols, the different groups were organized according to nationalities. The marchers continued to perceive of themselves in terms of national identities, thus mirroring a world divided into different states rather than a "global community" as such.[117] The activists realized themselves that the international movement would be meaningless without the national movements.[118] The activists themselves were very much aware of the many differences between the national movements. The more astute contemporary observers concluded that "non-violent resistance begins in one's own country."[119] In the same vein, the historian and New Left activist E. P. Thompson concluded that "internationalisation" should not imply the work of a "translation agency." Instead, it should establish a "discourse in which we participate."[120]

The discourses E. P. Thompson referred to did not always take place in face-to-face meetings or in correspondence between activists from different countries. They were mainly concerned with the emergence of a perception that protesters in different countries belonged together. The basis of this perception lay in the emotions that the language of "human brotherhood," outlined at the beginning of this chapter, and common actions could engender. And it could also be found in the mutual observation of the British and West German movements: for both movements, cross-cultural communication was primarily observation. Where communication took the form of mutual observation and where a fundamental agreement on cultural norms existed, such as in the networks linked to the WRI, cross-cultural communication succeeded, and the activists managed to create a transnational social space. Whenever activists tried to generate a common political message, such as in the EF and ICDP, it failed.

Historians who have assumed an "Americanization" of West German protests have not paid sufficient attention to the contested nature of transnational movement politics and have focused on specific intellectual voices that suggest a coherence which did not exist. Scholars have taken contemporary rhetoric for granted and have thus reproduced perceptions of the time, which defined "Americanism" as related to "mass society," "consumer society," and the "politics of the young."[121] Indeed, the "Americanization" paradigm appears to reflect more the fascinations, wishes, and dreams of a minority of activists and the assessment of the protests by some observers, rather than historical reality. These historians have identified the most prolific writers among the activists, but neglected the many seemingly voiceless local, regional, and national organizers who came to the protests through pacifist and Labour movement networks.

Concluding Remarks

The picture that emerges from this account is doubly paradoxical. First, the internationalist rhetoric of these movements and their organizational structures seemed to suggest successful cross-cultural communication between the two movements. But rhetoric did not reflect the conflictual reality. This, in itself, was not unusual. Even the national movements had problems defining a common agenda and their aims and strategies were constantly discussed while the British and West German activists sought to frame the problem of nuclear weapons with regard to the national contexts. The differences of national traditions of protests in general and the different effects the Cold War had on British and West German society, however, proved to be insurmountable obstacles on a transnational level in finding a common agenda and made it virtually impossible to set up new effective associations.

Second, the transnational relations between the two movements were nevertheless important. British and West German activists set up a transnational social space around the more traditionally pacifist organization of the WRI. As an extension of domestic networks of activists, the WRI proved very important for the domestic social movements and, indeed, for domestic social developments as a whole. While newly established groups such as the EF and ICDP were unable to cope with these differences under the pressures from the Cold War, the pacifist WRI managed to unite the different strands. This was not only because of the WRI's organizational and institutional capital, but also due to the fact that radical pacifism with its focus on superficially non-political issues like non-violence was able to unite disparate groups. Not least, the WRI was successful because it had well-established channels of communication. It also emphasised the importance of emotions and actions rather than ideas. WRI could thus avoid the acrimonious debates from which both the European Federation and the ICDP suffered.

This pacifist link was more important in West Germany than in Britain. Due to the constant competition between the GDR and the Federal Republic, the borderlines of what was acceptable and what was feasible were particularly narrow for the Left. In this scenario, the pacifist link was instrumental in helping the New Left to emerge. It was, at first, a network of activists and developed into a forum for theoretical discussion only during the mid 1960s. Many of the student protesters first came in contact with protest forms from Britain and the United States through the national pacifist networks such as the German branch of the WRI. The WRI contacts opened up the transnational social space in the first place. In conjunction with the increasing climate of détente of the mid and late 1960s, these structures were the preconditions for developments in West German extraparliamentary politics later on. Without the formation of these networks and their constant and dynamic evolution and reformation in the early 1960s, the history of the student and the West German anti-Vietnam protests of the later 1960s cannot be fully understood.

The double paradox which this chapter has revealed has two main implications for conceptualizing the relationship between culture and international history with regard to social movements. First, "culture" should not be regarded as a given, but as something which activists established and debated, thus creating both opportunities and limits for communication and cooperation across national boundaries. We therefore need to analyze the protesters' ideas in their own right, rather than imposing our own ideas onto the past. American forms of protests mattered surprisingly little in the discussions among British and West German protesters. Discussing these crucial developments in the early 1960s under the heading of an Americanization of protests thus appears rather problematic.

Second, merely referring to the transfer or diffusion of ideas between different movements does not suffice, as it ignores the self-evolving dynamic of protests in a given social situation. Although the transnational migration of ideas can account for developments to some extent, we cannot assume that ideas alone determine the ability to act. Analyzing which ideas travelled is thus only the first step for examining transnational protest movements. The second step has to be the analysis of the social spaces in which they were used. The fact that the structure of ideas alone allows them to be utilized by protesters is not realistic. For the protests movements in West Germany, this extension of their domestic networks into a developing transnational public space was of more fundamental importance: here, they could acquaint themselves both with the ideas and the realities of forms of protest and with a strategy that, in the West German context, could not yet be translated into actions. The groundwork for the more radical West German student protests was laid here. And it was here that the rhetoric of a "global community" became a complex reality.

In one of his contemporary essays, the historian and activist E. P. Thompson demanded that "internationalism should not be like a network of television stations, each beaming national programmes to passive viewers in alien lands. It should be a concourse, an exchange. Argument is its true sign."[122] Historians of transnational relations should take his advice seriously. Conversely, historians of protest movements around the world should realize that national social developments cannot be understood fully without reference to social interactions beyond borders.

Notes

I should like to thank Jessica C. E. Gienow-Hecht and Julia Moses for their insightful comments on earlier versions of this chapter.

1. On world society, see Rudolf Stichweh, "Zur Theorie der Weltgesellschaft," *Soziale Systeme: Zeitschrift für soziologische Theorie* 1 (1995): 29–45. The argument of a world society can already be found in Niklas

Luhmann, "Die Weltgesellschaft [1971]," in idem, *Soziologische Aufklärung 2* (Opladen: Westdeutscher Verlag, 1975), 103–33.
2. Toralf Staud, "Global Kids: Die Proteste gegen einen Irak-Krieg stehen erst am Anfang," *Die Zeit* 9 (2003).
3. Akira Iriye, "A Century of NGOs," *Diplomatic History* 23, 3 (1999): 421–35.
4. The numbers have been taken from Akira Iriye, "A Century of NGOs": 425, 426, 428; Margaret Keck and Kathryn Sikkink, *Activists Beyond Borders: Advocacy Networks in International Politics* (Ithaca, London: Cornell University Press, 1998), 11, table 1. For the developments before 1945, see Charles Chatfield, "Intergovernmental and Nongovernmental Associations to 1945," in *Transnational Social Movements and Global Politics*, eds. Jackie Smith, Charles Chatfield, and Ron Pagnucco (Syracuse: Syracuse University Press, 1997), 19–41. On the importance of the 1960s in promoting this development, see Sidney Tarrow, "Mentalities, Political Cultures, and Collective Action Frames: Constructing Meaning through Action," in *Frontiers in Social Movement Theory*, eds. Aldon D. Morris and Carol McClurg Mueller (New Haven and London: Yale University Press, 1992), 184.
5. See Philipp Gassert, "Atlantic Alliances: Cross-Cultural Communication and the 1960s Student Revolution," in *Culture and International History*, eds. Jessica C. E. Gienow Hecht and Frank Schumacher (New York, Oxford: Berghahn Books, 2003), 135–56; Wolfgang Kraushaar, "Die transatlantische Protestkultur: Der zivile Ungehorsam als amerikanisches Exempel und als bundesdeutsche Adapation," in *Westbindungen: Amerika in der Bundesrepublik*, eds. Heinz Bude and Bernd Greiner (Hamburg: Hamburger Edition, 1999), 257–84.
6. This perspective has also been criticized for the US. See Allen Smith, "Present at the Creation ... And Other Myths: The Port Huron Statement and the Origins of the New Left," *Peace & Change* 25 (2000): 339–62; Charles Chatfield, "At the Hands of Historians: The Antiwar Movement of the Vietnam Era," *Peace & Change* 29 (2004): 483–526.
7. See Carole Fink, Philipp Gassert, and Detlef Junker, eds., *1968: The World Transformed* (Cambridge: Cambridge University Press, 1998); Gerard J. DeGroot, ed., *Student Protest: The Sixties and After* (London and New York: Longman, 1998); Philipp Gassert, "Atlantic Alliances." For peace movement history more generally during this period, see Lawrence S. Wittner, *Resisting the Bomb: A History of the World Nuclear Disarmament Movement 1954–1970* (Stanford: Stanford University Press, 1997).
8. Akira Iriye, *Cultural Internationalism and World Order* (Baltimore: Johns Hopkins University Press, 1997, and Iriye, *Global Community: The Role of International Organizations in the Making of the Contemporary World* (Berkeley: University of California Press, 2002); Matthew Evangelista, *Unarmed Forces: The Transnational Movement to End the Cold War* (Ithaca: Cornell University Press, 1999).
9. See Jessica C. E. Gienow-Hecht, "Cultural Transfer," in *Explaining the History of American Foreign Relations*, 2nd ed., eds. Michael J. Hogan and Thomas G. Paterson (Cambridge: Cambridge University Press, 2004), 257–78.
10. Akira Iriye, "Culture and International History," in ibid., 241–56, here 242.
11. Frank Costigliola, "Reading for Meaning: Theory, Language, and Metaphor," in ibid., 241–56, here 290; William H. Sewell, Jr., "The Concept(s) of Culture," in *Beyond the Cultural Turn: New Directions in the Study of Society and Culture*, eds. Victoria E. Bonnell and Lynn Hunt (Berkeley and London: University of California Press, 1999), 35–61.

12. Peter J. Katzenstein, "Introduction: Alternative Perspectives on National Security," in *The Culture of National Security: Norms and Identity in World Politics,* ed. Katzenstein (New York: Columbia University Press, 1996), 4–6.
13. On theories of "framing," see Mayer N. Zald, "Culture, Ideology, and Strategic Framing," in *Comparative Perspectives on Social Movements: Political Opportunities: Mobilizing Structures, and Cultural Framings,* eds. Doug McAdam, John D. McCarthy, and Mayer N. Zald (Cambridge: Cambridge University Press, 1996), 261–74; Scott A. Hunt, Robert D. Benford, and David A. Snow, "Identity Fields: Framing Processes and the Social Construction of Movement Identities," in *New Social Movements: From Ideology to Identity,* eds. Enrique Laraña, Hank Johnston, and Joseph R. Gusfield (Philadelphia: Temple University Press, 1994), 195–208; Jürgen Gerhards and Dieter Rucht, "Mesomobilization: Organizing and Framing in Two Protest Campaigns in West Germany," *American Journal of Sociology* 98 (1992): 555–96; Ron Eyerman and Andrew Jamison, *Social Movements: A Cognitive Approach* (Cambridge: Cambridge University Press, 1991). On social movement theory more generally, see Donatella della Porta and Mario Diani, *Social Movements: An Introduction* (Oxford: Blackwell, 1999). On the importance of historical experiences, see Charles Tilly, *European Revolutions, 1492–1992* (Oxford: Oxford University Press, 1993), 14.
14. Donatella della Porta, "'1968' – Zwischennationale Diffusion und Transnationale Strukturen: Eine Forschungsagenda," in *1968: Vom Ereignis zum Gegenstand in der Geschichtswissenschaft,* ed. Ingrid Gilcher-Holtey (Göttingen: Vandenhoeck und Ruprecht, 1998), 131–50; Doug McAdam and Dieter Rucht, "The Cross-National Diffusion of Movement Ideas," *Annals of the American Association of Political and Social Science* 528 (July 1993): 56–74.
15. Niklas Luhmann, *Soziale Systeme: Grundriß einer allgemeinen Theorie* (Frankfurt: Suhrkamp Verlag, 1984), 196–98.
16. For brilliant examples of such an approach, see Leila J. Rupp, *Worlds of Women: The Making of an International Women's Movement* (Princeton: Princeton University Press, 1997), and Rupp, "Constructing Internationalism: The Case of Transnational Women's Organizations, 1888–1945," *American Historical Review* 99, 5 (1994): 1571–1600. From a political-science perspective, see Keck and Sikkink, *Activists beyond Borders.*
17. See John D. McCarthy and Mayer N. Zald, "Resource Mobilization and Social Movements: A Partial Theory," *American Journal of Sociology* 82 (1977): 1212–41. For a critique, see Sidney Tarrow, *Power in Movement: Social Movements and Contentious Politics,* 2nd ed. (Cambridge: Cambridge University Press, 1998), 16.
18. See Lawrence S. Wittner, *One World or None: A History of the World Nuclear Disarmament Movement Through 1953* (Stanford: Stanford University Press, 1993); Holger Nehring, "Cold War, Apocalypse, and Peaceful Atoms. Interpretations of Nuclear Energy in the British and West German Anti-Nuclear-Weapons Movements, 1955–1964," *Historical Social Research* 29, 3 (2004): 150–70. For a war studies perspective, see Beatrice Heuser, *The Bomb: Nuclear Weapons in their Historical, Strategic and Ethical Context* (Harlow: Longman, 2000), 135–91.
19. On the awareness of the destructive power of nuclear weapons, see the memorandum on "Die Wirkungen der Kernwaffen" [The Effects of Nuclear Weapons] by Karl Hagedorn, 10 August 1961, War Resisters' International

papers, WRI-235, International Institute for Social History, Amsterdam (hereafter IISG). On the development of public opinion, see Michael Geyer, "Cold War Angst: The Case of West-German Opposition to Rearmament and Nuclear Weapons," in *The Miracle Years: A Cultural History of Germany 1949–1968,* ed. Hanna Schissler (Princeton, Oxford: Princeton University Press, 2001), 376–408. For Britain, see George H. Gallup, ed., *The Gallup International Public Opinion Polls: Great Britain 1937–1975,* vol. 1: *1937–1964* (New York: Simon and Schuster, 1976).

20. See David Seed, "The Debate over Nuclear Refuge," in *Across the Blocs: Cold War Cultural and Social History,* eds. Rana Mitter and Patrick Major (London and Portland, OR: Frank Cass, 2004), 117–42; Paul S. Boyer, *By the Bomb's Early Light: American Thought and Culture at the Dawn of the Atomic Age* (New York: Pantheon, 1985); and Ilona Stölken-Fitschen, *Atombombe und Geistesgeschichte: Eine Studie der fünfziger Jahre aus deutscher Sicht* (Baden-Baden: Nomos Verlag, 1995).

21. See the title of a collection of essays by the philosopher Günter Anders, *Hiroshima ist überall* (Munich: C. H. Beck, 1982).

22. For a comparison of the two movements which highlights the differences with regard to their cultural assumptions, see my Oxford DPhil thesis, Holger Nehring, "The Politics of Security: The British and West German Protests against Nuclear Weapons, 1958–1964," (DPhil thesis, Oxford University, 2006), and the short summaries in Nehring, "Die Proteste gegen Atomwaffen in der Bundesrepublik und Großbritannien, 1957–1964 – ein Vergleich sozialer Bewegungen," *Mitteilungsblatt des Instituts für soziale Bewegungen* 31 (2004): 81–107, and Nehring, "The British and West German Protests against Nuclear Weapons and the Cultures of the Cold War, 1957–64," *Contemporary British History* 19, 2 (2005): 223–41. On the lack of a major movement in France, see Sudhir Hazareesingh, "Why No Peace Movement in France?" in *Political Traditions in Modern France,* Hazareesingh (Oxford: Oxford University Press, 1994), 178–206. On the American movement, see Milton S. Katz, *Ban the Bomb: A History of SANE, the Committee for a Sane Nuclear Policy* (Westport: Greenwood Press, 1986).

23. With precedents in the early 1950s.

24. For an overview of the history of CND, see Richard Taylor, *Against the Bomb: The British Peace Movement, 1958–1965* (Oxford: Oxford University Press, 1988), and Christopher Driver, *The Disarmers: A Study in Protest* (London: Hodder and Stoughton, 1964).

25. See Jost Dülffer, "The Movement against Rearmament 1951–55 and the Movement Against Nuclear Armament 1957/59 in the Federal Republic: A Comparison," in *Le pacifisme en Europe des années 1920 aux années 1950,* ed. Maurice Vaïsse (Brussels: Vaillant, 1993), 417–34. The standard works on the German movement are: Hans Karl Rupp, *Außerparlamentarische Opposition in der Ära Adenauer: Der Kampf um die Atombewaffnung in den fünfziger Jahren: Eine Studie zur innenpolitischen Entwicklung der BRD* (Cologne: Pahl-Rugenstein, 1970), and Mark Cioc, *Pax Atomica: The Nuclear Defense Debate in West Germany during the Adenauer Era* (New York: Columbia University Press, 1988).

26. See Karl A. Otto, *Vom Ostermarsch zur APO: Geschichte der ausserparlamentarischen Opposition in der Bundesrepublik 1960–1970,* 2nd ed. (Frankfurt and New York: Campus Verlag, 1982).

27. Henry Luce, "The American Century," reprinted in *Diplomatic History* 23, 2 (1999): 159–71. See, for another example, Wendell Wilkie, *One World*

(New York: Simon and Schuster, 1943). For the background, see Iriye, *Global Community*, 41.
28. Dexter Masters and Katharine Way, eds., *One World or None* (London: McGraw-Hill, 1946), 59. For the background, see Iriye, *Global Community*, 53–55.
29. Bertrand Russell, "Man's Peril," *The Listener*, 30 December 1954, 1135–36. On the intellectual context, see Ray Monk, *Bertrand Russell: The Ghost of Madness 1921–1970* (London: Jonathan Cape, 2000), 298–99 and 373ff.
30. See F. C. Hunnius, "Some Thoughts on the International Peace Movement," WRI 11th Triennial Conference, Stavanger (Norway), 27–29 July 1963: WRI-11, IISG; *Sanity*, December 1963, 6.
31. See paper by Ralph Hegnauer, "The 'Third Camp' and Voluntary Labour Services," WRI Conference, Paris 29 July–3 August 1954: IISG WRI-7/2; Victor Kiernan to Christopher Hill, 12 November 1956, John Saville papers (hereafter JS), JS-111, Brynmor Jones Library, Hull, United Kingdom (hereafter BJL).
32. CND Charter, n.d. [c. 1959], JS-7, BJL.
33. Robert Bolt, "Do you speak nuclear?" *New Statesman*, 24 December 1960.
34. "Who's going to be the Boss?" CND broadsheet, n.d. [c. 1958], JS-7, BJL.
35. Earl Russel and Rev. Michael Scott, "Act or perish: A Call to Non-violent Action," October 1960, JS-6, BJL.
36. Easter March Song Booklet, n.d. [c. 1962], uncataloged C100 collection, IISG.
37. *Peace News*, 11 April 1958, 8.
38. See Eric D. Weitz, "The Ever-Present Other: Communism in the Making of West Germany," in *Miracle Years*, ed. Schissler, 219–32; Anselm Doering-Manteuffel, "Im Kampf um 'Frieden' und 'Freiheit': Über den Zusammenhang zwischen Ideologie und Sozialkultur im Ost-West-Konflikt," in *Koordinaten deutscher Geschichte in der Epoche des Ost-West-Konflikts*, ed. Hans Günter Hockerts (Munich: R. Oldenbourg Verlag, 2004), 29–47.
39. Walter Lidl, "Kriegsbekämpfung in unserer Zeit: Beziehungen zwischen den Weltfriedensbewegungen," WRI Ninth Triennial Conference, Froebel Educational Institution, Roehampton, 15–20 July 1957, WRI-8, IISG.
40. See Alexander Gallus, *Die Neutralisten: Verfechter eines vereinten Deutschland zwischen Ost und West 1945–1990* (Düsseldorf: Droste Verlag, 2001), chs. 1–5.
41. See Siegward Lönnendonker, Bernd Rabehl, and Jochen Staadt, *Die Antiautoritäre Revolte: Der Sozialistische Deutsche Studentenbund nach der Trennung von der SPD*, vol. 1: *1960–1967* (Opladen: Westdeutscher Verlag, 2002), 44–95.
42. "Manifest der Deutschen Friedensgesellschaft zur Allgemeinen Abrüstung," 2 October 1960, Deutsche Friedensgesellschaft papers, RW 115 268/124-125, Hauptstaatsarchiv Düsseldorf (hereafter HstAD); Stefan Andres, "Der Glaube der Machtlosigkeit," in *Gegen den Tod: Stimmen deutscher Schriftsteller gegen die Atombombe*, eds. Gudrun Ensslin and Bernward Vesper (Stuttgart: Edition Cordeliers, 1964), 118–19.
43. "Perspektiven einer Mitteleuropäischen Friedenszone," RW 115-420/100-107, HstAD.
44. See Holger Nehring, "Apocalypse and Peaceful Atoms"; Michael Geyer, "Cold War Angst: The Case of the West-German Opposition to Rearmament and Nuclear Weapons"; Anson Rabinbach, "Restoring the German Spirit: Humanism and Guilt in Post-War Germany," in *German Ideologies*

since 1945: Studies in the Political Thought and Culture of the Bonn Republic, ed. Jan-Werner Müller (New York: Palgrave, 2003), 23–39.
45. On the general importance of this theme for German history, see Michael Geyer, "Das Stigma der Gewalt und das Problem der Nationalen Identität in Deutschland," in *Von der Aufgabe der Freiheit: Politische Verantwortung und bürgerliche Gesellschaft im 19. und 20. Jahrhundert,* eds. Christian Jansen, Lutz Niethammer, and Bernd Weisbrod (Berlin: VCH, 1995), 673–98.
46. Tony Smythe, "W.R.I. and the International Peace Movement," document 5, WRI 11th Triennial Conference, Stavanger (Norway), 27–29 July 1963, 2, WRI-11, IISG.
47. David A. Snow, et al., "Frame Alignment Processes, Micromobilization, and Movement Participation," *American Sociological Review* 51 (1986): 464–81, here 464.
48. See Dieter Rucht, "Transnationale Öffentlichkeiten und Identitäten in Neuen Sozialen Bewegungen," in *Transnationale Öffentlichkeiten und Identitäten,* eds. Hartmut Kaelble, Martin Kirsch, and Alexander Schmidt-Gernig (Frankfurt and New York: Campus Verlag, 2002), 327–51, here 331.
49. See Hunt, Benford, and Snow, "Identity Fields: Framing Processes and the Social Construction of Movement Identities"; Craig Calhoun, "Social Theory and the Politics of Identity," in *Social Theory and the Politics of Identity,* ed. Calhoun (Oxford, Cambridge, MA: Blackwell, 1994), 9–36.
50. Minutes of the SPD *Parteivorstand,* 24 January 1958, Archiv der Sozialen Demokratie, Bonn (hereafter AdsD). For Britain, see "Summary Report of the Meeting between the International Committees of the Labour Party NEC and the TUC General Council," Transport House, 10:30 AM, 6 March 1958, The Archives of the British Labour Party, Series One: National Executive Committee Minutes, part 5: 1956–59 inclusive (Microfiche edition, Harvester Press, Hassocks, 1976: Bodleian Library, Oxford).
51. See the folder "Tarnorganisationen," 2/PVAM000007, AdsD.
52. See Stefan Berger and Darren G. Lilleker, "The British Labour Party and the German Democratic Republic during the Era of Non-recognition, 1949–1973," *Historical Journal* 45 (2002): 433–58.
53. See Lönnendonker, et al., *Die antiautoritäre Revolte,* 44–95 on West Germany; Lin Chun, *The British New Left* (Edinburgh: Edinburgh University Press, 1993), 1–59, and Michael Kenny, *The First New Left: British Intellectuals after Stalin* (London: Lawrence and Wishart, 1995) on Britain.
54. See Chun, *New Left,* 60–64.
55. E. P. Thompson to John Saville, n.d. [1959?], JS-51, BJL. See also the circular "Notes for International Discussion," n.d. [c. 1960], JS-112, BJL; and the minutes of the meeting of the New Left Review editorial executive, 19 November 1960, JS-112, BJL.
56. Interview with Dr. Dorothy Thompson, Worcester, United Kingdom, 25 August 2003.
57. On Richter and the Gruppe 47, see Ingrid Gilcher-Holtey, "'Askese Schreiben, Schreib: Askese': Zur Rolle der Gruppe 47 in der Politischen Kultur der Nachkriegszeit," *Internationales Archiv für Sozialgeschichte der deutschen Literatur* 25 (2000): 134–67. On Richter's political activities directly after 1945, see Gallus, *Die Neutralisten,* 94–108.
58. Hans Werner Richter papers (hereafter HWR), 72.86.511, fol. 91ff., Stiftung Archiv der Akademie der Künste, Berlin (hereafter AKB).
59. Christopher Holme to Hans Werner Richter, 2 April 1958, HWR 72.86.512, fol. 55, AKB.

60. Statutes of the European Federation against Nuclear Arms [c. 1959], HWR 72.86.512, fol. 20ff., AKB.
61. Report about the European Congress against Nuclear Armaments, 6 February 1959, HWR, 72.86.512, fol. 158ff., AKB.
62. On West German anti-communism, see Detlef Siegfried, "Stalin und Elvis: Antikommunismus zwischen Erfahrung, Ideologie und Eigensinn," *Sowi* 28 (January–March 1999): 27–35.
63. Hans Werner Richter to Canon John Collins, 9 September 1961, HWR 72.86.512, fol. 303, AKB.
64. Strictly speaking, the ICDP was only founded one year later in Tyringe, Sweden. The Oxford conference led to the formation of a Continuing Committee.
65. ICDP, Constitution, Christel Küpper Collection, ED 702/52, Institut für Zeitgeschichte, Munich (hereafter IfZ).
66. *Sanity*, February 1963, 4.
67. See Statement of the Aims of the ICDP, ED 702/52, IfZ; Peter Cadogan, Minutes of the National Committee of 100 meeting, 23/24 February 1963, London, National Committee of 100 papers (hereafter C100), C100-1, IISG.
68. See letter by Diana Collins to *Peace News*, 29 March 1963; letter by Judith Cook to *Peace News*, 1 March 1963; Dora Russell in *Tribune*, 31 May 1963; *Sanity*, March 1963, 9; Barry Gorden, "After Oxford What?" *International Socialism* 12 (1963), 12–14.
69. ICDP, Report of Inaugural Congress held at Tyringe, Sweden, 9–13 January 1964, vol. 1: Working Sessions, 6, 27, ED 702-52, IfZ.
70. *Peace Information Bulletin*, various issues, starting in 1963, ED 702-53, IfZ.
71. Minutes of the National Committee of 100 meeting, London, 20–21 July 1963, C100-21, IISG.
72. The importance of this aspect is highlighted by Michael Geyer and Charles Bright, "World History in a Global Age," *American Historical Review* 100, 4 (1995): 1034–60, here 1056; and by Charles S. Maier, "Consigning the Twentieth Century to History: Alternative Narratives for the Modern Era," *American Historical Review* 105, 3 (2000): 807–31. On a network approach to social movement theory, see Mario Diani and Doug McAdam, eds., *Social Movements and Networks: Relational Approaches to Collective Action* (Oxford: Oxford University Press, 2003).
73. See Ludger Pries, ed., *New Transnational Social Spaces: International Migration and Transnational Companies in the Early Twenty-First Century* (London and New York: Routledge, 2001); Pries, ed., *Transnationale Migration* (Baden-Baden: Nomos Verlag, 1997); Edward W. Soja, *Postmodern Geographies: The Reassertion of Space in Critical Social Theory* (London: Verso, 1989). For the adaptation in historical research, see Jürgen Osterhammel, "Transnationale Gesellschaftsgeschichte: Erweiterung oder Alternative," *Geschichte und Gesellschaft* 27 (2001): 464–79, here 477–479, and Patel, "Überlegungen zu Einer Transnationalen Geschichte," 636–37.
74. See the suggestions in Thomas Welskopp, "Die Sozialgeschichte der Väter: Grenzen und Perspektiven der Historischen Sozialwissenschaft," *Geschichte und Gesellschaft* 24 (1998): 173–98, here 179 and 185; Welskopp, "Der Mensch und Seine Verhältnisse: 'Handeln' und 'Struktur' bei Max Weber und Anthony Giddens," in *Geschichte zwischen Kultur und Gesellschaft: Beiträge zur Theoriedebatte*, eds. Thomas Mergel and Thomas Welskopp (Munich: C. H. Beck Verlag, 1997), 39–70.

75. For the theoretical background, see Peter Berger and Thomas Luckmann, *The Social Construction of Reality* (Garden City, 1967), 61, and Herbert Blumer, "The Methodological Position of Symbolic Interactionism," in *Symbolic Interactionism: Perspectives and Method,* Blumer (Englewood Cliffs: Prentice-Hall, 1969), 1–60, here 19.
76. There is yet no detailed academic history on the WRI. For the West German section, see Guido Grünewald, *Die Internationale der Kriegsdienstgegner (IdK): Ihre Geschichte 1945–1968* (Cologne: Pahl-Rugenstein, 1982). On developments in the Weimar Republic, see Karl Holl and Wolfram Wette, eds., *Pazifismus in der Weimarer Republik* (Paderborn: Schöningh Verlag, 1981).
77. This is the interpretation of Kraushaar, "Die transatlantische Protestkultur."
78. See, for example, Pierre Martin, "Democracy and the WRI," document 4, WRI 11th Triennial Conference, Stavanger (Norway), 27–29 July 1963, WRI-11, IISG; Constitution and Rules (as agreed at the International Conference, 1957, and amended at the Conferences 1960 and 1963), WRI-11/VI, IISG.
79. See, for example, the document "Joining the Committee of 100," C100-8, IISG.
80. See Report from the WRI's 9th Triennial Conference, Roehampton, 15–20 July 1957, WRI-7, IISG.
81. Klaus Vack to the WRI, 10 March 1964; WRI to Vack, 16 March 1964, 31 March 1964 (quote), 13 April 1964, WRI-252, IISG.
82. H. G. Friedrich and Andreas Buro to the Executive Committee of the WRI, 3 September 1960, WRI-226, IISG, and the negative response by Tony Smythe, 21 September 1960, ibid.
83. See, for example, Hilda von Klenze, "Brief aus England," *Friedensrundschau* 14, 2 (1960): 15, and Hilda von Klenze, "Brief aus England," *Friedensrundschau* 17, 6 (1963): 15–16.
84. Reports from the 8th Triennial Conference, Paris 1954, WRI-7, IISG. See also the reports on the following Triennial Conferences in WRI-8, 9, 10, 11, WRI; and the exchange of letters between the WRI and Andreas Buro, WRI-226, IISG.
85. List of conference participants at the WRI's 8th Triennial Conference, Paris, 1954, WRI-7, IISG.
86. Andreas Buro to Tony Smythe, 3 September 1960, WRI-226, IISG.
87. Jochen Zimmer, "Das Abseits als vermiedener Irrweg: Die Naturfreundejugend in der westdeutschen Friedens- und Ökologiebewegung bis zum Ende der APO," in *Wir sind die grüne Garde: Geschichte der Naturfreundejugend,* eds. Heinz Hoffmann and Jochen Zimmer (Essen: Klartext Verlag, 1986), 93–170.
88. Letters by Vack to the WRI, WRI-252, IISG.
89. Proceedings of the 8th Triennial Conference, Paris 1954, WRI-7/VI, IISG.
90. On the West German "New Left," see Lönnendonker, et al., *Die antiautoritäre Revolte,* 44–95.
91. Andreas Buro to Tony Smythe, 3 September 1960, WRI-226, IISG; List of participants at the WRI Study Conference 1961, Blaricum near Amsterdam, 12–19 August 1961, WRI-63, IISG; List of participants at the 1963 11th Triennial WRI conference, Stavanger, Norway, 27–29 July 1963, WRI-11, IISG; Agenda for the WRI Study Conference 1964, Offenbach, 9–15 August

1964, WRI-64, IISG. For the links between the British Committee of 100 to the West German SDS through WRI relations, see the minutes of the National Committee of 100, International Sub-Committee, 4 April 1962, C100-29, IISG.
92. Tony Smythe to Klaus Vack, 12 October 1962, and Klaus Vack's reply, 15 October 1962, WRI-252, IISG.
93. See the complete lists of those attending the 1957 conference, London, WRI-7, IISG.
94. WRI to Herbert Stubenrauch and Klaus Vack, 5 June 1964, and Vack's reply, 15 June 1964, WRI-252, IISG.
95. Handwritten notes on the WRI Study Conference, Offenbach, 9–15 August 1964, and the document on the WRI Study Conference, "Non-violent Solution in Conflict with Special Reference to Germany and Berlin," WRI-64, IISG.
96. Minutes of the National Committee of 100, 20 June 1962, C100-2, IISG; invitation to the Conference on International Direct Action against War, Amsterdam, 10–12 November 1962, WRI-63, IISG.
97. Heinrich Kloppenburg and Herbert Stubenrauch attended for the West German Easter March Committee. See the report of the conference, C100-17, IISG.
98. Minutes of the International Sub-Committee, 10 March 1963, Cambridge, WRI C100-17, IISG.
99. See, for example, the details for the WRI Study Conference at Blaricum near Amsterdam, 12–19 August 1961, WRI-63, IISG.
100. George Clark, "Convenor's Notes," 27 March 1962, C100-2, IISG; Andreas Buro to Tony Smythe, 2 November 1960, WRI-226, IISG.
101. Andreas Buro to Tony Smythe, 11 May 1960; letters by Andreas Buro to Tony Smythe, 21 June and 13 July 1960, as well as Smythe's reply, 14 June 1960, WRI-226, IISG.
102. Klaus Vack to Devi Prasad, 6 September 1964, WRI-252, IISG.
103. Frank E. Myers, "Civil Disobedience and Organizational Change: The British Committee of 100," *Political Science Quarterly,* 86 (1971): 92–112; Taylor, *Against the Bomb,* 190–269.
104. Wolfgang Kraushaar's statement that Thoreau's pamphlet "On the Duty of Civil Disobedience" was first translated into German in 1966 is wrong. Various German translations circulated through the WRI's networks since at least the early 1950s. See Kraushaar, "Die transatlantische Protestkultur," 276.
105. Comments by Theodor Michaltscheff on a paper by Pierre Martin, WRI 11th Triennial Conference, Stavanger (Norway), 27–29 July 1963, WRI-11, IISG.
106. Report on the American-European March, 28 April 1961, WRI-235, IISG; Gerard Daechsel, "Amerikanisch-europäischer Marsch: Protest in Ost und West," *Friedensrundschau* 15, 6 (1961): 23, and Theodor Michaltscheff, "Der Marsch findet doch statt," *Friedensrundschau* 15, 7/8 (1961): 1–3.
107. Memorandum, "Weltfriedensbrigade," 2 May 1961, WRI-235, IISG. For the perception in the Federal Republic, see the report from the 15th Federal Conference of the IdK, Braunschweig, 29–30 September 1962, WRI-235, IISG; Andreas Buro and Helga Stolle, "Die Weltfriedensbrigade," *Friedensrundschau* 16, 3 (1962): 6–7 and 14.
108. See Hans Sinn, "Concluding Report: Vancouver-Berlin Peace Walk," background paper 1, Study Conference 1964, Offenbach, WRI-64, IISG.

109. For examples of such performative acts in a different campaign, see Michael S. Foley, *Confronting the War Machine: Draft Resistance during the Vietnam War* (Chapel Hill, London: University of North Carolina Press, 2003).
110. See, from a theoretical angle, Rucht, "Transnationale Öffentlichkeiten."
111. Tony Smythe, "W.R.I. and the International Peace Movement," WRI 11th Triennial Conference, Stavanger (Norway), document 5, 4, WRI-11, IISG.
112. ICDP, Report of Inaugural Congress held at Tyringe, Sweden, 9–13 January 1964, vol. 1: Working Sessions, 42–45, ED 702-52, IfZ.
113. Minutes of the National Committee of 100, Friends Institute, Birmingham, 6–7 April 1963, C100-1, IISG.
114. *CND Newsletter*, 8, 19 June 1958, JS-6, BJL. For the West German perception, see "Was bedeutet dieses Zeichen?" *Der Kriegsdienstgegner: Mitteilungsblatt der WRI Deutscher Zweig*, October 1963, 4/1963, 10, WRI-235, IISG.
115. See the collection of pamphlets and flyers in the private archives of Hans-Konrad Tempel, Ahrenburg (Germany). I would like to thank Mr. Tempel for making the material available to me.
116. Klaus Vack to the WRI, 28 September 1962, WRI-252, IISG.
117. *Peace News*, 12 April 1959.
118. Report from the anti-militarist conference, Amsterdam 1962, 10, C100-17, WRI.
119. Tony Smythe, Minutes of the National Committee of 100, Oxford, 21–22 September 1963, C100-1, IISG.
120. E. P. Thompson, "Where are We Now?" manuscript, n.d. [c. 1963], JS-109, BJL. See also his "Foreword," in *The Poverty of Theory and Other Essays* (London: Merlin Press, 1978), iv.
121. See Axel Schildt, *Moderne Zeiten: Freizeit, Massenmedien und "Zeitgeist" in der Bundesrepublik der 50er Jahre* (Hamburg: Christians, 1995), 324–50 and 398–423.
122. E. P. Thompson, "Foreword," iv.

Bibliography

Anders, Günter. *Hiroshima ist überall*. Munich: C. H. Beck, 1982.
Berger, Peter, and Thomas Luckmann. *The Social Construction of Reality*. Garden City: Doubleday, 1967.
Berger, Stefan, and Darren G. Lilleker. "The British Labour Party and the German Democratic Republic during the Era of Non-recognition, 1949–1973." *Historical Journal* 45 (2002): 433–58.
Blumer, Herbert. *Symbolic Interactionism: Perspectives and Method*. Englewood Cliffs: Prentice Hall, 1969.
Bonnell, Victoria E., and Lynn Hunt, eds. *Beyond the Cultural Turn: New Directions in the Study of Society and Culture*. Berkeley, London: University of California Press, 1999.
Boyer, Paul S. *By the Bomb's Early Light: American Thought and Culture at the Dawn of the Atomic Age*. New York: Pantheon, 1985.
Bude, Heinz, and Bernd Greiner, eds. *Westbindungen: Amerika in der Bundesrepublik*. Hamburg: Hamburger Edition, 1999.
Chatfield, Charles. "At the Hands of Historians: The Antiwar Movement of the Vietnam Era." *Peace & Change* 29 (2004): 483–526.

Calhoun, Craig, ed. *Social Theory and the Politics of Identity.* Oxford and Cambridge, MA: Blackwell, 1994.

Chun, Lin. *The British New Left.* Edinburgh: Edinburgh University Press, 1993.

Cioc, Mark. *Pax Atomica: The Nuclear Defense Debate in West Germany during the Adenauer Era.* New York: Columbia University Press, 1988.

DeGroot, Gerard J., ed. *Student Protest: The Sixties and After.* London and New York: Longman, 1998.

Della Porta, Donatella, and Mario Diani. *Social Movements: An Introduction.* Oxford: Blackwell, 1999.

Diani, Mario, and Doug McAdam, eds. *Social Movements and Networks: Relational Approaches to Collective Action.* Oxford: Oxford University Press, 2003.

Driver, Christopher. *The Disarmers: A Study in Protest.* London: Hodder and Stoughton, 1964.

Ensslin, Gudrun, and Bernward Vesper, eds. *Gegen den Tod: Stimmen deutscher Schriftsteller gegen die Atombombe.* Stuttgart: Edition Cordeliers, 1964.

Evangelista, Matthew. *Unarmed Forces: The Transnational Movement to End the Cold War.* Ithaca: Cornell University Press, 1999.

Eyerman, Ron, and Andrew Jamison. *Social Movements: A Cognitive Approach.* Cambridge: Cambridge University Press, 1991.

Fink, Carole, Philipp Gassert, and Detlef Junker, eds. *1968: The World Transformed.* Cambridge: Cambridge University Press, 1998.

Foley, Michael S. *Confronting the War Machine: Draft Resistance during the Vietnam War.* Chapel Hill and London: University of North Carolina Press, 2003.

Gallup, George H., ed. *The Gallup International Public Opinion Polls: Great Britain 1937–1975.* Vol. 1: *1937–1964.* New York: Random House, 1976.

Gallus, Alexander. *Die Neutralisten: Verfechter eines vereinten Deutschland zwischen Ost und West 1945–1990.* Düsseldorf: Droste Verlag, 2001.

Gerhards, Jürgen, and Dieter Rucht. "Mesomobilization: Organizing and Framing in Two Protest Campaigns in West Germany." *American Journal of Sociology* 98 (1992): 555–96.

Geyer, Michael, and Charles Bright. "World History in a Global Age." *American Historical Review* 100, 4 (1995): 1034–60.

Gienow-Hecht, Jessica C. E., and Frank Schumacher, eds. *Culture and International History.* New York and Oxford: Berghahn Books, 2003.

Gilcher-Holtey, Ingrid, ed. *1968: Vom Ereignis zum Gegenstand in der Geschichtswissenschaft.* Göttingen: Vandenhoeck & Ruprecht, 1998.

Gilcher-Holtey, Ingrid. "'Askese schreiben, schreib: Askese': Zur Rolle der Gruppe 47 in der politischen Kultur der Nachkriegszeit." *Internationales Archiv für Sozialgeschichte der deutschen Literatur* 25 (2000): 134–67.

Grünewald, Guido. *Die Internationale der Kriegsdienstgegner (IdK): Ihre Geschichte 1945–1968.* Cologne: Pahl-Rugenstein Verlag, 1982.

Hazareesingh, Sudhir. *Political Traditions in Modern France.* Oxford: Oxford University Press, 1994.

Heuser, Beatrice. *The Bomb: Nuclear Weapons in their Historical, Strategic and Ethical Context.* Harlow: Longman, 2000.

Hockerts, Hans Günter, ed. *Koordinaten deutscher Geschichte in der Epoche des Ost-West-Konflikts.* Munich: R. Oldenbourg Verlag, 2004.

Hoffmann, Heinz, and Jochen Zimmer, eds. *Wir sind die grüne Garde: Geschichte der Naturfreundejugend.* Essen: Klartext Verlag, 1986.

Hogan, Michael J., and Thomas G. Paterson, eds. *Explaining the History of American Foreign Relations.* 2nd ed. Cambridge: Cambridge University Press, 2004.

Holl, Karl, and Wolfram Wette, eds. *Pazifismus in der Weimarer Republik*. Paderborn: Schöningh Verlag, 1981.
Iriye, Akira. *Cultural Internationalism and World Order*. Baltimore: Johns Hopkins University Press, 1997.
———. "A Century of NGOs." *Diplomatic History* 23, 3 (1999): 421–35.
———. *Global Community: The Role of International Organizations in the Making of the Contemporary World*. Berkeley: University of California Press, 2002.
Jansen, Christian, Lutz Niethammer, and Bernd Weisbrod, eds. *Von der Aufgabe der Freiheit: Politische Verantwortung und bürgerliche Gesellschaft im 19. und 20. Jahrhundert*. Berlin: VCH, 1995.
Kaelble, Hartmut, Martin Kirsch, and Alexander Schmidt-Gernig, eds. *Transnationale Öffentlichkeiten und Identitäten*. Frankfurt and New York: Campus Verlag, 2002.
Katz, Milton S. *Ban the Bomb: A History of SANE, the Committee for a Sane Nuclear Policy*. Westport: Greenwood Press, 1987.
Keck, Margaret, and Kathryn Sikkink. *Activists Beyond Borders: Advocacy in International Politics*. Ithaca and London: Cornell University Press, 1998.
Kenny, Michael. *The First New Left: British Intellectuals after Stalin*. London: Lawrence and Wishart, 1995.
Laraña, Enrique, Hank Johnston, and Joseph R. Gusfield, eds. *New Social Movements: From Ideology to Identity*. Philadelphia: Temple University Press, 1994.
Lehmkuhl, Ursula. "Diplomatiegeschichte als internationale Kulturgeschichte: Theoretische Ansätze und empirische Forschung zwischen Historischer Kulturwissenschaft und Soziologischem Institutionalismus." *Geschichte und Gesellschaft* 27 (2001): 394–23.
Lönnendonker, Siegward, Bernd Rabehl, and Jochen Staadt. *Die antiautoritäre Revolte: Der Sozialistische Deutsche Studentenbund nach der Trennung von der SPD*. Vol. 1: 1960–1967. Opladen: Westdeutscher Verlag, 2002.
Luce, Henry. "The American Century." *Diplomatic History* 23, 2 (1999): 159–71.
Luhmann, Niklas. *Soziologische Aufklärung*. Opladen: Westdeutscher Verlag, 1975.
———. *Soziale Systeme: Grundriß einer allgemeinen Theorie*. Frankfurt: Suhrkamp Verlag, 1984.
Maier, Charles S. "Consigning the Twentieth Century to History: Alternative Narratives for the Modern Era." *American Historical Review* 105, 3 (2000): 807–31.
Masters, Dexter, and Katharine Way, eds. *One World or None*. London: McGraw-Hill, 1946.
McAdam, Doug, and Dieter Rucht. "The Cross-National Diffusion of Movement Ideas." *Annals of the American Association of Political and Social Science* 528 (July 1993): 56–74.
McAdam, Doug, John D. McCarthy, and Mayer N. Zald, eds. *Comparative Perspectives on Social Movements: Political Opportunities: Mobilizing Structures, and Cultural Framings*. Cambridge: Cambridge University Press, 1996.
McCarthy, John D., and Mayer N. Zald. "Resource Mobilization and Social Movements: A Partial Theory." *American Journal of Sociology* 82 (1977): 1212–41.
Mergel, Thomas, and Thomas Welskopp, eds. *Geschichte zwischen Kultur und Gesellschaft: Beiträge zur Theoriedebatte*. Munich: C. H. Beck Verlag, 1997.
Mitter, Rana, and Patrick Major, eds. *Across the Blocs: Cold War Cultural and Social History*. London and Portland, OR: Frank Cass, 2004.

Monk, Ray. *Bertrand Russell: The Ghost of Madness 1921–1970*. London: Jonathan Cape, 2000.
Morris, Aldon, and Carol McClurg Mueller, eds., *Frontiers in Social Movement Theory*. New Haven and London: Yale University Press, 1992.
Müller, Jan-Werner, ed. *German Ideologies since 1945: Studies in the Political Thought and Culture of the Bonn Republic*. New York: Palgrave, 2003.
Myers, Frank E. "Civil Disobedience and Organizational Change: The British Committee of 100." *Political Science Quarterly* 86 (1971): 92–112.
Nehring, Holger. "Cold War, Apocalypse, and Peaceful Atoms: Interpretations of Nuclear Energy in the British and West German Anti-Nuclear-Weapons Movements, 1955–1964." *Historical Social Research* 29, 3 (2004): 150–70.
———. "Die Proteste gegen Atomwaffen in der Bundesrepublik und Großbritannien, 1957–1964 – ein Vergleich sozialer Bewegungen." *Mitteilungsblatt des Instituts für soziale Bewegungen* 31 (2004): 81–107.
———. "The British and West German Protests against Nuclear Weapons and the Cultures of the Cold War, 1957–64." *Contemporary British History* 19, 2 (2005): 223–41.
———. "The Politics of Security: The British and West German Protests against Nuclear Weapons, 1958–1964," (DPhil thesis, Oxford University, 2006).
Osterhammel, Jürgen. "Transnationale Gesellschaftsgeschichte: Erweiterung oder Alternative." *Geschichte und Gesellschaft* 27 (2001): 464–79.
Otto, Karl A. *Vom Ostermarsch zur APO: Geschichte der ausserparlamentarischen Opposition in der Bundesrepublik 1960–1970*. 2nd ed. Frankfurt and New York: Campus Verlag, 1982.
Patel, Kiran Klaus. "Überlegungen zu einer transnationalen Geschichte." *Zeitschrift für Geschichtswissenschaft* 52, 7 (2004): 626–45.
Katzenstein, Peter J., ed. *The Culture of National Security: Norms and Identity in World Politics*. New York: Columbia University Press, 1996.
Pries, Ludger, ed. *Transnationale Migration*. Baden-Baden: Nomos Verlag, 1997.
———, ed. *New Transnational Social Spaces: International Migration and Transnational Companies in the Early Twenty-First Century*. London and New York: Routledge, 2001.
Rupp, Hans Karl. *Außerparlamentarische Opposition in der Ära Adenauer: Der Kampf um die Atombewaffnung in den fünfziger Jahren: Eine Studie zur innenpolitischen Entwicklung der BRD*. Cologne: Pahl-Rugenstein Verlag, 1970.
Rupp, Leila J. "Constructing Internationalism: The Case of Transnational Women's Organizations, 1888–1945." *American Historical Review* 99, 5 (1994): 1571–1600.
———. *Worlds of Women: The Making of an International Women's Movement*. Princeton: Princeton University Press, 1997.
Schildt, Axel, *Moderne Zeiten: Freizeit, Massenmedien und "Zeitgeist" in der Bundesrepublik der 50er Jahre*. Hamburg: Christians, 1995.
Schissler, Hanna, ed. *The Miracle Years: A Cultural History of Germany 1949–1968*. Princeton and Oxford: Princeton University Press, 2001.
Siegfried, Detlef. "Stalin und Elvis: Antikommunismus zwischen Erfahrung, Ideologie und Eigensinn." *Sowi* 28 (January–March 1999): 27–35.
Smith, Allen. "Present at the Creation ... And Other Myths: The Port Huron Statement and the Origins of the New Left." *Peace & Change* 25 (2000): 339–62.
Smith, Jackie, Charles Chatfield, and Ron Pagnucco, eds. *Transnational Social Movements and Global Politics*. Syracuse: Syracuse University Press, 1997.

Snow, David S., et al. "Frame Alignment Processes, Micromobilization, and Movement Participation." *American Sociological Review* 51 (1986): 464–81.
Soja, Edward W. *Postmodern Geographies: The Reassertion of Space in Critical Social Theory.* London: Verso, 1989.
Stichweh, Rudolf. "Zur Theorie der Weltgesellschaft." *Soziale Systeme: Zeitschrift für soziologische Theorie* 1 (1995): 29–45.
Stölken-Fitschen, Ilona. *Atombombe und Geistesgeschichte: Eine Studie der fünfziger Jahre aus deutscher Sicht.* Baden-Baden: Nomos Verlag, 1995.
Tarrow, Sidney. *Power in Movement: Social Movements and Contentious Politics.* 2nd ed. Cambridge: Cambridge University Press, 1998.
Taylor, Richard. *Against the Bomb: The British Peace Movement, 1958–1965.* Oxford: Oxford University Press, 1988.
Thompson, Edward P. *The Poverty of Theory and Other Essays.* London: Merlin Press, 1978.
Tilly, Charles. *European Revolutions, 1492–1992.* Oxford: Oxford University Press, 1993.
Vaïsse, Maurice, ed. *Le pacifisme en Europe des années 1920 aux années 1950.* Brussels: Vaillant, 1993.
Welskopp, Thomas. "Die Sozialgeschichte der Väter: Grenzen und Perspektiven der Historischen Sozialwissenschaft." *Geschichte und Gesellschaft* 24 (1998): 173–198.
Wilkie, Wendell. *One World.* New York: Simon and Schuster, 1943.
Wittner, Lawrence S. *One World or None: A History of the World Nuclear Disarmament Movement Through 1953.* Stanford: Stanford University Press, 1993.
———. *Resisting the Bomb: A History of the World Nuclear Disarmament Movement 1954–1970.* Stanford: Stanford University Press, 1997.

Part IV
CULTURAL VIOLENCE

Chapter 7

MISPERCEPTIONS OF EMPIRE
How Berlin and Washington Misread the "Ordinary Germans" of Latin America in World War II

Max Paul Friedman

Dreams of conquest and nightmares of helplessness fired the imaginations of certain officials in Germany and the United States when their minds turned to Latin America in the 1930s. Legend has it that Adolf Hitler himself indulged in thoughts of Latin America as a juicy, tropical fruit ripe for the picking: The endless, fertile fields of the Argentine *pampas*. The unexplored jungles of the Amazon. Vast, and undeveloped, a continent of *Lebensraum*. All it would take would be a well-disciplined band of solid German colonists to transform this torpid paradise into a rich outpost of the Third Reich. And they were already in place: over a million German settlers spread across the continent, biding their time, waiting for the word to strike from within. What did Adolf Hitler have to say about Latin America? "Our conquistadors have a more difficult task than the original ones," he remarked, according to one source, "and for this reason they have more delicate weapons."[1]

This image owes its longevity in part to wartime misperceptions of Latin America in Washington, in part to misunderstandings of the region widespread among German officials, and also to the inability of post-war scholars to decenter the United States when they look at the question of German nationals' behavior in Latin America. Adding a transnational dimension to

---

Notes for this section begin on page 270.

the study of perceptions of Latin America can help clarify and contextualize the nature of the German presence there in a half-way space between integration and cultural independence that was only somewhat vulnerable to Nazi appeals for purity and allegiance.

There was international alarm over the possibility of Nazi subversion in Latin America in the years before the Second World War. British intelligence circulated a secret map revealing Germany's plans to conquer South America and carve it into five satellite states under Nazi control. A series of books published in Europe, Latin America, and the United States with titles like "Hitler Conquers America" and "The Nazi Octopus" warned, in the words of a Uruguayan writer, that "the soldiers of the Third German Empire ... have been distributed by the thousands throughout the political underground of this continent."[2] US officials worried greatly about the power of Germany in the region: of one hundred meetings of the joint planning committee of the State, Navy, and War Departments in 1939 and 1940, all but six had Latin America at the top of the agenda.[3] Scholars writing in the post-war era, whether they sat at desks in East Germany, West Germany, Great Britain, France, or the United States, repeated statements allegedly made by Hitler as evidence that a German takeover of Latin America with the aid of ethnic Germans living in the region had been a nightmare scenario only narrowly avoided.

There was just one problem with this widely fostered view of the Nazi project to take over Latin America: it was an invention. The secret German map was a forgery. Hitler's dramatic quotations can all be traced back to a single source, the best-selling *Hitler Speaks,* published by a former member of the Nazi Party named Hermann Rauschning, which was a complete fabrication.[4]

Although the attention of top Nazis was focused elsewhere, the National Socialist German Worker Party's (NSDAP) office for foreign recruitment, the *Auslandsorganisation* (AO), launched a campaign to bring Latin America's Germans into its ranks. They largely failed in achieving their goals, because of a basic lack of appreciation of the true needs and circumstances of the unassimilated communities of German expatriates, who lived in a very different cultural context from the country they had left. Blinded by an ideology of racial superiority and inexperienced in the region, Nazi organizers engaged in self-defeating programs of action that alienated some of their potential supporters, offended their Latin American hosts, and brought down the wrath of the powerful neighbor to the north.

In the United States, diplomats, government officials, politicians, authors, and newspaper reporters retained many of their cherished beliefs about Latin American inferiority well into the era of Franklin Roosevelt's vaunted "Good Neighbor policy." The sense that Latin Americans were inherently incapable of managing their affairs made Americans predisposed to believe that the Germans to the south could easily overthrow governments and pave the way for an invasion through the "soft underbelly" of the United States.

These two sets of ideological blinders and assumptions of superiority, each in their own way, persuaded officials at the mid level in Berlin and all the way to the top in Washington that Latin America was a fertile field for the seeds of Nazi intrigue. As a result, the *Auslandsorganisation* ignored local conditions and tried to bully the region's German emigrants into line, producing a response that disappointed the organizers and should fascinate any historian interested in the behavior of "ordinary Germans" abroad. Ironically, because of their grounding in a culture that fostered beliefs about Latin America that were afflicted by the same kind of racism and disdain, many US officials were likewise convinced that the Latin Americans were hopeless and incompetent, and that the Germans of the region were lined up like stormtroopers ready to march at a signal from Berlin.

These misperceptions by the administrators of two empires produced a clash that resulted in the economic and social destruction of the expatriate communities and led directly to the roundup, expulsion, and internment in the Texas desert of some four thousand Germans taken from their homes in Latin America on suspicion of being Nazi subversives.[5] This essay emphasizes the cultural assumptions about Latin America that contributed to this sorry sideshow of the war by blurring the vision of policy makers in both Washington and Berlin.

For a decade or more, students of international history have paid growing attention to culture. They have endeavored to explain that such a focus need not come at the expense of attention to power relations. Instead, they call for a broader understanding of political history as "integrative" history that combines the material and the cultural.[6] To be sure, some scholars of international relations still bristle at this approach, objecting that the "new cultural history" at best distracts us from analyzing the state's preeminent role in determining events while we focus on colorful trivia, and at worst yields studies that obfuscate the mechanisms of power.[7] But power emanates not only from Mao's gun barrel or from the actions of the state; it is contained in symbols, identities, language, and everyday practices. To take a narrower focus would represent a lesser understanding.

One crucial element of the cultural analysis of international relations is the study of ideology, the set of learned assumptions and unspoken beliefs whose acquisition precedes, over a lifetime, any given crisis or other moment when policy decisions are taken. Ideologies greatly simplify the work of government officials in a changing world: rather than dedicate themselves to a lengthy, patient study of a given country, movement, or group of persons, and rather than developing expertise, language competence, and familiarity with many regions, they can fit all new players and events into a preexisting model of how the world works and act accordingly. For example, the Cold War-era American ideology that squeezed a multitudinous world into two categories, Communist or anti-Communist, greatly simplified policy decisions toward nationalist movements in developing countries (often with disastrous outcomes). Ideology is a shortcut to decision, if seldom an effective one.

In studying US policy toward Latin America, scholars have found it essential to consider the way in which the ideological views of policy makers, influenced by the culture in which they were raised, affected their decisions. For many US officials posted to or responsible for Latin America, stereotype and prejudice shape their thinking more than in-depth regional expertise, and interactions with Latin Americans are limited to those who can speak with them in English. Numerous studies have established a continuity in North American views of Latin Americans as inherently inferior and assigned to a station "Beneath the United States."[8] Without such an ideological framework, US officials would have been able to more accurately assess Nazi activities in the region for what they were: halfhearted attempts at political organization that failed on their own terms, and limited espionage efforts that were successfully countered by American intelligence. There was a danger posed by Germany's goals in the region, but these goals were far more limited than they appeared to US officials.

Less crucial a region geopolitically to Germany, Latin America has been less studied for its place in the German imagination.[9] One scholar even called Germans "the last discoverers" of Latin America[10]—this despite the enduring affection some Latin Americans felt for one of the earliest "discoverers," the scientist-explorer Alexander von Humboldt, exalted by Bolívar as "a great man who, with his eyes, pulled America out of her ignorance, and with his pen, painted her as beautiful as her own nature."[11] It was a long journey from Humboldt through a century of German emigration and experience to the Nazi ideology of strict racial hierarchy, and these interwoven tendencies, as will be shown, were reflected in the contradictions of German policy toward the region on the eve of the war.

In the period from 1938 until Pearl Harbor, the Nazi menace in Latin America seemed an imminent one to many Americans. President Franklin D. Roosevelt, in his private messages and his public statements, regularly warned of the danger. Several of his closest aides—including top assistant Harry Hopkins, Treasury Secretary Henry Morgenthau, and Assistant Secretary of State Adolf Berle—believed Nazi subversion in Latin America was likely. Officials as well acquainted with the region as Undersecretary of State Sumner Welles and his deputy Laurence Duggan would come to share this perspective for a time. If Latin Americans were too childlike, too insignificant to make important things happen, then when political unrest occurred, responsibility must lie elsewhere.

In this period, coup attempts and other forms of political unrest were routinely ascribed to Nazi machinations, despite the absence of evidence for such a link and the presence of local actors with their own agendas.[12] In Brazil in May 1938, a fascist group called the *integralistas*, led by Plinio Salgado, tried to overthrow the government of Getulio Vargas. US officials believed the Nazis had planned, funded, and orchestrated the plot. These claims were not based on evidence of German involvement, which was lacking; the presence of a few ethnic Germans at the lower ranks of the *integralistas* was enough to convince the US government that the Nazis called the tune. But an alliance between Nazis and *integralistas* was highly unlikely, because their goals were in contradiction: *integralismo*, the ideology of Salgado's group, stood for Brazilian nationalism and virtually forced assimilation of minority groups, while the NSDAP believed in German superiority and urged the immigrants to zealously guard their German identity. This conflict was apparent to the Brazilian press, which ascribed to the Nazi *Auslandsorganisation* a practice of *desnacionalização*, denationalizing, as opposed to the Brazilian nationalist program of *nacionalização,* the creation of a homogeneous, culturally united nation.[13] *Nacionalização* was actually the name for President Vargas' own policy of Brazilianization, not the program of the *integralistas,* who wished to carry it further. Both Brazilian positions were in direct conflict with Nazi aims; indeed, German Ambassador Karl Ritter, afflicted by his own version of great power blindness to small power initiative, assumed Vargas' policies were instituted at the behest of the United States. To representatives of both Berlin and Washington, the facts—that this was a conflict among Brazilians over Brazilian issues—did not fit their assumptions of Latin American inferiority and malleability.

No one in Washington could know exactly what Germany was planning in secret, and in the absence of reliable information, the Roosevelt administration assumed Hitler might use the *Auslandsdeutsche* to pave the way for a German invasion of the Americas. No record of any such planning by the German military has been found. Other evidence of trans-Atlantic military intentions—an on-again, off-again project to construct large battleships and long-range bombers, the search for naval bases on or near the North African coast—suggests Hitler expected to challenge the United States eventually, although he sometimes remarked that the confrontation might take place decades in the future, even as late as the 1970s.[14]

Hitler had plenty of opinions about the "degenerate" US democracy "enfeebled" by its influential population of Jews, but he evinced no interest in Latin America. He openly conceded that the region belonged properly in the US sphere of influence, and referred often to the Monroe Doctrine, asserting a comparable sphere for Germany under a "European Monroe Doctrine."[15] In strong contrast to his habitual micromanagement of foreign policy toward nations he was interested in, Hitler and his top aides left policymaking toward Latin America to the *Auswärtiges Amt*—so often cut out of important decisions elsewhere—and the foreign ministry left it to department heads.[16] Hitler took little notice of the potential of German-Latin American trade, although he once remarked that a German-dominated Europe could eventually displace the United States as principal trading partner with Latin America.[17] When Hitler did make a rare reference to Latin America in his so-called Second Book, it was merely to dismiss the region as the epitome of degenerate racial mixing.[18] He did not even remark upon the large German presence in South America—a telling omission, given his fervent interest in the ethnic Germans of Eastern Europe and the Soviet Union, and his vision of a worldwide *Volksgemeinschaft* (German racial community). Overall, German policy until December 1941 was to avoid provoking the United States, and thereafter to seek Latin American neutrality in the conflict.

Accounts in the US press warning of Hitler's designs on Latin America regularly referred to statements contained in the best-selling *Gespräche mit Hitler,* published in London as *Hitler Speaks* in 1939. The author, Hermann Rauschning, was Danzig senate president and a former member of the NSDAP who reluctantly broke with the Nazis over financial issues. He claimed to report the content of Hitler's bombast delivered at luncheons where he himself had been a guest, although he wrote the book years afterward. It presented dramatic statements purporting to be Hitler's, on the order of "if ever there is a place where democracy is senseless and suicidal, it is in South America" or the above-quoted claim to send German conquistadors to take over the continent. Rauschning is cited as a key source by scholars who argue that the Nazi regime sought to take over Latin America.[19] Unfortunately for proponents of this view, *Hitler Speaks* was demolished by subsequent investigations that showed that Rauschning had invented the quotations.[20]

Nevertheless, the legend of a Nazi plan to take over Latin America has been very long lived, and it turns on the actions of the German expatriates living in the region. There were indeed many of them; between one and two million people in Latin America were of German descent on the eve of the war. What they might do was misread by the few Nazi officials in Berlin who took an interest in them, and they were equally misunderstood by officials in Washington, who were much more interested in their actions—and highly alarmed by them. Were these footsoldiers of Hitler, waiting for a signal from home? Who were the Germans of Latin America? And why did both centers of power so completely misunderstand their condition?

Large-scale German migration to Latin America began in the middle of the nineteenth century, following the liberal revolutions of 1848; a larger wave followed in the last two decades of the nineteenth century. Of all European immigrants to Latin America, Germans received the warmest welcome. The influential writer and future Argentine president Domingo Sarmiento in 1860 praised "their proverbial honesty, their tireless devotion to work, and their pacific character."[21] Before Bismarck's unification of the German states in 1871, German arrivals had a special appeal, because they did not have the backing of a powerful colonial state—no France, Spain, Great Britain, or United States ready to send gunboats to Latin American ports to enforce the demands of their nationals. Latin American politicians tended to embrace European immigrants in general for bringing "sobriety" and "culture" as a necessary corrective to local "creole indolence"—a kind of racial flattery that would make German expatriates much more receptive to twentieth-century racist appeals.[22]

A vast array of separate cultural institutions hardened the immigrants' sense of their difference. "The first thing that two Germans do when they meet overseas is to found three associations," wrote an observer, and the Germans of Latin America proved this with enthusiasm, creating a profusion of *Vereine*, clubs or associations for recreational, educational, cultural, and charitable purposes. There were singing clubs, sports clubs, beer-drinking clubs, mutual aid societies, and volunteer fire brigades. The *Vereine* were sanctuaries of familiarity and the focal points of community. The emigrants' direct contact with the homeland tended to wane over time, vitiating any truly aggressive nationalism on their part. They knew where their own interests lay: in maintaining friendly relations with their Latin American neighbors, governors, and customers. Most German immigrants ultimately occupied an in-between space, loyal but apart, welcomed but unincorporated, in Latin America but not of it.

The end of the First World War and the economic collapse and political chaos that followed in Germany pushed a huge wave of demoralized and impoverished people out of the country. Branded as aggressors by the Treaty of Versailles, Germans were personae non gratae nearly everywhere, except on "the last free continent," as Latin America was called among those seeking a route out of national isolation. (Most Latin American countries remained neutral in World War I, and did not seek to retaliate against Germans afterward, instead welcoming immigrants with a reputation for hard work and access to European markets.) One hundred thousand new immigrants arrived in Latin America during the decade following the war.[23]

The new immigrants were as diverse as the population of Germany itself, but the post-war wave was characterized by its high proportion of young men alienated from the frail democracy of the Weimar Republic they had left and unimpressed by the societies they were joining. They included cashiered military officers and members of the *Freikorps,* right-wing veterans' clubs responsible for much of the brutal post-war violence in Germany.[24] Some of the post-World War I emigrants published travelogues, often printed in the hundreds of thousands of copies, laced with language that revealed a racist disdain for their Latin American neighbors. For example, travel writer Werner Hopp blamed the "idiocy" of the Quechua Indians on their "very low mental capacity" and innate inferiority to whites, which rendered them incapable of participating in modern life. Other writers routinely referred to *indios* as "louts" and "wild savages" with "eyes close together like apes." They dubbed *mestizos* "half-breeds" and described them as lazy, thieving, superstitious, and cowardly.[25]

Small, isolated Nazi groups sprouted in several Latin American capitals after 1929. But most German emigrants tried to ignore these first coarse, noisy upstarts. It was not merely their grating style that kept the Nazis from making many early converts. The conservative German expatriates abhorred the disorder, the acid partisan rivalries that hobbled the Weimar government and regularly spilled onto the streets of Germany's cities. Shrill local Nazis now threatened to import the same conflicts to the staid overseas communities. Extolling the supremacy of German culture and calling for defending the purity of German blood seemed to many emigrants to be in extremely poor taste where maintaining respectful relations with Latinos was crucial to their continued social and financial success.

The specificities of the Latin American context worked for and against the spread of Nazi ideology. Those immigrants whose worldview rested on popular social Darwinist, positivist, and racial determinist assumptions often saw their prejudices reinforced by the stratification of the Latin American societies they joined. They took their places in the *pigmentocracia,* the pigmentocracy, a hierarchy in which those with lighter skin tone advanced further up the social ladder. Some Germans managed rapidly to create sizeable plantations or thriving businesses, tangible achievements which some of them—and not a few of their Latino neighbors—interpreted in racial terms, overlooking the advantages of education, technical skill, and access to German capital and markets that they brought along with their renowned work ethic.

And yet those Germans who intermarried or had close social ties with Latin Americans were far less likely to welcome an ideology based on racial supremacy. The Nazis explicitly rejected a large segment of the German population—those who married non-Aryans, those who did not speak German in daily life, or who adopted Latin American citizenship. For this reason, the early Nazis alienated many Germans and wound up becoming not the unifying force they aspired to be, but a corrosive and divisive faction.[26]

Hitler's rise to power in 1933 changed the equation, and the influence of the Nazi Party in Latin America began to grow. Substantial open resistance in the first few years was stamped out by about 1937, as the Nazi Party moved to back up its transnational organizing efforts with the machinery of the state. The first targets were, naturally enough, the *Vereine,* the centers of community life. The *Auslandsorganisation,* the foreign organization of the Nazi Party, sought to enroll new members abroad and intimidate its opponents.

In country after country, Nazi officials marched into meetings with the boards of directors of German schools and German clubs to demand control as the true representatives of the Führer. If they were refused, the subsidies from Berlin were terminated. Where that was insufficient, physical threats and, occasionally, violence were used. Local Party organizations held demonstrations in uniform with all the paraphernalia of mass events in Nazi Germany—except for the masses. Their appeals could not overcome expatriate ambivalence. Party membership generally did not exceed 3 to 9 percent among German citizens, a tiny fraction of that among ethnic Germans.[27]

Nazi officials reported back to the *Auslandsorganisation* the disappointing results, and by the end of the 1930s, decided that Party activities were producing such a hostile reception, they should be suspended throughout the region. With the onset of the Second World War, the Nazi Party was banned by nearly every Latin American country. Ironically, in the very years when the Party was entering its steep decline in the region, the United States began to take notice. As Roosevelt administration officials planned for the inevitable conflict with Nazi Germany—and as they tried to persuade a reluctant American public that the war brewing in Europe affected them too—the most immediate security threat in the years preceding American entry into World War II seemed to be the possibility of German destabilization of Latin America.

Unassimilated German immigrants played a starring role in nightmare scenarios of the anticipated Nazi assault. The State

Department warned its missions in Latin America that the Germans living there were stockpiling weapons and were secretly organized into storm troop units, ready to seize territory and overthrow governments.[28] Senator Robert Reynolds of North Carolina believed that "Alien enemies, members of the [subversive] 'fifth column,' are coming from across the Atlantic." He declared: "They are coming north across the Rio Grande, and other[s] ... are already here by the hundreds of thousands.... The 'fifth column' is here and the Trojan horses in great herds are grazing upon the green, tender grasses of the pastures of America."[29]

If the Nazi Party in Latin America had made so few gains, why did it appear so powerful to Americans? Partly, to be sure, because of the real presence of several hundred German spies working in the region. Admiral Wilhelm Canaris had taken over the *Abwehr* (military intelligence) in 1935 with the aim of expanding the number of agents abroad. In a covert counterpart to the relatively public campaign of the *Auslandsorganisation*, Canaris recruited expatriates from business and commercial circles and built up a small network of spies in Latin America, some of them equipped with wireless communications kits for transmission back to Germany.[30] These groups were quickly identified by routine police work and radio intercepts, and did not contribute much to the German war effort.[31] But they did contribute to the image of the German menace.

So did the overheated press reports multiplying in the period before Pearl Harbor. Reporters sent by US newspapers to write about the German threat in Latin America contributed directly to the impressions held by policymakers in Washington. Many government officials and Roosevelt himself read the *New York Times* every morning.[32] There they saw their suspicions confirmed by a cycle of disinformation, as off-the-record briefings of correspondents by US embassies later appeared as dramatic stories in papers sold in the United States—and the articles duly made their way into government reports. "COLOMBIA'S NAZIS ARMED FOR ATTACK," blared the headline of a piece by *Times* reporter Russell B. Porter, who traveled through Latin America in 1940 writing overheated dispatches on the Nazis' ambitions. One of his stories reported that Germans had smuggled armored cars into Colombia disguised as tractors (a rumor then circulating in the US embassy in Bogotá) and estimated Nazi Party membership at fifteen hundred—a 500 percent exaggeration.[33] On another occasion Porter claimed that Germans could use the German airline in Ecuador, Sociedad Ecuatoriana de Tranportes Aéreos (SEDTA), to launch an attack on the Panama Canal—a most unlikely scenario given the defenses that would have to be overcome by the two lumbering, obsolescent JU-52 transport planes that made up SEDTA's entire fleet.[34] When the United Press reported that a US citizen flying over Haiti had discovered a German air base there, President Roosevelt forwarded the clipping to Sumner Welles with the question, "What do you know about this and what are we doing?" Welles immediately sent an embassy official to visit the site, who discovered that the "airfield" was a mineral water bottling plant run by refugees.[35] Cornelius Vanderbilt, Jr., breathlessly warned readers of *Liberty Magazine* that "German officers are training natives with German guns" in both Colombia and Costa Rica. "No one knows exactly how many Germans there are in either country," Vanderbilt wrote, "but all I talked with are sure that at least one tenth of the inhabitants have come from the Reich, and that fully 80 percent of these are Nazis."[36] (Actual figures for Colombia were 0.04 percent and 7.5 percent, respectively, and 0.1 percent and 6 or 7 percent for Costa Rica.)[37] The Colombian embassy in Washington, DC, regularly decried such "sensationalism." Ambassador Gabriel Turbay complained that "here in the United States, deliberately or unconsciously, official and semi-official declarations have exaggerated … the dangers of Nazi penetration."[38]

To meet the apparent danger posed by the German communities in Latin America, in June 1940, Roosevelt gave FBI director J. Edgar Hoover authority to send his agents south of the border. These FBI agents were designated "legal attachés" and assigned to US diplomatic missions throughout the hemisphere. Most lacked knowledge about the countries and communities they were supposed to spy on. Agent Donald Charles Bird recalled later that, in August 1941, he was given two weeks of language training—in Spanish—before being sent to Brazil.[39] Working together, the FBI and the embassies drew up lists of Germans they found suspicious on the thinnest of evidence. Anonymous denunciations were the rule. The US consul in Guayaquil, Ecuador, paid fifty dollars to anyone who would denounce a Nazi.[40] The FBI agent in Quito seems to have paid in whiskey.[41] It was the same story around the region. Rather than investigation, US agents engaged for the most part in transcription. They often saw only what they expected to see, based on their assumptions about Latin America, and since the US government had not taken the region seriously enough to invest in training more agents in the relevant languages and regional expertise, they were forced to rely on local volunteers who could pass along suspicions in English.

After Pearl Harbor, these lists were immediately put to use. The State Department pressured fifteen Latin American governments to hand over the potentially subversive Germans on their lists. Some four thousand people of German origin were delivered to the US military for transportation to the United States and internment in camps in Texas and other states.[42] The State Department used a combination of rewards and threats to achieve compliance from Latin American governments, from military aid under the Lend-Lease program to the warning that failure to deliver Germans would result in the boycott of key commodities such as coffee or sugar.[43]

Once interned, the alleged subversives turned out to be a motley crowd of German expatriates running the gamut from a minority of Nazi Party members to Social Democratic exiles, Spanish-speaking children of mixed marriages, and at least eighty Jewish refugees, all lumped together in the camps as Nazi prisoners. Again and again, post-war investigations would turn up "no evidence of any charges," "no indications of any reason" for many of the individual deportations. Such was the case of Walter Wolff, a Jewish butcher whose only offense was that he reportedly had "many German customers."[44] George Karliner, a Jewish refugee, was no stranger to barbed wire; he had been imprisoned in Buchenwald in 1938 along with his father, who was killed there by Nazi guards.[45] These people had been rounded up by US intelligence agents who knew as little about the region and its Germans as did Nazi officials in Berlin. The record of their behavior while in internment confirms the relative weakness of the Nazi organization, and shows that both sides had misjudged the nature of these expatriate Germans.

After receiving complaints from Jewish internees that they were being threatened by the Nazi inmates, camp guards at Stringtown, Oklahoma, interviewed them one by one. Many of the Jewish prisoners made statements that confirm the picture of a German internee group made up of a passive majority, with a small, coercive Nazi faction attempting to dominate the group. Erwin Klyszcz observed that "A lot of internees would be nice but do not associate with us because they are afraid of the Nazi element." Isidore Rosenberg, another Jewish internee, noted a change in the summer of 1942, after more

Germans arrived from Latin America. "Since the people from Costa Rica and Guatemala are here it is better," he said. "They are more intelligent ... [these] internees have been much nicer."[46]

Internee Emil Loewenthal's statement is especially intriguing: "I have heard [the Nazis] say that there are not enough of them to fight us but they are hoping that more will come and then they will take care of us." At that time there were only eighteen Jews, mostly older men, among a total internee population of 531 German adult males at the Stringtown camp. Despite the Nazi Party membership of a minority of prisoners, between 10 and 15 percent, Nazi activists evidently could not draw upon large numbers of adherents to carry out their schemes.[47]

Indeed, the number of the zealous willing to incur even a small risk for their beliefs seems to have been quite meager. When the internees at Stringtown were forbidden to give the Hitler salute, Nazis organized a group defiance of the regulation and were punished with thirty days in separate quarters. The protestors numbered fifteen—less than 3 percent of the internees were willing to follow Nazi orders.[48] This pathetic showing illustrates just how inoffensive were most of the allegedly dangerous Germans selected for internment.

The evidence from inside the camps and from the German communities in Latin America shows that acceptance of the Nazis among these German expatriates may have been broad, but it did not run deep. Had more of them been more enthusiastic, they would have expressed it not merely with occasional attendance at German holiday celebrations or other symbolic acts that might mean support for Nazism but might equally be traditional expressions of enthusiasm for German culture. A determination to aid the Nazi program would require the concrete commitment of time and resources—such as joining the Party and working for its goals. That between 90 and 97 percent were unwilling to do so speaks volumes. So does the behavior even of those selected as particularly dangerous and interned, Party members among them.

Without a doubt, the *Auslandsorganisation* failed to meet its own objectives. Its officials found the enrollment rates humiliating. Nazi activities produced widespread distrust and hostility toward Germany and the Germans, rather than drawing sympathy for the Nazi cause. The AO's wartime goal of promoting neutrality among Latin American states failed everywhere except Argentina, and a strong case can be made that

Argentina acted out of consideration for strategic relations with the great powers; local Party pressure was insignificant. Argentina had long aspired to the role of alternate pole to the United States in the Western Hemisphere. Argentine fascist leaders drew less on Hitler than Mussolini for inspiration, and promoted a particularly Latin American version of Catholic nationalism that did not have much in common with Nazi ideology. Finally, Argentine neutrality permitted some leeway for various forms of German espionage, propaganda, and financial schemes—just as other neutral countries such as Switzerland, Spain, and Turkey did. Strategic pursuit of self-interest had more to do with the choice for neutrality than did AO lobbying.[49] Even on its own terms, then, the Nazi Party never came close to achieving its ambitions in Latin America.

Perhaps that was partly because of the racially-inflected contempt top Nazi officials held for the entire region. Foreign Minister Joachim von Ribbentrop could not tell one South America country from another. Hermann Göring believed that cosmopolitan Argentina, whose capital evokes the architecture of Haussmann's Paris, was populated by Indian natives. Ernst Bohle, head of the *Auslandsorganisation,* had no interest in Latin American affairs and felt at a loss at diplomatic functions for visiting Latin American dignitaries. Not only could he not understand Spanish, but he could not seem to remember the odd-sounding names of the diplomats, and resorted to addressing them all as "Excellency." Bohle even felt alienated from German residents of Latin America, who on visits to Berlin would spend their time at the South American Club and speak Spanish among themselves. He complained that German citizens who settled in Latin America "tended to take on a very different outlook than was generally considered fitting for good [Germans]—they became much more lively and light-hearted, and often assumed a rather Latin attitude toward life which made them rather hard to handle at times."[50]

Nazi Germany's attitude toward Latin America and the Germans who lived there can be summed up largely as one of neglect rather than desire. The prejudices of top Nazis made the region uninteresting to them, and geopolitical considerations held their attention elsewhere. Lower-level Party hacks were stymied by their own racism. On the US side, similar prejudices were combined with a very different kind of desire for control in Latin America, and with the assumption, still at work today, that Latin Americans are inherently incapable of managing their own affairs. The strange treatment of German emigrants in the region by both sides during the war can be understood only in this light.

An accurate understanding of foreign cultures and contexts is always an elusive goal, but it seems safe to say that it is placed further out of reach when governments rely on officials who use stereotypes and bias to arrive at their clouded judgments. Uncovering these views is essential to understanding how such ineffectual policy could have been developed, and decentering the United States as the sole focus of inquiry more fully exposes the dilemmas faced by the German expatriate communities that were the focus of sputtering appeals for allegiance from ill-informed mandarins of the metropole. The experience of seeing what these kinds of misperceptions on both sides of the German-American rivalry did to the Germans of Latin America during the war should be instructive to other policymakers in other times, like those of our own, who are faced with decisions to make toward regions of the world about which they in truth know very little.

Notes

1. Hermann Rauschning, *Hitler m'a dit: confidences du Führer sur son plan de conquête du monde,* tr. Albert Lehman (Paris: Coopération, 1939). The quotation is my translation of the phrase "armes ... d'un maniement plus délicat" (80). The line is usually rendered in English as "more difficult weapons," a poor translation of the 1940 German version "diffizilere Waffen." The book was published in the US as *The Voice of Destruction* (New York: G.P. Putnam's Sons, 1940).
2. Hugo Fernández Artucio, *The Nazi Underground in South America* (New York: Farrar & Rinehart, 1942), 12.
3. Ernest May, "The Alliance for Progress in Historical Perspective," *Foreign Affairs* 41 (July 1963): 759–60, cited in Walter LaFeber, *Inevitable Revolutions: The United States in Central America* (New York: Norton, 1983), 82.
4. On Rauschning's fabrications see note 20 below.
5. For a fuller account of this episode and its implications for international relations, see Max Paul Friedman, *Nazis and Good Neighbors: The United States Campaign against the Germans of Latin America in World War II* (Cambridge: Cambridge University Press, 2003).
6. On "integrative" approaches, see Gilbert M. Joseph, ed., *Reclaiming the Political in Latin American History: Essays from the North* (Durham: Duke University Press, 2001).
7. Robert Buzzanco, "What Happened to the New Left? Toward a Radical Reading of American Foreign Relations," *Diplomatic History* 23, 4 (1999): 575–607. For a judicious assessment of the problems and potential of the new approaches, see Emilia Viotti da Costa, "New Publics, New Politics,

New Histories: From Economic Reductionism to Cultural Reductionism—in Search of Dialectics," in Joseph, *Reclaiming the Political*, 17–31.
8. For a comprehensive survey, see Lars Schoultz, *Beneath the United States: A History of U.S. Policy toward Latin America* (Cambridge, MA: Harvard University Press, 1998).
9. But see Nancy Mitchell, *The Danger of Dreams: German and American Imperialism in Latin America* (Chapel Hill: University of North Carolina Press, 1999); Stefan Rinke, *"Der Letzte Freie Kontinent": Deutsche Lateinamerikapolitik im Zeichen transnationaler Beziehungen, 1918–1933*, 2 vols. (Stuttgart: Hans-Dieter Heinz, 1996). On German schemes in Mexico during World War I, see Reinhard R. Doerries, *Imperial Challenge: Ambassador Count Bernstorff and German-American Relations, 1908–1917*, trans. Christa D. Shannon (Chapel Hill: University of North Carolina Press, 1989), 165–78.
10. Gustav Siebenmann, "Sind die Deutschen die letzten Entdecker Amerikas? Zur Rezeption der lateinamerikanischen Literaturen," in *Deutsche in Lateinamerika -Lateinamerika in Deutschland*, ed. Karl Kohut (Frankfurt: Vervuert Verlag, 1996), 297–314.
11. Bolivar's 1821 letter to von Humboldt quoted in Mary Louise Pratt, *Imperial Eyes: Travel Writing and Transculturation* (New York: Routledge, 1992), 112.
12. David Haglund, *Latin America and the Transformation of U.S. Strategic Thought* (Albuquerque: University of New Mexico Press, 1984), 69, 74–75, 99, 178, 182, 187–88; Braden to Welles, 9 August 1941, folder 12, Box 67, Sumner Welles Papers, Franklin D. Roosevelt Library, Hyde Park, NY (hereafter FDR Library).
13. See Dawid Bartelt, "'Fünfte Kolonne' ohne Plan: Die Auslandsorganisation der NSDAP in Brasilien, 1931–1939," *Ibero-Amerikanisches Archiv* 19, 1–2 (1993): 3–35; Stanley E. Hilton, "Acção Integralista Brasileira: Fascism in Brazil, 1932–1938," *Luso-Brazilian Review* 9 (1972): 3–29.
14. Norman J. W. Goda, *Tomorrow the World: Hitler, Northwest Africa, and the Path toward America* (College Station: Texas A&M University Press, 1998), 112, 170.
15. Jürgen Müller, "Hitler, Lateinamerika und die Weltherrschaft," *Ibero-Amerikanisches Archiv* 18, 1–2 (1992): 89–90.
16. Reiner Pommerin, *Das Dritte Reich und Lateinamerika: Die deutsche Politik gegenüber Süd- und Mittelamerika, 1939–1942* (Düsseldorf: Droste Verlag, 1977), 340.
17. Jochen Thies, *Architekt der Weltherrschaft: Die "Endziele" Hitlers* (Düsseldorf: Droste Verlag, 1976), 166–67.
18. Müller, "Hitler, Lateinamerika und die Weltherrschaft," 78.
19. See, for example, Manfred Kossok, "'Sonderauftrag Südamerika': Zur deutschen Politik gegenüber Lateinamerika 1938 bis 1942," in *Lateinamerika Zwischen Emanzipation und Imperialismus, 1810–1960*, eds. Kurt Büttner and Manfred Kossok (Berlin: Akademie Verlag, 1961), 234–55; Joachim Trotz, "Zur Tätigkeit der deutschen 5. Kolonne in Lateinamerika 1933–1945," *Wissenschaftliche Zeitschrift der Universität Rostock, Geschichtliche und sprachwissenschaftliche Reihe* 14 (1965): 119–32; Friedrich Katz, "Einige Grundzüge der Politik des deutschen Imperialismus in Lateinamerika von 1898 bis 1941," in *Der deutsche Faschismus in Lateinamerika, 1933–1943*, ed. Heinz Sanke (Berlin: Humboldt-Universität zu Berlin, 1966), 9–69.

20. See Müller, "Hitler," 74–78; Klaus Volland, *Das Dritte Reich und Mexiko: Studien zur Entwicklung des deutsch-mexikanischen Verhältnisses 1933–1942 unter besonderer Berücksichtigung der Ölpolitik* (Frankfurt: Peter Lang, 1976), 29–42; Fritz Tobias, "Auch Fälschungen haben lange Beine: Des Senatspräsidenten Rauschnings 'Gespräche mit Hitler,'" in *Gefälscht! Betrug in Politik, Literatur, Wissenschaft, Kunst und Musik*, ed. Karl Corino (Nördlingen: Greno, 1988), 91–105. Another former Nazi, Otto Strasser, published even more sensational, and even more dubious, "quotations" from Hitler in *The Gangsters around Hitler - with a Tropical Postcript: Nazi Gangsters in South America* (London: W.H. Allen & Co., 1942). But Strasser is rarely taken seriously as a reliable source.
21. Jean-Pierre Blancpain, "Des visées pangermanistes au noyautage hitlérien: Le nationalisme allemand et l'Amérique latine (1890–1945)," in *Revue historique* 281, 2 (1990): 437.
22. Jean-Pierre Blancpain, *Migrations et mémoires germaniques en Amérique latine* (Strasbourg: Presses Universitaires de Strasbourg, 1994), 70–72; Thomas Schoonover, *Germany in Central America: Competitive Imperialism, 1821–1929* (Tuscaloosa: University of Alabama Press, 1998), 149; Horst Nitschack, "La Recepción de la Cultura de Habla Alemana en Amauta," in *Encuentros y Desencuentros: Estudios sobre la recepción de la cultura alemana en América Latina* (Lima: Pontificia Universidad Católica del Perú, 1993).
23. Hermann Kellenbenz and Jürgen Schneider, "La emigración alemana a América Latina desde 1821 hasta 1930," *Jahrbuch für Geschichte von Staat, Wirtschaft und Gesellschaft Lateinamerikas* 13 (1976): 386–403; Stefan Rinke, *"Der letzte freie Kontinent": Deutsche Lateinamerikapolitik im Zeichen transnationaler Beziehungen, 1918–1933* (Stuttgart: Hans-Dieter Heinz, 1996), vol. 1, 294–95.
24. Blancpain, "Des visées pangermanistes," 468; Rinke, *"Der letzte freie Kontinent,"* vol. 1, 402.
25. Ursula Schlenther, "Rassenideologie der Nazis in der ethnographischen Literatur über Lateinamerika," in *Der deutsche Faschismus in Lateinamerika, 1933–1943*, ed. Heinz Sanke (Berlin: Humboldt-Universität zu Berlin, 1966), 75. For a bibliography of German travel writing on Latin America of the first quarter of the twentieth century, see Jürgen Kloosterhuis, *'Friedliche Imperialisten': Deutsche Auslandsvereine und auswärtige Kulturpolitik, 1906–1918* (Frankfurt: Lang, 1994), vol. 2, 908–12.
26. Marionilde Brepohl de Magalhães, *Pangermanismo e Nazismo: A trajetória alemã rumo ao Brasil* (Campinas, Brazil: Editora da UNICAMP/FAPESP, 1998), 158.
27. For figures as of June 1937, see Hans-Adolf Jacobsen, *Nationalsozialistische Außenpolitik 1933–1938* (Frankfurt: Alfred Metzner Verlag, 1968), 662–63, and compare to Michael Naumann, "Ausgewählte Daten zur Auslandsorganisation der NSDAP, Stand am 30.6.1939," based on Bundesarchiv document NSD 8/43 (Auslandsorganisation der NSDAP, Statistik, 30.6.1939, Geheim). Courtesy Michael Naumann, Institut für Zeitgeschichte, Aussenstelle Berlin-Lichterfelde.
28. Stetson Conn and Byron Fairchild, *The Framework of Hemisphere Defense* (Washington, DC: Office of the Chief of Military History, Department of the Army, 1960), 3–10, 32–35; Berle to Chiefs of the Diplomatic Missions in the Other American Republics, *The Pattern of Nazi Organizations and Their Activities in the Other American Republics*, 6 February 1941, pp.

22–25, 862.20210/414A, RG59, National Archives, College Park, Maryland (hereafter NA); Russell D. Buhite and David W. Levy, eds., *FDR's Fireside Chats* (Norman: University of Oklahoma Press, 1992), 192.

29. *Congressional Record—Senate,* vol. 86, pt. 1, 76th Congress, Third Session, pp. 681, 6773, 6775.
30. Stanley E. Hilton, *Hitler's Secret War in South America 1939–1945: German Military Espionage and Allied Counterespionage in Brazil* (Baton Rouge: Louisiana State University Press, 1981), 14–17.
31. Hilton, *Hitler's Secret War;* Maria Emilia Paz, *Strategy, Security, and Spies: Mexico and the U.S. as Allies in World War II* (University Park: Pennsylvania State University Press, 1997); Leslie B. Rout, Jr., and John F. Bratzel, *The Shadow War: German Espionage and United States Counterespionage in Latin America during World War II* (Frederick: University Publications of America, 1986).
32. Waldo Heinrichs, *Threshold of War: Franklin D. Roosevelt and the American Entry into World War II* (New York: Oxford University Press, 1988), 21.
33. Russell B. Porter, "Colombia's Nazis Armed for Attack," New York Times, 18 August 1940, 16. See note 32 below for Nazi Party membership figures.
34. Russell B. Porter, "Germans Maintain Losing Airline Inside Panama Canal Defense Zone," *New York Times,* 10 August 1940; William Burden, *The Struggle for Airways in Latin America* (New York: Arno Press, 1977), 67.
35. FDR to Welles, 21 January 1941, and Welles to President, 22 January 1941, "State: Welles, Sumner: Jan–May 1941," PSF 77, FDR Library.
36. Cornelius Vanderbilt, Jr., "Can Hitler Take Central America?" *Liberty Magazine,* 14 Nov 1940, 58.
37. Colombia's population was approximately nine million. Some 300 of the 4,000 resident Germans were Nazi Party members. Costa Rica's population was about 800,000. From a German population estimated between 850 and 1000, fewer than 60 joined the Party. Senate Committee on Military Affairs, *Nazi Party Membership Records,* Senate Committee Prints 79/2/46, Part 2, March 1946, and Part 3, September 1946, S1535-S1538 (Washington, DC.: US Government Printing Office, 1946); Robert H. Davis, *Historical Dictionary of Colombia,* 2nd ed. (London: Scarecrow Press, 1993), 404; Jacobo Schifter Sikora, *El Judío en Costa Rica* (San José: Editorial Universidad Estatal a Distancia, 1979), 82; [Duggan], *Latin America - Totalitarian Activities,* 1941, reel 45, Hull Papers (microfilm), Manuscript Division, LC; FBI, *German Espionage in Latin America,* p. 2, June 1946, 862.20210/6-1746, RG59, NA.
38. Alberto Vargas to MRE, 17 September 1940, in folder "Actividades Nazis 1940," Actividades Nazis 1940–1942, AMRE; Turbay to MRE, 25 July 1941, Embajada de Colombia en Washington, AMRE.
39. Rout and Bratzel, *The Shadow War,* 42.
40. Nester to secretary of state, *Request for allotment of $180.00 for Intelligence Information,* 4 December 1941, and Nester memo, 21 May 1942, in "Ultra-Confidential for Consul General Use Only," Ecuador: Guayaquil Consulate General, Records Re Payment of Funds for Intelligence Information, 1941–43, Box 1, RG84, NA; Eva Bloch, interview by author, Guayaquil, 18 Feb 1998; Gunter Lisken, interview by author, Guayaquil, 17 Feb 1998.
41. Nester to Guarderas, 5 January 1943, Serie B, Embajada de Estados Unidos, MRE, AHQ; Ickes to Nester, 18 March 1943, "711," Ecuador: Quito Embassy Confidential File, Box 10, RG84, NA.

42. See Friedman, *Nazis and Good Neighbors,* passim.
43. Friedman, *Nazis and Good Neighbors,* esp. chs. 3, 4, and 7.
44. Wolff folder in alphabetical Name Files of Enemy Aliens, Special War Problems Division (hereafter SWP), Boxes 31–50, RG59, NA.
45. Karliner folder in alphabetical Name Files of Enemy Aliens, SWP Boxes 31–50, RG59, NA.
46. Col. Bryan to Gufler, 14 September 1942, 740.00115EW1939/4525, RG59, NA.
47. Col. Bryan to Gufler, 14 September 1942, 740.00115EW1939/4525, RG59, NA; Max Habicht to Swiss Foreign Ministry, *Report on the Visit to Detention Stations for Civilian Intenees in the United States of America,* 18 Aug 1942, Band 1, E2200 Washington/15, Schweizerisches Bundesarchiv, Berne, Switzerland (hereafter SBA).
48. G. E. Martin (IRC), *Camp de Stringtown,* 22 September 1942, "Stringtown '42," Inspection Reports on War Relocation Centers, 1942–46, Box 20, SWP, RG59, NA.
49. On Argentina, see especially Arnold Ebel, *Das Dritte Reich und Argentinien: Die diplomatischen Beziehungen unter besonderer Berücksichtigung der Handelspolitik, 1933–1939* (Cologne: Böhlau, 1971); Michael Jackson Francis, *The Limits of Hegemony: United States Relations with Argentina and Chile during World War II* (Notre Dame: University of Notre Dame Press, 1977); Randall Bennett Woods, *The Roosevelt Foreign-Policy Establishment and the 'Good Neighbor': The United States and Argentina, 1941–1945* (Lawrence: Regents Press of Kansas, 1979); Mario Rapoport, *¿Aliados o Neutrales? La Argentina frente a la Segunda Guerra Mundial* (Buenos Aires: Editorial Universidad Buenos Aires, 1988); Guido di Tella and D. Cameron Watt, eds., *Argentina between the Great Powers, 1939–1946* (London: Macmillan, 1989); Joseph S. Tulchin, *Argentina and the United States: A Conflicted Relationship* (Boston: Twayne Publishers, 1990).
50. Bohle interrogation, State Department Special Interrogation Mission, 5–8 Sep 1945, pp. 12 and 20–21, 862.20210/3-446, RG59, NA.

Bibliography

Blancpain, Jean-Pierre. *Migrations et mémoires germaniques en Amérique Latine.* Strasbourg: Presses Universitaires de Strasbourg, 1994.

Brepohl de Magalhães, Marionilde. *Pangermanismo e nazismo: a trajetória alemã rumo ao Brasil.* Campinas, Brazil: Editora da UNICAMP/FAPESP, 1998.

Conn, Stetson, and Byron Fairchild. *The Framework of Hemisphere Defense.* Washington, DC: Office of the Chief of Military History, Department of the Army, 1960.

Corino, Karl, ed. *Gefälscht! Betrug in Politik, Literatur, Wissenschaft, Kunst und Musik.* Nördlingen: Greno, 1988.

Ebel, Arnold. *Das Dritte Reich und Argentinien: Die diplomatischen Beziehungen unter besonderer Berücksichtigung der Handelspolitik, 1933–1939.* Cologne: Böhlau, 1971.

Friedman, Max Paul. *Nazis and Good Neighbors: The United States Campaign against the Germans of Latin America in World War II.* Cambridge: Cambridge University Press, 2003.

Gaudig, Olaf, and Peter Veit. *Der Widerschein des Nazismus: Das Bild des Nationalsozialismus in der deutschsprachigen Presse Argentiniens, Brasiliens und Chiles 1932–1945.* Berlin: Wissenschaftlicher Verlag, 1997.
Goda, Norman J. W. *Tomorrow the World: Hitler, Northwest Africa, and the Path toward America.* College Station: Texas A&M University Press, 1998.
Haglund, David. *Latin America and the Transformation of U.S. Strategic Thought.* Albuquerque: University of New Mexico Press, 1984.
Hilton, Stanley E. *Hitler's Secret War in South America 1939–1945: German Military Espionage and Allied Counterespionage in Brazil.* Baton Rouge: Louisiana State University Press, 1981.
Hunt, Michael H. *Ideology and U.S. Foreign Policy.* New Haven: Yale University Press, 1987.
Jacobsen, Hans-Adolf. *Nationalsozialistische Außenpolitik 1933–1938.* Frankfurt: Alfred Metzner Verlag, 1968.
Johnson, John J. *Latin America in Caricature.* Austin: University of Texas Press, 1993.
Joseph, Gilbert M., ed. *Reclaiming the Political in Latin American History: Essays from the North.* Durham: Duke University Press, 2001.
Joseph, Gilbert M., Catherine C. LeGrande, and Ricardo D. Salvatore, eds. *Close Encounters of Empire: Writing the Cultural History of U.S.-Latin American Relations.* Durham: Duke University Press, 1998
Kießling, Wolfgang. *Exil in Lateinamerika.* Frankfurt: Verlag Philipp Reclam, 1984.
Kloosterhuis, Jürgen. *"Friedliche Imperialisten": Deutsche Auslandsvereine und auswärtige Kulturpolitik, 1906–1918.* Frankfurt: Peter Lang, 1994.
Kohut, Karl, ed. *Deutsche in Lateinamerika - Lateinamerika in Deutschland.* Frankfurt: Vervuert Verlag, 1996.
Kohut, Karl, and Patrik von zur Mühlen, eds. *Alternative Lateinamerika: Das deutsche Exil in der Zeit des Nationalsozialismus.* Frankfurt: Vervuert Verlag, 1994.
LaFeber, Walter. *Inevitable Revolutions: The United States in Central America.* New York: Norton, 1983.
Mitchell, Nancy. *The Danger of Dreams: German and American Imperialism in Latin America.* Chapel Hill: University of North Carolina Press, 1999.
Müller, Jürgen. *Nationalsozialismus in Lateinamerika: Die Auslandsorganisation der NSDAP in Argentinien, Brasilien, Chile und Mexico, 1931–1945.* Stuttgart: Verlag Hans-Dieter Heinz, 1997.
Newton, Ronald C. *The 'Nazi Menace' in Argentina, 1931–1947.* Stanford: Stanford University Press, 1992.
Paz, Maria Emilia. *Strategy, Security, and Spies: Mexico and the U.S. as Allies in World War II.* University Park: Pennsylvania State University Press, 1997.
Pommerin, Reiner. *Das Dritte Reich und Lateinamerika: Die deutsche Politik gegenüber Süd- und Mittelamerika, 1939–1942.* Düsseldorf: Droste Verlag, 1977.
Pratt, Mary Louise. *Imperial Eyes: Travel Writing and Transculturation.* New York: Routledge, 1992.
Rapoport, Mario. *¿Aliados o Neutrales? La Argentina frente a la Segunda Guerra Mundial.* Buenos Aires: Editorial Universidad Buenos Aires, 1988.
Rinke, Stefan. *"Der Letzte Freie Kontinent": Deutsche Lateinamerikapolitik im Zeichen transnationaler Beziehungen, 1918–1933.* 2 vols. Stuttgart: Hans-Dieter Heinz, 1996.

Rout, Leslie B., Jr., and John F. Bratzel. *The Shadow War: German Espionage and United States Counterespionage in Latin America During World War II.* Frederick: University Publications of America, Inc., 1986.

Sanke, Heinz, ed. *Der deutsche Faschismus in Lateinamerika, 1933–1943.* Berlin: Humboldt-Universität zu Berlin, 1966.

Schoonover, Thomas. *Germany in Central America: Competitive Imperialism, 1821–1929.* Tuscaloosa: University of Alabama Press, 1998.

Schoultz, Lars. *Beneath the United States: A History of U.S. Policy toward Latin America.* Cambridge, MA: Harvard University Press, 1998.

Schuler, Friedrich E. *Mexico between Hitler and Roosevelt: Mexican Foreign Relations in the Age of Lázaro Cárdenas, 1934–1940.* Albuquerque: University of New Mexico Press, 1998.

Volland, Klaus. *Das Dritte Reich und Mexiko: Studien zur Entwicklung des deutsch-mexikanischen Verhältnisses 1933–1942 unter besonderer Berücksichtigung der Ölpolitik.* Frankfurt: Peter Lang, 1976.

zur Mühlen, Patrik von. *Fluchtziel Lateinamerika: Die deutsche Emigration 1933–1945: politische Aktivitäten und soziokulturelle Integration.* Bonn: Verlag Neue Gesellschaft, 1988.

Chapter 8

RAPE AND MURDER IN THE CANAL ZONE
Cultural Conflict and the US Military Presence in Panama, 1955–56

Michael E. Donoghue

The years 1955 through 1956 were a time of crisis in US-Panamanian relations. A long and frustrating negotiating process to revise the infamous 1903 Hay-Bunau-Varilla Treaty that had established the US presence on the isthmus ended in January 1955 with an accord that pleased neither side. By the mid 1950s most Panamanians despised the original 1903 treaty that granted the United States the right to virtual sovereignty "in perpetuity" over the 10-mile-wide strip of the Canal Zone, "to construct, maintain, and defend" a transoceanic canal. The US enclave quickly developed into a "little America" on the isthmus, complete with its own police force, code of law, commissaries, post office, prison system, and counterinsurgency facilities. Panamanian nationalists grated under the constraints that such a colonial enclave imposed upon their nation, bisecting the republic physically, economically, and psychologically. Although the US-controlled enclave brought economic benefit to Panama via the canal's commercial activity, the Zone also reduced Panamanians to second-class citizens in their own land by establishing a foreign population of privileged workers, bureaucrats, and soldiers at the heart of the isthmus. An initial 1936 revision of the 1903 treaty ended the protectorate status of Panama and the US right to intervene unilaterally on the republic's territory, but still left Panamanian patriots frustrated. Likewise a younger generation of Panamanian students,

---

Notes for this section begin on page 301.

activists, and politicians viewed the 1955 accords as an unsatisfactory continuance of the US colonial system in Panama.[1]

Zonians, the US civilian inhabitants of the Canal Zone, saw even the modest American concessions in the 1955 accords as State Department appeasement to radical Panamanian nationalism. The agreed-upon compromises abolished the commissary purchasing rights of those Panamanians who worked for but lived outside the enclave as well as eliminated US-run bakery, dairy, and ice cream production within the Zone. After 1955 the enclave's inhabitants would have to purchase these products from Panama. The new treaty gave Panama the power for the first time to tax the incomes of the West Indian inhabitants of the Zone. Along with the Zonians, the US Defense Department expressed dismay at these small compromises to the US government's supreme position on the isthmus. A recent US-engineered coup in Guatemala against a perceived pro-Soviet regime combined with leftist guerrilla activity in Cuba increased the Pentagon's concern over the cold war security of its prize possession in Latin America: the Panama Canal and its military base complex. Any display of weakness from the US in the Caribbean basin or threat to the cozy military establishment of the Zone raised eyebrows among senior US officers. Throughout 1955, Panamanian anger intensified over US foot dragging in implementing the agreement and the Canal Zone government's hostile interpretation of numerous treaty clauses. In July 1956, nationalist emotion in Panama heightened when Egyptian President Gamel Abdel Nasser seized the Suez Canal from British control. Panamanian writers, students, and radicals called for a similar solution to their own "canal problem."[2]

While these larger events provided the bilateral and global context to the Panamanian nationalist struggle, a shocking series of assaults, rapes, and murders of Panamanian citizens by US military personnel in these same years of 1955–56 galvanized Panamanian popular opinion against the United States. This essay will examine two outrages in particular: the 1955 Helton-Mitchell rape case and the 1956 Harold Rose child-murder case, along with their cultural impact on the troubled US-Panamanian relationship. Such cultural conflicts registered "beneath the radar screen" of high-status diplomatic events yet resonated powerfully in the consciousness of the colonized, more so than any intellectual treaty debate or argument among distant officials. While historians of US-Latin American relations have ably researched the larger political-economic-strategic structure of the United States' and Panama's long association, less attention has been given to the social, cultural, and sexual interactions that helped shape this complex alliance. Historians and political scientists of international relations have increasingly turned to a cultural mode of analysis to examine the profound and multitudinous ways in which nations' citizens encounter one another and how these encounters reflect and influence policy, accommodation, representation, and resistance. In particular the Panamanian sex industry and the US practice of military concubinage played a key role in enforcing US gender hierarchies on the isthmus. Gender and sexuality proved central to the complex network of relationships between civilian and military cultures in Panama, as well as between the US and the Panamanian communities. Conflicts within the realm of sexuality exacerbated binational tensions especially during this historical period when the call for decolonization gained ascendance on both the Panamanian and on the world stage. Increasingly Panamanians began to connect the US colonization of Panama with the American military's subordination of Panamanian and Latina women on the isthmus.[3]

This chapter will explore two key acts of violence and what the different reactions to them tell us about the centrality of imperial culture in the US-Panamanian conflict. Vastly different concepts of race, gender, and sexual mores operated in relations between US servicemen from the First World and Panamanian women from a Latin American/Caribbean culture. Both incidents reflected two key cultural concepts at war on the isthmus: the US sense of paternalism and racial superiority and the Panamanian concept of national dignity and victimization in the face of US power. An analysis of the 1955 twin rape of two Panamanian sisters and the 1956 GI killing of a 2-year-old biracial Panamanian child help us to decipher the cultural and gendered significance of US colonialism in Panama during the post-war era. Both Zone and Panamanian officials regarded a tightly regulated prostitution industry as necessary to bolster US male soldiers' morale, to prevent the spread of sexually transmitted diseases, and to reassure Panama's white upper class and aspiring *mestizo* middle class that the GIs presence would not upset the local moral order. The US military strove to limit its soldiers' sexual relations to foreign prostitutes imported for the Panamanian sex industry and to working- and lower-class Panamanian women. Sexual relations with the latter group, which form the basis of this essay's analysis, would help foster binational accommodation and Panamanian subordination to US hegemony on the isthmus. But such strategies backfired on the US imperial project in unexpected ways and ignited Panamanian resistance during the crucial 1950s.

This essay also attempts to decenter our perspective on US-Latin American relations. Most scholarly works treat such relations from an overwhelmingly US viewpoint, emphasizing US sources, high-status actors, government agencies—that is conventional instruments of state power. Even when exploring "events on the ground" in other nations, these analyses tend to privilege US interpretations of meaning. In contrast, this study will move outside the realm of the White House, the State Department, and the Panamanian Presidential Palace to stress ordinary Panamanians' perceptions of the US presence in their midst. This essay takes a very street-level, "in-country" approach to the US-Panamanian alliance. Its inquiry moves beyond the geostrategic obsession with US power emanating from the metropole toward the "lived" and "felt" experience of local peoples and customs interacting with GIs stationed thousands of miles from home. Oddly enough, once they arrived on the isthmus, the center of the world for US servicemen was quickly transformed from their own bases in the Canal Zone to Panama—that cultural "other" on the "far side of the fence" that beckoned to their desires, needs, and illusions. Panamanian women also exoticized North Americans as objects of desire, danger, and liberation in the borderland that ran the length of the Canal Zone.[4]

On Friday night 16 April 1955, two enlisted men from the US Army, Sergeant William J. Mitchell, 25, and Corporal Vernon O. Helton, 24, met two young Panamanian sisters, 21 and 24, at a USO-sponsored dance at the Fort Amador NCO Club on the Pacific side of the Canal. After the dance, the two soldiers drove the women to the nearby Arraizona Bar in Arraijan just outside the Canal Zone for drinks. After leaving the bar separately, the soldiers later encountered them again at a bus stop nearby and offered them a ride home. Since it was near midnight and the buses had stopped running, the two women accepted. Instead of taking them home as promised, Sergeant Mitchell pulled off onto the jungle K-10 military road just inside the Canal Zone near Arraijan and parked in a clearing. According to the elder Panamanian woman's court testimony, Corporal Helton, who was seated in the back seat, grabbed her and attempted to have sexual intercourse with her in the car. She cried out that "she was a maiden" but he scratched her and forced himself upon her, pulling her by the hair. Her younger sister, sitting in the front seat with Mitchell, attempted to intervene despite Mitchell's attempts to restrain her. The younger sister hit Helton over the head with her shoe when he pounced on her sister. She then handed the shoe to her older sister to use as a weapon. Helton seized the older sister by the throat and dragged her out of the car where he tore her dress but failed in his efforts at penetration during a violent struggle on the ground. Meanwhile in the front seat, Mitchell raped the younger Panamanian sister. She ran into the jungle afterwards looking for her older sister who had already fled the scene.[5]

Following a heated argument, the two soldiers managed to convince the terrified women to get back in the car for transportation home. The soldiers' attorney later used this acquiescence against the women in court, suggesting that no sexual assault but rather consensual relations occurred that night. The women maintained that they only agreed reluctantly to accept a ride back to the city to avoid being abandoned in the jungle. In their traumatized condition they could not exercise proper judgment when they agreed to reenter the car. After driving only a few miles the soldiers' vehicle slowed when it encountered a Canal Zone police car parked at an intersection as a result of an accident. Screaming and weeping, the women leapt from the car and raced over to the accident scene. They told the two US police officers that they had been raped. The police officers noted the women's torn dresses, disheveled appearance, and swollen faces. They also observed the soldier's disorderly countenance and the scratches on their faces and arms. After listening to the sisters' story, the Canal Zone police officers arrested Helton and Mitchell and took them and the sisters back to the Balboa Police Station for further questioning and arraignment. The following afternoon, Panamanian newspapers carried the story of the assaults as front page news, pointedly warning readers of the perils of dating unknown *gringo soldados*.[6]

The US military community in Panama of approximately 20,000 (10,000 troops and 10,000 dependants in 1955) stationed on some fourteen bases within the Canal Zone traditionally maintained better relations with the Panamanian population than did the US civilian employees of the canal, the so-called

Zonians. The US military on the isthmus interacted more frequently with ordinary Panamanians than the US civilian enclave that tended to isolate itself from Panama in its day-to-day social life. Except for employer/employee relations with Panamanian and West Indian servants and service workers—bartenders, waiters, car washers, groundskeepers, and sales clerks—the majority of Zonians had limited contact with the Panamanian population. The Zonians lived in racially segregated communities and facilities separate from the Zone's West Indian inhabitants. This Jim Crow system had its roots in the gold/silver payment practices of the original canal builders that paid US workers in gold and West Indian black workers in silver. In 1947, under civil rights pressure from the Truman administration, the Canal Zone's gold/silver segregated structure changed to a US-rate/local-rate pay and facilities arrangement. But the apartheid nature of the system persisted in spite of a few cosmetic changes.[7]

In contrast to the Zonians, GIs had much higher rates of social and sexual contacts with Panamanians and intermarried frequently with Panamanian women. In the 1950s, Puerto Ricans made up over 30 percent of US military personnel in Panama. These Latin American recruits spoke Spanish, danced salsa, and appreciated the Caribbean culture of Panama. Puerto Rican recruits often served as mediators and translators for white ethnic US troops. While tension existed between the two groups, as one veteran remembered: "A Puerto Rican soldier was the best friend you could have in Panama. They spoke the lingo, could show you the ropes, introduce you to the girls, and teach you the dances, the whole nine yards."[8] Anglo-US soldiers also dated Panamanian girls in large numbers and bought highly prized PX food and clothing items for their Panamanian girlfriends' families. American military personnel "donated" construction materials, gasoline, tools, and auto parts "liberated" from US military warehouses to Panamanian friends and in-laws. In the racial hierarchy of Panama, darker local girls often prized "whiter" American soldiers even more than their Puerto Rican boyfriends. "They were *real* Americans," one recalled. Whatever the GIs' backgrounds, Panamanians welcomed generous US soldiers and their contraband into their homes, fiestas, and *ferias* (country fairs).[9]

US soldiers were also the prime customers of the thriving Panamanian sex industry, where the majority of prostitutes were Colombians, Dominicans, Nicaraguans, and Venezuelans in order to lessen nationalist anger over US exploitation of Panamanian women. The Panamanian government also used foreign women to shield their own female population from the spread of venereal disease. These houses of prostitution—such as the Gruta Azul, the Gloria, the Villa Amor, the Zamba, and the Phoenix—garnered enormous profits for their owners who sometimes included Panamanian government officials. Panamanian- and US-health officers regulated these establishments: they medically examined the prostitutes on a monthly basis and issued or withdrew sex worker visas from foreign *artistas* on the basis of their health and/or criminal records. US military officials cooperated fully with this regulation of the Panamanian sex industry. They issued latex condoms to servicemen and gave prophylaxis treatments to all soldiers, sailors, and airmen returning from the brothels.[10]

One key objective of the American military and the Zone government was to keep prostitution outside the enclave and in Panama. This exclusion of the vice industry from US-administered territory fit in with a long-standing American policy of assuring that the Zone remained a site of cleanliness, health, and order in opposition to the "barbarous" and "chaotic" Panama. The issue of disease and contamination from Panama preoccupied Zonian bureaucrats for generations, dating back to the yellow fever and malaria epidemics of the construction era (1904–14). A second objective centered on barring US personnel from those bordellos judged to be "off-limits" for their high rates of venereal disease and criminal offences against US personnel, typically the robbery or assault of drunken GIs. Occasionally, the Panamanian government moved to close such establishments, although their ownership by powerful local businessmen and Panamanian National Guard officers complicated such measures.[11]

US soldiers typically frequented these brothels for their first few months on the isthmus until they struck up a relationship with a local girl. The bordellos also did an enormous trade from US servicemen on furlough from ships transiting the Canal or on shore leave in the transit ports. Foreign sailors from merchant ships and Panamanian men comprised a significant portion of the brothels' clientele as well. Panamanian brothels also procured business from Zonian bachelors or those married Zonians estranged from their American wives. Male Zonian high school students partook of the trade on weekends. Several divorced and embittered soldiers whose marriages to Panamanian women had failed preferred the whorehouses of Panama to the emotional and financial complications of a new relationship with a Panamanian woman. "One thing you learn down here early: there is no such thing as free pussy," a cynical veteran of the Zone recalled. "Whether you're dating them, marrying them, or just going to the cathouses, when you're a *gringo* down here you pay and you pay and you pay." "I gave up on marriage a long time ago down here," another complained. "You have to remember that when you marry a Panamanian girl, you marry the whole family. First you get the wife and her kids, then the mother moves in, then the brother, a cousin, a nephew. Before you know it you're running a hotel for the homeless with a Panamanian on every couch." Such US attitudes and prejudices spoke volumes toward the colonial nature of US-Panamanian gender relations particularly within the context of military marriages and concubinage with poor or working class local women.[12]

Panamanians in general accepted the US military presence on the isthmus with a variety of attitudes that ranged from disgust to considering it a necessary evil or a bountiful client base. While many local males resented US servicemen striding the streets of their neighborhoods with attractive Panamanian women on their arms like trophies of war, hundreds of Panamanians made a good living shining soldiers' shoes, washing their cars, serving them drinks, finding women for them, coaxing them into red light establishments, driving them in taxis, and selling them street food. Panamanian service workers appreciated US military personnel's generosity in their tips, which were typically three times that of the local rate, and in their willingness to buy rounds of drinks for everyone when they entered an isthmian establishment on payday. While drunken members of the US military often provoked fights with Panamanian National Guardsmen, they proved less hostile toward the civilian population. The typical US soldier or airman served a two to three year hitch in Panama and did not have the same sense of proprietary rights or colonial superiority that second and third-generation Zonians demonstrated. Many US civilian canal workers felt that the Zone was—in the words of Ronald Reagan during the 1976 US presidential campaign—"as much American property as Louisiana or Alaska."[13]

The US military and the Zonian communities operated within the confines of the enclave in an atmosphere of barely repressed hostility. Middle-class Zonians forbade their daughters from dating lower- and working-class enlisted men. Classmates derided any Zonian high school girl who dated a GI as "rappy bait" (derived from Regular Army Personnel, or RAP), a potent insult within the close-knit Zone community. The Zonians reveled in their 25 percent tropical differential (hardship pay for serving in the tropics), eight weeks of paid vacation, and generous government benefits denied to ordinary soldiers. The two communities deployed two antagonistic police forces. The superiority of federal Canal Zone Police over US military police (MPs) chagrined the service constabulary as the former had the right to enter military bases to question and arrest GIs while military police could not arrest civilian Zonians. Zonian teenaged boys frequently taunted MPs when they raided "off-limits" Panamanian brothels. The uniformed police could arrest soldiers, sailors, and airmen for their presence but not Zonian kids who remained outside the MPs' jurisdiction.[14]

GIs resented the privileges of Zonians, not to mention their superior attitudes in general. As one veteran described the unique US social welfare system of the Zonians that afforded the canal workers free health care, education, and a generously subsidized lifestyle: "The government did everything for the civilians down here but wipe their asses."[15] Amicable relations only existed between middle-class officers and Zonians and outgoing Zonians and GIs who shared common interests like hunting, fishing, and visiting brothels. Given this background, it proved ironic that the gravest court cases involving US-Panamanian violence occurred over the actions of the US military and not the more-hated Zonians whose reputation among Panamanians was far worse than that of the GIs. Often the aloofness and exclusivity of the Zonians angered the local population more than the outright abuses suffered at that hands of the US military. One Panamanian remembered: "When people refuse to interact with you, it is like they are saying that you are not human; that you are not as good as I am."[16]

On 18 April 1955, Zone court officials held an initial hearing on the charges filed against Corporal Helton and Sergeant Mitchell in Balboa Municipal Court. A number of Zonian teenagers laughed during the Panamanian women's emotional testimony describing the GIs' attacks. US Judge Richard Altman admonished the spectators for making fun of the women, but the trial quickly became a magnet for controversy and cross-national anger. Gawking spectators, most of them US citizens, packed the small Zone courthouse. Meanwhile in Panama, Spanish-language radio and newspaper accounts dramatized the details of the assaults, warning young Panamanian girls and women of the dire consequences of associating with depraved *gringo soldados*.[17]

On 8 June 1955, Corporal Helton's attempted rape case came to trial in the US District Court of the Canal Zone in Balboa with Judge Guthrie Crowe presiding. Prominent Panamanian nationalists such as Ricardo J. Alfaro had long challenged the legitimacy of this court established in 1912 as a colonial instrument of extraterritoriality. But since the assaults occurred within the boundaries of the Zone, and the arresting officers had been federal Canal Zone policemen, the civilian US court claimed jurisdiction over Panamanian and US military courts. The court empanelled a twelve-member jury of all-white US citizens: ten men and two women. English-language newspapers described the prosecution's key witnesses—the two Panamanian women—as light-skinned *mesitzas* (women of mixed Spanish and Indian ancestry). In the first trial, the prosecutor instructed the jury that it had two choices: to convict Helton of attempted rape, which carried a maximum prison sentence of fourteen years; or to convict him of simple battery which called for a thirty-day sentence and a one hundred dollar fine.[18]

Panamanian accounts of the trial depicted Helton's assault in symbolic terms: as a US attack upon the nation. Panamanian journalists made much of Helton's hulking, overweight physique: 6-feet-2-inches tall and weighing 268 pounds. One Panamanian reporter referred to him as "a sadistic ape." During his opening remarks even the US prosecutor William Sheridan called Helton "a 268 pound blubber bag of lechery." In comparison, Helton's Panamanian victim was described as "slight, slender, innocent, and sweet-faced" in Panamanian dailies such as *La Hora* and *El Dia*. For Panamanian nationalists, the striking contrast between Helton and the young rape victim personified the entire US-Panamanian relationship: that of a dominant 268-pound gorilla and a small, slender innocent—the Panamanian nation—hoodwinked and exploited since 1903.[19]

In these accounts, Panamanian observers feminized their country as virtuous, dignified, and pure in the face of predatory and depraved US masculinity. This approach proved a startling contrast to the more masculine images of Panamanian resistance that would follow during the 1959 and 1964 anti-

American riots. In these celebrated uprisings, hordes of Panamanian protesters, almost all of them male, attempted to penetrate the Zone and plant the staff of the republic's flag in the sacred soil of the Canal Zone. They fired pistols and rifles at the hated *gringo* troops, overturned cars, smashed windows, and torched US symbols of power such as the Pan American Airways building. But in this earlier appeal to international justice, Panamanians preferred the notion of dignified victimhood as their chief stratagem.[20]

In the Balboa courtroom, Helton's Panamanian defense attorney Woodrow Castro immediately cast the young Panamanian women in an unflattering light. "They went onto the base unescorted not knowing the return bus schedule and went to pick up someone. They weren't prostitutes but they were out to seek contacts perhaps to get married eventually...." Castro spoke of women's "traditional attraction" to the military "in art and story as well as in life." "But the attraction is no longer epaulettes," he concluded, referring to the generous government stipends US military men and their Panamanian wives received for rent when living off base, "it is allotments." Speaking for the soldiers and the US community in Panama, Castro placed the two sisters in the hierarchy of sexual opportunism that had long operated in Panama as a result of the US colonial presence. Within this hierarchy, street walkers occupied the lowest rung, followed by *artistas,* officially licensed entertainer/prostitutes who worked the legal houses of prostitution in Panama City and Colón. Higher up in the hierarchy were the so-called "gate girls" who presumably included the two sisters.[21]

"Gate girls" or "gate spiders"—named for their gathering every weekend outside military base gates—were lower-, working-, and even lower-middle-class Panamanian women who entered the Zone every Friday and Saturday night to attend NCO dances in the hopes of establishing a relationship with a GI. Panamanian novelist Joaquin Beleño referred to these women, with their darker complexions and lower social status, as *rabicolorados* (colored birds), in contrast to the upper-class *rabiblancos* (white birds) that had long ruled the roost in Panama. Middle-class Panamanians attached a certain moral stigma to "gate girls," whom many saw as little more than prostitutes. However, "gate girls" comprised a broad range of Panamanian women, some certainly prostitutes that the military attempted to screen, some older women with previous relationships with and children by US servicemen, and many novices like the two sisters, curious to enter the Zone and meet Americans.

This latter group had its own moral code and would generally not sleep with a GI on the first date; rather they sought long-term relationships or even marriage. They were aware that giving in too quickly to soldiers' advances might mark them as "cheap" or "easy" in GI parlance, thereby damaging their chances for a more serious courtship. At the same time, opportunities to spark a relationship with a US soldier were rare and some Panamanian women felt pressure to give in to a serviceman's desires or else lose the chance to develop a deeper connection. Such stark choices left many Panamanian women at these dances in a difficult quandary. Despite North American stereotypes that branded all Panamanian women as naturally promiscuous and creatures of passion, many isthmian women came from strict religious backgrounds and were quite chaste in their personal deportment when meeting strangers. Sexual codes of conduct were never as strict in Panama—with its Caribbean culture—than, for example, in the Andean countries. Yet Panamanian women from the lower-middle class, such as the two sisters, knew the dangers of bringing dishonor to their families through an unwed pregnancy or the gossip that could develop through their publicly cavorting with *yanqui* soldiers.[22]

That said, impoverished Panamanian women suffered economic privation, and attaining a US soldier as a husband was the equivalent of winning the lottery—another obsession of Panama's poor. A senior US sergeant stationed in Panama in the mid 1950s earned more money than many Panamanian doctors and lawyers. Such economic distortions, typical of colonialism, shaped sexual and gender relations between the two nationalities. To have an American boyfriend meant that a Panamanian woman could spend every weekend in the nightclubs and resorts of Panama and the Zone, living a lifestyle most Panamaians could only live vicariously through *telenovelas* (soap operas). But it is important to note that the power differential between privileged US soldiers and economically deprived Panamanian women almost always placed GIs in the superior power position, with all its attendant dangers for abuse. US servicemen frequently impregnated Panamanian women and then abandoned them and their children when the soldiers were shipped stateside or rotated to another overseas posting. The section around Rio Hato, a US military base outside of the Zone near the Pacific became famous for its "blondish, blue-eyed negros," the result of many years of miscegenation between GIs and the local Afro-Panamanian population.²³

Another problem with US-Panamanian gender relations concerned the crossed signals the two parties often sent one another. Social space in Panama was customarily closer than in the United States. Individuals of the opposite sex sat, stood, talked, and danced with one another in much closer proximity than in North America. Panamanian women had long been acculturated to be more tactile and physically expressive of their emotions than many US women. It was quite common for Panamanian women to embrace and kiss male strangers on the cheek upon first meeting them, conduct rare in American society and sometimes misconstrued as provocative. Panamanian women typically danced very closely with American soldiers and constantly held the soldiers' hands and often stared into their eyes upon first meeting them. The rhythmic *salsa* dances of the isthmus intensified this feeling of easy intimacy between the sexes. US soldiers new to the isthmus frequently assumed that Panamanian women "were coming on to them" when this was not necessarily the case. At the same time, Panamanian women viewed ardor on the part of a North American suitor as similar to that of a Panamanian male. Such public passion comprised a key component in the theater of courtship and seduction so prevalent in Panamanian dances and celebrations. While cultural misunderstandings can never excuse sexual assault, they do help to explain how US men and Panamanian women often misread one another's intentions, leading to embarrassing and/or tragic consequences. Language added to the difficulties of these encounters.²⁴ While most upper-class Panamanians spoke English, few impoverished or working-class Panamanians were bilingual. And GI fluency in Spanish was generally abysmal.

During the first trial for Corporal Helton, US women in the courtroom again laughed and tittered at the victim's testimony and drew rebukes from Judge Crowe. Crowe later said that while he tried to prevent this laughter, he could not help it that "some people find sex funny," an odd comment since rape was the topic of the trial. Middle-class US women in the courtroom regarded the Panamanian women with contempt as little more than trollops who got what they deserved. American women also despised these women as possible sexual competition for US males in the Zone. For while Zonians prided themselves on maintaining a clean-living, family lifestyle, American bachelors, disgruntled husbands, and womanizers often drove into Panama on the weekend for discreet liaisons with local women. US women in the Zone were acutely aware that Panama always presented this alternative sexual playground for US males. Frustrated by the enclave's strict moral code, Zonian boys typically lost their virginity to Panamanian prostitutes. Some first entered these *casas de citas* at ages as young as twelve. The legality and availability of prostitution in the republic removed much of the moral stigma normally attached to adultery and promiscuity in 1950s America.[25]

Zonian girls, who made up the majority of the laughing American women in the courtroom, enjoyed the spectacle of seeing GIs in the dock with these questionable Panamanian accusers. Zonian girls had long shunned US servicemen as boyfriends, the one exception being during the Second World War when the US military drafted middle-class recruits and a heroic aura enveloped all servicemen. After 1945, however, middle-class Zonians returned to denigrating working- and lower-class enlisted men, a phenomenon common in many US military base towns as well. The trial thus presented a confirmation of the Zonians' negative view of both US servicemen and Panamanian women: the twin threats to the Zonian sense of propriety. A young recruit in the 1950s remembered asking a Balboa High School cheerleader out on a date at a Zone bus stop. The girl rolled her eyes and pointed toward the Fourth of July Avenue border with Panama. "The whores are down there," she told the GI.[26] Zonians viewed both Panamanian and US civilian women who dated enlisted men as little more than tramps "who should've known what they were in for." When GIs brought their *mestiza* and *mulata* girlfriends into the Zone in the 1950s for dates at the enclave's beaches and swimming pools, they often encountered stares from the color-conscious Zonians.[27]

Adopting an alternatively paternalistic and hostile attitude toward the women, the soldiers' attorney Woodrow Castro denigrated the sisters as either naïve and immature or as knowing seductresses. He questioned their judgment and veracity, implying that they either knew or should have known "the rules of the game" when it came to Panamanian women courting GIs. Castro played upon the Zonian jury's negative stereotypes about isthmian women as loose, promiscuous creatures willing to "throw themselves" at GIs if it might lead them to the altar and, eventually, US citizenship. He also alluded to the notorious reputation of US servicemen as womanizers and men of low character. In this manner, Castro shrewdly appealed to the Zonian jury's acculturated expectations of US-Panamanian sexual relations. According to Castro's weaving of events, such relations were always consensual and inevitably aligned the serviceman's desire for a good time with the Panamanian woman's goal of US wealth and citizenship. In other words, Castro was suggesting that "we know what *these people* are really like and what they are *really* after."[28]

The fact that Castro was of Latin American descent boosted the credibility of his argument. As a Panamanian, he understood isthmian society. By smearing the accusers and their motives through cultural disparagement, he lent a powerful authenticity to the jury's prejudices. Simultaneously, Castro reminded the Zonians that whatever their ethical failings the night of the alleged assault, both Helton and Mitchell had strong service records, the latter having served with distinction in the Korean War. Here Castro appealed to the US jury's chauvinism and to the tendency of all Americans to close ranks and support their fellow citizens when threatened by the cultural "other"—in this case, "barbarous" Panama.[29]

Castro's condescending portrait of the sisters struck a chord with the US jury. Despite strong corroborating testimony from the Canal Zone Police, torn dresses and undergarments, and photographed contusions as physical evidence, the jury found Helton guilty of only the lesser charge of battery and sentenced him to thirty days in jail and a one hundred dollar fine. Helton admitted in court that he had "rough sex" with the woman but that all the activity between them was consensual. Panamanian novelist and journalist Joaquin Beleño expressed his outrage over the verdict in the popular daily *La Hora*. Beleño contrasted the jury's finding with the infamous 1946 rape case of Panamanian West Indian, Leon Lester Greaves, who received a fifty-year sentence in the same US court for raping a white Zonian girl.[30] It proved no accident that Greaves' case gained power as a cause célèbre in Panama shortly after the Helton-Mitchell trials. Eventually Beleño would write Panama's most famous twentieth-century novel, *Los forzados de Gamboa* (Gambo Road Gang), recounting Greaves' plight and the endemic racism of the US-administered Zone.[31]

In a dramatic and telling turn of events, Judge Crowe cancelled the trial of Helton's codefendant Sergeant William Mitchell on the more serious charge of first-degree rape when the two Panamanian sisters refused to return to the US courtroom and testify after the first verdict. The mother of the women told Panamanian and US reporters that she would not permit her daughters to return to the court to again "face ridicule, laughter, and injustice." Her daughters concurred. Indeed, GIs had faced numerous rape charges against Panamanian women during the Second World War and afterward. These soldiers generally drew light or suspended sentences or even had their cases dismissed. Panamanian women had little faith in Canal Zone justice.

Judge Crowe called upon Panamanian detectives to bring the sisters in as reluctant witnesses, but the detectives were unable to persuade the women. Finally the Zone administration enlisted the commandant of the Panamanian National Guard, General Bolívar Vallarino, to convince the sisters to return. Despite his long association as a US ally in Panama and the Panamanian National Guard's close relationship with the US military, Vallarino pointedly refused to pressure the young women and their family. In the popular discourse of the Panamanian media, these women were defending the nation's dignity in their refusal to cooperate with the US court. Better to suffer an injustice with honor than to endure the ridicule and degradation of a US kangaroo court. For a nation long humiliated by US dominance, the concept of dignity held a special cultural import. Little wonder in the 1980s, Panamanian strongman Manuel Noriega referred to his street gang supporters as "dignity battalions."[32]

The 1955 Helton-Mitchell rape case had far reaching consequences in Panamanian society and cultural politics. Panamanian nationalists saw the event as one further example of the moral corruption that the United States and its cultural products, movies, magazines, television, as well as the troops—with their loose morals—had brought to Panama. Panamanian editorial writers compared the US military dances to *mercados de carne* (meat markets). On the heels of the trial, the government launched a crackdown on street and child prostitution, pornography, and the narcotics trade. The Panamanian National Assembly condemned juvenile delinquency and immorality in all its forms. Finally, Panamanian Archbishop Francis Beckman banned the wearing of bathing suits at Panamanian beauty contests. He threatened women who did so with excommunication and denial of the sacraments. "Such displays," according to the archbishop, "propagated vice and propagandized low passions and instincts." On 15 June 1955, days after the Helton trial, the Hotel Panamá canceled the Miss Panama Contest for that year and withdrew its participation from the Miss Universe Contest in Long Beach, CA, rather than defy the archbishop's dictum. No half-naked Miss Panama would parade in front of lascivious *gringos* in California and face the humiliation that the Panamanian sisters had endured in the Canal Zone court.[33]

The case also marked the failure of US-Panamanian collaboration in attempts to regulate the sexual behavior of US soldiers through the sex industry and sanctioned "gate girl" dances. The major focus of these efforts rested on channeling US sexual desire through official brothels and controlled army base events both aimed at limiting US enlisted men's relations to impoverished and lower-class isthmian women. As well as reinforcing the masculine imperial identities of US troops, this careful focusing of American sexual hunger for Panama represented an effort to evade criticism from Panama's upper and middle classes that the US military was corrupting the republic's *gente decente* (decent folk). Though they were still members of Panama's beleaguered working class, the sisters forcefully rejected the degradation that US servicemen and institutions meted out to them. They thus challenged the longstanding and mutually beneficial arrangement between the elites of Panama and the Canal Zone in subordinating lower-class Panamanian women to larger strategic designs. The Panamanian sisters' defiance of both the US court and Panamanian official efforts to coerce their compliance captured the imagination of Panama's popular classes. The Panamanian sisters had symbolically shouted to the US community and the elites of their own nation: "*We*, too are *gente decente*! *We*, too are human beings!" The increasingly anti-oligarchic and anti-American press played a role here in explaining the trial as a case of class and national— that is, not only personal—rape. Though vindicated by the biased US court, Corporal Helton and Sergeant Mitchell still stood condemned in the court of Panamanian public opinion for their atrocities against the Panamanian nation and its most vulnerable citizens.[34]

As crucial as the Helton-Mitchell rape case proved in inflaming Panamanian passions against the United States, perhaps the most shocking court case of an act of US-Panamanian violence took place the following year in November 1956. The Harold Rose child murder case proceeded against the backdrop of dramatic events in Suez that same month, with the Anglo-French intervention to retake the canal. Nasser's July 1956 seizure of the Suez Canal provoked an armed Anglo-French invasion three months later in conjunction with Israeli's conquest of the Sinai. The United States quickly intervened to halt the Western powers' occupation and to legitimate Nasser's sovereignty over the Canal. Suez led to a profound resurgence of Panamanian nationalism and provided the basis for a renewed campaign to assert Panamanian control over the Zone. The incident placed the United States in the dubious position of supporting the nationalization of the Suez Canal by local forces while opposing the same process in Panama. While critics and officials from both nations argued the merits of distant events and their consequences for Panama, on the afternoon of 22 November 1956, US Army Private Harold Rose, 19, hurled the 20-month-old son of his Panamanian girlfriend Blanca Maria Castillo against the cement wall of their apartment, killing the child. His trial later revealed that he did so out of anger after the child repeatedly cried as a result of soiled diapers.[35]

The death of "little Eduardo" Castillo remained front-page news for many days in all of Panama's newspapers with pictures of the small handsome boy and his frightened mother featured prominently on page one. Poignant photos of Eduardo's tiny corpse in the morgue highlighted these tabloid editions. The testimony of neighbors in the apartment building revealed that Private Rose had systematically tortured the infant for months before his death, beating him with a wet towel, whipping him with an electrical cord, and leaving him hanging from a high clothesline while the child begged for help. Initially Private Rose tried to blame the child's death on his mother, but she refused to go along with his contrived story that Eduardo had fallen off the kitchen table and struck his head on the floor. In an interview with reporters, Blanca admitted that Rose "frequently used a wide army belt to beat the boy." A second-degree burn on Eduardo's right upper arm noted by a US Army doctor during a 1 October 1956 medical examination (required in order for Rose to adopt Eduardo) confirmed these allegations of abuse as did the state of the boy's corpse.[36]

Further investigation exposed the source of Rose's hatred toward the boy: Eduardo was a *mulato*. His father—Blanca's previous lover before Rose—had been a black GI. According to witnesses, Rose would repeatedly verbally abuse Eduardo with racial insults such as "come here, you little nigger!" and, "I'll get you now, you black bastard!" before physically beating him. He would also furiously and roughly bathe him, in an apparent attempt to "whiten him." Panamanian accounts erroneously claimed that Rose was from Alabama, while he had actually been born in Maine. But in the anti-American discourse of the day, all racist Americans in Panama were perverted Southerners. As part of their criticism of the Canal Zone's segregation, Panamanian dailies gave intensive coverage to the 1955–56 Montgomery bus boycott led by Martin Luther King. "Little Eduardo" was thus presented as a victim of the United States' two principal vices: racism *and* imperialism.[37]

Since Private Rose killed Eduardo in Panama when he was out-of-uniform and not in the commission of his duties, the Panamanian courts held jurisdiction in the case. The US Army attempted to extradite Rose to the Canal Zone for court martial, but Panama refused. The case had aroused such public emotion that to do so might have provoked anti-government and anti-US riots. As it was, large groups of angry protesters gathered outside the Panama's Second Superior Tribunal. The Panamanian police could barely hold back the crowds that were demanding vigilante justice. Rose did not help matters by smirking nonchalantly for photographers in the courtroom. The photos of the unconcerned Rose in full US Army uniform infuriated ordinary Panamanians. The revelation that Rose also had a 7-month-old child Raquel with Blanca, and that Blanca was five months into a pregnancy with another of Rose's babies, further incensed the Panamanian public.[38]

Eduardo's mother came under considerable criticism as well and eventually faced charges as an unfit mother for her collaboration in Eduardo's torture and death. Panamanian accounts described Blanca as a *cholita interiorana* (Indian girl from the countryside). *Cholitas* frequently worked as maids in the Zone and for well-to-do Panamanians. These women proved the racial and social type most preferred by US servicemen as sexual partners. Allegedly docile and easy sexual conquests, these racially mixed women also had an exotic physical appeal for many white US soldiers. To Panamanian nationalists, life in the countryside, especially in Azuero peninsula and in Chiriqui, encompassed the true Panamanian identity and embodied a certain idealism and nostalgia for traditional Panama before the era of US domination and urbanization engendered by the canal. A strong moral lesson pushed in Panamanian accounts of the Rose case centered on the corruption of country girls like Blanca by the city life, with its pernicious North American influences, licentious soldiers, and nightclubs. According to these accounts, *gringo* soldiers and culture were destroying the innocent *cholita*, once the repository of the Panamanian soul.

In July 1955, the Panamanian daily *La Hora* ran a series of articles about the plight of Dora García, another young *cholita* caught up in a web of US sin. Twenty-three-year-old Dora created a sensation by abandoning her 2-year-old daughter Carmen and her 18-month-old son Juan. Dora left Carmen and Juan with a girlfriend in a dirty rundown room for three days while she drank and danced with American soldiers in the aptly named "Harem" and "El Mambo" cantinas where she worked as a bar girl. Authorities eventually rescued the near-starving children, who were able to survive thanks to heroic efforts at the Children's Hospital. Panamanian journalists portrayed Juan—like "little Eduardo"—as yet another casualty of the malevolent influence of North America on the isthmus.[39]

In July 1955, a series of front-page articles denounced Dora and then chronicled her and her children's state-sponsored rehabilitation. Photographers captured Dora's mother Norberta arriving in the capital by bus from the Chiriqui countryside. "A virtuous country woman," Norberta posted bail for her daughter's release from prison and then set forth to teach her the errors of her ways. Norberta packed up Dora's and her children's belongings and in the final installment of the serial took the family back to the healthy countryside. The fallen *cholita* returned at last to San Juan, Chiriqui, where she and the children, reconciled to their family, could live a decent life far from the wicked city and its perverted *yanquis*. According to the discourse of this story, urbanization destabilized the nation. Escape from US-frequented nightclubs and prostitution proved the family's salvation. As an ironic sidelight, the serial's final installment featured the happy family posing beneath an official photo of the recently assassinated President José Remón. Though enshrined as a hero, Remón had been the owner of numerous brothels similar to those where Dora had worked.[40]

The Panamanian government delayed Rose's trial, hoping to calm emotions in response to US concerns for a fair and balanced prosecution. Harold Rose's parents hired veteran Panamanian attorney José M. Faundes to defend their son. On 3 January 1958, after an anti-climatic trial, a Panamanian judge found Rose guilty of accidental manslaughter, not second-degree murder, the initial charge. Faundes was successful in convincing the judge that Eduardo's death had been a tragic mistake that a remorseful Rose now regretted. He introduced evidence of Rose's earlier attempts to adopt Eduardo and his now-legal marriage to Blanca who resided in the Canal Zone on base housing with their remaining children. Rose had spent less than fourteen months in a Panama prison before his quiet release after the January 1958 trial. The Panamanian government deliberately freed Rose with little fanfare lest it provoke public outcry. The Second Superior Tribunal of Justice sentenced Rose to twenty months, but the court released him four days after his conviction as a result of time already served and time off for good behavior since his November 1956 arrest.[41]

In their year-end editions, Panamanian newspapers listed the Rose case as one of the ten most important events of 1956 along with the Suez Crisis, the Soviet invasion of Hungary, and the election of Ernesto de la Guardia as president of the republic.[42] The Rose case generated a flood of anti-*gringo* sentiment against the US military as well as the US presence in Panama at just the moment when Suez reignited nationalist fervor. Eduardo Castillo came to symbolize small, racially-mixed Panama trampled by a racist and brutish United States. The Rose trial demonstrated how the continued presence of US troops in Panama brought Americans in uniform, many of them from disadvantaged, violent backgrounds themselves, into repeated conflict with the Panamanian population. The US military indoctrinated its troops into a culture of aggressive masculinity, violence, and national chauvinism. Such an atmosphere on the military bases helped foster crossnational antagonisms

The Rose murder trial and the Helton-Mitchell rape cases provided a key popular impetus to the resurgence of Panamanian nationalism in the mid 1950s. This ascendant nationalism had considerable breadth. Though a relatively small movement at the end of World War II, by the late 1950s protests against US control of the Canal Zone included more than just the leftist *Partido Socialista* (PC), the communist *Partido del Pueblo* (PDP), the student union *Frente Patriótico de la Juventud* (FPJ), and the traditionally anti-*gringo* Arnulfista party *Partido Revolucionario Auténtico* (PRA)—the "usual suspects," as the Central Intelligence Agency (CIA) called them. The movement also widened to the formerly accommodative Liberal Party *Partido Liberal Nacional* (PLN), Harmadio Arias' moderate *Partido Nacional Revolucionaria* (PNR), and the populist *Unión Popular* (UP).[43] Urbanization from the wartime boom and its aftermath fueled this nationalist resurgence as increasing numbers of Panamanians from the countryside grew politicized in their daily encounters with GIs, Zonians, and the Canal Zone's provocative presence amid a sea of poverty and red light districts.[44]

The US cultural and racial denigration of Panama drew a heated response from a broad range of Panamanians eager to maintain the republic's honor, traditions, and purity in the face of US colonialism, "Americanization," and cultural pollution. Panamanian nationalists of all stripes discovered a crucial and unifying weapon in their conflict with the North American hegemon: the concept of Panamanian dignity, the portrayal of Panama as an innocent and naive victim before a corrupt and lecherous United States. Both the Panamanian sisters in the Helton-Mitchell case and "little Eduardo" Castillo in the Rose case personified such virtuous, almost "saintly" victims of US arrogance and power.

These images would change quite dramatically in the 1959 and 1964 flag riots against the Zone. When the US concessions of the 1950s and early 1960s failed to mollify the more-radical opponents of the enclave, Panamanian students and workers turned to more "masculine" responses. The most famous of these confrontations occurred in January 1964. A group of Panamanian students entered the Zone to protest the illegal raising of a lone US flag at Balboa High School in the Zone by American students, violating the 1963 Kennedy-Chiari flag agreement. That accord designated fourteen locations in the Zone where both the American and Panamanian flags would fly jointly as an affirmation of Panamanian sovereignty over the enclave. Balboa High School was not among the assigned sites and Zone officials forbade the flying of a single US flag there as had been the practice for the decades prior. Such a glaring US concession provoked outrage from elements of the Zonian and American military communities. Encouraged by their chauvinistic elders, Panamanian and US students engaged in a shoving match at the Balboa High School flag pole when Panamanian youths sought to raise their nation's banner on the school's only flagpole. Panamanian students claimed that the American teenagers had torn their flag during the scuffle.[45]

Panamanian violence in the Zone quickly escalated with vandalism, arson, and the looting of US property. US Canal Zone police and Panamanians then began firing at one another respectively with modern service revolvers and antiquated rifles. By nightfall on 9 January, tens of thousands of Panamanians in the capital and Colón poured into the streets and rioted along the enclave's borders, requiring the deployment of US combat troops to prevent a full-scale invasion. Scores of US soldiers caught unawares in Panamanian brothels or in the apartments of their Panamanian girlfriends and wives had to dress quickly (in civilian clothes so as to not mark themselves as targets) and scurry back to the Zone. The strident violence of this uprising proved more in keeping with the *machista* image of Panama's young and growing male population. Nationalists demonstrated skill at reconfiguring those "images of resistance" most conducive to furthering their aims as the global decolonization movement intensified. In the wake of the Cuban Revolution and the Vietnam War, the popular role of Panama as victim waned and more forceful responses to US colonialism became prominent. Photographs and cartoons from the period showed a ferocious and animated Panamanian resistance against a barbaric foe.[46]

Still the most powerful nationalist image of the 1960s beyond that of young males scaling the Zone's boundary fence during the riots and attempting to raise their flag in the Zone was the vast funeral cortege of the twenty Panamanian victims of the January 1964 riots. The funeral procession stretched for three-quarters of a mile as nearly two hundred thousand citizens gathered for the last rites in the capital. While the ages of the slain ranged from a 6-month-old baby girl asphyxiated by tear gas to a 68-year-old man shot in the chest, the community portrayed them all as students, mere boys cut down by the most powerful military machine on earth. In fact, nine of the twenty victims were over the age of twenty-eight and at least six died of suffocation while caught in the burning Pan American Airways building. Here again, nationalist rhetoric returned to victimization, to the "young innocent sisters" and "poor little Eduardo" of the outrages in the 1950s, the atrocities that first caused the post-war generation to question the price of *gringo* hegemony in their homeland.[47]

The relationship between Panamanians and the US military reached its nadir in the 1964 riots that also claimed the lives of four US soldiers, destroyed numerous buildings, and left hundreds seriously wounded on both sides. Yet even throughout this crisis, the sexual bonds between US soldiers and Panamanian/Latina women persisted. When the Zone shut its borders for several months and forbade its inhabitants from entering Panama, the US military had to bus in prostitutes from Panamanian brothels in an attempt to maintain the sexual equilibrium between the Zone and Panama. Brothel owners cooperated in these efforts, temporarily ending the official taboo against prostitution in the enclave. Freelance sexual operations abounded as well, with US soldiers receiving oral copulation through the apertures of the Canal Zone's infamous chain-link border fence from kneeling Latina prostitutes. Such graphic images starkly demonstrated the US sexual hunger for Panama and the confluence of gendered/racial/colonial subordination inherent in the US-Panamanian relationship.[48]

Alarmed US soldiers who lived in Panama moved their Panamanian wives and children into the Zone to guarantee their safety in the aftermath of the 1964 riots. Enlisted men paid Panamanian boys to deliver love notes to their Panamanian girlfriends and common-law wives who did not merit asylum in the Zone due to their unofficial status. Throughout this crisis, official, individual, and communal concern for US sexual connections in Panama nearly equaled that of military/security considerations. Viewing the webs of prostitution and concubinage within the British Empire, Josephine Butler, the late nineteenth-century English moral crusader, wrote: "We had not realized that the women of a conquered race, in the character of official prostitutes, constituted one of the bulwarks of our great Empire!"[49] These were the same sexual/racial/gendered hierarchies existent in the American Empire in Panama, where the notion of the isthmus as a sexual paradise for GIs had always been one of the region's greatest attractions. Within that garden's paradise, however, laid the seeds of resistance, resentment, and hostility to the US imperial project. Cases such as the Helton-Mitchell rape trial and the Harold Rose child murder scandal helped unravel the US bonds of empire on the isthmus even as they drew impoverished and working-class local women into webs of dependency and accommodation. The racism, sexism, and chauvinism at the heart of US culture in Panama fatally damaged all efforts to build a lasting and just alliance.

In these events we can also perceive the decentering of US power in the hemisphere. Individual agents, US citizens, Panamanians, Puerto Ricans, and other Latinos on the ground, thousands of miles from Washington, DC, subverted, reshaped, and sabotaged the best-laid plans of empire. The networks of desire, prostitution, contraband, and resistance that operated in the Canal Zone borderland were as much a Panamanian as a US enterprise. Neither polity, the Canal Zone government, the Panamanian republic, nor the allegedly all-powerful center in Washington, DC, could effectively maintain control at the borders. Outbreaks at the margins of empire revealed the contradictions and hypocrisies that lay within. And as Panamanian nationalists loved to proclaim: "*Nosotros aqui en Panama somos el centro del mundo!*" (We here in Panama are the center of the world!).[50]

Notes

The author would like to thank the Fulbright Program and the Society for Historians of American Foreign Relations (SHAFR) for their support in funding my overseas research on this topic in the Republic of Panama.

1. For the best overviews of the 1955 treaty and US-Panamanian relations during the 1950s, see Walter LaFeber, *The Panama Canal: The Crisis in Historical Perspective* (New York: Oxford University Press, 1989), 89–102; John Major, *Prize Possession: The United States and the Panama Canal, 1903–1979* (New York: Cambridge University Press, 1993), 241–49; 274–79; Michael L. Conniff, *Panama and the United States: The Forced Alliance* (Athens: University of Georgia Press, 2001), 102–15.
2. For a jaundiced Zonian view of the 1955 treaty, see the aptly titled chapter, "The 1955 Giveaway Treaty Jammed Through – 'Mutual Consent' Is Only Way Out," from Earl Harding, *The Untold Story of Panama* (New York: Athene Press, 1959), 113–18. For the most comprehensive Panamanian accounts of the same period, see Ricardo J. Alfaro, *Medio siglo de relaciones entre Panamá y los Estados Unidos* (Panamá: Imprenta Nacional, 1959); Alfaro, *Los canales internacionales: Panamá* (Panamá: Imprenta Nacional, 1957); Ernesto Castillero Pimental, *Panamá y los Estados Unidos 1903–1953* (Panamá: ACP, 1999); Castillero Pimental, *Política exterior de Panamá* (Panamá: República de Panamá , 1961); Thelma King, *El problema de la soberanía en relaciones entre Panamá y los Estados Unidos* (Panamá: Ministerio de Educación, 1961); César Samudio, *El Canal de Panamá* (Panamá: Imprenta Universitaria, 1992); Celestino Andrés Araúz, *Panamá y sus relaciones internacionales* (Panamá: Universidad de Panamá, 1994); and Patricia Gelós and Celestino Andrés Araúz, *Estudios sobre el Panamá Republicano, 1903–1989* (Bogotá, Colombia: Manfer S. A., 1996).
3. For the importance of cultural, sexual, and racial interaction and images in foreign relations, see Amy Kaplan and Donald E. Pease, eds., *Cultures of United States Imperialism,* (Durham: Duke University Press, 1993); Michael J. Hogan and Thomas G. Paterson, eds., *Explaining the History of American Foreign Relations* (New York: Cambridge University Press, 2004), particularly the essays by Emily Rosenberg, Michael Hunt, and Akira Iriye;

Michael H. Hunt, *Ideology and U.S. Foreign Policy* (New Haven: Yale University Press, 1987); Emily S. Rosenberg, "Cultural Interactions," in *Encyclopedia of the United States in the Twentieth Century,* ed. Stanley I. Kutler, ed. (New York: Charles Scribner's Sons, 1996), 695–717; Gilbert Joseph et al., eds., *Close Encounters of Empire: Writing the Cultural History of U.S-Latin American Relations* (Durham: Duke University Press, 1998); Anne Stoler, "Making Empire Respectable: The Politics of Race and Sexual Morality in 20th Century Southeast Asia," in *Dangerous Liaisons: Gender, Nation, and Postcolonial Perspective,* eds. Anne McClintock et al. (Minneapolis: University of Minnesota Press, 1997); Katharine H. S. Moon, *Sex Among Allies: Military Prostitution in U.S.-Korean Relations* (New York: Colombia University Press, 1997); Ronald Hyman, *Empire and Sexuality: The British Experience* (New York: St. Martin's Press, 1990); Cynthia Enloe, *Bananas, Beaches, and Bases: Making Feminist Sense of International Politics* (Berkeley: University of California Press, 1990); Christian Appy, ed., *Cold War Cultural Constructions: The Political Culture of American Imperialism* (Amherst: University of Massachusetts Press, 2000); John W. Dower, *War Without Mercy: Race and Power in the Pacific War* (New York: Pantheon, 1986).
4. "Two GIs Jailed In Balboa Face Charge of Rape," *Panama American,* 18 April 1955. For an official account of the charges filed against the soldiers and the complete transcript of their trials, see *The Government of the Canal Zone vs. Vernon Omar Helton,* Case No. 4555, and *The Government of the Canal Zone vs. William Jerry Mitchell,* Case No. 4556, 17 April 1955, Ascension #21-76-44-17-7-48-4.3, District Court for the Canal Zone Records (hereafter DCCZR), Record Group 21 (RG 21), The Records of the District Courts of the United States, Box 47, Washington National Records Center (hereafter WNRC), Suitland, MD; "Girl Says 268 Pound GI She Was With Tried To Rape Her: Case Bound Over," *Panama American,* 23 April 1955.
5. "Two GIs Jailed In Balboa Face Charge of Rape," *Panama American,* 18 April 1955. For an official account of the charges filed against the soldiers and the complete transcript of their trials, see *The Government of the Canal Zone vs. Vernon Omar Helton,* Case No. 4555, and *The Government of the Canal Zone vs. William Jerry Mitchell,* Case No. 4556, 17 April 1955, Ascension #21-76-44-17-7-48-4.3, District Court for the Canal Zone Records (hereafter DCCZR), Record Group 21 (RG 21), The Records of the District Courts of the United States, Box 47, Washington National Records Center (hereafter WNRC), Suitland, MD; "Girl Says 268 Pound GI She Was With Tried To Rape Her: Case Bound Over," *Panama American,* 23 April 1955.
6. "Girl Says," *Panama American.*
7. For US military base structure in Panama and troop levels, see Suzanne P. Johnson, *An American Legacy in Panama: A Brief History of the Department of Defense Installations and Properties in the Former Panama Canal Zone* (Corozal, Panama: Directorate of Engineering and Housing, United States Army Garrison-Panama, 1995). For the lifestyle of the Zonians, see Herbert and Mary Knapp, *Red, White, And Blue Paradise: The American Canal Zone in Panama* (San Diego: Harcourt Brace Jovanovich, 1984); Jan Morris, *Destinations: Essays from the Rolling Stone* (New York: Oxford University Press, 1980), 111–43; R. M. Koster and Guillermo Sánchez, *In the Time of the Tyrants: Panama 1968–1990* (New York: W. W. Norton & Company, 1990), 174–82; Paul Theroux, *The Old Patagonian Express* (Boston: Houghton Mifflin, 1979), 201–30; Jules DuBois, *Danger Over Panama* (Indianapolis: Bobbs-Merrill, 1964), 343–61; David McCullough, *The Path Be-*

tween the Seas: The Creation of the Panama Canal, 1879–1914* (New York: Simon & Schuster, 1979), 555–88. For the most cogent analysis of the gold/silver Jim Crow system of the Canal Zone, see Michael F. Conniff, *Black Labor on a White Canal: Panama 1904–1981* (Pittsburgh: University of Pittsburgh Press, 1985). For the problems of racism and changes recommended in gold/silver system during Truman administration, see Frank McSherry, "Report to The Governor of the Panama Canal," Papers of John Mehaffey, Box 2, Folder: Panama Canal 7/1/47–9/30/47, Manuscript Division, Library of Congress, Washington, DC.

8. Interview with retired US Army Sergeant Robert Thrush, 12 August 2002, at his home in Panama City, Republic of Panamá (hereafter RP).

9. Interview with retired US Army Sergeant Wayne Bryant, 5 August 2003, at Niko's Café in Balboa, RP.

10. For the US military's regulation of prostitution in Panama in the 1950s, see "Report on Off-Limits Violations, 1950–1959," 19 February 1960, Adjutant Generals Office, Record Group 338, Records of the United States Caribbean Command 1947–49, File 203.5, Box 14, USNA. For comparisons to cases of the US Military in the Pacific and Korea, see Beth Bailey and Daniel Farber, *The First Strange Place: The Alchemy of Race and Sex in World War II Hawaii* (New York: Free Press, 1992), 95–130; and Katharine H. S. Moon, *Sex Among Allies*.

11. Interviews with Miranda Torres and Sonia Hernandez, 12 July 2002, at the Gruta Azul in Rio Abajo, RP. For the best studies of Panamanian prostitution, see Lana Lois Hyman, *Particularidades De La Prostitution En Panama* (Panamá: Universidad de Panama Escuela de Ley, 1978), and Carmen Anthony et al., *Rasgos De La Prostitution Feminina Adulta Y Minoril En Panama* (Panamá: Universidad de Panamá Instituto de Criminología, 1992).

12. Interview with Tom Carey, 11 May 2001, Albrook, RP; interview with Captain Jody Chamberlain, 20 December 2001, in his home in Piña, RP; interview with George Wheeler and Luke Palumbo, 21 December 2001, in Piña, RP.

13. Information regarding the informal US-Panamanian economy and US servicemen's participation in it is derived from: interview with Donald Philips, former US commissary vendor, 3 January 2002, at Elks Club Lodge 1414 in Balboa, RP; interview with Olmedo De Leon, 22 April 2001, at Bible Crossing Church in Cardenas, RP; and interview with José Rivera-Porras, 3 May 2001, in Ancon, RP. For frictions and benefits of US military presence in Panama, see 169, Harrington to Department of State, 14 February 1957, Foreign Relations of the United States 1955–57, the American Republics: Central and South America (Washington, DC, 1987), 327–36. For Reagan quote, see J. Michael Hogan, *The Panama Canal in American Politics: Domestic Advocacy and the Evolution of Policy* (Carbondale: Southern Illinois University Press, 1986), 79.

14. Herbert and Mary Knapp, *Red, White, and Blue*, 124–25. Information regarding the US Military-Zonian conflicts is derived from an interview with Kurt Chamberlain, 14 August 2002, at his father Captain Joseph Chamberlain's home in Piña, RP.

15. Interview with retired Sergeant Daniel Cooper, 21 July 2002, at Veterans of Foreign Wars Lodge in Curundu, RP.

16. Interview with retired US Corporal James Jenkins, who besides being a soldier in Panama, returned to work as a civilian for the Canal Zone Government and thus had experience in both camps, 21 July 2001, at Veter-

ans of Foreign Wars Lodge in Curundu, RP; interview with Panamanian taxi driver Issac Bonilla, who worked the US military bases in the 1950s and 1960s, 3 April 2002, in Curundu, RP; interview with Hernan DeJesus, former cantina owner, 7 April 2002, in Arraijan, RP.

17. "Packed CZ Court Hear Girl Tell of Fight, Rape," *Panama American,* 27 April 1955.
18. For historical critique of the Canal Zone justice system as an instrument of extraterritoriality, see Wayne D. Bray, *The Common Law Zone in Panama: A Case Study in Reception* (San Juan, PR: Inter American University Press, 1977).
19. "Helton Case Goes To Jury: Fourteen Year Minimum If Convicted As Charged," *Panama American,* 11 June 1955.
20. For other studies of gender constructions and national identity, see Robert D. Dean, "Masculinity as Ideology: John F. Kennedy and the Domestic Politics of Foreign Policy," *Diplomatic History* 22 (Winter 1998): 29–62; Frank Costigliola, *France and the United States: The Cold Alliance Since World War II* (New York: Twayne Publishers, 1992); Costigliola, "'Unceasing Pressure for Penetration': Gender, Pathology, and Emotion in George Kennan's Formation of the Cold War," *Journal of American History* 83 (March 1997): 1309–39; Andrew Jon Rotter, *Comrades at Arms: The United States and India* (Ithaca: Cornell University Press, 2000); Rotter, "Gender Relations, Foreign Relations, The United States and South Asia, 1947–1964," *Journal of American History* 81 (September 1994): 518–42.
21. "Helton Case Goes To Jury," *Panama American.*
22. For the honor/shame sexual paradigm in Latin American culture, see Marit Melhues and Kristi Anne Stolen, eds., *Machos, Mistresses, and Madonnas: Contesting Power of Latin American Gender Imagery* (New York: Verso, 1996).
23. Interview with Jose Miguel Moreno, former Panamanian Foreign Minister, ambassador to the United States, and ambassador to the Organization of American States (OAS), 17 April 2001, in his law offices in Panama City, RP.
24. For the differing cultural, gender, and sexual perceptions between North Americans and Panamanians, see John Biesanz, "Inter-American Marriages on the Isthmus of Panama," *Social Forces* 29 (December 1950): 159–63; John and Mavis Biesanz, *The People of Panama* (New York: Columbia University Press, 1955), 229–30; 311–14; 367–68 ; John Biesanz, Mavis Biesanz, and Luke M. Smith, "Adjustment of Inter-American Marriages on the Isthmus of Panama," *Sociological Review* 16 (December 1951): 76–80; Ramón Carillo and Richard Boyd, "Some Aspects of Social Relations Between Latin and Anglo-Americans on the Isthmus of Panama," *Boletín de la Universidad Interamericana de Panamá* 2 (1945): 703–84; and Herbert and Mary Knapp, *Red White and Blue,* 126–27, 174–76. For further insights into Latin American machismo, see Matthew C. Guttman, *Meaning of Macho: Being A Man in Mexico City* (Berkeley, Calif.: University of California Press, 1996).
25. For Judge Crowe's quote, see "Dismissal Denied in Rape Case: Trial Set For July 5th," *Panama American,* 16 June 1955. On Panama as a US sexual playground, interview with retired Canal Zone Police officer Kenneth Underwood, 12 May 2001, at his home in La Boca, RP; interview with retired Canal Zone Police officer Pablo Prieto, 21 May 2001, at the Autoridad del Canal Building in Balboa Heights, RP; interview with retired Canal Zone

Police officer Edgardo Tirado, 16 May 2001, at Amador, RP; interviews with Canal Zone pilot Captain Jody Chamberlain and retired US school teacher Luke Palumbo, 21 December 2001, at Captain Chamberlain's home in Piña, RP; interview with former Panamanian prostitute Ismela Ruiz, 12 November 2001, in Chorillo, RP; interview with former prostitute Bianca Iglesias, 13 November 2001, in Caledonia, RP; interview with retired Panamanian taxi driver Roberto Murillo, 5 December 2001, in Curundu, RP.

26. Interview with retired Sergeant James Thompson, 5 August 2001, at the Panama Canal Society of Florida Reunion in Orlando, FL.
27. Interview with retired US Army Sergeant Wayne Bryant, 5 August 2003, at Niko's Café in Balboa, RP.
28. Court transcript from The Government of the Canal Zone vs.Vernon Omar Helton, Case No. 4555, 17 April 1955, Ascension #21-76-44-17-7-48-4.3, DCCZR, RG 21, Box 47, WNRC.
29. Ibid.
30. The Canal Zone Government vs. Lester Leon Greaves, Case No. 3861, 24 February 1946, Ascension #55-K-2620, DCCZR, RG 21, Autoridad del Canal de Panama, División de Recuerdos, Corozal, RP.
31. "Jury Finds Helton Guilty of The Lesser Crime Battery," *Panama American,* 12 June 1955; Joaquin Beleño, "Propociones Astronomicas," from his column "Temas Aridos," *La Hora,* 14 June 1955; Beleño, *Los forzados de Gamboa* (Panamá: Impresora Nacional, 1961). For another angry Panamanian critique of both the Helton verdict and later dismissal of charges against Mitchell, see Mario J. Obaldía, "Dolorosa Readidad," *La Hora,* 6 July 1955.
32. "Dismissal Denied in Rape Case," *Panama American.* For the close alliance between the US military and Panamanian National Guard, see Robert C. Harding II, *Military Foundations of Panamanian Politics* (Somerset: Transaction Publishers, 2001); Carlos Guevara Mann, *Panamanian Militarism: An Historical Interpretation* (Athens: Ohio University Center for International Studies, 1996); David Vergara, *Acuerdos militares entre Panamá y los Estados Unidos* (Chitré, RP: Impresora Rios, 1995); Reymundo Gurdian Guerra, *La presencia militar de los Estados Unidos en Panamá* (Panamá: Universidad de Panamá, 1997). For CZ government attempts to persuade the sisters back into court through contacting General Bolívar Vallarino, see CZ Det. Juan Cazoria to C. T. McCormack, CZ Court Clerk, 28 June 1955, from The Government of the Canal Zone vs. William Jerry Mitchell, Case No. 4556, 17 April 1955, Ascension #21-76-44-17-7-48-4.3, DCCZR, RG 21, Box 47, WNRC; "Sisters Firm in Decision: No Testimony," *Sunday American,* 19 June 1955; and "Future A Mystery As Rape Charges Dismissed," *Panama American,* 5 July 1955. For the cultural importance of dignity in Panamanian politics, see Margaret E. Scranton, *The Noriega Years: U.S.-Panamanian Relations 1981–1990* (Boulder: L. Rienner Publishers, 1991), 16.
33. "800 Grabbed As RP Cops Spread Net Over Vice Operations," *Panama American,* 15 June 1955; "El Problema De Moralidad" and "Congresso Para Moralidad," *El Panama América,* 13 June 1955; "Panama Archbishop Beckman Bans Bathing Suits At Beauty Contests," *Star and Herald,* 15 June 1955; "Miss Panama Withdraws From Miss Universe Contest," *Panama American,* 16 June 1955. For Panamanian commentary on Miss Panama's withdrawal, see Fabían Velarde Jr., "Mediodia," *El Dia,* 15 June 1955.

34. For the theoretical constructs of military prostitution within a Third World society, see Cynthia Enloe, *The Morning After: Sexual Politics at the End of the Cold War* (Berkeley: University of California Press, 1993), 142–60, and Saundra Sturdevant and Brenda Stoltzfus, *Let the Good Times Roll: Prostitution and the U.S. Military in Asia* (New York: New Press, 1992). For the economic dependency of impoverished and working-class Latinas on First World white men, see Denise Brennan, *What's Love Got to Do With It? Transnational Desires and Sex Tourism in the Dominican Republic* (Durham: Duke University Press, 2004).
35. "El Soldato Relata El Bestial Asesinato De Niño de 20 Meses" [Soldier tells of His Bestial Murder of a 20-Month-Old Boy], *El Panama América*, 26 November 1956; "More Details of Rose's Atrocities In Panamanian Papers," *Panama American*, 27 November 1956.
36. "Mother Tells How GI Beat 20 Month Old Son," *Panama American*, 27 November 1956. For the US medical report on Eduardo before his death, see "Information re medical treatment for dependent – Harold Frederick Rose," Wilson to Cox, 17 February 1957, RG 338, the Records of the United States Army Caribbean Command, 1947–63, Box 92, Decimal Folder 250.3, "Correction and Punishment," January–December 1958, Box 92, United States National Archives (hereafter USNA), Orchard Park, MD.
37. "Asesinado Por Su Padrastro Con La Venia De Su Madre" [Murdered by His Stepfather with the Consent of His Mother], *La Hora*, 27 November 1956; "Another Soldier Was Father Of The Slain Boy," *Panama American*, 28 November 1956; "Ustedes Lo Mataron" [You Killed Him], and " El Pecado De Ser Negrito" [The Sin of Being a Little Negro], *La Hora*, 27 November 1956; "Declara Blanca María: Quien Mantiene A Mis Hijos?" [Blanca María Declares: Who will Support My Children?], *La Hora*, 28 November 1956.
38. The infamous photo of a smirking, nonchalant Rose can be seen on the first page of the *Panama American, El Panama América*, and the *Star and Herald* in their 26 November 1956 editions.
39. "El Niño Muriendose De Hambre Y La Madre Bailando El Mambo" [A Baby Boy Dying of Hunger and His Mother Dancing the Mambo], *La Hora*, 2 July 1955.
40. The series on Dora García, her daughter, and family ran from 2 through 23 July 1955 in *La Hora*: "Ahi Te Dejo Esa Vaina Y Tiro A Su Hija Menor" [So That You Will Leave this Crap and Tend to Your Young Daughter], *La Hora*, 5 July 1955; "El También es Panameño Abandonado!" [He Also is an Abandoned Panamanian!], *La Hora*, 5 July 1955; "Norbeta García Llega A Intervenir" [Norbeta García Arrives to Intervene], *La Hora*, 22 July 1955; and the final installment with the family posing in Chiriqui beneath the picture of President Remón, "Asi Se Cerro Ese Capitulo Doloroso" [Thus Ends that Sad Chapter], *La Hora*, 23 July 1955.
41. Transript and outcome of trial contained in CARCB 6636, USARCARIB to DEPTAIR Washington, DC, 3 January 1958, RG 338, Box 92, Decimal File 250.3, "Correction and Punishment," January–December 1958, USNA; also in "Rose Receives 15 Months For Manslaughter," *Star and Herald*, 4 January 1958.
42. "Diez Eventos Importantísimos de 1956" [Ten Most Important Events of 1956], *La Hora*, 31 December 1956. The Panamanian official's quote is from Mrs. Harold Rose Sr. to General Harold, 1 March 1957, RG 338, Box 92, Decimal File 250.3, "Correction and Punishment," January–December 1957, USNA.

43. For the best accounts of the sometimes-confusing political alignments and parties in Panama during the 1950s, see Larry LaRae Pippin, *The Remón Years: An Analysis of a Decade of Events in Panama, 1947–1957* (Stanford: Stanford University Press, 1964); Víctor F. Goytía, *Partidos políticos en el istmo* (Panamá: La Revista La Antigua, 1975); and Rubén Darío Souza et al., *Panamá, 1903–1970, nación-imperialismo: Fuerzas populares-oligarquía: Crisis y camino revolucionario* (Santiago, Chile: Talleres de la Sociedad Impresora, 1970).
44. Vilma N. Medina, *El crecimiento de la población panameña en el período 1950 a 1960* (Panamá: Dirección de Estadística y Censo, 1966); Medina, *Estimación de indicadores demográficos de la República de Panamá por el periodo 1950–1970* (Panamá: Contraloría General de la República, 1973); Robert W. Fox, *Population and Urban Trends in Central America and Panama* (Washington, DC: InterAmerican Development Bank, 1977), 176, 190.
45. For an outstanding analysis of the origins, course, and significance of the 1964 Panama Riots, see Alan McPherson, *Yankee No! Anti-Americanism is U.S.-Latin American Relations* (Cambridge: Harvard University Press, 2003), 77–116, and McPherson, "Courts of Public Opinion: Trying the Panama Canal Flag Riots," *Diplomatic History* 28 (January 2004): 83–112. See also William J. Jorden, *Panama Odyssey* (Austin: University of Texas Press, 1984).
46. For the most striking images of the 1964 Panama Riots, see Records Relating to the Events of January 1964, Photographic File, Box 1, RG 185, Records of the Panama Canal, USNA. For official descriptions of the riots, see United States Southern Command Chronology of Events – January 7–January 12, 1964: Report Submitted to Congress, 25 March 1964, Chronology of Events File, Box 1, RG 185, Records of the Panama Canal, USNA. See also *International Commission of Jurists: Report on the Events in Panama, January 9–12, 1964* (Geneva, Switzerland, 1964).
47. For powerful funeral cortege photos of the twenty dead Panamanians, see Records Relating to the Events of January 1964, Photographic File, Box 1, RG 185, USNA; also *Revista Lotería* 83 (Febrero 1964): 141–60. For the ages and identities of the dead, see "Lista de Muertos en los Sucesos de Enero 1964," *Recuerdos de los Sucesos de Enero 1964,* Tomo II, Folder 2, Archivos del Ministerio de Relaciones Exteriores, Quarry Heights, RP.
48. Interview with James Reid, 30 April 2001, at Elk Club 1414 in Balboa, RP; interview with Enrique Cantera, 6 April 2001; interview with Sergeant William Edwards, 21 November 2001, Ft. Lauderdale, FL; and interview with the author Joaquin Villarreal, 10 December 2001, Balboa, RP.
49. For the Butler quote, see Enloe, *Bananas, Beaches, and Bases,* 84.
50. Interview with Cesar Cedeno, 12 April 2003, Curundu, RP.

Bibliography

Alfaro, Ricardo J. *Medio siglo de relaciones entre Panama y los Estados Unidos.* Panama: Imprenta Nacional, 1959.
———. *Los canales internacionales: Panamá.* Panamá: Imprenta Nacional, 1957.
Andrés Araúz, Celestino. *Panamá y sus relaciones internacionales.* Panamá: Universidad de Panamá, 1994.

Anthony, Carmen, et al. *Rasgos De La Prostitution Feminina Adulta Y Minoril En Panamá*. Panamá: Universidad de Panamá Instituto de Criminología, 1992.

Appy, Christian, ed. *Cold War Constructions: The Political Culture of U.S. Imperialism, 1945–1966*. Amherst: University of Massachusetts Press, 2000.

Armbrister, Trevor. "Panama: Why They Hate Us - More than One Torn Flag." *Saturday Evening Post* (7 March 1964), 237.

Beleño, Joaquin. *Los forzados de Gamboa*. Panamá: Imprenta Nacional, 1961.

Bailey, Beth, and David Farber. *The First Strange Place: The Alchemy of Race and Sex in World War II Hawaii*. New York: Free Press, 1992.

Biesanz, John. "Cultural and Economic Factors in Panamanian Race Relations." *American Sociological Review* 14 (1949): 772–79.

———. "Race Relations in the Canal Zone." *Phylon* 11 (1950): 23–30.

———. "Inter-American Marriages on the Isthmus of Panama." *Social Forces* 29 (December 1950): 159–63.

Biesanz, John and Mavis. *The People of Panama*. New York: Columbia University Press, 1955.

———. "Adjustment of Inter-American Marriages on the Isthmus of Panama." *Sociological Review* 16 (December 1951): 76–80

Bray, Wayne D. *The Common Law Zone in Panama: A Case Study in Reception*. San Juan, PR: Inter American University Press, 1977.

Brennan, Denise. *What's Love Got to Do With It? Transnational Desires and Sex Tourism in the Dominican Republic*. Durham: Duke University Press, 2004.

Brock, Rita Nakashima, and Susan Brooks Thistlethwaite. *Casting Stones: Prostitution and Liberation in Asia and the United States*. Minneapolis: Fortress Press, 1996.

Cahill, Anne J. *Rethinking Rape*. Ithaca: Cornell University Press, 2001.

Calzadilla, Carlos G. *Historia Sincera de la Repúblic (Siglo XX)*. Panamá: Editorial Universitaria, 2001.

Carillo, Ramón, and Richard Boyd. "Some Aspects of the Social Relations between Latin and Anglo Americans on the Isthmus of Panama." *Boletín de la Universidad Interamericana de Panamá* 2 (1945): 703–84.

Castillero Pimental, Ernesto. *Panamá y los Estados Unidos 1903–1953*. Panamá: ACP, 1999.

———. *Política exterior de Panamá*. Panamá: Imprenta Nacional, 1961.

Conn, Stetson, and Byron Fairchild. *Guarding the United States and Its Outposts: The U.S. Army in World War II: The Western Hemisphere*. Washington, DC: Government Printing Office, 1964.

Conniff, Michael L. *Black Labor on a White Canal: Panama, 1904–1981*. Pittsburgh: University of Pittsburgh Press, 1985.

———. *Panama and the United States: The Forced Alliance*. Athens: University of Georgia Press, 2001.

———. "Panama Since 1903." In *The Cambridge History of Latin America,* vol. 7, ed. Leslie Bethel. New York: Cambridge University Press, 1990, pp. 603–42.

Costigliola, Frank. *France and the United States: The Cold Alliance Since World War II*. New York: Twayne Publishers, 1992.

———. "'Unceasing Pressure for Penetration': Gender, Pathology, and Emotion in George Kennan's Formation of the Cold War." *Journal of American History* 83 (March 1997): 1309–39.

Darío Souza, Rubén, et al. *Panamá, 1903–1970, nación-imperialismo: Fuerzas populares-oligarquía: Crisis y camino revolucionario*. Santiago, Chile: Talleres de la Sociedad Impresora, 1970.

Dean, Robert D. "Masculinity as Ideology: John F. Kennedy and the Domestic Politics of Foreign Policy." *Diplomatic History* 22 (Winter 1998): 29–62.
De Conde, Alexander. *Ethnicity, Race, and American Foreign Policy: A History.* Boston: Northeastern University Press, 1992.
Dower, John W. *War Without Mercy: Race and Power in the Pacific War.* New York: Pantheon, 1986.
DuBois, Jules. *Danger over Panama.* Indianapolis: Bobbs-Merrill, 1964.
Ealy, Lawrence. *Yanqui Politics and the Isthmian Canal.* University Park: Penn State University Press, 1971.
Enloe, Cynthia. *Bananas, Beaches, & Bases: Making Feminist Sense of International Politics.* Berkeley: University of California Press, 1989.
———. *The Morning After: Sexual Politics at the End of the Cold War.* Berkeley: University of California Press, 1993.
Farnen, Russell F., ed. *Nationalism, Ethnicity, and Identity: Cross National and Comparative Perspectives.* New Brunswick: Rutgers University Press, 1994.
Gilderhus, Mark T. *The Second Century: U.S.-Latin American Relations Since 1889.* Wilmington: Scholarly Resources, 2000.
Goytía, Víctor F. *Partidos políticos en el istmo.* Panamá: La Revista La Antigua, 1975.
Guevara Mann, Carlos. *Panamanian Militarism: An Historical Interpretation.* Athens: Ohio University Center for International Studies, 1996.
Gurdian Guerra, Reymundo. *La presencía militar de los Estados Unidos en Panamá.* Panamá: Universidad de Panamá, 1997.
Guttman, Matthew C. *Meaning of Macho: Being A Man in Mexico City.* Berkeley: University of California Press, 1996.
Harding, Earl. *The Untold Story of Panama.* New York: Athene Press, 1959.
Harding II, Robert C. *Military Foundations of Panamanian Politics.* Somerset: Transaction Publishers, 2001.
Hershatter, Gail. *Dangerous Pleasures: Prostitution and Modernity in Twentieth Century Shanghai.* Berkeley: University of California Press, 1997.
Hogan, J. Michael. *The Panama Canal in American Politics: Domestic Advocacy and the Evolution of Policy.* Carbondale: Southern Illinois University Press, 1986.
Hogan, Michael J., and Thomas G. Paterson, eds. *Explaining the History of American Foreign Relations.* 2nd ed. New York: Oxford University Press, 2004.
Hunt, Michael H. *Ideology and U.S. Foreign Policy.* New Haven: Yale University Press, 1987.
Hyam, Ronald. *Empire & Sexuality: The British Experience.* New York: St. Martin's Press, 1992.
Hyman, Lana Lois. *Particularidades De La Prostitución En Panama.* Panamá: Universidad de Panama Escuela de Ley, 1978.
James, Joy. "US Policy in Panama." *Race and Class,* 32 (1990): 17–32.
Johnson, Suzanne P. *An American Legacy in Panama: A Brief History of the Department of Defense Installations and Properties in the Former Panama Canal Zone.* Corozal, Panama: Directorate of Engineering and Housing, United States Army Garrison-Panama, 1995.
Jorden, William J. *Panama Odyssey.* Austin: University of Texas Press, 1984.
Joseph, Gilbert, et al., eds. *Close Encounters of Empire: Writing the Cultural History of U.S-Latin American Relations.* Durham: Duke University Press, 1998.
Kaplan, Amy, and Donald E. Pease, eds. *Cultures of United States Imperialism.* Durham: Duke University Press, 1993.

Kennedy, Dane. *Islands of White: Settler Society and Culture in Kenya and Southeastern Rhodesia, 1890–1939*. Durham: Duke University Press, 1987.
Knapp, Herbert and Mary. *Red, White, and Blue Paradise: The American Canal Zone in Panama*. San Diego: Harcourt Brace Jovanovich, 1984.
King, Thelma. *El problema de la soberanía en relaciones entre Panamá y los Estados Unidos*. Panamá: Ministerio de Educación, 1961.
Koster, R. M., and Guillermo Sánchez. *In the Time of the Tyrants: Panama 1968–1990*. New York: W. W. Norton, 1990.
LaFeber, Walter. *The Panama Canal: The Crisis in Historical Perspective*. New York: Oxford University Press, 1989.
Lindsay-Poland, John. *Emperors in the Jungle: The Secret History of the U.S. in Panama*. Durham: Duke University Press, 2003.
Major, John. *Prize Possession: The United States and the Panama Canal, 1903–1979*. New York: Cambridge University Press, 1993.
Mastellari Navarro, Jorge E. *Zona del Canal: analogía de una colonia*. Panamá: n.p., 2003.
McCullough, David. *The Path Between The Seas: The Creation of the Panama Canal, 1870–1914*. New York: Simon and Schuster, 1977.
McFerson, Hazel M. *The Racial Dimension of American Overseas Colonial Policy*. Westport: Greenwood Press, 1997.
McPherson, Alan. *Yankee No! Anti-Americanism is U.S.-Latin American Relations*. Cambridge: Harvard University Press, 2003.
———. "Courts of Public Opinion: Trying the Panama Canal Flag Riots." *Diplomatic History* 28 (January 2004): 83–112.
Medina, Vilma N. *El crecimiento de la población panameña en el período 1950 a 1960*. Panamá: Dirección de Estadística y Censo, 1966.
———. *Estimación de indicadores demográficos de la República de Panamá por el periodo 1950–1970*. Panamá: Contraloría General de la República, 1973.
Melhues, Marit, and Kristi Anne Stolen, eds. *Machos, Mistresses, and Madonnas: Contesting Power of Latin American Gender Imagery*. New York: Verso, 1996.
Moon, Katharine H. S. *Sex Among Allies: Military Prostitution in U.S.-Korean Relations*. New York: Columbia University Press, 1997.
Morris, Jan. "Panama, An Imperial Specimen." In *Destinations: Essays from Rolling Stone*, Morris. Oxford: Oxford University Press, 1980, 55–79.
Ortner, Sherry, and Harriet Whitehead, eds. *Sexual Meanings: The Cultural Constructions of Gender and Sexuality*. Cambridge: Cambridge University Press, 1991.
Pike, Fredrick. *The United States and Latin America: Myths and Stereotypes of Nature and Civilization*. Austin: University of Texas Press, 1992.
Pizzurno Gelós, Patricia, and Celestino Andrés Araúz. *Estudios sobre el Panamá Republicano, 1903–1989*. Bogotá, Colombia: Manfer S. A., 1996.
Price, A. Grenfell. "White Settlement in the Canal Zone." *Geographical Review* (1935): 1–11.
Rabe, Stephen G. *Eisenhower and Latin America*. Austin: University of Texas Press, 1988.
———. *The Most Dangerous Area in the World: John F. Kennedy Confronts Communist Revolution in Latin America*. Chapel Hill: University of North Carolina Press, 1999.
Ramírez C., Luis E. *Panama y su historia: una vision diferente de la historía nacional*. Panamá: Imprenta Articsa, 2002.

Rotter, Andrew Jon. *Comrades at Arms: The United States and India.* Ithaca: Cornell University Press, 2000.

———. "Gender Relations, Foreign Relations, the United States and South Asia, 1947–1964." *Journal of American History* 81 (September 1994): 518–42.

Rosenberg, Emily S. "Cultural Interactions." In *Encyclopedia of the United States in the Twentieth Century,* ed. Stanley I. Kutler. New York: Charles Scribner's Sons, 1996, pp. 695–717.

Rudolf, Gloria. *Panama's Poor: Victims, Agents, and Historymakers.* Gainesville: University of Florida Press, 1999.

Samudio, César. *El Canal de Panamá.* Panamá: Imprenta Universitaria, 1992.

Scott, James C. *Domination and the Arts of Resistance: Hidden Transcripts.* New Haven: Yale University Press, 1990.

———. *Weapons of the Weak: Everyday Forms of Peasant Resistance.* New Haven: Yale University Press, 1985.

Scranton, Margaret E. *The Noriega Years: U.S.-Panamanian Relations 1981–1990.* Boulder: L. Rienner, 1991.

Soler, Ricaurte. *Fundación de la nacionalidad panameña.* Caracas, Venezuela: Biblioteca Ayacucho, 1982.

———. *Panama: nación y oligarchía, 1925–1975.* Panama: Ediciones Revistas Tareas, Imprenta Cervantes, 1976.

Stoler, Anne. *Race and the Education of Desire: Foucault's History of Sexuality and the Order of Things.* Durham: Duke University Press, 1995.

———. "Making Empire Respectable: The Politics of Race and Sexual Morality in 20th Century Southeast Asia." In *Dangerous Liaisons: Gender, Nation, and Postcolonial Perspective,* eds. Anne McClintock et al. Minneapolis: University of Minnesota Press, 1997, pp. 344–73.

———. "Carnal Knowledge and Imperial Power: Gender, Race, and Morality in Colonial Asia." In *Feminism and History,* ed. Joan Wallach Scott. New York: Oxford University Press, pp. 209–68.

———. "Sexual Affronts and Racial Frontiers: European Identities and the Cultural Politics of Exclusion in Colonial Southeast Asia." In *Tensions of Empire: Colonial Cultures in a Bourgeois World,* eds. Frederick Coope and Ann Laura Stoler. Berkeley: University of California Press, 1997.

———. "Rethinking Colonial Categories: European Communities and the Boundaries of Rule." In *Colonialism and Culture,* ed. Nicholas B. Dirks. Ann Arbor: University of Michigan Press, 1992.

Sturdevant, Saundra, and Brenda Stoltzfus. *Let the Good Times Roll: Prostitution and the U.S. Military in Asia.* New York: New Press, 1992.

Theroux, Paul. *The Old Patagonia Express: By Train Through the Americas.* Boston: Houghton Mifflin, 1979.

Vergara, David. *Acuerdos militares entre Panamá y los Estados Unidos.* Chitré, RP: Impresora Rios, 1995.

White, Luise. *The Comforts of Home: Prostitution in Colonial Nairobi.* Chicago: University of Chicago Press, 1990.

Part V
DECENTERING THE WORLD? THE CULTURE OF DIPLOMACY

Chapter 9

THE MARRIAGE OF THAMES AND RHINE
Reflections on the English-Palatine Relations 1608–32 and the Culture of Diplomacy in Early Modern Europe

Magnus Rüde

After 350 years of secular diplomacy dominated by state interests, religion is back as a central factor on the stage of world affairs. For the first time since the end of the Thirty Years' War, religious fanatics have shaped international relations with the devastating attacks on 11 September 2001. US authorities have alleged that the conflict had a partly religious logic: After the attacks, the Bush administration publicly declared that they are now fighting the ultimate battle of good versus evil.

Several studies on international history—such as Seth Jacobs' and Andrew Rotter's analysis of US foreign policy in Southeast Asia—have now and then addressed the role of religion and the individual religious background of leading politicians and diplomats in Cold War diplomacy.[1] What has changed with the emergence of global terrorism in world affairs is that the present religious turn in foreign policy now runs in tandem with a new role of the nation-state. In the recent conflicts in Afghanistan and Iraq, we can observe a belligerent combination of state failure and religious radicalization. Today's hot spots of world affairs in Africa and Asia are characterized by eroding state power, the terror of warlords, and a religious overtone. Herfried Münkler hence speaks of the "privatization

Notes for this section begin on page 337.

of warfare," comparing the atrocities of Third World warlords with marauding mercenaries during the Thirty Years' War.[2]

By analyzing Anglo-Palatine relations between 1608 and 1632, this essay sheds light on this complex relationship of foreign policy, state making, and the role of religion as a cultural dimension of diplomacy.[3] At the same time, I will broaden the approach of this volume—decentering America—in a genuine historical sense by applying this twentieth-century concept to early modern history. Focusing on processes, structures, and cultural aspects at the starting point of international relations, I wish to contextualize the history of American international relations. This is particularly true for the power of religion and the political dimensions of militant dogmatism. Both are emerging again as an international issue in the Muslim world after they were superseded by secular ideologies in the nineteenth and twentieth centuries.

When approaching the history of religion and international relations in early modern history, students of nineteenth- and twentieth-century history ought to bear in mind a variety of issues raised by Wolfgang Reinhard and Heinz Schilling. Their "confessionalization" paradigm employs the religious quarrels between Catholics, Lutherans, and Calvinists in the sixteenth and seventeenth centuries as an explanation for both the appearance of the modern confessional churches and the modernization of the European state system. Reinhard and Schilling consider the merger of secular politics and religion in the sixteenth century as more than just the starting point of the rational administrative state. From an international perspective, the birth of the "confessional state" also made religion a decisive force in early modern diplomacy, competing with secular forces like dynasty and state interest as exclusive categories in world affairs.[4]

The confessionalization paradigm constitutes an important aspect of the cultural approach to early modern diplomacy. Religion and dynasty represent two significant factors in the early modern state system that did not only influence the general social structures of early modern society, but also shaped the cultural identity of diplomats, councilors, and princes. By reducing the complexity of world affairs, both forces accommodated rulers (as well as their subjects) with biased interpretations that served to guide their actions. Availing the results of the so-called "cultural turn in international history," I will describe religion and dynasty as a repertory of effective action in early modern world politics. Both forces dominated seventeenth-century diplomacy and together created a dangerous conglomeration of belligerent factors on the eve of the Thirty Years' War.[5]

Applying this paradigm to the case of Anglo-Palatine relations, this chapter combines three different perspectives on early modern international affairs. The first section focuses on the macrohistorical structures of early modern international relations in general. Turning to the tradition of diplomatic history, the following section describes the role of the Palatinate in the seventeenth-century state system and the different political concepts of European politics that were designed by Palatine diplomats. Having described these structural and diplomatic surveys, the main section of this chapter deals with the public performance and perception of Anglo-Palatine relations and examines the role of religious, early modern nationalist, and dynastic concepts of "identity" and "enemy" as issues in pamphlet literature and court festivities from 1613–24.

Structural Conditions of Early Modern International Relations

In Early Modern Europe the concept of a pluralist state system replaced the traditional struggle between papacy and the Empire for universal rule over the Christian realm. The powers gradually agreed that all participants were equal. This development was not paramount to an era of peace and stability in European affairs. Early modern international relations remained in a state of violent flux until they reached their full development in the so-called "classical period" following the Thirty Years' War.[6]

The early modern state itself experienced a time of fundamental change. Since late-medieval times, the feudal state, based on fealty, gradually developed into the modern territorial state. It exerted power over the population with the help of the bureaucracy and the prince's broad sovereignty as supreme legislator, governor, and judge. This process culminated in the emergence of a more or less effective system of tax collecting and the establishment of a military administration in the face of permanent international threats and warfare.[7]

But despite these improvements, the early modern state differed considerably from the twentieth-century nation-state. The main protagonist of early modern international relations was not the "billiard ball" in the international field, proposed by Arnold Wolfers' model of twentieth-century international relations, in which "every state represents a closed, impermeable, and sovereign unit, completely separated from all other states."[8] Instead, lacking clearly defined boarders and a total sway over people and resources, early modern territories rather resembled an amorphous Leviathan similar to the failing states in Africa or Asia today. The merger of the atavistic family interests and the modern reason of state in the person of the ruling prince made the early modern state an unstable hybrid. Due to its unbroken desire for expansion, the state was the driving force of permanent warfare between 1500 and 1800.[9]

In addition to these structural deficits resulting from imperfect state building, religion and dynasty contributed much to the dynamism of sixteenth- and seventeenth-century international relations. Operating on the basis of different rationalities, both these forces of early modern foreign policy shaped, in different ways, the character of the state system.

Scholars arguing for the confessionalization paradigm stress that the emergence of Lutheranism, Calvinism, and Catholicism exerted a huge influence on international relations.[10] The most visible effect of religious divisions in late sixteenth and early seventeenth century was the birth of a bipolar world system, sharply divided between two religious blocks. Europe now experienced a pitiless ideological confrontation between Protestants and Catholics. Between 1550 and 1650, sovereign princes preferred political as well as dynastic alliances with adherents of their own religion and even avoided diplomatic relations with those courts belonging to the opposing religious party. This development culminated in the formation of military pacts comparable to NATO and the Warsaw Pact during the Cold War era. At the same time, the common concept of religion as an indisputable truth of general validity for the human race fostered the idea of spiritual exclusivity even among diplomats and politicians. All of this hampered peaceful settlements in European affairs.[11]

Dynasty represents another, more traditional force in European politics. It adopted an ambivalent position, simultaneously detaching itself from religion but also preserving an autonomous status. On the basis of strategic marriages among other elite families, the European nobility sought to augment its territorial property as well as its social rank in case of succession. This phenomenon of optimized family policy strongly influenced diplomacy from medieval times until the early twentieth century. It shaped international relations by promoting the dynastic state as the dominant model of political order. Dynastic interest, interpreted by the prince as head of both the ruling family and the state, was tantamount to the interest of the state.[12]

The dominance of the dynastic state favored dynasty as a force of diplomacy and changed European politics into a monopoly for a limited number of noble families. At the same time, the dynastic issue destabilized the early modern state and the entire state system. Every crisis within a noble family generated a state crisis and threatened the international system. Facing a plethora of succession conflicts between 1500 and 1900, European affairs suffered mainly from wars of succession.[13]

Besides these structural dimensions, religion and dynasty also represent cultural aspects of early modern international relations. Both were important sources of distinctive social identity for broad parts of the population as well as for elite groups, such as noble families. In this context, religion and dynasty worked as toolkits for individual and collective interpretations of world affairs and led indirectly to social action and reaction in foreign policy.[14] It is therefore useful to examine the cultural dimension of religion and dynasty in the area of early modern communication.

Rüdiger Brandt argues that the public sphere of the sixteenth and seventeenth centuries was the sophisticated negotiation between different individuals and social groups on each stage of the feudal hierarchy. All aspects of daily life, including foreign policy, were part of these negotiations which also could assume a critical dimension and challenge the princely policy.[15] Religion and dynasty represented two important issues for those negotiations. As I will show below, both comprised different contents and were used in a complex communications system.[16]

The Palatinate in Early Modern State System

Despite its small size and lack of economic and military means, the Palatinate temporarily represented an influential agent in the seventeenth-century state system. The development of this south-west imperial estate into a comprehensive territorial state was by no means straightforward. Its traditional dominions in the lower Rhine valley resembled a patchwork consisting of dozens of different regions in which the prince shared power with local knights.[17]

This late semi-feudal character of Palatine territory did not correspond with the astonishing successes in establishing a modern administration.[18] The conversion of the Electoral family to Calvinism in the 1560s was another modernizing force in the princely administration. The Elector Palatine Friedrich III (1515–76), a prince of deep spiritual convictions, took the Lutheran reformation in a more radical direction and opened his boarders for well-trained Protestant refugees from Counter-Reformation countries, like the Spanish Netherlands and France. The new citizens pressed for political responsibility and joined the Electoral council in alliance with Calvinist scholars at the university.

The introduction of Calvinism and the employment of Protestant servants from foreign countries led to considerable social heterogeneity within government. Traditional councilors from neighboring Lutheran knighthoods were now partly displaced by Calvinist French-speaking servants. A large number of them had experienced religious persecution during the Counter Reformation and many had an interest in European affairs. The majority of the councilors took a militant and uncompromising view toward the European state system.[19]

These social peculiarities of Heidelberg's foreign politicians fell on fertile ground in the Palatinate itself. Since the introduction of Calvinism, the Electorate faced a high degree of legal insecurity concerning its constitutional status within the Empire. Until the Treaties of Westphalia in 1648, it was uncertain whether Calvinism belonged to the religious settlement negotiated between Lutherans and Catholics in Augsburg in 1555. Both representatives of Counter-Reformation Catholicism and dogmatic Lutherans doubted that the Electorate formed a part of the peace treaty of 1555 and thus questioned its protection by the imperial constitution.[20]

Besides the juridical insecurities concerning the Palatinate's religious and legal status, the Calvinist religion itself represented a source of unrest and political conflict. Two important dogmatic aspects of Calvinism fostered a kind of militant foreign policy. The first was the theology of predestination, which promised adherents of the church that they were destined to eternal salvation. This doctrine strengthened the widely shared attitude among the Palatine councilors that they were God's elected children and that their actions were sanctioned by

God's will.[21] The second feature of Calvinism was its apocalyptic stance toward history. The apocalyptic interpretation of world history found its all-important end in an imminent crisis of the present world order and a decisive triumph over evil that was part of a divine plan. The combination of this apocalyptic tradition and the theology of predestination promoted a militant style of foreign policy. With these ideological underpinnings, the Palatinate pursued an active policy of international alliances with other Calvinist powers that sought a showdown with the inimical forces of the Counter Reformation.[22]

In addition to militant Protestant influence, the Palatinate also suffered from a dynastic threat. The Electorate was traditionally ruled by the House of Wittelsbach, a venerable imperial dynasty dating back to early medieval times.[23] Due to a specific succession order, the House of Wittelsbach disintegrated in several different branches, of which the Palatine, Bavarian, and Neuburg parts presented the most important dynastic members. The Palatine part claimed the highest rank within the dynasty on the basis of its dignity as both Elector of the Holy Roman Emperor and imperial vicar during an interregnum.[24]

The relationship between the different branches of the house was aggravated by severe internal conflicts. The Bavarian cousins traditionally competed with Heidelberg for the electoral dignity, whereas the Palatine branch had intended to incorporate major parts of the Bavarian territories during the war of succession at the beginning of the sixteenth century. These conflicts were aggravated in the aftermath of Reformation. The Bavarian branch excelled as the avant-garde of Counter Reformation in Germany, whereas Neuburg introduced Lutheranism and intensely opposed Heidelberg's Calvinist reformation. Therefore, a religious dimension permeated traditional conflicts within the House of Wittelsbach during the late sixteenth century.[25]

In sum, due to the specific territorial, constitutional, and political development in the late sixteenth and early seventeenth centuries, the Palatine political elite had to cope with a high degree of religious and dynastic insecurity. These insecurities shaped the individual and collective perception of German and European affairs within the Palatine council, for which both religion and dynasty came to represent two important issues that determined the range of options for Palatine foreign policy.

Palatine foreign policy constantly sought to intervene in the neighboring religious conflicts and civil wars in France and the Netherlands. Although the Electorate could not afford the means to raise powerful troops without foreign help, it excelled in organizing subsidies and the recruitment of mercenaries to relieve the French Huguenot leader and future king Henri de Navarre (1553–1610) in his fight against the Catholic Guise party.[26] But despite some astonishing military victories, the Palatinate soon realized that the small territory lacked the means to maintain an active, interventionist foreign policy. Desiring a more powerful basis for its political designs, the council in Heidelberg made great efforts to unite all Protestant territories and cities in Germany at the beginning of the seventeenth century. The founding of the Protestant Union in 1608 as a reaction to Catholic infringements of the imperial constitution represented a major victory of Palatine policy. Initiated and headed by the Elector Palatine and financed by an impressive number of Lutheran and Calvinist estates, the alliance represented an appealing ally both within and outside the Empire.[27]

Soon after its creation, the Protestant Union entered into serious negotiations with important powers of the anti-Habsburg bloc. Several local conflicts on the eve of the Thirty Years' War pushed forward an international alliance of those nations opposing the offensive policy of Counter-Reformation Spain. After the regicide of the French King Henri IV—the key figure of the international anti-Habsburg party—the alliance developed into a purely Protestant military association.[28] Thanks to the initiative of the Palatine politicians, the Protestant Union concluded a defensive alliance with the English king in 1612. That was further strengthened by the marriage between the young Elector Friedrich V and the English royal Princess Elizabeth Stuart (1596–1662) on Valentine's Day in 1613.

The second important project favored by the Palatine council was a closer alliance with the Protestant noble opposition in Bohemia, which was in constant conflict with its Habsburg rulers. The Bohemian estates' struggle for more religious and constitutional liberties brought them into conflict with the extremist Catholic policy of the Habsburg dynasty. The conflict culminated in the dethroning of the Austrian Archduke Ferdinand as King of Bohemia, symbolized in the famous Defenestration of Prague on 23 May 1618. The Palatinate regarded the Bohemian uprising as an opportunity to strike a decisive blow against the House of Habsburg and weaken the Catholic party.

It was therefore no coincidence that the Palatinate's ambitious policy culminated in the acceptance of the Bohemian crown by the Elector Palatine Friedrich V in 1619, undoubtedly the key event leading to the Thirty Years' War.[29] Unfortunately, the Palatine rule in Bohemia ended in catastrophe. Imperial and Bavarian troops defeated the Palatine-Bohemian forces at the battle of White Mountain on 8 November 1620 and the Spanish army invaded the Elector's home countries. In this desperate situation, Friedrich V and his wife fled to the Netherlands. It was not until the Westphalian Peace Conference of 1648 that their son was reestablished as Elector Palatine in Heidelberg.[30]

At first glance, the Electorate pursued a coherent and uncompromising foreign policy, often labeled as militant Calvinism. It entailed military support for religious allies.[31] Nonetheless it would be misleading to regard religion as the only decisive force in Palatine foreign policy. More accurately, the Electorate's foreign policy represented a sophisticated combination of religious and dynastic interests. Bearing in mind the developments that put the ruling house of the Electorate under heavy dynastic pressure, dynastic issues of reputation and rank also influenced political designs. The Palatinate's role as head of the Protestant Union should therefore be considered a logical continuation of Heidelberg's traditional anti-Habsburg policy, symbolizing the Palatinate's claim to royal dignity, even though dating back to late medieval times the election of the German emperor seemed to be monopolized by the House of Habsburg, and the Wittelsbach dynasty still considered itself a potential candidate for imperial dignity.[32]

Thus, the Electorate's early engagement in the Bohemian troubles not only represented the traditional policy of religious solidarity. As part of the Palatinate's designs on royalty, it also entailed a two-fold dynastic dimension. By replacing the Habsburg dynasty in the Bohemian royal succession, the Palatinate would have acquired a second Electoral dignity. With two of the seven possible votes within the assembly that elected the Emperor, Heidelberg would have substantially improved the prospects of a Wittelsbach candidate for the Imperial crown. Besides these strategic considerations, a successful election of Friedrich V as King of Bohemia would also have increased the reputation of the Electoral family and strengthened its position in the fierce internal conflicts with its Neuburg and Bavarian cousins.

Finally, a similar connection can be observed in the case of Anglo-Palatine relations. The Palatine efforts to negotiate an alliance with the English kingdom and to strengthen it by the marriage of the Elector Palatine with the English royal Princess demonstrate the power of dynastic issues in early modern international relations. Like the Bohemian case, this alliance with a royal house was especially suited to increase the reputation and the social rank of the Electoral house. This was an important advantage given the dynastic pressure the Palatinate faced at the beginning of the seventeenth century. The following study of the public aspects of Anglo-Palatine relations will show this strong influence of dynastic issues on Palatine foreign policy.

Identity and Conceptions of the Enemy in the Public Communications of Anglo-Palatine Relations 1613–24

Public discussions concerning the state system represented an important aspect of seventeenth-century foreign policy, for public interest in international relations involved more than just the surprisingly broad general knowledge concerning events and processes in European affairs. A strenuous public debate on foreign policy also affected the identity of individuals and larger groups.[33]

Thus international relations were not limited to diplomatic actions between two or more powers. They also represented a sophisticated analysis of one's own role and that of others in the state system. Unfortunately, there is no simple connection or mechanism between the image of self and other. Instead, historians must deal with a complex process characterized by competing modes of perception of world affairs. This competition prevented the dominance of any one single identity or concept of the enemy and ensured a high degree of flexibility, regardless of the success of some durable national stereotypes.[34]

Nevertheless it is also plain that public judgments about foreign nations often comprised prejudices and distorted images. Concepts of "attitude" and "identity" as forces in international politics presuppose no realistic or neutral view on world affairs. In fact diplomats and politicians often act on the basis of biased images and attitudes that indirectly influence the decision-making process. It can be said that imperfect and incomplete perspectives on world affairs and their participants constitute a vital mechanism for reducing social complexity and thus enabling action.[35]

In international relations, concepts of the enemy make for striking examples of identity and images of the others. Contrary to simple national stereotypes and prejudices, concepts of the enemy hamper the communication between international rivals and therefore frustrate a peaceful settlement with the foe. This happens due to a relatively stable and highly emotional structure, including the fantasy or actual destruction of the perceived adversary.[36]

Such highly emotional concepts of the enemy also characterized the pamphlet literature dealing with Anglo-Palatine relations in the early seventeenth century. An impressive number of militant, mostly English Protestant authors used a traditional concept of the enemy to publicly assist the Palatine cause at the beginning of the Thirty Years' War. The support culminated in the severe defeat of the allied Palatine-Bohemian forces in the battle of White Mountain and in the capture of Heidelberg by Spanish and Bavarian troops in the fall of 1622. This concept of the enemy was based on the so called *leyenda negra* (black legend), a flat denunciation of the Spanish nation as brutal and immoral. Going back to the early years of the Dutch uprising against the Spanish rulers and the infamous Duke of Alba (1507/08–82), this legend provided the basis for a successful Protestant enemy image that attributed negative and highly emotional prejudices to the Spanish nation.[37]

The English broadsheets and leaflets employed the Spanish theme as code for a brutal, dangerous, and almighty enemy threatening the Electoral family and their fellows in the Palatinate. Yet, the authors varied the black legend. It is possible to discern two major strategies in which the Spanish concept of the enemy was used: an early nationalist and therefore secular polemic operating with generally chauvinist stereotypes concerning Spanish culture and mentality, and a distinctively religious strategy with an apocalyptic interpretation of the Spanish Antichrist.

A prominent example for the first type of anti-Spanish attacks is the theologian and diligent author Thomas Scott (1580–1626). Having fled from Jacobean censorship to the Netherlands in the early 1620s, he produced a plethora of leaflets for the English public in which he resorted to nationalist hispanophobic propaganda. In his leaflets he called on the reluctant English government to attack the Spanish navy in order to relieve the Palatine forces in Bohemia and the Electoral home country.[38]

Scott's major concern was the *monarchia universalis*. In most of Scott's writings, he accused Spain and its Habsburg allies of striving for universal monarchy and therefore hegemony in Europe.[39] This imperialist policy was attributed to the immoral national character of the Spanish nation. Besides zealous Catholicism, Scott also considered the Arabic influence of the Moors a source for the wicked Spanish mentality as illustrated by the brutal missionary work of Spanish conquerors in overseas colonies.[40]

In order to give his writings a personal dimension, Scott frequently employed the infamous figure of Diego Sarmiento de Acuña, Count of Gondomar (1567–1626). The Count resided as Spanish ambassador at the English court from 1613 to 1622 and became the target of anti-Spanish uprisings among radical Protestant groups. In his fictitious leaflet, "Essex's Ghost," written in 1624, Scott confronted Gondomar with Robert Devereux, earl of Essex (1567–1601) and famous victor of the battle of Cádiz (1596). Scott attacked Gondomar for his unscrupulous character and his Machiavellian designs, portraying him as the personification of the vicious Spanish politician.[41]

Fiction remained Scott's favored medium. No clear distinction between political information, comment, and literary fabrication can be detected in his writings. In the first part of "Vox Populi," Scott reported on a meeting of the Spanish secret council, a mere invention of a consultation concerning Madrid's ferocious political plans to oust the Protestant religion from Europe.[42] This case shows the complex relationship between ruler and subject in the early modern communication process. Giving a fictive account of a secret political meeting, Scott publicly infringed on the idea that foreign policy belongs to the so-called *arcana imperii,* those secrets of state from which the common people had to be excluded. Thus despite the biased and fabricated character of this kind of political information, Scott challenged the royal foreign policy by publicly disparaging the king's Spanish allies. Furthermore, Scott weakened the royal prerogative in the field of foreign policy as, for example, in the case of the "Spanish Match": After fierce public upheavals between 1621 and 1624—fueled by Scott's militant writings—James I gave up on his plan to marry his son Charles to a Spanish princess.[43] Royal foreign policy could neglect neither the religious nor the nationalist feelings of the common people any more.

In the long run, such radical examples of anti-Spanish writings shaped the general perception of world affairs in Protestant countries. Another author on foreign policy, John Reynolds (1580?–1626), illustrates the popularity of the concept of the Spanish enemy in the early 1620s. Taking up Scott's contents and style, Reynolds named Spain—but not Bavaria or Vienna—as England's and the Palatinate's greatest enemy.[44] He considered the Spanish government the perfidious intriguer, foiling all negotiations between England and the imperial court. At the same time, he ignored the fact that, besides the total obstinacy of Friedrich V, it was also due to Bavarian and Austrian blockades that a peaceful settlement of the Palatine question failed. This example shows the ways in which an intransigent concept of the enemy distorted the public perception of world affairs. It is highly likely that this extremely pejorative attitude toward Catholic adversaries also influenced the world view among diplomats and finally hampered an otherwise effective diplomatic strategy.

The lion's share of anti-Spanish propaganda employed a clearly religious—that is, anti-Catholic—rhetoric. Contrary to the more secular writings examined above, radical Protestant libels bore witness to an apocalyptic interpretation of international relations and therefore generated a distinctive religious identity concerning one's community, the course of history, and international enemies.

A prominent case of an early modern religious identity is the English kingdom in the aftermath of Tudor Reformation. The introduction of Protestant theology brought deep and often bloody conflicts to England, culminating in religious persecutions during the reign of Mary Tudor (1553–58). These experiences fostered apocalyptic world views within extremist religious groups on the isle. They perceived themselves as warriors in the decisive struggle against the antichrist, represented by the pope and the Spanish.[45] Moreover they soon called themselves martyrs of the Counter Reformation and at the same time God's elected nation, comparable to the people of Israel in the Old Testament.[46]

Appalled by an apparently victorious Counter Reformation, especially after the battle at White Mountain, English theologians and Protestant authors now applied these Mosaic and apocalyptic myths to the case of the Palatinate and to the fate of the Electoral family. In his sermons, Thomas Gataker (1574–

1654) called the Palatinate the new people of Zion, beleaguered by Spanish and Bavarian armies. An anonymous newspaper even drew a parallel between the capture of Heidelberg by Catholic troops in 1622 and the devastation of the Old Temple in Jerusalem by Roman forces in A.D. 70.[47]

The biblical story of Meroz's curse represented the most successful code in English public discourse on the Palatine's destiny during the first years of the Thirty Years' War. The biblical town Meroz refused to assist the people of Israel in its struggle against the infidel and therefore suffered God's eternal malediction (Iudex 5.23). After the first news of the Bohemian uprising and the election of Friedrich V as King of Bohemia arrived in the British Isles, Protestant authors employed Meroz's curse to encode their public critique of James' I indecisiveness. John Harrison began his account of Friedrich's and Elizabeth's departure from Heidelberg for the coronation in Prague with a report of the sermon given by the Electress's chaplain, in which the topic of Meroz was used to criticize the lack of English and international solidarity for the Bohemian and Palatine cause: "Curse ye Meros (said the angel of the lord), curse ye bitter lie the inhabitants thear of because they came not to help the Lord, to help the Lord against the mightie, to help the Lord. I say it is the Lords cause: yea and it is everie mans particular cause that feareth god; for if religion be put to the worst, and suffer, so of consequence must everie one that professeth the same lykewise, of what nation or condition soever."[48]

Biblical codes were also used to stigmatize the international enemy. For example, visions of Spain and the Roman pope as antichrist were inflated dramatically during the matrimonial ceremonies in 1613 and the beginning of the Thirty Years' War. Radical Protestants celebrated the dynastic alliance between Heidelberg and London as "another terror, to the Whore of Babylon," whereas they welcomed Friedrich's election as King of Bohemia as Babylon's fall.[49] Thus, apocalyptic and Mosaic myths as well as biblical codes joined with early nationalist prejudices against Catholic Spain and generated a concept of the international enemy that deeply influenced English perceptions of Anglo-Palatine relations.

Evidence of religious, early modern nationalist, and dynastic identity and conceptions of the enemy as factors in Anglo-Palatine relations can be found not only in public writings and pamphlet literature; it also occurred in the public performances and court festivities accompanying the marriage in 1613. In particular the splendid celebrations and magnificent solemnities in London and Heidelberg represent a collection of historical sources that exemplify those factors guiding and influencing the policy of these two participants in early modern international relations. By examining these cultural sources closely, we can analyze English and Palatine identity as factors in the early modern state system, as well as the Protestant concept of the enemy in world affairs.

Extraordinary celebrations accompanied the Anglo-Palatine marriage in London in February 1613. The kingdom had not seen a royal wedding for many years and the court spared no expense. A variety of public shows, such as sea fights on the river Thames and fireworks combined with theatrical displays were performed to honor the young couple. The festivities culminated in several elaborate court masques in Whitehall, such as Francis Beaumont's (1584–1616) "The Marriage of Thames and Rhine."

The wedding displays communicated a complex system of contents varying from the celebration of peace and unity—symbolized by love and marriage—to the demonstration of martial Protestantism and anti-Catholic sentiments.[50] These different contents reflected the fierce dispute between the adherents of a more conciliatory policy toward the Catholic bloc at the English court and the militant Protestant court faction. Whereas the former regarded the marriage of Friedrich V and Princess Elizabeth as one aspect of peaceful diplomacy, hopefully followed by a Catholic match for Prince Charles, the latter celebrated the Anglo-Palatine alliance as the crucial attempt to topple the assumed Catholic supremacy in Europe.[51]

Thomas Campion (1567–1620) embodied these two different approaches to the Anglo-Palatine marriage in his courtly spectacle "The Lord's Maske," performed on the wedding day in Whitehall. In this masque, English courtiers appeared in antique costumes to celebrate James I alias Jupiter as patron of the arts. At the same time, one courtier, disguised as Prometheus, addressed the young couple to represent his expectations concerning the result of the dynastic alliance: "So be it ever, joy and peace/ And mutual love give you increase;/ That your posteritie may grow / In fame, as long as seas doe flow."[52]

Over the course of the masque, this peaceful statement took on martial overtones in a Latin prognostication by a sibyl addressing Princess Elizabeth, "the future mother of kings, of emperors": "Let the British strength be added to the German: can anything equal it? One mind, one faith, will join two peoples, and one religion, and simple love. Both will have the same enemy, the same ally, the same prayer for those in danger, and the same strength. Peace will favor them, and the fortune of war will favor them; always God the helper will be at their side."[53] In this courtly masque, dynastic ideals concerning a hopeful noble posterity perfectly merged with religious statements longing for a joint Protestant war against the anti-Catholic enemy.

After the marriage in London, the young Elector and his royal bride started their journey to the Elector's countries. A large procession of approximately three hundred servants and over one thousand soldiers accompanied the young couple, underlining their high social rank and reputation. The escort's journey through the Netherlands and the Rhine valley was "performed" as a splendid royal entrée into the Empire, mimicking the example of triumphal processions that victorious generals and emperors held in ancient Rome. With the help of triumphal arcs, battle displays, and exciting fireworks, the Palatine councilors played on the early baroque fashion of celebrating the arrival of royalty.[54]

These luxurious shows formed a vital instrument in representing the Palatinate's status as both a sovereign state and an important actor on the international stage. But it was not only a pretentious show of wealth. The festivities also deployed a sophisticated system of symbols and codes that stood for a heterogeneous group of ideas.[55] Consistent with other court festivities of the early baroque age, the Palatine Electorate used antique topics and motives to bestow the mythical splendor of an idealized antique past upon its noble house and upon its prince. During a procession of masques on 19 June 1613, the Elector Palatine entered his capital Heidelberg disguised as Jason in the search of the Golden Fleece. In this display, Friedrich V used Greek mythology to represent his voyage to England and the marriage of Princess Elizabeth, idealizing himself as an antique hero and his wife as a legendary hoard.[56]

The young Elector used the festivities in the Palatinate to communicate his identity, his concept of the Palatine's role in the European state system, and a clear concept of those enemies threatening Heidelberg's position on the international stage. This concept of the enemy was closely linked to religious statements in the public celebrations of the dynastic alliance. Several triumphal arcs and festive elements clearly branded

Catholic Spain and Rome as dangerous enemies of the Palatinate. Before entering Heidelberg, the Elector Palatine and his wife visited the city of Frankenthal, a Palatine settlement for French and Dutch refugees fleeing from Spanish persecution. Citizens welcomed the couple with two triumphal columns at the market place. The inscriptions on these columns reiterated the common Protestant legend of the sinister Spaniard, characterizing the Spanish nation as the bloodthirsty Catholic persecutor of the Protestants. The burghers hailed Friedrich V and his ancestors as the protectors of the Protestant religion.[57]

Furthermore, the Palatine festivals in Heidelberg in June of 1613 also used scornful elements to denigrate the religious enemy. On a rainy day, the Palatine court interrupted the fes-

Figure 9.1
"Triumphal column erected by the city of Frankenthal to welcome the Elector Palatine Friedrich V and his wife Elizabeth, June 1613." Source: *Beschreibung der Reiss: Empfahun[n]g dess Ritterlichen Ordens: Vollbringung des Heyraths: vnd gluecklicher Heimfuehrung: [...]: Des Herrn Friederichen dess Fuenften/ [...]. Mit der Princessin/ Elisabethen[n]/ [...]* (Heidelberg: Vögelin, 1613).

tivals and organized a comical tournament of fools and jesters using baskets as helmets and straw bales as armor. On a printed leaflet the organizer coined the slogan for the comedy, calling it "Don Quixote de la Mancha's adventures, a tournament for all foolish knights."[58] In this curious early German reading of Cervantes's famous novel from 1605, Heidelberg transformed the legend of the brutal Spaniard into one of a silly Spanish jester who was fooled by Palatine diplomacy: an indicator of the new Palatine self-assurance after sealing the dynastic alliance with England.

Martial and militant tones extended these rather passive and reserved descriptions of the Catholic enemy. During the celebrations of 1613, English and Palatine authors expanded the trope of a decisive fight against the Spanish and Roman Catholic enemy into a more apocalyptic interpretation. The English poet George Wither (1588–1667) expressed the hopes he invested in the Anglo-Palatine marriage in the following fighting verse: "Happy they, and we that see it, / For the good of Europe be it. / And heare Heaven my devotion, / Make this Rhyne and Thame an Ocean: / That it may with might and wonder, / Whelm the pride of Tiber under." [59]

The procession of masques in Heidelberg tied into this apocalyptic interpretation. Friedrich V alias Jason entered Heidelberg in his ship Argo. On the top of the ship's mast the oracle of Delphi promised that the Elector Palatine was destined to fight and destroy the town of Babylon, like "Tiber" another prominent metaphor for Rome as the center of the Counter Reformation. The oracle threatened that Catholic adversaries would wade in their own blood.[60]

Besides this martial tone, celebrations in Palatine towns also employed an abundance of allusions to the royal rank of the new Electress and the new reputation that the house of the Elector Palatine had gained by this dynastic alliance. Given that the entire reception in the Electorate resembled the triumphal entrance of an antique emperor, a great number of royal signs appeared on the engravings and inscriptions of the triumphal arcs. The very moment when Elizabeth's coach passed the arc erected by the University of Heidelberg, a golden crown descended to symbolize the coronation of the only daughter of the English king.[61] In addition, the inscription of a triumphal arc in Oppenheim emphasized that former dynastic alliances between England and the Palatinate had produced numerous famous emperors and kings, a subtle hint to the young couple.[62]

Figure 9.2
"Friedrich V alias Jason on his ship Argo during a procession in Heidelberg, June 1613." Source: *Beschreibung der Reiss: Empfahun[n]g dess Ritterlichen Ordens: Vollbringung des Heyraths: vnd gluecklicher Heimfuehrung: [...]: Des Herrn Friederichen dess Fuenften/ [...]. Mit der Princessin/ Elisabethen[n]/ [...]* (Heidelberg: Vögelin, 1613).

Contrary to the militant, religious topics described above, more peaceable dynastic themes emphasized the importance of harmony and concord. One prominent example was the triumphal arc in the city of Oppenheim. One side of the building was covered with bushes of roses joined at the peak of the arc. The flowers symbolized the two houses of York and Lancaster, famous rivals in the fight for the English crown during the Wars of the Roses (1455–87). The city of Oppenheim used this historical metaphor to state that the union of two houses could settle even the bloodiest dynastic conflict.[63]

A display in the Palatine capital Heidelberg provided a more direct allusion to the conflict within the House of Wittelsbach. A triumphal arc at the entrance of the princely castle celebrated the historical figure of Heinrich the Lion (1129/30–95) as the ancestor of the different Wittelsbach branches.[64] Therefore, not all dynastic displays in 1613 were used in a militant or radical manner. Whereas the religious theme always emphasized the inevitable destruction of the Catholic antichrist,

Figure 9.3
"Frontispiece of a triumphal arc erected by the city of Oppenheim to welcome the Elector Palatine and his wife, June 1613." Source: *Beschreibung der Reiss: Empfahun[n]g dess Ritterlichen Ordens: Vollbringung des Heyraths: vnd gluecklicher Heimfuehrung: [...]: Des Herrn Friederichen dess Fuenften/ [...]. Mit der Princessin/ Elisabethen[n]/ [...]* (Heidelberg: Vögelin, 1613).

the dynastic issue occasionally served to celebrate common interests and ancestry. It offered negotiations and peaceful settlements as alternative perspectives within the international state system.

Conclusion

The examination of religious, early nationalist, and dynastic issues in the pamphlet literature and court festivities 1613–24 reveals the specific English and Palatine concept of the enemy and modes of identity. Writings and public displays reveal a stable and highly emotional concept of the religious adversary, as well as a great degree of dynastic insecurity, especially on the Palatine side. In order to justify the radical means necessary to fight a brutal enemy, broadsheets and court festivities dehumanized the other party. English and Palatinate's concepts of the enemy reduced the complexity of international relations to structure the state system in Manichean terms of good and evil. Conjuring up an imminent international threat and providing a coherent religious and proto-national identity, they also served the interests of political stabilization.

Nevertheless, it is important to qualify the general function of concepts of the enemy in the early modern state system. Religious and dynastic concepts of the adversary varied in their goals. In the case of religious concepts of the enemy, a remarkable increase in biased judgment led to an overestimation of international adversaries. Linked to an apocalyptic interpretation of world affairs, this concept of the religious enemy acquired diabolic proportions in order to comfort domestic religious communities in the face of victorious enemies. The earthly antagonist seemed almost invincible due to his alliance with evil forces, so that in the long run he could only be beaten by a broad alliance of "Godly people," determined to die for a religious cause. Thus, the enemy assumed apocalyptic dimensions and therefore had to be confronted using radical means, including his extermination. This exaggeration of the religious adversary prevented any peaceful settlement.

Contrary to religious concepts of the enemy, the dynastic concepts did not insist upon the destruction of the adversary. Instead, dynasty relied on the existence of other noble families as competitors in the struggle for the limited resources of reputation and honor. Thus, the existence of the other was vital for dynastic concepts of the enemy, because the adversary's judgment and reaction indicated the success of one's own aristocratic claim. Parts of the matrimonial displays in the Palatinate reflected this dynamic. Unlike the polemical anti-Spanish utterances, the Palatine branch of the House of Wittelsbach endeavored to integrate its Catholic competitors in Bavaria by celebrating a common history.

Appallingly, in the case of Anglo-Palatine relations, the dynastic and religious concepts of the enemy merged on the eve of the Thirty Years' War. Due to the specific religious and dynastic insecurity of the Palatine side, the Electorate combined the contest for reputation and honor with its uncompromising fight against the religious adversary. The religious dimension expanded the dynastic idea of fair competition between two opponents to include the ultimate battle between two foes. This merger of different belligerent factors served as a breeding ground for the bloody conflicts in the European state system. It took thirty years of warfare and, finally, intensive negotiations at the peace conference in Münster and Osnabrück to solve this conflict and to commence a new period of international relations.

What can scholars of American and international history learn from the Anglo-Palatine relations between 1608 and 1632? For one thing, it is insufficient to confine one's perspective to purely diplomatic history when dealing with enemy images in international history. The present survey suggests that a combination of traditional diplomatic history, macrohistorical analysis, and a cultural approach to world affairs demonstrates the timeless importance of cultural aspects of the state system, above all religion and dynasty. Both forces represent not only two macrohistorical factors shaping the overall structure of early modern world affairs; they were also cultural powers that influenced identity and generated distinctive, ultimately destructive concepts of the enemy.

Second, this volume's approach—decentering America—would be insufficiently covered if it remained restricted to a mere geographical dimension. Prior eras offer rich historical resources supporting the analyses of atavistic phenomena in contemporary international relations. By utilizing these resources carefully, and by avoiding the methodological traps of eclecticism or anachronism, scholars of international history can improve their analytical toolkits even when dealing with modern diplomacy. They gain deeper understanding of an international system lacking the territorial or nation-state as the sole actor, a system that we can observe today in many contemporary conflicts outside the Western world. For instance, one finds striking similarities between early modern condottieri perfectly represented by the Austrian Duke Albrecht von Wallenstein and the growing market for contemporary private military contractors, such as the South African-based enterprise "Executive Outcome," fighting as modern mercenaries in several African civil wars on account of local warlords. Following this perspective, the preponderance of the territorial state in world affairs represents merely an intermezzo in modern history.

Third, using the evidence of early modern history, scholars can also take a closer look at supposedly irrational motives of diplomacy, as we can currently retrace in the religious harangues of politicians in the Muslim world planning for a global holy war. In doing so, we discover the significance of religion as a power of international relations which cannot be discounted as mere rhetoric confined to underdeveloped societies. In the end, early modern international relations sensitize us for epochal developments such as, perhaps, the twilight of a supreme power straining its might in an asymmetric struggle with determined religious fanatics.

Notes

1. Seth Jacobs, "'Our System Demands the Supreme Being': The U.S. Religious Revival and the 'Diem Experiment', 1947–54," *Diplomatic History* 25 (2001): 589–624; Andrew Rotter, "Christians, Muslims, and Hindus: Religion and US-South Asian Relations, 1947–54," *Diplomatic History* 24 (2000): 593–613.
2. Herfried Münkler, *Die neuen Kriege* (Hamburg: Rowolth Verlag, 2003), 65.
3. Magnus Rüde, *England und Kurpfalz im werdenden Mächteeuropa (1608–1632). Konfession, Dynastie, kulturelle Ausdrucksformen* (Stuttgart: W. Kohlhammer, 2007).
4. Wolfgang Reinhard, "Gegenreformation als Modernisierung? Prolegomena zu einer Theorie des konfessionellen Zeitalters," *Archiv für Reformationsgeschichte* 68 (1977): 226–52; Heinz Schilling, "Confessionalization in the Empire: Religious and Societal Change in Germany between 1555 and 1620," in *Religion, Political Culture and the Emergence of Early Modern Society: Essays in German and Dutch History* (Leiden: Brill, 1992), 205–245.
5. Ursula Lehmkuhl, "Diplomatiegeschichte als internationale Kulturgeschichte: Theoretische Ansätze und empirische Forschung zwischen Historischer Kulturwissenschaft und Soziologischem Institutionalismus," *Geschichte und Gesellschaft* 3 (2001): 394–423; Anja Jetschke and Andrea Liese, "Kultur im Aufwind: Zur Rolle von Bedeutungen, Werten und Handlungsrepertoires in den internationalen Beziehungen," *Zeitschrift für Internationale Beziehungen* 5 (1998): 149–79.
6. Heinz Duchhardt, "Grundmuster der internationalen Beziehungen in der Frühen und Späten Neuzeit," in *Strukturwandel internationaler Beziehungen: Zum Verhältnis von Staat und internationalem System seit dem Westfälischen Frieden,* eds. Jens Siegelberg and Klaus Schlichte (Wiesbaden: Westdeutscher Verlag, 2001), 85.
7. Charles Tilly, "War Making and State Making as Organized Crime," in *Bringing the States Back Inn,* eds. Peter Evans et al. (Cambridge: Cambridge University Press, 1985), 182; Michael Mann, *The Sources of Social Power,* vol. 1, *A History of Power from the Beginning A.D. 1760* (Cambridge: Cambridge University Press, 1986), 476. For the recent debate on the evolution of the modern territorial state, see Charles Maier, "Consigning the Twentieth Century to History: Alternative Narratives for the Modern Era," *American Historical Review* 105 (June 2000): 807–31. Maier, however, dates the takeoff of the industrial nation-state in the 1860s, its descent since the 1960s.
8. Arnold Wolfers, *Discord and Collaboration: Essays on International Politics* (Baltimore: John Hopkins Press, 1962), 19.

9. Johannes Burkhardt, *Der Dreißigjährige Krieg* (Frankfurt: Suhrkamp, 1992), 20.
10. Holger Th. Gräf, *Konfession und internationales System: Die Außenpolitik Hessen-Kassel im konfessionellen Zeitalter* (Darmstadt: Hessische Historische Kommission, 1993), 43; Schilling, "Confessionalization in the Empire," 208.
11. Heinz Schilling, "La confessionalisation et le système international," in *L'Europe des traités de Westphalie: Esprit de la diplomatie de l'esprit*, ed. Lucy Bély (Vendôme: Presses Universitaires de France, 2000), 414.
12. Samuel Clark, *State and Status: The Rise of the State and Aristocratic Power in Western Europe* (Montreal: McGill-Queens University Press, 1995), 182.
13. Johannes Burkhardt, "Die Friedlosigkeit der Frühen Neuzeit: Grundlegung einer Theorie der Bellizität Europas," *Zeitschrift für Historische Forschung* 24 (1997): 509.
14. Ann Swidler, "Culture in Action: Symbols and Strategies," *American Sociological Review* 51 (1986): 273.
15. Rüdiger Brandt, *Enklaven – Exklaven: Zur literarischen Darstellung von Öffentlichkeit und Nichtöffentlichkeit im Mittelalter: Interpretationen, Motiv- und Terminologiestudien* (Munich: Fink, 1993), 301.
16. Axel Schmitt, "Inszenierte Geselligkeit: Methodologische Überlegungen zum Verhältnis von 'Öffentlichkeit' und Kommunikationsstrukturen im höfischen Fest der frühen Neuzeit," in *Geselligkeit und Gesellschaft im Barockzeitalter*, vol. 2, ed. Wolfgang Adam (Wiesbaden: Harrassowitz, 1997), 721.
17. Heinz–Dieter Heimann, *Hausordnung und Staatsbildung: Innerdynastische Konflikte als Wirkungsfaktoren der Herrschaftsverfestigung bei den wittelsbachischen Rheinpfalzgrafen und den Herzögen von Bayern: Ein Beitrag zum Normenwandel in der Krise des Spätmittelalters* (Paderborn: Schöningh, 1993), 288.
18. Henry Cohen, "The Territorial Princes in Germany's Second Reformation, 1559–1622," in *International Calvinism 1541–1715*, ed. Menna Prestwich (Oxford: Clarendon Press, 1985), 144; Volker Press, *Calvinismus und Territorialstaat: Regierung und Zentralbehörden der Kurpfalz 1559–1619* (Stuttgart: Klett, 1970), 19.
19. Claus Peter Clasen, *The Palatinate in European History 1559–1660* (Oxford: Blackwell, 1963), 33; Friedrich Hermann Schubert, *Ludwig Camerarius 1573–1651: Eine Biographie* (Kallmünz: Lassleben, 1955), 52.
20. Martin Heckel, "Reichsrecht und 'Zweite Reformation': Theologisch-juristische Probleme der reformierten Konfessionalisierung," in *Die reformierte Konfessionalisierung in Deutschland: Das Problem der "Zweiten Reformation": Wissenschaftliches Symposion des Vereins für Reformationsgeschichte 1985*, ed. Heinz Schilling (Gütersloh: Bertelsmann, 1986), 22.
21. Robert M. Kingdon, "Der internationale Calvinismus und der Dreißigjährige Krieg," in *1648 – Krieg und Frieden in Europa*, vol. 1, *Politik, Religion, Recht und Gesellschaft*, eds. Klaus Bußmann and Heinz Schilling (Münster: Westfälisches Landesmuseum für Kunst und Kulturgeschichte, 1998), 232.
22. Clasen, *The Palatinate in European History*, 33.
23. Andreas Kraus, "Das Haus Wittelsbach und Europa: Ergebnisse und Ausblick," *Zeitschrift für Bayerische Landesgeschichte*, 44 (1981): 425–52.
24. Volker Press, "Reich und Habsburger Monarchie im europäischen Mächtesystem," in *Die Bildung des frühmodernen Staates – Stände und Konfessionen*, ed. Heiner Timmermann (Saarbrücken-Scheidt: Dadder, 1989), 342.

25. Karl-Friedrich Krieger, "Bayerisch-Pfälzische Unionsbestrebungen vom Hausvertrag von Pavia (1329) bis zur Wittelsbachischen Hausunion vom Jahre 1724," *Zeitschrift für Historische Forschung* 4 (1977): 397.
26. Bernhard Vogler, "Die Rolle der Pfälzischen Kurfürsten in den französischen Religionskriegen (1559–1592)," *Blätter für pfälzische Kirchengeschichte und religiöse Volkskunde* 37/38 (1970/71): 235–66.
27. Axel Gotthard, *Konfession und Staatsräson: Die Außenpolitik Württembergs unter Herzog Johann Friedrich (1608–1628)* (Stuttgart: Kohlhammer, 1992), 32.
28. Friedrich Beiderbeck, "Heinrich IV. von Frankreich und die protestantischen Reichsstände, vol. 2," *Francia* 25 (1998): 20.
29. Joachim Bahlcke, "Theatrum Bohemicum: Reformpläne, Verfassungsideen und Bedrohungsperzeptionen am Vorabend des Dreißigjährigen Krieges," in *Friedliche Intentionen – kriegerische Effekte: War der Ausbruch des Dreißigjährigen Krieges unvermeidlich?* ed. Winfried Schulze (St. Katharinen: Scripta Mercaturae Verlag, 2002), 12.
30. Brennan C. Pursell, *Frederick V of the Palatinate and the Coming of the Thirty Years' War* (Aldershot, Burlington: Ashgate, 2003), 123.
31. Simon L. Adams, "The Protestant Cause: Religious Alliance with the West European Calvinist Communities as a Political Issue in England, 1585–1630" (PhD diss.: University of Oxford, 1973), 425.
32. Heinz Duchhardt, *Protestantisches Kaisertum und altes Reich: Die Diskussion über die Konfession des Kaisers in Politik, Publizistik und Staatsrecht* (Wiesbaden: Steiner, 1977), 108.
33. Peer Schmidt, *Spanische Universalmonarchie oder "teutsche Libertet": Das spanische Imperium in der Propaganda des Dreißigjährigen Krieges* (Stuttgart: Steiner, 2001), 23.
34. Gottfried Niedhart, "Selektive Wahrnehmung und politisches Handeln: Internationale Beziehungen im Perzeptionsparadigma," in *Internationale Geschichte: Themen – Ergebnisse – Aussichten,* eds. Wilfried Loth and Jürgen Osterhammel (Munich: Oldenbourg, 2000), 141.
35. Kenneth Boulding "National Images and International Systems," *Journal of Conflict Resolution* 3 (1959): 120.
36. Ragnhild Fiebig-von Hase, "Introduction," in *Enemy Images in American History,* eds. Ragnhild Fiebig-von Hase and Ursula Lehmkuhl (Providence and Oxford: Berghahn Books, 1997), 8.
37. William S. Maltby, *The Black Legend in England: The Development of Anti-Spanish Sentiment, 1558–1660* (Durham: Duke University Press, 1971).
38. Peter Lake, "Constitutional Consensus and Puritan Opposition in the 1620s: Thomas Scott and the Spanish Match," *The Historical Journal* 25 (1982): 805–25.
39. Thomas Scott, *The Spaniards perpetuall designes to an universall monarchie: Translated according to the French* (London: N.p., 1624).
40. Thomas Scott, *The Second Part of Vox Populi [...]* (London: N.p., 1624).
41. Thomas Scott, *Earl of Essex's Ghost: Sent from Elysium, to the Nobility, Gentry, and Commonalty of England* (London: N.p., 1624).
42. Thomas Scott, *Vox Populi; or Newes from Spayne, translated according to the Spanish Copie, which may serve to forwarn both England and the United Provinces how far to trust Spanish pretences* (London: N.p., 1620).
43. Thomas Cogswell, "England and the Spanish Match," in *Conflict in Early Stuart England: Studies in Religion and Politics,* eds. Richard Cust and Ann Hughes (London and New York: Longman, 1989), 110.

44. John Reynolds, *Vox coeli, or Newes from heaven [...]* (London: N.p., 1624).
45. Matthias Pohlig, "Konfessionskulturelle Deutungsmuster internationaler Konflikte um 1600 – Kreuzzug, Antichrist, Tausendjähriges Reich," *Archiv für Reformationsgeschichte* 93 (2002): 281; Robin B. Barnes, "Varieties of Apocalyptic Experience in Reformation Europe," *Journal of Interdisciplinary History* 33 (2002): 274.
46. Ronald G. Asch, "An Elect Nation? Protestantismus, nationales Selbstbewußtsein und nationale Feindbilder in England und Irland von zirka 1560 bis 1660," in *"Gottes auserwählte Völker": Erwählungsvorstellungen und kollektive Selbstfindung in der Geschichte*, ed. Alois Mosser (Frankfurt: Lang, 2001), 118; Philip S. Gorski, "The Mosaic Moment: An Early Modernist Critique of Modernist Theories of Nationalism," *American Journal of Sociology* 105, 5 (2000): 1452.
47. Thomas Gataker, *A Sparke toward the Kindling of Sorrow for Sion: Mediation on Amos 6.6, Being the Summe of A Sermon preached at Sergeants Inne in Fleet-Street* (London: N.p., 1622); *More Newes From the Palatinate; and More Comfort to every true Christian, that either favoureth the cause of Religion, or wisheth well to the King of Bohemia's proceedings. [...]* (London: N.p., 1621).
48. John Harrison, *A short Relation of the departure of the high and mightie Prince Frederick King Elect of Bohemia: With his royall & vertuous Ladie Elizabeth; And the thryse hoefull yong Prince Henrie, from Heydelberg towards Prague, to receive the Crowne of that Kingdome* (Dort: G. Waters, 1619).
49. George Wither, *Epithalamia or Nuptiall Poems upon the most blessed and Happie Mariage betweene [...] Frederick [...] and [...] Elizabeth [...]* (London: N.p., 1620); *Babilon is fallen [...]* (London: N.p., 1613).
50. Graham Parry, *The Golden Age Restor'd: The Culture of the Stuart Court 1603–1642* (Manchester: University Press, 1981), 107.
51. David Norbrook, "'The Masque of Truth': Court Entertainment and International Protestant Politics in the Early Stuart Period," *Seventeenth Century* 1 (1986): 98.
52. Thomas Campion, "The Description, Speeches, and Songs of The Lords Maske, presented in the Banquetting-house on the mariage night of the high and mightie Count Palatine, and the royally descended the Ladie Elisabeth," in *The Works of Thomas Campion: Complete Songs, Masques, and Treatises with a Selection of the Latin Verse*, ed. Walter R. Davies (Garden City, New York: Doubleday, 1967): 255.
53. See ibid., 260.
54. James Mulryne, "Marriage Entertainments in the Palatinate for Princess Elizabeth Stuart and the Elector Palatinate," in *Italian Renaissance Festivals and their European Influence*, eds. James Mulryne et al. (Lewiston: Edwin Mellen Press, 1992), 173–206; Georg Schmitz, "Die Hochzeit von Themse und Rhein: Gelegenheitsschriften zur Brautfahrt des Kurfürsten Friedrich V. von der Pfalz," *Daphnis* 22 (1993): 265–309.
55. Schmitt, "Inszenierte Geselligkeit"; Gerrit Walther, "Adel und Antike: Zur politischen Bedeutung gelehrter Kultur für die Führungselite der Frühen Neuzeit," *Historische Zeitschrift* 266 (1998): 359–85; Jean Seznec, *Das Fortleben der antiken Götter: Die mythologische Tradition im Humanismus und in der Kunst der Renaissance* (Munich: Fink, 1990).
56. *Paladis Posaun vom Triumph Jasonis [...]* (Heidelberg: N.p., 1613), 14.
57. See fig. 9.1; *Beschreibung der Reiss: Empfahun[n]g dess Ritterlichen Ordens: Vollbringung des Heyraths: vnd gluecklicher Heimfuehrung: [...]: Des*

Herrn Friederichen dess Fuenften/ [...]. Mit der Princessin/ Elisabethen[n]/ [...] (Heidelberg: Vögelin, 1613), 117.
58. Ibid., 199.
59. Wither, *Epithalamia or Nuptiall Poems*.
60. *Paladis Posaun,* 17; see fig. 9.2.
61. *Churfürstlicher Hochzeitlicher HeimführungsTriumph* [...] (Heidelberg, N.p., 1613), 10.
62. *Beschreibung der Reiss,* 109.
63. Ibid., 107; see fig. 9.3.
64. Ibid., 142.

Bibliography

Adams, Simon L. *The Protestant Cause: Religious Alliance with the West European Calvinist Communities as a Political Issue in England, 1585–1630.* PhD diss. Oxford: University of Oxford, 1973.
Asch, Ronald G. "An Elect Nation? Protestantismus, nationales Selbstbewußtsein und nationale Feindbilder in England und Irland von zirka 1560 bis 1660." In *"Gottes auserwählte Völker": Erwählungsvorstellungen und kollektive Selbstfindung in der Geschichte,* ed. Alois Mosser. Frankfurt: Lang, 2001, pp. 117–41.
Babilon is fallen. [...]. London, 1620.
Bahlcke, Joachim. "Theatrum Bohemicum: Reformpläne, Verfassungsideen und Bedrohungsperzeptionen am Vorabend des Dreißigjährigen Krieges." In *Friedliche Intentionen – kriegerische Effekte: War der Ausbruch des Dreißigjährigen Krieges unvermeidlich?* ed. Winfried Schulze. St. Katharinen: Scripta Mercaturae Verlag, 2002, pp. 1–20.
Barnes, Robin B. "Varieties of Apocalyptic Experience in Reformation Europe." *Journal of Interdisciplinary History* 33 (2002): 261–74.
Beiderbeck, Friedrich. "Heinrich IV. von Frankreich und die protestantischen Reichsstände, vol. 2." *Francia* 25 (1998): 1–32.
Beschreibung der Reiss: Empfahun[n]g dess Ritterlichen Ordens: Vollbringung des Heyraths: vnd gluecklicher Heimfuehrung: [...]: Des Herrn Friederichen dess Fuenften/ [...]. Mit der Princessin/ Elisabethen[n]/ [...]. Heidelberg: Vögelin, 1613.
Boulding, Kenneth. "National Images and International Systems." *Journal of Conflict Resolution* 3 (1959): 120–31.
Brandt, Rüdiger. *Enklaven – Exklaven: Zur literarischen Darstellung von Öffentlichkeit und Nichtöffentlichkeit im Mittelalter: Interpretationen, Motiv- und Terminologiestudien.* Munich: Fink, 1993.
Burkhardt, Johannes. "Die Friedlosigkeit der Frühen Neuzeit: Grundlegung einer Theorie der Bellizität Europas." *Zeitschrift für Historische Forschung* 24 (1997): 509–74.
———. *Der Dreißigjährige Krieg.* Frankfurt: Suhrkamp. 1992.
Campion, Thomas. "The Description, Speeches, and Songs of The Lords Maske, presented in the Banquetting-house on the mariage night of the high and mightie Count Palatine, and the royally descended the Ladie Elisabeth." In *The Works of Thomas Campion: Complete Songs, Masques, and Treatises with a Selection of the Latin Verse,* ed. Walter R. Davies. Garden City, New York: Doubleday, 1967, pp. 249–77.
Churfürstlicher Hochzeitlicher HeimführungsTriumph [...]. Heidelberg 1613.

Clark, Samuel. *State and Status: The Rise of the State and Aristocratic Power in Western Europe.* Montreal: McGill-Queens University Press, 1995.
Clasen, Claus Peter. *The Palatinate in European History 1559–1660.* Oxford: Blackwell, 1963.
Cogswell, Thomas. "England and the Spanish Match." In *Conflict in Early Stuart England: Studies in Religion and Politics,* eds. Richard Cust and Ann Hughes. London and New York: Longman, 1989, pp. 107–33.
Cohen, Henry. "The Territorial Princes in Germany's Second Reformation, 1559–1622." In *International Calvinism 1541–1715,* ed. Menna Prestwich. Oxford: Clarendon Press, 1985, pp. 135–65.
Duchhardt, Heinz. "Grundmuster der internationalen Beziehungen in der Frühen und Späten Neuzeit." In *Strukturwandel internationaler Beziehungen: Zum Verhältnis von Staat und internationalem System seit dem Westfälischen Frieden,* eds. Jens Siegelberg and Klaus Schlichte. Wiesbaden: Westdeutscher Verlag, 2001, pp. 74–85.
———. *Protestantisches Kaisertum und altes Reich: Die Diskussion über die Konfession des Kaisers in Politik, Publizistik und Staatsrecht.* Wiesbaden: Steiner, 1977.
Fiebig-von Hase, Ragnhild. "Introduction." In *Enemy Images in American History,* eds. Ragnhild Fiebig-von Hase and Ursula Lehmkuhl. Providence and Oxford: Berghahn Books, 1997, pp. 1–40.
Gataker, Thomas. *A Sparke toward the Kindling of Sorrow for Sion: Mediation on Amos 6.6, being the Summe of A Sermon preached at Sergeants Inne in Fleet-Street.* London: N.p., 1621.
Gorski, Philip S. "The Mosaic Moment: An Early Modernist Critique of Modernist Theories of Nationalism." *American Journal of Sociology* 105, 5 (2000): 1428–68.
Gotthard, Axel. *Konfession und Staatsräson: Die Außenpolitik Württembergs unter Herzog Johann Friedrich (1608–1628).* Stuttgart: Kohlhammer, 1992.
Gräf, Holger Th. *Konfession und internationales System: Die Außenpolitik Hessen-Kassel im konfessionellen Zeitalter.* Darmstadt: Hessische Historische Kommission, 1993.
Harrison, John. *A short Relation of the departure of the high and mightie Prince Frederick King Elect of Bohemia: With his royall & vertuous Ladie Elizabeth; And the thryse hoefull yong Prince Henrie, from Heydelberg towards Prague, to receive the Crowne of that Kingdome.* Dort: G. Walters, 1619.
Heckel, Martin. "Reichsrecht und 'Zweite Reformation': Theologisch-juristische Probleme der reformierten Konfessionalisierung." In *Die reformierte Konfessionalisierung in Deutschland: Das Problem der "Zweiten Reformation": Wissenschaftliches Symposion des Vereins für Reformationsgeschichte 1985,* ed. Heinz Schilling. Gütersloh: Bertelsmann, 1986, pp. 11–44.
Heimann, Heinz-Dieter. *Hausordnung und Staatsbildung: Innerdynastische Konflikte als Wirkungsfaktoren der Herrschaftsverfestigung bei den wittelsbachischen Rheinpfalzgrafen und den Herzögen von Bayern: Ein Beitrag zum Normenwandel in der Krise des Spätmittelalters.* Paderborn: Schöningh, 1993.
Jacobs, Seth. "Our System Demands the Supreme Being: The U.S. Religious Revival and the Diem Experiment, 1954–54." *Diplomatic History* 25 (2001): 589–624
Jetschke, Anja, and Andrea Liese. "Kultur im Aufwind: Zur Rolle von Bedeutungen, Werten und Handlungsrepertoires in den internationalen Beziehungen." *Zeitschrift für Internationale Beziehungen* 5 (1998): 149–79.
Kingdon, Robert M. "Der internationale Calvinismus und der Dreißigjährige Krieg." In *1648 – Krieg und Frieden in Europa,* vol. 1, *Politik, Religion, Recht*

und Gesellschaft, eds. Klaus Bußmann and Heinz Schilling. Münster: Westfälisches Landesmuseum für Kunst und Kulturgeschichte, 1998, pp. 229–35.
Kraus, Andreas. "Das Haus Wittelsbach und Europa: Ergebnisse und Ausblick." *Zeitschrift für Bayerische Landesgeschichte* 44 (1981): 425–52.
Krieger, Karl-Friedrich. "Bayerisch–Pfälzische Unionsbestrebungen vom Hausvertrag von Pavia (1329) bis zur Wittelsbachischen Hausunion vom Jahre 1724." *Zeitschrift für Historische Forschung* 4 (1977): 385–414.
Lake, Peter. "Constitutional Consensus and Puritan Opposition in the 1620s: Thomas Scott and the Spanish Match." *The Historical Journal* 25 (1982): 805–25.
Lehmkuhl, Ursula. "Diplomatiegeschichte als internationale Kulturgeschichte: Theoretische Ansätze und empirische Forschung zwischen Historischer Kulturwissenschaft und Soziologischem Institutionalismus." *Geschichte und Gesellschaft* 3 (2001): 394–423.
Maier, Charles. "Consigning the Twentieth Century to History: Alternative Narratives for the Modern Era." *American Historical Review* 105 (June 2000): 807–31.
Maltby, William S. *The Black Legend in England: The Development of Anti-Spanish Sentiment, 1558–1660.* Durham: Duke University Press, 1971.
Mann, Michael. *The Sources of Social Power,* vol. 1, *A History of Power from the Beginning A.D. 1760.* Cambridge: Cambridge University Press, 1986.
More Newes From the Palatinate; and More Comfort to every true Christian, that either favoureth the cause of Religion, or wisheth well to the King of Bohemia's proceedings. [...]. London: N.p., 1622.
Mulryne, James. "Marriage Entertainments in the Palatinate for Princess Elizabeth Stuart and the Elector Palatinate." In *Italian Renaissance Festivals and their European Influence,* eds. James Mulryne et al. Lewiston: Edwin Mellen Press, 1992, pp. 173–206.
Münkler, Herfried. *Die neuen Kriege.* Hamburg: Rowolth Verlag, 2003.
Niedhart, Gottfried. "Selektive Wahrnehmung und politisches Handeln: Internationale Beziehungen im Perzeptionsparadigma." In *Internationale Geschichte: Themen – Ergebnisse – Aussichten,* eds. Wilfried Loth and Jürgen Osterhammel. Munich: Oldenbourg, 2000, pp. 141–57.
Norbrook, David. "'The Masque of Truth': Court Entertainment and International Protestant Politics in the Early Stuart Period." *Seventeenth Century* 1 (1986): 81–110.
Paladis Posaun vom Triumph Jasonis. [...]. Heidelberg: N.p., 1613.
Parry, Graham. *The Golden Age Restor'd: The Culture of the Stuart Court 1603–1642.* Manchester: University Press, 1981.
Pohlig, Matthias. "Konfessionskulturelle Deutungsmuster internationaler Konflikte um 1600 – Kreuzzug, Antichrist, Tausendjähriges Reich." *Archiv für Reformationsgeschichte* 93 (2002): 278–316.
Press, Volker. *Calvinismus und Territorialstaat: Regierung und Zentralbehörden der Kurpfalz 1559–1619.* Stuttgart: Klett, 1970.
———. "Reich und Habsburger Monarchie im europäischen Mächtesystem." In *Die Bildung des frühmodernen Staates – Stände und Konfessionen,* ed. Heiner Timmermann. Saarbrücken-Scheidt: Dadder, 1989, pp. 331–51.
Pursell, Brennan C. *Frederick V of the Palatinate and the Coming of the Thirty Years' War.* Aldershot, Burlington: Ashgate, 2003.
Reinhard, Wolfgang. "Gegenreformation als Modernisierung? Prolegomena zu einer Theorie des konfessionellen Zeitalters." *Archiv für Reformationsgeschichte* 68 (1977): 226–52.
Reynolds, John. *Vox coeli, or Newes from heaven. [...].* London: N.p., 1624.

Rotter, Andrew. "Christians, Muslims, and Hindus: Religion and US-South Asian Relations, 1947–54." *Diplomatic History* 24 (2000): 593–613.

Rüde, Magnus. *England und Kurpfalz im werdenden Mächteeuropa (1608–1632). Konfession, Dynastie, kulturelle Ausdrucksformen*. Stuttgart: W. Kohlhammer, 2007.

Schilling, Heinz. "Confessionalization in the Empire: Religious and Societal Change in Germany between 1555 and 1620." In *Religion, Political Culture and the Emergence of Early Modern Society: Essays in German and Dutch History*. Leiden: Brill, 1992, pp. 205–45.

———. "La confessionalisation et le système international." In *L'Europe des traités de Westphalie : Esprit de la diplomatie de l'esprit*, ed. Lucy Bély. Vendôme: Presses Universitaires de France, 2000, pp. 411–28.

Schmidt, Peer. *Spanische Universalmonarchie oder "teutsche Libertet": Das spanische Imperium in der Propaganda des Dreißigjährigen Krieges*. Stuttgart: Steiner, 2001.

Schmitt, Axel. "Inszenierte Geselligkeit: Methodologische Überlegungen zum Verhältnis von 'Öffentlichkeit' und Kommunikationsstrukturen im höfischen Fest der frühen Neuzeit." In *Geselligkeit und Gesellschaft im Barockzeitalter*, vol. 2, ed. Wolfgang Adam. Wiesbaden: Harrassowitz, 1997, pp. 713–34.

Schmitz, Georg. "Die Hochzeit von Themse und Rhein: Gelegenheitsschriften zur Brautfahrt des Kurfürsten Friedrich V. von der Pfalz." *Daphnis* 22 (1993): 265–309.

Schubert, Friedrich Hermann. *Ludwig Camerarius 1573–1651: Eine Biographie*. Kallmünz: Lassleben, 1955.

Scott, Thomas. *Vox Populi; or Newes from Spayne, translated according to the Spanish Copie, which may serve to forwarn both England and the United Provinces how far to trust Spanish pretences*. London: N.p., 1620.

———. *The Second Part of Vox Populi [...]*. London: N.p., 1614.

———. *Earl of Essex's Ghost: Sent from Elysium, to the Nobility, Gentry, and Commonalty of England*. London: N.p., 1624.

———. *The Spaniards perpetuall designes to an universall monarchie: Translated according to the French*. London: N.p., 1624.

Seznec, Jean. *Das Fortleben der antiken Götter: Die mythologische Tradition im Humanismus und in der Kunst der Renaissance*. Munich: Fink, 1990.

Swidler, Ann. "Culture in Action: Symbols and Strategies." *American Sociological Review* 51 (1986): 273–86.

Tilly, Charles. "War Making and State Making as Organized Crime." In *Bringing the States Back In*, eds. Peter Evans et al. Cambridge: Cambridge University Press, 1985, pp. 169–91.

Vogler, Bernhard. "Die Rolle der Pfälzischen Kurfürsten in den französischen Religionskriegen (1559–1592)." *Blätter für pfälzische Kirchengeschichte und religiöse Volkskunde* 37/38 (1970/71): 235–66.

Walther, Gerrit. "Adel und Antike: Zur politischen Bedeutung gelehrter Kultur für die Führungselite der Frühen Neuzeit." *Historische Zeitschrift* 266 (1998): 359–85.

Wither, George. *Epithalamia or Nuptiall Poems upon the most blessed and Happie Mariage betweene [...] Frederick [...] and [...] Elizabeth [...]*. London: N.p., 1613.

Wolfers, Arnold. *Discord and Collaboration: Essays on International Politics*. Baltimore: John Hopkins Press, 1962.

Chapter 10

Self-Perception, the Official Attitude toward Pacifism, and Great Power Détente
Reflections on Diplomatic Culture before World War I

Friedrich Kießling

> When the historian of the future writes about our days, he will perhaps admit that the quiet and unobtrusive activity of diplomacy has done some good, if only perhaps in gaining time when popular feeling is running high, in narrowing down certain irritating questions to their real limits—sometimes infinitely smaller than they appear in the excitement of public discussion—and working in this way in the interest of the peace of the world and the harmony of nations which must be the chief aim of all statesmen and diplomatists of our age.[1]

Count Mensdorff-Pouilly-Dietrichstein expressed this hope in a speech delivered in London in May 1914, a few weeks before the Sarajevo assassinations. Today, he would be disappointed. Historians have not praised diplomatic activity before World War I in the way the Austrian ambassador to Great Britain expected. On the contrary, after the war the secret diplomacy of the years before 1914 was thought to be a major, if not the main reason for World War I. And historical judgement has not turned more positive since then. No doubt, methods of diplomacy used before 1914 proved unfit to handle international relations at the beginning of the twentieth century in an ade-

---

Notes for this section begin on page 369.

quate way and to prevent the breakdown of European peace. Nevertheless Mensdorff's statement is worthwhile for historical analysis. The Austrian ambassador does not tell us much about the course of events before 1914 and, as far as I can tell, his speech has never been quoted in the vast amount of work published on the outbreak of World War I. However, with regard to a different aspect of international relations before 1914, Mensdorff's speech is extremely revealing. By expressing a diplomat's view of the world, it provides insight into what we might call "diplomatic culture" before 1914.

There are several different ways of integrating cultural factors into the history of international relations.[2] In the context of diplomatic culture one distinction is especially interesting: studies like those of Emily Rosenberg or Anders Stephanson describe and explain foreign policy as being an integral part of existing cultural entities.[3] Other historians, such as James Der Derian, Jürgen Osterhammel, or Johannes Paulmann, analyze international relations as a cultural phenomenon in its own right. They are primarily concerned with concepts and self-perception of the decisionmakers, the rules and customs they followed, and the way in which they interacted. This chapter contributes to the considerations introduced by Osterhammel and others.[4]

Interconnections between culture and the history of international relations have been traced principally for the Cold War when the United States became a major player in the bipolar struggle. Fredrik Logevall, for example, studies the specific style of US diplomacy after 1945 (which he refers to as a "nondiplomacy") and contrasts it with a European approach to international negotiations.[5] In this context the study of diplomatic culture during the pre–World War I era contributes to the emerging debate in the field of International History concerning the description and comparison of distinct diplomatic epochs in modern history. The analysis of "old diplomacy" before 1914—when from a European point of view, US diplomats were still outsiders—deepens our understanding of Cold War diplomacy and of American "exceptionalism"—not in the sense of America's superiority, but in the sense of its distinctiveness.[6]

By presenting some reflections on diplomatic culture before 1914 this chapter particularly highlights three aspects of the political landscape during those years: the first concerns the self-perception and the memories of the foreign policy decisionmakers throughout Europe; the second deals with basic values and concepts—in other words with the underlying logic of international relations before 1914; the third describes the rules diplomats and politicians followed and the instruments they used as well as the various meanings of these diplomatic forms. Finally, on a more theoretical level, I will ask whether this cultural approach can deliver new insights into the political relations between the major European powers, the so-called "high politics."

The starting points and guiding principles are the official reactions to alternative models of international order, expressed, above all, by the European peace movements. These reactions do not only reveal self-perceptions and fundamental ideas of diplomats and politicians but also help to clarify the mechanisms of foreign policy before 1914. The international system was characterized on the one hand by the increasing importance of non-governmental factors such as public opinion, the emergence of mass media, or pressure groups, and on the other hand by a continued preponderance of a relatively small circle of men. In many ways these men formed a "world apart"[7] with its own rules, customs, and a set of meaningful instruments that we will have to decipher if we want to understand politics in Europe before World War I.

Self-Perception and Memories

The nineteenth century was not only the century of nationalism. It was a century of internationalism as well. During the last decades of the nineteenth and the beginning of the twentieth century international cooperation and interconnections in the fields of trade, science, or sports increased tremendously—even between alleged enemies such as France and Germany.[8]

This growing internationalism affected politics in several ways. Traffic and trade required international standards regarding weights, measures, or postal services. Disputes between companies of different countries had to be solved by politicians and led to the call for an international law. Finally—and most importantly for us—internationalism produced new concepts regarding foreign affairs and the ways in which international relations could or should be organized.

The international peace movement is probably the most striking example of the search for a new international order at the beginning of the twentieth century. This movement comprised a wide range of different groups and organizations: there were national peace associations, the Interparlamentary Union, and several so-called "understanding committees," including an Anglo-German and a French-German committee. There were also religious and private initiatives, such as the famous Carnegie Peace Foundation. Although quite different in size, social structure, and their degree of radicalism, most of these groups shared a number of fundamental aims, such as universal arbitration, arms control, and the development of a supranational organization, a union of nations.[9] In pursuing such objectives the peace movement tried to influence public opinion as well as government policies. Hundreds of letters campaigning for international peace and understanding reached the foreign ministries and the European monarchs. In the last years before World War I many of these correspondences were addressed to Wilhelm II, the German kaiser, whom many pacifists regarded as an ally. How did diplomats, politicians, and monarchs react to these initiatives?

In light of Mensdorff's attitude regarding the aim of foreign policy, it was quite apparent that the Austrian diplomat would have quickly come to terms with the peace movement. But neither he nor his European colleagues held pacifism in high regard. Although widely recognized by diplomats and statesmen, the peace movement was considered useless and utopian, possibly even undermining national interest. Moreover, experts viewed the "amateur diplomacy" of the various non-governmental groups with considerable arrogance.[10]

A senior official of the Foreign Office described the Interparlamentary Union, which advocated universal arbitration, as an "undesirable body."[11] An Austrian diplomat derided their efforts as the work of "humanitarian phrasemongers."[12] When receiving a telegram from the *New York Times* advocating arbitration, Wilhelm II himself commented: "May the devil take arbitration + all who prate about it."[13]

To be sure, there were some statesmen in Europe, for example in the British cabinet, who regarded certain pacifist ideas with sympathy, and most governments could not avoid occasional contact with representatives of the peace movement. But almost none of the European diplomats and statesmen who held important positions in foreign affairs took the pacifists' ideas seriously.

If they considered the peace movement at all, it was because they considered it part of the diplomatic game, not because they valued its contribution to European peace. In April 1913, the German ambassador in Paris was afraid that substantial German participation in an "understanding meeting" with the French in Switzerland might weaken the international position of the German government.[14] Similar fears were expressed by several British diplomats in view of the Anglo-German understanding committee. The English minister to Munich, for example, held the private efforts for détente in the British-German relationship to be dangerous because they could be interpreted in Germany as signs of weakness.[15]

At the same time alternative notions of regulating international order peacefully had already found their way into official foreign policy. Arbitration treaties and international law had been part of foreign policy routine since the last third of the nineteenth century. Smaller states, above all, saw this development as a reasonably good chance to strengthen their influence.[16] For sure, this development had not yet reached the level of decisions on war, peace, and "vital interests." It was exactly this weakness that the US Secretary of State William Jennings Bryan had in mind when in the spring of 1913, he proposed binding arbitration agreements between the United States and all states with which the nation maintained diplomatic relations. However, the reaction of the European Great Powers proved to be reticent. The British government showed polite interest, but a relevant treaty was only signed after the outbreak of the First World War.[17] In diplomatic circles Sir Arthur Nicolson, permanent under-secretary and number two in the Foreign Office, called the proposal "dilettantish."[18] In Austria both the US initiative and private efforts to sponsor new forms of conflict agreements likewise achieved little. Whereas at first Bryan was mocked as a pacifistic caricature in the reports of the Austrian ambassador,[19] the Austrian foreign ministry finally made the suggestion part of a classic diplomatic quid pro quo: it used Bryan's proposal to negotiate a US compromise in other matters in return for agreeing to a relevant treaty. A military conflict with the United States in which an arbitration treaty would come into force seemed as good as impossible.[20]

Particularly at the Hague Conference the governments of the Great Powers became deeply involved in new concepts of conflict regulation. There, too, the development of international law played an important role. But none of the European powers really supported this option emphatically.[21] Governments handled the continuation of the process in a dilatory fashion since at least the second Hague Conference of 1907. At its close, a third conference was projected for 1915. The government committees should have begun preparations at least two years before the event. But official interest remained nil. Internal consultations about the program of the next conference had indeed begun in Vienna in the spring of 1913,[22] but decisionmakers preferred not to reveal any activity to the outside. The German imperial leadership feared a resumption of the discussion about arbitration. Due to the Germans' intransigent attitude, this discussion had almost completely isolated the country at the second Hague Conference. And when the International Arbitration and Peace Association asked the Foreign Office in autumn 1913 whether the planned committee for the preparation of the next Hague conference had already been established, the association received an abrupt and frank answer from the Foreign Office: the situation in Europe was too precarious to bother the governments with such unimportant questions such as how the peace could be saved by means other than the classic diplomacy. "[N]o doubt owing to the fact," the Office wrote, "that the attention of many of the governments has been engrossed by other political questions of grave international import, it has not so far been found possible to make any progress in the constitution of such a committee."[23] All in all, governments took notice of the peace movement's activities to a quite considerable extent. Some alternative forms of foreign policy even found their way into interstate relations. But at the same time the basic reserve endured. Why?

It would be misleading to attribute this rejection of alternative concepts of foreign relations to a lack of interest in innovation. The foreign offices throughout Europe did not lack conceptional consciousness, nor did they lack a vision; they simply did not see any need for change. When diplomats and politicians looked back at the previous decades they saw an unprecedented epoch of peace between the European Great Powers. There had been no war among them for over forty years, although military conflict had threatened more than once.[24] All diplomats ascribed this development to their own efforts; the traditional methods seemed to work. Even shortly before the outbreak of war, this self-perception remained intact.

This assessment of the international situation on the eve of World War I originated in the memories of the behavior of all government officials shortly before 1914 and the lessons they believed they could learn from their own experiences. Particularly since the notable success of the crisis management in the Balkan crisis of 1912–13, ambassadors, ministers, and heads of state brought back to mind that war had been successfully avoided and they assured each other that this experience was still "valid." The Russian Foreign Minister Sazonov spoke in August 1913 of the growing "need for peace of all the Powers."[25] In January 1913 the French president Raymond Poincaré thought that the benefit of the oriental crisis was that the will for peace of all the Powers had become clearer—and even more importantly, the German ambassador believed him.[26] Kaiser Wilhelm II wrote, when looking back on the Balkan conflicts, that the crisis had shown that the "need for peace among the Great Powers is more important than had been foreseen and that different poses might be described as bluff."[27] Already in April 1913 Nicolson, in the face of new crises, referred to earlier experiences: "However, it is of no use to anticipate evil events, and we have on former occasions passed through crises successfully which at first sight looked almost so bad as the present one."[28] And in a similar situation during May 1914 he noted: "Fortunately *all* Powers were anxious for peace."[29]

In a famous essay on the "Topos of Inevitable War in Germany in the Decade before 1914" Wolfgang J. Mommsen has argued that war seemed increasingly unavoidable prior to World War I.[30] That is, however, only half the truth. There was another "topos", increasingly predominant, the longer the war remained prevented: the topos of a continually avoided war. From the point of view of diplomats and foreign policymakers, their own methods had already avoided a world war. The rejection of the peace movement and its ideas, then, can by no means be attributed to a lack of conceptual thought.

Sociohistorical factors likewise assumed a salient significance. The representatives of official foreign policy formed a relatively homogeneous group in terms of background, upbringing, and education. This was true even for republican France.[31] But the memories of the real and fictional success of secret diplomacy in particular and its role in maintaining peace during difficult times contributed to the self-confidence of a professional elite. New methods seemed unnecessary to these men. The rejection of alternative models of foreign policy also cannot be attributed to an underdeveloped awareness of the problem of European peace. On the contrary, official foreign policy circles at the beginning of the twentieth century were well aware that the question of war and peace was highly explosive.

Values and Concepts: The Inherent Logic of International Relations before 1914

At the center of considerations within the peace and understanding movement was the preoccupation with peace; and even Count Mensdorff in his speech did not mention national interests or power as the principal aim of all statesmen and diplomats, but rather "the peace of the world and the harmony of nations." This is perhaps not surprising and we do not have to take him at his word. Nevertheless there is no doubt that the question of war and peace was central to international politics before 1914. The very mention of this in May 1914 is extremely significant. In order to understand the role that the problem of war and peace played in the logic of international relations before 1914, further factors must also be taken into consideration. These factors illuminate a number of fundamental ideas in official foreign policy before 1914. In other words: When governments argued over the Balkans, Turkey, or North Africa at the beginning of the twentieth century, what was it all about?

Notwithstanding a number of pioneering studies in this field,[32] we are not well informed about how foreign policy decisionmakers before 1914 believed the international order should work. The development of a security policy founded on rigid alliances in the last two decades before 1914 stands at the center of most observations.[33] But things are decidedly more complicated. The practice of interstate relations before 1914 was based on a whole range of basic ideas about the inner workings of international relations. Some were developed only in the last decades before World War I; others had a much longer tradition. Some complemented and reinforced one another; others seemed to compete. The most important of these represented the combination of antagonistic or even socio-Darwinist notions[34] and those that still reckoned with the basic solidarity of the Great Powers. The notion of nation-states globally competing in all fields (economy, technology, culture, or biological) coexisted with cooperative ideas. These ideas held that the Great Powers had a common aim, creating order in Europe and the bordering regions. These different interpretations of foreign policy could be found simultaneously in one and the same person. The most outstanding example is perhaps again the German kaiser who was aware of biological assertion but also convinced of the Great Powers' function: maintaining order.

During the Balkan War he spoke out in favor of the "young" nations testing their strength while simultaneously advocating that the Powers should form a ring around the crisis region to guarantee European peace.[35]

The assumed hierarchy of power is also important for the era of imperialism and contemporaries' ideas on world empires.[36] While England and Russia carefully guarded their status as world powers and Germany strove to enter this league, Austria-Hungary chose an altogether different path. In the final years before World War I, Vienna and Budapest gradually lost sight of the level of relations between the Great Powers. We can observe here the decline of a Great Power, which underwent an almost complete change of perspective. For some actors in the Donau monarchy, international relations no longer meant Russia, France, and Italy, but rather, Romania, Serbia, and the minor state Montenegro. Confusing ideas about the hierarchy and importance of states uprooted all traditional concepts of international relations before World War I. This was reflected in the monarchy's behavior.[37]

For example, in the course of the second Moroccan crisis one conceptual alternative came into the foreground. What began as a German-French dispute gradually turned into a general conflict involving all European powers. Immediately the great problem of alliance politics became visible. Great Britain, Russia, and Austria-Hungary feared having to intervene in a possible Franco-German war, even though the origin of the altercation was not of vital interest for them. The security dilemma was already known to contemporaries by 1911 at the latest: alliances did not only offer more security for the individual members but also increased the number of serious conflicts. Maintaining or regaining flexibility in an otherwise rigid block system became an important factor in the conceptual thinking of European governments in the next few years. The alternatives of "Group Politics" and "Flexibility" very quickly found their way into the actions of cabinets. The Austrian government made efforts to save or even strengthen its own contacts with London or Paris, even during the Moroccan crisis.[38] Shortly after the climax of the quarrel, Paris and Berlin, as well as London and Berlin entered into a conciliation dialogue, which was never completely broken off even during the July crisis. And when, in the following three years, governments repeatedly applied the mechanisms of the old European concert in new crises, they attempted to combine the concept of alliance politics with other forms of international politics to increase national security.

We can indeed believe Mensdorff's peaceful affirmation. The enormous demands placed on the policy of the Great Powers by the Moroccan crisis and to which they also reacted can nevertheless not be understood without another factor in international relations before 1914: the assessment, from the diplomats' and statesmen's point of view, of significantly more precarious risks compared to earlier periods. The stakes seemed extremely high to the participants, whom often felt overstretched. British diplomats argued in the "alliance debate" following the crisis of 1911 that they feared losing India and thus England's world position; Germany saw itself "threatened with life or death"; Austrians were confronted with their decline as an independent Great Power.

This feeling of risk percolating diplomats' worldviews had to do with several circumstances. It went along with an increased speed of foreign policy. This was partly the consequence of a second novelty: the ever-growing importance of the general public. Diplomacy and public opinion moved at quite different speeds. It was also a result of technical developments. Because means of communication were becoming faster, international relations also seemed to be accelerating and crises seemed to follow in quick succession. Diplomats often remarked with surprise how the acceleration of communication and world events at large influenced diplomatic practice.[39] They often complained about the growing workload: in times of crises, carefully written reports were rapidly outdated. "It is really hardly any use writing dispatches or private letters, as the situation changes so quickly that they are ancient history by the time they arrive," complained the British ambassador to Russia Buchanan in April 1913.[40] Sometimes diplomats gave each other tips on how they could organize their work more efficiently. But by and large they kept to their own way of working despite everything. Kajetan Mérey von Kapos-Mére, the Austrian ambassador to Rome, did not want to give up his habit of taking care of all the political work himself, even though he felt "from week to week more like an overheated boiler under extreme pressure" and noticed in himself "symptoms of nervous overwork and exhaustion."[41]

The disposition toward war and peace also contributed to the increased feeling of risk, and it was exactly the perceptions and the expectations of war that underwent great changes in the decades before 1914. The fact that Mensdorff strongly recommended the maintenance of peace especially to diplomats and statesmen of his time ("of our age") already constituted a hint. The development of war technology and the requirements of mobilizing modern society at the beginning of the twentieth century raised the question of whether there could still be a winner in a future world war. In any case, in the view of many contemporaries, the absolute costs rose to such an extent that war could hardly be afforded.[42] This herald of total war had already reached the diplomats and foreign policymakers before 1914.[43] Without question a "little" war in which perhaps no more than one Great Power took part, or a colonial war raised no second thoughts. The question was: would there be a "great" war or even a "world war"? Conversely there was a question of the value of "European peace."

There can be no doubt about the political leadership elite's view of war before 1914. Research into the German imperial leadership has shown that most politicians and even military elites were thoroughly aware of the extent and horror of a modern world war.[44] The way in which European diplomacy spoke about a war confirms this view. In the July crisis, Count Mensdorff for example foresaw "the greatest catastrophe in world history."[45] His German colleague Prince Lichnowsky pointed out a year-and-a-half before to the German Chancellor how "substantial" the losses would be "even in a victorious war."[46] "[I]f there was a great war," said the English Foreign Secretary Sir Edward Grey in conversation with the German ambassador in June 1912, it was "not likely to profit anyone."[47] There is no reason to doubt the credibility even of the public statements of the German Chancellor Bethmann Hollweg, who said in the Reichstag, in the spring of 1913, that the wars of the past would be "probably a child's game" in comparison to the future war: "Nobody can imagine the dimension of a world conflagration, the misery and the destruction that it would bring upon the people."[48] Or to doubt the credibility of a well-known passage from Grey's memoirs: "Each time that there had seemed to be danger of war I had been more and more impressed with the feeling of the unprecedented catastrophe that a war between the Great Powers of Europe must be under modern conditions."[49]

Now it can be argued that the resulting esteem of peace has above all to do with fear of war, but then it also remains true that this view of war significantly determined the attitude to war and peace. For people living at that time it seems subjectively to have raised the threshold for the use of force in conflicts between the Great Powers considerably. "I think 20 years ago," wrote the English diplomat and later ambassador to Vienna Maurice de Bunsen in January 1913 about the Balkan crisis, expressing a widespread sentiment, "there w[ould] have been war before now, in such a crisis, but people are now not so ready to plunge into war."[50]

The question of the accepted grounds for war within the diplomatic worldviews is likewise interesting. Let us thus return to a central aspect that played a particular role in the logic of international relations before 1914. What was important enough to justify the decision for war in a certain phase of diplomatic history? In order to investigate such questions we need to analyze serious international crises. In the reports and commentaries of European diplomacy during the second Moroccan crisis, diplomats often discussed whether and why the present crisis could lead to a European war.[51] Hardly anyone saw serious material interests involved.[52] A different argument marked the discussions: the national "honor" of the countries involved. In November 1911, looking back on the past crisis, Grey spoke in the House of Commons about "British interests" and the necessity of "honorably" defending treaty obligations. An "honorable" settlement had to be reached between France and Germany.[53] According to Sir Francis Bertie, the French desired above all an "honorable peace."[54] As rumors arose that the French government also wanted to send a warship to Agadir if the French and the Germans would not reach an agreement, Kaiser Wilhelm II saw "a question of honour for our Fatherland" in this French "menace" and threatened to break off negotiations.[55] The assertion of honor was important both publicly and internally before 1914, so important that it could trigger a war. Apart from national interests or the question of European peace, the question of "national honor"[56] topped the worldview of the foreign policy elite before 1914.

These perceptions of Europe, interest politics, honor, and the value of peace were naturally not the same in every country. Although the British government also carried out realpolitik, London perceived the German variant as brutal and false. In a similar vein, orientation to alliance politics did not come through at the same time in all places, not to mention the different meanings of a term such as the "Balance of Power."[57] With regard to the disposition to war, Joachim Radkau has detected a kind of "desire for fear" *(Angstlust)* in Germany.[58] A similar emotion could be found in France, but scarcely in Great Britain.

There were also differences among the foreign policy decisionmakers of one country. Further "models" of international relations are to be examined, such as the role of the monarchs.[59] But taken together the foreign policy models and values of the politico-diplomatic elites were rather homogeneous. Regarding the question of peace and war, many decisionmakers took the danger of a European war to be real. But at the same time they feared unprecedented horrors and burdens on society and therefore assumed that governments would shy away from the risk of a modern war. Thus, in the years between the second Moroccan crisis and World War I, the Great Powers took the outlook on war and the expectations of war into account in at least three ways. They prepared and armed themselves; they entertained ideas of deterrence; and finally, the views on war and risk assessment increased their desire for détente.

Rules and Instruments, Language and Meanings

The peace movement set its hopes on the effects of cultural, economic, and legal interaction between the nations. Awareness of the value of peace was expected to arise from these manifold contacts and many pacifists already believed they could observe such a development. During the Bosnian annexation crisis of 1908–09, the Austrian pacifist Bertha von Suttner wrote to Kajetan Mérey von Kapos-Mére, later Habsburg ambassador to Rome: "The present situation in Europe is very alarming; but I find that it shows that there will soon be a Europe with a desire for peace which will slowly work through to unity."[60] Suttner's fellow pacifist and founder of the German Peace Association Alfred Fried wrote triumphantly after the settlement of the second Moroccan crisis that this was a "victory for pacifism." According to Fried, "the number of unfought wars has been increased by one new very important case."[61]

The place of the peace movement in the perception of the cabinets was quite different. In addition to all other reservations, pacifism seemed, above all, part of national public opinion. But it was not only Mensdorff who held no high regard for its influence on international relations. Mensdorff's superior, Count Berchtold, likewise never overcame his apprehensiveness when he had to address the common parliament of Austria-

Hungary *(die Delegationen)*. His unpublished memoirs are full of anger and aversion directed toward the disruptive influence of the press. Like Mensdorff, he understood diplomacy at the beginning of the twentieth century largely as the art of minimizing the influence of the public.[62] Although Alfred v. Kiderlen-Waechter, German foreign secretary from 1910–12, did not share the fears of his Austrian counterparts, he too failed to accept the impact of public opinion and the emerging mass media on politics in the early days of the twentieth century. As Ralf Forsbach and Thomas Meyer have shown, his policy either neglected public opinion completely or tried to treat it as a calculable diplomatic factor.[63] Even Sir Edward Grey, the English foreign secretary, was no exception to the rule. According to Keith Robbins and Zara Steiner: "Sir Edward Grey, of course, believed that 'public opinion' existed.... But he eschewed public speaking whenever possible." To him, "any form of public discussion appeared as a form of implied criticism."[64] And so he did not alter his belief that foreign policy had an urgent "need for secrecy and discretion."[65]

Therefore, in their efforts at understanding, governments followed strategies quite different from those of the peace movement. Supported by their professional self-confidence and self-perception, their methods of détente were determined by traditional foreign policy concepts as well as the enduring models of behavior and rules of diplomacy. Very rarely did public opinion enter their considerations as a constructive factor.

The forms of European Great Power diplomacy had developed and re-developed over centuries. At the eve of World War I these forms continued to be based predominantly on the rules of the Vienna Order following the European congress of 1814–15.[66] Most important were the sets of instruments with the help of which the Great Powers pursued their goal of discussing and settling all questions of international politics without outside interference. Even in the years before 1914 the Great Powers reserved the right to intervene in any question of international politics if they deemed it necessary by means of conferences, congresses, ambassadors' meetings, or any sort of démarche. For those concerned in governments and ministries, foreign policy was carried out in this area of diplomatic form and its conventional meanings to a much greater extent than may be clear at first sight to today's analysts. Historians must know the various instruments available and especially the accompanying possibilities of interpretation at hand if they do not want to overlook one of the most important aspects of international relations before 1914. Foreign policy before the First World War was predominantly made by men for whom these forms were quite self-evident. These men drew a great part of their identity from the use of these rules. Specific terms and the institutionalized manner of speaking constituted part of these forms of foreign policy.

Three instruments were available to the Great Powers to canvass their positions. The normal case was consultation through the usual diplomatic channels. One government invited the others to an exchange of views on a specific question in the name of "Europe." This invitation typically took the form of a circular to their representatives in the other capitals. Then followed a set of protracted and highly complicated consultations across the continent. Special conferences took place, covering questions of higher significance and complexity. There existed two principal forms of conventions. Special delegates could be sent, as happened for instance at the famous Algeciras Conference in 1906. Alternately, so-called ambassadors' conferences convened, during which the accredited representatives of the Great Powers in a capital simply gathered together in meetings. The number of these sessions probably rose into the hundreds during the entire nineteenth century up to 1914.[67] The last and most formal possibility was the great European congress in which the leaders responsible for foreign relations came together. The congresses following Vienna, the Paris Congress of 1856 and the Berlin Congress of 1878, exemplify this point. The choice of the respective form of communication was naturally no small matter. This was also true for the various kinds of démarches that the European Great Powers used to inform the small and medium states about the "will of Europe." Here, the Great Powers used a similarly differentiated and meaningful set of instruments. (Among themselves, however, they followed different rules.) The variety of démarches was wide. These could be delivered simultaneously and with identical text, with identical text but consecutively, by one Power in the name of others, as a collective démarche, and much more. The relative form was selected depending on how strong the presentation should be or how united the Powers basically were. It was also important from which government the initiative originated or appeared to originate. Indeed these forms could decide on success or failure. The form therefore also had its meaning not only for the government to which the respective démarche was addressed, but also for relations among the Powers.

When governments carefully set out to make bilateral agreements or improve the situation in Europe in the last years before the First World War, they quite naturally made use of this set of instruments. In view of the suggestive wording of foreign policy forms, this was no easy undertaking. The choice of methods already took the form of extended consultations. For instance, until the London ambassadors' conference for the settling of the Balkan crisis could meet in December 1912, months of almost daily discussions among the governments concerned passed. The form of the conference was to be defined, but also its agenda or the location of the talks. Was Paris the suitable town, or London, or even Berlin? And if they wanted to meet in the British capital, then where in London should they get together? In a separate building or simply in the Foreign Office (which was what they finally decided)? It was imperative to find a form that was flexible enough to maintain the room for negotiation of the individual governments, but nevertheless sufficiently rigid to exercise a certain amount of pressure on them to compromise. In order to ensure room for negotiation, pains were taken to give the discussions as informal a character as possible. Thus, the ambassadors met in the "normal" rooms of the Foreign Ministry. For a short time people started talking about a "congress," but even the word "conference" seemed to be too dangerous to some diplomats and they regretted ever having mentioned it.[68] But even the fact that they were sitting together in a conference—whatever form it took—completely achieved the desired function. Nobody could now afford simply to leave the conference and thus be visibly responsible for the failure of the discussions. The arrangement worked in this case. The London ambassadors' conference proved to be a suitable vehicle for preventing the tension from escalating into open conflict. The carefully chosen form was therefore of decisive significance.

Even the arranging of démarches could be a very difficult task. During the Italian-Turkish War it took over four months until spring 1912 for a démarche to the Ottoman Empire to come about. Officials needed to clarify which power would take the initiative and what form the step should take. If an identical but separate procedure had been decided, it still remained to be negotiated which of the Great Powers should apply it first. Each possibility represented a certain measure of commitment within the highly developed diplomatic techniques and therefore had to be exactly weighed within the overall political calculation, since repercussions on bilateral relations were expected or even the position of the country in the whole European system might become jeopardized. Negotiation was of utmost importance and it was carried out in most cases by foreign ministers and state secretaries.

Was the London meeting of ambassadors a "conference"? Was a collective note or merely a note with identical text required? The exact term was also important because the word "conference" in 1912 was still connected with the diplomatic defeat of the German Empire in Algeciras in 1906. This also explains how fastidiously the word was handled. Similar mechanisms worked in the case of the concept "détente." Détente at first meant the improvement of relations below the level of concrete binding agreements. The matter was thus initially well defined. When the English Secretary of State for War Lord Haldane was staying in Berlin for political soundings at the beginning of 1912, the French ambassador in the city literally asked if it was a question of détente or "entente":[69] he wanted to know whether some agreement had already been reached or was purposed. But détente too was bound up with specific foreign policy experiences before the First World War. At the beginning of the century the Anglo-French relationship had evolved from a détente to an entente created by a special agreement, which in the meantime seemed to have become almost an "alliance" between the two states. In the years around 1910 the German Empire had tried to break up a similar development between London and St. Petersburg by means of a German-Russian détente. In other words, détente, under the conditions of international relations before 1914, meant the start of a process which ran through to the overthrow of diplomatic groupings and alliances. This specific meaning of détente considerably burdened even those efforts before 1914, which were by no means intended to be tactical. There were, indeed, attempts to work against this problem and to establish other possibilities of interpretation. But they could never be carried out.

Whoever wants to decipher the highly formalized terminology of international politics prior to 1914 must turn to the many statements of officials, communiqués, and public speeches. Here, too, the apparently stereotypical turns of phrase carry explosive information for the professional observer of politics and diplomacy. Parliamentary speeches, formal audiences on entering or leaving office, and press announcements at the end of summit meetings were all occasions when such messages were almost expected. The formulae used in them could confirm successes achieved, awaken expectations, or prepare, strengthen, or end diplomatic initiatives. For the diplomats and politicians, they clarified the current state of international relations. To this extent, they belonged to the most important "actions" of a country's foreign policy.[70]

In public speeches, diplomats and politicians looked carefully at a rhetorical triad of recollections of the past development of relations on both sides, an up-to-date description of the state of affairs and a view of the future. If one element was missing, it left room for interpretation and the completeness with which each aspect was dealt with also carried meaning. Besides that, the exact wording played a decisive role. This can be observed, for example, in German-English relations. Parallel to the slow improvement of relations between Berlin and London, the terms with which the respective heads of government or foreign ministers publicly described the bilateral relations also changed.[71] When the new German ambassador to London Marschall von Bieberstein, however, spoke about "friendly" relations in his first conversation with Sir Edward Grey in the summer of 1912, this was more than the confirmation of an achievement. It was an advance. Grey understood at once and rejected it immediately with a reference to his own "real" friends.[72] Grey himself on the other hand fairly tenaciously tried to impose his new idea of détente in the ever-repeated formula of "separate" but not "hostile" "groups" in public speeches.[73] The success was only moderate. But the Austrian Foreign Minister Leopold von Berchtold at once took up on them. It was not pure coincidence that he did this at a time when he himself was trying to achieve a rapprochement with Great Britain.[74]

How important this institutionalized language could be may perhaps have become clear during the French-American—respectively the German-American tensions—during the Iraq crisis of 2002–03. Suddenly observers paid attention to every word that the French or US president or the German chancellor spoke. Before 1914, the attention of politicians and diplomats focused on such nuances in an almost paranoid way. Graf Thurn, Austrian ambassador to St. Petersburg, saw in Nichola's II choice of words at the 1912 New Year's Reception, and in the Russian Foreign Minister's statements on his entry into office or in his reaction to a speech by his Austrian colleague, signs of "eminent political significance." Thurn observed a "web of highly personal considerations and courtesies" as well as "political remarks and insinuations," that altogether "unmistakably" pointed at a "long-term initiative towards closer relations on both sides."[75]

No doubt, occasionally the major European powers honestly tried to improve things in Europe. Before and after the Balkan Wars the governments sent several collective notes to the Balkan states to convey the "will of Europe." They gathered in ambassadors' conferences. They negotiated problems of minor importance hoping that such step-to-step-diplomacy could improve relations in the long run. Thurn and many of his European colleagues on the eve of World War I found themselves faced with a mesh of efforts at détente and symptoms of détente. Moreover, in important points relations in Europe seemed to improve compared to the years before 1911.[76] The methods with which this seemed to have been achieved were the long-practiced diplomatic ones. At the same time, the new conditions of foreign policy at the beginning of the twentieth century did not go unnoticed. Considerations about the press, political parties, and the peace movement abound in the diplomatic reports of those days. But in their routine diplomacy, foreign ministries tried to block any interference from outsiders. They refused to consider new concepts of international relations developed by the peace movement. In their opinion such new visions did not live up to their traditional standards. Despite the changing context, governmental foreign policy largely followed its traditional rules, customs, and behaviors.

The consequences of this policy were considerable. For the diplomatic success of this kind of effort at détente had a serious side effect: it worked, or seemed to work—that is, until the results had to be presented to the public or the public discovered them on their own. Then the well-considered plans threatened to collapse. Exposed to public scrutiny, carefully negotiated results and carefully chosen methods suddenly assumed altogether different meanings. The diplomacy described here needed discretion, carefully calculated signs, and gestures. Above all, it needed time. Once things became public, in the view of diplomats, public opinion ruined everything. Things scarcely considered by diplomats were openly discussed in the papers. The meeting of an ambassador with a monarch was suddenly understood as the starting point of a change of the

European alliance system. The goals of diplomatic action, calculated for months or even years, suddenly became the expectation of a whole nation—a nation that tends to lose patience within only a few weeks. In that context, symptoms of détente were easily transformed into symptoms of increasing tension because nothing else happened after the first step and because after a short time the press interpreted the lack of further information as a sign of new misunderstandings between the governments.

As Johannes Paulmann has pointed out,[77] governments occasionally tried to manipulate public opinion to gain control of how things were understood. Sometimes they even used the public for their own purposes. But without changing their diplomatic style they had to fail. The misunderstandings between diplomacy on the one hand and the public on the other hand persisted. In 1914 the German government refused to publish the English-German agreement on the future of the Portuguese colonies because Berlin feared "that publication of an agreement made to improve relations would cause such an outcry that any improvement actually reached by means of diplomacy would be lost."[78]

It might be a stretch to describe these different views on foreign policy problems as a clash of two cultures—the culture of diplomacy and the culture of public opinion. Still, the incident shows quite clearly how individual aspects of international relations before 1914 can be interpreted with great benefit in terms of a cultural approach to history. On the one hand such episodes are an expression of the tangled situation before 1914. In addition they give an insight into the mechanisms of interstate relations in those years. The foreign policy decisionmaking elites shared common concepts and values. They recalled international politics of the previous years in a similar way. They could be sure that their negotiating partners would understand them "correctly." In a way they in fact formed "a world apart," which followed independent laws.

The best evidence for the relevance of this element in international relations before World War I are the many cases in which foreign politicians and diplomats cooperated beyond their national contexts. The London ambassadors' conference worked because it triggered solidarity among diplomats and governments of different countries. The question of a resolution of the Balkan crisis was consciously referred to a body of experts whose members consisted of (partly related) nobles.

These aristocrats cherished their own thoughts in regard to the expression "conference." They also had their difficulties with public opinion and they could sense the overthrow of the European alliance system in the form of a single démarche in Cetinje. Sir Edward Grey and Bethmann Hollweg coordinated their speeches to parliament in autumn 1911 in order to exercise moderate influence on public opinion in both their countries.[79] The French and German governments agreed to take steps against chauvinistic plays in the spring of 1913 and thus to combat the excesses of nationalism in public opinion.[80] Naturally this diplomatic world was not the only one to which the protagonists felt they belonged. There were the national or nationalistic or aristocratic spheres and multiple interactions and restrictions among these affiliations.[81] In interstate practice, however, the unifying force of this diplomatic world was enormous. Even newcomers like the often-changing French foreign ministers or the German chancellor Bethmann Hollweg, inexperienced in foreign affairs, soon fit in.[82]

Conclusion

In his "genealogy" of foreign policy practice, James Der Derian defines "diplomatic culture," a concept crucial to his work, only after demonstrative hesitation. "Diplomatic culture," says Der Derian finally, "will be studied as the mediation of estrangement by symbolic power and social constraints."[83] More generally, according to Der Derian, diplomatic culture constitutes the way in which estrangement and alienation have been handled within Europe. In a similar vein, Jürgen Haacke examines the origin and development of a set of "norms and related practices" in the relations among ASEAN countries in his study of diplomatic culture and "security culture."[84]

Such approaches differ in two ways from many other attempts to integrate cultural aspects into the history of international relations. For one, they interpret foreign policy not primarily as dependent on or closely connected with the culture of a country, a region, or a group of people.[85] Instead, Der Derian, for example, is interested in the cultural history of the diplomatic or foreign policy contacts proper. Here we can also detect another difference between those studying diplomatic culture and many other studies of the cultural approach in the field of international history. For Der Derian, various forms of "mediation" are not a matter of contacts between different cultural entities. Instead, they are part of the development of European diplomacy, that is mediation and conflict management within one civilization.[86]

This chapter centers on both the sphere of state negotiation and contacts within a cultural circle. I have examined how far foreign policy negotiations of governments of the European powers before 1914 can be analyzed as an independent cultural practice. My concern was not to retrace foreign policy behavior to an original culture. In this sense culture does not function as a "foundation" or an "explanation"[87] of foreign policy. Nor did I wish to study contacts between cultures as scholars of intercultural communication do.[88] At the center of this chapter stood classic European diplomacy. The concrete subject has been traditional: relations between the European Great Powers in the last years before 1914; diplomats and foreign policy makers of the European great powers; what they wrote, said to one other, or stated in public.[89]

At the same time, my examination was guided by a series of questions which generally have received high attention by cultural historical research: the self-perception of diplomacy as articulated in its dealing with pacifism and public opinion; contemporary foreign policy concepts and values; the communicative side of official foreign policy, the interaction process with its rules and its meanings. Using linguistic theories or discourse analysis, political scientists have long recognized the significance of such aspects in official foreign policy.[90] Historians have been a bit more reserved. Above all, relevant research exists for the Middle Ages and early modern history.[91] Additionally, there is a growing interest in the "subjective side" or internalized rules in the history of state systems.[92] Concerning the late nineteenth and early twentieth centuries, however, we are not particularly well informed about any of those three aspects. We have only recently discovered more details about foreign policy elites' perceptions of war. Their image of Europe, for example, still remains largely obscure. Some scholars have raised questions about communicative practice in intercultural diplomacy in the age of imperialism, but very seldom about the situation within Europe.[93]

Noticing gaps in research is one thing. But is it even worth the effort to fill them? Asked in a different way: where is the added value of investigation such as the one suggested, what new perspectives does a cultural analysis offer? In case of great power détente before 1914, I think, the answer is actually easy to provide. Cultural questions open up aspects in international history, which according to conventional interpretations simply should not exist. Attempts at détente, for example, have so far been examined only as individual phenomena.[94] Only the systematic analysis of perceptions makes the meaning of bilateral or multilateral détentes for the worldviews and expectations of diplomacy and politics clear. Détente has undoubtedly become relevant as perception and expectation in the history of events.[95] But the analysis of self-images or diplomatic systems of meaning also offers new explanations. In cases of bilateral détente, this analysis can help us understand the choice of diplomatic instruments in the last years before 1914 and so deepen our knowledge of why bilateral détente did not serve to avoid the Great War. On the systematic level, one outcome is that the détente strategies forming the Triple Entente up to 1907 could not work any more in the altered European system of the following years. Détente, in the experience of the protagonists, was clearly bound up with the reshaping of international relations in the first decade of the twentieth century. It could never be as successful in the unstable bloc system of the immediate pre-war years. Instead, it contributed considerably to sharpening the security dilemma. Furthermore it becomes clear how differing expectations and interpretations in diplomacy on the one hand and public opinion on the other thwarted official efforts at détente. The location of the London ambassadors' conference is significant: it was held as far away as possible from reporters and journalists. Governments shied away from the open market in important cases because they feared (or knew) that they would otherwise lose control over the negotiations. Without the participation of public opinion, they had hoped to keep control over diplomatic activities. But their efforts at détente also lost their full effectiveness under the conditions of modern foreign policy.

An examination oriented toward a cultural approach to official foreign policy before 1914 moreover gains value by describing the connection between form and content in foreign policy contexts.[96] In a highly formalized interaction process such as European diplomacy before the First World War, positions and intentions were articulated and interpretations were yielded by the use—or modification—of certain institutionalized ways of speaking, gestures, or the choice of a certain diplomatic instrument out of a number of possible alternatives.

The semantic interpretation of such repeated foreign policy formulae represents an important area of communication. This is true not only for intercultural communication or forms of communication in the middle ages, but also for the diplomacy of the "long nineteenth century" as well as the twentieth century. The form of foreign policy cannot be separated from its content. The communicative or symbolic aspect is not to be disentangled from the aspect of power.

I will close with two points indicating new research perspectives. In his "genealogy," Der Derian aims at deconstructing the perception of a continuous history of diplomacy based on common sense. Der Derian quotes Michel Foucault in saying, "The search for descent is not the erecting of foundations; on the contrary, it disturbs what was thought unified; it shows the heterogeneity of what was imagined consistent with itself."[97] In a similar way, Jürgen Osterhammel describes the refinement of differences between the various epochs of diplomatic history as one of the tasks of a "new history of diplomacy."[98] Both authors thus touch upon the problem of change in "diplomatic culture." Theoretically speaking, the question arises of whether and how diplomats entangled in patterns of interpretation and customs could react to new needs.[99] Our case illustrates possible alternatives. The failure of many efforts at détente before 1914 was the result of long practiced anachronistic behaviors and interpretations. At the same time, the protagonists were thoroughly able to recognize this problem and they also tried to react on a case-by-case basis. English Foreign Secretary Sir Edward Grey tried to establish another pattern of détente before 1914. Publicly and in diplomatic correspondences he spoke persistently of détente despite bloc confrontation. In doing so, he set up a new pattern in opposition to the traditional model of détente as a prelude to an entente. Détente should thus be compatible with the changed conditions of international relations. Sadly, this model of negotiation did not become common practice before 1914.

My second point concerns the place of the history of diplomacy in international history. The more traditional history of diplomacy regards the history of international relations embedded in the actions of diplomats. On the other end of the spectrum, historians argue that the examination of diplomatic practices is only relevant for an enriched social history of diplomatic personnel.[100] Following a third course,[101] it seems to me that the description of diplomatic forms for the years before 1914 can lead to the center of the history of international relations of this period. It may have been different before and after; and the challenges to the traditional practices of diplomats and foreign policymakers have certainly become obvious in the present study.

The outbreak of World War I shattered the belief in diplomacy as a force dedicated to the preservation of peace. In the epoch after 1918 common perceptions, values or interpretations long held by the decisionmaking elites of foreign policy ceased to exist. World War II and the Cold War inspired another break with diplomatic traditions and customs throughout Europe and the West.

But also with a view to the epochs after 1918 respectively 1945, one task of the history of international relations is to take the inevitable "lack of familiarity"[102] with its subject seriously when describing and interpreting state contacts. Especially when studying highly formalized state foreign policy, historians can profit from the so-called cultural turn with its new heed for the importance of rules and forms, for the worldviews and webs of interpretation found in history. In this context comparing different diplomatic epochs will be one of the important fields of future research. After 1945, notably, in the United States, cultural diplomacy and public diplomacy—specifically designed to keep audiences at home and abroad abreast of American viewpoints—became key instruments of the diplomatic process. No doubt, the analysis of "old diplomacy" helps us to frame our understanding of this Cold War diplomacy and the peculiarity of American foreign relations.

Notes

Thank you to Nicolas Jaspert, Andreas Lorenczuk, Birgit Neuhold, and Jessica C. E. Gienow-Hecht.

1. 7 May 1914, Haus-, Hof- und Staatsarchiv Vienna, Mensdorff Papers, Box 3 (original in English).
2. Eckart Conze, Ulrich Lappenküper, and Guido Müller, eds., *Geschichte der internationalen Beziehungen: Erneuerung und Erweiterung einer historischen Disziplin* (Cologne: Böhlau, 2004); Jessica Gienow-Hecht and Frank Schumacher, eds., *Culture and International History* (New York: Berghahn Books, 2003); Michael J. Hogan and Thomas G. Paterson, eds., *Explaining the History of American Foreign Relations* (Cambridge: Cambridge University Press, 1991).
3. Emily S. Rosenberg, *Financial Missionaries to the World: The Politics and Culture of Dollar Diplomacy, 1900–1930* (Cambridge, MA: Harvard Univer-

sity Press, 1999); Anders Stephanson, *Manifest Destiny: American Expansionism and the Empire of Right,* 4th ed. (New York: Hill and Wang, 1999).
4. James Der Derian, *On Diplomacy: A Genealogy of Western Estrangement* (Oxford and New York: Blackwell, 1987); Jürgen Osterhammel, "Internationale Geschichte, Globalisierung und die Pluralität der Kulturen," in *Internationale Geschichte: Themen—Ergebnisse—Aussichten,* eds. Wilfried Loth and Jürgen Osterhammel (Munich: Oldenbourg, 2000), 387–408, especially 399–402; Johannes Paulmann, *Pomp und Politik: Monarchenbegegnungen in Europa zwischen Ancien Régime und Erstem Weltkrieg* (Paderborn: Schöningh, 2000). See also Friedrich Kießling: "Der 'Dialog der Taubstummen' ist vorbei: Neue Ansätze in der Geschichte der internationalen Beziehungen des 19. und 20. Jahrhunderts," *Historische Zeitschrift* 275 (2002): 651–80, and Kießling, *Gegen den "großen Krieg"? Entspannung in den internationalen Beziehungen 1911–1914* (Munich: Oldenbourg, 2002).
5. Fredrik Logevall, "A Critique of Containment," *Diplomatic History* 28 (2004): 474–99.
6. Ibid., 498.
7. Valerie Cromwell, "'A World Apart': Gentlemen Amateurs to Professional Generalists," in *Diplomacy and World Power: Studies in British Foreign Policy 1890–1950,* eds. M. L. Dockrill and Brian McKercher (Cambridge: Cambridge University Press, 1996), 1–18.
8. On internationalism in the "long" nineteenth century, see Martin H. Geyer and Johannes Paulmann, eds., *The Mechanics of Internationalism: Culture, Society and Politics from the 1840s to the First World War* (Oxford: Oxford University Press, 2001); Gabriele Schirbel, *Strukturen des Internationalismus: First Universal Races Congress London 1911: Der Weg zur Gemeinschaft der Völker,* 2 Teile (Münster and Hamburg: Lit, 1991). On the history of German-French trade, see, for example, Robert Frank, "L'Allemagne dans le commerce français, ou la tendance séculaire à l'entente franco-allemande (1910-1965)," in *France and Germany in an Age of Crisis 1900–1960,* ed. Haim Shamir (Leiden: Brill, 1990), 30–42.
9. There is a comprehensive literature on the international peace movement at the beginning of the twentieth century. Relevant among others are Sandi E. Cooper, *Patriotic Pacifism: Waging War on War in Europe 1815–1914* (New York and Oxford: Oxford University Press, 1991); Wilfried Eisenbeiß, *Die bürgerliche Friedensbewegung in Deutschland während des Ersten Weltkriegs: Organisation, Selbstverständnis und politische Praxis 1913/14–1919* (Frankfurt: Lang, 1980); Keith Robbins, *The Abolition of War: The "Peace Movement" in Britain, 1914–1919* (Cardiff: University of Wales Press, 1976).
10. On the attitude of official foreign policy to the peace movement, see Solomon Wank, ed., *Doves and Diplomats: Foreign Offices and Peace Movements in Europe and America in the Twentieth Century* (Westport: Greenwood Press, 1978).
11. Treasury to Mr. Tyrrell, 1 January 1912, minute Villiers, 19 January, PRO/FO 371/1555.
12. Report from Bern, 11 October 1912, Haus-, Hof- und Staatsarchiv, Administrative Registratur, Fach 60/95.
13. Tel. NYT, 1 January 1912, minute William II, Auswärtiges Amt/Politisches Archiv, Europa Generalia 37 secr., Bd. 3 (original in English).
14. Report from Paris, 18 April 1913, Auswärtiges Amt/Politisches Archiv, Europa Generalia 37, Bd. 14.

15. Report by Sir Vincent Corbett, 21 September 1912, PRO/FO 371/1378.
16. Madeleine Herren, *Hintertüren zur Macht: Internationalismus und modernisierungsorientierte Außenpolitik in Belgien, der Schweiz und den USA 1865–1914* (Munich: Oldenbourg, 2000). On arbitration, see Richard Langhorne, "Arbitration: The First Phase 1870–1914," in *Diplomacy and World Power,* 43–55.
17. G. P. Gooch and Harold Temperley, eds., *British Documents on the Origins of the War 1898–1914,* 11 vols. (London, N.p., 1926–38), vol. 8, ed. note, 648.
18. 2 May 1913, Auswärtiges Amt/Politisches Archiv, Europa Generalia 37, vol. 14.
19. See, for example, Report from Washington, 16 May 1913, Haus-, Hof- und Staatsarchiv/Politisches Archiv, XXXIII/51.
20. Report from Washington, 19 May 1913, Haus-, Hof- und Staatsarchiv/Politisches Archiv, XXXIII/51. However, the German government balked at such a line of action. Since a distinct procedure had been agreed to between Vienna and Berlin on this question, as a result there were no Austrian–American negotiations in any event.
21. Jost Dülffer, *Regeln gegen den Krieg? Die Haager Friedenskonferenzen von 1899 und 1907 in der internationalen Politik* (Berlin: Ullstein, 1981).
22. Letter to the Ministry of War, plan, 28 May 1913, Haus-, Hof- und Staatsarchiv, Administrative Registratur, Fach 60/92.
23. International Arbitration and Peace Association to Foreign Office, 31 October 1913, minute Crowe, 3 November 1913, PRO/FO 372/450. Crowe's minute was adopted virtually unchanged in the Foreign Office reply of 7 November (ibid.). Moreover, no committee had yet assembled even by spring 1914. A concrete date, June 1915, was considered only shortly before the beginning of the First World War. Thus it was clear that the next conference could not have taken place before 1917. Cf., on the slow preparations for a third Hague conference, Jost Dülffer, "Efforts to Reform the International System and Peace Movements before 1914," *Peace and Change* 14 (1989): 25–45.
24. A collection of such crises is offered in Jost Dülffer, Martin Kröger, Rolf-Harald Wippich, *Vermiedene Kriege: Deeskalation von Konflikten der Großmächte zwischen Krimkrieg und Erstem Weltkrieg 1856–1914* (Munich: Oldenbourg, 1997).
25. 15 August 1913, Haus-, Hof- und Staatsarchiv, Berchtold Papers, Memoiren, Box 2.
26. Report from Paris, 9 January 1913, Auswärtiges Amt/Politisches Archiv, Frankreich 105 1a, Bd. 24 u. tel. from Paris, 21 February 1913, ebd.
27. Johannes Lepsius et al., eds., *Die Große Politik der Europäischen Kabinette 1871–191: Sammlung der Diplomatischen Akten des Auswärtigen Amtes, im Auftrag des Auswärtigen Amtes,* 40 Bde, (Berlin, N.p., 1922–27), Bd. 36/1, Nr. 13781.
28. PRO/FO, Nicolson Mss., 800/364.
29. Goschen to Grey, 4 May 1914, PRO/FO 371/1990, minute Nicolson (emphasis in the original).
30. Wolfgang J. Mommsen, "The Topos of Inevitable War in Germany in the Decade bevor 1914," in *Germany in the Age of Total War. Essays in Honour of Francis Carsten,* eds. Volker R. Berghahn and Martin Kitchen (London: Croom Helm, 1981), 23–45.
31. M. B. Hayne, *The French Foreign Office and the Origins of the First World War 1898–1914* (Oxford: Clarendon Press, 1993); Lamar Cecil, *The German Dip-*

lomatic Service: 1871–1914 (Princeton: Princeton University Press, 1976); Zara S. Steiner, *The Foreign Office and Foreign Policy 1898–1914* (Cambridge: Cambridge University Press, 1969); Erwin Matsch, *Geschichte des Auswärtigen Dienstes von Österreich(-Ungarn) 1720–1920* (Vienna: Böhlau, 1980).

32. Pioneering work has been done by, e.g., Heinz Gollwitzer, *Geschichte des weltpolitischen Denkens,* 2 Bde. (Göttingen: Vandenhoeck & Ruprecht, 1972–82); Carsten Holbraad, *The Concert of Europe: A Study in German and British International Theory 1815–1914* (London and Southampton: Longman, 1970); James Joll, *1914: The Unspoken Assumptions* (London and Southampton: Weidenfeld and Nicolson, 1968).

33. Klaus Hildebrand, "Julikrise 1914: Das europäische Sicherheitsdilemma: Betrachtungen über den Ausbruch des Ersten Weltkrieges," *Geschichte in Wissenschaft und Unterricht* 36 (1985): 469–502.

34. For the German imperial leadership, see Thomas Lindemann, *Die Macht der Perzeptionen und Perzeptionen von Mächten* (Berlin: Dunker & Humblot, 2000).

35. Cf. *Große Politik,* 33, Nr. 12297, and ibid., Nr. 12225.

36. Sönke Neitzel, *Weltmacht oder Untergang: Die Weltreichslehre im Zeitalter des Imperialismus* (Paderborn: Schöningh, 2000).

37. On Austria, see Günther Kronenbitter, "'Nur los lassen': Österreich-Ungarn und der Wille zum Krieg," in *Lange und kurze Wege in den Ersten Weltkrieg: Vier Augsburger Beiträge zur Kriegsursachenforschung,* Johannes Burkhardt et. al. (Munich: Vögel, 1996), 159–87.

38. Cf. Alois Lexa von Aehrenthal, *Aus dem Nachlaß Aehrenthal: Briefe und Dokumente zur österreichisch-ungarischen Innen- und Außenpolitik 1885–1912,* ed. and introduced by Solomon Wank with contributions from M. Grafinger und Franz Adlgasser, 2 vols. (Graz: Neugebauer, 1994), 174f.; private correspondence Aehrenthal an Mérey, 1 November 1911.

39. E.g., *Österreich-Ungarns Außenpolitik von der Bosnischen Krise 1908 bis zum Kriegsausbruch 1914: Diplomatische Aktenstücke des österreichisch-ungarischen Ministeriums des Äußern,* selected by Ludwig Bittner et al., ed. by Ludwig Bittner and Hans Uebersberger, 9 Bde. (Vienna and Leipzig, 1930), Bd. IV, Nr. 4347 u. 4455.

40. Buchanan to Nicolson, 3 April 1913, PRO/FO, Nicolson Mss., 800/365; Nicolson to Goschen, 21 January 1913, ibid., 362; Forgách to Mérey, 1 April 1914, Haus-, Hof- und Staatsarchiv, Mérey Papers, Box 10.

41. Mérey to Szápáry, 17 April 1913, Haus-, Hof- und Staatsarchiv, Szápáry Papers, Box 1. Also on the problem of foreign policy and speed, see Stephan Kern, *The Culture of Time and Space: 1880–1918* (Cambridge, MA: Harvard University Press, 2000). Also interesting is Joachim Radkau's diagnosis of a "nervous" German world policy which can be traced back to the sense of the speed of time: Joachim Radkau, *Das Zeitalter der Nervosität: Deutschland zwischen Bismarck und Hitler* (Munich and Vienna: Hanser, 1998). On the connection between diplomatic forms and technical development, see also Richard H. Solomon, "Political Culture and Diplomacy in the Twenty-first Century," in *The Political Culture of Foreign Area and International Studies: Essays in Honor of Lucian W. Pye,* eds. Richard J. Samuels and Myron Weiner (Washington, DC: Brassey's, 1992), 141–54. Solomon sees an unprecedented personalization of Great Power relations going along with the technical development achieved today.

42. Richard Ned Lebow, "Windows of Opportunity: Do States Jump Through Them?" *International Security* 9 (1984): 155f.

43. On the origin of the term, see Stig Förster, ed., *On the Road to Total War: The American Civil War and the German Wars of Unification 1861–1871* (Washington, DC: German Historical Institute, 1997).
44. Jost Dülffer, "Die zivile Reichsleitung und der Krieg: Erwartungen und Bilder 1890–1914," in *Gestaltungskraft des Politischen: Festschrift für Eberhard Kolb,* eds. Wolfram Pyta and Ludwig Richter (Berlin: Duncker & Humblot, 1998), 11–28; Stig Förster, "Der deutsche Generalstab und die Illusion des kurzen Kriegs, 1871–1914: Metakritik eines Mythos," in *Lange und kurze Wege in den Ersten Weltkrieg,* 115–58. Additionally, taking into account the situation above all in France, Dieter Storz, *Kriegsbild und Rüstung vor 1914: Europäische Landstreitkräfte vor dem Ersten Weltkrieg* (Herford: Mittlos, 1992).
45. Diary entry, 31 July 1914, Haus-, Hof- und Staatsarchiv, Mensdorff Papers, Box 4.
46. *Große Politik,* 34/I, Nr. 12561.
47. *British Documents,* VI, No. 591.
48. *Stenographischen Berichte über die Verhandlungen des Deutschen Reichstages* (Berlin, N.p., 1871), Bd. 289, 4513 C.
49. Sir Edward Grey, *Twenty-Five Years 1892–1916,* 2 vols. (London: Hodder and Stoughton, 1925), vol. 1, 302.
50. Bunsen to his daughter Hilda, 5 January 1913, Bodleian Library Oxford, Bunsen Papers, Box 9.
51. Nevertheless it is still astonishing how vast the difference in talking about war and peace even immediately before the First World War is compared to, for example, the negotiations of the European Powers in the second half of the 1930s. This comparison would be worth an examination of its own.
52. The German State Secretary seems to have chosen Morocco as an international conflict point just for this reason. See Alfred von Kiderlen-Wächter, *Kiderlen-Wächter der Staatsmann und Mensch: Briefwechsel und Nachlaß,* ed. Ernst Jäckh, 2 Bde. (Berlin and Leipzig: Deutsche Verlagsanstalt, 1924), Bd. 2, 128ff.
53. Sir Edward Grey, *Speeches on Foreign Affairs 1904–1914,* selected with an introduction by Paul Knaplund (London: Allen & Unwin, 1931), 171.
54. Bertie to Grey, 29 August 1911, *British Documents,* VII, No. 497.
55. William II to Kiderlen, 9 August 1911, *Große Politik,* 29, Nr. 10686.
56. On international honor in international relations, see Barry O`Neill, *Honor, Symbols, and War* (Ann Arbor: University of Michigan Press, 1999). O`Neill certainly points out that the argument of honor is still common today in foreign policy contexts. The content and dissemination of the term, however, is, of course, different.
57. Michael Sheehan, *The Balance of Power: History and Theory* (London and New York: Routledge, 1996), 1–23.
58. Radkau, *Das Zeitalter der Nervosität,* 423.
59. Roderick R. McLean, *Royalty and Diplomacy in Europe 1890–1914* (Cambridge: Cambridge University Press, 2001).
60. Suttner to Mérey, 15 October 1908, Haus-, Hof- und Staatsarchiv, Mérey Papers, Box 16.
61. Alfred Fried, "Das Marokkoabkommen," *Die Friedens-Warte* 13 (1911): 313. The research on the peace movement is fairly agreed on the point that the peace movement in all countries before 1914 was convinced that the mood was swinging more and more their way. Cf. Robbins, *The Abolition*

of War, 26; Karl Holl, *Pazifismus in Deutschland* (Frankfurt: Suhrkamp, 1988), 103. Richard R. Laurence, "The Peace Movement in Austria, 1867–1914," in *Doves and Diplomats*, 32ff.; Klaus Wilsberg, *"Terrible ami— aimable ennemi": Kooperation und Konflikt in den deutsch-französischen Beziehungen 1911–1914* (Bonn: Bouvier, 1998), 337.

62. Under 3 December 1912, e.g., it says in his memoirs that he was continuing to pursue "a peace policy taking into account the international situation" against a great part of public opinion: Haus-, Hof- und Staatsarchiv, Berchtold Papers, Box 1.
63. Ralf Forsbach, *Alfred von Kiderlen-Wächter (1852–1912): Ein Diplomatenleben im Kaiserreich,* 2 vols., (Göttingen: Vandenhoeck & Ruprecht, 1997); Meyer, *"Endlich eine Tat, eine befreiende Tat…"*
64. Zara S. Steiner, *Britain and the Origins of the First World War* (Basingstoke and London: Macmillan Press, 1995), 174 (first published in 1977).
65. Cf. Keith Robbins, "Public Opinion, the Press and Pressure Groups," in *Politicians, Diplomacy and War in Modern British History,* ed. Robbins (London: Hambledon Press, 1994), 127.
66. On the development of the state system in the nineteenth and twentieth centuries or the development of diplomacy among others, see Anselm Doering-Manteuffel, "Internationale Geschichte als Systemgeschichte: Strukturen und Handlungsmuster im europäischen Staatensystem des 19. und 20. Jahrhunderts," in *Internationale Geschichte,* 93–115; Peter Krüger and Paul W. Schroeder, eds., *"The Transformation of European Politics, 1763–1848": Episode or Model in Modern History?* (Münster: Lit, 2002); M. S. Anderson, *The Rise of Modern Diplomacy* (London: Longman, 1993); Keith Hamilton and Richard Langhorne, *The Practice of Diplomacy: Its Evolution, Theory and Administration* (London and New York: Routledge, 1995).
67. A partial listing can be found in Winfried Baumgart, *Vom europäischen Konzert zum Völkerbund: Friedensschlüsse und Friedenssicherung von Wien bis Versailles* (Darmstadt: Wissenschaftliche Buchgesellschaft, 1974).
68. See, e.g., *British Documents,* IX/II, No. 292 u. 296.
69. Gordon A. Craig and Alexander L. George, *Force and Statecraft: Diplomatic Problems of our Time* (Oxford: Oxford University Press, 1988), 248.
70. Examples of how seriously the wording of communiqués was taken would be too numerous to mention here. As an indication, the German Foreign State Secretary von Kiderlein once complained that the communiqué issued by both governments after the German–Russian Monarchs meeting in Baltic Port in July 1912 unnecessarily assured the French and English governments by its formulation. Jäckh, Bd. 2, S. 152 u. *Große Politik,* 31, Nr. 11543, Marginal note Kiderlen. The State Secretary had not taken part in the meeting.
71. It went, for example, from "normal" to "good" to "hearty" relations.
72. *British Documents,* VI, No. 591; cf. *Große Politik,* 31, Nr. 11433.
73. Cf., e.g., speech to the lower house of 10 July 1912, Grey, *Speeches,* 206f.
74. Speech Berchtold to the Austrian delegation, 29 April 1914, *Schulthess' Europäischer Geschichtskalender* 55 (1914/I), S. 456f.
75. ÖUA III, Nr. 3256.
76. In other points not. Thus it came to a mixture of optimism and pessimism which became significant in the July crisis. On this effect of détente, see Kießling, *Gegen den "großen Krieg"?*
77. Paulmann, *Pomp und Politik,* 343.

78. Richard Langhorne, *The Collapse of the Concert of Europe: International Politics 1890–1914* (New York: St. Martins Press, 1981), 105.
79. See, e.g., *British Documents,* VII, No. 657 and 659.
80. Report from Paris, 14 May 1913, Auswärtiges Amt/Politisches Archiv, Frankreich 102, Bd. 57 and report from Paris, 5 July 1913, ibid., Bd. 59.
81. Valerie M. Hudson, "Culture and Foreign Policy: Developing a Research Agenda," in *Culture and Foreign Policy,* ed. Hudson (Boulder and London: Rienner, 1997), 16 poses the question of different "cultures" in different foreign policy areas.
82. That was typically no longer the case in the years between the wars. Now politicians succeed in getting their rules through against the diplomats. Cf. Gordon A. Craig, "The Professional Diplomat and His Problems, 1919–1939," in *War, Politics and Diplomacy: Selected Essays,* ed. Craig (London: Weidenfeld and Nicolson, 1966), 207–19.
83. Der Derian, *On Diplomacy,* 42.
84. Jürgen Haacke, *ASEAN's Diplomatic and Security Culture: Origins, Developments and Prospects* (London and New York: Routledge, 2003).
85. Once more, see Rosenberg, *Financial Missionaries to the World*; Anders Stephanson, *Manifest Destiny.* See, in addition, studies which are dedicated to examining the connection between national political culture and the foreign policy of the respective country: e.g., Jürgen Bellers, *Politische Kultur und Außenpolitik im Vergleich* (Munich and Vienna: Oldenbourg, 1999); Roland H. Ebel, Raymond Taras, James D. Cochrane, *Political Culture and Foreign Policy in Latin America: Case Studies from the Circum-Caribbean* (New York: State University of New York Press, 1991); Samuels and Weiner, eds., *The Political Culture of Foreign Area and International Studies.*
86. Culture and international relations have obviously been connected in other ways: cultural diplomacy or certain aspects of culture transfer, to name but two. See, e.g., the stimulating volume Reinhold Wagnleitner and Elaine Tyler May, eds., *"Here, There and Everywhere": The Foreign Politics of American Popular Culture* (Hanover and London: University Press of New England, 2000).
87. Frode Liland, *Culture and Foreign Policy: An Introduction to Approaches and Theory* (Oslo: Institute for Forsvarsstudies, 1993), 8 or 13.
88. Raymond Cohen, *Negotiating Across Cultures: Communication Obstacles in International Diplomacy* (Washington, DC: United States Institute of Peace Press, 1991).
89. Concentration on the foreign policy process within a culture does not mean that intercultural contact plays no part in emergence and stabilization. This point is strongly made by Beate Jahn, *The Cultural Construction of International Relations: The Invention of the State of Nature* (Basingstoke: Palgrave MacMillan, 2000). The courtly nucleus should certainly also not be forgotten in the emergence of western diplomatic forms: see, e.g., Der Derian, *On Diplomacy,* 111.
90. Paul A. Chilton, *Security Metaphors: Cold War Discourse from Containment to Common House* (New York: Lang, 1995); Henrik Larsen, *Foreign Policy and Discourse Analysis: France, Britain and Europe* (London and New York: Routledge, 1997); Barry O'Neill, *Honor, Symbols, and War* (Ann Arbor, 1999). The general question of "how to deal theoretically with general beliefs to which actors adhere" (Larsen, *Foreign Policy an Discourse Analysis,* 1) has surely already been raised in the most various variants.

With reference to behaviourist models, see J. W. Burton, *Systems, States, Diplomacy and Rules* (Cambridge: Cambridge University Press, 1968). With emphasis on psychological aspects, see Richard Little and Steve Smith, eds., *Belief Systems and International Relations* (Oxford and New York: Blackwell, 1988). For institutionalistic approaches, see Christian Reus-Smit, *The Moral Purpose of the State: Culture, Social Identity, and Institutional Rationality in International Relations* (Princeton: Princeton University Press, 1999).

91. Gerd Althoff, "Rituale—symbolische Kommunikation: Zu einem neuen Feld der historischen Mittelalterforschung," *Geschichte in Wissenschaft und Unterricht* 50 (1999): 140–54; Karl Leyser, *Communication and Power in Medieval Europe: The Carolingian and Ottonian Centuries* (London: Hambledon Press, 1994); Christina Lutter, *Politische Kommunikation an der Wende vom Mittelalter zur Neuzeit: Die diplomatischen Beziehungen zwischen der Republik Venedig und Maximilian I (1495–1508)* (Vienna and Munich: Oldenbourg, 1998).
92. See Kießling, "Der 'Dialog der Taubstummen,'" 658f.
93. In a certain segment of Great Power diplomacy, see Paulmann, *Pomp und Politik*.
94. Richard J. Crampton, *The Hollow Detente: Anglo-German-Relations in the Balkans, 1911–1914* (London: Prior, 1979); Hanns Christian Löhr, "Für den König von Preußen arbeiten? Die deutsch-französischen Beziehungen am Vorabend des Ersten Weltkriegs," *Francia* 23 (1996): 141–54; Gregor Schöllgen, "Richard von Kühlmann und das deutsch-englische Verhältnis 1912–1914: Zur Bedeutung der Peripherie in der europäischen Vorkriegspolitik," *Historische Zeitschrift* 230 (1980): 293–337; Klaus Wilsberg, *"Terrible ami—aimable ennemi."*
95. Cf. Kießling, *Gegen den "großen Krieg"?* 281–324.
96. So far this has been undertaken above all for the connection between courtly ceremonial and external relations. Besides Paulmann, *Pomp und Politik,* see David Cannadine and Simon Price, eds., *Rituals of Royalty: Power and Ceremonial in Traditional Societies* (Cambridge: Cambridge University Press, 1987). In another area, see Robert A. Rubinstein, "Cultural Aspects of Peacekeeping: Notes on the Substance of Symbols," in *Culture in World Politics,* eds. Dominique Jacquin-Berdal, Andrew Oros, Marco Verweij (Basingstoke: Palgrave MacMillan, 1998), 187–205.
97. Der Derian, *On Diplomacy,* 200. Quotation from Michel Foucault, *Language, Counter-Memory, Practice,* ed. D. Bouchard (Oxford: Blackwell, 1977).
98. Jürgen Osterhammel, "Internationale Geschichte, Globalisierung und die Pluralität der Kulturen," in *Internationale Geschichte,* 399f. Osterhammel expressly mentions the differentiation between "new" and "old diplomacy."
99. Cf. Christian Windler, "Tribut und Gabe: Mediterrane Diplomatie als interkulturelle Kommunikation," *Saeculum* 51 (2000): esp. 25f. and 35.
100. In this sense Mette Boritz describes diplomatic practices only from the point of view of the status-consciousness or career chances of diplomats: Boritz, "The Hidden Culture in Diplomatic Practice: A Study of the Danish Foreign Service," *Ethnologia Scandinavia* 28 (1998): 48–61.
101. Cf. Osterhammel, "Internationale Geschichte," note 56.
102. Glifford Geertz, "Thick Description: Toward an Interpretive Theory of Culture," in *The Interpretion of Cultures: Selected Essays* (New York: Basic Books, 1973), 13.

Bibliography

Althoff, Gerd. "Rituale—symbolische Kommunikation: Zu einem neuen Feld der historischen Mittelalterforschung." *Geschichte in Wissenschaft und Unterricht* 50 (1999): 140–54.
Anderson, M. S. *The Rise of Modern Diplomacy*. London: Longman, 1993.
Bellers, Jürgen. *Politische Kultur und Außenpolitik im Vergleich*. Munich and Vienna: Oldenbourg, 1999.
Boritz, Mette. "The Hidden Culture in Diplomatic Practice: A Study of the Danish Foreign Service." *Ethnologia Scandinavia* 28 (1998): 48–61.
Buzzanco, Robert. "Commentary: Where's the Beef? Culture without Power in the Study of U.S. Foreign Relations." *Diplomatic History* 24 (2000): 623–32.
Cannadine, David, and Simon Price, eds. *Rituals of Royalty: Power and Ceremonial in Traditional Societies*. Cambridge: Cambridge University Press, 1987.
Cecil, Lamar. *The German Diplomatic Service: 1871–1914*. Princeton: Princeton University Press, 1976.
Cooper, Sandi E. *Patriotic Pacifism: Waging War on War in Europe 1815–1914*. New York and Oxford: Oxford University Press, 1991.
Conze, Eckart, Ulrich Lappenküper, and Guido Müller, eds. *Geschichte der internationalen Beziehungen. Erneuerung und Erweiterung einer historischen Disziplin*. Cologne: Böhlau, 2004.
Craig, Gordon A. "The Professional Diplomat and His Problems, 1919–1939." In *War, Politics and Diplomacy: Selected Essays*, ed. Craig. London: Weidenfeld and Nicolson, 1966, pp. 207–19.
Craig, Gordon A., and Alexander L. George. *Force and Statecraft: Diplomatic Problems of our Time*. 3rd ed. Oxford: Oxford University Press, 1995.
Crampton, Richard J. *The Hollow Detente: Anglo-German-Relations in the Balkans, 1911–1914*. London: Prior, 1979.
Cromwell, Valerie. "'A World Apart': Gentlemen Amateurs to Professional Generalists." In *Diplomacy and World Power: Studies in British Foreign Policy, 1890–1950*, eds. Michael Dockrill and Brian McKercher. Cambridge: Cambridge University Press, 1996, pp. 1–18.
Der Derian, James. *On Diplomacy: A Genealogy of Western Estrangement*. Oxford and New York: Blackwell, 1987.
Dülffer, Jost. *Regeln gegen den Krieg? Die Haager Friedenskonferenzen von 1899 und 1907 in der internationalen Politik*. Berlin: Ullstein, 1981.
———. "Die zivile Reichsleitung und der Krieg: Erwartungen und Bilder 1890–1914." In *Gestaltungskraft des Politischen: Festschrift für Eberhard Kolb*, eds. Wolfram Pyta and Ludwig Richter. Berlin: Duncker & Humblot, 1998, pp. 11–28.
Dülffer, Jost, Martin Kröger, and Rolf-Harald Wippich, eds. *Vermiedene Kriege: Deeskalation von Konflikten der Großmächte zwischen Krimkrieg und Erstem Weltkrieg 1856–1914*. Munich: Oldenbourg, 1997.
Ebel, Roland H., Raymond Taras, and James D. Cochrane, eds. *Political Culture and Foreign Policy in Latin America: Case Studies from the Circum-Caribbean*. New York: State University of New York Press, 1991.
Eisenbeiß, Wilfried. *Die bürgerliche Friedensbewegung in Deutschland während des Ersten Weltkriegs: Organisation, Selbstverständnis und politische Praxis 1913/14–1919*. Frankfurt: Lang, 1980.
Förster, Stig. "Der deutsche Generalstab und die Illusion des kurzen Kriegs, 1871–1914: Metakritik eines Mythos." In *Lange und kurze Wege in den Ersten Weltkrieg: Vier Augsburger Beiträge zur Kriegsursachenforschung*, ed. Johannes Burkhardt. Munich: Vögel, 1996, pp. 115–58.

———. "Im Reich der Absurden: Die Ursachen des Ersten Weltkrieges." In *Wie Kriege entstehen: Zum historischen Hintergrund von Staatenkonflikten,* ed. Bernd Wegner. Paderborn: Schöningh, 2000, pp. 211–52.
Geertz, Clifford. *The Interpretation of Cultures: Selected Essays.* New York: Basic Books, 1973.
Geyer, Martin H., and Johannes Paulmann, eds. *The Mechanics of Internationalism: Culture, Society and Politics from the 1840s to the First World War.* Oxford: Oxford University Press, 2001.
Gienow-Hecht, Jessica, and Frank Schumacher, eds. *Culture and International History.* New York: Berghahn Books, 2003.
Gollwitzer, Heinz. *Geschichte des weltpolitischen Denkens.* 2 vols. Göttingen: Vandenhoeck & Ruprecht, 1972–82.
Haacke, Jürgen. *ASEAN's Diplomatic and Security Culture: Origins, Developments and Prospects.* London and New York: Routledge, 2003.
Hamilton, Keith, and Richard Langhorne. *The Practice of Diplomacy: Its Evolution, Theory and Administration.* London and New York: Routledge, 1995.
Hamilton, Richard F., and Holger H. Herwig, eds. *The Origins of World War I.* Cambridge: Cambridge University Press, 2003.
Hayne, M. B. *The French Foreign Office and the Origins of the First World War 1898–1914.* Oxford: Clarendon Press, 1993.
Herren, Madeleine. *Hintertüren zur Macht: Internationalismus und modernisierungsorientierte Außenpolitik in Belgien, der Schweiz und den USA 1865–1914.* Munich: Oldenbourg, 2000.
Hildebrand, Klaus. "Julikrise 1914: Das europäische Sicherheitsdilemma: Betrachtungen über den Ausbruch des Ersten Weltkrieges." *Geschichte in Wissenschaft und Unterricht* 36 (1985): 469–502.
Holbraad, Carsten. *The Concert of Europe: A Study in German and British International Theory 1815–1914.* London and Southampton: Longman, 1970.
Hudson, Valerie M. "Culture and Foreign Policy: Developing a Research Agenda." In *Culture & Foreign Policy,* ed. Hudson. Boulder and London: Rienner, 1997, pp. 1–24.
Jahn, Beate. *The Cultural Construction of International Relations: The Invention of the State of Nature.* Basingstoke: Palgrave, 2000.
Joll, James. *1914: The Unspoken Assumptions.* London and Southampton: Weidenfeld and Nicolson, 1968.
Kern, Stephan. *The Culture of Time and Space: 1880–1918.* 10th ed. Cambridge, MA: Harvard University Press, 2000.
Kießling, Friedrich. *Gegen den "großen Krieg"? Entspannung in den internationalen Beziehungen 1911–1914.* Munich: Oldenbourg, 2002.
———. "Der 'Dialog der Taubstummen' ist vorbei: Neue Ansätze in der Geschichte der internationalen Beziehungen des 19. und 20. Jahrhunderts." *Historische Zeitschrift* 275 (2002): 651–80.
Kronenbitter, Günther. "'Nur los lassen': Österreich-Ungarn und der Wille zum Krieg." In *Lange und kurze Wege in den Ersten Weltkrieg: Vier Augsburger Beiträge zur Kriegsursachenforschung,* eds. Johannes Burkhardt et al. Munich: Vögel, 1996, pp. 159–87.
Krüger, Peter, and Paul W. Schroeder, eds. *"The Transformation of European Politics, 1763–1848": Episode or Model in Modern History?* Münster: Lit, 2002.
Larsen, Henrik. *Foreign Policy and Discourse Analysis: France, Britain and Europe.* London and New York: Routledge, 1997.
Leyser, Karl. *Communication and Power in Medieval Europe: The Carolingian and Ottonian Centuries.* London: Hambledon Press, 1994.

Liland, Frode. *Culture and Foreign Policy: An Introduction to Approaches and Theory.* Oslo: Inst. for Forsvarsstudier, 1993.

Lindemann, Thomas. *Die Macht der Perzeptionen und Perzeptionen von Mächten.* Berlin: Duncker & Humblot, 2000.

Logevall, Fredrik. "A Critique of Containment." *Diplomatic History* 28 (2004): 474–99.

Löhr, Hanns Christian. "Für den König von Preußen arbeiten? Die deutsch-französischen Beziehungen am Vorabend des Ersten Weltkriegs." *Francia* 23 (1996): 141–54.

Lutter, Christina. *Politische Kommunikation an der Wende vom Mittelalter zur Neuzeit: Die diplomatischen Beziehungen zwischen der Republik Venedig und Maximilian, 1495–1508.* Vienna and Munich: Oldenbourg, 1998.

Matsch, Erwin. *Geschichte des Auswärtigen Dienstes von Österreich-Ungarn 1720–1920.* Vienna: Böhlau, 1980.

McLean, Roderick R. *Royalty and Diplomacy in Europe 1890–1914.* Cambridge: Cambridge University Press, 2001.

Neitzel, Sönke. *Weltmacht oder Untergang: Die Weltreichslehre im Zeitalter des Imperialismus.* Paderborn: Schöningh, 2000.

O'Neill, Barry. *Honor, Symbols, and War.* Ann Arbor: University of Michigan Press, 1999.

Osterhammel, Jürgen. "Internationale Geschichte, Globalisierung und die Pluralität der Kulturen." In *Internationale Geschichte: Themen—Ergebnisse—Aussichten,* eds. Wilfried Loth and Jürgen Osterhammel. Munich: Oldenbourg, 2000, pp. 287–308.

Paulmann, Johannes. *Pomp und Politik: Monarchenbegegnungen in Europa zwischen Ancien Régime und Erstem Weltkrieg.* Paderborn: Schöningh, 2000.

Radkau, Joachim. *Das Zeitalter der Nervosität: Deutschland zwischen Bismarck und Hitler.* Munich and Vienna: Hanser, 1998.

Robbins, Keith. *The Abolition of War: The "Peace Movement" in Britain, 1914–1919.* Cardiff: University of Wales Press, 1976.

Rubinstein, Robert A. "Cultural Aspects of Peacekeeping: Notes on the Substance of Symbols." In *Culture in World Politics,* eds. Dominique Jacquin-Berdal, Andrew Oros, and Marco Verweij. Basingstoke: MacMillan, 1998, pp. 187–205.

Samuels, Richard J., and Myron Weiner, eds. *The Political Culture of Foreign Area and International Studies: Essays in Honor of Lucian W. Pye.* Washington, DC: Brassey's, 1992.

Schöllgen, Gregor. "Richard von Kühlmann und das deutsch-englische Verhältnis 1912–1914: Zur Bedeutung der Peripherie in der europäischen Vorkriegspolitik." *Historische Zeitschrift* 230 (1980): 293–337.

Sheehan, Michael. *The Balance of Power: History and Theory.* London and New York: Routledge, 1996.

Solomon, Richard H. "Political Culture and Diplomacy in the Twenty-first Century." In *The Political Culture of Foreign Area and International Studies: Essays in Honor of Lucian W. Pye,* eds. Richard J. Samuels and Myron Weiner. Washington, DC: Brassey's, 1992, pp. 141–54.

Steiner, Zara S. *The Foreign Office and Foreign Policy 1898–1914.* Cambridge: Cambridge University Press, 1969.

———. *Britain and the Origins of the First World War.* Basingstoke and London: Macmillan, 1995 (first published in 1977).

Storz, Dieter. *Kriegsbild und Rüstung vor 1914: Europäische Landstreitkräfte vor dem Ersten Weltkrieg.* Herford: Mittler, 1992.

Wank, Solomon, ed. *Doves and Diplomats: Foreign Offices and Peace Movements in Europe and America in the Twentieth Century.* Westport: Greenwood Press, 1978.

Wilsberg, Klaus. *"Terrible ami—aimable ennemi": Kooperation und Konflikt in den deutsch-französischen Beziehungen 1911–1914.* Bonn: Bouvier, 1998.

Windler, Christian. "Tribut und Gabe: Mediterrane Diplomatie als interkulturelle Kommunikation." *Saeculum* 51 (2000): 24–56.

INDEX

A

Abwehr, 265
Adenauer, Konrad, 79, 81, 97, 215, 218, 230
Advertiser's Weekly, 38
advertising, 23–57; *See also* American advertising; British advertising; European advertising
    American, 8
    as Americanization, 23–24
    brand image, 44–47
    European invention, 32–33
    fallacies of Americanization thesis, 30–37
    in Germany, 52–56
    as global culture, 56–57
    globalization of, 24
    globalized by 1920s, 55
    and international history, 23–26
    modernization in United Kingdom, 57
    and motivational studies, 47
    Orwell's view of, 29
    retail, 33
    transatlantic exchange of ideas, 43–47
advertising agencies, 25–26, 44–47, 48–56
    British-American competition, 55
    effect of Great Depression, 53–55
advertising films, 33
advertising postcards, 33
advertising war, 27
Advertising World, 28, 41
Afghanistan, 194
African Queen, 81
Agent Orange, 176, 178
Aguilar, Manuela, 78
Air Craft Stories (Law), 5
Alba, Duke of, 325
Alfaro, Ricardo J., 286
Algeciras Conferfence of 1906, 359
Alka-Seltzer, 86
Allende, Pedro Humberto, 139
All German People's Party, 229
alliance debate, 354
Allied High Commission, 79
Almeng, Victor, 176
Altman, Richard, 285–286
Alvarega, Oneyda, 149
ambassadorial congresses, 359–360
American advertising, 8
    aggressiveness in United Kingdom, 26–30
    British opposition to, 28–29
    as cultural imperialism, 26
    dominant European view of, 30
    Europeanization of, 35–37
    extent of influence in Europe, 31–32
    global growth of, 57
    of tobacco in United Kingdom, 27–28
American Ballet Caravan, 148–149
American Century thesis, 24, 26
American Congress on Intellectual Cooperation, 139
American consumers
    desire for European products, 34
    European influences, 34–35
    global spread of, 26
    impact of British advertising, 37–47

American Council of Learned
  Societies, 85, 147, 150–151
American culture
  diversity of, 31
  and foreign relations, 98–99
  global spread of, 26
  global success of, 95–96
  historiography of, 3–4
  transnational perspective, 5
American-European anti-nuclear
  march, 233
American exceptionalism, 346
American history
  decentering as means to
    understanding, 13
  internationalizing, 4–5
  means of decentering, 7–8
American imperialism, and Vietnam
  War, 89
Americanism, 98
  definitions of, 236
Americanization
  advertising agencies in Europe,
    47–56
  and Americanism, 98
  of anti-nuclear protests, 211
  assumptions for public
    diplomacy, 95–101
  assumptions in W. German
    protests, 236
  of British consumer culture, 26
  concept of, 8
  and cultural imperialism, 24
  fallacies of advertising influences,
    30–37
  of German advertising, 48
  and globalization of advertising, 24
  and international relations, 26–30
  inverted, 9
  and modern advertising, 23–24
  political rhetoric of, 26–30
  sender-receiver thesis, 30
  of West Germany, 89–90
Americanization studies, German-U. S.
  intercultural relations, 76
American Musicological Society, 144
American Nationalist Confederation,
  77
American Tobacco Company, 27–28
Amin, Ash, 6
anarchism, 109
Anderson, Craig W., 177
Andreatta, Glenn, 177

Anglo-American cultural relations, 31
Anglo-German peace committee, 348
Anglo-Palatine relations, 12; *see also*
  Palatinate
  celebration of dynastic marriage,
    329–334
  complexity of foreign policy, 316
  concepts of the enemy
    anti-Catholic propaganda,
      327
    denunciations of Spain,
      325–327
    John Reynolds's attack on
      Spain, 327
    Thomas Scott's attacks on
      Spain, 325–326
  conclusions on, 334–338
  English Reformation, 327
  fate of Palatinate, 327–328
  identity concept, 324
  lessons from, 336–337
  marriage of Friedrich V and
    Elizabeth Stuart, 328–334
  nature of international relations,
    324–325
  perspective on international
    relations, 317
  religious/dynastic concepts of
    emery, 335–336
anti-Americanism, in United Kingdom,
  28–29
anti-Catholic rhetoric, 327
Anti-German wave in United States
  American resistance to, 87–90
  background to, 73–76
  Cold War context, 87–90
  Fischer controversy, 85–86
  German public relations in U. S.
    under Kaiser Wilhelm II,
    76–77
    in Nazi era, 77–78
    post-World War II, 78–81
  German reasoning about, 84
  German responses to, 84–87
  importance of public diplomacy,
    100–101
  and *Judgment at Nuremberg* film,
    90–94
  in movies and television, 80–84
  onset and sources of, 81–84
  and study of public diplomacy,
    95–101
  survey results on, 87

and U. S. civil rights movement, 93–94
anti-Habsburg bloc, 322
anti-nuclear protest movement, 10, 210–238
   Americanization issue, 236
   American perspective, 211
   Bertrand Russell on, 217–218
   British-West German communications, 233–235
   civil disobedience, 230–233
   conclusions on
      conflictual reality, 236
      culture and, 237–238
      pacifist links, 237
      self-evolving dynamic, 238
      success of War Resisters' International, 236–237
   context of, 214–216
   cross-cultural communication problems, 220–225
   and culture, 212–213
   emotions in, 233
   focus on British/West German protests, 211
   fundamental disagreements, 224
   Hans Werner Richter on, 223–224
   internationalist rhetoric, 216–220
   multilateral disarmament, 221
   One World idea, 217
   origin of British movement, 214–215
   origin of West German movement, 215–216
   preserving national identities, 235
   radical pacifism, 226–227
   and Soviet peace propaganda, 220–221
   transnational perspective, 212
   transnational social space concept, 226, 233
   unilateral disarmament, 219
   War Resisters' International work, 225–236
anti-Vietnam War movement, 177–178
Apocalyptic tradition, 321
arbitration treaties
   in pre-World War I diplomacy, 349–350
   Wilhelm II's disregard of, 348
Arcana imperii, 326
Archive of American Folk Song, 142–143
Archive of Folklore, Colombia, 155
Argentina
   fascist leaders, 268–269
   Federal Commission on Folklore and Natives, 141
   inspired by Mussolini, 269
Arias, Harmadio, 298
Art Deco advertising style, 35–37
Art Nouveau advertising style, 35
arts, decentering in, 6–7
Asia, non-governmental influence, 10
Association of Southeast Asian Nations, 365
Atkinson, G. A., 28
Atlantic Monthly, 80
atomic bombs
   dropped on Japan, 214
Au Bonheur des Dames (Zola), 33
Aufhagen, Friedrich E. F., 77
Augsburg Lutheran-Catholic settlement, 320
Auslandsorganization, efforts in Latin America, 256–257, 259–260, 264, 268–269
Austin & Nichols, 38
Austria-Hungary, view of foreign policy, 353
Automobile industry, British advertising, 39–41
avante-garde
   Brazilian, 137–138
   Europe, 137
Azevedo, Luiz Heitor Correa de, 141, 151–153, 154, 155

B

Bailey, Richard D., 177
Balanchine, George, 149
Balboa High School, Panama, 298
Balkan crisis of 1911-12, 351
   London conference of 1912, 360–361
Balkan Wars, 363
Ballet Folklorico, Mexico, 140
Barilla, John Michael, 177
Battle of the Bulge, 83
Beardsley, Aubrey, 35
Beaumont, Francis, 329
Beckman, Francis, 292–293
Beggarstaff brothers, 35
Beleño, Joaquin, 287, 291
Bender, Thomas, 4

Berchtold, Leopold von, 357–358, 362
Berghahn, Volcker, 95
Berle, Adolf, 259
Berlin Congress of 1978, 359
Berlin Wall, 74
Bernhardt, Sarah, 33
Berrien, William, 148, 151
Bertie, Francis, 356
Bethmann Hollweg, Theobald von, 355, 365
Bieberstein, Marschall von, 362
Billiard ball concept of international relations, 317–318
Bipolar world system, 318
Bird, Donald Charles, 266
Bismarck, Otto von, 261–262
Blackbourn, David, 7–8
Black legend, about Spain, 325
Bloody Sunday 1965 (US), 93
Blue Max, 83
Blumenthal, Roy, 79
Boas, Franz, 137
Boeke, Kees, 226
Boggs, Ralph Steele, 143, 145, 154
Bohemia
   Defenestration of Prague, 32
   Friedrich V named king, 323
   king dethroned, 322
   Protestant-Catholic conflict, 322–323
   start of Thirty Years' War, 323
Bohle, Ernst, 269
Boletin Latinamercana Musica, 141–142, 148
Bolivar, Simon, 259
Bolshevik Revolution, 12
Bolt, Robert, 217
Bourdet, Claude, 229
Bradley, Will, 35
brand image, 44–47
Brandt, Rüdiger, 319
Brandt, Willy, 73, 75, 92
Brave New World (Huxley), 29
Brazil
   avant-gardists, 138
   Center for Folklore Research, 152–153
   cultural identity, 137
   failed fascist coup of 1938, 269–260
   folklore research in, 137–138
   nationalist program, 260
Brigham, Robert, 186–188

British advertising
   for auto industry, 39–41
   global growth of, 57
   impact on U. S. consumer culture, 37–47
   internationalization of, 56–57
British anti-nuclear protests
   annual fifty-mile march, 215
   Campaign for Nuclear Disarmament, 214–215, 217–218, 221, 228, 234–235
   civil disobedience, 230–233
   Committee of 100, 215
   conclusions on, 236–228
   cultural assumptions, 232–234
   cultural norms, 212–213
   and International Confederation for Disarmament and Peace, 225
   Labour Party stance, 214–215, 221
   leading figures in, 217–218
   links to West German movement, 220–225
   origin of, 214–215
   as response to threat of thermonuclear war, 211
   rhetoric of internationalism, 216–218
   symbolic internationalism, 234–235
   War Resisters' International, 225–236
   and World Peace Council, 224–225
British Brewers Association, 50
British consumer culture
   fallacies of American influence, 30–37
   perception of Americanization of, 26
   receptiveness to U. S. advertising, 25–26
   warnings against American marketing, 26–27
British empire, marketing of, 37–38
British historiography, and U. S. influences, 23–24
British Market Research Bureau, 52
Broadley, Herbert, 52
Brockway, Fenner, 229
Brown, William, 172
Bryan, William Jennings, 349
Bühler, Charlotte, 47

Bunsen, Maurice de, 356
Bunyo, Ishikawa, 176
Buro, Andreas, 229
Bush, George H. W., 171
Butler Josephine, 300
Buy British campaign, 40–41

C

Cádiz, battle of, 326
Calvinism
    apocalyptic tradition, 321
    influence in international
        relations, 318
    introduced into Palatinate, 320
    predestination theology, 320–321
Cambodia, Pol pot regime, 193
Cameron, James, 82
Campaign against Atomic Death, 215, 223
Campaign for Democracy and Disarmament, 215
Campaign for Nuclear Disarmament, 214–215, 217–218, 221, 223, 228, 234–235
Campion, Thomas, 329
Canal Zone Police, 285, 292, 299
Canaris, Wilhelm, 265
Cancionera Pan Americana, 132
Canclini, Nestor Garcia, 140
Can Dao, Vietnam, 176
Carnegie Endowment, 147
Carter, April, 231
Carter, Jimmy, 191–193
Casten, Sam, 178
Castillo, Blanca Maria, 294–296
Castillo, Eduardo, killing of, 294–295
Castro, Woodrow, 287, 290–291
Catholicism
    anti-Catholic rhetoric, 327
    influence in international
        relations, 318
    Lutheran settlement at Augsburg, 320
CBS televsion, 82–83
Center for Folklore Research, Brazil, 152–153
Central Intelligence Agency, 297–298
Cervantes, Miguel de, 332
Chamberlain, William H., 89
Chang, Carson, 121
Charles F. Higham Advertising Agency Ltd., 37–38

Charles F. Higham agency, 43
Charles I of England, 326, 329
Chavez, Carlos, 141
Chen Duxiu, 113–114
Chéret, Jules, 32
Cherrington, Ben, 143
Chiang Kai-Shek, 117
Chile
    cowboy books, 140
    folklore research, 138–139
    Institute of Musical Extension, 150–151
    music traditions, 139
    nativist writers, 138
    Popular Front government, 139
Chilean Commission on Intellectual Cooperation, 139
China
    abolition of Confucian examinations, 115
    advantages over Europe, 126
    diversity of ideologies in 1914, 12
    effects of Versailles Peace Treaty, 119
    embrace of Western values, 109–116
    European stereotypes of, 111–112
    Europe learning from, 123–125
    failure to restore monarchy, 111
    interpretations of World War I, 118–126
    marginalized in world order, 117–118
    modernity as perceived danger, 120–122
    modernity debate, 9
    national essence processes, 117
    national humiliation, 112
    new urban intellectuals, 113
    presence of Japan and Western powers, 119
    pro-Western forces, 113
    revolutionary changes in, 111–112
    sense of nationalism, 112
    Social Darwinism in, 121
    speech by Bertrand Russell, 121–122
    spread of modernity, 110–112
    traditionalism/conservatism, 116–118
    viewed as backward, 113–114
    Western-style education, 110–111
    youth movements, 114–116

Chinese intellectuals
  Cau Yuankei, 119
  Chen Duxiu, 113–114
  commitment to Western values, 119
  conservatives, 117–118
  diverse ideologies of, 112
  doubts about progressivism, 120
  Gao Yihan, 114
  Hu Shi, 119
  Liang Qichao, 111, 117, 121, 123–125
  Li Dazhao, 115, 120
  Liu Shuya, 119
  New Culture Movement, 125–126
  New Youth Movement, 114
  post-1918 visits to Europe, 121–122
  post-World War I, 119–121
  pro-Western, 113–114
  Shen Yi, 120
  traditionalists, 116–117
  urban-based, 113
  view of European revolutions, 114
  view of World War I, 119
  Wei Siluan, 119–120
  Yan Fu, 121
  Young China, 114–116
  Zhang Junmai, 121, 122–123
  Zhu Xi, 117
  Zong Zhikui, 115
Chinese Revolution of 1911, 110, 117
Christian Democratic Party (W. Germany), 215
Chrysler Corporation, 52
Cinematograph Films Act of 1927 (UK), 39
civil disobedience
  Gandhian methods, 229, 230–231
  and Martin Luther King, 232
  in United States, 231
civil rights movement, 189, 231
  Selma, Ala., march, 93
  and War Resisters' International, 226
Classical period in Europe, 317
Clay, Lucius, 73
Clay, William, 175
Coca-Cola Company, 98
Coca-colonization and the Cold War (Wagnleitner), 95
Colburn, Lawrence, 177
Cold War, 74, 75
  anti-nuclear protests, 10
  context of anti-German wave, 87–90
  diplomatic culture studies, 346
  effect on diplomacy, 369
  public diplomacy in, 96
  religion in diplomacy of, 315
  rhetoric of internationalism, 216–220
  and Soviet nuclear weapons, 214
  and West Germany, 230
Cold War ideology, 258
Collier's magazine, 80
Collins, Canon, 224–225
Colombia
  Archive of Folklore, 155
  National Folklore Commission, 140
Colonized societies, 119
Combat!, 84, 87
Comite 1952 voor de Vrede, 231
comment books, in War Remnants Museum, 190–196
commercialization of folklore, 140
Committee of 100, 215, 231, 232
Communist Party
  banned in West Germany, 230
  USSR, 230
Conference on the Inter-American Relations in the Field of Music, 144
confessionalization paradigm, 316–317, 318
confessional state, 316
Conflict regulation concept, 349–350
Confucianism
  and German idealism, 122
  Lu-Wang school, 117
  as religion, 117
  system of education, 110
Confucian state examinations, abolition of, 115
Congress of Vienna of 1915, 359
conservatism in China, 117–118
Constantinou, Marios, 6
consumer culture, Americanized, 30
Consumerism, 47
consumers
  impact of British advertising in U. S., 37–47
  impact of Hollywood films in United Kingdom, 39
cosmic race concept, 137
Costigliola, Frank, 98
Counter-Reformation
  in Bavaria, 321

versus Bohemian Protestants, 322–323
versus Calvinism, 321
Protestant reactions to, 327–328
refugees from, 320
in Spain, 322
Crawford, William, 55
"Crisis of European Culture" (Zhang), 122
cross-cultural communication
diffusion of ideas, 213
framing processes, 212–213
problems for anti-nuclear protesters, 220–225
at symbolic level, 234
Crowe, Guthrie, 286, 291–292
Cuba
congress on music, 137
guerrilla activity in, 278
Cultural diplomacy, 2
Cultural diplomacy of United States
after World War II, 153–154
benefits from, 155
denounced in Latin America, 133
on eve of World War II, 143–147
and Good Neighbor Policy, 133–134, 153
in Great Depression, 142–143
and Latin American cooperation of folklore research, 147–153
misuse of Latin American folklore, 133
music conference of 1939, 144
Office of the Coordinator of Inter-American Affairs, 133–134
overall outcome, 155–156
Pan American Songbook of 1942, 132
Pan American Union Music Division, 144–145
politically motivated, 154
realistic reassessment of, 146–147
shift away from Latin America, 153–154
by State Department, 143–144
during World War II, 153
Cultural Division of U. S. State Department, 134, 143–144, 145, 147, 155
cultural emancipation, 135
cultural identity
Brazil, 137
Latin American research for, 134–135
cultural imperialism, 8
of American advertising, 26
and Americanization, 97
Americanization as, 24
denounced in Latin America, 133
cultural initiatives, and public diplomacy, 99
cultural nationalism
Brazil, 138
Chile, 138–139
from folklore research, 137–138
in Latin America, 136–142
cultural norms, 212
cultural policies of United States, 9
cultural relations, postcolonial theory, 134
cultural transfer
direction of Americanization, 98
German-U. S. intercultural relations, 76
U. S. - West Germany, 95–101
culture
and Americanization, 31
and anti-nuclear protests, 10, 220–225
decentering U. S., 1–3
and diplomacy, 12–13
and diplomatic history, 346–347
dynamic definition of, 212–213
European crisis of, 122–123
folklore as means of analyzing, 141
and foreign policy, 366
of Germany
imperial era, 76–77
Nazi era, 77–78
sidelined by Federal Republic, 78–81
and international history, 257–258
in international relations, 212
mass culture, 4
Panama-U. S. conflict, 278–279
and power, 96
public diplomacy as means of studying, 100
U. S. as recipient and exporter of, 8

D

Daily Express, 28, 38
Darío, Ruben, 136

de Andrade, Mario, 138, 141
de Andrade, Oswald, 137–138
decentering
   of American history, 7–8
   approach to U. S. culture/history, 1–3
   in arts, 6–7
   in deconstructionist thought, 6
   in ethnicity, 6
   in geography, 6
   in historiography, 7
   in humanities, 5–6
   by internationalization, 11–12
   meaning of, 2
   origin of term, 5
   in postmodernist thought, 6
   and poststructuralism, 6
   and risk of new dogma, 13–14
   U. S. from anti-nuclear protests, 211
   U. S. power in Panama, 280, 300–301
   to understand American history, 13
   uses of term, 7
Decentering Music (Korsyn), 6
Deconstructionist thought, 6
Deer Hunter, 190
della Porta, Donatella, 213
Denny, Ludwell, 23
Department of Culture of Sao Paulo, 138
Department stores, 33–34
Der Derrien, James, 346, 365, 368
Derrick, Paul E., 48
Desert Fox, 81
détente, 362
   Edward Grey on, 368
   German-Russian, 361
   and security dilemma, 367
   serious side effects of, 363
deutschstum, 77
Devereux, Robert, 326
Diamond, Sander, 78
Dichter, Ernest, 47
Dickinson, G. Lowe, 28
Diem, Ngo Dinh, 193
diffusion theories, 213
diplomacy; *see also* foreign policy; international relations
   based on Vienna Order of 1815, 358
   as cultural phenomenon, 12–13
   deconstructing history of, 358
   effect of Cold War, 369
   effect of World War I, 369
   European, 12–13
   gaps in research, 366
   institutionalized language of, 362–363
   in international history, 368
   irrational motives in, 336–337
   old, 346
   purpose of cultural analysis, 366–368
   and religion, 12
   religion and dynasty and, 316–317
   religion as factor in, 315
   secret, 351
   self-perceptions of, 366
   of United States after 1945, 346
diplomatic consultations, 359
diplomatic culture
   approaches to study of, 365–366
   and Cold War, 346
   definition, 365
   pre-World War I, 346–347
   problem of change in, 358
   versus public opinion, 364
   purpose of analysis, 366–368
   studies of, 346
diplomatic historians, 2
diplomats
   homogeneous group, 351
   self-confident elite, 351
diplomats, pre World War I
   disdain for public opinion, 358
   pre-1914 war risk assessment, 354–355
   self-perception before 1914, 350–351
   shared values, 364–365
   speed of communication, 354
   view of arbitration treaties, 349
Discoteca Publica Municipal, Brazil, 138
Disney, Walt, 133, 153
Domino Doctrine, U. S., 178
Donoghue, Michael, 11
Don Quixote, 332
Dorfman, Ariel, 133
Dorland agency, 48, 53, 55
Doyle, Seamus, 148–149
Duara, Prasenjit, 4
Duff, Peggy, 225
Duggan, Laurence, 259

Duke, James Buchanan, 27
Dunlop tires, 40
Durén, Gustavo, 153
Dutch radical pacifists, 231
dynastic threat, in Palatinate, 321
dynasty
    in early modern diplomacy, 316–317
    in European politics, 318–319

E

early modern state
    in bipolar world system, 318
    compared to nation state, 317–318
    as confessional state, 316
    dynasty as force in, 318–319
    ideological confrontations, 318
    importance of dynasties, 318–319
    international relations, 317–319
    international relations in, 324
    monopoly of noble families, 319
    Palatinate, 319–324
        alliance with Bohemia, 322–323
        alliance with England, 323–324
        in anti-Habsburg bloc, 322
        development of, 319–320
        dynastic threat, 321
        foreign policy, 322–324
        founding or Protestant Union, 322
        influence of Calvinism, 320–321
        introduction of Calvinism, 320
    political alliances, 318
    role of religion, 318, 319
    seen in Manichean terms, 335
    strategic marriages, 318–319, 328–334
    structure of, 317–318
Easter marches of antinuclear groups, 228
    British, 218
    immediate goals, 234
    Munich, 229
    national identities preserved in, 235
    and pacifist groups, 230
Easter March of Nuclear Weapons Opponents, 215–216
Eastman Kodak, 52
Eastman School of Music, 145
East Timor genocide, 193
education, changes in China, 110–111
Eichmann, Adolf, trial, 74, 75, 81, 84, 87–88
Eisenhower, Dwight D., domino doctrine, 178
El Salvador, folklore research, 139–140
Empire Marketing Board, 37, 40
Enemy, concepts of, 326–328
English-German agreement on Portuguese colonies, 364
English Reformation, 327
Enola Gay controversy, 188
entente, 362
Erwin, Wasey & Company, 48
"Essex's Ghost" (Scott), 326
Etheridge, Brian, 8–9
Eucken, Rudolf, 122
eugenics, 91
Europe; *see also* early modern state; Great Powers of Europe
    Chinese view of revolutions in, 114
    culture crisis of World War I, 122
    department stores, 33–34
    design movements, 33
    diplomacy, 12–13
    dominant view of American advertising, 30
    early modern international relations
        cultural aspects, 319
        dynasties, 318–319
        ideological conflicts, 318
        monopoly of noble families, 319
        papacy *versus* Empire, 317
        political alliances, 318
        religious blocs, 318
        strategic marriages, 318–319
        structure of states, 317–318
    learning from China, 123–125
    Nazi propaganda in, 77
    non-governmental influence, 10
    political landscape before 1914, 346
    pre-World War I foreign policy
        accepted grounds for war, 356–357
        ambassadorial congresses, 359–360

arbitration treaties, 349–350
assumed hierarchy of power, 353
Austria's view of, 353
Balkan crisis of 1911-12, 351
based on Vienna Order of 1815, 358
basic ideas underlying, 352–353
blocking outside interference, 363
Bosnian annexation crisis, 357
conflict resolution concept, 349–350
cultural factors, 346–347
détente or entente, 361
diplomatic assumptions, 351
diplomatic consultations, 359
diplomatic culture and, 365–366
and diplomatic history, 368–369
diplomatic perceptions, 350–35`
diplomatic solidarity, 364–365
disregard of peace movement, 357–358
effect of public opinion, 363–364
effect of war on diplomacy, 369
expectations of war, 354–355
failure of bilateral détente, 367
form *versus* content, 367–368
fundamental ideas, 352–357
Great Powers' view of, 353
institutionalized language, 362–363
internationalism factor, 347
London conference of 1912, 360–361, 364–365
manipulating public opinion, 364
Mendorff's assessment, 345–346, 348, 352, 354
minimizing public opinion, 357–358
nationalism of public opinion, 365

new 20th century conditions, 363
official speeches and communiqués, 361–362
and peace movement, 347–350
and postwar views, 345
preoccupation with peace, 352
problem of changing diplomatic culture, 368
question of total war, 355
rights of Great Powers, 358–359
second Moroccan crisis, 353–354, 356
security based on alliances, 352
sociocultural factors, 351
war risk assessment, 354–355
rise of fascism in, 134
societal model for Latin America, 136–137
stereotypes of China, 111–112
traditionalism/conservatism, 116
visits by Chinese scholars, 121–122
World War I and China, 118–126
European advertising
Art Deco style, 35–37
Art Nouveau style, 35
extent of American influence, 31–32
influence on American consumers, 34–35
invention of modern techniques, 32–33
posters, 32–33
European Enlightenment, 114
European Federation against Nuclear Arms, 213, 223–224, 224, 228, 234, 237
European intellectuals
meetings with Chinese scholars, 121
post-World War I pessimism, 124
European International Commission on Folk Arts and Folklore, 154
European Monroe Doctrine, 260
Evans, Harold, 26
Exhibition House of Aggression, Vietnam, 173–174

Exhibition House of American and Chinese War Crimes, Vietnam, 173
Exposition Internationale des Arts Décoratifs et Industriels Modernes, 35–37

F

Faiendes, José M., 297
Faller, Herbert, 229
Farley, Christopher, 231
fascism, in Latin America, 134
Federal Bureau of Investigation, agents in Latin America, 266–267
Federal Commission on Folklore and Natives, Argentina, 141
Federal Press and Information Office, West Germany, 79
Federal Republic of Germany; see also West Germany
    and cold War, 74
    Fischer controversy, 83–84, 85–76
    German Information Office, 85
    image-building in U. S., 78–81
    image rehabilitation, 74
    Liaison Department to Allied High Commission, 79
    at onset of anti-German wave, 81–84
    public diplomacy of, 95–96
    public relations by Roy Bernard Co., 79–81
    public relations efforts in U. S., 78–81
    response to anti-German wave, 84–87
Fehrenbach, Heide, 30
feudal state, 317
Fischer, Fritz, 83, 85–86
flag riots, Panama, 298–301
Flechtheim, Ossip K., 231
Fluck, Winfried, 4
Fodor's Exploring Vietnam, 183–184
Fodor's Gold Guide, 184–186
folklore
    and analysis of regional/national cultures, 141
    Latin American, 9
    musical Americanism, 141
    reasons for appeal of, 140–141
Folklore Americana, 154
Folklore Americas, 154
Folklore Congress, 155

folklore research
    American condescension on, 147–148
    at American universities, 143
    Boletin Latinamercana Musica, 141–142, 148
    Brazil, 137–138
    Chile, 138–139
    Colombia, 140
    commercial dimensions, 130
    and cultural emancipation, 135
    and cultural nationalism, 137–138
    El Salvador, 139–140
    exchanges and collection projects, 154
    extent of Latin American cooperation, 147–153
    during Great Depression, 142–143
    international networking, 154–155
    lack of funding after World War II, 154
    Mexico, 137
    transnational nature of, 135–136
    in U. S. 1939-1945, 143–146
    Venezuela, 140
folk music
    Chilean, 139
    Conference on the Inter-American Relations in the Field of Music, 144
    Cuban congress on, 137
    emergence in United States, 142
    in U. S. cultural diplomacy, 145–147
Folk Music of the Americas series, 152
Footprint travel guide, 186–188
Ford Foundation, 154
Ford Motor Company, 52
Foreign Office, West Germany, 79
foreign policy; see also diplomacy; international relations
    arbitration treaties, 349
    Austria *versus* Great Powers on, 353
    clash of cultures in, 364
    diplomatic culture, 365–366
    fundamental ideas before 1914, 352–357
    independent cultural practice, 366
    of Palatinate, 322–324
    pre-1914 speed of communications, 354
    secret diplomacy, 351
    shared value of elites in, 364–365

foreign relations
    and American culture, 98–99
    broadening study of, 2
Forsbach, Ralf, 358
Foucault, Michel, 6, 368
framing processes, 212-2–13
Franco, Jean, 133
Frank, Anne, 81
Frederick the Great, 76
Freikorps, 263
French-German peace committee, 348
Frente Patriótico de la Juventud, Panama, 297
Freyre, Gilberto, 149
Fried, Alfred, 357
Friedman, Max, 11
Friedrich III Elector Palatine, 320
Friedrich V Elector Palatine, 12, 327
    marriage to Elizabeth Stuart, 322, 328–334
    named king of Bohemia, 323
Friends of Nature, 229

G

Gambo Road Gang (Beliño), 291
Gandhi, Mahatma, 232
García, Dora, 296
Garrida, Pablo, 139
Gatekar, Thomas, 326–328
General Electric, 86
General Motors, 41, 49–50, 52
Geneva Accords of 1954, 176, 186
geography, new, 6
George VI of England, 142
German-American Bund, 77–78
German Americans, number of, 77
German Anti-Defamation League, 84
German historiography, and Americanization, 23
German idealism, 122
German Information Center, 85
German intellectuals, view of United States, 76
German Library of Information, 77
German National Railway, 77
German Peace Association, 357
German-Russian détente, 361
Germans, Latin American, 11
    alleged subversive in Latin America, 267–268
    American misperceptions about, 257
    banning of Nazi party, 264
    disappointing Nazi results, 264
    diversity of, 262–263
    economic success of, 263
    emigration after 1918, 262–263
    exaggerated press reports about, 265–266
    and failed Brazil coup of 1938, 269–260
    founding of associations, 262
    immigration after 1848, 261–262
    intermarriage of, 263–264
    interned by U. S. in 1940s, 257, 267–268
    investigated by Federal Bureau of Investigation, 266–267
    Nazi organizing efforts, 264
    network of spies among, 265
    number of, 261
    and pigmentocracy, 263
    racist attitudes, 263
    small Nazi groups, 263
    U. S. illusions about, 264–265
"Germans, The" (TV program), 82
German Tourist Information Office, 77
Germany; *see also* Nazi Germany; Nazi Party
    advertising industry, 47–48
    and anti-German wave in U. S., 8–9
    desire for empire, 353
    diplomatic defeat at Algeciras, 362
    Europeanizing history of, 7–8
    and Iraq War of 2002, 362
    peace movements, 350
    public relations in U. S.
        under Federal Republic, 78–81
        under Kaiser Wilhelm II, 76–77
        in Nazi era, 77–78
    study of Latin America, 258–259
    W. S. Craford agency in, 52–56
Gibson, Mel, 175
Gienow-Hecht, Jessica C. E., 30, 76, 95, 97, 99
Gittelson, Bernard, 79
Gleason, Abbott, 88, 89
global community language, 217–220
global hierarchies, 119
globalized advertising service market, 56–57
globalized world, 210
global mass marketing, 57

global terrorism, 315
Godfrey Phillips, 27
Goebbels, Joseph, 77
Goeffe, Petra, 95
Gondomar, Count of, 326
Good Neighbor Policy, 133–134, 153, 257
Göring, Hermann, 269
Goro, Nakamura, 176, 179
Grace Line, 132
Great Depression
    effect on advertising agencies, 53–55
    interest in folklore during, 142–143
Greatest Show on Earth, 81
Great Powers of Europe
    Algeciras conference of 1906, 359
    ambassadorial congresses, 359–360
    arbitration treaties, 349
    assumed hierarchy, 353
    basic solidarity before 1914, 352
    basis of diplomacy, 358–359
    conflict regulation concept, 349–350
    diplomatic consultations, 359
    London conference of 1912, 360–361
    preparations for war, 357
    pre-1914 policy assessment, 350–351
    right of intervention, 358–359
    in second Moroccan crisis, 353–354
    success in Balkan crisis, 351
    total war concept, 355
    view of foreign policy, 353
    view of international peace movements, 358
    war risk assessment, 354–355
Greaves, Leon Lester, 292
Grey, Edward
    on détente, 362
    influence on public opinion, 365
    pattern of détente, 368
    on public opinion, 358
    on treaty objectives, 356
    on war, 355
Griff nach der Weltmacht (Fischer), 83, 85
Gruppe 47 literary circle, 223–224
Gruson, Edward, 81
Guardia, Ernesto de la, 297

Guarneri, Camargo, 141
Guatemala, United States coup in, 279
Guénon, René, 121
Guggenheim Foundation, 154
Guinness, 50
Guise faction in France, 322
Guthrie, Woody, 142–143

H

Haacke, Jürgen, 365
Habsburg, House of, 322, 323
Hague Peace conferences, 349–350
Haiti, alleged German air base, 266
Haldane, Richard Burton, 361
Hanke, Lewis, 144, 148, 156
Hanoi Hilton, 190
Hanson, Howard, 145
Harding, Sandra, 6
Harrison, John, 328
Hathaway Shirts, 43
Havinden, Ashley, 55
Hay-Bunau-Varilla Treaty of 1903, 277
    revisions of, 277–278
Heck, Michael, 177
Heinrich the Lion, 333
Helton, Vernon O., 280; *see also*
    Helton-Mitchell rape case
Helton-Mitchell rape case, 30
    consequences of, 292–293
    the crime, 278
    Helton trial, 280–281, 289–291, 385–287
    impetus for Panamanian nationalism, 297–298
    Mitchell trial canceled, 291–292
Henri of Navarre (Henry IV of France), 322
Hewitt, Ogilvy, Benson & Mather, 46
Higham, Charles, 37–38, 40–41, 48–49
Hinckle, Warren, 93
Hiroshima, 214
historiography
    of American culture, 3–4
    decentering in, 7
    diverse American views of, 193
    Germany and Americanization, 23
    United Kingdom and Americanization, 23–24
    of Vietnam War, 193–196
history
    decentering U. S., 1–3
    internationalization of, 11–12

Hitler, Adolf, 78, 92, 134
    alleged hopes for Latin America, 255–256
    expected confrontation with U. S., 260
    lack of interest in Latin America, 260–261
    on Monroe Doctrine, 260
    and Nazi growth in Latin America, 264
    view of American democracy, 260
    vision of worldwide German racial community, 261
Hitler Speaks (Rauschning), 256, 261
Hixson, Walter, 96, 98
Ho Chi Minh City, 10
Hodier, Catherine, 6
Hoehn, Maria, 95
Hogan's Heroes, 84, 87
Hoganson, Kristin, 34
Holiday magazine, 80
Hollywood films
    anti-German themes, 81
    impact on British consumers, 39
    on Vietnam War, 190
Holmes, Oliver Wendell, 91
Holocaust, 91–92
Holy Roman Empire
    versus papacy, 317
    status of Palatinate in, 320
holy war, 336–337
Hoover, J. Edgar, 266–267
Hopkins, Harry, 259
Hopper, Hedda, 85
How to Read Donald Duck (Dorfman & Mattelart), 133
Huet, Henri, 178
human brotherhood, 210–220
humanities, 5–6
Humboldt, Alexander von, 259
Hungary, Soviet invasion of 1956, 230
Hunnius, F. C., 217
Huxley, Aldous, 29
hydrogen bomb, 214

I

ideologies/ideology
    in China in 1914, 12
    of Cold War in U. S., 258
    conservatism in China, 117–118
    in international relations, 258
    of racial superiority, 256
    of religion in early modern state, 318
    traditionalism in China, 116–117
    of Twentieth Century, 109
    of U. S. on Latin America, 158
Imperial Tobacco Company, 27–28
Impressions of Travels in Europe (Liang), 123, 125
Indian Tea Growers' Association, 37
Indonesian genocide, 193
In Retrospect (McNamara), 175
Institute of Motivational Research, 47
Institute of Musical Extension, Chile, 150–151
Inter-American Institute of Indigenous Studies, Mexico, 150
Inter-American Institute of Musicology, 148
Inter-American Musical Center, 148
intercultural relations, and Americanization, 96–98
International Arbitration Peace Association, 350
International Confederation for Disarmament and Peace, 213, 223, 225, 228, 237
international design
    Art Deco, 35–37
    Art Nouveau, 35
International Folklore Music Council, 155
international history
    and advertising, 23–26
    cultural turn in, 316–317
    lessons from Anglo-Palatine relations, 336–337
    place of diplomacy in, 368
    and study of culture, 257–258
internationalism, 9
    effect on politics, 347
    rhetoric of, 216–220
internationalization
    of anti-nuclear movement, 233–234
    of history, 11–12
"Internationalizing the Study of American History," 4
international order; *see* world order
International Peace Brigade, 233
international peace movement
    arbitration treaties, 348–349
    and conflict regulation concepts, 349–350

diplomats' attitudes toward,
    348–350
  Hague Peace conferences, 349–350
  organizations involved in, 348
  as perceived by governments, 358
  pre-1914 hopes, 357
international relations; *see also*
  diplomacy; foreign policy
  based on Vienna Order of 1815,
    358
  billiard ball concept, 318
  concept of identity, 324
  concepts of the enemy, 325–328
  conduct of
      by ambassadorial
        congresses, 359–360
      by diplomatic consultations,
        359
      London conference of 1912,
        360–361
  confessionalization paradigm, 316
  diplomatic culture studies,
    346–347
  early modern Europe, 317–319
      classical period, 317
      dynastic states, 318–319
      religion and negotiations, 319
      religious blocs, 318
      structure of states, 317–318
  in early modern state, 324
  lessons from Anglo-Palatine
    relations, 336–337
  perspective of Anglo-Palatine
    relations, 317
  political rhetoric of
    Americanization, 26–30
  pre-World War I
      accepted grounds for war,
        256–257
      ambassadorial congresses,
        359–360
      arbitration treaties, 348–350
      Austria's view, 353
      Balkan crisis of 1911-12`351
      based on Vienna Order of
        1815, 358
      basic ideas underlying,
        352–353
      blocking outside
        interference, 363
      Bosnian annexation crisis, 357
      changes in diplomatic
        culture, 368
      as clash of cultures, 364
      closed cultural circle, 366
      conflict resolution concept,
        348–350
      cultural factors, 346–347
      cultural historical research,
        366–368
      détente or entente, 361
      diplomatic assumptions, 351
      diplomatic consultations, 359
      diplomatic history, 368–369
      disregard of peace
        movement, 357–358
      effect of public opinion,
        363–364
      expectations of war, 354–355
      failure of détente, 367
      form *versus* content in,
        367–368
      fundamental policy ideas,
        352–357
      institutionalized language,
        362–363
      internationalism factor, 347
      London conference of 1912,
        360–361, 364–365
      manipulation of public
        opinion, 364
      Mensdorff's assessment,
        345–346, 352, 354
      minimizing public opinion,
        357–368
      nationalism of public
        opinion, 365
      new 20th century conditions,
        363
      official speeches and
        communiqués, 361–362
      and peace movements,
        347–350
      political elite's view of war,
        355–356
      postwar evaluation of,
        345–346
      preoccupation with peace,
        352
      question of total war, 355
      questions of protocol,
        360–361
      rights of Great Powers,
        358–359
      second Moroccan crisis,
        353–354, 356

security based on alliances, 352
sociocultural factors, 351
solidarity among diplomats, 364–365
speed of communications, 354
war risk assessment, 354
religion as power in, 337
religion in early modern state, 316
secrets of state, 326
and study of culture, 257–258
and study of ideology, 258
in twentieth century, 317–318
Interparliamentary Union, 348
Inverted Americanization, 9
Iraq War of 1991, 171, 194
Iraq War of 2002, 171, 362
Iriye, Akira, 212
Isamitt, Carlos, 139
Is Paris Burning?, 83
Italian-Turkish War, 360

J

J. Walter Thompson, 26, 47–56, 53
    advertising in United Kingdom, 40–41
    in London, 47–52
Jacobs, Seth, 315
James I of England, 12, 326, 328
Japan, atomic bombing of, 214
Jaumain, Serge, *33*
Jews
    and anti-German wave, 84
    interned with Germans in U. S., 267–268
Jim Crow system in Panama, 282
Johnson, Lyndon B., 87
Johnson, Nunnally, 81
Johnson, Walter, 4
Jordan, Michael, 98
Journey Down the Rainbow (Priestly), 29
Judgment at Nuremberg premiere, 83, 87–88
    and anti-German wave, 90–94
    attempts to prevent, 74–75
    conflicting narratives in, 75
    historical context of, 73–76
    in San Francisco, 92, *93*
    West German reaction, 93
    Willy Brandt speech, 73

K

Karliner, George, 267
Kauffer, Edward McKnight, 55
Keep the Aspidistra Flying (Orwell), 29
Kennedy, John F., 73
Kennedy-Chiari flag agreement of 1963, 298
Kerber, Linda, 5
Kettle, George, 48
Khmer Rouge, 193
Khruschev, Nikita, secret speech of 1956, 222, 230
Kiderln-Waecher, Alfred von, 358
Kiesinger, Kurt G., 86
Kiessling, Friedrich, 12–13
King, Martin Luther, Jr., 231, 232, 295
Kirstein, Lincoln, 148–149
Kirstein Ballet, 133
Kloppenberg, James, 5
Klyszcz, Erwin, 267
Knights of the White Camellia, 77
Kopp, Werner, 263
Korsyn, Kevin, 6
Kosovo, 194
Kramer, Stanley, 73–74, *90*, 92, 93
Krekeler, Heinz, 79, 80
Kroes, Rob, 4, 30, 31, 98
Kronfeld, Chana, 13
Kuhn, Fritz, 78
Kuisel, Richard, 30
Kupperman, Karen Ordahl, 4
Küster, Ingeborg, 229

L

Labour Party (UK), 29, 221–222
    and anti-nuclear protests, 214–215
Lange, Francisco Curt, 141, 146, 148
Langer, William, 85
La Petra Report, 4
LaPorte, Roger, 178
Latin America; *see also* Germans, Latin American
    Americanism in, 136–142
    appreciation of German immigrants, 262
    attempts to create national cultures, 134–135
    cosmic race concept, 137
    and cultural diplomacy of U. S. 1939-1945, 142–146
    cultural extension projects, 134

cultural nationalism in, 136–142
effects of U. S. cultural
   diplomacy, 153–156
efforts of Nazi recruitment,
   256–257, 264, 268–269
emancipation from European
   views, 134–135
European societal models,
   136–137
extent of cooperation of folklore
   research, 147–153
failed fascist coup of 1938,
   269–260
failure of Nazi Party in, 263–267
Federal Bureau of Investigation
   in, 266–267
folklore misused by U. S., 132–133
folklore/popular culture, 9
German and U. S. misperceptions,
   255–256
German immigration patterns,
   261–263
Germans in, 11
German view of, 258–259
Hitler's alleged hopes for, 255–256
Hitler's lack of interest in,
   260–261
lack of German planning for, 260
nativist cultural movements,
   136–137
Nazi Party view of, 11
pigmentocracy, 263
post-colonial theory, 134
quest for identity, 136–137
reasons for Nazi failure in,
   269–270
U. S. alarm over Nazi subversion,
   256
U. S. fear of Nazi menace in,
   259–261
U. S. stereotypes of, 258
viewed as inferior by U. S., 257
Laugh-In, 87
Law, John, 5
Lawler, Vanett, 153
Lazarsfeld, Paul, 47
Leadbetter, Huddie William, 143
League of Nations, 120
Lenin, V., 120
Levin, Carlos, 139
Levi's, 43
Leyenda negra; *see* Black legend
Lez, Rudolf, 138

Liang Qichao, 111, 117, 123–125
liberalism, 109
Liberty Magazine, 266
Library of Congress, 135–136, 147
Library of Congress Archive of
   American Folk Song, 142–143, 149,
   150, 151
Lichnowsky, Karl Max, 355
Life magazine, 80
Lindner, Michael A, 177
Lipton's teas, 41
literary critics, 5
local order, 109
Loewenthel, Emil, 268
Logevall, Fredrik, 346
London conference of 1912, 360–361,
   364–365, 367
London Press Exchange, 49
Lonely Planet Vietnam travel guide,
   182
Lord & Thomas, 48
Los forzados de Gamboa (Beliño), 291
Lowenthal, Richard, 82
Luce, Henry, 217
Lutheran-Catholic settlement of
   Augsburg, 320
Lutheranism, influence in
   international relations, 318
Lu-Wang school of Confucianism, 117

M

MacLeish, Archibald, 148
Macy's Department Store, 33
Mann, Abby, 90–91
Mann, Thomas, 121
Mariátequi, José Carlos, 137
marketing
   of British Empire, 37–38
   by U. S. in United Kingdom, 26–30
market research, and motivational
   studies, 47
Marlboro Cowboy, 44
Martí, José, 136
Mary Tudor, 327
mass culture, 4
   of U. S. in United Kingdom, 28
Massey, Dorien, 6
mass marketing
   global, 57
   social interactions, 24
mass media, diplomats' criticisms of,
   358

Mather & Crowther, 44–45, 49
Mattelart, Armand, 133
May Fourth Movement, China, 114, 119
McCann-Erickson, 48
McDonald's, 98
McNamara, Robert S., 175
Mendoza, Vicente T., 143
Mensdorff-Pouilly-Dietrichstein, Count, 357, 358
　on coming of war, 355
　on pre-World War I diplomacy, 345–346, 348, 352, 354
Mérey von Kapos-Mére, Kajetan, 354, 357
Meroz curse, 328
Metro-Goldwyn-Mayer, 81, 153
Mexico
　Ballet Folklorico, 140
　folklore research in, 137
　Inter-American Institute of Indigenous Studies, 150
Meyer, Thomas, 358
Microsoft Corporation, 43
militant Protestantism, 12
Milward, Frith, 28
Minh, Ho Chi, 177
Ministry of Popular Enlightenment and Propaganda, Germany, 77
Miranda, Carmen, 145
Miss Panama Contest, 293
Miss Universe Contests, 293
Mitchell, William J., 280; *see also* Helton-Mitchell rape case
modernity
　as danger for China, 120–122
　debate in China, 9
　spread of, in China, 110–112
　traditionalist reaction to, 116–117
Mondale, Walter, *94*
Monroe Doctrine, 260
Montague Burton men's wear, 32
Montgomery, Ala., bus boycott, 295
Monuments of Music in the Western Hemisphere project, 147
Morgenthau, Henry, 259
Moroccan crisis, second, 353, 356, 357
Morris, Stuart, 229
Morrison, Norman, 178
Morse, Richard, 136
Mort, Frank, 31–32
motivational studies, 47
movie industry
　anti-German films, 80–84

Hollywood films, 39
　in United Kingdom, 38–39
　Vietnam War films, 190
　Walt Disney films, 133
multilateral disarmament, 221
Munich Committee against Nuclear Armaments, 223–224
Munich Easter marches, 229
Münkler, Herfried, 316–316
Museum of Vietnamese Revolution, Hanoi, 177
music, Chilean, 139
Musical America, 153
Musical Americanism, 141, 146
Music Education Research Council, 147
Music Educators' National Conference, 145–146, 147
musicologists, 6
Muslim world, 316, 336–337
Muste, A. J., 229–230
My Lai massacre, 176

N

Nagasaki, 214
Narayan, Uma, 6
Nasser, Gamal Abdel, 11, 278, 294
National Air and Space Museum, 188
National Committee for Folklore Research, El Salvador, 139–140
national culture
　creation of, in Latin America, 134–135
　public diplomacy as means of studying, 100
Nationaldemokratische Partei Deutschlands, 82
National Folklore Commission, Colombia, 140
national historiography, 3
national honor, 356
nationalism
　in Brazil, 260
　in China, 112
　combating excesses of, 365
　revival in West Germany, 82
National Liberation Front, Vietnam, 180, 188
National Museum of American History, 188, 200
National Service for Folklore Investigation, Venezuela, 155

National Socialism, 92; *see also* Nazi Germany; Nazi Party
nation state, in twentieth century, 317–318
Nativist cultural movements, Latin America, 136–137
Nava, Mica, 44
Nazi Germany
    alleged air base in Haiti, 266
    compared to Selma, Alabama, 93
    lack of planning for Latin America, 260
    and Latin America, 143
    military intelligence, 265
    misperceptions of Latin America, 255–256
    reasons for failure in Latin America, 269–270
    spy networks in Latin America, 265
Nazi Party
    Auslandsorganization, 256–257, 259–260, 264, 268–269
    ignorance of Latin America, 269
    in Latin America
        American illusions about, 264–265
        banned after 1939, 264
        emergence after 1929, 263
        exaggerated press reports, 265–266
        Federal Bureau of Investigation and, 266–267
        growth after 1933, 264
        rejected by most German immigrants, 263–264
    propaganda in Europe, 77
    propaganda in United States, 77–78
    and racial superiority, 256
    view of Latin America, 11
Nehring, Holger, 10
new cultural history, 257–258
New Culture Movement, China, 116, 125–126
New Left
    British, 215, 222
    in United States, 89
    West German, 222, 229
New Left Review, 222
New Song movement, 156
Newsweek, 201
New Wave, 115
New York Times, 81, 265, 348

New York Times Magazine, 82
New York University, 4
New York World's Fair of 1939, 37
New Youth, 113, 114
New Youth Movement, China, 114, 116
Nicholas II of Russia, 362–363
Nicholson, William, 35
Nicolson, Arthur, 349, 351
Nike, Inc., 43, 98
Ninkovich, Frank, 98
nondiplomacy, 346
non-governmental organizations, 10
    Association of Conscientious Objectors, 228
    Campaign against Atomic Death, 215, 223
    Campaign for Nuclear Disarmament, 214–215, 217–218, 221, 228, 234–235
    century of, 210
    Comite 1952 voor de Vrede, 231
    Committee of 100, 215, 231
    European Federation against Nuclear Arms, 213, 223, 224, 228, 234, 237
    Friends of Nature, 229
    German Peace Association, 357
    International Arbitration Peace Association, 350
    International Confederation for Disarmament and Peace, 213, 223, 225, 237
    International Peace Brigade, 233
    Japanese Zengakuren group, 231
    May Fourth Movement, China, 114, 119
    Munich Committee against Nuclear Armaments, 223–224
    New Culture Movement, China, 116
    New Youth Movement, China, 114, 116
    number of, 210
    in peace movement, 348
    Socialist German Student Federation, 222
    Socialist Youth, 229
    Society for the prevention of World War II, 78
    War Resisters' International, 213, 217, 225–236, 237
    World Peace Council, 224–225
    Young China Association, 119–120

Noriega, Manuel, 292
North Atlantic Treaty Organization, 318

O

Office of Coordinator of Inter-American Affairs, United States, 133–134
Ogden's, 27
Ogilvy, David, 43–46, 47
Ogilvy & Mather, 46
One World idea, 217
One World or None, 217
Oppenheimer, Robert, 217
Organization of American Historians, 4
Organization of American States, 153–154, 197
Orwell, George, 29
Osterhammel, Jürgen, 7, 346, 358

P

pacifism, 231; *see also* War Resisters' International
    regarded as utopian, 348
    Wilhelm II of Germany on, 348
Packard, Vance, 47
Palatinate; *see also* Anlgo-Palatine relations
    defeat at battle of White Mountain, 323
    dynastic threat, 321
    early development, 319–320
    effects of dogmatic Calvinism, 320–321
    Elector Friedrich III, 320
    foreign policy
        anti-Habsburg, 322–323
        founding or Protestant Union, 322
        Friedrich V named king of Bohemia, 323
        interventionist, 322
        proposed alliance with England, 323–324
        proposed dynastic marriage, 322
        relations with Bohemian Protestants, 322–323
        religious/dynastic motives, 323
    Heidelberg-Bavaria tensions, 321
    internal conflicts, 321
    introduction of Calvinism, 320
    legal insecurity in Empire, 320
    in Protestant sermons, 326–328
Panama Canal Zone
    flag riots, 298–301
    Kennedy-Chiari flag agreement of 1963, 298
    segregation in, 295
Panamal Canal Zone, 11
Panamanian National Assembly, 292
Panamanian National Guard, 283, 284
Panamanian nationalists
    flag riots, 298–301
    opposition to U. S. courts, 286
    reaction to Suez crisis, 278, 294, 297
    resentment of U. S. controls, 277
    resurgence in 1950s, 297–298
Panamanian sexuality, 279, 282–284
Panamanian women; *see also* Helton-Mitchell rape case
    acculturation of, 289
    American stereotypes of, 288
    class divisions, 287–289
    prostitution, 282–284
Panama - United States relations
    and American racism, 298
    class divisions, 287–289
    cultural and racial denigration, 298
    cultural conflict, 279–280
    decentering U. S. power, 300–301
    flag riots, 298–301
    flourishing sex industry, 282–284
    gender relations, 279, 282–284, 287–291, 293
    Harold Rose child murder case, 278, 294, 295, 296–297
    Hay-bunau-Varilla Treaty, 277
    Helton-Mitchell rape case, 278, 280–281, 285–287, 286–287, 289–291, 291–292, 292–293
    military-Panamanian interactions, 282–284
    Panamanian nationalism, 297–298
    prostitution and U. S. military, 282–284
    and Suez Canal crisis, 278
    treaty revisions, 277–278
    U. S. sovereignty and enclave, 277
    U. S. stereotypes of women, 288
    and U. S. coup in Guatemala, 278
    Zonians (U. S. civilians)
        opposed to treaty revisions, 278
        vs. U. S. military, 281–285

Pan American Institute of Geography and History, 154
Pan American Songbook, 132
Pan American Union, 135–136
Pan American Union Music Division, 132, 144–145, 147, 150, 151, 153
Papacy *versus* Holy Roman Empire, 317
Paramount Studios, 81
Paris Congress of 1856, 359
Parra, Violeta, 156
Partido del Pueblo, Panama, 297
Partido Liberal Nacional, Panama, 298
Partido Nacional Revolucionaria, Panama, 298
Partido Revolucionario Auténtico, Panama, 297
Partido Socialista, Panama, 297
Paulmann, Johannes, 7, 346, 364
peace
    at center of pre-1914 politics, 352
    Mendorff's recommendation, 355
    versus total war concept, 355
Peace News, 228
Pells, Richard, 96, 99
Pernet, Corinne, 9
Persian Gulf War, 201
photojournalists, in Vietnam War, 178–179
pigmentocracy, of Latin America, 263
Poiger, Uta, 30, 56–57, 95
Poincaré, Raymond, 351
popular culture
    American, 26
    Latin American, 9
Popular Front government, Chile, 139
Porter, Russell B., 265–266
postcolonial theory, 134
poster advertising, 32–33
    Art Nouveau, 35
postmodernist thought, 6
poststructuralism, 6
power, and culture, 96
predestination, 320–321
Premdas, Ralph, 6
Priestly, J. B., 29
prisoners of war, in Vietnam, 189–190
privatization of warfare, 316–316
Problem of Life (Euken & Zhang), 122
propaganda
    by Nazi Party in Europe, 77
    by Nazi Party in United States, 77–78
    by Roy Bernard Company for Germany, 79–80
    by Soviet Union, 220–221
Prostitution in Panama, 282–284
Protestantism, militant, 12
Protestant Union
    alliance with James I, 322
    anti-Habsburg policy, 323
    founding of, 322
Pryde, James, 35
public diplomacy
    Adenauer's understanding of, 79
    and Americanization, 96–100
    as Americanization process, 96–97
    and anti-German wave, 95–101, 100–101
    in Cold War, 96
    culture-power relationship, 96
    German post-war goals, 78
    by Germany in United States
        under Federal Republic, 78–81
        under Kaiser Wilhelm II, 76–77
        Nazi propaganda, 77–78
    impact of cultural initiatives, 99
    one-directional, 98
    study of national culture, 100
    U. S.-German campaign, 97–98
    of United States, 96–101
    of West Germany, 95–96
public opinion, pre-World War I
    attempts to influence, 365
    and diplomacy, 354
    versus diplomatic culture, 364
    and failure of détente, 363–364
    manipulation of, 364
    minimizing influence of, 358
public relations, by Germany in U. S.
    under Federal Republic, 78–81
    hiring of Roy Bernard Company, 79–80
    in Nazi era, 77–78
    under Wilhelm II, 76–77
public relations firms
    of Germany in United States, 78–81
    Roy Bernard Company, 79–80
Puerto Ricans, in Panama, 282

Q

Qing dynasty, 115
Quechua Indians, 263

R

racism
    of Germans in Latin America, 263
    Jim Crow system in Panama, 282
radical pacifists
    British, 232–233
    Dutch, 231
    West German, 232–233
Radkau, Joachim, 356
Rambo: First Blood Part II, 190
Ramparts, 93
Rappaport, Erika, 33–34
Rat Patrol, 84, 87
Rauschning, Hermann, 256, 261
Reagan, Ronald W., 175, 193, 284
Reinhard, Wolfgang, 316
religion
    in cold War diplomacy, 315
    confessionalization paradigm, 316–317, 318
    Confucianism as, 117
    and diplomacy, 12
    in early modern diplomacy, 316–317
    in early modern state, 318
    as factor in diplomacy, 315
    global holy war, 336–337
    Muslim world, 316
    as power in international relations, 337
    quarrels of 16th-17th centuries, 316
Republic of Vietnam, 179–180
retail advertising, 33
Retail Grocers' Association, 38
Rethinking American History, 4–5
Revista Brasileira de Música, 152
Reynolds, David, 31, 34
Reynolds, John, 327
Reynolds, Robert, 265
Ribbentrop, Joachim von, 77, 269
Richards, Nelly, 6
Richter, Hans Werner, 223–224
Richter, Linda, 173
Rincón, Carlos, 6
Rise and Fall of the Third Reich (Shirer), 75, 83, 87
Ritter, Karl, 260
Robbins, Keith, 358
Rockefeller, Nelson A., 133–134, 144, 150–151
Rodgers, Daniel, 4
Rodó, Enrique, 136
Rolland, Romain, 121
Rolls-Royce, 43
Rommel, Erwin, 81
Roosevelt, Franklin D., 142, 257, 259, 265, 266
Roosevelt administration, 260, 264
Rope of Sand, 81
Rorty, Richard, 6
Rose, Harold, child murder case, 30, 278
    background to, 294–295
    impetus for Panamanian nationalism, 297–298
    the killing, 293–294
    trial, 295
Rosenberg, Emily, 98, 346
Rosenberg, Isidore, 267–268
Rotter, Andrew, 315
Roy Bernard Company, 79–80, 85, 88, 94, 97
Rüde, Max, 12
Russell, Bertrand, 217–218, 223–224
    icon of anti-nuclear protests, 234
    speech in China, 121–122
Rustin, Bayard, 231

S

S. H. Benson Ltd., 46, 49
Sachsenmaier, Dominic, 9
Salas, Eugenio Pereira, 149, 150
Salat, Rudolf, 79
Salgado, Plinio, 259
Sanity, 228
Santa Cruz, Domingo, 149, 150
Sarajevo assassinations of 1914, 345
Sarmiento, Domingo, 261
Sarmiento de Accuña, Diego, Count of gondomar, 326
Saunders, Douglas, 50
Schilling, Heinz, 316
Schmid, Peter Andre, 6
Schroeter, Harm, 47
Schug, Alexander, 48
Schwarzkopf, Stefan, 8
Schweinitz, Graf, 87
Schweppes, 43
scoialism, 109
Scott, Michael, 218
Scott, Thomas, 325–326
second Moraccan crisis; *see* Moroccan crisis, second
secret diplomacy, 351

secrets of state, 326
security culture, 365
Seeger, Charles, 132, 142, 144–145, 146, 147, 148, 150, 156
segregation, in Panama Canal Zone, 295
Selfridge, Gordon, 33
Selfridge's Department Store, 33–34
Selma, Alabama, civil rights debacle, 93
semi-colonized societies, 119
Shell Tiger, 44
Shen Yi, 120
Ship of Fools, 83
Shirer, William, 75, 83, 86
Silver Burdett Company, 132
Silver Shirts, 77
Smith, Carleton Sprague, 145, 146, 151, 152
Smythe, Terry, 231
social Darwinism, 112
    in China, 121
    in pre-1914 foreign policy, 352
    spread of, 125
Social Democratic Party (W. Germany), 215, 230
    anti-nuclear protests, 221–222
Socialist German Student Federation, 222
Socialist Youth - The Falcons, 229
social movements
    diffusion of ideas between, 213
    and perceptions of crisis, 212
social movement theories, 212
Sociedad del Folklore Chileno, 138
Sociedad Ecuatoriana de Transportes Aéreos, 266
Society for Ethnography and Folklore, Brazil, 138
Society for the Prevention of World War II, 78
Son My, Vietnam, 176
    massacres, 177
Sound Archive of Sao Paulo, 150
Southern Christian Leadership Conference, 93
Soviet Union
    breakup of, 210
    invasion of Hungary, 222–223, 230
    peace propaganda, 220–221
Spain
    accused of universal monarchy, 326
    anti-Catholic rhetoric against, 327
    black legend about, 325
    Count of Gondomar, 326
    and Duke of Alba, 325
    as enemy of Palatinate, 325
    propaganda against
        by John Reynolds, 237
        by Thomas Scott, 325–326
"Spanish Match," 326
Stalinism, Khruschev's secret speech, 222
state power
    erosion of, 315–316
    hypocrisy of, 199
Stead, William Thomas, 28
Steiner, Zara, 358
Stephanson, Anders, 346
Stolle, Helga, 229
Storey, Robert, 184
Stuart, Elizabeth, 12
    marriage to Friedrich V, 322, 328–334
student protests of 1960s, 10; *see also* Anti-nuclear protests
Suez Canal crisis of 1956, 11, 230
    Panamanian reaction to, 278, 294, 297
Suri, Jeremi, 5
Suttner, Bertha von, 357

T

Tai, Hue-Tam Ho, 176
television, anti-German programs, 84
Tempel, Hans-Henry, 215
Tempel, Hans-Konrad, 229
terrorist attack of 2001, 315
Thieu, Nguyen Van, 193
Third Camp theory, 229–230
Thirty Years' War, 12, 315, 316, 317
    battle of White Mountain, 323, 325, 327
    classical period following, 317
    conflicts on eve of, 322
    Spain *vs.* Palatinate, 325–328
Thomas, Joseph, 82, 85, 87
Thompson, E. P., 235, 237
Thompson, Hugh, 177
Thompson, Stith, 145, 155
Thoreau, Henry David, 232
Thurm, Graf, 362–353
Tiersten, Lisa, *33*
Time Machine (Wells), 214

tobacco advertising war, 27
Tono Bungay (Wells), 27
Toscanini, Arturo, 133
totalitarianism, 88
total war concept, 355
Toulouse-Lautrec, Henri de, 32
Tracy, Spencer, 74
traditionalism, in China, 116–117
Trans-cultural folklore movement, 9
transnational history, 110, 212
transnationalism, in folklore research, 135–136
transnational social space, 233
Treaties of Westphalia, 320
Triple Entente, 367
Trommler, Frank, 76
Turbay, Gabriel, 266
Tyrrell, Ian, 4

U

Ullstei Presse, 53
Uncommon Valor, 190
understanding committees, 348
UNESCO, 153, 155
unilateral disarmament, 219
Union Carbide, 86
Unión Popular, Panama, 298
United Artists, 81
United Kingdom
    advertising war, 27
    aggressive American marketing in, 26–30
    alliance debate, 354
    American ad agencies in, 47–56
    American advertising of tobacco, 27–28
    American department store in, 33–34
    American mass culture in, 28
    anti-American attitudes, 28–29
    anti-nuclear protests, 10
    Empire Marketing Board, 37
    impact of Hollywood movies, 39
    men's wear industry, 32
    modernization of advertising in, 57
    movie industry, 38–39
    New Left, 222
United States, 197; *see also* Anti-German wave in U. S.
    aim of public diplomacy, 97–98
    alarm over Nazi subversion in, 256
    anti-German wave, 8–9
    attitudes toward Germany 1950s–1960s, 75
    belief in Latin American inferiority, 257
    central position in culture/history, 2
    changing attitudes in 1960s, 93–94
    civil rights movement, 89, 93–94
    cold War ideology, 258
    cultural diplomacy and Latin America, 123–133, 142–147
    cultural policies, 9
    decentering culture and history of, 1–3
    diplomacy after 1945, 346
    disinformation on Nazis in Latin America, 265–266
    emergence of folk music movement, 142
    exporter and recipient of culture, 8
    Federal Bureau of Investigation agents in Latin America, 266–267
    Hitler's expected confrontation with, 260
    Hitler's view of, 260
    imagined Nazi menace in Latin America, 259–261
    impact of Shirer's book, 83
    impressions of Germany
        under Federal Republic, 78–81
        Nazi era, 77–78
        Wilhelmine era, 76–77
    internment of Germans, 257, 267–268
    misperceptions of Latin America, 255–256
    Monroe Doctrine, 260
    and Nazi hopes for Latin America, 143
    New Left, 89
    number of German Americans, 77
    occupation of Panama Canal Zone, 11
    in Panama
        American sovereignty, 277
        consequences of rape case, 292–293
        cultural-racial denigration, 298
        flag riots, 298–300
        gender relations, 279, 282–284, 287–291, 293

and Guatemala coup, 278
Harold Rose child murder
  case, 278, 293–297
Hay-Bunau-Varilla Treaty, 277
Helton-Mitchell rape case,
  278, 280–281, 285–287,
  289–292
Jim Crow system, 282
outcome of flag riots, 300–301
Panamanian nationalism,
  297–201
paternalism and racism, 279
Puerto Rican soldiers, 282
reaction to U. S. racism, 298
size of military community,
  281
social space, 289
status of Panamanians, 277
stereotypes of women, 288
treaty revisions, 277–278
U. S. military and sex
  industry, 282–284
Zonians (U. S. civilians), 278
Zonians vs. military, 281–285
perception of Nazi efforts in Latin
  America, 261
persistence of Vietnam
  syndrome, 171–172
popularity of European
  advertising, 35
and post-colonial theory in Latin
  America, 134
pro-Nazi organizations, 77–78
public diplomacy of, 96–101
remembrance of Vietnam War, 10
responses to *Judgment at
  Nuremberg*, 90–94
stereotypes of Latin America, 258
target of Hate Germany
  campaign, 89
terrorist attack of 200, 315
visit of British monarchs, 142
United States Department of Defense,
  278
United States foreign policy
  bloodless war concept, 194
  contrition for Vietnam War,
    191–196
  Domino Doctrine, 178
  Guatemala coup, 279
  Hay-Bunau-Varilla Treaty of 1903,
    277
  interventions 1980s to 1990s, 193
  support for dictatorships, 193

and 21st century ambitions, 199
war against terrorism, 194
United States military; *see* Panama -
  United States relations
United States National Committee for
  Intellectual Cooperation, 143
United States State Department, 136;
  see also Cultural Division of U. S.
  State Department
  resentment of concessions to
    Panama, 278
universal monarchy, 326

V

Vack, Klaus, 229, 230
Vallarino, Bolívar, 292
Vanderbilt, Cornelius, Jr., 266
Vargas, Getulio, 134, 138, 259–260
Vasconcelos, José, 137, 141
Vega, Carlos, 143, 149–150, 155
Venezuela
  folklore research, 140
  National Service for Folklore
    Investigation, 155
Verband des Kriegsdienstverweigerer,
  228, 235
Vereine, in Latin America, 262
Versailles Peace Treaty, impact on
  China, 119
"Victory of the People" (Li Dazhao),
  120
Vienna Order of 1815, 358
Viereck, George Sylvester, 77
Vietnam National Administration of
  Tourism, 184
Vietnam syndrome, persistence of,
  171–172
Vietnam travel guidebooks, 183–188
Vietnam Veterans Memorial Wall, 186
Vietnam War, 10, 89; *see also* War
  Remnants Museum
  Agent Orange use, 176
  American atrocities, 176
  antiwar movement in U. S.,
    177–178
  conservative *vs.* liberal views,
    171–172
  critical historiography, 193–196
  Hollywood films, 190
  National Liberation Front, 180
  number of casualties, 176
  one-sided portrayals, 186–189
  prisoners of war, 189–190

Republic of Vietnam forces, 179–180
varying assessments, 175
Villa-Lobos, Hector, 133, 138, 140, 141, 146
Volksgemeinschaft, 261
Von Thadden, Adolf, 82

W

W. S. Crawford agency, 26, 47–56
   in Berlin, 52–56
Wagnleitner, Reinhold, 30, 95
Wallenstein, Albrecht von, 336
Wall Street Journal, 89
Walt Disney films, 133
War Remnants Museum of Vietnam, 10, 171–201
   alleged historical inaccuracies, 184–188
   American antiwar display, 177–178
   And American memory, 183–184
   comment books, 190–196
   compared to Museum of American History, 188–189
   Fodor Guide criticisms, 184–186
   Historic Truths room, 175
   as history, 174
   and hypocrisy of state power, 199–200
   incomplete narrative, 176–177
   justification of Vietnam insurgents, 180
   mediated by travel books, 180–190
   minimizing awareness of, 184
   as multinational dialogue, 196–200
   need for balance, 189–190
   number of visitors, 174
   and postwar U. S. policies, 194–196
   purpose, 172
   as shared history, 200–201
   tourist complaints, 179–180
   tourist responses, 172–173
   U. S. views on, 178
   and U. S. contrition for war, 191–194
   versus U. S. accounts of war, 175–176
   use of Western sources, 175
   works of photojournalists, 178–179

War Resisters' International, 213, 217, 225–236, 237
   and American civil rights movement, 230–231
   Anglo-German cooperation, 225–226
   and civil disobedience, 230–233
   communication resources, 228
   demand for iconic figures, 235
   and Easter marches, 228–229, 230, 234–235
   founded in 1921, 226
   German branches, 228
   links to American civil rights movement, 226–227
   preserving national identities, 235
   reasons for efficiency of, 227
   symbolic internationalism, 234
   Third Camp theory, 229–230
   transnational networks, 229
   transnational social space concept, 226, 233
   Triennial Conferences, 227–231
Warsaw Pact, 318
Wars of the Roses, 333
war/warfare
   accepted grounds for, 356–357
   and assertions of national honor, 356
   avoided in Balkan crisis, 351
   at center of pre-1914 politics, 352
   conflict regulation concept, 349–350
   danger regarded as real, 357
   European risk assessment, 354–355
   pre-1914 diplomats' view on, 355
   privatization of, 315–316
   and rejection of peace movements, 351
   technological developments, 355
Watson, Albert, 73
Watson, Clement, 50
Weimar Republic, 262
Welles, Orson, 133
Welles, Sumner, 147, 259, 266
Wells, H. G., 27, 214
Welsh, David, 93
West, Douglas, 50
West Berlin, 80
   and Cold War, 88
West German anti-nuclear protests, 10
   in American perspective, 211
   civil disobedience, 230—233

cross-cultural communication
  problems, 220–225
cultural assumptions, 233–234
disagreements with British, 224
Easter marches, 215–216
founding of European Federation
  against nuclear Arms, 223
goals, 219
and Khruschev's secret speech,
  222–223, 230
language of global community,
  219–220
links with British, 221–223
Munich Committee, 223–224
origin of, 215–216
pacifist groups, 230
proximity to Eastern bloc, 230
and rhetoric of internationalism,
  218–220
symbolic internationalism, 234
and War Resisters' International,
  225–236
and World Peace Council, 225
West Germany
  aim of public diplomacy, 97
  Americanization of, 89–90
  British, 222
  in Cold War consensus, 89
  political parties and nuclear
    protests, 215
  radical pacifists, 232–233
  reaction to *Judgment at
    Nuremberg,* 93
  revival of nationalism, 82
Westphalian Peace Conference of
  1648, 323
We Were Soldiers, 175–176
White Mountain, battle of, 32–33, 325,
  327
White supremacist organizations, 77
Whitmore, Terry, 177
Wiener Werkstétte movement, 33
Wilhelm II of Germany, 76
  on accepted grounds for war, 356
  on arbitration treaties, 348
  on Balkan crisis, 351
  on function of Great Powers,
    352–353
  on pacifism, 348
Willet, Ralph, 95
William H. Rankin Agency, 48–49
Williams, Francis, 29
Winchell, Walter, 80

Wither, George, 332
Wittelsbach, House of, 321, 323, 333
Wolfers, Arnold, 318
Wolff, Walter, 267
Woolworth, 33
Work Program Administration, 142
world order
  competing visions of, 109–110
  debates on, 109
  and international peace
    movement, 347–350
  marginalization of China in,
    117–118
  policy ideas before 1914, 352–353
World Peace Council, 224–225
world society, 210
World War I; *see also* Europe; Great
  Powers of Europe; International
  relations
  Chinese interpretations, 118–126
  German emigration after, 262–263
  in Hegelian terms, 120
  impact of diplomacy, 369
  prewar risk assessment, 354–355
  revising understanding of, 83
World War II
  atomic bombs, 214
  as global moment, 126

Y

Yan Fu, 121
Young, Andrew, 93
Young, Marilyn, 4
Young China, 114–116
Young China Association, 119–120
Young China journal, 115, 120
youth movements, in China, 114–116
Yuan Shikui, 111

Z

Zeilin, Jonathan, 30
Zengakuren (Japanese radical
  organization), 231
Zhang Junmai, 121–123
Zhu Xi, 117
Zola, Emile, 33
Zonians (U. S. civilians in Panama)
  contempt for U. S. military,
    281–285
  resentment of treaty changes, 279
Zunz, Oliver, 26

www.ingramcontent.com/pod-product-compliance
Lightning Source LLC
Chambersburg PA
CBHW071329080526
44587CB00017B/2775